AN INTRODUCTION TO
SOCIOLOGY

By

CARL A. DAWSON

PROFESSOR AND CHAIRMAN OF THE DEPARTMENT
OF SOCIOLOGY AND ANTHROPOLOGY,
MCGILL UNIVERSITY

and

WARNER E. GETTYS

PROFESSOR AND CHAIRMAN OF THE DEPARTMENT
OF SOCIOLOGY, UNIVERSITY OF TEXAS

THIRD EDITION

THE RONALD PRESS COMPANY ⋅ NEW YORK

PREFACE

Since the revised edition of *An Introduction to Sociology* appeared in 1935, the world has gone through the agony and social disorganization of another conflict. The authors are hopeful that this Third Edition, which has been reorganized and largely rewritten, bears adequate witness, in text and in research documentation, to the important developments in sociology during this fateful decade. They are conscious of the fact that it may also reflect some of the temper of these times, when man is struggling to rebuild, and perhaps to reorient, his shattered world.

The reorganization of chapters in this edition will, it is believed, serve to make the text even more teachable. The authors recognize that a textbook for the introductory course in sociology gives most students their first, and some students their only, contact with sociology. This being so, they feel that the text should set forth, first, a clear and adequate concept of sociological theory. Most students, they have found, are surprised when confronted with the perspective of sociology. They expect it to be reformatory, or to tell them what, as persons, they ought to be and ought to do. The initial emphasis in this text on the basic components and processes of our social life respects this point of view, but strives to give students a new orientation. It describes the fundamental social situations in which they find themselves and, in a great many instances, explains the recurrent problems we all face in our daily lives. In so doing the text forms a background for the individual decisions these students will be called upon to make during their lives.

The authors have no apology to make for the fact that *An Introduction to Sociology* contains no blueprints for institutional, community, national, or world planning. Nor does the text make any attempt to determine the motivations of social planners, although it does have an indirect and scientific concern with the problems of social planning. The authors' responsibility has been to set forth the basic structure of human relations and thereby aid those who may wish to bring about needful changes in this structure.

Part I, then, is devoted to a discussion of the fundamental factors of Group, Culture, and Personality. Teachers who have used earlier editions of the book will find that the treatment of Personality has here been considerably expanded. Part II retains the emphasis on

iii

the ecological approach to the study of man and his institutions which, the authors feel, formed such a distinctive feature of earlier editions of the text. Its chapters on the distribution of peoples and cultures, on the community, and on social institutions have been brought fully up to date by taking account of the newer trends in sociological study.

Part III, on Interaction, supplies a clear presentation of this vital social concept, and treats of the whole process, in all its phases. Especial emphasis is given to how differences in ecological position and social status enter into and affect interaction between persons and groups. Part IV carries the function of Interaction into the broad field of Social Change, where full attention is given to its ecological and cultural dynamics, to social unrest and types of collective behavior, to the mechanisms of social control, and to the trends of present-day social movements.

Part V is essentially the two-chapter summation of the history of the sociological movement and of the theory, methods, and applications of sociology as a science, which formed such an important element in earlier editions. But it, too, has been largely rewritten.

Stress should be put on the retention, in this edition, of much illuminating documentary material, which gives the reader considerable firsthand acquaintanceship with the research activities of many specialized social scientists. A few of the most helpful documents in the earlier editions have been retained, but most of them are new. They truly reflect the ferment of sociological research since 1935. Collective and appreciative acknowledgment is here made to the many publishers whose cooperation has made possible the extensive use of this documentary material. Individual sources have been acknowledged in footnotes. Limitations of space have permitted the introduction of no more than a tiny fraction of this vast and significant literature. The authors have therefore felt themselves under obligation to give the reader something more than a cursory idea of the extent of this research and have, consequently, implemented their chapters with ample, though not exhaustive, bibliographies.

The authors are conscious of the fact that they could not have prepared this revision without the counsel of many colleagues in the field, some of whom may be surprised at the use which has been made of their good advice. They wish to record, in particular, their indebtedness to Professors Forrest LaViolette, Oswald Hall, Nathan Keyfitz, and William Kelly of McGill University, and to Professor Walter I. Firey of the University of Texas. Mrs. Joan Currie

Jackson, research assistant in the McGill Department of Sociology and Anthropology, did some of the original writing and has been associated with the work of proofreading. Her competency is reflected on every page of this edition.

CARL A. DAWSON
WARNER E. GETTYS

September 8, 1948

CONTENTS

PART I

Group, Culture, and Personality

PART II

The Ecological Approach to the Study of Man and His Institutions

PART III

Social Interaction

CONTENTS

PART IV

Social Change

PART V

Lines of Sociological Development

ILLUSTRATIONS

TABLES

PART I

GROUP, CULTURE, AND PERSONALITY

INTRODUCTION

THE ORIGINAL NATURE of man contains the potentialities of mental development to which the primates below man cannot aspire. In human society, alone, does language develop. In consequence, mind, thought, and plans for the future are the restricted possessions of human societies. The associative memory of animals permits them to react to immediate but not future stimuli. They do not lack memory but, without language, they do not have imagination. The animals' memory permits only the backward look. Man can use his past reconstructively to visualize his future.

Man's group life means that he can, through language communication, organize his past experience with others in cumulative fashion. He can compare his present problems with those of preceding generations and with those of alien cultures. With such a vantage ground he can speculate about the future and plan to meet its possibilities. Not only are "stock" plans included but also the flexible alternatives that unforeseen situations call for. In a last analysis, the imaginative reconstruction of man's past in meeting new situations is his greatest resource. This reconstruction is primarily social.

In the chapters that follow, the collective life of man is given central consideration. The individual is studied in relation to his group relations and the cultural heritages which result from continued social interaction. Group life is varied in nature and content. One item is held constant, the tendency everywhere for men to reach common objectives at the levels of sentiment and rational prevision, although such objectives are never isolated from each other. Consequently, a culture (or the integral patterning of a society's past experience) is always the basis of its present and future collective activities. Men face the unknown future in terms of what they have already experienced.

Personality, starting with the inherited and random impulses at birth, is organized in relation to the immediate exigencies of group life and is constantly related to the cultural traditions that have come down from past generations. No new generation takes over these cultural ways intact. They are revamped to meet the needs of new individuals and new social situations. The point of view of the chapters on personality is applicable to all societies, but the illustrations are drawn primarily from our own society. The person and

3

his social adjustment require above everything else a knowledge of the factors that have made him what he is. Group, culture, and special personality-making situations work in conjunction in the making and remaking of man. In society a man becomes a human personality; apart from it, he remains an animal.

Chapter 1

THE SOCIAL GROUP

Sociology is the study of people living in groups. This science is interested in how groups arise, in their similarities and differences, in the effects of groups on individuals and the individual's effect on the group, as well as in the products of group interaction.[1] Thus the concept of the social group is basic to sociology.

By definition, a social group is "a sociological designation for any number of people, larger or smaller, between whom such relations are discovered that they must be thought of together. The 'group' is the most general . . . term used in Sociology for combinations of persons. A family, a mob, a picnic party, a trade union, a city precinct . . . the civilized or uncivilized population of the world may be treated as a group. Thus a 'group' for Sociology is a number of persons whose relations to each other are sufficiently impressive to demand attention. The term is merely a commonplace tool. It contains no mystery." [2]

In later chapters, the emergence of groups, the comparison of groups, the interaction of groups, the individual's effect on the group and the group's effect on the individual will be dealt with in some detail. At this point we are primarily interested in noting man's relationships to specific groups. Particular emphasis will be placed on those groups with which men have relationships, regardless of where they live in the world.

Society.—The largest social group with which a person has relationships is a *society*. By definition, a society is "the largest relatively permanent group who share common interests, common territory, a common mode of life and a common 'esprit de corps' or 'belongingness' whereby they distinguish themselves from outsiders." [3] As a rule, the person acquires membership in a society by virtue of birth. However, as in the case of an immigrant, membership is sometimes acquired by adoption. As all men live within a society and as the

---

[1] E. D. Monachesi, "Sociology and Culture," in E. P. Schmidt (Ed.), *Man and Society*, New York, Prentice-Hall, Inc., 1938, p. 9.

[2] Albion W. Small, *General Sociology*, Chicago, University of Chicago Press, 1905, p. 495.

[3] John Gillin, *The Ways of Men*, New York, Appleton-Century-Crofts, Inc., 1948, p. 340.

society determines their goals, their behavior, and their attitudes, it would be well to examine the nature of this social group at some length before continuing.

A society is made up of a group of people who have been together long enough to work out a common way of life, or, in other words, patterns of behavior. Some of these patterns are related to the solution of recurrent problems which the group experiences. Examples of such recurrent problems are birth, the care of children, death, food, shelter, and protection. Other patterns of behavior emerge to regulate the interaction of the members of a society in such a way that conflict between the individuals who compose it is kept at a minimum. For example, in every known society a division of labor has been developed in accordance with which certain tasks are allotted to males and others to females. In simple and relatively stable societies, the division of labor has not progressed beyond this point but, in our more complex American civilization, the division of labor has become much more complex, factors other than sex playing an extremely important part in determining who is to execute specific tasks.

Other patterns of behavior have arisen which define the rights and duties of every member of the society with respect to every other member and regulate their interaction. The close interrelationship of these patterns has tended to make the members of a society very dependent upon one another. The existence of these ways of acting and the adherence of the members of a society to them increase the predictability of behavior. When behavior becomes predictable (to at least a limited degree) cooperation between the members of a society becomes effective.[4]

Group life is possible only when the individual members suppress many of their personal interests and desires for the sake of the survival of the group as a whole. Unless this can be done, the patterns of mutually adaptive behavior cannot operate. In addition, individuals must be able to cooperate voluntarily, without continual supervision. This voluntary cooperation develops most easily when the members of a group develop a strong feeling of psychological and emotional unity, that is, "esprit de corps." When a feeling of unity develops, individuals feel that the group should be put ahead of themselves at all times and that, in a group crisis, they would be willing to lay aside their personal wishes, ideas, and even their lives for the sake of group survival. Esprit de corps emerges through the inter-

---

[4] Ralph Linton, *The Study of Man*, New York, Appleton-Century-Crofts, Inc., 1936, p. 93.

action of the members of a group. Living together in the same area, sharing the same language, having a multitude of common interests, the group members reinforce one another's ideas and emotions. The more the members share these ideas and emotions, the more the group comes to believe that its way of thinking is the right way.[5]

In transmitting its way of life to new members, a society relies on the human capacity for learning. One generation expresses patterns verbally or acts them out in behavior which implies the pattern and, from these expressions, the new generation learns and comes to participate in the patterns. These constitute the known way of dealing with problems which have arisen in the history of the society. As these patterns exist in the society at the time the individual becomes a member, he tends to take them for granted and to accept them without objective evaluation.

However, the patterns do not remain static down through time. An individual can learn a pattern only when it is expressed. Hence patterns which are no longer in use tend to drop from the society's configuration of patterns of behavior. They are also expressed in a variety of ways, according to the circumstances or personality of the individual who is interpreting them. For example, an employer in a large corporation and an employer in a small business will express employer-employee relations differently. A neurotic person interprets mother and son relationships in a manner different from a normal mother. As the new member of a society learns the pattern from the individual who expresses it, and as individuals differ greatly, there is a wide range of ways in which any one may be expressed. In addition, the new member of the society interprets the pattern as he sees it, in keeping with his own circumstances and his own personality, which makes the pattern still more varied. When there is a sufficiently large number of individual deviations from the ideal pattern in actual behavior, the ideal pattern itself changes.

The range of expression in patterns of behavior is kept within socially defined limits. The ideal patterns are the society's idea of what behavior is appropriate and, although allowance is made for variations, social disapproval is exercised upon the individual who transgresses the socially acceptable limits.

The ideal patterns represent the knowledge of the group concerning problems which have arisen in history and the means of solving them and are closely interrelated with one another. The patriarchal

---

[5] The tendency of groups to feel that their way of thinking and acting is the right and only way is known as "ethnocentrism." This concept will be of vital importance in later chapters dealing with group interaction.

father lives within his position as a wage earner and his other positions in the functioning of a community. The integration of these mutually adjusted ideal patterns of behavior is the *social system* of a society.[6]

In a social system the patterns of reciprocal behavior which are an integral part of any position within the society are known as statuses. The *status* of an individual is an ideal pattern which outlines the rights and duties in relation to other members of a society of a person holding a given position. When the person with a status exercises these rights and duties, he is said to be playing a *role*. The combined status and role represent the minimum of attitudes and behavior which a person must take on if he is to fill the position adequately. It should also be noted that the ideal patterns of rights and duties which constitute a status continue even though the persons occupying the position come and go. The society's idea of behavior appropriate to a teacher remains, even though the position of teacher is occupied by a succession of persons over a long period of time.[7]

Let us take the example of a fraternity. The social system of such a group consists of an organization of ideal patterns of behavior for those who occupy the positions of president, secretary, treasurer, through to member. Rights and duties are most obvious in the case of the executives and less obvious in the case of the member. However, if the ideal patterns of behavior appropriate to a member are analyzed, it is clear that the member has rights and duties just as do the executives. The member elects the executives. The member owes them his cooperation. Yet the executive is responsible to the member for his conduct while occupying the position to which he has been elected. When the executive has completed his term of office, someone else takes his place. The rights and duties implicit and explicit in the executive position now belong to his successor. The members of the fraternity also have a preconceived idea of how they expect the executive to perform his duties, that is, how they expect him to play his role by putting into action the rights and duties implicit in his position. They may permit the executive to vary from their interpretation of his status within certain limits, but, if he deviates too far from what is expected of him, pressure will be brought to bear upon him or he will be removed from his position.

"Status and role serve to reduce the ideal patterns for social life into individual terms."[8] They serve as the models for the individual

---

6 Linton, *The Study of Man*, p. 253.
7 *Ibid.*, pp. 113-114.
8 *Ibid.*, p. 114.

so that he can recognize his behavior and attitudes to be congruous with the behavior of other individuals engaged in acting out the pattern. Linton gives the following example:

Thus, if we are studying football terms in the abstract, the position of quarterback is meaningless except in relation to the other positions. From the point of view of the quarterback himself, it is a distinct and important entity. It determines where he shall take his place in the lineup and what he shall do in various plays. His assignment to this position at once limits and defines his activities and establishes a minimum of things he must learn.[9]

A society functions smoothly or otherwise in proportion to how well its members are adjusted to their statuses. As the new member of the society forms his habits and attitudes from the time of birth onward, it follows that the earlier status training begins, the more successful it will be. Fortunately, people are mutable. Hence almost any person can be trained to fill almost any status position adequately. However, a society usually makes use of the talents and differences of its members by providing them with status positions that can be acquired by persons with special capabilities or special limitations.[10]

It should be noted that there are a large number of societies in the world today all of which have worked out their own ways of life. The social systems of the world's societies are widely varied and range from the highly complex patterns of behavior found in the society of America to the simpler patterns of the Zuñi and Kwakiutl Indians of North America, the Kaingang Indians of South America, and the Maori of New Zealand.

The relationship which exists between the individual and his society is a reciprocal one. Society provides an individual with an accumulation of knowledge from past generations in the form of patterns of behavior which are appropriate for meeting the vast majority of the problems which he will face throughout life. These patterns of behavior provide him with the means of satisfying not only his basic physical needs but also of working with the other members of his group without whose support survival would be exceedingly difficult, if not impossible. In return, the individual members of a society express the behavior patterns to the best of their abilities, adjust them to meet new situations, and transmit them to new members. Thus the continuation of the society is ensured and its social system kept at a high level of efficiency for meeting the needs of its members.

Within the society are smaller divisions and groups with which the individual has relationships. In many countries, for instance, the

9 *Ibid.,* p. 114.
10 *Ibid.,* Ch. 8.

society is broken into class divisions which have a monopoly of certain of the patterns of behavior of the society as a whole. A person is usually a member of a social class by virtue of birth or his occupation. Some societies are divided into geographic areas which have a segment of the patterns of behavior of the society as a whole. For example, in the United States, although the attitudes toward the Negro in both the North and the South are a part of the social system of America, each division has a different point of view on this matter. The individual will act according to the pattern of behavior laid down by the subsection of society to which he belongs. The individual will also be a member of a community, of a number of institutions, of interest groups and informal groups such as clique and friendship groups. Many of these will be dealt with at greater length elsewhere in the text.

Group Relationships.—It is through their participation in the groups which make up a society that individuals find their status and role and participate in the social system. The relationships of individuals with these groups have been broadly classified in many different ways in sociology. One of the most convenient classifications has been that put forth by Professor Cooley, the concept of primary and secondary group relationships.[11]

PRIMARY RELATIONSHIPS. All individuals within a society have primary relationships: with a family, a neighborhood group, a friendship group. It is because they are the first relationships an individual has and because they remain his most important relationships throughout life that they are termed *primary relationships*. They are characterized by intimacy and the sentiments of sympathy and identification. It is through such relationships that the newborn child experiences the patterns of the society of which he is to become a member. Through these relationships he first experiences the roles which he can copy. Through this experience he gradually comes to know what will be expected of him in most of the situations with which he will be confronted throughout life.

In the modern, industrialized world, with its extensive methods of transportation and communications, primary relationships are no longer limited to the immediate geographic neighborhood and to persons whom he can meet face to face. The primary relationships of the young child are in the immediate neighborhood of his home, but as he grows older these relationships include widespread areas of

---

[11] C. H. Cooley, *Social Organization*, New York, Charles Scribner's Sons, 1909.

urban and rural communities. For example, at the age of eighteen, the youth may have close friends in his immediate neighborhood, in a fraternity which is composed of boys from widespread areas of the country, and, if he is a radio enthusiast, he may have friends whom he has never seen but whom he contacts by short wave.

In primitive societies, nearly all the relationships of members to one another are of the primary type. All members of the community are well known to one another and contacts are satisfying and frequent. It is only when the membership of a society becomes too large that primary relationships diminish and relationships of the secondary type predominate. In our society, formal relationships have tended to succeed the informal.

SECONDARY RELATIONSHIPS. Secondary relationships are impersonal, brief, and anonymous. They are secondary from the point of view of being of less importance to the individual in his personal life than the primary. Examples of secondary relationships are found in the contacts of the individual with institutions. A man may go into a store to purchase a tie. In so doing, he goes into the store as an anonymous person, broadly categorized as a "customer." He meets a person who is one of a group broadly classified as "salesmen." This salesman shows him a tie. He purchases it and leaves the store. The contact has been extremely brief. It has been for a definite purpose and is terminated once the purpose has been fulfilled. Neither the customer nor the salesman has experienced more than one aspect of the personality of the other; neither has seen the other as a person; neither knows more about the other than what was seen during this particular transaction.

All the more formal aspects of human activity in our society take on this characteristic of anonymity. Individuals are classified by the majority of the members of a society under broad headings, as it is only in primary relationships that individuals are partially freed from group stereotypes. The broad categories into which individuals are placed become symbols which guide thinking and acting. Individuals have a general idea of how a policeman, a workman, a politician, and a minister should look and act, and they govern their thinking by these general ideas or "stereotypes," with little knowledge of what the persons filling these statuses are really like. These stereotypes are based on those aspects of the role which can be readily seen during brief and impersonal contacts with others.

The individuals who function within the institutional structure of a society hold certain statuses and, in accordance with them, they play out their roles. Through the secondary relationships of the individual with these formal groups, he becomes acquainted with a much wider variety of roles than is possible for him in his primary relationships. However, these roles and statuses are seen by the outsider only in part. For example, he sees the role which the sales-girl plays when dealing with a customer, but he rarely sees the role she plays in relation to her employer and her family.

IN-GROUP AND OUT-GROUP RELATIONSHIPS. On the basis of loyalty and a feeling of belonging, the relationships of the individual may be classified as in-group and out-group relationships. Due to the transient character of the loyalty of individuals who can be mobilized in different permutations and combinations around differ-ent issues, this is a less satisfactory division than primary and sec-ondary. There are, however, many occasions when this means of classification permits better understanding of a situation, for ex-ample, in conflict situations.

The relationship of the individual to an in-group is characterized by a conviction that he and the members of the in-group share com-mon aims and interests, a feeling of social unity, cooperation, sym-pathy, and identification. When speaking of the in-group, the individual refers to them as "we." The out-group is composed of all those who are not members of the in-group, and especially those who actively disagree. His relationships with these people are the opposite of those with the in-group and he thinks of the out-group as "they."

From the foregoing it would seem that primary relationships and in-group relationships are very similar. What distinguishes them is that the in-group does not necessarily consist of people who have face-to-face relationships, or with whom contact is maintained. In-cluded in the in-group may be people one has never seen and whose names are unknown. For example, in the Second World War, for the individual in America, the peoples who belonged to the Allied group constituted the in-group, the "we," while those who made up the Axis powers were the out-group, the "they." The in-group may vary in size from a family or friendship group, to an ethnic group, a church society, a nation or group of nations. It might include groups with whom the individual had primary relationships or it might cut across them. At times the children of the family constitute an in-group and each of them thinks of his parents as members of the out-group in certain typical situations. In Nazi Germany, the members of a family who were members of the Nazi Party were an in-group and their relationships with the non-party members of the family were of an out-group type.

The person thinks of his in-group as "right" and gives it uncritical loyalty. Such an attitude is known as *ethnocentrism,* that is, the tendency of a person or group of persons to judge other groups by the standards of judgment prevailing in their own group.[12] For example, the Hebrew thinks of himself as one of the "chosen people"; the Nazi thought of himself as one of the "master race." The upper-class American regards the lower-class American as irresponsible and coarse. The white man regards the colored person as childlike and inferior. Thus do the members of countries, races, communities, families, institutions, and other groups pay tribute to their own inner sanctities.[13]

Relationships of the Individual with Specific Groups.—It is through the relationships of the individual with the subgroups of his society that he learns the acceptable patterns of behavior of that larger social group. At birth, he has not the requisites of group status. The newborn infant is merely an organization of constitutional or biological qualities, characterized by undefined and inchoate impulses. However, the human infant differs from the newborn animal in that he is mutable and has the ability to learn a wide range of responses. As Professor Cooley says,

Animal conduct, as broadly contrasted with human, is a system of fixed hereditary responses to fixed stimuli; the instinct is like a hand organ which will play certain tunes whenever you turn the crank, and will play no others no matter what you do. . . .

The distinctive thing in human evolution, on the other hand, is the development of a process which is not fixed but plastic, which adapts itself directly to each particular situation, and is capable of an indefinite number of appropriate and successful modes of action. . . . The hereditary tendencies, instead of remaining definite and fixed, have to become vague and plastic in order that they may be moulded into the infinitely various forms of human conduct. The hand-organ has become a piano, which will yield no tune at all except under the touch of a trained player, but under such a touch, it is capable of infinite melody.

The player, to carry out the analogy, is the human intelligence trained by working with the social environment. This is the agent through which situations are understood and hereditary tendencies organized to meet them.[14]

---

12 John F. Cuber, *Sociology: A Synopsis of Principles,* New York, D. Appleton-Century Co., Inc., 1947, p. 82.
13 Kimball Young, *Personality and the Problems of Adjustment,* New York, F. S. Crofts & Co., 1940, p. 129.
14 C. H. Cooley, *Social Processes,* New York, Charles Scribner's Sons, 1922, pp. 198-199.

It is clear that the infant finds the pattern for the release of his impulses already in operation in group life. These patterns give definition and direction to his original nature potentialities with respect to food, elimination, sex, and movement. On learning these patterns, the child fits into the established ways of life which his society requires. If, for example, he belongs to Balinese society, he is fed at any time during the day or night that he desires. If, however, he is born into American society, he is quite likely to be fed only at those times specified by a medical adviser. Even with regard to such matters as the child's freedom of movement, different societies have varying definitions of what is appropriate. The Kwakiutl Indians strap him to a board, which makes movement impossible until after the first six months to a year. The Balinese infant is hung in a sling on the side of his sister, from which position he is forced to adjust to all her movements as she plays. In America, the child is left unhampered, free to move his limbs as he chooses. Each of these definitions of what is appropriate in child rearing forces the infant into the pattern which is acceptable to his society. Such adjustments become organized into stable ways of meeting specific problems.[15]

As he goes through life, the person learns an increasing number of the patterns of behavior which his society approves. As he passes from childhood to adulthood and to old age, his statuses change and with each change he assumes different rights and obligations, behaves differently, and thinks differently. However, the basic organization of his personality, which is mainly formed in childhood, acts as a central theme throughout his life around which status changes, behavior changes, and attitude changes are organized.

THE FAMILY. The group which plays the most important part in the life of an individual is the family. The function of this social group is basically the same everywhere and has changed but little down through time. It is composed of persons who are responsible for the physical security of the child, and for transmitting to him the patterns of behavior appropriate to his society.

During the early years of the child's life, the family is the only group with which he has continuous contact. This is especially true of American society. Through this social group, he is introduced to

---

[15] H. Blumer, "Social Psychology," in E. P. Schmidt (Ed.), *Man and Society*, pp. 152-155; Margaret Mead and Gregory Bateson, *Balinese Character*, Spec. Pubs. of the New York Academy of Sciences, Vol. 2, 1942; Ralph Linton, *The Cultural Background of Personality*, New York, D. Appleton-Century Co., Inc., 1945, p. 50; Clellan S. Ford, *Smoke from Their Fires*, New Haven, Yale University Press, 1941; J. Dollard, L. W. Doob, N. E. Miller, O. H. Mowrer, and R. T. Sears, *Frustration and Aggression*, New Haven, Yale University Press, 1939; Linton, *The Study of Man*, p. 69.

the way of life of his society. One of the first patterns of behavior with which he comes into contact is the form of marriage which his society approves. If he is a member of our society, his family will probably be monogamous, that is, it will consist of one man and one woman and their children. If he is born into some other society, the definition of what constitutes a family group might be very different. Each society has worked out a pattern of marriage in keeping with the necessities of its life. For example, polyandry is usually correlated with hard economic conditions and the need for limiting the population. Polygyny is found usually where there is a shortage of men.[16] The child might also be born into a society where the family does not form a biological unit. In some societies, if paternity is indeterminate, the mother's husband is recognized as the social father of the child and acts as if the relationship were real. Such a situation is to be found among the Kaingang Indians of South America.[17] Among the Nayar, the family consists of the mother and children and there is no place in their arrangement for husbands and fathers. Although families consisting of biologically related persons are most frequent, there are many variations existing in the world today. However, the main function of the family—that is, the raising of children to biological and social maturity—persists regardless of the form of marriage or the structure of the family group.

It is within the family group that the child finds his status in his community and his society. Through participation in family life he discovers that he has certain rights and securities and certain obligations. As he passes through more and more situations, he discovers the roles he is expected to play and his status in the family. For example, if an American child breaks his mother's favorite vase, the situation is defined for him as "not permissible," the mother is defined as the source of authority, and the child's status is defined as being subordinate to the authority of the mother.

Through constant intercommunication, close contact, and similar interests, the child comes to share in the esprit de corps of the family and gains a strong emotional attachment to its members. Within the first years of his life, he learns to organize and manage these emotions of affection, hostility, aggression, and dependence. If this is not done early in life, the unmanaged emotions interfere with his stable personality development.[18]

---

16 Linton, *The Study of Man*, pp. 182-187.
17 Jules Henry, *Jungle People*, Richmond, The William Byrd Press, 1944; Linton, *The Study of Man*, p. 154.
18 W. A. Davis and R. J. Havighurst, *Father of the Man*, Boston, Houghton Mifflin Co., 1947, p. 35.

In the family, the child is also introduced to some of the material objects of which his society makes use. Toward these objects and in relation to them, he develops the approved attitudes and habits of his society. An American child who is accustomed to sitting in chairs develops very different habits and attitudes from the Balinese child who is accustomed to squatting on his haunches or sitting on the ground. The American child who has been taught to sleep in a bed would find it very uncomfortable to sleep on mats on the floor as does the Samoan child. The American child, taught to eat with implements, would feel ill at ease and rather crude eating food with his fingers as even adults do in Samoa, because his society defines such a method of eating as "ill bred." [19]

The child also comes to participate in the subgroups of his society, of which his family are members. In Western civilization,[20] one of the most important of such social groupings is the *social class*. In America, the social class to which a family belongs is usually determined by income and the occupation of the family wage earner. Each social class has characteristic patterns of behavior. The family, because of its membership in one of the three major classes, limits the primary contacts of the child to those of its own class. Rarely, for example, does the child of a laborer play with the child of a bank manager in the urbanized American society. Through the family and his other primary contacts, the child finds his place in the community and adopts the patterns of behavior appropriate to those with whom he spends the majority of his time.[21]

In simpler societies, the contacts of the child are also limited, although often not as rigidly as in the more complex urban life of Western societies. For example, the French-Canadian child of a habitant family spends most of his time with relatives until he has reached adulthood.[22]

In a basic sense, the family gives the individual his first conception of himself as a person, his position in his community and social class. It also sets the problems which he must face in enhancing his social security and his status. In our society, the child acquires a place in the community by being born into a family to which the community has ascribed a status. The problems of enhancing social security and

---

[19] Linton, *The Study of Man*, p. 468; Margaret Mead and Gregory Bateson, *Balinese Character;* Margaret Mead, *Coming of Age in Samoa*, New York, William Morrow & Co., Inc., 1928, p. 10.

[20] By "civilization" is meant a society in which social groupings and patterns of behavior are more complex than in a simple society such as the "folk society."

[21] W. L. Warner and P. S. Lunt, *The Social Life of a Modern Community*, New Haven, Yale University Press, 1941; Linton, *The Study of Man*, pp. 468-469.

[22] Horace Miner, *St. Denis*, Chicago, University of Chicago Press, 1939, p. 177.

status derive almost directly from the status of his family and the means provided by his society for rising or falling from that social position. In American society, there are many opportunities for the individual to climb socially. This society allows many desirable statuses to be filled by those with initiative or a good education. Even in America, however, certain statuses are limited to a single sex, to certain age groups and ethnic and racial backgrounds, or by heredity. Among many other societies, birth is the major determinant of the individual's status. However, all societies leave some openings for those with special talents. Among the Zuñi Indians, although most advances in social position are determined by birth and family membership, some positions are open by virtue of special abilities or ambitions. For example, ritual means are provided for entering the highly respected Medicine Society or the War cult. For both American and Zuñi children the problems of enhancing their status and security are set almost entirely by the position of their families in the social order of their society.[23]

The family is also of primary importance to the new member in the interpretation of the aims and interests of the community. In our society, many conflicting opinions and objectives are prevalent at all times. In the midst of these conflicting objectives and opinions, the family is the chief adjudicator for its members. Its interpretation of social goals is given priority through the strong emotional ties which bind the members of the family together. In addition, in our society, the adult members of the family are always ready to go into play against the wayward member. In more primitive societies, the conflicts in the ideologies of their composite families are much less severe, and the use of authority in controlling children is much less necessary as the community's controls come into operation to back up the family.[24]

THE NEIGHBORHOOD. In teaching the child the ways of his society, the neighborhood is next in importance to the family. It exerts a strong degree of social control on the families living within its boundaries.[25] The *neighborhood* is composed of those families which know a great deal about each other's affairs, borrow from one another, visit back and forth, and come under the rule of sentiment

23 Mead, *Growing Up in Samoa*, pp. 237-238; R. S. Lynd and H. M. Lynd, *Middletown*, New York, Harcourt, Brace & Co., Inc., 1929, p. 132; Linton, *The Study of Man*, pp. 126-129; Ruth Benedict, "The Western Pueblos," in *Patterns of Culture*, Boston (copyright Houghton Mifflin Co.), 1934, pp. 52-119.

24 Mead, *Growing Up in Samoa*, p. 241; Lynd and Lynd, Middletown, p. 133; Davis and Havighurst, *Father of the Man*, p. 44.

25 Peter Blos, *The Adolescent Personality*, New York, D. Appleton-Century Co., Inc., 1941, p. 8.

and gossip. It is not necessarily made up of those who live within a limited geographic area.

The neighborhood sets the standards of behavior which are expected from the families within its boundaries and exerts pressure upon those who deviate from its norms. Whatever may be the tendencies for any family to become eccentric or marginal, the neighborhood observes and, in subtle ways, makes known its social expectations. Direct pressure may be brought to bear on the deviant family by ostracizing it. This family may also feel an indirect pressure to conform to others in the neighborhood when its children begin to compare their way of life with that of other families and find their own lacking. In a sheerly material sense, this situation was described by E. L. Koos in his book *Families in Trouble.*[26] He tells of one family of very low income which was attempting to pay its way without going into debt. They bought no new furniture but kept the old possessions spotlessly clean and in good repair. The children of the family, who had been in most of the other homes in the neighborhood—these other homes being garishly decorated with time-payment furniture—refused to bring their friends home for fear of being laughed at. The difference in the furnishing of the houses posed an acute problem for the children of the deviant family, who tended to withdraw gradually from social relationships. After the individual's sense of self in the immediate family, the most important consideration to him is the social position of his family in the eyes of its neighbors, regardless of whether that neighborhood is in the immediate geographic vicinity or is more widely distributed.

Of equally great importance to the child are those play groups which are linked to the immediate geographic neighborhood. In the more stable residential areas, these play groups are composed of the children of physically proximate families. As can be seen from the preceding paragraph, the children within a given local area play together and are notable participants in a trend to bring their families under a common form of living and a common way of looking at things.

Through his family, the urban child has contacts with neighborhood institutions which exert considerable influence on the behavior of their members. The church influences the religious viewpoint of the adults and children who attend, and in many ways affects their behavior toward one another through its ethical teachings. The schools, in addition to teaching the child reading and writing, play

---

[26] E. L. Koos, *Families in Trouble*, New York, King's Crown Press, 1946, p. 38.

a great part in orienting the child's viewpoint to that considered acceptable by his society and thus helping him through his difficulties in socialization.

The members of the family find their status and role in the neighborhood and area institutions. The father of the family may be active in the local veterans' group and through this affiliation derive prestige. This affiliation also conditions what is expected of him by the community. They will look to him for aid in matters which pertain to his special interests. Similarly the child finds his status and role through the church, the school, and the Y. M. C. A. or equivalent types of institutions. The members of the family exercise the statuses they have derived from their neighborhood institutions to influence the behavior and attitudes of those with whom they have primary relationships.[27]

THE FRIENDSHIP GROUP OF CONTEMPORARIES. Beyond these intimate group affiliations of the family, the neighborhood, and the neighborhood play group lie the relationships of the individual with comrades, buddies, chums, friends, and others. Through intimate contact the child finds these latter groups to be dynamic forces in introducing him to the ways of his society. One function of the primary relationships of close friends is the transmission of certain patterns of behavior within the same age group. Although the family transmits most of the patterns to its children, there are certain aspects which it does not know or will not pass on to the child. The child tends to learn such patterns of behavior as games, skipping rhymes, and slang expressions from his contemporaries. These are patterns which his parents do not know or have forgotten. In addition, there are behavior patterns which the family will not transmit. For example, in American society, parents are reticent in giving their children knowledge of sexual behavior. The child tends to learn the "facts of life" and the norms for relationships between the sexes from his own age group. Frequently the parents are completely ignorant of their children's knowledge of such matters or become extremely upset concerning it.[28]

Another function of the intimate groupings of those of the same age is the sharing of experience and the emotional support given to the individual by members of a group with whom he has common interests and behavior. Such groups tend to have values and appreciations distinctive to themselves. In American society, where

---

27 *Ibid.*, p. 86; Warner and Lunt, *The Social Life of a Modern Community*, pp. 128-201.
28 Koos, *Families in Trouble*, p. 40; Blos, *The Adolescent Personality*, p. 251.

there is such a marked gap between the interests and activities of parents and children, the role played by the child's intimate friendship group is extremely important in lending support to the behavior of the child. The wish to be approved by his own age group becomes a dominant force in his life, and his actions tend to follow the definitions of his group, rather than those of his family.[29]

It is also of primary importance that the individual learn to get along with those outside of his immediate family group. Belonging to a play group or gang helps the child to do this and prepares him for the new behavior which will be expected of him in adult life. Family behavior and attitude patterns are gradually modified in favor of those approved by his own group.[30]

SECONDARY RELATIONSHIPS OF THE PERSON. As the person reaches adulthood, he exercises more self-determination in group relationships. Through his contacts at school, the current printed page, the radio, special friends, and other influences he becomes more individually aggressive in selecting the groups with which he wishes to have contacts. This does not necessarily mean that his primary relationships have been effaced. Indeed, the primary relationships have conditioned to a large extent the way he reacts to other groups.[31] With wider contacts and experience he can see other aspects of the teachings of his earlier groups which permit him greater choice of the new groups in which he now wishes to participate. In the meantime, his struggle for a place in the group into which he was thrust primarily by birth, race, or locality has changed and become extended to the wider community and the world. At this point the individual has become a participating member of his society.

There are, however, certain factors which will inhibit full participation in societies. For example, in America, if the person is a member of a minority group—and especially if he possesses racial physical characteristics or has patterns of behavior identified by the majority as belonging to the minority group—he finds his social participation limited. For the majority group, these characteristics are symbolic of the individual belonging to an "out-group" and call forth crystal clear value-judgments which favor either group entrance or rejection. For example, a person who has only recently come to America from the British Isles is marked by his accent for what he is, but the attitudes called forth on the part of the majority group would

29 Blos, *The Adolescent Personality*, p. 251.
30 *Ibid.*, pp. 250-253.
31 Blos, *The Adolescent Personality*, p. 6; Davis and Havighurst, *Father of the Man*, pp. 43-44.

probably be favorable to group acceptance. In the south of the United States, a person with Negroid characteristics evokes immediate attitudes of superior status in the majority group. It should be pointed out, however, that in any given area these majority group attitudes concerning acceptance or rejection of a minority group may be modified by special conditions. In general, however, the cultural definitions of the accepted and rejected racial elements prevail. Much of the modification of these attitudes rests on the luck and behavior of the "exceptional" member of the minority group.

The processes which have been broadly outlined above hold, along with certain variations which exist in any given area, regardless of the culture to which the individual belongs and regardless of the ideologies of those cultures. Among the Samoans and the Zuñi, the family plays an even greater part in the socialization of the individual than does the family in the modern Western industrial world, but the basic process is unaltered. The process of socialization may also be varied in the great ideological divisions of the present world, of which the two poles are collectivist Russia and individualistic North America with vast interstitial areas influenced by both ideologies.

Group Relationships and Social Control.—The socialization of the person occurs through his relationships with a variety of the subgroups of his society. If, as in a small town, contacts are with a limited number of groups whose membership is relatively constant, the person is able to form a relatively clear and consistent picture of his status and the roles which he is required to play. His status is even more clearly defined if mobility has been slight and his family has lived in the same place for three or four generations. If such is the case, the pattern for the person's life and the expectations of the community concerning his roles are clearly defined. An example of this control of the person through the expectations of the community on the basis of family background is found in Warner and Lunt's study of Yankee City.[32] Miss Elizabeth Breckenridge, a member of the upper class and of a family which had maintained that position in Yankee City for generations, was expected to act the part of the traditional Breckenridge lady. Following the expectations of the family meant certain unhappiness, but the controls and pressures to make her conform to the expected behavior were so strong that she could not break away.

In America, the tendency has been to move to new areas, with a resultant reduction of the influence of family heritages on the roles

---

32 Warner and Lunt, *The Social Life of a Modern Community*, pp. 135-137.

and status of the average citizen. In this country, the individual's status is determined not so much by birth as by occupation and income. The roles he plays are expected to be in accordance with his economic position rather than his family heritage. When meeting new people, Americans tend to ask, "What does he do for a living?" rather than "Who were his family?" while older societies are more likely to follow the latter pattern. As mobility in economic positions is also high, the person must have a wide diversity of roles at his command.[33]

Through high mobility, the person's affiliations with neighborhood groups and institutions are also in a state of flux and suffer reductions. Church memberships become less or cease entirely, clubs change membership at a rapid pace, and all groups lose their control upon the behavior of the individual. As he moves from group to group, the strong emotional ties which held his behavior under their control are weakened. The outcome of such a situation is that the person becomes responsible to himself alone for his behavior. With no strong group controls and no definitions of appropriate behavior which are absolute, the person improvises new definitions for the situations which lack group definition. As a result, he tends to come under the control of current aims and sentiments.[34]

The high mobility so characteristic of America has given rise to a new idea of appropriate behavior for the person. Whereas social control in more static societies is effected through the group membership of the person, the group defining the appropriate behavior and disciplining the individual who does not conform,

The only limitation placed on his [the American's] magnificent independence and mastery of his personal destiny, is that imposed by his conscience, by the personal rights of others and by the law. Thus the social group impinges on this symbolic American and modifies his independence. Whether the rights of others exert their pressure internally as the force of conscience or externally as the law, the effect is the same, and personal liberty must thereby be curbed.[35]

Society's controls have become indirect, rather than direct. Group membership controls the person from a distance, through definitions and values learned mainly in childhood which retain their emotional connotations in later life. Through participation in the broader

---

[33] Margaret Mead, *And Keep Your Powder Dry*, New York, William Morrow & Co., Inc., 1942, p. 65.
[34] *Ibid.*, p. 74; Linton, *The Study of Man*, p. 95.
[35] R. Grinker and J. P. Spiegel, *Men Under Stress*, Philadelphia, The Blakiston Co., 1945, p. 445.

society, only those values which are characteristic of the society as a whole remain as compulsives to govern the behavior of the individual member.

Group Unity

On what basis does any group, whether its membership is stable and continuous or highly mobile and constantly changing, become a unit? How do its members become motivated by common goals, whether these goals be implicit or explicit?

The school of instinct psychology answers these questions by saying that man is by nature gregarious. Those who upheld this view felt that man's social alignment with others was determined by his biological inheritance, which only abnormal conditions could prevent.[36]

This general notion fell apart with the fall of instinct psychology, which was given its greatest blow by Professor John Dewey when his book *Human Nature and Conduct* was published in 1922.[37] Dewey and a host of his followers maintained that man inherits a bundle of undefined impulses and that at birth random behavior is most obvious to all observers. Even Watson's primary emotions of fear, rage, and love succumbed to the general onslaught on instinct psychology. More recent research, with its careful control of laboratory conditions, has backed up the theories Professor Dewey put forward.[38]

The explanation for group unity lies in the individual's taking over, from birth onward, the social habits of which his society approves. From his interaction with others with whom is he in constant contact, the new member learns the established ways of his society. These group ways are accepted as absolutes and gradually, through learning an increased number of these ways, the person becomes a full-fledged member of the society, acting out his roles and transmitting the proper behavior patterns to other newer members of the society.

The ability of the person to learn these group ways is based on his capacity for language and abstract thought. This subject will be given a more detailed treatment in a later chapter. Suffice it to say here that language arises from group interaction. It could not

[36] W. Trotter, *Instincts of the Herd in Peace and War*, New York, The Macmillan Co., 1916; William McDougall, *Introduction to Social Psychology*, Boston, John W. Luce & Co., 1909.

[37] John Dewey, *Human Nature and Conduct*, New York, Henry Holt & Co., Inc., 1922.

[38] G. Murphy and L. Murphy, *Experimental Social Psychology*, New York, Harper & Bros., 1931; Carl Murchison (Ed.), *Handbook of Social Psychology*, Worcester, Mass., Clark University Press, 1935; M. Sherif and H. Cantril, *The Psychology of Ego-Involvements*, New York, John Wiley & Sons, Inc., 1947.

develop within a social vacuum. And language is basic to the ability to think.[39]

A language system requires the continued presence of other persons in order to stimulate and organize it. A babble of sounds is given group definition, is organized into words and sentences, and becomes a homogeneous language. Speech is taken over by the new members of a society in much the same manner as other social habits.[40]

The importance of language to the unity of the social group is that it extends enormously the means of interacting with others. Through speech, radio, and the printed page, members of the society put forward and repeat its norms and, through constant repetition, reinforce them. It enhances social solidarity in this way and greatly broadens the numbers of persons who can feel common interests, who can share common experiences and seek common goals. Esprit de corps is on a much wider scale and the unity of society is consequently more complete.

QUESTIONS

1. Define social group. Discuss the sociologist's interest in social groups.
2. What are some of the more important social groups in the life of the individual?
3. Distinguish between primary and secondary relationships and give examples of each. What is their importance to the individual?
4. What is meant by a division of labor? What is its role in society? Give examples of the division of labor in America, based on age, sex, and race.
5. What forms of human behavior are necessary for group living? How do they emerge?
6. How are the society's patterns of behavior transmitted down through time? How do changes come about in these patterns?
7. What are ideal patterns of behavior?
8. Define social system.
9. What is the relationship of the individual to his society?
10. Define society.
11. Discuss the importance of esprit de corps to a society.
12. Define status and role. What is meant by the statement that "status and role serve to reduce the ideal patterns for social life into individual terms"?
13. "Individuals find their status and role through participation in groups." Discuss.

---

[39] Davis and Havighurst, *Father of the Man*, pp. 167-215; Young, *Personality and the Problems of Adjustment*, p. 139.
[40] Young, *Personality and the Problems of Adjustment*, pp. 155-159.

14. What are in-group and out-group relationships? How are these relationships determined? Give examples.
15. "At birth the infant does not possess the requisites of group status." Discuss.
16. What does Cooley say about animal conduct as contrasted with human conduct?
17. Why is the family the most important group in the life of an individual?
18. What is the importance of the neighborhood, the play group, the friendship group of contemporaries, and secondary relationships in introducing the person to the ways of his society?
19. What part do group relationships play in controlling individual behavior?
20. What effect does mobility have on group affiliations? on social control?
21. Outline briefly some of the theories used in the past to explain how the social group comes to act as a unit.

BIBLIOGRAPHY

ARNOLD, THURMAN. *The Folklore of Capitalism.* New Haven, Yale University Press, 1937.

BENEDICT, RUTH. *Patterns of Culture.* Boston (copyright, Houghton Mifflin Co.), 1934.

BLOS, PETER. *The Adolescent Personality.* New York, D. Appleton-Century Co., Inc., 1941.

BLUMER, H. "Social Psychology," in E. P. Schmidt (Ed.), *Man and Society.* New York, Prentice-Hall, Inc., 1938.

BODENHAFER, WALTER B. "The Comparative Role of the Group Concept in Ward's *Dynamic Sociology* and Contemporary American Sociology." *Am. J. Sociol.,* Vol. 26, No. 3, November, 1920, pp. 273-314; No. 4, January, 1921, pp. 425-474; No. 5, March, 1921, pp. 588-600; No. 6, May, 1921, pp. 716-743.

BROWN, B. WARREN. *Social Groups.* Chicago, The Faithorn Co., 1926.

BURGESS, E. W. *Personality and the Group.* Chicago, University of Chicago Press, 1929.

BURGESS, E. W., AND COTTRELL, L. S. *Predicting Success or Failure in Marriage.* New York, Prentice-Hall, Inc., 1939.

COOLEY, C. H. *Human Nature and the Social Order.* New York, Charles Scribner's Sons, 1902.

COOLEY, C. H. *Social Organization.* New York, Charles Scribner's Sons, 1909.

COOLEY, C. H. *Social Processes.* New York, Charles Scribner's Sons, 1922.

COYLE, G. L. *Social Processes in Organized Groups.* New York, Richard R. Smith, 1930.

CUBER, J. F. *Sociology: A Synopsis of Principles.* New York, D. Appleton-Century Co., Inc., 1947.

DAVIS, W. A., AND HAVIGHURST, R. J. *Father of the Man.* Boston, Houghton Mifflin Co., 1947.

DEWEY, JOHN. *Human Nature and Conduct.* New York, Henry Holt & Co., Inc., 1922.

DOLLARD, J., DOOB, L. W., MILLER, N. E., MOWRER, O. H., AND SEARS, R. T. *Frustration and Aggression.* New Haven, Yale University Press, 1939.

FARIS, E. "The Primary Group: Essence and Accident." *Am. J. Sociol.,* Vol. 38, No. 1, July, 1932, pp. 41-50.

FORD, CLELLAN S. *Smoke from Their Fires.* New Haven, Yale University Press. 1941.

GILLIN, JOHN. *The Ways of Men.* New York, Appleton-Century-Crofts, Inc., 1948.

GRINKER, R., AND SPIEGEL, J. *Men Under Stress.* Philadelphia, The Blakiston Co., 1945.

HENRY, JULES. *Jungle People.* Richmond, The William Byrd Press, 1944.

HILLER, E. T. *Social Relations and Structures.* New York, Harper & Bros., 1947.

HUGHES, E. C. *The Growth of an Institution: The Chicago Real Estate Board.* Chicago, The Society for Social Research of the University of Chicago, 1931.

KARDINER, A. *The Individual and His Society.* New York, Columbia University Press, 1939.

KOOS, E. L. *Families in Trouble.* New York, King's Crown Press, 1946.

LINTON, RALPH. *The Study of Man.* New York, Appleton-Century-Crofts, Inc., 1936.

LINTON, RALPH. *The Cultural Background of Personality.* New York, D. Appleton-Century Co., Inc., 1945.

LIPPMANN, WALTER. *Public Opinion.* New York, The Macmillan Co., 1941.

LUNDBERG, G. A. *Foundations of Sociology.* New York, The Macmillan Co., 1939.

LYND, R. S., AND LYND, H. M. *Middletown.* New York, Harcourt, Brace & Co., 1929.

McCLENAHAN, BESSIE AVERNE. *The Changing Urban Neighborhood.* Los Angeles, University of Southern California Press, 1929.

McDOUGALL, WILLIAM. *Introduction to Social Psychology.* Boston, John W. Luce & Co., 1909.

MEAD, MARGARET. *Coming of Age in Samoa.* New York, William Morrow & Co., Inc., 1928.

MEAD, MARGARET. *And Keep Your Powder Dry.* New York, William Morrow & Co., Inc., 1942.

MEAD, MARGARET, AND BATESON, GREGORY. *Balinese Character.* Spec. Pubs. of the New York Academy of Sciences, Vol. 2, 1942.

MINER, HORACE. *St. Denis.* Chicago, University of Chicago Press, 1939.

MONACHESI, E. D. "Sociology and Culture," in E. P. Schmidt (Ed.), *Man and Society,* New York, Prentice-Hall, Inc., 1938, pp. 1-54.

MURPHY, G., MURPHY, L. B., AND NEWCOMB, T. M. *Experimental Social Psychology.* New York, Harper & Bros., 1935.

PLANT, J. S. *Personality and the Culture Pattern.* New York, The Commonwealth Fund, 1937.

SHERIF, M., AND CANTRIL, H. *The Psychology of Ego-Involvements.* New York, John Wiley & Sons, Inc., 1947.

SPENCER, H. *The Principles of Sociology, II.* London, Williams & Norgate, Ltd., 1893.

SPYKMAN, N. J. *The Social Theory of Georg Simmel.* Chicago, University of Chicago Press, 1925.

SUMNER, W. G. *Folkways.* Boston, Ginn & Co., 1906.

TROTTER, W. *Instincts of the Herd in Peace and War.* New York, The Macmillan Co., 1916.

WARNER, W. L., AND LUNT, P. S. *The Social Life of a Modern Community.* New Haven, Yale University Press, 1941.

WHYTE, W. F. *Street Corner Society.* Chicago, University of Chicago Press, 1943.

YOUNG, KIMBALL. *Personality and the Problems of Adjustment.* New York, Appleton-Century-Crofts, Inc., 1947.

ZNANIECKI, F. "Social Groups as Products of Cooperating Individuals." *Am. J. Sociol.,* Vol. 44, No. 6, May, 1939, pp. 799-811.

Chapter 2

CULTURE

The preceding chapter described the relationship which exists between the person, his society, and the groups which compose it. It traced the process whereby the person develops from a biological organism at birth into a socialized person through his relationships with the groups which make up his society. Through his participation in group life, he is acquainted with the tools and material objects of his society; he learns and acts out the patterns of behavior which his society approves and transmits them to the next generation; he comes to hold ideas and points of view which his society condones or rewards; he accepts the institutional organization of his society and participates in and adds to his society's methods of adjusting to its environment. These things which the person learns can be broadly grouped under the heading of culture.

Characteristics of Culture.—The culture of a society is the *means by which that group has solved its problems*—biological, environmental, and social. Each society experiences different problems in its evolution and meets them in its own characteristic way. Thus it is that historically no two societies have ever developed the same culture. Each has its own means of training the individual to participate in, to believe in, and to be controlled by the patterns of behavior which it considers appropriate.

Culture is a *social phenomenon,* that is, it is a means of dealing with the problems of a group of men, which those men have worked out themselves.[1] The tools which men use may be physical objects but they are also social in that they were invented by men, ascribed specific uses by men, and surrounded with man-made ideas concerning the means of manipulation and their importance. Man himself is a biological organism with basic physical requirements, but the means by which his physical requirements are met are social.

The culture of a society is an *abstract*. It cannot be seen. However, it can be deduced by observing the ways in which people act, the

---

[1] John Gillin, *The Ways of Men,* New York, Appleton-Century-Crofts, Inc., 1948, p. 176.

thoughts they express, and the tools they use. In the words of Kluckhohn and Kelly:

> . . . culture is like a map. Just as a map isn't the territory but an abstract representation of the territory, so also a culture is an abstract description of trends toward uniformity in the words, acts, and artifacts of human groups.[2]

The culture of a society is an *integration* of all the patterns of behavior, attitudes, and artifacts which are to be found within that society. In the previous chapter it was pointed out that within a society there are many subdivisions which, as it were, have a priority on certain of these patterns of behavior, attitudes, and artifacts. The members of the other subdivisions of the society might not be aware that these even exist. Even if they do know, however, they would probably never have occasion to put their knowledge to use. For example, there are many patterns of behavior, attitudes, and artifacts in occupational groups which those outside these groups know little about. The manner of using, for instance, the pneumatic drill and the ideas associated with it are a part of American culture, yet it is a part which is known by only a very small segment of the total membership of that society.

The culture of a society is *selectively cumulative*. One generation finds a solution to a new problem which has arisen and when the solution has been accepted by the group as the appropriate means of dealing with that problem, it has become a part of the culture. The solution is transmitted to subsequent generations. In this way, culture is cumulative. However, if the problem ceases to exist, and there is no longer a need for the solution, it is dropped and the next generation will be ignorant of it. No way of acting is taken over or perpetuated in the group unless it is of value in the adaptation or adjustment of individuals.[3] In this way, culture is selective.

However, there are culture patterns and artifacts which persist even though the usefulness of the pattern for adjustment seems to have passed. Upon investigating the reasons for such *cultural survivals,* as they are called, it is usually found that they have changed their function and have come to fulfill a need different from that for which they were originally intended. For example, in Montreal, although the automobile, bus, and streetcar have replaced the horse and buggy for all practical purposes of transportation, a certain number are still used in the city. But now, instead of being primarily a

[2] C. Kluckhohn and W. H. Kelly, "The Concept of Culture," in Ralph Linton (Ed.), *The Science of Man in the World Crisis*, New York, Columbia University Press, 1945, p. 93.
[3] *Ibid.*, p. 86.

means of transportation, they serve the purpose of making the city more "picturesque" in answer to the need for novelty in order to attract a tourist trade.

Although culture is basically the solution to man's needs, certain patterns have been *overelaborated,* that is, developed far beyond the point where increased efficiency results. Every society elaborates some aspects of its culture beyond the level of necessity while other aspects remain barely efficient for meeting its needs. No two societies tend to elaborate the same aspects. For example, the courtesy systems of the Chinese and Japanese are elaborated far beyond the requirements for smooth social intercourse. The Christian religion has been elaborated far beyond the requisites for faith and the adequate solution of individual crises. Such overelaborations as these satisfy esthetic needs or give prestige but only because these are the values which the society has attached to them.

Some of these overelaborations are carried to the point where they even endanger the continued existence of the group. For example, the Kaingang Indians of South America developed their feuding system to the point where it threatened to wipe out the whole tribe. The Kwakiutl Indians of British Columbia developed the lending and destruction of property to the extent that the Canadian Government felt it necessary to pass legislation against it. The Cocopa Indians of the United States developed their death ceremonies to the extent that burial of a family member impoverished the relatives. However, even though survival is threatened, such overelaborations persist because they perform a function within the culture, even though the need they satisfy is one which has been socially created.[4]

Not only does culture tend to satisfy man's basic needs, but it also *creates needs.* For example,

If the lore of a people states that frogs are dangerous creatures, or that it is not safe to go about at night because of were-animals or ghosts, threats are posed which do not arise out of the inexorable facts of the external world.[5]

The culture has created a fear of frogs, were-animals and ghosts, and also provides a means of resolving the fear which has been socially created. In American life, an example of a socially created need is

[4] Ralph Linton, *The Study of Man,* New York, Appleton-Century-Crofts, Inc., 1936, pp. 87-90; Jules Henry, *Jungle People,* Richmond, The William Byrd Press, Inc., 1941; Clellan S. Ford, *Smoke from Their Fires,* New Haven, Yale University Press, 1941; W. H. Kelly, "Culture and Civilization," Lecture delivered at McGill University, Montreal, Canada, as fourth in a series entitled "Lectures on Living," November 12, 1947.
[5] Kluckhohn and Kelly, "The Concept of Culture," *op. cit.,* p. 81.

the strong drive to "keep up" with the members of one's social class, even though hardship is incurred to do so. Such a pattern of behavior has no physical survival value but is as serious a matter to a group of Americans as fulfilling the actual survival requirements of eating and finding shelter.

The culture of a society is at one and the same time both *rewarding and frustrating*. It satisfies the majority of man's needs and is, in this sense, rewarding. However, it also denies expression to many of men's impulses, and is, in this sense, frustrating.[6] It places tabus on many of the aspects of behavior which man might wish to use. To cite an extreme case, an American upper-class male has been ruined in business by the dishonest tactics of another man, who has also eloped with his wife. The ruined man may have a strong inclination to kill his enemy. However, American culture does not permit this, but it does give him an opportunity for revenge by recourse to courts of law. Less sensational but more widespread evidence of the frustrating nature of culture is to be found in the prevalence of neuroses in our society.[7]

Culture is *dynamic*, that is, it is constantly changing. Even in the simple, isolated folk societies, culture is never static. In such folk societies, change may be slower and therefore more difficult to see, except by long-term observation. The slow rate of change can be partially accounted for by the limited means of communication. No writing exists and thus communication is possible only through direct contact, by word of mouth, or by example. All knowledge must be transmitted directly from one generation to the next. This knowledge consists of the accumulation of experience gained in a lifetime and those aspects which were transmitted from past generations. Under such circumstances, the older members of the society are the group who are revered as being very wise. They receive much respect and exert a great amount of influence on the life of the group. These older individuals tend to be conservative and resistant to change, and the influence they exert tends to reflect these tendencies. Social change is therefore slow.

Nor is there any opportunity for the members of such a group to compare their way of life with that of another group, or even with the culture of their own society at a different point in time. The patterns of culture which exist during their own lifetimes are the known ways and they cling to them tenaciously. To each generation,

---

6 *Ibid.*
7 Karen Horney, *The Neurotic Personality of Our Time,* New York, W. W. Norton & Co., Inc., 1937.

the existing patterns of behavior seem to be the only means of solving the problems at hand and they cannot conceive of the possibility of experimentation with new methods. Being emotionally tied to their culture, they accept it, without objective consideration of its nature, its traditions, its beliefs, and its practices.[8]

However, even in such a folk society, change does occur. As culture patterns are transmitted to new members of the group, they tend to undergo some degree of modification. A pattern may be interpreted differently by several individuals, each interpretation fitting into the needs of the person concerned, but the needs in each individual case being different. Also, as each person judges what he sees in terms of what he knows—that is, in terms of the accumulation of his past experience—and, as the members of a society have a wide range of different experiences, each individual tends to make unique interpretations of the pattern. The process whereby the interpretation of the pattern varies between individuals is somewhat parallel to what goes on in one of our American parlor games. A sentence of twenty words is whispered to the first person in a chain of ten or more people. Each, in turn, whispers to the next what he understood the sentence to be. By the time it has been reinterpreted by all present, it is rarely anything like the original statement. Similarly, culture patterns may be altered in transmission from one generation to the next. In such a manner, the culture affects the individual by giving him patterns of behavior, but the individual also affects the culture by changing these patterns to suit his personal and contemporary needs.

The other extreme in the speed of cultural change is found in our American society. Writing exists, whereby new ideas can be readily circulated and debated. Tradition has bowed to rational thinking to a large extent. There is constant experimentation, classification, and systematization of knowledge. The emphasis of our society is on youth, and older people exercise a decreasing amount of influence; thus our culture is receptive to new ideas. Through increased knowledge and the use of modern mechanisms of transportation and communication, there is constant cultural contact with other nations and peoples which facilitates the exchange of ideas. The new and the unique are constantly sought after. As Margaret Mead states, "We are dominated by the idea of progress, the idea that we can find a new and better way of life." [9] As a result, Americans tend to dis-

---

8 Robert Redfield, "The Folk Society," *Am. J. Sociol.*, Vol. 52, No. 4, January, 1947, pp. 293-309.
9 Margaret Mead, *And Keep Your Powder Dry*, New York, William Morrow & Co., Inc., 1942, p. 134.

card the old for the new, frequently without an adequate evaluation of the merits of each. They want the newest make of car, the newest style of clothes, the newest gadgets in their kitchens, the most "modern" homes, the newest type of weapons. Under such conditions as these social change is extremely rapid.

The culture of a society is a *continuum*, that is, it represents the whole social heritage of the group. An anthropologist, in studying a culture, takes a cross section at one point in time. Some changes are beginning and some are ending, but the culture is centered around and integrated with certain main themes. Yet the patterns found in the culture at the time it is studied are the result of the development of that culture since life began among men. Down through history changes and modifications have occurred constantly until today the culture of any group is very different than what it was 6,000 years ago. Yet each custom and trait that ever entered the culture has left its mark, and some repercussion of that trait exists in the present-day culture.[10]

The culture of a society is also *independent of the individuals who compose it*. It can survive any who participate in it at a given point in time. The child is born into the society and is brought up in the culture of his group. Its patterns, which were external to him at birth, become internalized by the time he is a functioning member of the society. He then transmits the culture patterns he has learned to the next generation. Culture, therefore, is perpetuated by a constantly changing group of people. It continues to exist as long as there are people alive who participate in it.[11]

These, then, are the main characteristics of culture. It is a solution of men's problems while at the same time it creates problems for men. It is an abstract which is made up of an integration of the modes of behavior which find expression in the activities of the men who share it. Through them it is transmitted from one generation to the next. Culture forms personalities and is, at the same time, formed by them. It is selectively cumulative yet characterized by so-called survivals and an uneven elaboration and overelaboration of patterns. It is rewarding and frustrating. It is a continuum, dynamic and independent of the individual. The question of why culture has arisen and how remains to be examined.

Origins of Culture.—Due to his biological characteristics, man needs the support of an organized group in order to survive. Possessing unintegrated impulses, he must learn or invent every response

10 Linton, *The Study of Man*, pp. 294-298.
11 *Ibid.*, pp. 290-294.

he uses. He can learn and invent because of his capacity for remembering and forming connections between old and new experiences.[12] Man can also learn from other people. In combining what he has learned from his own experience and what he has learned from others man has a much greater chance of survival than if he were alone.[13] In addition, man's maturation period, which is longer than that of other animals, requires that the mother and child be given protection for a certain period of time. Not only is the child helpless but the mother, during her period of pregnancy and while the child is still dependent upon her, is also hampered from carrying out many of the exigencies of life such as searching for food. Man's survival is then dependent on group life.

Culture emerges from the experiences of the group while living together and represents the means they have worked out for dealing with recurrent problems. Concerning the origins and nature of culture, Malinowski says:

. . . [T]he satisfaction of the organic or basic needs of man and of the race is a minimum set of conditions imposed on each culture. The problems set by man's nutritive, reproductive, and hygienic needs must be solved. They are solved by the construction of a new, secondary or artificial environment, which is neither more nor less than culture itself, has to be permanently reproduced, maintained, and managed. This creates what might be described in the most general sense of the term as a new standard of living, which depends on the cultural level of the community, on the environment and on the efficiency of the group. A cultural standard of living, however, means that new needs appear and new imperatives or determinants are imposed on human behavior. Clearly, cultural tradition has to be transmitted from each generation to the next. Methods and mechanisms of an educational character must exist in every culture. Order and law have to be maintained, since cooperation is the essence of every cultural achievement. In every community there must exist arrangements for the sanctioning of customs, ethics, and law. The material substratum of culture has to be renewed, and maintained in working order. Hence, some forms of economic organization are indispensable, even in the most primitive cultures.[14]

Among men, the ability to develop language has been a vital factor in their ability to develop culture. Possessing language, men can communicate with others. Language enables them to think about and to solve their problems on a conceptual basis, rather than by trial

12 Ralph Linton, *The Cultural Background of Personality*, New York, D. Appleton-Century Co., Inc., 1945, pp. 13-16.
13 Linton, *The Study of Man*, pp. 69-79.
14 Reprinted from *A Scientific Theory of Culture and Other Essays* by Bronislaw Malinowski, by permission of the University of North Carolina Press. Copyright, 1944, by the University of North Carolina Press.

and error or by accident. It is this attribute which has been responsible for the vast wealth of culture by which they live. Many minds have collaborated on the solutions of problems down through the centuries, and have been able to transmit their knowledge to the generations which followed them.

CULTURE AS A SOLUTION TO MAN'S ORGANIC NEEDS. Culture provides the satisfactions to man's most urgent needs, for example, the need for shelter, food, reproduction, and hygiene. In satisfying such physical needs, the combined efforts of many persons are required. Techniques of hunting and fishing and farming are worked out and many people work together to utilize these techniques in getting food for the group. In the rearing of children, it is usually necessary for the mother to stay near the young infants while other members of the group provide her with adequate food, shelter, and protection.

In any culture there is rarely a one-to-one relationship between the physical need and culture's satisfaction of it. For example, the need for food is bound up with hygienic practices, with the organization of the family, religion, and with many other factors. The fulfillment of a cultural need usually involves, in varying degrees, the whole range of that culture's institutions. The explanation of this lies in the tendency of culture to be integrated. In other words, every pattern of culture ties in with all other patterns and helps to define, organize, and satisfy the need.

The integration of culture arises from its development during which the patterns are built, one upon another. It seems probable that in the beginning basic needs formed recurrent problems for a group of people living together. Methods of solving these problems were worked out. If magic, for example, was of aid in their solution, it is probable that magic was used as a part of the solution of subsequent problems. Over a long period of time these solutions became embodied in the tradition of the group through intercommunication between the members of the group about the problem. As the traditional means of meeting the problems was biased in one direction— in this case, in the direction of magic—the means of solving the problems became closely interrelated. One part of the culture was, however, overelaborated, that of magical practices. What began as only a bias in the method of meeting a recurrent problem of the society had, through constant use in a variety of problems, become the main theme and integrating aspect of the culture.[15] For example,

---

[15] Ruth Benedict, *Patterns of Culture,* Boston (copyright Houghton Mifflin Co.), 1934, p. 43; Redfield, "The Folk Society," *op cit.*

in Dobu, all new situations are met in terms of sorcery; among the
Zuñi they are met in terms of religion; and among the Kwakiutl in
terms of a distribution of property.[16]

It should be pointed out that such problem solving and subsequent
integration did not take place on a conscious level. Problem solving
was more a matter of finding a type of solution satisfactory for one
problem and trying it out again on the next problem, in hopes that
it would prove efficient in this field also. We should also note that
such culturally created patterns as religion, magic, and knowledge,
which reaffirm the values of the culture in emotional and rational
form, facilitate the trend toward cultural integration and coherence
which already exist.

A coherent culture, whatever the dominant elements in its integration, has become the chief factor in the survival of any group
of human beings:

> In human life the society rather than the individual has become the primary
> unit in the struggle for existence. Men confront nature, not as isolated units,
> but as members of organized cooperative groups. The incorporation of the
> individual into the group and his training in one or another of the specialized
> activities necessary to the group's well being has thus become the primary
> function of man's social heredity. As a result, every culture must and does
> include a series of techniques for group living and the training of young
> individuals to such a life.[17]

The ways in which man's basic needs have been defined and
satisfied by culture have been grouped by Malinowski [18] into a series
of categories which show the need and the cultural response:

A	B
Basic Needs	*Cultural Responses*
1. Metabolism	1. Commissariat
2. Reproduction	2. Kinship
3. Bodily Comforts	3. Shelter
4. Safety	4. Protection
5. Movement	5. Activities
6. Growth	6. Training
7. Health	7. Hygiene

(a) *Metabolism.* Taking these categories one at a time, metabolism is listed first. Metabolism includes the partaking of food, digestion, and the elimination of waste. Every culture has worked out

---

16 Benedict, *Patterns of Culture*, pp. 52-205.
17 Linton, *The Study of Man*, p. 86.
18 Malinowski, *A Scientific Theory of Culture*, p. 91.

some procedures whereby these closely related physical needs can be met. The patterns for eating and drinking tend to vary as widely from culture to culture as do the type of food produced by the environment and the religious beliefs of the group.

As was stated earlier, there is rarely a one-to-one relationship between a basic need and the culture's means of meeting that need. Under modern conditions, the products of the world are utilized at the family table. Their production and distribution involve a vast network of economic institutions in addition to the organization of the household. These are linked with other phases of the culture which outline the reasons for production and consumption of food, such as religious tabus, standards of living, medical practices, technical knowledge, and government regulation. To these must be added the family's concern for its status in the community. This involves not only the definition of what should be eaten but also the close observance of cultural expectations connected with preparation, serving, and consumption. Additional demands within and without the family circle appear on those days which are fraught with family, religious, or national significance. To illustrate:

A member of the American middle class acts as an individual in feeling and satisfying hunger. However, he unconsciously chooses food which is accepted by his culture. It is unlikely that he would consider ordering fried snake or candied cockroaches or antique eggs, all of which are acceptable to other groups in the world. He may choose the following meal: tomato juice, roast beef, potatoes, carrots and peas, with a dessert of pineapple pie and coffee. This choice is dictated by his tastes which have been strongly influenced by his culture. In our society, beef is permissible from a religious viewpoint to the vast majority of the population, whereas pork of all types is tabu for Jewish Americans and meat is tabu on Fridays for American Roman Catholics. His choice is probably influenced also by the teachings of medicine which prescribe a certain number of vitamins and calories each day in order to maintain optimum health. The government has probably regulated whether he will use margarine or butter on his bread and the quality of the food.

In order to bring all this food to the table of the middle class American, a great network of producing and distributing institutions has been at work which involves vast sums of money, hires millions of individuals, uses modern technical knowledge, and often involves the relationships existing between nations of the world.

Once the food is in the house, however, the story is not ended. If it is an ordinary day of the week, the family may feel content with the food. It is prepared by hired help or some organization of family members in the kitchen. It is served in a way prescribed by the culture in the dining room on a table set with linen, china, and silverware, all of a type used by the culture. Father probably carves and mother serves the vegetables. Children are served according to age and sex. Either before or after dinner, depending on the religious beliefs of the family, father will say grace. Throughout the meal great emphasis is placed on politeness and good table manners in accordance with the requirements of the middle-class status of the family. It has been stated that the family is probably pleased with this meal if it is an average day. However, should it be a religious and family day such as Christmas, the family will feel unhappy and that they have lowered their status in not being able to have the culturally prescribed Christmas dinner of roast turkey and plum pudding.[19]

The above example shows the multitude of cultural factors which can intervene between the physical impulse and its satisfaction. What we require, when we shall partake of it, and in what manner are defined by our cultural heritage, regardless of how static or dynamic that culture may be.

The release of tensions relating to the elimination of body wastes is also in accordance with the established social patterns of society. In his earliest years, the child learns to manage these tensions under the guidance of persons who are socially mature. In our own society, special rooms are set aside in order to give the individual privacy and assure the hygienic disposal of the waste product. In Dobu, privacy is also prescribed but for the purpose of preventing the use of bodily wastes by sinister sorcerers seeking to harm the individual. In other parts of the world, little privacy is felt to be necessary.[20]

(b) *Reproduction.* The pairing of human beings in partnerships for sexual relations, pregnancy, birth and care of children, are matters of concern for all social groups. The long period of dependency which the human infant passes through requires that some obligation be felt by the parents or their substitutes. Social arrangements for the care of children form an integral part of cultures everywhere. The obligations are mainly set within the framework of marriage, regardless of how varied the forms of marriage may be. Within this framework are set the rights and obligations of the family and kinship group, backed by tradition and law. The community and special functionaries keep the family under continual observation to see that these obligations are carried out. In our own society, to cite an extreme case, the neighbors may note that a family is not caring for its children adequately. Through their intervention, the Society for

---

19 Unpublished document.
20 Gontran de Poncins, *Kabloona*, New York, Reynal & Hitchcock, 1941; Clellan S. Ford, *Smoke from Their Fires;* Reo F. Fortune, *Sorcerers of Dobu*, New York, E. P. Dutton & Co., Inc., 1932; Margaret Mead and Gregory Bateson, *Balinese Character*, New York, Spec. Pubs. of the New York Academy of Sciences, Vol. 2, 1942.

the Prevention of Cruelty to Children may be called in or the laws for the prevention of child labor or those concerning non-support may be brought into play.

The care of children is obviously dependent also upon the economic organization and wealth of the group. If, as in Alor, the mother is required to work all day to help provide sustenance for the family, the care of the child may be left to an old woman or a brother or sister. If economic conditions are difficult for the group, female infanticide may be practiced in order to regulate the number of females who mature to produce children.[21] Birth and care of children are also closely linked with the educational aspects of group life, with religious sanctions, and with all other parts of the culture.

The social channelization of the reproductive processes is further evidence of the fact that the biological continuity and survival of human beings depend on safeguarding culture. As the solution of any one need is dependent upon the solutions of all other needs, culture as a whole must be kept intact. However useful it may be to single out one aspect of culture for analysis, it is soon realized how closely it is bound up with other aspects. Culture is an entity which cannot be broken down into separate parts.

(c) *Biological Comforts and Health.* The need for protection from the extremes of heat and cold, moisture, and contamination is as widespread as man's distribution on the face of the earth. Standards and forms are dependent on the cultural setting and the environment. The demands of bodily comfort and health call for houses, clothing, sanitation, a potable water supply, and medical practices. Houses may vary from the modern house, oil or coal heated, to mere three-sided lean-tos which the Kaingang Indians use as shelters from the wind. Clothing may run the gamut from little or none, as among the Kaingang, to the silk robes of the Chinese aristocrats and the many layers of furs of the Eskimo, or may be of the type worn in our own society, with the emphasis on non-utilitarian factors. Sanitation may give rise to a vast amount of organized behavior as in America, involving public health functionaries in federal and civic administrations, street cleaners, plumbers, garbage collectors, and factories for the manufacturing of equipment; or sanitation may be taken care of by the simple expedient of keeping dogs or pigs to act as scavengers. Medical practices range from the magic of North American Indian shamans or the folk medicine of peasant

---

[21] Cora DuBois, *People of Alor,* Minneapolis, University of Minnesota Press, 1944; Linton, *The Study of Man,* p. 183.

groups as depicted by Miner and Ferencz to the highly rational, scientific medical practices of western industrial civilization.[22]

The fulfillment of these needs has reached its zenith in American civilization and is at the center of a vast, organized network. Whether in home, club, shop, factory, hunting or trading expedition, hospital, church, or theater, the facilities affording bodily comfort, safety, and health are to be found in some stage of their development. On having suitable cultural responses to these basic bodily needs, man's continued existence depends.

(d) *Safety, Movement, and Growth.* Man acquires protection from the vicissitudes of nature, hostile animals, and hostile men in accordance with his culture. The statement "in accordance with his culture" is important. For example, man builds himself a house to protect himself against nature. Lapland, Switzerland, Northern Japan, and Southern Canada are all in the North Temperate Zone. The shelter requirements are quite similar. Yet the houses built in each of these areas are extremely different in form. Culture rather than environment determined their form.[23]

The need for protection against animals and hostile men is achieved by choosing suitable building sites, by erecting walls around villages and cities, and by maintaining some force of men bearing arms. Our own society, with its high degree of technological development, relies upon such weapons as the atomic bomb, the airplane, the tank, and the battleship against other men. The threats from nature and hostile animals have been brought under control to a large degree, and we feel it necessary to protect ourselves only against other men. We also rely on rational approaches in this striving for protection. We put our faith in the ability of such organizations as the League of Nations or the United Nations to secure cooperation between nations who would otherwise be hostile to one another. Here again, however, economic organization, apprenticeship and educational means, no matter how crude, are present.

For protection against a hostile environment, be it men, animals, or nature, man also tends to use religion, invoking his god to aid him. In times of crisis the necessity of placating his god is felt and a search is made for those presumed to have been the cause of deistic anger. Pacifying his deity may run the gamut from human sacrifices to a mending of ways.

---

22 Henry, *Jungle People;* de Poncins, *Kabloona;* Mead and Bateson, *Balinese Character;* DuBois, *People of Alor;* Horace Miner, *St. Denis,* Chicago, University of Chicago Press, 1939; Agnes Ferencz, *The Impact of Urbanization on French-Canadian Medical Attitudes,* M. A. Thesis, McGill University, 1945. (Unpublished.)

23 Gillin, *The Ways of Man.*

Man's cycle of activities varies from those employed in the work of defense, winning a livelihood, and placating deities, to actions of relaxation such as we find in art and play. Finally, the growth of the body and mind to maturity has found a response in special kinship and wider communal agencies. If physical and mental retardation happens to occur to more than a small minority of the group, its survival is jeopardized. Every phase of any given cultural heritage, whether life within the immediate family, initiation rites, schooling, apprenticeship, is linked with this vital matter of physical and mental growth and with the movements which facilitate it.

CULTURE AS THE CREATOR AND SOLVER OF SOCIAL NEEDS. Social needs do not depend on physical requirements. They are derived needs, some of which emerge in order that a culture may survive in competition with other cultures. These needs have been socially created. For example, culture must be transmitted from generation to generation in order that the society may survive. Hence education emerges as a social need. Other social needs of this kind are government and economic systems which organize the life of the society and maintain internal order.[24]

There are other social needs, however, which are difficult to explain on the grounds of the survival of the species or of the culture. The origins of this class of needs, although it seems probable that they were culturally created, are obscure. Examples of these needs are man's wish for emotional response from others, his wish for security, for novelty of experience, and for prestige among his fellow men.[25] Another need could be described as the need for aesthetic satisfaction from such things as music and art.

Definition of Culture.—Up to this point a definition of culture has not been given. While it is irregular to discuss a subject without an exact understanding of what it constitutes, any definition given before this point would have been merely enumerative, that is, it would have stated broad categories which go to make up culture. The list would have been long and incomplete.

On the basis of the foregoing discussion, however, it is now possible to define culture as *"those historically created definitions of situations which individuals tend to acquire by virtue of participation in or contact with groups which tend to share ways of life which are*

---

[24] George Peter Murdock, "The Common Denominator of Cultures," in Linton, *The Science of Man in the World Crisis*, pp. 134-135.

[25] Linton, *The Cultural Background of Personality*, pp. 7-11; W. I. Thomas and F. Znaniecki, *The Polish Peasant in Europe and America*, New York, Alfred A. Knopf, 1927, pp. 1831-1914.

in some way distinctive . . . and which channel men's relations both to internal and external stimuli." [26]

Questions

1. Contrast the meaning given to the word culture by laymen with that given to it by the sociologist.
2. Culture is a social phenomenon. Discuss.
3. What is meant by saying that culture is selectively cumulative?
4. Give examples of overelaboration of culture to be found in our society.
5. Compare the rate of social change found in a folk society with that found in America. Can you account for the difference?
6. What is a cultural survival? Can you give examples of cultural survivals other than those found in this text?
7. The population of the Western World is aging rapidly. What effect do you think that this will have on American culture?
8. How does culture change come about?
9. Distinguish between society and culture.
10. What are socially created needs? Give examples.
11. Culture is man's solution of recurrent problems. Discuss.
12. How does culture emerge?
13. A culture persists only as long as there are people alive who have been brought up in its ways. Do you agree? Support your opinion.
14. Culture acts as a screen between man and his physical environment. Explain.
15. What is meant by the statement that there is rarely a one-to-one relationship between a need and the culture's solution of that need?
16. What is meant by the statement that culture is a continuum?
17. How does cultural integration come about?
18. What are some of the dominant themes in American culture? Show how the American emphasis on youth, on wealth, on science, the debunking of heroes, and quiz programs are tied in with American cultural themes.

Bibliography

The combined bibliography for Chapters 2-4 will be found on pages 77-79.

---

26 Kluckhohn and Kelly, "The Concept of Culture," *op. cit.*, p. 84. Italics by present authors.

Chapter 3

CULTURAL INTEGRATION IN SPECIFIC SOCIETIES

In order to demonstrate the concepts concerning the nature of culture which were put forward in the last chapter, the next two chapters will be devoted to a description of the cultures of the Kwakiutl Indians of British Columbia and the Zuñi Indians of New Mexico. Because the cultures of these societies are less complex than our own, have a much slower rate of social change, are relatively isolated, and because we are in no way emotionally involved in them, their social processes and social forms can be observed under conditions as near to those of the laboratory as the social scientist can usually get.

It is only in very recent years that the study of custom has challenged the social theorist. He looked at the world through eyes which had been conditioned by his own culture and saw the customs of others as primitive, barbarian, or pagan. He felt that his own ways were the right ways; his behavior he thought of as Behavior. He interpreted the range of personality accepted by his own culture as Human Nature; his own motivations and goals he thought of as the universal motives and goals of mankind. The white man in particular has been guilty of this way of thinking, largely due to the extensive spread of white culture throughout the world. In the words of Ruth Benedict:

He has never seen an outsider, perhaps, unless the outsider has been already Europeanized. If he has travelled, he has very likely been around the world without ever staying outside a cosmopolitan hotel. He knows little of any ways of life but his own. The uniformity of custom, of outlook, that he sees spread about him seems convincing enough, and conceals from him the fact that it is after all an historical accident. He accepts without much more ado the [idea of the] equivalence of human nature and his own cultural standards.[1]

Before an adequate study of culture was possible, it was necessary that the investigator come to weigh his own society and his own ways of life against those of other societies, that he observe dispassionately, accepting the solutions of other societies as adequate means of dealing

[1] Ruth Benedict, *Patterns of Culture*, Boston (copyright, Houghton Mifflin Co.), 1934, p. 5.

with their problems, but neither better nor worse than the solutions of his own society. Having examined other cultures, the investigator came to realize that he too was the product of his culture. Only then was he able to turn in his examination and look objectively at the ways of his own society. Through the observation of these other groups with whom his own society is unrelated and with whom he has no emotional attachment to cloud his thinking, he was able to observe the diversity of human institutions and derive much illuminating material on cultural forms and processes. The cultures of these primitive societies were ideally suited for such study. Not only does their isolation limit the number of external forces to be taken into consideration, but their cultures are also often sufficiently simple to be contained within the knowledge of the individual adults of the group. The anthropologist is thus able to see a well-defined pattern to which manners, behavior, thoughts, and goals are molded and with which they are integrated.

The careful study of primitive societies is important today rather, as we have said, because they provide case material for the study of cultural forms and processes. They help us to differentiate between those responses that are specific to local cultural types and those that are general to mankind. Beyond this, they help us to gauge and understand the immensely important role of culturally conditioned behavior. Culture, with its processes and functions, is a subject about which we need all the enlightenment we can achieve, and there is no direction in which we can seek with greater reward than in the facts of preliterate societies.[2]

Before continuing with our discussion of the Kwakiutl and Zuñi cultures, we will summarize briefly what was said in the previous chapter concerning cultural integration.

The culture of any society is more than the sum of all the traits which go to make it up. In addition to these, there is a consistent purpose or orientation, in accordance with which all the traits of the culture are organized. From an almost infinite number of possible solutions to situations, somewhere back in time, a few at most were chosen and all subsequent solutions were fitted into the frame of reference which these established. There is nothing at all mystical about this idea. It is somewhat similar to a man with a set of ideals and interests. Once these have emerged, they channel his life into certain directions and determine what he will find acceptable. Any new problem which arises in his life he solves in terms of his ideals and interests. Any behavior in which he engages he rationalizes in

---

2 *Ibid.*, p. 18; see also Margaret Mead, *And Keep Your Powder Dry*, New York, William Morrow & Co., Inc., 1942, p. 4.

terms of his interests and ideals so that it seems acceptable to him. Similarly, a culture which has become oriented in a certain direction in prehistory makes all additions to its content in the light of this main frame of reference. It accepts only those new traits which fit into its purposes or those which can be reshaped and made to conform. In accordance with this main orientation, all behavior is integrated until the end result is a high degree of consistency.

However, not all societies have achieved this consistency or integration. Just as there are people alive who have many different interests which govern their behavior in different situations, so too there are cultures which have several or a great number of themes. Just as some persons can incorporate into their personalities many conflicting points of view, so too are there cultures which have themes which contradict one another. In our own society this is very true. We believe in brotherly love and the equality of all men and yet at the same time can be thoroughly prejudiced against a minority group in our population and deny them the means of a satisfactory life. However, as these conflicting views are limited to specific situations, we can still manage to carry on.[3]

In the following examples, the main orientations of the cultures, known as *themes,* are quite clear.[4] In Kwakiutl society, the main theme is rivalry, the desire to excel over all others in the possession of the titles and prerogatives which give the individual of that society prestige. The potlatch is "a congregation of people ceremoniously and often individually invited to witness a demonstration of family prerogative," [5] and is thus the institutionalized aspect of this central theme, or, in the words of Opler, "the formalized expression of the theme." [6] As such, the potlatch was an institution of great importance in Kwakiutl society. It entered into every phase of the lives of the people, into their system of heredity, into their rivalries, into their marriage and death ceremonies and in order to help the individual Kwakiutl over many of the other crises in his life. As A. R. Radcliffe-Brown commented when the Canadian Government passed a law against these ceremonies,

[3] Benedict, *ibid.;* Mead, *ibid.;* Margaret Mead, *Coming of Age in Samoa,* New York, William Morrow & Co., Inc., 1928, pp. 234-248; C. Kluckhohn and W. H. Kelly, "The Concept of Culture," in Ralph Linton (Ed.), *The Science of Man in the World Crisis,* New York, Columbia University Press, 1945, pp. 95-96; Karen Horney, *The Neurotic Personality of Our Time,* New York, W. W. Norton & Co., Inc., 1937.

[4] The concept of "themes" is dealt with by M. E. Opler, "Themes as Dynamic Forces in Culture," *Am. J. Sociol.,* Vol. 51, No. 3, November, 1945, pp. 198-206; W. H. Kelly, *Culture and Civilization,* lecture delivered at McGill University, Montreal, Canada, in a series entitled "Lectures on Living," November 12, 1947; Kluckhohn and Kelly, "The Concept of Culture," *op. cit.,* pp. 95-96.

[5] H. G. Barnett, "The Nature of the Potlatch," *Am. Anthrop.* Vol. 40 (New Series), 1938, pp. 349-350.

[6] Opler, "Themes as Dynamic Forces in Culture," *op. cit.,* p. 199.

For the politicians of Canada the potlatch of the Indians of the northwest of America was simply wasteful foolishness, and it was therefore forbidden. For the anthropologist, it was the machinery for maintaining a social structure of lineages, clans and moieties, with which was combined an arrangement of rank defined by privileges.[7]

In Zuñi society, the main theme of the culture was group participation and the subservience of the individual for the greater good of the group. This social relaxation of the will to supremacy and individual power is seen most clearly in their religious rituals. These rituals are group activities which are highly formalized and unemotional, and the whole interest of the members of the society is focused upon them. The religious life of the society gives meaning to all their other behavior.

Although the main accent in the following examples is on the main themes of the cultures, it is also important to note individual *culture traits,* that is, the smallest units which go to make up the culture. Examples of culture traits are the Zuñi prayer sticks, a set of objects around which a pattern of behavior and attitudes is focused. This particular culture trait forms a part of a larger *culture-complex,* that is, a larger group of traits around an object or aim, in this case religious ritual. The potlatch of the Kwakiutl, with its use of many means and many occasions to forward one end and all the behavior and attitudes which accompany it, is a kind of super culture-complex.

The main emphasis should be placed on studying the culture as a whole. However, when fragmentation seems desirable for analysis, the social institutions and their various aspects might then dominate the center of attention. However, the interdependence of all parts of the culture should not be overlooked and their constant reflection of the main cultural themes should be always kept in mind. For example, in Kwakiutl life, the functionaries in the secular life of the group are also the functionaries in their religious life, and positions in both these fields are competed for in the potlatch system and are bound up with the struggle for power and prestige. The economic life of the group is strongly tied to enhancing the prestige of the chiefs.

The education of the young is for participation in the fight for status in adulthood. Even marriage, the family, and death are intricately bound up in this dominant cultural theme.

---

[7] A. R. Radcliffe-Brown, "On Social Structure," *J. R. Anthrop. Inst.,* Vol. 70, Part 1, 1940, p. 8.

THE KWAKIUTL INDIANS OF BRITISH COLUMBIA

The Kwakiutl Indians were one of a number of Indian tribes which were formerly scattered along the central part of the British Columbia Coast. During the last century, the cultures of all the coastal tribes have changed or become disorganized until today very little is known of these pre-European cultural systems. In the case of the Kwakiutl culture, most of the knowledge we have has been compiled from reports and studies made several generations ago.

The Kwakiutl culture was based on a fish and cedar economy. The protected inlets and harbors of the British Columbia coastline favored the development of sea travel and the exploitation of the almost inexhaustible supply of ocean products. Salmon was abundant. Clams could be obtained from the beaches. Sea mammals were obtainable by those who had the necessary skills, prerogatives, and supernatural sanctions. The dense forest which began on the other side of the beaches inhibited land travel and the exploitation of the products of the land, but did provide giant cedars from which the Kwakiutl fashioned huge sea-going canoes which could hold as many as sixty men. This tree, which the Kwakiutl referred to as "Mother Cedar," was also used to make clothing, utensils, dancing masks, and for the construction of their lodges. Very little use was made of land products otherwise and agriculture played but a very negligible part in their lives. Only small fields of cinquefoil and clover were tended. There was some hunting but, in the main, their livelihood came from the sea.

The Kwakiutl lived in permanent villages, built on the beaches where their canoes could be beached easily and perhaps clams dug for food. Each village was organized around a number of households, each of which was headed by a chief. The households were composed of the relatives of the chief, a number of commoners, and some slaves; over them the chief ruled absolute. The slaves were his to deal with as he saw fit; commoners had slightly more freedom and the relatives of the chief even more. In each community there was one chief who was the leader of all these lesser chiefs. Although the head chief had a general power as his household was highest in rank because of wealth, birth, or some other consideration, his power was modified by the necessity of taking into consideration the wishes of his subchiefs in coming to any decision. The prestige which was accorded to him by the lesser chiefs was of the same nature as that accorded to them by their own families.

Although there was no ranking of commoners and slaves, the chiefs themselves were very rigidly ranked. This ranking was expressed at feasts where the chiefs were seated according to their importance, in the order in which the chiefs received invitations to potlatches and in the order in which they were given gifts, as well as in the size of the gift. Through these expressions of rank, the community knew what prestige should be accorded to them and noted any changes. In a folk society such as that of the Kwakiutl, where certain types of behavior were prescribed toward individuals holding certain positions, the knowledge of the rank a chief held was very important in social relationships.

Among the members of a village, there was a strong feeling of kinship, expressed in the terms of relationship used in referring to one another, and according to the folk tales and legends which claimed that all members of a village had a common ancestor, and that all members of a clan originally came from the same village. Each tribe was composed of from three to five clans, the membership of which was determined by tracing patrilineal descent from the traditional father of the clan. Clan membership carried with it the right to live in a particular tribal district and determined one's loyalties in a potlatch contest. Otherwise it had little significance, as kinship was traced bilaterally for most other purposes.

The lodges of the Kwakiutl were built in a row with their entrances facing the beach. In front ran a wide, level road. Across the road were the huts for the infirm, the widows, and the sick people of the tribe as well as menstruating women.

In each communal lodge, there usually lived four or five families between whom there were usually some bonds of relationship. Each family group owned its own furniture and utensils, had a private fireplace, and had its own bed compartment which was shut off from the main room of the lodge by sliding doors. Although there was little privacy when the families were in the main room, once they entered the sleeping compartments no one was ever disturbed, as privacy was highly respected. The families shared many of their tasks. With such a mode of life a high degree of intercommunication was a natural result.

The technology of the Kwakiutl was very simple. Natural power was not used nor was there any knowledge of making metal into tools. Most tools were of wood, stone, shell, or bone, but with these they were able to fell huge trees, build lodges and canoes, and become renowned for their skill at woodwork. Dishes and spoons were carved, and also door posts, to look like animals or human figures.

The wheel was unknown and travel was almost entirely by water. The Kwakiutl very rarely walked. As in other folk cultures, there was little experimentation with new ways and all things were done in the manner of their forefathers until the time when contact with the white man became close. The Kwakiutl took into their culture those aspects of the white culture which were of obvious and immediate benefit and utility, and which could be incorporated into their way of life without placing too much strain on their culture. Traits adopted were the gasoline boat, the use of factory-made lumber for the building of houses, and the use of woolen blankets in their potlatch system.

The culture of the Kwakiutl was self-sufficient and the division of labor simple and unspecialized to any great extent. Men hunted, fished, and carved while the women took care of household tasks, cared for the small plots of clover near the house, and gathered roots and shellfish. The women were also famous for their textiles, cordage, and basketry. Among the men some degree of specialization existed, as those who did woodcarving especially well were paid for their labors and gained prestige from this ability. Canoe building was also a specialized task, as was the hunting for sea mammals, which was permitted only to those with the necessary skills, prerogatives, and supernatural sanctions. The children were trained very early in life in the tasks which they would be expected to perform as adults. In the play period, as in our own society, adult life was imitated and, when the children became old enough to be of use, they helped their parents in the activities which were appropriate to their sex.

There was much visiting among the tribes up and down the coast. They traveled back and forth in their canoes through the sheltered inlets of the coast, inviting one another to feasts and potlatches and arranging marriages between the nobility. In this intermingling with "outsiders," the Kwakiutl were unlike most other folk cultures, the majority of which tend to remain homogeneous groups, marrying within their own tribe and rarely contacting others. Contact between the coastal tribes was made relatively easy because of the intermarriage between them. As the Kwakiutl recognized kinship with the families of both their mothers and fathers, a visitor was assured of hospitality from relatives up and down the coast. This extension of hospitality to outsiders through the obligations imposed by kinship ties performed the function of reinforcing the bonds between the tribes which had been set up by intermarriage. In addition, visiting was easy because nearly all the surrounding tribes had the same cultural orientation as the Kwakiutl and the same goals. Hence contacts between them were of somewhat the same nature as those between Canada and the United States in the present day; that is, between cultures which, although they are separate and distinct, still center their lives around the same goals, such as "democratic government" and an economic system of "free enterprise."

The personality of the Kwakiutl Indian was highly competitive, individualistic, and megalomaniacal. The will to superiority over rivals was the main motivation behind the actions of the members of the society. Everything in life was seen as a threat which had to be overcome. The stormy winters—strong tidal currents and winds which often blew against or across tidal currents—could not foster a trust of nature. There was a constant threat to survival which had to be overcome. On the other hand, the abundant food supply and the almost inexhaustible supply of materials for their potlatch system made possible the strongly competitive system which they evolved, giving an intense and rather paranoid cast to almost all Kwakiutl institutions.

From the almost infinite number of possible motivations and behavior patterns of which human beings are capable, the Kwakiutl selected and emphasized intense competition and the will to superiority as the central theme of their culture, expressing it in their institutions and overelaborating it to what we would consider a fantastic degree. The choice came about unconsciously in the distant past through the intercommunication of the ancestors of the Kwakiutl about recurrent problems. Gradually a system of meeting these problems had evolved and, over a period of time, had become the traditional manner of solving them. The method of dealing with certain problems of status and rank by means of a potlatch and a show of force proved satisfactory and became the central theme of their social organization, many other subsequent problems being met in the same manner. As new problems emerged and new traits were added to the culture, they were all oriented toward and given meaning in terms of the central theme. Ultimately the Kwakiutl culture emerged as "an integration of conventional understandings and the acts and objects in so far as they express and maintain these understandings." [8]

The Kwakiutl Indians were members of a folk society, that is, a society ruled in its behavior and thinking by tradition. All problems

---

[8] Robert Redfield, "The Folk Society," *Am. J. Sociol.*, Vol. 52, No. 4, January, 1947, pp. 293-309.

were met in terms of the folkways and mores.[9] The members of the tribe all agreed in their acceptance of the traditional ways of solving problems. If any objective was stated, every member of the group knew how that objective was to be reached and the method used was in accordance with the means used by their ancestors. This agreement on objectives and the ways of obtaining them gave a considerable degree of stability to the society, as well as high morale and close cohesion, which were further enhanced by the common activities in which the group engaged and in which each member had a well defined part to play. In the case of the potlatch, although the men of nobility played the leading roles, there was an opportunity for all members of the group except slaves and sluggards to take part at least indirectly and to share in the prestige and wealth. Even women and children could take part. Everyone involved knew why the potlatch was being held and what behavior was expected of them.

In a society such as that of the Kwakiutl, which is dominated by sacred attitudes and where rule is by tradition, where there is little experimentation or questioning but merely an acceptance of the past, legends, techniques, skills, and the mores of the society are passed down from father to son and from mother to daughter. In his autobiography, a Kwakiutl chief recalled lying by his father at night and being educated in tribal traditions. His father told him the myths of the tribe and clan, the deeds of his forefathers, the "musts" and "must-nots" in conducting a potlatch, and the correct behavior toward the elite of the tribe. Throughout this education, his father constantly admonished him to remember very carefully what he had been told.[10] Had this Kwakiutl chief not taken over so many of the white ways, he would have passed this tribal knowledge on to his own son in the same way.

In the Kwakiutl culture, the potlatch expressed the central theme of their culture, the strong competitive drive and self-glorification. It enabled the individual to assemble an appreciative and purposeful audience outside his immediate localized kinship group to hear his

---

[9] *Folkways* are elementary patterns of action which take form through intercommunication and are followed unreflectively by the members of a group. Since their origin and maintenance represent so much more than the efforts of any one individual, they are typical of group rather than individual behavior. However, they do become part of the habit system of a new group member as a result of their collective demonstration. Shaking hands upon meeting a friend would be an example of a folkway in our society. It seems to us the natural thing to do in such a situation, and we do not reflect on it. It is the pattern of behavior our society follows for greeting.

Mores are folkways which have added to them, through some reflection, the judgment that group welfare is particularly dependent upon them. In our society, the confining of sexual intercourse to individuals united by a marriage ceremony is part of the mores.

[10] Clellan S. Ford, *Smoke from Their Fires*, New Haven, Yale University Press, 1941, p. 55.

claims to new rank, titles, and prerogatives, judge them and give them validity. By this means he could raise his own status, or that of his clan and tribe, and could release aggressive tendencies in a way which was not a threat to the tribe's existence.

Wealth among the Kwakiutl was not a means of acquiring comforts in the usual sense but, rather, was used to gain social prestige. Property was gathered only that it might be given away again. To the Kwakiutl it was unthinkable that wealth should be amassed for any other purpose.

Two kinds of property were of importance to this Indian group, and, as in most societies, the property was transmitted within the kinship group from generation to generation. The first type of property was the hunting and fishing grounds which were strictly owned in family lines. Even though a family might scatter many miles from this property over a space of time, they still retained their rights to it and trespassing was severely dealt with.

The second type of property, which was vastly more important in the eyes of the Kwakiutl, were nobility titles, ceremonial rights, the privilege to use certain myths and songs, the right to named house posts and spoons with heraldic crests. All these were owned and used individually and transmitted in family lines. The claims to this type of property were the most frequent reasons behind the potlatches. Inheritance was usually from father to eldest son and from father to son-in-law to be held in trust for his grandson. If there were no male heirs a brother or daughter might inherit the prerogatives. In the latter case, she did not usually exercise them but merely held them in trust for her sons.

Of prime importance were the nobility titles, and all other prerogatives were connected with these. Each family and religious society had a series of such titles which individuals assumed as their birthright or due to their competitive ability in the potlatch system. The titles, which had remained unchanged down through the ages, were used as personal names. When a person acquired one of these titles, he assumed all the traditional greatness of those who had borne the name before him, and when he passed it on to his heir he gave up not only the title itself but also the prerogatives and legendary fame which were attached to it.

The prerogatives and titles belonging to any one chief were not necessarily transmitted to the same heir but could be passed down, in whole or in part, as the chief saw fit. Rank was not a permanent status which [was] expressed in a number of absolute ways, but rather the resultant standing attained by the inheritance of a considerable number of theoretically independent privileges which [did] indeed tend in most cases to be associated in certain ways but may, nevertheless, be independently transmitted from generation to generation.[11]

For example, privileges which were connected with a certain locality usually remained there. If their holders did move, however, the privilege was never lost to its locality in that it retained its local reference over generations.

As previously mentioned, the assumption of a given name depended partly on birth, the eldest son usually acquiring it. The other children were regarded by the tribe as commoners while the holder of the title was considered nobility. From time to time, however, the claim to the title had to be reasserted by the giving of a potlatch.

"In its formal aspects, the potlatch is a congregation of people ceremoniously and often individually invited to witness a demonstration of family prerogative." [12] How many guests were invited and how many of the donor's group were involved in giving the potlatch depended on the importance of the occasion. However, there was always a minimum of the "numaym," or the patrilineal kinship group. This group pledged support to the person giving the potlatch and lent him property for the occasion, but they did not participate in its distribution. All those who supported the donor shared in the prestige derived from the cooperative nature of the enterprise. This was true of commoners also, although the prestige which they gained was of a more indirect nature. The potlatch enabled the person concerned to assemble an appreciative and purposeful audience outside his own kinship group to hear and judge his claims to prestige. He and his heirs benefited directly as the publicity kept their rank and prerogatives in the public eye. Even when the potlatch was ostensibly given for another purpose, reassertion and the announcement of claims played a major part. The potlatch system was such a firm organization that no claim could be made without the distribution of property to formally invited guests. The goods distributed to the guests were in the nature of gifts to repay those who had acted as witnesses to the claim. The amount of wealth given away on such an occasion was in keeping with the self-conception of the person giving the potlatch and was consciously aimed at enhancing his status. Even the type of food served was not of the types regularly used by the society for everyday consumption but was food calculated to

---

11 E. Sapir, "The Social Organization of West Coast Tribes," *Proc. and Trans. Royal Soc. of Canada*, Third Ser., Vol. 9, May, 1915, p. 362.
12 Barnett, "The Nature of the Potlatch," *op. cit.*, p. 349.

enhance the prestige of the donor. The formal recognition of his right to the claims he put forward came later when one of the guests gave a potlatch, and he was given a gift of the size suitable to his new prestige and in the order which befitted his new position. If he were given the wrong kind of a gift at this subsequent potlatch, or if his rival to the claim were given a gift before him, or if he were seated at the feast in an inferior position, it was obvious to them that his claim to the title or prerogative had not been accepted.

The most highly valued property given at potlatches was the "copper," which was a flat piece of copper that had been pounded out, and which was valued at the number of blankets it had represented the last time it had changed hands. The whole tribe knew the name and value of each copper and was very interested in their distribution. In giving it away, the chief could break it up or give it as a whole.

Every male entered the potlatch system very early in life. As early as a few days after the birth of the child, forces were at work to bring him into the system. When the umbilical cord dropped from the baby, the father placed it with his best copper in order to assure the success of the grown child. At birth the baby was merely given the name of the place where he had been born. At ten months of age, it was given formal recognition as a new addition to the tribe. Ford explains this delay in terms of the high mortality rate among Kwakiutl children. At ten months it seemed that the child had a good chance of growing into adulthood and hence its recognition at this time. On this occasion the father invited the men of the tribe into his house. There the baby's hair was singed and he was given arm and ankle bands and a new name. Each man present was given a small gift on behalf of the child for witnessing the giving of his new name.

When the child became older and it was time for him to enter the life of the tribe, he was given yet another new name at a potlatch held for this purpose. This potlatch marked the formal entry of the child into the adult life of the tribe. The older members of his patrilineal kinship group gave him blankets to distribute among the guests. These guests then made certain that within a short time they had occasion to give him gifts of blankets of greater value. At the end of a year, the boy repaid his family for their original outlay with 100% interest. The remainder he retained and these usually amounted to the equivalent of the original loan. After he had engaged in a number of potlatches with those of his own age group, he was ready to receive his first potlatch name. All the extended family gathered together for this occasion and he made his claim to a new name before guests to whom property was distributed.

From this time onward, the boy's main occupation was taking part in potlatches and holding a traditional position among the nobility of the tribe. At each potlatch he made greater and greater claims, gave away more and more property and, if he were successful in convincing his audience, he assumed greater and greater names. These names indicated his family connections, his wealth, and his position in the tribe. Whatever the occasion for the potlatch, the host used it as an occasion to make greater claims to prestige for himself.

If the person in the Kwakiutl society wished a status higher than he possessed or could hope to inherit, there were certain ritual channels through which he might achieve it. One way was through marriage, which could take one of two forms.

The first form of marriage was similar to that in our own society, that of a man to a woman. It was customary for the father-in-law to transfer a large number of his prerogatives to the man who married his daughter. These did not usually become the property of the son-in-law but were usually held in trust for his children. Other prerogatives, however, were given to the son-in-law at the birth of his children, at their coming of age, and as a return upon the property which he had given to his wife's family as a bride price.

The Kwakiutl Indians followed a pattern which is common to a great many societies in acquiring a wife, that is, the male paid a bride price to the family of the female. The function of such a payment was that it repaid the girl's family for the loss of her labor and also established the rights of each family involved in the transaction, the family of the girl relinquishing all rights to her children. Even in the event of her death or the death of her husband, the children remained with the husband's family. If the husband died, the girl might return to her family but, in such a case, her family was obligated to pay the family of her husband in order that she might return. The bride price gave social support to the union as the honor and finances of both families were involved if the couple separated.[13]

The bonds of marriage, as the rights to a title, were expressed time and time again by an exchange of property as long as the marriage lasted. The bride's family was obliged to repay the original bride price, with interest, to the husband at the birth of the first child.

---

13 Ralph Linton, *The Study of Man*, New York, Appleton-Century-Crofts, Inc., 1936, pp. 172-178.

Frequently, however, this payment was delayed in order to finance the potlatch given when the child became ready to enter adult society. The son-in-law, in due course, had to repay the father-in-law in order to retain his wife. Until he had done so it was said that his wife was living with him without being paid for, which was considered by the society as not quite correct. The exchange of property continued throughout life. The father-in-law gave the son-in-law wealth and prerogatives and the son-in-law repaid the father-in-law, thus constantly reasserting the kinship ties between them.

Marriage was not according to romantic love or to attraction. As in most folk societies, and many more complex societies, marriage was an arrangement between two families of equal rank. Means were provided by the society for the people involved in the marriage to satisfy their desires for happiness outside the family circle if the marriage were not successful. Adultery was permissible as long as it was not discovered. In contrast to the situation which exists in our own society, extramarital sexual behavior was not regarded as sinful but merely as highly amusing. Among a people as sensitive to ridicule as the Kwakiutl, this was a highly effective means of social control. Also in marked contradiction to our own culture, but in keeping with the ideas of the Kwakiutl, was the custom of paying the loved one for her favors. No value was placed upon sexual relations with a woman who did not expect a substantial gift.

The other type of marriage which was permitted was the marriage of a man with a part of another man's body. This was, in part, a technique for extending the kinship group outward. The Kwakiutl used this ritual means for acquiring wealth and prerogatives from a person who had no heirs to whom he wished to transmit his wealth. Thus one man would pass on his wealth to the man who had married his arm or his leg. The ceremony by which the marriage was carried out was in all respects the same as if the marriage had been real.

Another means of acquiring higher status was by marriage to a woman of higher rank. This, however, was extremely difficult to do. The man was usually unable to pay the proper bride price and hence the marriage was considered to be of the nature of a common-law relationship and the children were considered illegitimate. If the husband received any prerogatives from the father-in-law, it was a source of shame as he was said to have received them for nothing.

Prerogatives could also be acquired by the murder of their owner. The murderer would inherit them as a matter of course. However, before killing the owner, it was necessary that the murderer know the ceremony, the words of the song, or the use of the sacred object which he wished to possess as unless these were perfectly known, the title to them would be meaningless.

Power could also be acquired from the gods by killing them. The Kwakiutl regarded their gods as their rivals and sought to shame them and outdo them. In thinking in this manner about the supernatural, the Kwakiutl merely followed the trend of all cultures which project the behavior upon which they place most reliance in life into their picture of the supernatural.[14]

Prerogatives could also be obtained by becoming a shaman, that is, a religious practitioner. Shamans were supposedly given titles by supernatural beings, in recovering from a serious illness while alone in the woods. These titles were treated in much the same way as secular titles. The person returned from the woods, declared himself a shaman, and proved his claim by curing someone who was ill. He then gave a potlatch to announce his new name formally. Shamans competed with other shamans, attempting to show more power and to prove themselves in possession of better tricks. Tricks were acceptable behavior for shamans, but only so long as they were not found out to be tricks. The audience judged which shaman was best, in much the same manner as they judged which contender for a title was to be acknowledged at a potlatch. When a shaman cured a patient, he was given payment in proportion to the wealth of his patient.

Ritual means were provided for becoming a shaman without first being cured of an illness. A person might pay a recognized shaman to teach him the necessary knowledge. The title of shaman could also be passed down to an heir.

Religious titles were treated in the same way as the secular. They were passed along in family lines or were one of the most important aspects of the dowry of a daughter. Each inheritor put forth his claims to the title at a potlatch ceremony. Those who held secular titles tended also to possess religious titles. As the secular rule of the society was only for six months of the year, during that season when the Kwakiutl were preoccupied with collecting food, and as the religious powers were exercised during the remaining six months, the fact that the same men held both secular and religious titles enabled the society to carry on with a minimum of disruption.

The system of claiming titles at a potlatch and then exercising the accompanying prerogatives was the main preoccupation of the Indians along the northwest coast of British Columbia, including

---

[14] E. D. Monachesi, "Sociology and Culture," in E. P. Schmidt (Ed.), *Man and Society*, New York, Prentice-Hall, Inc., 1938, pp. 1-3.

tribes other than the Kwakiutl. The reasons behind the potlatch were summarized by Ruth Benedict:

The ultimate reason why a man of the Northwest Coast cared about the nobility titles, the wealth, the crests and the prerogatives, lays bare the mainspring of their culture: they used them in a contest in which they sought to shame their rivals.[15]

Each individual, according to his means, vied with another. No one could refuse to accept gifts or sidestep a return potlatch without admitting defeat. If he did this, his rival's position was further enhanced and his own possessions lost much of their prestige and value. If the winner were lucky he claimed greater and greater titles, giving larger and larger potlatches. Unless his rivals could give return potlatches and honor him with an appropriate gift, they were defeated. The object of the system was to show oneself superior to one's rivals. This will to superiority was shown in a most uninhibited fashion, verging on megalomania in self-glorification and ridicule of others. On all occasions, the retainers of the chief sang his praises and these songs are among the most characteristic expressions of their culture. They recognized no other motivation save the will to superiority and most of their institutions were channels for its expression.

Although the dominant pattern which prevailed in the society was one of aggression, within each group there were mechanisms for keeping the hostility within control. Members of the same clan or the same family did not conduct potlatches against one another except on ritual occasions, and there was a set alignment of clans within each tribe for potlatching. Thus, clans 1 and 2 did not potlatch against one another but rather with clans 3 and 4. When the head chief was engaged in a potlatch against the chief of another tribe, individual and clan potlatches were dropped and support rendered to the chief.

Within the groups where primary relationships predominated, there was much leeway for the expression of genuine affection and comradeship. There were many sincere and easy-going friendships among men and women, and within the family affection was warm and genuine. Children were cared for mainly by the mother or an older daughter but the whole family played with them and took great pleasure in fondling them. There was also a tremendous amount of loyalty within the family group and its members supported one another in all difficulties. However, even though the family would

---

[15] Benedict, *Patterns of Culture*, p. 174.

support and protect a wayward member in difficulty, they would severely discipline him.

In addition, the culture put checks on the chief so that his tribe could not be ruined by his personal ambitions. The Kwakiutl believed that if the chief went too far his luck would leave him. When the supporters of the chief felt that he had overdone it, they withdrew from him. In Kwakiutl life, the chief was by necessity arrogant and tyrannical and the limits to which he could go before this cultural check was applied would be considered fantastic by our culture.

Sorcery was another mechanism of social control. The Kwakiutl used it a great deal and sincerely believed in its efficacy. Those who were sorcerers were paid fees for bewitching enemies, but it was necessary that they keep their actions and identity a secret. If a sorcerer were caught while in the process of bewitching he was immediately put to death. However, even if a man were strongly suspected of being a sorcerer but was never caught in action, he could go unpunished. Those who credited the sorcerer with power through evil magic had no criteria by which to judge the effectiveness of his actions or to decide whether the magic was actually responsible for what seemed to be its results. If a woman took ill after she had been unfaithful to a lover, the assumption of the group was that the abandoned man was using sorcery against her and from that time onward he was carefully watched for suspicious behavior. This belief in sorcery acted as a social control to such a degree that even the most powerful Kwakiutl chief feared to transgress the mores to the detriment of any member of his tribe, for fear of retaliation through sorcery.

Notwithstanding these social controls, however, potlatching was a culture trait which was fantastically overelaborated. Great amounts of property were accumulated and given to other mighty chiefs but, as the property usually eventually made its way back to the group from which it had originally come, the system in this respect did not prove too disruptive. However, it became dangerous to the welfare of the group in the great feasts, where the chiefs destroyed all the property which they had gathered from the tribe in order to show their utmost contempt for wealth. This was considered the peak of potlatching. The chief against whom the potlatch was conducted was then obligated to destroy a similar amount of property or to accept defeat. Such behavior greatly enhanced the prestige of one individual but, at the same time, impoverished his tribe.

The potlatch, as previously stated, was used for all possible occasions: in the relations between the sexes, on religious occasions, marriage, the investiture of an heir, the acquisition of titles, and sometimes as a substitute for warfare. It was also used to overcome accidents, as a ritual means of wiping out shame. Any affront received by the Kwakiutl required a potlatch to reinstate his name. The Kwakiutl regarded any accident that happened to him as an affront and a slur on his name. If he injured his foot, he would give a potlatch. If he tipped in his canoe, he would give a potlatch. At all costs, he felt he had to prevent the tribe from laughing at him. Such an accident constituted an emergency for the person and he followed the techniques of his society in dealing with the situation. However, if for any reason these techniques could not be used, his only recourse was suicide. If he lost all his property in a potlatch with a rival and could not give a return potlatch, it was probable that he would kill himself.

Death was the greatest event to be dealt with in terms of shame. It was the greatest affront which a Kwakiutl recognized, regardless of the cause of death and it, too, was dealt with by potlatches. The shame of death could also be wiped away by killing a person of another tribe but of the same rank as the deceased. The murdered person was not in all likelihood in any way connected with the death of the first person who might have died by drowning, from drinking bad whiskey, or from disease. However, by killing another of equal rank, the mourner had acted nobly because he had struck back in return rather than allowing himself to be shamed.

Such a reaction to the death of a member of the family does not imply that sincere grief was not felt. Almost every society provides techniques for helping its members to meet the recurrent crises of life, one of the most important of these being the crisis of death. The Kwakiutl's view of death was consistent with his beliefs that the gods and other men were trying to defeat him. The death of a family member was the greatest affront which the universe could deal him and he acted as toward any other insult but with an intensity proportionate to his feelings for the deceased.

The man who got ahead in Kwakiutl society was one who could live in these terms. Every event was a threat to his ego's security and definite steps had to be taken to reinstate him after the blow. Everything in life was staked upon retaining a grandiose self-conception and, if self-esteem were threatened, the person had nothing to fall back upon. His relationships with men and his gods were of the same nature. He constantly glorified himself and insulted them in order to break down their pretensions and to protect his own. He ran the gamut of emotions from triumph to shame and magnified them to their utmost proportions. Triumph was an uninhibited indulgence in delusions of grandeur and shame was a cause of death. Knowing but one gamut of emotions, he used it for every occasion, no matter how unlikely. The Kwakiutl society institutionalized extreme aggressiveness and uninhibited self-glorification, which is considered abnormal by some societies. They made it an essential attribute of the ideal man.[16]

BIBLIOGRAPHY

The combined bibliography for Chapters 2-4 will be found on pages 77-79.

---

[16] Adapted from Benedict, *Patterns of Culture;* E. Sapir, "The Social Organization of West Coast Tribes," *op. cit.;* Ford, *Smoke from Their Fires;* F. Boas, "Ethnology of the Kwakiutl," *Thirty-Fifth Annual Report of the Bureau of American Ethnology,* 1913-14, pp. 43-1388; Barnett, "The Nature of the Potlatch," *op. cit.;* Barnett, "The Coast Salish of Canada," *Am. Anthrop.,* Vol. 40 (New series), 1938, pp. 118-141.

Chapter 4

CULTURAL INTEGRATION IN SPECIFIC SOCIETIES
(Continued)

The Zuñi Indians of New Mexico

The Zuñi are a tribe of Western Pueblo Indians who live in New Mexico, in villages along the Rio Grande. Although their villages are easily accessible to any American traveler, Zuñi culture has not disintegrated under the impact of surrounding white culture, as have the cultures of Indian tribes in other parts of America. When the Zuñi contact another culture, either that of present-day America or that of former Indian tribes, they have shown themselves to be highly selective about the aspects of the alien culture which they adopt. Any culture traits taken from other societies have been integrated with their own way of life, these forms being divested of the central core of emotion and ideas which they held for the group from which they originated. Thus the Zuñi have adopted many of the dance forms used by other Indian tribes, but in Zuñi culture these dance forms have lost their frenzied character, have ceased to be an expression of the quest for individual power through visions, and have become orderly, slow, and a medium of group participation. As the Zuñi way of life values inoffensiveness and sobriety above all else, these adopted forms tended to enrich the culture rather than contribute to its disorganization.

The Zuñi, like the Kwakiutl, are members of a sacred folk culture. The division of labor is simple, mainly differentiated as to male and female tasks. Although they are a small group, they do not leave their tribe for the outside world to marry beyond its boundaries. As a result they are biologically homogeneous.

All members of the group share the same way of life, the same beliefs, and the same daily activities. Since they never question their culture or think about it in objective terms, they are also homogeneous ideologically. Each man thinks similarly to the next man on most issues which arise because both share the same cultural definitions. All behavior is governed by tradition and accepted. Only in

61

a *crisis situation,* that is, at a time when the known way of life in the society ceases to function well enough to care for the recurrent needs of its members, is the traditional way of life questioned. Even at such a time, unless the members of the society can compare their way of life with another culture, the questioning is not likely to go further than wondering why the gods have been angered and how to pacify them again. As there is no questioning, no experimentation or classification of culture, and as no writing exists by means of which the present could be compared with the past, social change in a folk society such as that of the Zuñi is relatively slow. However, their culture is not static. No culture ever is. People change almost every hour and, as they are the medium through which the culture is expressed and transmitted, any change in them will be reflected in the culture itself. In addition there are always new situations to which the culture must adjust.

In Zuñi and other folk cultures there is not the great variability of personality types which we find in our own society. The personality of an individual is formed by the interaction of the physical organism with the environment and personal experiences and, as the environment and personal experiences of one member of a folk culture are very much the same as those of all other members, only a small variation is found in personality types. Their similarity is still further enhanced in that society rewards and accords prestige to the individuals who most nearly approach the type of personality idealized by that culture, and penalizes the deviant or places him in a status position distinct from the rest of the group. In Zuñi the ideal man is one who is calm at all times and is not easily stirred to anger. He shuns authority and has never tried to lead. He strives never to call forth comment from his neighbors or become involved in any conflict, regardless of its justification. In brief, he strives to be moderate in all things at all times.

In Zuñi, group behavior and its expression in the ceremony and ritual of their religion is the central theme of their culture. All problems are solved in accordance with their religious beliefs. The road to prestige is through religious participation. The education of the child is preparation for taking part later in ceremonies. Government is carried out by the priests. Wealth is of no importance save as a means of acquiring religious prerogatives. One of the main functions of the family is to take care of religious possessions. The need of controlling the supernatural is also met by religious activity.

All activity in Zuñi is group activity, and all group activity is religious. Although men are the actual participants in ceremonies, religious life holds the interest of all. It is a vital matter in the minds of these Indians, who conceive of it as contributing to their welfare. Thus, if a chief misplaces a feather in his headdress and thus threatens the efficacy of the ceremony in which he is participating, the welfare of the group is at stake and the people are interested. On the other hand a subject such as divorce is not considered interesting by them. It is a matter which does not affect the group but rather only individuals and is a matter for individual solution.

Ceremonial occasions abound in Zuñi. These occasions are breaks in the ordinary routine of life, sufficiently marked to call for an appropriate form of observance. Such ceremonies were originally emotionally disturbing and characterized by random behavior but have now become crystallized into a set body of ritual with functionaries in charge to initiate the ritual and carry it through to a successful conclusion. These ceremonies are very impressive to the group, by virtue of being a break in the routine of life and because they focus attention and thought on certain aspects of Zuñi life. Completion of the ritual enhances group solidarity and security due to the mutual participation of the members of the society in the ritual and through the reassertion and reacceptance of the group values with which a specific ceremony deals.

The *functionaries* in Zuñi ceremonials have their roles prescribed by tradition. All the members of the group have common expectations of how a functionary should act. How well he performs his role in the eyes of the group is manifest in the degree of his prestige. The adequacy of his performance also accounts for the success of the ceremony itself and the prestige accorded to the status he holds.

The explicit duties of the functionaries are expressed in many of the prayers which are used in the Zuñi ceremonies. These prayers are not similar to our own. They are not an outpouring of the human heart, nor demands for favors from the supernatural. They are mere formulae, the effectiveness of which comes from the accurateness of the prayer's recital. The society possesses almost innumerable prayer forms. These recount in ritualistic language the whole course of the reciter's ceremonial obligations leading to the ceremony. They tell of each detail in the ceremony: how the official was chosen, his family line, how the prayer sticks were gathered and the bird feathers bound, the content of the offering to the gods, the pre-ceremonial obligations which the functionary has already performed. These prayers also state the ceremonial objective of the occasion and display the Zuñi's point of view in connection with achieving it. They show, in the manner in which they are spoken—quietly and ceremoniously—as well as in their content, the Zuñi love of order, pleasantness, and lack of violence. Even the war priests end their prayers with a request for order and safety for tribal members.

The functionary in any ceremony must be a man with an administrative sense. He must be able to perform all the details which are explicit in any ceremony but he must also have the ability to interpret what is implicit in his position. It is not sufficient for him to carry out the ritual mechanically; he must be able to put the spirit of the occasion into it in order to make it effective for his listeners. Implicit in the duties of a functionary in Zuñi is a great concern for detail. As religious practices are effective in their own right, the people feel that the gods will answer their wishes. Hence the functionary must be sure that every step of the ceremony is perfect according to tradition.

He must also be able to perform imitative magic. The Zuñi believe that this is effective with the gods. Large stones rolled around on a stone floor make the sound of thunder and bring rain. Suds are whipped up from a native plant to imitate clouds for the same purpose.

The functionary must not, at any time during the performance of his ceremonial duties, feel any anger. The Indians feel that absence of anger is a sign of concentration upon the supernatural and that it is pleasing to the gods. They feel that if a priest is polite the gods will answer any request.

The functionary must direct the ritual and express what is implicit in his own status, without having any actual authority except that derived from the group. He must initiate a ceremony but he can do so only at the traditional time and for the traditional purpose. Other members of the ceremony act with him in carrying out the ceremony but he has no authority with which to make them conform to his wishes.

The emphasis on detail, on group ceremony, and on traditional behavior is a means of deterring individual initiative in favor of group decisions and group rule. The religious activities of the community carry out the main theme on which the Zuñi culture is based and, by giving it constant expression, reinforce the common understandings of aims and the means of achieving them. These ceremonies thus give an orientation to Zuñi behavior which can be seen in all their institutions. The *institutions* in any society reflect the culture and social organization and the functionaries of the institutions interpret to the people the particular phases of culture in which their institution is most interested. In Zuñi there is a minimum of

formal institutions and most activities have been organized upon religious lines.

The governing body of the community consists of the heads of the
various major priesthoods. The Tribal Masked Gods deal with the
relationship of the people to the supernatural. The War Society
members are the Zuñi police force and the Medicine Society takes
care of Zuñi health. Each of these societies has its own observances,
its own sacred objects, prayers, retreats, and program. The Winter
Solstice ceremony brings all the different groups together and focuses
their functions. This ceremony marks the beginning of the separate
programs of the different societies.

The three major societies of Zuñi are the Priesthoods, the Tribal
Masked-God Society, and the Medicine Society. Membership in any
one of these does not preclude membership in the others. Very often
a man is a member of all three for the greater part of his life. Each
gives him sacred possessions, demands duties and obligations, and
gives him rights.

The priesthood is the most sacred of all Zuñi societies. These
men are in charge of the behavior of the people and are looked upon
as holy men. They derive their power from their medicine bundles,
which are of the utmost sanctity. These medicine bundles are kept
in separate rooms of the priest's house and are carefully tended by
the eldest woman of his household or the youngest girl. No one else
except the priest and the tender of the bundles can enter the room
where they are kept.

As previously stated, the priests do not decide on when the ceremonies are to be held. Each ceremony must occur at a particular time
in the calendar and the priest's function is to take the initial step in the
ceremony and to participate in the rites. Before the ceremonies
the priests go into a retreat, the four major priesthoods first and for
the longest period of time, and the eight minor priesthoods next for a
shorter time. Retreats are sacred and cannot be interrupted. During
them the priests sit motionless before the sacred bundles and think
on religious and ceremonial matters. If the desired end is achieved
during any retreat, whatever priesthood was in at that time is thanked
by the people for achieving it.

The ruling body of Zuñi is composed of the heads of the major
priesthoods with the chiefs of the War Cult and Sun Cult. However,
their power is exceedingly limited in that no dispute which is likely to
cause anger or a split decision will ever be brought before them. This
is in keeping with the Zuñi belief that priests must not feel anger.
Their function is merely to make ritual appointments, to give judg-

ment where witchcraft is suspected, and to initiate and take part in ceremonies. Disputes between individuals are settled by the people concerned and are felt to be personal matters. Only disputes involving groups necessitate action by authority. However, such disputes rarely arise. As in most sacred cultures, control is through the mores. All members of the group share the same beliefs and the same definitions of appropriate behavior. As these mores are usually surrounded by prohibitions and threats of ill luck if deviated from, few authoritative measures are necessary in order to control behavior. It is only when a society becomes secularized and experimental behavior is therefore prevalent that the controlling force of the mores is lessened and procedures akin to legal control are needed.

The most popular cult is that of the Masked Gods. This is made up of the masked gods, known as the kachinas, and the kachina priests. The kachina priests are the heads of the supernatural world and are impersonated by the mortal Zuñi who wear the masks of the gods. When a man puts on the mask of a god he becomes, for the time being, the god himself. He must assume all the tabus connected with being a sacred individual and go into retreat before the dance, plant prayer sticks, etc. The kachinas themselves are conceived of by the Zuñi as happy, dancing supernaturals who live in the bottom of a lake in an empty desert to the south of Zuñi. What they like best is to return to Zuñi to dance. Hence the kachina priest, who becomes the god while he wears his mask and dances, gives the real kachina the greatest pleasure he could wish for. Each god has his own dance, his own costume, his own legends and certain special ceremonies which he expects. As there are well over a hundred such gods, these ceremonies provide participation in ceremonial life for a good many males in the Zuñi society. Men are the usual participants in such dances. Rarely are more than three women members of the Masked-God Society at any one time.

The conception of the supernatural, which members of any culture hold, is usually a reflection of their main cultural themes. The Zuñi attribute to their gods the same characteristics which they themselves possess. Life in Zuñi is calm and benevolent and filled with a richness of ritual and ceremonial behavior. Therefore, the Zuñi think of their gods as being similar. The people of Zuñi are interested in group activity and this characteristic is also attributed to the gods, who, although supernaturals, are still participating members of the Zuñi society and protectors of Zuñi welfare.

The Masked-God Society is divided into six groups, each with its own kiva or ceremonial chamber and functionaries, its own rituals and membership. It is through one of these societies that the male child in Zuñi makes his first entrance into the ceremonial aspect of Zuñi culture. It is his first ritual recognition as a member of the group, that is, the first *rite de passage*. Which kiva is chosen for the boy is determined by the kiva membership of the boy's ceremonial father who was selected for him at the time of the boy's birth. The preliminary initiation of the child takes place when he reaches an age of about five or six. This first initiation only establishes a bond between him and the masked gods. It does not give him membership in the society. The children are whipped by the kachina priests "to drive off bad happenings," and to give them good luck in the future. The children are supposed to be frightened and they are permitted to cry out. The whippings are never severe. In Zuñi whipping as a means of correcting children is unheard of.

At about fourteen years of age, the actual initiation takes place. The boy is again whipped by stronger masked gods and then it is revealed to him that the masked gods are only members of his own tribe in reality. This revelation usually terrifies the boys. When the masks are put on, the boys themselves are allowed to whip the kachinas who had whipped them: "It is the first object lesson in the truth that they, as mortals, must exercise the functions which the uninitiated ascribe to the supernaturals themselves." [1] They are not permitted to tell of this revelation outside of their own kiva. If they do they are severely punished, as divulging of this secret is the most serious crime which can be committed in Zuñi. After this initiation, the boys are formal members of the cult.

As yet, however, the boys do not possess masks. They must first grow up, marry, and accumulate economic wealth sufficient to give a huge feast for the kiva to which they belong and to those who dance at the accompanying ceremony. They must build a house within which to keep the mask. This mask honors his house and makes it valuable. When he dies, it is buried with him in order that he may join the dancing kachinas in the Sacred Lake.

Wealth, however, is of little importance for participation in Zuñi life. Any individual may borrow the mask of another at any time without obligation. He may paint it to represent any kachina he chooses. Hence, even a poor man can participate.

The criteria for choosing officials for the Zuñi ceremonies also take wealth into but very little account. If an individual shows himself interested and capable of reciting long prayers in accurate de-

---

[1] Ruth Benedict, *Patterns of Culture*, Boston (copyright, Houghton Mifflin Co.), 1934, p. 63.

tail, and is of the proper lineage, he may be chosen as a priest. The society provides for the acquisition of status positions for individuals which are partly determined by birth and partly by aptitude. The acquisition of each new status position is marked by a ceremonial group observance.

The masks of the kachina priests cannot be borrowed or made up on request. They are permanent and are second in sanctity only to the medicine bundles. They are owned in family lines and are kept in the dwellings which have housed them as long as anyone can remember. The man who dons such a mask must know the ritual which goes with it. Otherwise, the mask has no power. In this manner, again, individualism is discouraged as the power goes with the mask only when it is used by the individual whom the group has delegated to use it and only when it is used according to tradition. Such a kachina priest does not dance at the ceremonies but goes to perform definite prescribed acts in the calendric rituals.

The Medicine Society is the third important part of the structure of Zuñi society. The patrons of this society are animals. The chief patron is the bear, whom the medicine societies imitate. The bear is felt to have powers of healing which are derived through the use of his bodily substances. The membership of the society is made up of those who have been cured of a serious illness. Such a cured person is obligated to join the cult to which his doctor belonged.

The power which the successful doctor uses is not thought of as belonging to him exclusively. Hence no prestige accrues to him as an individual. All prestige goes to the group whose power was channelled through him. The cured person must belong to the group who cured him because the return of his life puts him under an obligation to aid in the work of the group. As both men and women are ill and are cured, both sexes belong to the Medicine Society.

Every society provides its members with ritual ways in which to enter certain groups when they otherwise lack the necessary requirements. This provides an outlet for individual initiative. Hence there are ritualistic means provided for becoming a member of the Medicine Society without the necessity of becoming ill. In a society where membership in most organizations is based on birth and special abilities, the Medicine Society offers an opportunity for those with more individualistic tendencies.

However, to become a doctor through ritualistic or traditional means takes many years of learning and some knowledge is withheld until the individual has been initiated into higher orders of other societies. The doctors also have their sacred objects and altars. Their personal fetish is a perfect ear of corn, covered with beautiful and valuable feathers and set in a fine basket. This is kept on the altar of the society to which the doctor belongs during his life and on his death is buried with him, but divested of its feathers and base. The doctors have their special ceremony at the end of the Winter Solstice when the members of the tribe come in to the Medicine Society's rooms to have illnesses removed from them for the year to come.

The war, hunting, and clowning cults are grouped with the Medicine Society in the minds of the people. To become a member of the war cult, one must kill another individual. The circumstances around the killing are irrelevant, but the killing has usually taken place outside the tribe. It is necessary for the murderer to join the war cult as he is considered to be in great danger. This cult has charge of the scalp house and also the policing of the village. Only men are members. Thus the war cult also permits an individual to gain a group membership, regardless of family membership.[2]

Although the family holds a very important position in Zuñi life, marriage is thought to be a matter for the two individuals concerned and the group is disinterested. As the girls are heavily chaperoned from an early age and as their activities from about ten years of age onward are along domestic lines, while the boys in the same age group are concerned with religious matters, little opportunity exists for a young man and young woman to become closely acquainted. The society makes no provision for a courtship period and hence marriage follows on only slight acquaintance. Custom requires that the request for the girl's hand be made to the father by the suitor. The father, however, merely refers the matter to his daughter. If she is willing, the mother goes into the girl's room, makes up the pallet, and the couple retire together. With very little other activity they are considered married, and the young man comes to live in the home of his mother-in-law.[3]

This system of marriage marks the Zuñi as very different from most folk cultures where marriage between two individuals is looked upon as a union between two families. In such cases the families are greatly interested in the matter, which assumes the nature of a contract between them involving loyalties and obligations and an exchange of wealth. Marriage partners are usually chosen for their children by parents and any disruption of the marriage is somewhat

2 *Ibid.*, pp. 52-119.
3 Ruth Bunzel, "Introduction to Zuñi Ceremonialism," *Forty-Seventh Annual Report of the Bureau of American Ethnology*, 1929-30, pp. 467-547; A. L. Kroeber, "Zuñi Kin and Class," American Museum of Natural History, *Anthropological Papers*, Vol. 18, Parts 1-5, 1919.

like a breach of contract and involves financial loss and the lowering of the honor of the families involved.

However, in Zuñi, where families have no interest in the matter, if the couple does not get along together, the wife goes out to serve at a ceremonial feast where she has an opportunity to meet eligible men. As there are more men than women in Zuñi, and as it is considered more dignified to live with a wife than one's mother, the men are always willing to marry. When the woman finds a man who is willing to become her second husband, she places all her former husband's possessions on the doorstep. This constitutes a divorce. The husband must return to the home of his mother. Little interest is taken in the matter by the community and there is very rarely any violence, as both the husband and the wife abide by the rules. Despite the easy techniques provided for the dissolution of the marriage, most endure for a lifetime.

The endurance of marriage in Zuñi is all the more amazing in view of the fact that it is not backed by institutions and the mass of tradition which exists in most societies. Rather, it cuts across the most strongly institutionalized social bond in Zuñi, the matrilineal family.[4]

Persons in Zuñi belong to the kin of their mother but feel that they are connected with the kin of their father. The house belongs to the women of the society and the men of the household work for them. The women own outright all the products of their husbands' and sons' labors. On this ownership of the house rests the woman's place in Zuñi society. The matrilineal customs of the tribe rest upon the permanent occupancy of one house by a woman. The mother and her daughters and their families have the right to live in the mother's house. However, after a time, the daughters very often move away to a home of their own. Other than in this permanent residence of the matriarch of the family, relationship is bilateral. All relatives on both sides of the family are thought of with affection and are blindly loyal to one another. The male child in the Zuñi family can inherit privileges from either the father or mother or from both.

All Zuñi belong to clans, which, however, play only a minor role in their lives. The clans are named after animals but, contrary to the findings in most other North American Indian cultures, there is no idea of descent from that animal nor any tabus connected with it. The clan is important only in connection with the choice of a mate, who cannot be from the clan of one's mother and is not supposed to

---

[4] Benedict, *Patterns of Culture.*

be—but sometimes is—from the clan of one's father. It also plays a part on certain ceremonial occasions, when the functionary must be a member of a specific clan. Otherwise, the clans impose no obligations and offer no privileges to the members of the community.

The women in the Zuñi society have very few prerogatives. Although they own the land and the products of all the work done, the husband has all the authority within the house as long as he lives there. If he leaves, however, he has no further claim upon the household of his former wife. She keeps the fruits of his work and the children belong to her. Any succeeding husband will exercise control, both over the accumulated wealth and the family. This pattern has become so deeply ingrained into the culture and the individuals who compose it that resentment is never shown at the relinquishing of family wealth and control.[5]

All sacred objects are kept in the home of the matriarch of the family, which is considered their permanent abode. The men return to this house on all ceremonial occasions. The women, although they cannot participate in religious events, are often the holders of a great amount of religious knowledge and some have become authorities on prayers and procedures. Even priests frequently consult such women on points about which they are in doubt. A woman, too, has certain ceremonial obligations toward the child of her brother. For fulfilling these obligations, she is usually compensated.

For all men in the community, there is a double allegiance. They are husbands in one group and brothers and sons in another. Their role of brother is the more important of the two statuses and derives, not from being a wage earner, but from the relation of the man to the religious objects in his maternal household. The women usually unite against them as husbands in any conflict, and it is only as fathers of children that they begin to derive any appreciable status.

Economic affairs in Zuñi are not regarded as being of any great importance. Zuñi is wealthy in comparison with the other Pueblos and food is not a matter which causes great concern. Wealth is of little importance, giving prestige only when it is used to acquire ritual prerogatives. Even in this area of interest it is not necessary, as most ritual possessions are kept within clearly defined family lines. A poor man may be sought after as much as a rich man in the religious life of the society because he is of the required lineage. In such a case, the kiva to which the man belongs would provide the ritual necessities for him. They would feel that the participation of

---

5 Bunzel, "Introduction to Zuñi Ceremonialism," *op. cit.*; Kroeber, "Zuñi Kin and Class," *op. cit.*

the individual of the proper lineage in the ceremony would give prestige and blessing to their kiva.

The women own the maternal home and the land which belongs to it. This land is inalienable. A limited amount of land also belongs to the men and this can be bought and sold. Men also own sheep. The tending of these sheep points up the cooperative aspect of Zuñi culture. Brothers take turns tending them throughout the year. All products of the men's labor, be it agricultural produce of their own fields or those of their wives, go into the common storehouse. The women draw on this storehouse for supplies and sell the surplus. The profit from the shearing of sheep is spent by the men to provide clothing for their fathers and mothers, their wives and children, whether the children belong to their present marriage or an earlier one.[6]

The Zuñi always act as a group. They keep to the middle of the road and cling to the known way. Influences which are uncongenial to this outlook are ignored or minimized. They have come into contact with other cultures which have stressed individualism. Probably the most frequent contact was with other Indian tribes who sought individual power through visions induced by fasting, torture, drugs, or alcohol. The Zuñi do not accept visions as indications of supernatural power, but rather fear them as a sign of death. For them all supernatural power is derived from membership in one of their cults. Even then the power belongs to the group, not to an individual member. The Zuñi avoid going beyond the bounds of sobriety and self-control.

However, the Zuñi have borrowed some of the forms which exist in other cultures and have adapted them to their own. The Zuñi go into the woods and listen for voices. But, in Zuñi culture, it is not a search for supernatural power, but merely for an omen of good or bad luck. Unlike the cultures from which they borrowed this pattern, it is not necessary to be courageous when in the forest, and most Zuñi are very frightened during the whole process.

The Zuñi have also taken over the pattern of fasting. Here again they have divested the pattern of its implications of vision-seeking and masochism, and have made it merely a part of their obligations before a ceremony. Fasting is a means to ritual cleanliness.

Drugs and alcohol, which were widely used among the North American Indians in their vision quest, do not play a part among the Zuñi. Drugs are used to ascertain the name of a criminal and also

---

6 Kroeber, "Zuñi Kin and Class," *op. cit.*

on ceremonial occasions. In the latter, however, they are not used in a manner which would have any effect on the sobriety of the individual. Drugs which would have to be swallowed to be effective are used as a kind of dusting powder to achieve ceremonial ends. Alcohol was never adopted and the Zuñi are distinctive in being the only American Indians who have caused the United States Government no concern in this respect.

Torture, which was prevalent in surrounding tribes, has always been rejected in Zuñi. It is not even understood. The whipping which goes with a child's initiation into the ranks of the kachinas is a ceremonial matter and is never harsh. The Zuñi would be horrified if the whipping were severe enough to raise welts.

Many other aspects of the surrounding tribal cultures have been completely rejected by the Zuñi. Most Indians surround their menstruating women with tabus and some even place them in isolation. The Zuñi pay no attention at all to the matter. The surrounding tribes' greatest fear is witchcraft. They regard their priests with fear and suspicion. The Zuñi have no reason to fear or be suspicious of their priests because they consider their priests to be merely the organs through which group will is put into action. Witchcraft, although it is known, is mainly on the level of folklore.

They have borrowed many of the elements of the dance from other cultures, but have rejected the excesses which are associated with it in other tribes. For the Zuñi, magical efficacy is derived from moderation, and the repetition of minutely correct ritual. Hence there is nothing wild about them and men never lose their self-control. The love of moderation in the Zuñi society acts to outlaw all expressions of individualistic power through frenzy, intoxication, or drugs.[7]

In the day-to-day life of the society, individualism is also discouraged. The means of acquiring status are prescribed by tradition. One must memorize word-perfect ritual, must pass up through the required orders, and serve for a set time in certain societies before becoming the incumbent of a high status position. Even should one become a very high priest, he has no power which can be used for his own ends. Priests can never act, except when sanctioned by tradition and the group. Personal authority is very widely disparaged, so much so that a man who is asked to assume a position in the Zuñi structure must show himself unwilling to accept the office until it has been pressed upon him for a long time. When he finally accepts he must seem to be exceedingly unwilling. Nor is any recog-

---

7 Benedict, *Patterns of Culture*.

nition given to the individual for special talents and ability. In contests of skill, if a man wins habitually, he is debarred from further
contests. The Zuñi are interested in games that can be played with
even chances and are not concerned with who wins them.

This lack of personal authority is not only a characteristic of the
priesthood; it is consistently absent throughout the society. The
priesthood has no power except what it derives from the group. Decisions which might cause anger are never brought before it. Only
the war cult has any measure of what our society would term authority. This derives from their position as community policemen.
However, they have little to do. Crimes are few. Theft rarely occurs and when it does it is a private matter. In a society where all
know one another and where there is little privacy for the individual
member, the chances of a person's stealing and not being discovered
are very small. In addition, when women own most of the produce,
there is little point in a man's stealing. As the group cares for its
members in time of need, poverty rarely enters as a motivating factor
for theft. As the group sanction must go along with any religious
prerogative before it is powerful, and as masks can always be borrowed without asking, there is no reason for theft in this field either.
Adultery is no crime and is dealt with by divorce if the two individuals involved wish it. The only case of homicide which can be
remembered was dealt with by a payment between the two families.
The kachina priests take care of those who have given away kiva
secrets. Thus the authority of the war priests is very limited and is
expressed mainly in their power to proclaim a hunt or dances, or
summon the priests.

Nor are personality problems very prevalent in Zuñi. Everyone
is affectionate toward children. The growing child finds no situation
in which authority is exercised and hence feels a minimum of rebellion. Throughout his growing period, he experiences cooperation
from all. His initiation rites are an easy granting of status to the
individual without divorcing him from his family and hence have
no traumatic effects on his sense of security. He has at all times
the authority of his family and his group behind him. Any mis-
deeds of his as an individual do not make him the focus of attention
or bring punishment because the group is simply disinterested.
Hence there is no seeking for status in deviant behavior. The individual realizes that by adhering to custom he has much greater rewards and a more satisfactory life than in rebellion. Being reared in
a culture where all men believe alike and the mores are clear-cut and
uncontradictory, little conflict is caused in the individual. Having

no basis for comparison of his way of life with that of another group, he accepts his culture as the only way possible in which to act.

Nor does the attitude toward sex, upon which the psychoanalysts lay great stress in our culture, play any part in personality disorganization. The Zuñi attitude is most closely akin to what we would call Puritanical except that, where the latter attitude flows from a sense of sex as sin, the Zuñi have no familiarity with the concept of sin. Chastity throughout life is extremely undesirable, and it is thought that if a girl chooses this way of life the gods will contrive a means of leading her from it. Pleasant relations between the sexes, to the Zuñi, are merely another element of getting along well with other people. Sex to them is merely an incident in a full and happy life.

In all activities the group acts as a unit. It has responsibility and power but these are always distributed so that the group is a smoothly functioning unit. The only means of acquiring any desire in life is through group participation. No power can be used individually, as individually no power exists. Everything done is done in the name of the group, the individual merely carrying out the group will and retaining as much anonymity as possible in the process.

No situation ever is met by violence. An example of this is found in the case of the woman who knew that her husband was having an extramarital love affair. She did nothing about it until a white trader, with his American cultural background, convinced her that she should take a stand and assert her rights. Suddenly the husband ceased to see the other woman and confined his attentions to his wife. However, there was no indication that any conflict had occurred in the family group to achieve this. Upon inquiry it was discovered that the wife had never mentioned the other woman to her husband. She had merely stopped washing his clothes. He then realized that she knew of the affair and ceased to see the other woman. Thus the wife had handled the situation in a manner in keeping with her culture. The traditional method of handling adultery is divorce. If a wife whose husband is adulterous does not divorce him, her family usually brings pressure to bear on her. They do this because they are ashamed that she is not abiding by the rules laid down for her by her culture.

Although emotions such as jealousy can be minimized, death and sorrow over the death of a loved one are inescapable. All societies provide their members with some mechanism for meeting the recurrent problem of death. Death is a threat to the solidarity of the group and calls for readjustments in living, especially if it is an adult who has died. There is also loneliness for the survivors who were closest to the deceased. The Zuñi provide a ritualistic means of minimizing grief and of cutting the ties of the deceased with the group. In cutting the group's ties with an individual, the ceremonies surrounding his death form a kind of final *rite de passage* of the individual.

The Zuñi do not deny death. They treat bereavement realistically as an important loss. However, they place the emphasis of their ritualistic techniques on making the mourner get over the situation as quickly as possible. The funeral rites are the simplest of the society and no priests officiate. The dead are buried quickly and quietly. The grief felt by the survivor is conceptualized as danger and the fear that the deceased may come back for him. The more the survivor grieves, the greater his danger. Thus he is treated with all the precautions usually given to an individual in danger. For four days he goes into a retreat and follows prescribed ritual while there. At the end of the four days he recites a prayer to the dead one and the danger is considered as minimized, but it is not entirely over until a year has passed. At that time, the widower may take another wife and is considered free, and the same procedure is followed in the case of a widow.

In Zuñi a man who slays another is treated in the same manner as a surviving spouse, but his retreat is in a ceremonial kiva under the supervision of priests. This retreat is considered as his initiation into the war cult and from then onward he must assume responsibilities in that group. The scalp of the slain enemy is initiated into the tribe and becomes one of the sacred symbols, important in the ceremonies for rain. Thus the enemy becomes a member of the Zuñi dead and of benefit to the group.

In their views of the supernatural, the Zuñi do not fear death or evil. They feel that the gods are like themselves and like what men like. Thus the gods will help them if they give them pleasure. Nor do they see life as a span between birth and death. Life is always present and so is death. One is no denial of the other. Death merely changes the form of the individual from a man to a god or part of the universe. They feel that their dead are still interested and participating group members. Thus they have a strong sense of man's oneness with the universe.[8]

---

[8] Benedict, *Patterns of Culture*; Bunzel, "Introduction to Zuñi Ceremonialism," *op. cit.*; Kroeber, "Zuñi Kin and Class," *op. cit.*; Hutton Webster, *Magic*, Stanford University, Stanford University Press, 1948.

QUESTIONS

1. Why are sociologists interested in studying primitive groups? Why was an objective study of these groups impossible until recent years?
2. Give examples of contradictions in culture. How do you explain the presence of these contradictions in culture? Can you think of examples other than those given in this text?
3. Discuss the culture complex and culture trait. Can you illustrate by examples drawn from discussions of the Kwakiutl and Zuñi Indians?
4. Compare the personality of the average man in Zuñi society with that of the average man in Kwakiutl society. Why are they so different? In what ways are they similar? Why?
5. What are the central themes of Zuñi and Kwakiutl culture? Show how these themes serve to integrate the culture.
6. What is true and moral depends on the culture in which a person has been raised. Do you agree? Defend your point of view.
7. The sudden abolition of the Kwakiutl potlatch by the Canadian Government brought about cultural disorganization. Discuss.
8. Can you account for the fact that Zuñi culture has remained relatively uninfluenced by the American culture which surrounds it?
9. The introduction of a new culture trait may have repercussions on the whole of the culture. Do you agree? Defend your point of view.
10. Evaluate the effectiveness of the manner in which the Zuñi or Kwakiutl cultures meet the following problems: prestige, crime, marriage, acquisition of wealth, the according of status to a child, death, disgrace. Compare their methods with those utilized in our own society.
11. What are the American culture patterns regarding marriage, courtship, authority, death, enhancing of status, religion?
12. The religion of a group is a projection of their culture. Do you agree? Give examples to support your point of view.
13. What is meant by the statement that culture is often unevenly integrated? Can you give examples in American culture?
14. Lack of understanding between groups is partly due to culture. Discuss. What present-day misunderstandings between nations arise from cultural differences? Would a Zuñi Indian and a Kwakiutl be able to live together peacefully? Defend your point of view.
15. Of what value is the study of culture?

BIBLIOGRAPHY

BARNETT, H. G. "The Nature of the Potlatch." *Am. Anthrop.*, Vol. 40 (New Series), 1938, pp. 349-358.

BARNETT, H. G. "The Coast Salish of Canada." *Am. Anthrop.*, Vol. 40 (New Series), 1938, pp. 118-141.

BENEDICT, RUTH. *Patterns of Culture.* Boston (copyright, Houghton Mifflin Co.), 1934.

BERNARD, JESSIE. "Culture as Environment." *Sociol. and Soc. Res.,* Vol. 15, September-October, 1930, pp. 47-56.

BLUMENTHAL, ALBERT. "The Nature of Culture." *Am. Sociol. Rev.,* Vol. 1, No. 6, December, 1936, pp. 875-894.

BOAS, F. "Ethnology of the Kwakiutl." *Thirty-Fifth Annual Report of the Bureau of American Ethnology,* 1913-1914, pp. 43-1388.

BOAS, F. *Race, Language and Culture.* New York, The Macmillan Co., 1940.

BUNZEL, RUTH. "Introduction to Zuñi Ceremonialism." *Forty-Seventh Annual Report of the Bureau of American Ethnology,* 1929-1930, pp. 467-545.

DuBOIS, CORA. *People of Alor.* Minneapolis, University of Minnesota Press. 1944.

EUBANK, EARLE E. *Concepts of Sociology.* Boston, D. C. Heath & Co., 1931.

FERENCZ, AGNES. *The Impact of Urbanization on French-Canadian Medical Attitudes.* M. A. Thesis, McGill University, 1945. (Unpublished.)

FORD, CLELLAN S. *Smoke from Their Fires.* New Haven, Yale University Press, 1941.

FORTUNE, REO F. *The Sorcerers of Dobu.* New York, E. P. Dutton & Co., Inc., 1932.

GILLIN, JOHN. *The Ways of Men.* New York, Appleton-Century-Crofts, Inc., 1948.

GILLIN, JOHN. "The Configuration Problem in Culture." *Am. Sociol. Rev.,* Vol. 1, No. 3, June, 1936, pp. 373-387.

HENRY, JULES. *Jungle People.* Richmond, The William Byrd Press, Inc., 1941.

HILL, G. "The Use of the Culture Area Concept in Social Research." *Am. J. Sociol.,* Vol. 47, No. 1, July, 1941, pp. 39-48.

HILL-TOUT, CHARLES. "The Origin of Totemism of the Aborigines of British Columbia." *Proc. and Trans. Royal Soc. of Canada,* Second Ser., Vol. 7, May, 1901, pp. 3-15.

HORNEY, KAREN. *The Neurotic Personality of Our Time.* New York, W. W. Norton & Co., Inc., 1937.

KARDINER, A. *The Individual and His Society.* New York, Columbia University Press, 1939.

KELLY, W. H. "Culture and Civilization." Lecture delivered at McGill University, Montreal, Canada, as fourth in a series entitled: "Lectures on Living," November 12, 1947. (Unpublished.)

KLUCKHOHN, C., AND KELLY, W. H. "The Concept of Culture," in Ralph Linton (Ed.), *The Science of Man in the World Crisis.* New York, Columbia University Press, 1945, pp. 78-106.

KROEBER, A. L., AND WATERMAN, T. T. *Source Book in Anthropology.* New York, Harcourt, Brace & Co., Inc., 1931, Chs. 32, 33, 37.

KROEBER, A. L. "Zuñi Kin and Class." American Museum of Natural History, *Anthropological Papers,* Vol. 18, Parts 1-5, 1919.

LINTON, RALPH. *The Study of Man.* New York, Appleton-Century-Crofts, Inc., 1936.

LINTON, RALPH. *The Cultural Background of Personality.* New York, D. Appleton-Century Co., Inc., 1945.

LOWIE, R. *An Introduction to Cultural Anthropology.* New York, Farrar & Rinehart, Inc., 1940.

MALINOWSKI, BRONISLAW. *Coral Gardens and Their Magic.* New York, American Book Co., 1935.

MALINOWSKI, BRONISLAW. *A Scientific Theory of Culture and Other Essays.* Chapel Hill, University of North Carolina Press, 1944.

MEAD, MARGARET. *And Keep Your Powder Dry.* New York, William Morrow & Co., Inc., 1942.

MEAD, MARGARET. *Coming of Age in Samoa.* New York, William Morrow & Co., Inc., 1928.

MEAD, MARGARET, AND BATESON, GREGORY. *Balinese Character.* New York, Spec. Pubs. of the New York Academy of Sciences, Vol. 2, 1942.

MEAD, MARGARET. "Culture and Personality." *Am. J. Sociol.,* Vol. 42, No. 1, July, 1936, pp. 84-87.

MEAD, MARGARET. "Custom and the Mores." *Am. J. Sociol.,* Vol. 47, No. 6, May, 1942, pp. 971-981.

MINER, HORACE. *St. Denis.* Chicago, University of Chicago Press, 1939.

MONACHESI, E. D. "Sociology and Culture," in E. P. Schmidt (Ed.), *Man and Society.* New York, Prentice-Hall, Inc., 1938, pp. 1-54.

MURDOCK, GEORGE PETER. "The Common Denominator of Cultures," in Ralph Linton (Ed.), *The Science of Man in the World Crisis.* New York, Columbia University Press, 1945.

OPLER, M. E. "Themes as Dynamic Forces in Culture." *Am. J. Sociol.,* Vol. 51, No. 3, November, 1945, pp. 198-206.

PONCINS, GONTRAN DE. *Kabloona.* New York, Reynal & Hitchcock, 1941.

REDFIELD, ROBERT. "The Folk Society." *Am. J. Sociol.,* Vol. 52, No. 4, January, 1947, pp. 293-309.

REDFIELD, ROBERT. "The Folk Society and Culture." *Am. J. Sociol.,* Vol. 45, No. 5, March, 1940, pp. 731-743.

SAPIR, E. "The Social Organization of West Coast Tribes." *Proc. and Trans. Royal Soc. of Canada,* Third Ser., Vol. 9, May, 1915, pp. 355-374.

SOROKIN, PITIRIM A. *Social and Cultural Dynamics.* New York, American Book Co., Vols. 1-3, 1937; Vol. 4, 1941.

THOMAS, W. I., AND ZNANIECKI, F. *The Polish Peasant in Europe and America.* New York, Alfred A. Knopf, 1927.

THURNWALD, R. C. "Civilization and Culture." *Am. Sociol. Rev.,* Vol. 1, No. 3, June, 1936, pp. 387-396.

THURNWALD, R. C. "Progress Viewed as a Component in the Configuration of Culture." *Am. Sociol. Rev.,* Vol. 1, No. 4, August, 1936, pp. 604-614.

WEBSTER, HUTTON. *Magic.* Stanford University, Stanford University Press, 1948.

WISSLER, C. *Man and Culture.* New York, T. Y. Crowell & Co., 1923.

WOODARD, J. W. "The Relation of Personality Structure to the Structure of Culture." *Am. Sociol. Rev.,* Vol. 3, No. 6, October, 1938, pp. 637-652.

Chapter 5

PERSONALITY

As used in everyday speech, the word "personality" is somewhat different in meaning from its sociological definition. Whereas the average person may remark that Mary has a "wonderful personality," the sociologist might well consider such a statement merely a description of one aspect of Mary's personality, that is, her ability to form friends among her own social group. Personality, to the sociologist, is an integration of all the traits and characteristics which make up a person. Included in this definition are a person's physical characteristics, behavior, and attitudes which enable him to adjust to his physical and social environment. Personality cannot be quantified or qualified. No person has a "good" or "bad" personality, except in relation to the mores, and no person has "more" or "less" personality than any other person. Personality is judged by the sociologist only as well integrated or as poorly integrated, depending upon its effectiveness in helping the person to acquire a satisfactory adjustment to his environment.

At birth, the individual is merely an organization of constitutional qualities and of potentialities for behavior which differ from those of all other individuals.[1] These constitutional qualities and potentialities interact with his environment and, from the integration of his experiences, his personality is formed. Although personality change is most rapid during the very early years of life, it never ceases. As the individual goes through life, he has new experiences which modify his personality.

The wide variety of personality types can be accounted for by the interaction of different constitutional qualities and potentialities with different environments. The effect of these can be noted by holding the factor of environment constant. If it were possible for two persons to have exactly identical environments, the manner in which they are experienced would be very different for an intelligent person and for a dull one. Similarly, it would be different for a person who could see and for one who was blind; for a person whose glandular makeup predisposed him to excitability and for one who was predisposed to

[1] Gardiner Murphy, *Personality: A Biosocial Approach to Origins and Structure,* New York, Harper & Bros., 1947, p. 51.

passivity; for an attractive person and for an ugly one.[2] These
rather extreme examples serve to illustrate the possibility of wide
personality variations on the basis of constitutional differences alone.

In considering the wide range of personality differences, however,
environment is even more important than constitutional organization.
At all times environment dominates experience.[3] The meaning of this
statement will become clearer when we consider what is meant by the
word "environment." Ralph Linton defines it as "the whole of the
individual's surroundings; the personalities as well as the objects and
natural phenomena with which he is in contact." [4] Through the environment culture influences experience and, therefore, personality.[5]
If constitutional factors were to be held constant, the effect of environment on them could be noted. The meaning of dullness to a
child brought up in an intellectual family would be markedly different
from its meaning to a dull child brought up in a family of about the
same I.Q. The meaning of epileptic fits to a person in our society,
which regards the disease as horrible and tinges it with an aura of
disgrace, would differ greatly from the meaning of epilepsy to a person of the Shasta or Zulu societies, for these peoples revere and honor
the epileptic, and believe him to be a miracle man.[6] Thus it can be
seen that although constitutional factors can influence the experience
of the individual, the environment plays an even greater part, in that
it defines the meaning of his constitutional makeup for him.

Culture, whether it be that of Dobu, Zuñi, or America, influences
the environment and, through it, the personality of the person. The
other individuals in the environment of a person have personalities
formed in the same way as his own. The objects which he experiences
are usually those with which his culture is familiar. Even the physical
environment is influenced by culture. In this latter case, the cultural
environment is like a screen between the person and the physical natural environment.[7] It determines to a large extent what the individual
will see in the natural environment and how he will interpret what he
sees. The American sees beauty in a tree while the Andaman Islander
sees a potential canoe.[8] The meaning of a rainstorm is different to a

---

2 Ralph Linton, *The Study of Man*, New York, Appleton-Century-Crofts, Inc., 1936,
p. 466.
3 *Ibid.*, p. 467.
4 *Ibid.*
5 *Ibid.*
6 Ruth Benedict, *Patterns of Culture*, Boston (copyright, Houghton Mifflin Co.), 1934,
pp. 245-250.
7 C. Kluckhohn and W. H. Kelly, "The Concept of Culture," in Ralph Linton (Ed.), *The
Science of Man in the World Crisis*, New York, Columbia University Press, 1945, p. 90.
8 A. R. Radcliffe-Brown, *The Andaman Islanders*, New York, The Macmillan Co., 1933,
pp. 22-48.

city-dweller and a farmer. The geologist sees a volcano far differently from the superstitious natives who live near its base.

The other persons in the environment of any individual are participants in the social system of their society. Each of them occupies a position in the society, that is, each has a *status*. In connection with this position, each plays *roles,* that is, each person puts into effect the rights and duties which go with his position in the social system. The combination of a person's status and roles constitutes for him the minimum of behavior and attitudes which he must possess in order to act effectively in his position. They are the models on which he bases his behavior so that it will not be in conflict with other statuses in the system. Hence, if a person wishes to be a banker in America, in order to fill that status successfully he must have the requisite training and experience, must dress in conservative but well-tailored clothes, must own a certain type of house, drive a car, and entertain only conservative political ideas. He must do nothing which will reflect adversely upon his stability. These are some of the pertinent factors in the ideal pattern our culture contains for a banker —ways in which he should conform if he is to fill his position successfully. Each individual banker will, of course, vary somewhat from the ideal pattern which is set for him, and when enough bankers deviate, the pattern itself may be modified.[9]

The cultural environment presents to the young child a wide variety of statuses and roles which he can observe in action and which, later in life, he will be required to imitate. In the family, he is introduced to the roles of brother, sister, mother, father, and corresponding in-law situations. To these may be added others outside the primary group, such as the businessman, skilled laborer, policeman, fireman, doctor, lawyer, teacher, philanthropist, politician, and prophet. Early in life he comes to realize that many of these roles can be played only by those of appropriate age, sex, economic and social class. It is also obvious that one man may play many of these roles during an average day. For example, consider the table at the top of the opposite page.

This table has included only those roles which were dominant in the situations in which this one man was participating. However, a person must always know many more roles than those which occupy a place of central dominance in his personality. He is required to know what others expect of him in order to play any role in his society.

---

[9] Linton, *The Study of Man,* Ch. 8.

	Time	Activity	Roles
A.M.	7.30— 8.30	Dresses and eats breakfast	Father and husband
	8.30— 9.00	Drives to office with neighbor	Friend
	9.00—12.00	Answers business letters	Manager, employer
P.M.	12.00— 2.00	Has lunch at club of which he is president and to which his brother belongs. Gives speech.	Brother, politician, president of club, prophet, friend, employer
	2.00— 3.30	Conference with company union	Manager, employer, conciliator, tyrant
	3.30— 5.30	Meeting with government officials	Manager, citizen, employer
	6.00— 9.30	Takes wife and children to dinner at home of wife's mother	Husband, father, son-in-law, guest

Although all cultures require the knowledge of many and complex roles, this is particularly true of our own society. Roles and statuses are changing with such rapidity that persons frequently do not know what others expect of them. Such role uncertainties frequently lead to social instability and personal disorganization. However, regardless of the rate of change, these roles represent the general patterns of group expectations for behavior which the child in any culture meets.

As the roles an individual plays in various situations in life represent the minimum of attitudes and types of behavior which he must possess in order to play his part adequately in society, and as all individuals must possess a wide variety of roles, personality can also be defined as the integration of a person's roles. This is merely a different way of stating the definition given earlier that personality is the integration of all the traits and characteristics which make up the person.

It should be emphasized again that status and role in the abstract are the ideal patterns. However, no growing individual experiences them in their ideal forms. The child sees roles played with individual variations. For instance, his father may approximate the ideal father of the society or may deviate from it in varying degrees. Special factors in the situation, such as illness, may distort the playing of the father or mother role in the family; or, as in broken families, the child may never have experience with the father role. As these roles are the examples placed before him of how he is expected to behave when he comes to playing these roles himself, in adulthood, he is placed in the embarrassing situation of trying to play a role he has experienced in a distorted fashion, or has never experienced. Furthermore, he must play the role in a manner which is acceptable to those whose father-mother conceptions have been more in accordance with the ideal patterns. Great emotional disturbances arise within such a person, upsetting his adequate relationships with others. Frequently his role conceptions disintegrate into bits and parts. These segments tend to organize into a secondary personality which frequently collides with the society's expectations for the person and he becomes a pathological personality.

The question arises as to how the child bridges the gap between infancy and adulthood. How does an organization of constitutional qualities become a socialized role-playing man or woman? C. H. Cooley, George Herbert Mead, and Gardiner Murphy present theories which explain the genesis of role-playing activity, and the manner in which these roles become organized into a basic personality structure which George Herbert Mead calls "the self." [10]

The Genesis of the Self in Society.—At birth the infant is merely an organization of constitutional qualities which reacts to the environment. He has no conception of his body as organized, or of its being separate from the environment. Gradually he discovers his leg, his bedpost, his sheets, his mother's hands, and his own arms, but he experiences them as separate entities, having no particular connection, one with the other. His behavior at this time is mainly on the physiological level of satisfying basic needs. His reactions to his environment become increasingly complicated as more and more observations take place. In order to satisfy his needs more adequately he is forced to make changes in his behavior. Growth and experience tend to mark off for him objects which cling together functionally and, as he discovers that this increasing differentiation helps him to satisfy his basic needs more fully, he retains these in memory. The way he reacts to stimuli depends increasingly on association and memory. He tends to respond in the manner he found most satisfactory for meeting the situation the previous time. Gradually he develops the capacity for deciding the type of behavior in which he will engage, that is, what his need is and the behavior which will lead most effectively to its satisfaction.[11] Thus he comes to associate his own wants with the responses they bring from those upon whom he is dependent. In order to call forth effectively the desired response

[10] George Herbert Mead, *Mind, Self and Society,* Chicago, University of Chicago Press, 1934.

[11] Gardiner Murphy, *Personality: A Biosocial Approach to Origins and Structure,* pp. 480-487; Kimball Young, *Personality and Problems of Adjustment,* New York, Appleton-Century-Crofts, Inc., 1947, p. 168.

from others, he must know what they think he is and act accordingly. In other words, his self must become an object to him. He must be able to view himself as he observes others.

This idea of himself as an object, which begins very early in life, becomes integrated in childhood, and changes as new experiences demand throughout life, is what George Herbert Mead has called the "self." The "self" is the central core of the individual's personality. From his conception of the self come all the person's attitudes and behavior throughout life.

As the idea of the "self" emerges from what others think of him, the attitudes of his family and primary group are exceedingly important. Until language is developed the only indication which the child has of these attitudes is from the way his family acts toward him. This is clearly indicated by C. H. Cooley's conception of "the looking glass self."

The reflected looking-glass self ... seems to have three principal elements: the imagination of our appearance to the other person; the imagination of his judgment of that appearance; and some sort of self-feeling, such as pride or mortification. The comparison with a looking glass hardly suggests the second element, the imagined judgment, which is quite essential. The thing that moves us to pride or shame is not the mere mechanical reflection of ourselves, but an imputed sentiment, the imagined effect of this reflection upon another's mind. This is evident from the fact that the character and weight of that other, in whose mind we see ourselves, makes all the difference with our feeling. We are ashamed to seem evasive in the presence of a straightforward man, cowardly in the presence of a brave one, gross in the eyes of a refined one, and so on. We always imagine, and in imagining, share, the judgments of the other mind.[12]

The conception which the child has of the "self" is, therefore, his own notion of what he is and the ideas he thinks that others have about him.

In order to form such a notion for himself, he must observe others. That he does so is shown in numerous childhood situations. The child imitates her mother when playing with a doll, which she treats in the same manner as her mother treats her. Thus she can be said to be playing the role of mother. In the imagined behavior of the doll she is seeing herself as an object through the eyes of her mother, taking over the mother's attitudes toward the child as the latter has interpreted them. This is the first stage of the self when it is composed of "an organization of the particular attitudes of other

---

12 C. H. Cooley, *Human Nature and the Social Order*, New York, Charles Scribner's Sons, 1902, pp. 152-153.

individuals toward himself . . . in the specific social acts in which he participates with them." [13]   At this first stage the child has yet no well defined personality. He plays a succession of roles, passing quickly from one to the other. He takes childish parts in adult life situations. One moment he is the street-car conductor selling a ticket; then he is the purchaser of the ticket; and following this he may be any one of a number of remembered personages who have come into his experience. The child takes into his inner life each of these parts as he plays them. The various selves flow in his memory as autonomous and disconnected.

In internalizing these roles, the use of language is of central importance. While he is playing the role he speaks to himself. He talks as one person and, as the other imaginary person, he hears himself and replies. His reply serves as a stimulus to himself as the first imaginary person and thus the conversation goes on developing within him. At first this activity is overt and verbal. As time goes on, however, he can carry on this process mentally. Thus he takes over the habits, attitudes, and ideas of others and reorganizes them into his own system. Such a process is fundamental to the child's learning to behave as others anticipate that he should. In brief, this is the process of socialization.[14]

In time the child faces a more critical situation in which in order to play the roles of child, father, mother, street-crossing policeman, fireman, and solicitous neighbor, his various roles must converge in a more unified conception of self. Many of his imagined roles overlap. Partly due to this they begin to become organized into a larger pattern of response.

. . . out of a wide range of specific roles of "others" which he has played, there emerges in time a generalized and more or less integrated pattern of the total role of the child. This becomes a part of the integrated self which grows up in everyday interaction with hundreds of specific persons whose attitudes and habits get woven into the child's own.[15]

The importance of such organization in social situations is shown by Professor Mead, who takes the example of a child playing an organized game. In such a game as baseball the child must have an organization of roles or he cannot play the game.[16]   He has a specific part to play but this part is qualified by the roles his teammates are expected to play.

---

13 Mead, *Mind, Self and Society*, p. 158.
14 Young, *Personality and Problems of Adjustment*, p. 170.
15 *Ibid.*, p. 171.
16 Mead, *Mind, Self and Society*, p. 152.

... in order to carry out his own part, he must know what every member of his team is supposed to do or is going to do. He must also anticipate the actions of the opposing team's members. He does not, of course, have to carry all the possible patterns of action in mind at once, but he may have to have a dynamic picture of two, three or four other individuals present in consciousness at the same time. Thus the first baseman's actions will be effective for making a particular play only if he can in imagination assume the ideas and attitudes of the pitcher, the catcher, and the man at bat. The successful ball player is just that one who is able to imagine the actions of others and thus in his own inner forum of thought and imagination be able to anticipate what they will do. Mechanistically he does actually experience in his own neuromuscular system incipient responses like those of the other players, both those of his own team and those of the opposing side.[17]

In playing a game, the action is organized in terms of rules. As Mead points out, rules are often made on the spot, when difficulties arise for which no rule exists. These rules represent a set of responses which a particular attitude calls forth. If a child takes a specific attitude, he can demand a specific response from others. These responses of others are also within himself in that he must be able to put himself in their place in order to be able to predict how they will react.[18] "The game," says Mead, "represents the passage in the life of the child from taking the role of others in play to the organized part that is essential to self-consciousness in the fullest sense of the term." [19]

This game situation can be taken into the relationships of the child and his family. As he obeys rules in baseball, so must he obey the rules of his family. He must be able to imagine the acts of his parents and siblings and be able to put himself in their places. He must, in other words, learn to play his general role of child in the family.[20]

In order to understand how a child organizes the self into a pattern which is in keeping with his social situation, Mead has postulated "The Generalized Other." It is at this point that the attitudes of the social group to which the child belongs come upon the stage. To return to the example of the baseball game, it has been pointed out that the child must be able to put himself in the place of everyone else on the team. Thus he controls his own actions by playing the part of everyone else on the team, at least in taking those attitudes which affect his own particular response. The organization of the

---

[17] Young, *Personality and Problems of Adjustment*, pp. 171-172.
[18] Mead, *Mind, Self and Society*, p. 152.
[19] *Ibid.*
[20] Young, *Personality and Problems of Adjustment*, p. 172.

attitudes he thinks his teammates have toward him is the "generalized other" in this particular situation.

However, the concept, as usually used, is somewhat broader than this would imply. The "generalized other" of the child is the attitude of his whole community and all those he may meet. As the attitudes of his teammates toward his role in the game modify his responses to that specific situation, so does the attitude of the community condition the way he acts in any community situation. He must also take unto himself the attitudes of other individuals toward one another and to various aspects of activity in which they are engaged. From these he must generalize so that all situations of a certain kind call forth the appropriate response which he learned from experiencing only one situation like this.[21] As Mead says,

This getting of the broad activities of any given social whole or organized society as such within the experimental field of any one of the individuals involved or included in that whole is, in other words, the essential basis and prerequisite of the fullest development of that individual's self: only in so far as he takes the attitudes of the organized social group to which he belongs toward the organized, cooperative social activity or set of such activities in which that group as such is engaged, does he develop a complete self.[22]

It is in this situation of self-maturity that the individual can adjust his behavior with respect to what is expected of him by all others whose attitudes have contributed to his self-conception. As he goes through life he plays his roles as schoolboy, wage earner, husband, father, etc., in the manner of which his community approves. In all situations, the role he plays is related to and is modified by all the other roles which are being played or could be played in his society. Having internalized the expectations of others concerning any role he might play, he is under the social (or moral) compulsions of the "generalized other," that is, the other members of his society. This "generalized other" keeps the interests of the larger society omnipresent in all life's decisions.

The importance of Mead's concept of the "generalized other" is well stated by Kimball Young:

G. H. Mead's concept of the generalized other is basic to an understanding of the integration of the self. It rests upon the ability of the individual to develop general attitudes and ideas out of a wide variety of specific and concrete experiences. . . . Apparently an individual may have a range from specific attitudes and habits to general attitudes and habits. So, too the individual may play more or less specific roles in some instances and

---

[21] Mead, *Mind, Self and Society*, pp. 153-155.
[22] *Ibid.*, p. 155.

yet in others may develop the generalized or integrated self. The child is characterized by specific roles, the mature, integrated adult by a generalized self. More or less generalized roles may become linked to concepts of given primary or secondary groups, to those of a larger society or nation, or to humanity or mankind in general. Just how broad and all-inclusive the generalized other may become depends in part on one's capacity to identify himself with a participating role with reference to such human associations as may be considered units in themselves.[23]

While an individual may play many roles in many different situations throughout his life, these are organized into a self which is consistent and predictable. This consistency is based on the similarity between social situations, on broad cultural definitions of appropriate behavior which he has incorporated in the "generalized other," and to his basic self-conception, which defines for him what he is and what he feels is expected of him.

Up to this point in our discussion of the emergence of the self, it would appear that the individual was rather passive, merely accepting roles which were played by those with whom he was in contact. Whereas the "generalized other" is omnipresent in all behavior of individuals, another concept is involved to explain the person as dynamic. In this connection, Mead postulates an "I" and a "me." The self, as it acts, consists of both the "I" and the "me." The "I" is that with which we identify ourselves.

The "I" is the response of the organism to the attitudes of the others; the "me" is the organized set of attitudes of others which one himself assumes. The attitudes of others constitute the organized "me," and then one reacts toward that as an "I." [24]

As Kimball Young states the matter,

The unique character of the "I" is a most important feature of the personality organization. Its roots appear to lie (1) in the organic or constitutional foundations of activity itself, the wants or impulses in connection with which feelings, emotions, fatigue, energy organization and glandular and other bodily functions play a part; (2) in the so-called unconscious associations which have been so well exposed by psychoanalysis; and (3) in the conscious but uncontrolled mental associations depending upon exposure to a wide variety of social experiences. It represents the creative, flexible aspect of the personality. It serves as a basis of that autonomous, individualized form and activity which distinguishes one person from another.[25]

---

23 Young, *Personality and Problems of Adjustment*, p. 173.
24 Mead, *Mind, Self and Society*, p. 175.
25 Young, *Personality and Problems of Adjustment*, p. 178.

The combination of the "I" and the "me" makes up the individual's personality as seen in social situations. "The 'I' is the unpredictable, the unique, the novel element in our thought processes and in overt action." [26] It is subject to modification by the "me," which is, in turn, modified by the social situation. When the "I" has come under the influences of the society's various "me's" the person tends to lose his spontaneity and individuality as the "me's" represent internalized social control or, as it is called by the layman, "conscience." [27]

There are situations in which the "I" and the "me" fuse completely. At such times, self-consciousness is absent or nearly so. "The self under these circumstances is the action of the 'I' in harmony with the taking of the role of others in the 'me.' " [28] Examples are moments of mob behavior, when the person "loses his head," in "losing onself in one's work," and in all-engrossing, mystical, religious, or patriotic behavior.

Language and The Self.—Language and the self develop together within social situations. As Mead points out,

selves must be accounted for in terms of the social process, and in terms of communication. . . . The body is not a self as such; it becomes a self only when it has developed a mind within the context of social experience. . . . Mind arises through communication by a conversation of gestures in a social process or context of experience—not communication through mind.[29]

. . . The language process is essential for the development of the self.[30]

The importance of language in the development of the self can be partially clarified by comparing man with other animals. For example, the dog has no way of indicating yesterday's cat chase to another dog. The only means by which he can communicate any aspect of this experience to the other animal is by chasing another cat. At that point, the other dog can be drawn into the chase. The first dog's behavior in chasing the cat is based on instinct and associated memory, rather than on insight. He does not anticipate finding a cat to chase and intentionally search for one. It is only when the cat appears that his chasing response is again called into action.

The human being, on the other hand, is capable of planning his actions to bring forth a desired response. The infant learns very early in life to think of its own acts in terms of the responses these acts elicit from others. The infant reaches and cries out for objects

---

[26] *Ibid.*, p. 176.
[27] Mead, *Mind, Self and Society*, p. 210.
[28] *Ibid.*, p. 277.
[29] *Ibid.*, pp. 49-50.
[30] *Ibid.*, p. 135.

beyond its grasp and these acts serve to indicate its desire to the adults who can complete it. In an elementary way, this behavior is a use of signs which are associated with ideas.[31]

Human beings constantly adjust their actions to those of others. Each person, before acting, imagines how his conduct will appear to others, and modifies it in keeping with the expectations of the observers. By acting in this way, the person becomes an object to himself even as he is to others. Among animals, however, there is no self-consciousness of behavior. The dog never becomes an object to himself. He modifies his behavior not on the basis of what others expect of him, but rather on a conditioned fear of punishment. Nor does he become an object to another dog unless they are together. Consequently, a dog's behavior remains automatic and, when away from people, uninhibited.

The important difference between human and animal behavior is that the human being has the capacity for developing language and using symbols, which facilitates his communication with other humans. The animal, on the other hand, can communicate with other animals only by setting an example for them to imitate or by the use of a variety of sounds, which are understood by others of their species and which serve only to communicate simple wants and emotional states, but which cannot describe objects or indicate abstract ideas.[32]

Language begins in a "conversation of gestures" between two or more persons in a social act which is initiated by a gesture. Let us call the two persons involved A and B. A makes the initial gesture. B sees this gesture and interprets it, that is, he ascertains what A meant by the gesture. B then reacts to his interpretation of A's gesture. A then interprets B's reaction to his initial gesture and reacts to what he considers B's response meant. In order that A and B can carry on this "conversation of gestures" each must be able to put himself in the place of the other and view the gesture as the other views it.[33] At every stage in the developing social act, each is aware of the common meaning of the gestures they make. This goes on until the act is completed, whereat a new social object, objective, or idea has emerged. To state it more simply, at the completion of the act, an understanding or undertaking has been agreed upon.

In a social act involving two or more persons, the gestures are vocal sounds which become words or symbols of a language system. Whereas there are other gestures in communication—a shake of the

31 E. T. Hiller, *Principles of Sociology*, New York, Harper & Bros., 1934, p. 91.
32 *Ibid.*, p. 93.
33 H. Blumer, "Social Psychology" in E. P. Schmidt (Ed.), *Man and Society*, New York, Prentice-Hall, Inc., 1938, pp. 171-172.

head, a frown, movements of the hands, posture of the body—the vocal sounds are of central importance in that they do not interfere with major forms of physical activity and in that meaning can be conveyed more speedily and more exactly and in wider variety. As language grows up in a social situation, those who share the same language also share the meanings of the symbols they employ, or have enough meanings of other symbols in common to come to an agreement concerning the significance of a word with two or more interpretations. Hence, although the American sociologist and the American layman have different interpretations of the word "personality," they share common meanings of enough other words so that if a layman decided to study sociology he could come to an agreement with the sociologist about the meaning of this other term.

The function of symbols is to pick out those aspects of an act which are pertinent and meaningful in the experience of the individuals concerned. This limiting of the procedure to the most pertinent stimuli permits the various responses to organize themselves into a form of action.

> The symbol is more than a mere substitute stimulus ... conditioned reflexes plus consciousness of the attitudes and meanings they involve are what constitute language ... and thence lay the basis ... for thought and intelligent conduct. Language is the means whereby individuals can indicate to each other what their responses to objects will be and hence what the meanings of objects are. . . .[34]

It has been pointed out that language has its beginnings in an overt "conversation of gestures," which involves taking the place of the other person, in imagination. While the external actions of the individual remain important throughout life, the development of the self and the ability to take the role of the other person in imagination accentuates the growing importance of the mind or "inner forum" in personality development. Within this "inner forum" the person can use the words and ideas associated with the many roles he has to play in life's social situations. He can review or anticipate the responding attitudes and ideas of others to any of his roles. For example, the child who is late for supper tries to figure out how to act on arriving home so as to meet the least possible punishment from his mother. In his mind he tries out the various possibilities. He sees himself entering the door and anticipates what his mother will be doing and how she will react to his late entrance. He anticipates what he will say and how she will react to his words. He decides

---

[34] Mead, *Mind, Self and Society*, pp. 122-123.

what he will say next and how she will react and so on until he hits upon what he considers will be the best way to meet the ensuing situation. He is then ready to meet the problem of entering the house.

By such a rehearsal of the person's roles and his interpretation of what the responses of others would be to his behavior, the content of the mind becomes orderly. The person can solve problems and crises and can modify his personality in keeping with the expectations of others. To illustrate the latter, Brown uses the example of Mary, whose sloppy manner of dressing made her unpopular. One day she overheard the girls of her class talking about her. Although she was made unhappy by their remarks, she rehearsed them in her mind and thus saw herself from their point of view. In her mind she rehearsed their reactions to her as a tidy, attractive person and decided to change herself to fit in with their ideas of what she should be like.[35]

Symbols and language are the mechanisms by which meanings can be conveyed to others. With the evolution of vocal symbols into sight symbols, the number of persons with whom communication is possible has been greatly increased. Books, newspapers, and other media which use the printed word have made it possible to share experiences with others who have very different backgrounds and who interpret experience in another way. Such inventions as the telegraph, telephone, radio, and television have enlarged the number of communicants still further. Through such inventions the individual is enabled to participate in social situations occurring at great distances from him, and can incorporate these social situations into his own experience.[36]

This, then, is the social-psychological background from which the chief insights into man as a thinking and planning animal can be gained. Language and the self grow up in a social situation due to the interaction of the individual and his environment. From his experiences in this interaction, his personality is formed.

Questions

1. What is personality? Under what conditions does it come into existence?
2. What is meant by role and status? How do these concepts enter into the organization of personality and behavior?
3. "The person acquires a family, a social world." Discuss.

[35] L. G. Brown, *Social Psychology*, New York, McGraw-Hill Book Co., Inc., 1934, pp. 499-500.
[36] *Ibid.*, p. 504.

4. What does Cooley mean by "the looking-glass self"?
5. Discuss the emergence of the self in social interaction.
6. Differentiate between the "I" and the "me."
7. What is meant by the "generalized other"? What part does it play in the formation and control of personal behavior?
8. What is the relationship between personality and culture?
9. Most human problems turn out to be problems of status. Do you agree?
10. Is there any evidence to support the contention that a baby would not develop human behavior or personality if permanently isolated from others?
11. What role does language play in the development of personality?
12. Playing the role of the other is the underlying factor in our private thinking. Explain.
13. What part does the concept of playing the dual role play in determining our ability to understand people of cultural groups different from our own?

BIBLIOGRAPHY

The combined bibliography for Chapters 5-6 will be found on pages 130-133.

Chapter 6

PERSONAL ADJUSTMENT

The preceding chapter has discussed the emergence of personality through the interaction of the biological characteristics of the human organism with his culture, as transmitted to him through the social groups with which he has had relationships. Other chapters have dealt with the nature of social groups and culture. In the present chapter we shall concern ourselves with the manner in which the basic personality structure of the individual enables him to meet the problems which arise during the course of his life. It is not our intention to attempt to deal with all the adjustments people have to make. We are interested here only in those problems which affect the majority of people in our own society. The less common areas of adjustment will be left for later sections of this text, for example, the problems in adjustment arising from membership in ethnic, racial, or ideological groups.[1]

Personality and Culture.—The personalities of all members of a society are representative of that society's culture. Regardless of the wide range of variation which exists among the individual members in biological heritages, environments, and experiences, the society expects all its members to conform to its standards of appropriate behavior and personality type. The culture of the society helps them to do so by offering certain ready-made solutions for many of the problems which will arise during their lives. The person incorporates many of these solutions into his personality in the form of habits and attitudes which are called forth automatically by the situations with which they are designed to cope, requiring little thought on the part of the person. However, there are other situations for which the culture has no clear-cut solution. Some of these are unique and new and others are situations for which the society offers a wide range of alternative patterns from which the individual may choose the solution which is most congenial to him. Some persons manage to solve these latter types of situations in a manner which is in keeping with their own personalities and, at the same time,

---

[1] See Chapters 15 and 19.

in a manner which is acceptable to their culture. Others fail in their attempts. However, regardless of whether the person succeeds or fails, his personality is still representative of his culture. It is the culture of the society to which he belongs which gives rise to and patterns both the conforming and non-conforming personality.

In addition to being representative of a culture, each personality is also unique, for no two persons have exactly the same biological inheritance. Great differences in intelligence, temperament, strength, health, and appearance enter into the process of personality development to give rise to distinct and individual personalities. The uniqueness of personality is still further enhanced by the fact that no two persons ever have exactly the same experiences, exactly the same environment, or take part in exactly the same social groups. Thus distinctly different personalities are developed through the interaction of different biological characteristics with different interpretations of the same culture, as transmitted by a wide variety of social groups made up of a great number of different personalities. The number of distinct personalities which arise from such a process is infinite.

What is surprising is not that personalities are different but that they tend to have so many characteristics in common, falling within a range typical of the culture to which they belong. The majority of the Zuñi Indians are quiet, cooperative, friendly, and unassuming. The Kwakiutl tend to be aggressive, individualistic, hostile, and megalomaniacal. The personalities of the members of these groups are all distinct and unique entities, yet the number of persons in these societies whose personalities are markedly divergent from the average types are very few and are looked upon by the society as abnormal.[2]

Although each society tends to organize its social system around the average personalities existing in the culture, provisions are also made for those with personality differences. Few cultural patterns exist as absolutes, permitting no deviation on the part of individuals. Customarily, alternatives are offered which are acceptable as long as they are kept within the range defined by the culture as permissible. For those with special interests and aptitudes, each social system provides a choice of statuses for which a person may compete. Thus the society is able to make use of his special talents and interests and, at the same time, the person is given a congenial status.

The social systems of societies, however, tend to be built around the average personality. The person with no special gifts and no

---

[2] See Chapters 3 and 4.

particular disabilities can be trained to occupy almost any status and to perform the associated roles adequately for the purpose of the continuance of the society. As talents and special interests are unpredictable, the society tends to rely upon the average person to conduct most of the routine tasks of living. The training of members of the society for their future statuses begins at birth and, as talents do not usually become apparent until adolescence or even later, most persons are trained in a similar manner during their early years, the society assuming that they will be average. Differential training and the assignment of special statuses for the gifted members of a society begin when the talent or interest becomes apparent.

Each society has stages around which it organizes its roles and statuses. These stages are usually outlined in terms of chronological age. In addition, each stage is usually subdivided according to sex. Within each of these particular stages and sex divisions, the individual not only has to act in a manner acceptable to his own particular group, but is also preparing to move on to the next stage. Parents give the infant training for childhood; the adolescent learns the roles which will be appropriate for his status as an adult.[3] In this chapter, the development of the individual's personality as he passes through these stages will be dealt with at some length.

Personality Adjustment and Maladjustment.—In every society individuals have varying degrees of difficulty in orientating their personalities to the requirements of their new status positions. The transition from one stage to the next brings new situations to be met, new degrees of responsibility, and new duties. Unless the training for the new status has been adequate, it is difficult for the person to adjust his earlier roles to the new situation. Some of these roles may become fixed and rigid, and may continue to play a major part in forming his attitudes and behavior long after they have ceased to be appropriate for his age and sex group and his status position in this group. Such fixated roles are resistant to change and frequently interfere with his adjustment to new situations and new statuses, disturbing the balance and healthy integration of his personality. Such a person is said to be maladjusted.

The well-adjusted person is one "whose various social activities are in substantial reciprocal balance. . . . his various life processes are integrated into a smoothly functioning whole."[4] He thinks and acts

---

3 Ralph Linton, *The Study of Man*, New York, Appleton-Century-Crofts, Inc., 1936, Ch. 8.
4 M. A. Elliott and F. E. Merrill, *Social Disorganization*, New York, Harper & Bros., 1941, p. 75.

in accordance with his group's definition of the normal. In contrast, the maladjusted person is "essentially uncoordinated. For one reason or another he becomes one-sided, devoting too much time and energy to one group of activities and ignoring others equally important in his life scheme. Even if he does not become so maladjusted as to be adjudged undesirable, . . . he is regarded as definitely unnatural, or out of balance." [5]

In our society, the high mobility of the population and the greatly accelerated rate of social change make it difficult to train a person adequately for new status positions. New situations are constantly arising which make demands on the person in any status position. These are often situations for which he has received no training and for which no patterns of appropriate behavior have been laid down by the culture. Parents and teachers find it difficult, if not impossible, to prepare the child for a world which is very different from the one in which they grew up and from which they derived a major part of their knowledge of how to train him. In addition, the social system itself is in flux. New positions are constantly being created and the old ones are becoming less meaningful or are altering their character. The person in the new status position must find his way alone and must build up patterns of reciprocal behavior which make his position meaningful to and well integrated with the society as a whole.

However, the situation is not quite as black as it appears at first glance. Although the conditions existing in our society make status training difficult, parents are still aware that there are fundamental qualities which, if instilled into the child, will make his path easier and will help him to retain a well-integrated and well-adjusted personality. If he is taught independence of thought and action, responsibility for his own behavior, and acceptance of the values of the society, he will be able to evaluate and act in new situations in a manner which is considered appropriate by his social group and which is congenial to his personality.

The underlying factors in personality maladjustment are legion. The majority of maladjustments, however, arise from inadequate training during the processes of personality development in primary and secondary relationships as the person passes from one age group to the next, from personal crises which disrupt his habitual patterns of behavior, and from maladjustments in his culture, arising from its uneven integration and the high rate of social change. In reality, the underlying factors making for personality maladjustment are so

---

[5] *Ibid.*, pp. 75-76.

intricately interrelated that it is only for the purpose of analysis that they can be separated arbitrarily in this fashion.

PERSONALITY ADJUSTMENT AND DEVELOPMENT IN PRIMARY AND SECONDARY RELATIONSHIPS

The preceding chapter has dealt at some length with the emergence of personality in the human infant through his participation in primary relationships. Later, as a child, his personality becomes organized and integrated through the playing of socially defined roles and through interaction with other members of his society. By learning to play the dual role, and acquiring the ability to see himself as others see him, he is able to regulate his behavior to conform to the expectations of those about him. His behavior becomes consistent and to some degree predictable. Still later he acquires what G. H. Mead has termed the Generalized Other which helps him to act in a manner which his society considers suitable for a person of his status.

The motivation behind learning and performing social roles is the necessity of learning to manage one's social world in order to survive. In infancy the social world which must be managed is the family into which the child was born, particularly the adult members upon whom the child depends for even his most elementary needs. In childhood, he must learn to manage a world composed of his family and other children of his own age. In adolescence and adulthood, his social world broadens out to its maximum boundaries, to shrink again to a smaller size in old age. In this section we are primarily concerned with the adjustment of personality to these different stages of life.

Personal Adjustment in Infancy.—In order to survive, the infant must acquire techniques for dealing with the adult world upon which he depends for the satisfaction of his most elementary needs and for protection during his maturing years, as well as for training for self-sufficient adulthood. He must learn to manage the psychological and physiological tensions associated with feeding, sleeping, elimination, and movement. He must learn to play social roles and to see himself as others see him in order to act in a manner which is acceptable, first to those upon whom he depends and later to the larger society. He must learn to generalize behavior learned in specific situations to other areas of action to which it is applicable. He must learn to achieve the satisfactions of his basic needs even when his parents reject or overprotect him or in spite of their inconsistent treatment. He must learn responsibility and independence. Without this knowledge he will be unable to manage the adult world upon which he is forced to depend during his maturing years or to become self-sufficient when he himself grows to adulthood.

The techniques which the child develops or learns for solving his problems and gaining his wishes during the period of dependence upon his family shape his basic attitudes, which are retained as permanent parts of his mental equipment,[6] and are altered only when they prove to be inadequate in providing him with the satisfaction of his needs. Some of the techniques learned at this stage of life become so strongly reinforced through repetition in the family situations with which they deal successfully that they are never amenable to change. Personality maladjustment occurs when they no longer prove satisfactory, although some of these maladjustments prove to be only temporary. The person is often in a confused state only until his personality becomes sufficiently reorientated to deal with the new situation. Other maladjustments are more permanent and interfere with the adjustment of the person from infancy to old age.

The very early training of the infant in eating, sleeping, and elimination lays the groundwork upon which orderly and predictable patterns of behavior and a well-integrated personality can be built. The parents deal with the child according to certain culturally established techniques of child training and the child is forced to learn to satisfy his needs within this framework. Other restrictions are placed upon the techniques which he acquires for dealing with the adult world by his own innate biological heritage. His intelligence, temperament, strength, and appearance all play a part in the development of his patterns of response. In addition, the attitudes of his parents toward him condition the forms of behavior which prove most efficient in achieving the desired responses to his demands. If the child knows that he is to be fed only at specific times, he learns to adjust to that situation. However, if there is disagreement because of a parent's whim, the interference of others living in the household, or the conflict of culture patterns (for example, the mother's wish to feed the child when he cries as against the doctor's instructions to feed him only at specified hours), the child will be hampered in developing orderly response patterns. Behavior which one time brings forth food may not, the next time, bring any response from the mother. The child has no basis for understanding the reasons behind the

6 Abram Kardiner, "The Concept of Basic Personality Structure," in Ralph Linton (Ed.), *The Science of Man in the World Crisis*, New York, Columbia University Press, 1945, pp. 107-122.

inconsistency of treatment and has difficulty in building up patterns of behavior which will unfailingly solve that situation.

However, whether or not he understands the reasons behind his mother's behavior, action on the part of the child is imperative. He must learn to manage the adult world because his very existence depends upon it. If treatment is consistent, he will fall in with the pattern laid down as he realizes that it is the best way to achieve his ends. However, if this path is not open to him, due to inconsistency on the part of the adults, he will discover other methods. He frequently shows at a very early age an amazing knowledge of how to play off one parent against the other. Often he gives way to temper tantrums, which are a strictly biological reaction to frustration.[7] This latter form of behavior makes him the center of attention, frequently leaving his parents without any way of dealing with his outbreak and ultimately getting him the desired wish when the parents, unable to cope with the situation, give in to his demands. He may also take the path of withdrawal, stubbornly standing his ground. This behavior is equally difficult for the parent and often gets the child what he wants. These latter two forms of behavior are often the reaction of the child to a situation with which he disagrees but has not the command of language required to explain. Depending on the treatment meted out in these situations, the child will "grow out of it," or it will become an habitual and immature reaction pattern.

In learning to manage the adult world, the first object of fixation and identification for the child is his mother, and, as a result, a great number of his responses get tied in with her behavior toward him. His attitude toward her is frequently ambivalent. Discipline gives an unpleasant tone to a relationship which is, at other times, pleasant in that she satisfies his demands. Through her he learns to inhibit some of his wishes in order to gain social approval. He learns to classify his wishes as acceptable and not acceptable. She is the first "other" to the child.

To a great extent, he forms his self-conception in keeping with what she and the other members of the family feel about him. If he is subjected to ridicule, abuse, or sarcasm, an unwanted feeling may develop and inferiority feelings emerge which frequently have serious effects when carried into other areas of life when the child leaves the family circle. On the other hand, if his mother is oversolicitous, the child may develop a culturally unacceptable degree of dependence

---

7 Kimball Young, *Personality and Problems of Adjustment*, New York, F. S. Crofts & Co., 1947, p. 386.

upon her and be unable to cope with life situations when she is not present to help him. If he is overpraised, he may develop an inflated idea of his own worth which, if it persists, will make him incapable of competing successfully with others at a later date. If the mother pushes him to do tasks which are beyond his abilities, a sense of inferiority and failure may develop. The reaction of the child to this situation may be to withdraw into a world of fantasy in which he is able to manage his problems successfully; to react with anger and aggression, by which he tries to compensate for his feelings of inferiority. Or, he may try unself-confidently to conform to what is expected of him and constantly be haunted by fear and anxiety, feelings inimical to a healthy personality development.

In developing his self-conception, the average child does not run into these extremes of behavior. The parents are usually aware that they are training the child for adulthood and behave toward him in a manner which is conducive to the development of a self-conception based on self-confidence and a feeling of worth tempered by a realization of shortcomings. Parents who are overprotective, who reject the child, or set too high standards for him, are usually those who have some inadequacy in their own personalities, the demands of which assume ascendency over their wishes for the child's healthy personality development.

In the family group, the child finds satisfaction for his needs for security and safety. A feeling of security develops when he finds that he can satisfy his wishes by his behavior. Consistent treatment on the part of parents plays a major role in building up this feeling in the child. It enables him to predict and use definite patterns of behavior in order to bring forth desired responses. It gives him a sense of being able to manage his own world. On the other hand, if he is treated inconsistently, a feeling of insecurity arises because he cannot formulate any pattern of behavior which will bring forth the desired response from his parents.

Security also arises from stable family relationships. The child is certain of a lasting group of adults upon whom he can depend. He is able to identify himself with these adults and, through observing their behavior, learn new roles and acquire appropriate attitudes. However, if there is constant bickering between the parents, uncertainty arises as to the durability of the family unit. The child does not know on which parent to depend for the satisfaction of his needs. The resultant insecurity is intensified as the child is often unable to differentiate between rage caused in one parent by the actions of the other and that which he brings about by unacceptable behavior. The parents who are not compatible are also likely to involve him in their disagreements, treating him in a highly emotional and inconsistent manner and seeking to gain his allegiance by criticizing one another to him. Such behavior is emotionally very upsetting to the child, who does not know how to feel about or how to behave toward his parents. It breaks down his feelings of identification with them, and thereby injures his personality development.

The child must also learn responsibility and independence. He must learn to manage his own needs in relation to those needs rather than in relation to parental wishes. If the parents impose their solutions upon the child, he is unable to understand what is involved in solving the problem, which makes it difficult for him to generalize the solutions and apply them to other problems of a similar nature. In addition, he is not learning to act independently or to accept responsibility for his behavior. If he is overprotected by the parent and shielded from failure, he will not learn to fail and try again and will be unable to act independently of the parent in situations which arise away from home.

Usually, however, parents realize that they will not always be present to solve the problems of their child. They are aware of the need for independence and a feeling of responsibility for behavior in the child, if he is to live a satisfactory adult life. As a result, the child usually learns early in life to stand on his own feet to the degree which is possible at his stage of development.

Personal Adjustment in Childhood.—Many of the learning processes begin in infancy, are carried over into childhood, and from childhood are continued throughout adult life. However, childhood is the time when the individual really begins to learn to manage social relationships with others outside his family group.

Normally, at about five years of age, the child begins to break away from his family and become incorporated into a group of children about his own age with whom he spends several hours each day. Among his playmates he learns to manage responsibilities which are not connected with the family. He learns to find his way in interpersonal relationships and to acquire a status in his own group. In doing so the patterns of response learned in the family situation play an important part. If he is a secure person, he is able to adjust to this new situation and adapt his patterns of behavior in a manner acceptable to his play group. As a rule he is relatively free of his parents in this situation and, even when the parents do enter in, the other children define the meaning of such interference for him. New interaction patterns arise and the child begins to free himself of his emotional dependence upon his mother. However, if he has been overprotected at home and if the parents continue to be oversolicitous in shielding him in his play group, he is severely handicapped in deriving satisfactory patterns of interaction, in learning responsibility, and in breaking his emotional attachment to his parents. It is in the play group that the child also learns the cultural rules of fair play, of loyalty to a group, how to manage antagonism, rivalry, and emulation. He also learns many of the roles appropriate to his sex.

If the child has been a member of a family containing other children, he has already learned many of the behavior patterns which will help him to adjust to those children of his own age outside the home. He has probably learned to manage rivalry and the benefits of mutual give and take. Where rivalry has been balanced by love and help among children, the chances that a well-balanced personality will emerge are excellent. However, if jealousy and envy are present, if favoritism is shown, or if the child is rejected by the other children in the family, insecurity and inferiority feelings may result which will color his responses to his play group.

As the child grows older, he begins to participate in other institutions in his society, for example, the church and the school, and, from this participation, he enlarges his experience. The community and its institutions provide goals for the child which the family interprets until he is old enough to judge for himself. Always the child has before him the example of his parents, as well as their verbal behavior. If the parents act in keeping with the community and institutional goals, the child is able to incorporate these into his way of thinking without conflict. However, if their verbal interpretations and actual behavior fail to coincide, confusion results for the child. He finds it difficult to form a well organized "Generalized Other," that is, a consistent idea of what the community regards as acceptable behavior on his part.

In later childhood and early adolescence the child frequently joins a gang. This is especially true if he is a boy. In these relationships, he breaks more of his emotional ties with his family. Above all he desires the approval of his gang, even when it conflicts with gaining the approval of his family. The friendships formed in the gang are based on common interests, on a common age and sex, and on loyalty to one another. Many of the tensions created in the family by taboo subjects can be released by discussing these with members of the gang. Much information which the family refuses him can be acquired. At all times the gang assures him of understanding and help in solving his problems and provides a sympathetic listener or group of listeners. Through his gang activity, he learns cooperation in joint undertakings, and the elementary patterns for participating in a formal organization. He also learns to enhance his status by competitive activity and to be able to subjugate his own wishes to the authority of his own age group. Often he learns for the first time to respond to reason rather than to commands.

In these play groups and the gang relationships of the child, feelings of worth and of emotional support may be derived. If his family has been oversolicitous, if they have given him an inflated self-conception, if they have failed to provide him with a feeling of independence and responsibility, the child may find himself unsuccessful in these group relationships. On the other hand, these groups may teach him what his family has failed to give him. If the child finds himself unsuccessful in the mutual give and take of gang and play group relationships, he may become aggressive or he may withdraw into isolation. The latter is inimical to future adjustment. However, if, in his aggression, he learns to play a dominant role in his group and is able to see others in his mind as being submissive and therefore understand them, he may become an effective leader. If this is the case, he may develop a healthy and independent personality.

In closing, one might wish to consider the special case of the only child who does not have the same opportunities as the average young person for socializing his egotistical impulses. This problem is becoming increasingly important in the western world. With the greater degree of urbanization, one-child families are becoming more and more prevalent and can be expected to increase still further in keeping with the trend toward city living.

Ideally, the young child should be in contact with other children of his own age from about eighteen months onward. However, under conditions of urban living this is often very difficult. The apartment-dwelling family tends to keep the child within its confines except for brief periods of outdoor activity when the mother watches the child at play. It is not, as a rule, feasible for the child to play out of doors by himself without supervision as streets are dangerous playgrounds and apartment areas are not overly supplied with gardens and parks where the young child can play by himself in safety.

The only child may be handicapped in his relations with those of his own age group as the only roles which are available to him to learn are those of adults. He is unable to learn from other children the roles which are more simplified and appropriate to his age group. He tends to develop a strong identification with adults and, as he is

usually the center of attention in a small family group, his conception of himself and his importance is often out of line with reality.
Being very small and dependent upon adults, he may develop inferiority feelings instead. In either event, his personality often has
too great an emphasis on self-attitudes and self-concern.[8]

While the only child may be handicapped in his relations with
those of his own age group, he is not necessarily inadequately trained
for the adult world. He has learned adult roles early in life and this
may become an advantage in his own adulthood. In addition, with
the increasing number of only children in the western world, his
personality may eventually become the norm.

As we have seen, the behavior patterns laid down in childhood are
those which equip the person for eventual adulthood. Certain roles
and responses may become fixated, with harmful effects on the future
adjustment of the person. However, a large number of these fixated
roles are likely to be called forth only by specific situations and may
not harm his adjustment to the ordinary routine of living. But they
always remain as potential threats. Overdependence upon a parent
may result in the person not marrying and in having difficulty in establishing normal heterosexual relationships. If the parent dies there
is always the danger that the person will be unable to manage his
life without parental support. In the last war fixations and dependence upon mothers interfered with the adjustment of many men to
combat situations. Many other situations may arise in which the
person with fixated roles may be unable to meet the expectations of
the adult world. However, maladjustment is often only a potential.
It may be realized in childhood, in adolescence, in adult life, or never,
according to the circumstances which arise.

Personal Adjustment in Adolescence.—In our society adolescence
is looked upon as a period of life which is very upsetting for the young
person. However, anthropologists have discovered that adolescence
in other societies poses few or no problems for the growing person.
Although the behavior characteristic of adolescence in our society
has been explained by greatly accelerated physical growth, extensive
physiological changes, and the transition from dependent childhood
to responsible adult status, it is now more generally agreed, on the
basis of anthropological findings, that ambivalence of attitudes and
treatment, rather than biological changes, is the basis of the confusion felt at this period of life. Our society has no clear idea of what

---

[8] Louis Taylor, "The Social Adjustment of The Only Child," *Am. J. Sociol.*, Vol. 51, No. 3,
November, 1945, pp. 227-232.

to do about the adolescent and provides no place for him. His physical changes impress themselves upon our minds and we can no longer think of him as a child in this respect. However, his social immaturity is such that neither can we think of him as an adult. He is too old for many childish forms of behavior and yet too young to go to work, to marry, and to accept other adult responsibilities. Our behavior toward him reflects the ambivalence of our attitudes and gives rise to confusion in his attitudes toward himself. Because of our society's uncrystallized attitudes about the appropriate status of adolescents, a wide range of behavior is permitted to them. Only when they go beyond the limits of this range is action taken to force them to conform.

Each stage in the life of the person is preparation for the next stage, and adolescence is a preparation for adulthood. In infancy and in childhood, the person has a status and is given training for assuming a new status when he gets older. However, little training is given to the adolescent to prepare him for adulthood. The child is protected and guided by the parents until, at adolescence, he is expected to begin to assume adult statuses without any knowledge of how to assume the responsibilities involved or how to make the necessary and important decisions upon which the remainder of his life may depend. Having been brought up in the parents' idea of what is in keeping with their status, it is difficult for him to decide upon occupational or educational opportunities which do not conform to their desires and expectations. Presumably free to choose and act freely, he is frequently termed "ungrateful," "unworthy of love and support," or even "wicked," when he goes against parental wishes. He is torn between the desire and necessity of being independent and retaining his emotional ties with his family. Having no training for his new adult status, he frequently resorts to trial and error methods to solve his problems. Some adolescents rebel against their parents and break free of them, others are helped by their parents to stand on their own feet and others give up the fight for independence in favor of retaining their emotional ties with the family. There is no uniform pattern on which they can base their behavior in our society.

In many other societies the situation at this time of life is very different. The society provides statuses and sets a time or age level for the acquisition of each. Training precedes taking over the new status. In addition, the rights and duties of each status are clearly defined and well understood by all members of the group. Once the person has been initiated into the new status, either formally or informally, he is expected and permitted to exercise the prerogatives which go with it to the best of his ability. His mistakes are tolerated or severely disciplined until he learns to feel his way. However, in the mind of the adolescent there exists no confusion as to whether he is a child or an adult, as to whether he is responsible for his own actions or is still dependent upon parental authority. The status he occupies makes his position clear to himself and to others. The relatively rigid nature of the social order of such a group delineates for him only a few possible life courses and he is, therefore, not faced with the multiple and confusing choices which confront the adolescent of our own society.[9]

Other problems for the adolescent center around the facing of impersonal economic competition for the first time; around the necessity of reconciling cultural ideals with reality; in retaining his feeling of worth in the face of unemployment and occupations which are not suited to his interests, abilities, and self conception; and in finding new values when some of the old values prove inadequate. He also has the problem of adjusting his heterosexual relations to the demands of his society and his own personality, despite the obscure attitudes in which he has been indoctrinated during his maturing period.

In relatively stable, primitive societies even these problems do not face the adolescent. There is little impersonal and harsh competition in a society where economic and social status are determined by family membership or ritual requirements. Cultural ideas and reality are closely coordinated with little apparent discrepancy to cause confusion and disillusionment. Each person is given the task which he expected and unemployment is non-existent. Hence the person's feeling of worth is rarely threatened in the economic field. If he does not succeed in his ascribed task, blame is not thrown upon him but on some external force or the job is modified in keeping with his capabilities. Lacking the emphasis placed upon economic success and the accumulation of wealth, the economic activities of the person do not tend to become a matter of deep concern to the group.

An adolescent in a primitive society shares a set of values with his whole society. These values rarely cause him emotional turmoil as they are not open to question and hence are infrequently, if ever,

---

[9] Ruth Benedict, "Continuities and Discontinuities in Cultural Conditioning," *Psychiatry*, Vol. 1, 1938, pp. 161-167; Cora DuBois, *People of Alor*, Minneapolis, University of Minnesota Press, 1944; John Gillin, "Personality in Preliterate Societies," *Am. Sociol. Rev.*, Vol. 4, No. 5, October, 1939, pp. 681-702; Margaret Mead, *Coming of Age in Samoa*, New York, William Morrow & Co., Inc., 1928; Margaret Mead, *Growing Up in New Guinea*, New York, William Morrow & Co., Inc., 1929.

proved inadequate. They are the values of his group and he accepts them as absolutes without feeling any need for considering them further. Lacking the wide variety of values which exist in our society, there is no ground for comparing them with the values of others and they remain strong and firm.

Living in large families, in close proximity to persons of all ages, sexual intercourse, pregnancy, and birth are without mystery and are merely aspects of living. Thus sex poses no problem and the integration of this part of life into the personality is smooth, without confusion or feelings of guilt so prevalent in our own society.

The small size of the family and the high rate of social change in our society complicate life still further for the adolescent in the transition period between childhood and adulthood. In America the household tends to be made up of adults and children, between whom there is an age gap of twenty years or more. The rapidity of social change widens the gap psychologically even more than the actual number of years would indicate. Parents and children live in somewhat different social worlds and find it difficult to understand one another. The parent cannot put himself in the position of his child in order to understand the behavior of the latter in many situations, as he has little personal experience which would enable him to do so. The only guide by which he can hope to understand his son or daughter is comparison with other children of about the same age.[10] Conflict and lack of understanding between the viewpoints of adults and adolescents are therefore inevitable in our society. The result is often confusion and mental upset for the adolescent who has come to see the deficiencies of his parents' views and yet has no satisfactory definitions by which to guide his behavior.

The small size of the family group also intensifies emotional feeling among its members. Family sentiment is directed toward so few persons that complexes and fixations frequently develop. With the sheering away of the kinship group and a large number of common family activities, these emotional ties are extremely tenuous and unstable. For the adolescent this situation is difficult to deal with because any behavior defined by his parents as inappropriate is seen by them as a threat to their ties with their child and its seriousness is magnified in proportion to their emotional attachment to him. Because these ties are so intense and because parents and children are so closely identified with one another, the adolescent finds it difficult to assert himself. When, in addition, the parents have been

---

10 Margaret Mead, *And Keep Your Powder Dry*, New York, William Morrow & Co., Inc., 1942.

dissatisfied with their own lives and have set for their child the goals which they themselves failed to achieve, the situation becomes even more difficult for the young person.[11]

In other societies, where the larger kinship group is the family unit, generations overlap and there is no discrepancy in ages as in our society's family group. The slow rate of social change tends to minimize the psychological gap between the age groups. These two factors contribute to the provision of patterns of appropriate behavior for the adolescent, who can watch either those in the next age group to his own or his parents whose experiences at adolescence were very similar to his. Thus this period of life does not constitute a crisis but is merely a continuation of life and personality development from which little maladjustment develops.

The large size of the family group tends to spread out the emotional ties and lessen their intensity. In addition, the large number of activities in which the family group as a whole is engaged operates to hold the person to his group for other than emotional reasons. As the expectations of what life will offer are always closely allied to reality in a stable society, there is no tendency for the parents to project their thwarted desires upon the child. All his relatives are responsible for his behavior and his welfare, and the child feels less hesitant to break away from any parental demands upon him which he feels he is unable to fulfil.

In our society, the lack of any clear-cut expectations of adolescent behavior are reflected in the institutions to which the young person belongs. The different institutions make varying demands upon his maturity. Thus the roles which he plays in these institutions show different degrees of maturity. The adolescent may show himself capable of taking over adult responsibility in his first job or in the educational institution to which he belongs, while retaining many infantile patterns of response in the family situation. In addition, the demands made upon him by the various groups may not be consistent with one another. Business may require cutthroat methods while the family, church, and friendship groups require consideration of others. As the person plays roles in each of these institutions, a certain inconsistency of personality may develop. In managing to act in the face of inconsistent attitudes learned in these institutions, the person has two alternatives. First, he may segregate his roles in such a manner that they are called forth only by the situations for

---

[11] Kingsley Davis, "Sociology of Parent-Youth Conflict," *Am. Sociol. Rev.*, Vol. 5, No. 4, August, 1940, pp. 523-535; Young, *Personality and Problems of Adjustment*, Ch. 16; Elliott and Merrill, *Social Disorganization*, Ch. 3.

which they are appropriate without any attempt being made to relate them to one another or make them consistent. This is poor mental hygiene and behavior is often paralyzed when situations arise which are not defined in terms of one attitude or another. The other alternative is to require a mature self-control based on consistent ideals and principles with the realization that, in order to be successful in human relationships, he must see himself in relation to others. He must plan and control his behavior accordingly, and be willing to accept responsibility for his actions. Unless he has received training in childhood, in the habits and attitudes prerequisite to this new maturity, he may suffer maladjustment as a result of his lack of personality integration.

After adolescence, the person is an adult. Although his personality will continue to change as circumstances change throughout life, certain of the main trends within it are relatively set: for example, his vocational interests, his ability to get along with other persons, whether he is introverted or extroverted, and whether he is self-sufficient or not. From adolescence onward, the person must make his own choices, establish his own interpersonal and heterosexual relationships, take responsibility for his actions, and acquire mature self-control.

Personal Adjustment in Adulthood

Occupational Adjustment.—In our society, one of the major problems for the young person is finding suitable employment. His future status in the social system, his own self-conception and the manner in which he will adjust to many of his future problems are dependent, to a large extent, upon the nature of his occupation. The importance of a person's job in achieving status for him has been stated by Moore.

Occupation combines to a fairly high degree a number of the more important criteria of class membership. Thus gradations in wealth and income are ideally closely related to occupational position and achievement, and in fact the correspondence is rough but important. Although even less closely related, there is a notable tendency for the level and types of living ... to follow occupational lines. The same correspondence is to be observed in regard to common interests ... and social affiliations, including intermarriage.

... [It] may be noted that to a large degree the primary criterion of social status in our society is the economic worth of the individual.... [The] emphasis upon reward for useful labor is a basic part of our culture even in regard to occupations not so neatly rewarded by the operation of the market.

In fact, one of our most frequent, and usually the first, method of placing a person in social space is to determine what he ... does for a living.

... [It] is understandable that shifting occupational position has been the chief avenue of class mobility. This is, as we shall see, significant in two respects: the factual possibility of class mobility by means of occupational ladders, and the general conviction that the possibility is real and extensive, whatever the facts.[12]

For the person brought up in most countries of the Western World, and particularly the United States, the problem of deciding upon an occupation is one fraught with confusion and uncertainty. Parents have been unable to give the young person very much concrete training for an occupational status as they do not know where he will fit into the economic order. This situation is in marked contrast to primitive societies, where there is little specialization and occupation is determined by age and sex. In Zuñi, for example, all adult males care for sheep, till the fields, and take part in the religious life of the community. Also in contrast to the United States are other more stable societies where occupation is determined by family membership or social class. For example, in Victorian Britain, sons tended to follow the occupations of their fathers. However, in the United States, there are no set patterns to follow. The parents expect that their children will enter an occupation which is accorded more prestige than their own but, beyond this, the young person has little guidance.[13] His parents can help him little more than this because they do not know, any more than does their child, what opportunities are open or the amount or nature of the training required. They are further restricted in helping him as they are often unable to provide the financial backing required for specialized training.

Theoretically, the American can choose any occupation for which he has an aptitude and interest. In actuality, however, this freedom of choice is severely curtailed. Aside from the lack of parental guidance and financial backing, there are many other limitations placed upon him in his search for a job. His family's self-conception narrows the range of his occupational choice. For example, if he is a member of the middle class, his family probably will try to direct him into a white-collar or professional job, rather than into a skilled laboring occupation, regardless of where his interests and abilities lie. For the middle-class family, retaining their status in a social class is extremely important and they feel that a drop on the oc-

---

12 From Wilbert E. Moore, *Industrial Relations and the Social Order.* Copyright, 1946, by The Macmillan Company and used with their permission, pp. 483-484.
13 Mead, *And Keep Your Powder Dry.*

cupational ladder by one of the children is a threat to their own status, around which their personalities have been organized.

If the young person chooses to go into a profession and his family is able to back him financially, he runs into other difficulties. Most professions limit the numbers which they admit for training in order to keep the prestige and value of their services high. Some of the criteria for admission or restriction are race, ethnic group, religion, social class, family background, "connections," intelligence, appearance, and type of personality. Thus a young person seeking admission to a profession may be severely handicapped by the demand for personal qualifications over which he has little or no control.[14] This limiting of admissions to occupational groups is not the sole prerogative of the professions, although it is perhaps most obvious here. Unions and occupational groups which require apprenticeship also limit membership to a degree. For example, the Negro in the United States finds it difficult to receive apprenticeship training or to be admitted to many unions.

In order to get a job, the person must be at the right place at the right time. Even presuming that there is an adequate circulation of information about opportunities, this is frequently impossible. In the United States, it often requires that the person be highly mobile, able to move from one area to another. Many factors control mobility, for example, home ownership or living accommodations in one community with an uncertainty of their availability in another, lack of money with which to travel, and hesitation about leaving friends, to mention just a few.

The complexity of the industrial order raises still other complications. If he has received adequate training, there is still no guarantee that management will make the best use of it or even realize where his skill fits into their organization. The high rate of technological change operates to make some skills obsolete while creating new occupations which require completely unrelated skills. This has severe implications for the worker in that, once he has received one kind of specialized training, he is often not amenable to new training or is financially unable to undertake it. When he has finally settled into some occupation, the problems of the worker are not over. There are many conditions typical of his occupational group to which he is forced to adjust.

The occupational status of the person, like any other status he holds, is a collection of rights, duties, and patterns of behavior re-

14 See Chapter 11.

quired by social expectations. His status is not isolated but rather closely interrelated with the statuses of others. The person who goes into a job situation must ascertain what his status is and must learn to act in the manner expected so that he can fit into the organization. He must adjust his skill to the job on hand and his behavior and attitudes to those with whom he works. Depending on the basic personality structure of the person, he will find this adjustment easy or difficult to make. If the occupation is in line with his expectations, the path will prove easier than for the person who feels that the job is less than he deserves or wants.

In our society, there are many aspects of industrial employment which require major adjustments in personality on the part of the young worker. He faces some of the problems almost immediately while others may not be met until middle age or later. In the primary relationships of childhood he has come to feel that he is a person of some worth. His opinions are usually heard and have some relation to the outcome of any given situation. He often believes in the myth that he controls his own destinies and that by work and ability he can climb in the social scale. When he enters a job in industry, he must adjust to the impersonality of the organization.[15] Even if he has original ideas about how to improve his own job or factory techniques, any prestige which results rarely goes further than his own unit of fellow-workers. The community or his primary groups, whose opinions of him are what count to the person, are unaware of what is involved in his work and cannot share his pride. Hence his status is not enhanced and his pride seems meaningless, even to himself.[16] On the whole, however, he has no control over working procedures. His work is frequently so specialized and its relation to the whole so obscure that the worker is unable to determine for himself the techniques or the standards required by any new task. He must depend on his immediate superior for instructions and for approval. This often gives rise to anxiety concerning the relationship of the worker to his foreman or other superiors, lessens his own feeling of worth, and diminishes his interest in the task over which he has no control.[17]

Frequently it seems to the worker that the machine is more important than he is. This attitude is reinforced by periodic shut-downs

---

15 Burleigh B. Gardner, "The Factory as a Social System," in William Foote Whyte (Ed.), *Industry and Society*, New York, McGraw-Hill Book Co., Inc., 1946, p. 7.
16 Moore, *Industrial Relations and the Social Order*, p. 293; Chester I. Barnard, "Functions and Pathology of Status Systems in Formal Organizations," in William Foote Whyte (Ed.), *Industry and Society*, p. 58.
17 Gardner, "The Factory as a Social System," *op. cit.*, p. 11.

or the stretching out or speeding up of work. He must adjust his habits and behavior to the demands made upon the machine rather than in relation to what he himself wishes or is capable of doing. When technological improvements are introduced or when his specific task is changed, the effect on the workman is not given consideration. That these alterations have made it necessary for him to adjust his routines, his habits, his relationships with other workers, that they may mean a drop in status, is of no importance to the foreman or manager who believes that the worker's only interest in his job is his pay envelope.[18]

There is also a kind of social isolation to which the industrial worker must adjust. "The worker's orientation to the machine takes precedence over his position in a group of workmen."[19] His location in relation to equipment is often the only criterion for the assignment of any task to him. His abilities, interests, or social relationships are not taken into consideration.

Insecurity frequently develops as a result of this social isolation, from the feeling that he is subservient to the machine, from his inability to relate his working relationships to his social relationships, and from the high rate of technological change which may vary the demand for his skill or make it obsolete at any time. Other factors which give rise to insecurity in the worker are his inability to control his employment, as it is based on impersonal laws of supply and demand in the outside world rather than on his abilities and needs; the fact that he is competing for his job with social change as often as with other workmen,[20] and that, in a society such as ours which lays such great emphasis on youth, as he grows older, his chances of remaining employed steadily diminish.

Other adjustments must be made to monotony and fatigue, which give rise to tensions which incapacitate the worker in the adequate performance of his job and in his social relationships.[21] The minute subdivision of tasks destroys his self-reliance and his pride in his work. The environment in which he works has an effect both on the quality of his performance and on his self-conception. Individual specialization makes the person increasingly dependent upon society and yet he is too far removed from the common values toward which his activity is directed and too little aware of his place in the social structure to be well integrated with society.[22]

---

[18] *Ibid.*, p. 14.
[19] Moore, *Industrial Relations and the Social Order*, p. 294.
[20] *Ibid.*, p. 306.
[21] D. Ewen Cameron, *Life Is for Living*, New York, The Macmillan Co., 1948, Ch. 11.
[22] Moore, *Industrial Relations and the Social Order*, p. 65.

In a society such as ours where a satisfactory status, feelings of security, and recognition are tied in with the nature of a person's occupation, the roles surrounding a person's employment form a central part of his personality organization. His family's personalities are also organized around his job since it affects their membership in a social class. The attitudes and adjustments which a man makes in industry affect his life outside the working situation and any maladjustment which occurs in the former has repercussions in the latter. Hence his adjustment to his job is of major importance in determining how satisfactory his life will be and how well his personality is integrated.

Unemployment.—Unemployment is a special situation in the life of a person which precipitates a crisis situation to which his personality must make some adjustment. Although unemployment is sometimes due to personal inadequacies, it is more frequently due to a disruption in the economic system of our society. Even when personal inadequacy is the reason behind unemployment in any specific case, the inadequacy is frequently one defined as such in culture, as, for example, being over forty years of age, belonging to a religious or racial minority, or having physical handicaps which might or might not interfere with the task to be done.[23]

In a society such as ours, which stresses individualism and makes job success and self-support synonymous with self-respect and a high status, unemployment for any length of time suggests personal inadequacy to the person concerned. Having derived his self-conception and status (and that of his family) in the community on the basis of being a wage earner, when his job fails and another cannot be found, the person finds that his earlier roles cannot be performed in the new situation. First comes a loss of his feelings of security. Having been reared with the idea that it is a man's personal inadequacies which cause him to be unemployed, and only vaguely realizing that it is the economic order which is at fault, he tends to blame himself for what he feels to be his personal failure. His insecurity and sense of guilt are further intensified by his family's feeling that he is to blame. Being around home more than usual requires a reorganization of family relationships. If the child or wife gets work, patterns of authority and status within the family are changed. The whole situation gives rise to a feeling of futility and sometimes desperation.

---

[23] Joan Jackson, *Rehabilitation: A National, Institutional and Individual Crisis*, M. A. Thesis, McGill University, 1947. Unpublished.

To some extent, the manner in which the person has reacted to other crises in the past determines his adjustment to unemployment. If he has always been able to surmount these he is more likely to be able to retain his personality integration in the face of lack of work. However, unemployment is a situation in which he has no basis on which to rebuild his sense of worth as an individual. Some of the more common reactions to this situation by those whose personalities cannot adjust are: (a) aggressiveness and antagonism, (b) withdrawal and a complete loss of morale, (c) escape into fantasy, (d) the use of drugs or alcohol as a release from the situation, (e) physical or mental illness, (f) for a very small number, criminal behavior and, (g) for an even smaller number of the most desperate, suicide.[24]

Personal Adjustment to Courtship and Marriage.—Upon assuming adult status, the decisions and adjustments which have the most far-reaching effects on the life and personality of the person are those in relation to his job and in choosing his mate. His self-conception, his feeling of security and worth, his status in the community are bound up with these two. Any crisis in his work situation is felt in his marriage, and any dissatisfaction with the latter has repercussions in the performance of his economic duties. The major roles which he plays in life are those derived from these two situations and his personality is organized around them.

In our society, romantic love and free choice of a mate are regarded as the basis of a successful marriage. This culture pattern, to be effective, demands that opportunities exist for contact between the sexes. In the Western World, the high mobility and the greater participation of women in business and educational institutions, as well as in the professions, afford opportunities for young people to meet and become acquainted. Although theoretically there is freedom to choose a mate, in actuality there are limitations. A man can choose only from among those women with whom he is acquainted and his range of acquaintances is usually curtailed by his occupation, his place of residence, his social class, and his age. The culture of Western society imposes further restrictions on his theoretical freedom. Men frequently hesitate to marry older or better educated women, or those from a higher social class. The women reinforce this pattern by aspiring to husbands who are older, better educated, more intelligent, and superior to them in social class.[25] In addition

---

[24] Elliott and Merrill, *Social Disorganization*, Chs. 26 and 27.
[25] Paul Popenoe, "Mate Selection," *Am. Sociol. Rev.*, Vol. 2, No. 5, October, 1937, pp. 735-743.

to, and associated with the high degree of mobility in our society, are secondary types of relationships which are impersonal and fleeting and which often do not afford a basis on which to build a more lasting relationship.

Courtship usually commences after a preliminary period of acquaintance. However, in keeping with our cultural idea of "love at first sight," which is looked upon as highly desirable, courtship frequently begins immediately upon meeting. During this period, the two people involved assess one another's attitudes, values, appearance, background, and behavior. This evaluation is carried on in an atmosphere divorced from everyday life. Both young people are on their best behavior and their time together is spent in leisure-time activities. There is an emphasis on lavish spending, on thrills and lyrical expressions of devotion; they tend to idealize one another and indulge in fantasies concerning marriage and the future which often have little or no relation to actuality. However, in their behavior at this time, the young people are playing the roles laid down by the culture as appropriate for courtship.

The roles learned in courtship rarely coincide to any great extent with those called into action in marriage. The fantasies, the emphasis on sentimentality, and the over-idealization often pose adjustment problems for the realities of marriage. The "romantic" sentiments and stated evaluations of each young person about the other tend to become incorporated into their self-conceptions and, during courtship, each tries to live up to what is expected of him, even though this may be foreign to certain aspects of his personality. In marriage, however, it is impossible to keep up the pretense indefinitely, due to the close and continuous interaction between them. The young persons face adjusting to the realities of one another rather than to the rather fictitious conceptions they built up during courtship.

After the marriage ceremony comes the honeymoon. This is a period of readjustment carried on in an aura of romance somewhat akin to that of the courtship period. The couple begins to find their respective statuses and roles for the new arrangement of their lives. The majority of the roles called forth in adjusting to one another are those developed in childhood and adolescence and these must be altered and fitted into a pattern of reciprocal relationships. The average person has at his command, not one set of roles, but a variety, which may be called forth in different situations.

Cases seem to indicate a multiplicity of roles. For example, a wife may play a much depended upon mother-role, a hated sister-role, and a loved brother-role at different times for her husband. The husband may in turn be

for his wife her distantly respected father, her hated younger brother, and her
loved older sister. The startling ambivalence frequently displayed by married
persons for one another may not be true ambivalence in the strict Freudian
sense. It may actually be the result of corresponding attitudes for different
role patterns derived from early family relations. Thus a husband may call
out affectionate as well as hostile responses from his wife by playing roles of
members of her family who earlier called out different responses. Of course
it is not at all necessary nor even likely that either husband or wife will be
aware that he is playing such roles.[26]

Although roles developed in childhood and adolescence are brought
into the marriage situation, behavior may be reorientated or altered,
as long as the personality is sufficiently flexible. In addition, new
roles may be created. Adjustment in roles and attitudes must take
place in relation to appearance, manners, money, values, and interests.
The culture of the society contains broad, general rules about the
roles and statuses of marriage partners which are of help to the young
people in their adjustment and organization of a new way of life.
However, these are patterns which are in flux in our society and subject to a great amount of individual interpretation within the range
which our society considers permissible.

The adjustment of two young people to sexual relations is stressed
by our society. A good adjustment in this area of life is considered
to be of the greatest importance to a happy marriage. For both, but
more often for the bride, it is frequently a new experience, and one for
which little positive training has been given in earlier life. The attitudes concerning sex which have been inculcated in the young couple
prior to marriage often make this adjustment exceedingly difficult.
In adolescence and even before, sex has been too often regarded as
nasty, sinful, and crude. The young man has been told that women
should be treated as mothers and sisters. The young woman has been
warned of man's bestiality and depravity. In the marriage situation
these attitudes must change, if a successful sexual adjustment is to
be achieved. The lack of information about sex and its elementary
biological foundations complicates attempts at adjustment still
further.

Burgess and Cottrell cite the following factors as being of importance to marital happiness. (a) The parents of the young couple were
happily married. (b) The young couple prior to marriage had a close
relationship with their parents with a minimum of conflict between
them. (c) The young couple were well socialized prior to marriage,

---

[26] L. S. Cottrell, "Roles and Marital Adjustment," *Pub. Am. Sociol. Soc.*, Vol. 27, 1933,
pp. 107-115.

as measured by their level of education, the evidence of religious activity, the number and sex of friends, participation in social organizations, residence in a stable neighborhood of single-family dwellings. (d) They had moderate economic security. (e) They achieved a good sexual adjustment, although this seems to arise largely as a result of previous cultural conditioning about sex and a stable personality development.[27]

From the above-mentioned factors it can be seen that the majority which make for a successful marriage are dependent on earlier personality development. The roles of the parents, as observed in the families of the two partners, are brought into their own marriage pattern. The close identification with parents has taught them response patterns toward love objects. Their participation in social, educational, and religious activities has furnished them with patterns of cooperation, organization, and loyalty.

Maladjustments in personality arising from the marriage situation seem to be caused by the following: different cultural backgrounds which make understanding and common goals and values difficult to achieve; clashing of personalities which is frequently due to incompatibility of the roles brought by each partner to the marriage; and difficulties brought about by lack of sexual adjustment. Basically, however, the personalities of the two partners are of the greatest importance, determining their ability to adjust to one another and their definitions of what constitutes a conflict situation.

If the marriage is unhappy, much damage can be done to the personalities of the people involved. Our society puts a premium on success, and a person who fails in marriage tends to feel anxiety and guilt and a sense of failure. The conflict situations involved in an unhappy marriage are frequently damaging to self-conceptions, giving rise to feelings of isolation, inferiority, loss of self-esteem and self-confidence, and cynicism and disillusionment which may carry over into other areas of their lives from that time onward or be remedied when a more satisfactory life organization is achieved.[28]

Bereavement.—Death is one of the recurrent crises for which each culture has made provision. The funeral and the necessary arrangements which must be made are cultural rituals which serve to convince the living that the death is real. The expression of grief is also channelled into forms which the culture has laid down as ap-

---

[27] E. W. Burgess and L. S. Cottrell, *Predicting Success or Failure in Marriage*, New York, Prentice-Hall, Inc., 1939, pp. 341-347.

[28] See Young, *Personality and Problems of Adjustment*, Chs. 20, 21; and Elliott and Merrill, *Social Disorganization*, Chs. 24-27.

propriate. For a time the family is the center of attention, and sympathy and aid are given them by friends and members of the larger family group. These culture patterns are provided to help the family over the initial shock and to help them reorganize their lives on a new basis.

Then follows a period of reorganization for all the family members. The remaining parent is forced to take over many of the roles of the deceased in order to manage the family. Some of the children may also be allocated certain of the roles of the dead person as when, with the death of the father, the eldest son takes over the exercising of authority and the role of breadwinner.

In the small family group of our society, where ties between its members are highly charged with emotion and where the roles of all members are in close reciprocal relationships, the death of a parent and spouse gives rise to a crisis situation. After the initial shock, the members of the family must reorganize their lives and personalities in keeping with the new form of family organization. A large segment of the roles played by the children and the remaining parent can no longer operate and must be directed toward a person other than the deceased or be cut off completely. The affectional and emotional needs which were filled by the deceased must find satisfaction elsewhere.

These affectional ties which have been spread out over the complete family must be reorientated. Sometimes these emotional needs are met by persons outside the immediate family group—by an uncle, an aunt, or a favorite teacher. More frequently, however, they concentrate around the remaining parent, who makes additional demands on the children as a result of his or her own need for response. Such a solution often leads to maladjustment in the personalities of the children, who find it difficult to break free of the emotional demands of the parent without crippling feelings of guilt.

The children must also revise their identifications. The boy of a fatherless family must learn his masculine roles from men outside the family group. If he fails to do so, and switches his identification to his mother, the effect on his personality is one which frequently makes the later development of heterosexual relationships impossible. This is especially true where the mother finds in her son a substitute husband. The same situation is likely to be true, with some degree of modification, for the daughter-father relationship. The father usually has business activities around which to center his readjustment and is unlikely to make the same emotional demands upon his daughter.

For the remaining parent, the readjustment is more difficult than for the children. The roles which were organized around the deceased partner are of longer duration and are a central part of the person's personality structure. Between the two parents, there was a division of labor in keeping the family a going concern. Their roles in this field were mutually adjusted and closely interrelated. With the death of one partner, the other must exercise all these roles or allocate them elsewhere. The need for emotional response must be satisfied in some manner, by a member of the extended family, from persons in the social circle, or from the children. The need may also be sublimated by idealization of the deceased or by an absorbing occupation. The other alternative is remarriage.

Where remarriage occurs, another adjustment in personalities and the life organization of family members takes place. Problems in the relationship of the children to the step-parent arise. If, in the interval between the death of one parent and the remarriage of the other, one of the children has taken over the roles of the deceased, conflict and confusion of roles result from the new family organization in which many of these roles must be relinquished to the new parent. If there are children by the second marriage, the problem of sibling relationships arises. The children of the first marriage may become to the new partner a symbol of their parent's previous marriage and be rejected and resented.

However, many successful adjustments are made to bereavement by children and their parents. Much depends, as in any crisis situation, on the personalities involved, on the nature of the family organization before the bereavement, and on the amount of security which it afforded its individual members.[29]

Divorce and Desertion.—The effects of divorce and desertion upon the personalities of family members are in some way similar to those of bereavement. However, due to the nature of the crisis caused by the former, the effects on personality are frequently more severe. Usually conflict has preceded the final break and the loyalties and affections of the children have been demanded and manipulated by the two contestants. Each parent has sought to disillusion the children about the other and to align their sympathies. Even when the family ties have finally been severed, the battle for the affections of the children does not stop. The parent who leaves the family

---

[29] Young, *Personality and Problems of Adjustment*, pp. 536-541; Thomas Eliot, "The Bereaved Family," *Annals Am. Acad. Pol. and Soc. Sci.*, Vol. 160, March, 1932, pp. 184-190; Elliott and Merrill, *Social Disorganization*, pp. 759-760.

group leaves behind a feeling in the children that he or she does not care for them—something which is often difficult for them to accept. The remaining parent finds it necessary to bolster his or her own self-conception and control over the family by laying the blame for the break on the absent partner.

After the desertion or divorce, the adjustment of the family follows the same general lines as after bereavement, but with some unique patterns typical of the situation. Idealization of the absent partner very rarely occurs. The remaining partner must overcome any feelings of guilt which have accrued due to his or her part in the conflict. In the case of divorce, the support of friends and the larger family group in helping the partner to surmount the crisis is not as unreserved as in bereavement. Even the children do not tend to rally around the remaining parent to the same extent. In addition to being forced to reorganize the family into a new and satisfactory working relationship, the parent must rebuild his or her own diminished ego. Readjustment is more difficult than after bereavement. Lingering legal ties make the social relationships of the deserted and the deserting unsatisfactory and remarriage impossible. For the divorced, the social stigma which is attached by many self-righteous citizens makes normal social relationships difficult.[30]

Personal Adjustment to Old Age.—Although in most societies old age is a period of withdrawing from active community life and the time of sloughing off responsibilities, our society is one of the few in which it is a period of isolation, of lowered prestige and, frequently, of dependency. In other societies, the aged are accorded great prestige and are honored as extremely wise due to the knowledge they have acquired through long living. The withdrawal from toil and economic production is looked upon as their due by their society and by themselves. With their retired status go new roles which keep alive their interest in life. The group as a whole, or their own families, care for them as a matter of course rather than as a matter of "duty." In a few societies, where the means of subsistence are hard and there is no place for the aged in the social structure, they are put to death suddenly and without warning. In the latter case, this is regarded as merciful treatment in that the aged person will not be infirm in his next life.

In our society, the adjustment in self-conception and life organization which comes with age is one of the most difficult transitions

---

[30] Young, *Personality and the Problems of Adjustment*, Ch. 21; Elliott and Merrill, *Social Disorganization*, Ch. 27.

a person has to make. It is made more difficult because there is little future left to engage hope. Life is behind and there is little in front of them to challenge their interests and efforts. In addition, the aged are no longer capable of adjusting readily to new situations. Their personalities and their attitudes have become rigid and strains placed upon them by the necessity of change are often so great that senility or even death results. They, unlike any other age group which meets a crisis, have no in-group with whom to share their experiences. Friends of their own age are usually either dead or scattered. This fact, plus the physical infirmities which accompany age, tend to force attention upon themselves or give them an increasing preoccupation with death.

The aged, as a general rule, have been adequately successful. This means that they have married, raised their families, and until old age have been self-supporting. It is difficult for such persons to accept the idea that they are cast-offs in an economic system which stresses specialization, speed, and youth, and that they have no useful roles to play in society. In a society which stresses economic self-sufficiency as a criterion of success, it is difficult to think of themselves as "failures," and to accept a state of dependency. After a life organized around a schedule of work and leisure, it is difficult to adjust to retirement and enforced leisure, to the idea that they can no longer compete with youth for employment opportunities.

For the aged who become dependent upon their children, other difficulties in adjustment arise. They are regarded in the light of economic burdens. When they attempt to do their share of the work or to help in the rearing of their grandchildren, they come into conflict with the ideas of their children on how things should be done and are often regarded as interfering. They no longer exercise authority; instead, they are subject to the authority of their own children, to whom they must account for their comings and goings. Once financially independent, now they must ask for money for their most trivial needs. Having lived a successful life, it is frequently difficult for them to accept treatment from their grandchildren which implies mere tolerance, some amusement, some hostility, and an attitude on the part of the latter that their grandparents are something of children themselves.

The difficulties of the aged in our society center around an adjustment of their personalities to a status which is inferior and dependent, compared with that to which they have been accustomed during life. The process of adjustment is still further complicated by the fact that the change in the status of the aged is imposed upon them by society without regard for their capacities and needs. The roles they are permitted to play in their new status are prescribed by younger age groups. These adjustments would be difficult for a person of any age, even for those whose personalities were still mutable. For the aged, whose personalities have become relatively rigid, a satisfactory adjustment is almost impossible of achievement.

The problems of the aged are of steadily mounting importance in our society. The proportion of aged persons in the population of the western world is rapidly increasing, due to the marked trend toward a lowered birth rate and the prolongation of life by medical discoveries. As the proportion increases, some adjustment will have to be made in our social system to provide more adequately for them.[31]

Adjustment to Personal Crises.—A personal crisis is brought about when any situation or condition arises which disturbs the life organization of the person. If he is unable to reorganize his life, personality maladjustment is very likely to occur. Some personal crises have been dealt with earlier in this chapter, for example, unemployment, divorce, desertion, and bereavement.

As has been noted in the previous chapter, the personality of the individual is formed in his group relationships. Through these he learns to play roles which enable him to participate in the society and these roles become internalized and integrated to form his personality. From the judgments of others as to how well he is playing his part in his group relationships he derives a status and his self-conception. In each social situation in which he takes part, a segment of his personality is revealed. If the situation is one which recurs regularly, the roles which he plays in it are a permanent and central part of his life organization.

When a personal crisis occurs, the person is faced with amputating certain of his roles from his personality organization, or with redefining them in keeping with the new situation. For the person with a rigid personality organization this is frequently difficult or impossible to accomplish. Even for the pliable personality, if the crisis strikes at an aspect of his life around which he has organized a major part of his personality, maladjustment may be difficult to avoid.

------

31 Mirra Komarovsky, Discussion on L. S. Cottrell, Jr., "The Present Status and Future Orientation of Research on the Family," *Am. Sociol. Rev.*, Vol. 13, No. 2, April, 1948, pp. 123-136; G. V. Hamilton, et al., *Problems of Aging*, Baltimore, The Williams & Wilkins Co., 1939; G. Lawton, "The Study of Senescence," *Am. J. Sociol.*, Vol. 44, No. 2, September, 1938, pp. 280-281; G. P. Murdock, *Our Primitive Contemporaries*, New York, The Macmillan Co., 1934; Joan Jackson, *Survey on the Problems of the Aged at the Provincial Mental Hospital*, Essondale, British Columbia, 1947. (Unpublished.)

To a degree, the manner in which the person has adjusted to crises in the past determines how he will be able to meet the most recent one. If he has always been able to face and accommodate himself to the smaller crises of life, he will be more capable of overcoming those of major importance. If, on the other hand, he is a dependent person who has had a tendency to seek escape from minor disruptions in life, the major crisis will probably cause maladjustment in personality.

Other factors of importance in the manner in which he meets crises are economic and cultural resources and personal intelligence. A secure economic background can militate against maladjustment caused from illness or injuries. A person who is economically secure can, to a degree, manipulate his environment and thus lessen many of the tensions which a poorer person cannot alter. The cultural level of his social group is also of importance in increasing or decreasing the possibility of maladjustment. The definition of the crisis by his group and the means provided by the group for overcoming the difficulty are of importance. In our society, for example, bereavement constitutes a crisis fraught with more factors which might give rise to personality maladjustment than it is in other societies, where sincerely believed ritual means are provided to help the person overcome the crisis and reorganize his life. A high level of intelligence is also of aid in helping the person to view the situation objectively and to evaluate the factors giving rise to the crisis and the steps which he can take to overcome it.[32]

Organic or Functional Disorders and Adjustment.—For the person who has been leading a well-rounded and active life, playing a wide variety of roles in many different social situations from which he has derived a satisfactory status, the onset of illness or injury may constitute a crisis. If the crisis is merely temporary, maladjustment is not difficult to avoid. However, if it is permanent or of long duration, the person is forced to reorganize his life in keeping with the new situation and to alter his self-conception. Personality maladjustment may occur or the person may be successful in surmounting his difficulties. In either case, personality change may take place. The person must learn new roles in keeping with the situation and integrate them into a new personality organization. He must gain a new status based on abilities and interests which may never before have been called forth in the situations in which he has participated. If some of the roles which were used in previous situations are still

---

[32] Elliott and Merrill, *Social Disorganization*, p. 79.

possible in the new situation, personality readjustment and change are less difficult.

The attitudes of others, and particularly of his primary group toward the infirmity, are important in determining the person's self-conception and what his illness means to him. If his group treats him as helpless and as a burden, he is likely to take over these attitudes or to feel rebellion and resentment against them. If, on the other hand, new interests are encouraged and bases for the acquisition of a new and satisfactory status are presented, the person is likely to achieve a more satisfactory adjustment.

If the person has previously been flexible, if he has been rational rather than emotional in his reactions to past crises, and if he has a range of interests independent of physical abilities, he is more likely to be able to reintegrate his personality and find new goals in life than if the opposite is true. However, so many factors are involved in such a situation that it is difficult to predict, except in general terms, how any person will react to such a crisis.[33]

Adjustment to the Nature and Integration of Culture.—Our culture is one which contains a mass of contradictory beliefs which have been internalized into the personalities of those who have been trained in its ways. Values and beliefs change from one generation to the next and certain of the old values always persist alongside the new. A part of the population retains one set of values, while another segment adheres to the other. Frequently these values are in marked contradiction to reality. Fundamentalists in religion who reject the theory of evolution exist alongside the more liberal people who accept it. The norms of sexual behavior as expressed verbally by the people of our society are very different from the behavior in which these people indulge.[34]

Another reason for the divergent beliefs which exist in our culture is that immigrants from many lands have come to our shores, bringing with them cultures of widely varying beliefs which have contributed to our heritage. This variety of beliefs, along with the rapidity of social change, makes the integration of our culture very difficult to achieve.

The development of a well-integrated personality is difficult for the person in an unintegrated society. He incorporates the conflicting views prevalent in the culture into his personality. When a

---

33 *Ibid.*, pp. 77-81; Young, *Personality and Problems of Adjustment*, Ch. 26.
34 Alfred C. Kinsey, Wardell B. Pomeroy, and Clyde E. Martin, *Sexual Behavior in the Human Male*, Philadelphia, W. B. Saunders Co., 1948.

personal situation arises which calls forth beliefs which are inconsistent one with the other, behavior is paralyzed and the integration
of the personality threatened. The members of our society have been
partially able to manage this lack of integration by defining situations
in terms of one attitude or another. Honesty is an admirable trait
to be used in all areas of life but one often forgotten in business. In
the latter sphere "sharp" practices are frequently condoned and justified. Examples of some of our conflicting beliefs are: We believe
in competition and success, and in brotherly love and humility. We
believe in the equality of all men and in the inferiority of the Negro;
in democracy and that an individual is powerless to affect government; in control by reason and in the use of non-rational authoritarian and emotional methods of raising children; in the ability of a
man to go from rags to riches and that man is the victim of the economic order. Some of these contradictory beliefs have or have had a
basis in fact. Some of them have or have had, at some time, social
utility.

There is another class of beliefs which is a threat to the stable
personality. These beliefs are carry-overs from another era, when
they served a purpose or had a basis in truth. Usually close to the
central core of personality and protected by an emotional glaze from
objective consideration, they threaten personality stability by their
effects on the person's outlook on life or give rise to crisis situations
when the person comes face to face with the reality they have clouded.
Because such a myth is so frequently an important component of the
person's roles, its collapse when faced with reality leaves the personality in an anxiety-ridden state. If the myth is retained and the
reality rejected, anxiety will surround those situations in which the
myth comes into play and will distort the person's outlook. Examples of such myths are: a pauper can be president; sex is sinful
and disgusting; a boy should treat all women like his mother or his
sister; man is born in sin; man is completely free and the master of
his own destiny; all mothers are self-sacrificing and children owe
them a great debt; parents should be respected and obeyed regardless
of their character and their demands; certain things should be done
merely for the sake of doing them; any situation can be mastered by
"will power"; human nature cannot change.

In their attempts to make their behavior conform to the ideals and
aspirations which these myths expound, the majority of persons are
forced to resort to methods which, from the viewpoint of mental
hygiene, are unhealthy for the personality. They "put things out of
their minds," refuse to make decisions, or to accept responsibility

for their behavior, or they follow authoritarian leaders who tell them how to act.[35]

The person who attempts to see through this haze of unreality, in a rational and objective fashion, finds himself crippled by his own indoctrination into these beliefs at an early age and by the emotional overtones which cloud them, as well as by an inability to see what the reality of the situation is in a society which pays lip service to these unrealities and contradictions.[36] Those who do manage to analyze the situation for themselves find that they have no patterns left by which to guide their behavior, and that they have a difficult and tension-filled period to face before they can formulate new and satisfactory values which are consistent with each other and reality, and yet not in conflict with the social order. Very few succeed in this effort.

QUESTIONS

1. The personality of a person, while unique, is at the same time representative of the culture to which he belongs. Explain.
2. The majority of statuses within a society are suitable for the average person. Why? Discuss. What provisions are made for those members of a society who have special talents?
3. What is meant by the statement that a society organizes its statuses and roles around stages? Of what importance are these stages to personality development?
4. Differentiate between well adjusted and maladjusted personality.
5. What techniques does the infant normally develop for managing the adult world? What restrictions limit the types of techniques which he can develop?
6. What effects are overprotection and inconsistency of treatment likely to have on personality development and adjustment in infancy, childhood, adolescence, and adulthood? What are some of the techniques developed by the individual for dealing with these forms of parental behavior?
7. Of what importance is the mother to the infant in the development of his personality?
8. How does the child find satisfaction for his need for safety and security?

---

35 D. Ewen Cameron, *False Values,* Montreal, 1948. (Unpublished.)

36 In recent years a few of these myths have been evaluated and explored. A. C. Kinsey, in his book *Sexual Behavior of the Human Male,* has shown the actual sexual behavior of the American male in contrast to what it is said to be. Thurman Arnold, in his book *The Folklore of Capitalism,* New Haven, Yale University Press, 1938, has explored the myths surrounding our economic institutions. See also Cameron, *Life is for Living;* Mead, *And Keep Your Powder Dry;* Karen Horney, *The Neurotic Personality of Our Time,* New York, W. W. Norton & Co., Inc., 1938; Gunnar Myrdal, *An American Dilemma,* New York, Harper & Bros., 1944; Young, *Personality and Problems of Adjustment.*

9. Of what importance to the developing personality is the play group? the institutions in which the individual participates? the gang?

10. Why does the only child in our society lack the opportunities of children from larger families for socializing his egotistical impulses? Is this a help or a hindrance to him in his adjustment to adult life?

11. Compare the period of adolescence in our society with adolescence in more stable societies.

12. How does adolescence prepare the person for adulthood? What difficulties does the adolescent in our society encounter in attempting to assume full adult status?

13. What difficulties does the young person of our society have in obtaining a suitable occupation?

14. What are some of the adjustments to their jobs which America's industrial workers are forced to make?

15. What effect does unemployment tend to have on personality? What factors determine the adjustment of the person to this crisis? What form do the adjustments to this situation sometimes take?

16. The courtship period provides a good basis for successful marriage. Do you agree? Defend your point of view.

17. What are some of the major adjustments which two marriage partners must make during their early years of living together?

18. Name five factors which Burgess and Cottrell feel are important to a successful marriage.

19. What adjustments must be made by members of a family to bereavement, divorce, and desertion? What effects do these situations have on personality?

20. Contrast the treatment of the aged in preliterate societies with that accorded them in America.

21. What adjustments does personality have to make to old age? What special factors make these adjustments difficult?

22. What constitutes a personal crisis?

23. What factors determine the success or failure of adjustment to traumatic injuries or illnesses with long-term effects? What are some of the adjustments which the person must make to such disabilities?

24. Why do contradictory beliefs persist in our society? How do they emerge? What effect does their existence have on the types of personality formed within the culture?

BIBLIOGRAPHY

ANDERSON, JOHN E. "The Development of Social Behavior." *Am. J. Sociol.*, Vol. 44, No. 6, May, 1939, pp. 839-857.

ARNOLD, THURMAN. *The Folklore of Capitalism.* New Haven, Yale University Press, 1938.

BARNARD, CHESTER I. "Function and Pathology of Status Systems in Formal Organizations," in William Foote Whyte, *Industry and Society.* New York, McGraw-Hill Book Co., Inc., 1946.

BENEDICT, RUTH. *Patterns of Culture.* Boston, Houghton Mifflin Co., 1934.

BENEDICT, RUTH. "Continuities and Discontinuities in Cultural Conditioning." *Psychiatry,* Vol. 1, 1938, pp. 161-167.

BLOS, PETER. *The Adolescent Personality.* New York, D. Appleton-Century Co., Inc., 1941.

BLUMER, HERBERT. "Social Psychology" in E. P. Schmidt (Ed.), *Man and Society.* New York, Harper & Bros., 1931.

BLUMER, HERBERT. *An Appraisal of Thomas and Znaniecki's "The Polish Peasant in Europe and America."* New York, Social Science Research Council, 1939.

BOLLES, N. M., METZGER, H. F., AND PITTS, M. W. "Early Home Background and Personality Adjustment." *Am. J. Orthopsychiatry,* Vol. 11, 1941, pp. 530-535.

BRIDGES, K. M. B. *The Social and Emotional Development of the Pre-School Child.* London, Kegan Paul, Trench, Trubner & Co., Ltd., 1931.

BROWN, L. G. *Social Psychology.* New York, McGraw-Hill Book Co., Inc., 1934, Ch. 25.

BROWN, L. G. *Social Pathology.* New York, F. S. Crofts & Co., 1942.

BURGESS, E. W. *Personality and the Social Group.* Chicago, University of Chicago Press, 1929.

BURGESS, E. W., AND COTTRELL, L. S. *Predicting Success or Failure in Marriage.* New York, Prentice-Hall, Inc., 1939.

BURGESS, E. W., AND LOCKE, H. S. *The Family.* New York, American Book Co., 1945.

CAMERON, D. EWEN. *Life Is for Living.* New York, The Macmillan Co., 1948.

CHAVE, E. J. *Personality Development in Children.* Chicago, University of Chicago Press, 1937.

COOLEY, C. H. *Human Nature and the Social Order.* New York, Charles Scribner's Sons, 1902.

COTTRELL, L. S. "Roles and Marital Adjustment." *Pub. Am. Sociol. Soc.,* Vol. 27, 1933, pp. 107-115.

COTTRELL, L. S., JR. "The Present Status and Future Orientation of Research on the Family." *Am. Sociol. Rev.,* Vol. 13, No. 2, April, 1948, pp. 123-134.

CUBER, J. F. *Sociology: A Synopsis of Principles.* New York, D. Appleton-Century Co., Inc., 1947.

DAVIS, K. "Extreme Social Isolation of a Child." *Am. J. Sociol.,* Vol. 44, No. 4, January, 1940, pp. 554-565.

DAVIS, K. "Sociology of Parent-Youth Conflict." *Am. Sociol. Rev.,* Vol. 5, No. 4, August, 1940, pp. 523-535.

DAVIS, K. "Adolescence and the Social Structure." *Annals Am. Acad. Pol. and Soc. Sci.,* Vol. 236, 1944, pp. 8-16.

DOLLARD, JOHN. *Criteria for the Life History.* New Haven, Yale University Press, 1935.

DOLLARD, JOHN, DOOB, L. W., MILLER, N. E., MOWRER, O. H., AND SEARS, R. T. *Frustration and Aggression.* New Haven, Yale University Press, 1939.

DOLLARD, J., AND DAVIS, A. *Children of Bondage.* Washington, American Council on Education, 1940.

DUBOIS, CORA. *People of Alor.* Minneapolis, University of Minnesota Press, 1944.

ELIOT, THOMAS. "The Bereaved Family." *Annals Am. Acad. Pol. and Soc. Sci.,* Vol. 160, March, 1932, pp. 184-190.

ELLIOTT, M. A., AND MERRILL, F. E. *Social Disorganization.* New York, Harper & Bros., 1941.

FARIS, E. "The Social Psychology of George Herbert Mead." *Am. J. Sociol.,* Vol. 43, No. 3, November, 1937, pp. 391-403.

FOLSOM, J. K. *The Family and Democratic Society.* New York, John Wiley & Sons, Inc., 1943.

GARDINER, BURLEIGH B. *Human Relations in Industry.* Chicago, Richard D. Irwin, Inc., 1946.

GARDINER, BURLEIGH B. "The Factory as a Social System," in William Foote Whyte, *Industry and Society*. New York, McGraw-Hill Book Co., Inc., 1946.

GESSEL, A., AND ILG, F. L. *Infant and Child in the Culture of Today*. New York, Harper & Bros., 1943.

GILLIN, JOHN. "Personality in Preliterate Societies." *Am. Sociol. Rev.*, Vol. 4, No. 5, October, 1939, pp. 681-702.

GILLIN, JOHN, AND RAIMY, V. "Acculturation and Personality." *Am. Sociol. Rev.*, Vol. 5, No. 3, June, 1940, pp. 371-380.

HAMILTON, G. V., ET AL. *Problems of Aging*. Baltimore, The Williams & Wilkins Co., 1939.

HILLER, E. T. *Principles of Sociology*. New York, Harper & Bros., 1934, Chs. 6-9.

HORNEY, KAREN. *The Neurotic Personality of Our Time*. New York, W. W. Norton & Co., Inc., 1938.

HORST, P. *The Prediction of Personal Adjustment*. New York, Social Science Research Council, 1941.

HUNT, JOSEPH MCVICKER (ED.). *Personality and Behavior Disorders*. New York, The Ronald Press Co., 1944.

JONES, H. E. *Development in Adolescence*. New York, D. Appleton-Century Co., Inc., 1943.

KARDINER, ABRAM. *The Individual and His Society*. New York, Columbia University Press, 1939.

KARDINER, ABRAM. "The Concept of Basic Personality Structure," in Ralph Linton (Ed.), *The Science of Man in the World Crisis*. New York, Columbia University Press, 1945, pp. 107-123.

KINSEY, ALFRED C., POMEROY, WARDELL B., AND MARTIN, CLYDE E. *Sexual Behavior in the Human Male*. Philadelphia, W. B. Saunders Co., 1948.

KLUCKHOHN, C., AND KELLY, W. H. "The Concept of Culture," in Ralph Linton (Ed.), *The Science of Man in the World Crisis*. New York, Columbia University Press, 1945, pp. 78-107.

LAWTON, G. "The Study of Senescence." *Am. J. Sociol.*, Vol. 44, No. 2, September, 1938, pp. 280-281.

LINTON, RALPH. *The Study of Man*. New York, Appleton-Century-Crofts, Inc., 1936.

LINTON, RALPH. *The Cultural Background of Personality*. New York, Appleton-Century-Crofts, Inc., 1945.

LINTON, RALPH (ED.). *The Science of Man in the World Crisis*. New York, Columbia University Press, 1945.

MEAD, G. H. *Mind, Self and Society*. Chicago, University of Chicago Press, 1934.

MEAD, MARGARET. *Coming of Age in Samoa*. New York, William Morrow & Co., Inc., 1928.

MEAD, MARGARET. *Growing Up in New Guinea*. New York, William Morrow & Co., Inc., 1929.

MEAD, MARGARET. "Culture and Personality." *Am. J. Sociol.*, Vol. 42, No. 1, July, 1936, pp. 84-87.

MEAD, MARGARET. *And Keep Your Powder Dry*. New York, William Morrow & Co., Inc., 1943.

MEAD, MARGARET. "Adolescence in Modern and Primitive Societies," in T. M. Newcomb and E. L. Hartley, *Readings in Social Psychology*. New York, Henry Holt & Co., 1947.

MOORE, WILBERT E. *Industrial Relations and the Social Order*. New York, The Macmillan Co., 1946.

MOWRER, E. R. *Disorganization: Personal and Social*. New York, J. B. Lippincott Co., 1942.

MOWRER, E. R. "A Study of Personal Disorganization." *Am. Sociol. Rev.*, Vol. 4, No. 4, August, 1939, pp. 475-488.

MUMFORD, LEWIS. *Technics and Civilization.* New York, Harcourt, Brace & Co., 1934.

MURDOCK, G. P. *Our Primitive Contemporaries.* New York, The Macmillan Co., 1934.

MURPHY, GARDINER. *Personality: A Biosocial Approach to Origins and Structure.* New York, Harper & Bros., 1947.

MURPHY, G., AND MURPHY, L. *Experimental Social Psychology.* New York, Harper & Bros., 1931.

MYRDAL, GUNNAR. *An American Dilemma.* New York, Harper & Bros., 1944.

NIMKOFF, M. F., AND OGBURN, W. F. *A Handbook of Sociology.* London, International Library of Sociology and Social Reconstruction, 1947.

PLANT, JAMES. *Personality and the Cultural Pattern.* New York, The Commonwealth Fund, 1937.

POPENOE, P. "Mate Selection." *Am. Sociol. Rev.,* Vol. 2, No. 5, October, 1937, pp. 735-743.

RADCLIFFE-BROWN, A. R. *The Andaman Islanders.* New York, The Macmillan Co., 1933.

ROETHLISBERGER, W. J., AND DICKSON, W. J. *Management and the Worker.* Cambridge, Harvard University Press, 1937.

SCHEINFELD, A., AND SCHWEITZER, M. D. *You and Heredity.* Philadelphia, Frederick A. Stokes Co., 1939.

SCHETTLER, C. "Topical Summaries of Current Literature: Personality Traits." *Am. J. Sociol.,* Vol. 45, No. 2, September, 1939, pp. 234-259.

STONEQUIST, E. V. *The Marginal Man.* New York, Charles Scribner's Sons, 1937.

TAYLOR, LOUIS. "The Social Adjustment of the Only Child." *Am. J. Sociol.,* Vol. 51, No. 3, November, 1945, pp. 227-232.

TROYER, W. L. "Mead's Social and Functional Theory of Mind." *Am. Sociol. Rev.,* Vol. 11, No. 2, April, 1946, pp. 198-202.

WALLER, W. *War and the Family.* New York, The Dryden Press, 1940.

WARNER, LLOYD W., AND LOW, J. O. *The Social System of the Modern Factory.* New Haven, Yale University Press, 1947.

WHYTE, WILLIAM FOOTE. *Industry and Society.* New York, McGraw-Hill Book Co., Inc., 1945.

WOODARD, J. W. "The Relation of Personality Structure to the Structure of Culture." *Am. Sociol. Rev.,* Vol. 3, No. 5, October, 1938, pp. 637-652.

WOODARD, J. W. "Social Psychology," in G. Gurvitch and Wilbert E. Moore (Eds.), *Twentieth Century Sociology.* New York, The Philosophical Library, 1945.

YOUNG, KIMBALL. *Studies in Personality.* New York, McGraw-Hill Book Co., Inc., 1942.

YOUNG, KIMBALL. *Personality and Problems of Adjustment.* New York, Appleton-Century-Crofts, Inc., 1947.

PART II

THE ECOLOGICAL APPROACH TO THE STUDY OF MAN AND HIS INSTITUTIONS

HOWEVER CONSCIOUS we may be of freedom to move and make decisions, we live in a "web of life" in which selective factors operate below the level of self-consciousness. In human communities we are aware of much that has happened to us and that may happen to us. In a plant community, such awareness is entirely absent. We need to re-emphasize that, while plants are completely subject to impersonal selection as to place and function, we share some of this aspect with them. It will appear that, while we are aware of many things, there are other aspects of our existence which result from a type of interaction that is just as impersonal as that of the plant world. A heavy industry like steel thrives at a point where coal, iron ore, and limestone may be assembled most cheaply and from which point markets for the steel are most easily penetrated. Financial streets find their location and persist in it because they occupy a place in the urban structure in which the selective tests have been met successfully. Few persons could give adequate reasons for the location of such streets. Special studies of financial streets, as you will see, tell why they are to be found in a similar position in all our cities. But, even in more personal situations, some such factors operate. With the best of training and the acme of will power, the athlete's success is not assured. His stamina and other physical resources over which he has no control enter into the determination of a winner. In all areas of life, such uncontemplated phenomena are present.

The processes of natural selection operate on a world-wide scale, placing human beings in areas and occupations wherein life is tolerable. In this way, there has come about an unplanned distribution of peoples, great cities, lesser communities, and their institutional establishments. This impersonal selection may be brought under control at those points where men become aware of the factors involved. But this awareness is always partial. Consequently, the selective distribution of human beings and items of their cultures have to run the gantlet of an experimental test of fitness to survive, and perchance thrive.

That section of sociology which has to do with such impersonal patterning of regions and communities is called *human ecology*. Prominent in making this point of view available to students were Mukerjee, Park, McKenzie, and Burgess. More recently, Hollings-

137

head, Quinn, and many others have taken an active part in testing and redefining ecological concepts for greater usefulness in sociology. Human ecology, as sociologists conceive it, has something in common with phases of human geography, plant ecology, and part of biology. However, sociologists have worked out their own definitions and procedures. Quinn has defined human ecology (or, as he terms it, interactional ecology) :

. . . as a specialized field of sociological analysis which investigates (1) those impersonal sub-social aspects of communal structure—both spatial and functional—which arise and change as a result of interaction between men through the medium of limited supplies of the environment and, (2) the nature and forms of the processes by which this sub-social structure arises and changes.[1]

As thus defined, human ecology is concerned with location of cities, towns, villages, their relation to hinterland areas, and their patterned structure in space and time. Typical invasions and successions of populations are phases of ecological analysis,[2] as succeeding chapters will demonstrate.

The approach to human ecology is applied in the first instance to the distribution of world population with particular emphasis on those parts of the world in which the Industrial Revolution has had its greatest influence. The active roles of the great cities in organizing world markets, developing new divisions of labor between regions, and placing men in a new system of highly specialized occupations are worthy of careful attention by the student.

Then follows a detailed analysis of the ecological processes in relation to the development and structural differentiation of urban communities. The discussion analyzes the expansion of the city outward from its central business district. Burgess has made use of the hypothesis that cities may be divided into five circular zones: (1) the Central Business District; (2) the Zone of Transition; (3) the Zone of Workingmen's Homes; (4) the Zone of Better Residences; and (5) the Commuter's Zone.[3] This concept has stimulated the interest of students and was used at length in previous editions of this text. Recently Burgess' zone hypothesis has come under much-needed criticism, which has led to a more careful statement of this zonal scheme of studying the spatial and temporal pattern of the city. Quinn has pointed out in detail that if time-cost

[1] J. A. Quinn, "Human and Interactional Ecology," *Am. Sociol. Rev.*, Vol. 5, October, 1940, p. 721.

[2] *Ibid.*

[3] R. E. Park and E. W. Burgess (Eds.), *The City*, Chicago, University of Chicago Press, 1925, pp. 47-62.

rather than linear distance is used, the concept of zones as stated by Burgess can readily be defended.[4] In this edition of the text, *sector analysis,* that is, pie-shaped sectors extending from the center outward, is used in presenting the differentiated structure of the city. This concept complements but does not conflict with the notion of concentric zones as established by Burgess.

The human ecological approach to the location and functioning of social institutions with particular reference to the city, follows in the chapter on urban patterning. This, in turn, is followed by a study of institutions at the level of social interaction. For the sake of analysis, the ecological processes can be distinguished from the social processes and, moreover, a study of these subsocial processes affords a most effective basis for understanding social interaction.

---

[4] J. A. Quinn, "The Burgess Zonal Hypothesis and Its Critics," *Am. Sociol. Rev.,* Vol. 5, April, 1940, pp. 210-218.

Chapter 7

SELECTIVE DISTRIBUTION OF PEOPLE AND CULTURES

Introduction.—A discussion of the interrelated concepts of the social group and culture would be incomplete without a knowledge of the distribution of people in the world and of the factors which organize population elements into the particular formations they take in time and space. Just as impersonal laws have been discovered which govern the emergence and organization of social groups and culture, other equally impersonal laws have been found which regulate the location of people on the earth, their patterns of growth or decline, and their mobility.

The interest of the sociologist in population studies is derived from his concern with all factors involved in the growth of culture, the interaction of social groups, and the products of this interaction. He is interested in where people live, in the density of their settlement, in their resources, and in their adjustment to these factors. He is also concerned with how, why, and where people move, because such movement is a vital aspect of intergroup and intragroup interaction. The study of population has become increasingly important because of the greater interdependence of the countries of the world due, in large measure, to improvements in transportation and communication.

Global Population Distribution.—The masses of mankind are concentrated into four continental clusters. Most notable for its density is the cluster in southeastern Asia, particularly in Java, in the lower valleys of the Hwang Ho and Yangtze rivers of China, and on the islands of Japan. Ranking second in density is the subcontinent of India, the greatest concentrations being in the valleys of the Ganges and lower Brahmaputra rivers. The European concentration of population along the fiftieth parallel of latitude from Great Britain to the lower Dnieper in Soviet Russia is third in rank according to density. The fourth cluster is found in the northeastern United States, north of the Ohio River and east of the Mississippi. The northern margin of this latter region includes areas along Lake Erie and Lake Ontario and the upper St. Lawrence Valley.

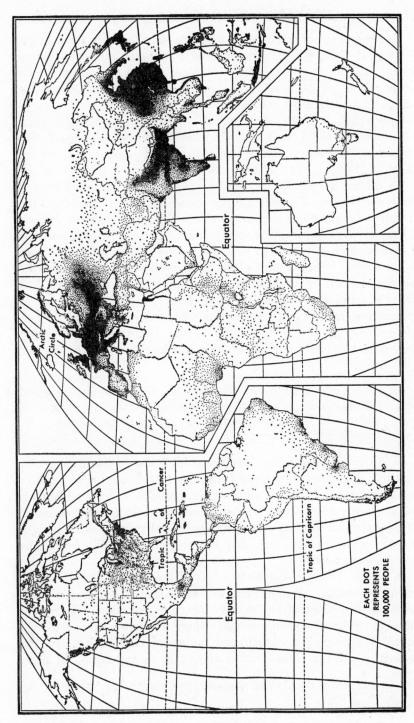

Figure 1. Distribution of Population

EACH DOT REPRESENTS 100,000 PEOPLE

By permission, from *Elements of Geography*, p. 613, by V. C. Finch and G. T. Trewartha, Copyrighted 1936, 1942. Published by McGraw-Hill Book Co., Inc.

Lesser concentrations of population are to be found in the districts of Buenos Aires, Rio de Janeiro, and São Paulo, and the eastern "hump" of Brazil. Also worthy of mention are the valley of the Lower Nile, the Mediterranean borderlands, Western Sudan, the Guinea Coast, the East African uplands, and portions of the south-eastern coast of Africa. In Australia the chief nucleus of population extends along and inland from its southeast coast. In Australasia, the most marked concentration of population is on the island of Java.

To fill out the picture of global population distribution, Figure 2 shows the density of population per square mile. In this figure, the tendency of populations to move out from the major and minor areas of heaviest concentration to occupy suitable and accessible portions of surrounding regions is to be noted. This type of settlement goes on, extending outward until physical barriers such as mountains or seas are reached or until land becomes marginal in its utility. Migrants generally avoid these areas or those in which the hazards of temperature, rainfall and transportation become excessive. For such reasons, only 15 per cent of mountainous Japan is cultivated and more than half the continent of Asia has less than two people per square mile.

The entire northern half of Siberia, Mongolia, Tibet, most of Arabia, and much of Turkestan . . . [have] a paucity of inhabitants. These areas of sparse population lie for the most part in high isolated plateaus, arid regions, or cold, forbidding subpolar areas.[1]

In Australia, climate has been the chief factor in confining settlement to limited parts of the coastline. Its vast, central desert within semi-arid borders, has been an insurmountable obstacle to settlement. The strikingly low population density of Africa is largely accounted for by extensive deserts, steaming equatorial rain forests, a high, rugged, unbroken coastline, and rivers generally unfit for unobstructed navigation.[2]

In North America, the eastern half of the United States is quite heavily populated. A more detailed study shows, however, that it has isolated sections of low density where mountainous topography limits agricultural expansion and where the absence of suitable natural resources has discouraged industrial exploitation. In the western half of the United States, mountainous and semi-arid areas

---

[1] George T. Renner (Ed.), *Global Geography*, New York, Thomas Y. Crowell Co., 1945, p. 388.
[2] *Ibid.*, p. 389.

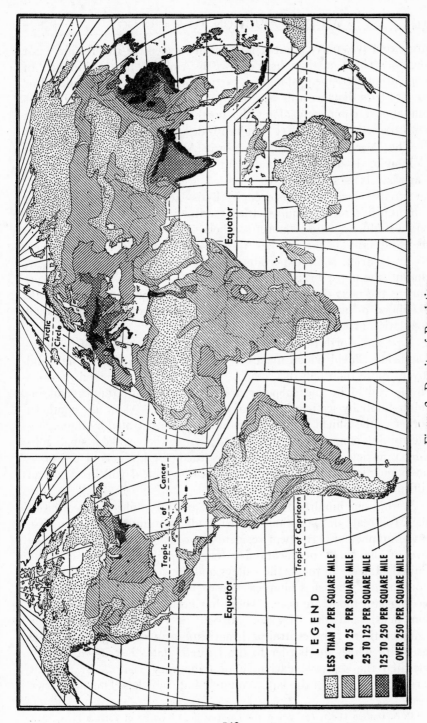

Figure 2. Density of Population

By permission, from *Elements of Geography*, p. 625, by V. C. Finch and G. T. Trewartha, Copyrighted 1936, 1942. Published by McGraw-Hill Book Co., Inc.

LEGEND

LESS THAN 2 PER SQUARE MILE

2 TO 25 PER SQUARE MILE

25 TO 125 PER SQUARE MILE

125 TO 250 PER SQUARE MILE

OVER 250 PER SQUARE MILE

are extensive, making for a low density except in the Pacific coast region. The Canadian half of North America has a thin belt of population settlement along the forty-ninth parallel of latitude. For much of its distance this belt is three hundred miles wide. It fades out almost completely along the northern shore of Lake Superior but broadens again to five hundred miles in the prairie region.

The Peace River Region, partly in Alberta and partly in British Columbia, is the most important northern settlement pocket in Canada. It is separated from settled areas in southern Canada by an extensive area which is occupied by isolated agricultural or fishing communities. This thinly settled territory is crossed by a railroad and a highway which connect southern Alberta with Dawson Creek, the southern anchor of the Alaska Highway. Beyond the Peace River District, some expansion of settlement northward to and including the upper branches of the MacKenzie River may take place during the next decade. Beyond that point, however, there is little likelihood of any great addition to the present scatter of very small population groups.[3]

East and north of this territory lies the vast expanse of the Pre-Cambrian Shield which makes a wide sweep toward the south and covers more than half of Canada. On the northern rugged portions of the Shield lie the subpolar areas, covered with tundra and inhabited only by scattered tribes of native people. Along the southern border of the Shield, certain areas have been penetrated by lumbering and mining companies which have drawn in their wake a small subsidiary agricultural population. Any further additions to the present population scatter of the Pre-Cambrian Shield will be slow and difficult.

Within one hundred to one hundred and fifty miles north of cities like Montreal, an expanding tourist trade is stimulating an increase in the number of permanent residents who have moved there to take care of the needs of vacationists from southern Canada and the United States. In the fertile valleys and the coastal region of scenic, mountainous British Columbia, the extension of settlement is proceeding at a moderate pace. There has been little change in population density in the Maritime Provinces since 1867, when the confederation of the central and maritime provinces occurred. The ease with which the border to the United States is crossed has accelerated the seasonal exchange of temporary visitors in a great variety of regions in the latter country and Canada. This and other

---

[3] C. A. Dawson (Ed.), *The New Northwest*, Toronto, University of Toronto Press, 1947.

population movements across the border have left permanent settlers in both countries.

A population distribution map of the world shows the exceedingly irregular spread of population. It might be felt that lack of agricultural or other resources, coupled with inaccessibility, keeps man away from the unsettled portions of the globe. While this is in a large measure true, much should be said by way of qualification. There are those who wish to live on the frontiers of civilization, but the vast majority of mankind settles in or close to the familiar and established nuclei of settlement. The great pioneers in geographic discovery can be counted on the fingers of very few hands, while those who stayed close to the communities of their birth take in the majority of mankind. Thousands have moved from their ancestral homes in the wake of the discoverers, and millions in the "new worlds" have grown from the loins of the thousands who migrated. The habitual inclinations of men keep them close to the gods, culture, land and other material resources of their fathers which offer them a continuation of the known way of life.

In our time many artificial restraints curb the wishes of the more restless human beings who desire new scenes and freer opportunities. Current nationalistic imperatives demand that nationals stay at home to develop and defend their countries' interests. In contrast to this policy is the clamor to keep out those whose race, culture, and political ideology seem to clash with the familiar securities of those who close the door in varying degrees to the aliens from another social world. At present artificial barriers to movements of population are high, but it should be remembered that even when they scarcely affected population movements in the western world, the natural tendency of population to press close to well known and highly accessible habitats prevailed. This continues to be true within the United States, where population movements are generally free from governmental controls.[4]

Table 1 reveals that more than half the world's population lives in Asia, nearly one quarter in Europe, and about one fifth in North America, Africa, and South America. Among individual countries, China leads with nearly one quarter of the earth's population, followed by India with just under one sixth.

The countries of one of the major population areas, Europe, may be compared as to population in relation to its land base. (See Figure 3, page 147.)

---

4 D. H. Davis, *The Earth and Man*, New York, The Macmillan Co., 1943, p. 32.

TABLE 1

Population Statistics, 1939

Continents

Asia	1,254,000,000
Europe	472,000,000
North America	184,878,000
Africa	158,000,000
South America	88,500,000
Oceania	10,800,000
Total	2,168,178,000

Countries

China	450,000,000
India	382,000,000
Soviet Russia	172,000,000
United States	131,416,000
Japan	72,520,000
Germany	69,700,000
United Kingdom	47,928,000
Italy	43,864,000
France	41,200,000

Estimates, from League of Nations Statistical Year Book, 1940-1942.

TABLE 2

Political Distributon of Population in Europe, 1900, 1920, and 1939

Country	1900		1920		1939	
	Population (000's)	Per Cent of Total	Population	Per Cent of Total	Population (000's)	Per Cent of Total
Soviet Union	138,987	136,900	(000's)	28.3	173,800	30.1
Germany	56,367	32.3	61,153	12.7	69,640	12.1
Austria-Hungary	46,995	13.1	—	—	—	—
United Kingdom and Ireland	41,471	10.9 9.6	47,127	9.8	50,924	8.8
France	38,962	9.1	39,210	8.1	41,950	7.3
Italy	32,475	7.6	37,929	7.8	43,864	7.6
Great Powers	355,257	82.6	322,319	66.7	380,178	65.9
Small Western Countries	25,106	5.8	30,054	6.2	34,565	6.0
Spain and Portugal	24,017	5.6	27,336	5.7	33,259	5.8
Balkans	24,752	5.8	39,329	8.1	51,698	9.0
Succession States	—	—	63,039	13.0	75,720	13.1
Other States	73,875	17.2	159,758	33.1	195,242	33.9
Minor Areas	711	.2	1,162	.2	1,305	.2
Total Europe and U. S. S. R.	429,843	100.0	483,239	100.0	576,725	100.0

From Kirk, *Europe's Population in the Interwar Years*, p. 27.

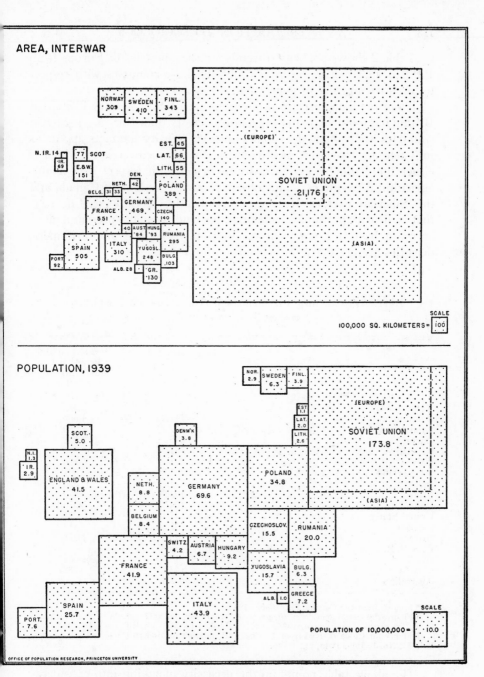

Figure 3. Area and Population of European Countries Contrasted

Schematic map of Europe and the Soviet Union with areas of countries proportioned to territorial size, and to population size, the total area within the squares being the same in both panels. From Dudley Kirk, *Europe's Population in the Interwar Years,* League of Nations Pub., 1946, p. 12. By permission, Department of Social Affairs, United Nations, and Office of Population Research, Princeton University.

Table 2 shows population trends for the countries of Europe from 1900 to 1939 while Figure 3 contrasts those countries with respect to territory and size of population.

From the data just given, it can be seen that a country like Great Britain has a much greater population density than Russia. If certain countries are compared as to arithmetical density the facts appear as in Table 3. However, most countries have much territory which is either uninhabitable or decidedly marginal with respect to available agricultural resources. This observation is very true of Canada and the Siberian part of Russia. Consequently, physiological density, that is, density per square mile of arable land, seems to present a more accurate basis for comparison. Both physiological and arithmetic densities are presented in Table 3:

TABLE 3

ARITHMETICAL AND PHYSIOLOGICAL DENSITIES OF POPULATION
FOR SELECTED COUNTRIES

	ARITHMETICAL * People per Square Mile	PHYSIOLOGICAL † People per Square Mile of Arable Land
Netherlands	716.57	2,085
Belgium	711.99	1,664
United Kingdom	507.24	2,080
Japan	495.72	2,532
Germany	381.98	793
Italy	372.07	798
Switzerland	261.80	2,007
India	245.97	533
France	193.99	463
China	104.97	378 ‡
United States	45.10	221
Sweden	37.63	413
Norway	23.67	1,071
U. S. S. R.	20.85	—
Brazil	13.00	1,661
Canada	3.32	88
Australia	2.43	—

* Figures from the *Canada Year Book*, 1947.
† Figures by permission from *Elements of Geography*, pp. 622-623, by V. C. Finch and G. T. Trewartha, Copyrighted, 1936, 1942. Published by McGraw-Hill Book Co., Inc.
‡ Figure for China derived from Ta Chen, "Population in Modern China," *Am. J. Sociol.*, Vol. 52, No. 1, July, 1946, pp. 1-126.

The above table points up the necessity of taking into consideration factors other than population and total area when judging whether a country is overpopulated or underpopulated. Where the economy is based primarily on agriculture, a calculation of physiological density of population gives a fair picture; the Indian sub-continent, for example, has a population of 533 people per square mile of arable land. However, in the case of a highly industrialized country such as Great Britain, still other factors must be studied, such as local resources, advantages for manufacturing and trade, and access to the raw materials and markets of a colonial empire.

Growth of World Population Since 1800.—During the past one hundred and fifty years the population of the world has more than doubled. Asia's totals have expanded steadily but even more spectacular has been the growth of population in Europe and the two Americas.

TABLE 4

POPULATION OF THE WORLD BY CONTINENTS, 1800-1939 *

(in millions)

Continent	1939	1900	1850	1800
World	2,080	1,527	1,091	919
Asia	1,097	839	664	600
Europe	542	390	266	188
Africa	157	141	100	100
North and Central America	184	110	39	15
South America	89	41	20	14
Oceania	11	6	2	2

*Data for 1800 and 1850 are from Walter F. Wilcox, *Studies in American Demography* (Ithaca, N. Y., Cornell University Press, 1940), pp. 30, 45; those for later years are from a number of official yearbooks and the *Aperçu de la démographie des divers pays du monde, 1929-1936* (La Haye, Office Permanent de l'Institut Internationale de Statistique, 1939).

From W. S. Thompson, *Population and Peace in the Pacific*, Chicago, University of Chicago Press, 1946, p. 23.

The main factors which stimulated population growth in the western world were the Industrial Revolution and the great migration to the Americas. Although these two continents and other lands were discovered in earlier centuries, heavy migration did not begin until the mid 1700's. However, after that time large numbers of people came to the new countries to exploit their abundant resources. This, in turn, gave great impetus to industrial expansion and population growth in Europe. As Kirk says,

Three centuries ago there were only about a hundred million persons of European stock, these being almost wholly confined to the European continent. . . . The number of Europeans living outside of Europe was negligible in 1650; it has been estimated that since that time some 60 million Europeans have sought homes overseas, chiefly in the Americas. Millions more crossed the low barrier of the Urals to settle Siberia and the interior of Asia. Some

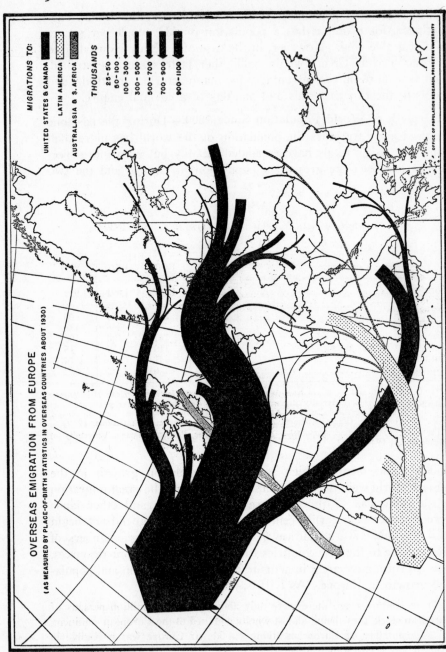

Figure 4. Overseas Emigration from Europe, as measured by place of birth statistics in overseas countries, about 1930

From Dudley Kirk, "European Migration Postwar Trends and Future Prospects," in *Postwar Problems of Migration*, New York, Milbank

of these emigrants returned to Europe, but those who remained abroad have since multiplied several times.[5]

Less than one fifth of the world's population was European in 1650, compared with one third at present, this one third including Europeans in Europe and those mainly descended from them abroad.

By 1930 transoceanic migration had pretty well ceased. In its wake it left 20,000,000 persons in overseas countries who were born in Europe. 12,000,000 of these were in the United States, 5,000,000 in Latin America, and 3,000,000 in the British Dominions. As shown in Figure 4, these immigrants were drawn from all parts of Europe.

Zones of Active and Passive Concentration.[6]—*Concentration* is the tendency of population to show a high density in certain areas as compared with a scattered distribution elsewhere. There are two main types, active and passive. These two types of concentration are rarely, if ever, present in their pure forms. In each type, certain characteristics predominate which permit countries to be classified as areas of active or passive concentration. However, in the modern world, there are numerous intermediate mixtures of both types.

Southeastern Asia is an area which can be designated as a *passive concentration*. For the most part the productive effort of the people is based on manpower rather than on the mechanization of agriculture such as one sees, for example, in western Europe. Abundant rain, plenty of sunshine, and great fertility make possible enormous agricultural production with much less effort than in regions less favored by nature. This does not mean that the inhabitants of this type of region have no struggle for life or that they lack knowledge and techniques for winning a livelihood from the soil. It merely means that the inhabitants can rely to a great extent on nature's bounty and can be more leisurely in the struggle for existence. Furthermore, they reap the advantages of mass aggregation without experiencing the drive of competitive enterprise which is found in the West. In such an area of passive concentration, an appropriate culture has developed which stabilizes the passivity in the midst of abundance.

Until the beginning of the nineteenth century such regions were not a part of the world market. Penetration of this southeastern mass and its more remote hinterlands by the production and market-

---

[5] Kirk, *Europe's Population in the Interwar Years*, p. 17.
[6] J. Brunhes and C. Vallaux, *La Géographie de l'histoire*, Paris, Librairie Félix Alcan, 1921, pp. 120-192.

ing system of the industrialized western world has been difficult. Inertia has been widespread, and these areas have not become a part of the way of life which emerged with the spread of the Industrial Revolution with its new inventions, increased division of labor, and its efficient and widespread network of transportation and communication. However, with the increased use of the seaboard, the main inland waterways, railroad extensions, along with the exigencies of war, contacts have been extended to this vast area which is now being drawn into world markets. The result of this will be that sections of this great land will become ever less passive in their struggle for existence and will gradually take over some of the more active characteristics of the invading Western economy.

The term *active concentration* denotes those parts of the world in which the struggle with nature for a livelihood makes initial concentration difficult. Physical density depends but little on the physical resources of the area but more upon physical energy and inventiveness. For example, England's use of the sea enabled its people to obtain capital for trade which, when coupled with special transportation advantages, led to an extensive concentration based on commerce and industry. An elaboration of the factors in active concentration will be found in a later part of this section. Since England and the rest of western Europe afforded the population base for the Industrial Revolution, many of the interrelated factors involved will receive detailed analysis.

These two contrasted types of concentration must bear the documentation of this phase of the study of world population. Although space does not permit an extension of data of this kind, it should be noted that there are many marginal concentrations of population which bear some of the characteristics of both these types. The Eskimo represent active population concentration of a minor sort. Geographic and climatic barriers have kept them out of the world market and they still live under conditions of self-sufficiency. At some points, however, their mode of life is also being modified by the northern extension of industrialized culture, for example, at Aklavik.

GLOBAL ORGANIZATION

Certain non-political factors play a part in the emergence of world organization and in determining where heavy concentrations of people arise. For example, the Industrial Revolution changed the distribution of peoples in the areas which we have discussed under the heading of active concentration, that is, England, western continental Europe, and northeastern United States. The Industrial Revolution is misnamed, as it was not a revolution but rather a series of inventions leading eventually to a factory system and mass production which reached its zenith in present-day North America. However, it also includes all regions in which human labor has been replaced by mechanized industry. One of the most recent and remarkable examples of mechanization of the means of production is modern Russia.

This new industrial and trading system emerged out of the historical development of trade across western Europe, from the Mediterranean Sea to the British Isles. It was further stimulated by a series of new inventions, the most important of which was the harnessing of steam power for manufacturing and for transportation. With this use of steam, the Industrial Revolution introduced a new era of factory production into western Europe. Manufactured goods were exchanged for raw materials from distant regions. Ultimately there emerged an organized world market, with its headquarters in a few great cities. New divisions of labor were created, not only between manufacturing and extractive regions but also in the more passive raw-material areas, where specialization occurred in the production of only a few commodities for the world market. Some regions specialized in cotton, some in wool, others in lumber, cattle, tea, coffee, jute, gold, coal, diamonds, iron ore, and many other commodities. As manufacturing spread beyond Europe, regional specialization resulted, for example, in shipbuilding on the Clyde, in carpets in the countries of the Near East, and in precision instruments in continental Europe.

This expansion of the division of labor along regional lines was infinitely greater with respect to occupations and to social institutions. The extension of specialization brought about a reorganization of customary ways of life and created increased consensus and interdependence between countries. London, and later New York, became the dominant centers in the world, and the spearheads of these changes.

The methods of mass production had their first demonstration in London. Due to certain natural advantages, London became the center of a new mode of production which brought about a new way of life. Ultimately the repercussions extended far beyond Great Britain, her colonies and Dominions, as the factors at work were of a non-political nature. This new impersonal system of producing and marketing resulted in the breakdown of older cultural systems. However, the change operated throughout within cultural controls.

The nature of the change can be explained by giving central attention to the concept of dominance.

The Concept Center of Dominance.—All spatially distributed aspects of the structure of communities or regions, such as roads, homes, shops, factories, and other institutions are integrated into a pattern of dominance and subordination. A *center of dominance* may be defined as the focal point of transportation and communication where are assembled the specialized agencies which are most active in integrating with it outlying centers and their constituencies, on the basis of subordination and division of labor. Somewhat similar in function is the brain of man, the physiological center which, by means of the principle of dominance and subordination, integrates all parts of the body. The physiological center of dominance emerges at the point of greatest sensitivity to internal and peripheral stimuli. By means of the coordinating functions of its higher center, the body can respond as an organic unit.[7] Ecological or physiological centers of dominance are the points where the community or the body is most alive.

While a center of dominance, such as the downtown business center, the major city in a region, or the world's chief city, is at a focal point of transportation and communication, the speed of the latter over the former has been most significant in widening the area of subordination. It now requires just a few moments to send a message from New York, which sets in motion the wheels of a factory in Shanghai. Thus, by means of modern devices of communication, a few great centers have become the foci in receiving and transmitting information. As a result they have become the centers of intelligence where persons with special aptitudes are congregated, where businesses have their head offices, and where plans affecting distant enterprises are made. Centralization of information and management have been accompanied by decentralization of operation to immediate and far distant hinterlands.

Dominance in the ancient empires of China and Rome, being military and political, centered in fortified cities. Tribute rather than trade defined the relation of subordinate territory to the dominant center. Modern centers of dominance have grown up in relation to trade and commerce, and present-day political organization is an adjustment to this newer type of dominance. The shift came with the rise of trade centers on the Mediterranean, Baltic, and other

---

[7] R. D. McKenzie, "The Concept of Dominance and World-Organization," *Am. J. Sociol.*, Vol. 33, No. 1, July 1, 1927, pp. 29-30.

European seaboards. Each was successful in so far as it was able to maintain efficient lines of communication with other ports of the world. Spanish, Portuguese, Dutch, French, and English strove to extend their commercial relations with Asia, Africa, and America. England became supreme because she succeeded in developing the most efficient system of communication between her home and foreign ports.[8]

London, strategically located as the center of England's coastwise trade, through its expansion became the world center of dominance. This city had great natural advantages in its immediate hinterland. England's extensive coastline and rich fishing grounds stimulated the development of a seafaring population. Her battle with the sea prepared the way for later commercial and industrial expansion. Then, too, the English hinterland was not only fertile but rich in iron and coal. England had made great advances in the days of wooden ships, but when the time came to build coal-burning steel ships, the country not only had seafaring tradition and skill but also possessed other great natural advantages over her competitors. Previously she had developed the most powerful navy; under its protection she developed the world's greatest merchant marine. These, in turn, led to the extension of world trade, which was greatly facilitated by laying cables and by the development of agencies of communication not the least of which was Lloyds, the great marine insurance corporation. The latter depended on quick and constant communication. Cumulatively, one factor leading to another, London came into the position of world dominance with respect to market and exchanges, head offices of great corporate enterprises, and quick information.

The activities of the many specialized agencies of a center have far-reaching effects in outlying areas which become subordinate to it. Consequently, London became the point of reference in respect to widespread industrial and commercial reorganization at home and abroad. This reorganization was not planned like the military campaign of a Roman general. The flag now followed trade into regions where new political loyalties emerged. Trading and transportation companies penetrated new and old countries in an effort to extend their markets for manufactured products and to obtain raw materials. This was the procedure of competitors who knew little of, or reflected less upon, the reordering of the world which their competition was bringing about. Their competition was impeded by national and cultural boundaries, but today most of these have been penetrated to

---

[8] *Ibid.*, p. 33.

an important degree, and the various regions of the world are brought into closer competition with each other. The result was the emergence of new regional divisions of labor, wherein a region specialized in the production of cotton, wheat, rubber, or some other product. Changes in production and consumption, accompanied by regional developments in transportation and communication, brought one of its cities into a position of dominance in relation to others. However, before such a closely integrated constellation of a region's centers takes place, each center may have more direct contacts with a distant center of dominance like London than with other centers within the region.

Old countries, too, may be considered frontiers from the point of view of the spatial redistribution of people and institutions which result from the penetration of organizations which have their head offices in a distant center of dominance like London. Household and domestic industries of Oriental countries, for instance, gradually yielded to the competition of the factory and cheaper lines of imported merchandise. Lines of modern transportation and communication displaced age-old modes of travel, and populations were partially redistributed to rising industrial centers and to new occupations. The old regions and their cities received a new ecological structure similar to that of industrialized regions of the western world.

Thus, world hinterlands were reorganized in relation to main and subsidiary centers of dominance. All regions, as they become integrated through their chief cities, are linked successively to a series of larger centers with wider tributary areas until London or some other world center is reached, which stands at the head of an ecological constellation that includes them all. Taken together, this series of centers comprises a symbiotic unity which tends to encompass the world. Nevertheless, there are large sections of the world, especially in the Orient, which have not yet been closely integrated with Eastern or Western centers of dominance. The immense expansion of the system of spatial relationships during the past century and a half, just described, indicates that it may yet include every region from the center to the periphery. As integration about great centers becomes more complete, commodities travel by more direct routes from one outlying region to another, although such transactions may be arranged in dominant centers such as London or New York.

NEW CENTERS OF DOMINANCE. Centers of world dominance are fixed only for a time. Some of their powers and earlier advantages may come into the possession of their competitors. The United

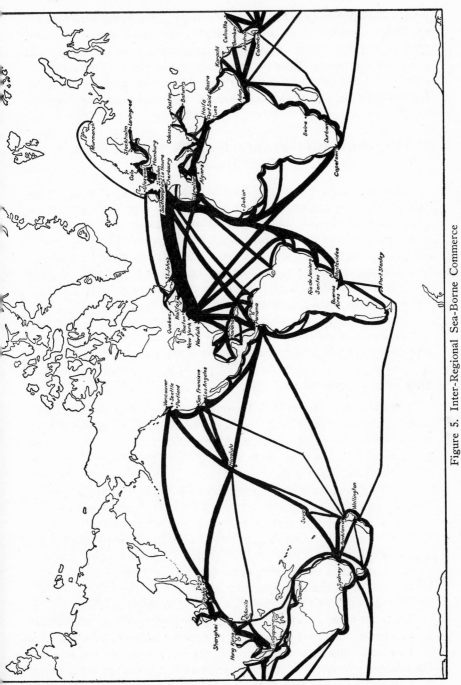

Figure 5. Inter-Regional Sea-Borne Commerce

Redrawn from *Encyclopaedia Britannica World Atlas*, 1945, p. 3-s. By permission.

States of America began as a series of frontier colonies of European nations, chiefly England, and now has become a great world power. Thus a frontier colony may emerge as a competitor of the original center of dominance. Today New York has succeeded London as the center of dominance in the western world. Other great centers play their specialized roles in a London-New York-centered world mechanism.

The Mechanisms Involved in London's Rise to a Position of World Dominance

We may think of metropolitan economy as an organization of people having a large city as nucleus, just as town economy had a town as its center. Or we may put it this way: metropolitan economy is the organization of producers and consumers mutually dependent for goods and services, wherein their wants are supplied by a system of exchange concentrated in a large city, which is the focus of local trade and the center through which normal economic relations with the outside are established and maintained.

As a town, London had at one time approximately 17 per cent of the total foreign trade of England. But when the town became a metropolis, the percentage was almost doubled. Probably its share of foreign trade never was over 45 per cent, which is, of course, a very large proportion.

Location and Hinterland Resources.—The district from which London drew its supplies in the home territory was increased from a narrow circuit of but twenty to fifty miles in radius, which had been sufficient in the town stage, to a wide area comprehending almost all of England. Not only was the coast traffic more extensive, but also an overland trade was opened up which had not existed before. The grain, cattle, and dairy products of the Midlands were brought to London and, later, textiles and iron and steel products in great volume. The externals (the growth of population, expansion of the area of the metropolis itself and of the district from which it drew its supplies, and even the volume of trade) are significant only in so far as they point to the new function performed by the metropolis, the function of organizing business for a wide metropolitan area.

The towns that developed into economic metropolitan communities had to possess marked advantages over their fellows. The situation had to be healthful, not only for a small town population but also for a larger group. The town located on the seacoast or a tidal river had an advantage in that refuse would be carried off twice daily by tides. Facilities for shipping are, of course, necessary, and by shipping we mean here primarily loading and unloading, for land as well as water transportation. Position, or location, between large groups of consumers and producers is vital for commercial growth and metropolitan economy. London lies between the rich European market and the developing markets of the Orient and America. Much of its success has been due to this fact. And yet this middle position is not in itself enough. The Phoenician cities along the shores of the Mediterranean had it in antiquity, Italian cities had it in the Middle Ages, and Flemish cities in the modern period. One further qualification is absolutely necessary. The aspiring town or city must possess a "hinterland," a tributary adjacent territory, rich in natural resources, occupied by a productive population and accessible by means of transportation.

The Area of the Metropolitan Market.—The large area of many communities, or rather the population, may be called a "metropolitan market," and the organization that sustains it "metropolitan economy." It is true that in studying this organization we are inclined to emphasize the great metropolitan center, but to forget the large dependent district would be fatal to a correct understanding of the subject. Perhaps, indeed, it is somewhat incorrect to speak of the area as dependent upon the center, for, though that is true, the center is also dependent upon the outlying area with its towns, villages, and scattered homesteads. Interdependence of the parts is really the key to the whole situation.

First Phase: Organizing the Market [9]

Such a wide area of mutually dependent communities required a well-organized marketing system. In this first phase, we discover, there were developed most, or all, of the institutions and practices necessary to supply the large agglomeration of people. In later phases we find that these were improved and elaborated.

In the stage of town economy there had been wholesalers, merchants who "sold to the trade," that is, to other dealers rather than to the consumers. But apart from those handling a few commodities, wholesalers as a group were not well developed. In the Middle Ages, at least, those who dealt in foodstuffs were generally compelled to sell to consumers direct. For example, the importing merchant had

---

[9] Much of the material on the development of the "first phase" and "second phase" (to page 167) has been adapted from N. S. B. Gras, *An Introduction to Economic History*, New York, Harper & Bros., 1922, pp. 183-269.

to sell his wine directly to the agents of noblemen. The peasant was forced, during the early hours of the day, to sell grain directly from his cart to the housewife, before the grain retailer was given any chance at all. Indeed, the only place where there was full freedom to buy and sell by wholesale was at fairs, and these came only occasionally and lasted only a few days. But when some one town grew into metropolitan proportions, the wholesaler came into his own. Every day was fair-day, and every merchant might sell to whomsoever he would. Of course, there were fitful returns to old-time restrictions, but the general development was in the direction of free trade for wholesalers. And indeed, we can readily see the point when we consider that as the metropolitan center grew, the area for supplying it grew likewise. Accordingly, it was necessary to have one class of traders specialize in bringing goods into the center and taking them out, while another handled them when they arrived.

Wholesalers.—At first these wholesalers, like their predecessors of the town period, performed several functions. They not only bought and sold, but they also stored their goods, notably in the metropolis itself, and acted as their own carriers. Further progress meant a separation of these functions, so that the merchant could devote all his attention and his capital to purchase and sale, leaving to other specialized dealers the business of transporting the goods, and storing them for whatever period was necessary. Gradually such specialists arose in answer to the need, men who owned the pack horses, carts, wagons, and coaches, required to carry the goods, and who charged so much for each article carried. They were open for service to anyone who wished to hire them, hence the term "common carrier." The advent of common-carrier steamship lines, with their great liners, resulted in the decline and gradual disappearance of the merchant's steamship business. The railroads, of course, have now become the most important common carriers. At first they often used the coaches and wagons of the merchants, but in time they came to provide substantially all of the carrying facilities (only a little over half the wagons in England, however), and even assumed the risk involved in transportation.

The wholesale merchants, having long distances to go and accordingly bearing great risks, and having a business peculiar to themselves, formed various associations and combinations for their own benefit, and ultimately for the benefit of all concerned. The exchange, one of the most notable of these associations, is a public place, established at first on the street and later in some inclosure or building, where traders congregate to do business.

The Metropolitan Exchange.—But the metropolitan exchange was somewhat different. Consumers were eliminated entirely, leaving the exchange a wholesalers' market, although near at hand, perhaps in the same building, consumers were catered to by enterprising retailers who saw them gravitate toward the exchange. More and more was the trade confined to goods that could be sold by grade or by sample—that is, spices, silk, and precious metals. And finally, many kinds of securities were bought and sold like other commodities.

In London proposals were early made to have the merchants withdraw from Lombard Street to a place where rain and mud would not hamper business, in fact, to found a bourse. Finally, Sir Thomas Gresham proposed to build an exchange, provided the city of London would supply the land. This became the Royal Exchange, twice burned, but still doing business—in the third building. The Royal Exchange consisted of a square and colonnade in which the merchants assembled twice daily, shops above for retailers, and cellars below for storing goods. Besides being a great center for business, it was the scene of a good deal of social intercourse, at a later date of a rather boisterous and illicit kind. At various prominent places topping the Exchange was the sign of the grasshopper—not of the purse—the sign that Gresham's own house bore in Lombard Street. The building, in general plan and in many details, was modeled after the bourse at Antwerp, where Gresham had done much business both for himself and for his country. Although the Royal Exchange nowadays reflects but faded memories of its past, it still stands as a monument to the metropolitan merchant (mercer) and financier, who, dying childless, made the public his heir not only to the Royal Exchange but to Gresham College. When exchanges have been founded in America, they have usually been patterned after the London institution. In colonial days Boston had its Royal Exchange where there were walks for merchants and around which there were several booksellers' shops.

Specialized Bourses.—As metropolitan centers have gone on developing, a third kind of exchange has come into existence—specialized bourses. Instead of one general exchange there came to be many, one for securities, the stock exchange; one for some single merchandise, such as the cotton, the coffee, or the corn exchange; and one for a group of related commodities such as the produce exchange, handling grain, meat, eggs, hay, and the like. In London the Royal Exchange is left with one of its original functions, the sale of foreign bills of exchange.

It should not be thought that exchanges exist only in metropolitan centers, for only the great ones are there. Minor exchanges are found in metropolitan centers near the place of production or near the consuming market. Examples of the former are the cotton exchange at Alexandria, Egypt, the grain exchanges at Duluth and Peoria, and of the latter the coffee exchanges at Le Havre and Bremen. Stock exchanges exist in provincial towns, but neither in number of members nor in volume of business are they important. Such towns merely approximate the position of Antwerp, Amsterdam, and London in the 16th century when the first metropolitan exchanges were established.

The same merchants that were founding exchange associations were establishing joint-stock companies, notably for colonization and trade. Although the joint-stock company was used before the metropolis existed, it was not an important factor in trade till the metropolitan stage. Any venture that required much capital and encountered great risk was difficult for one man even though rich. Accordingly, a joint-stock company was formed. When well developed, it was made up of a specified number of shares of equal value, and available for sale. Although the first joint-stock company in English commerce was probably the Russia Company, the earliest of importance was the East India Company, founded chiefly by London merchants, to trade directly with India, Ceylon, and the East Indian islands. Shortly after this, the Virginia Company was created to colonize and develop Virginia. English noblemen and London merchants were the backers of the company and sank a good deal of money in their venture, which was financially unprofitable. Besides gain, the founders hoped for a conversion of the heathen natives of America and for relief from overpopulation in London. Vagrant children were to be sent out as colonists, and indeed were so sent. A similar company was established by London merchants for the plantation of Ireland. The merchants invested in this enterprise not directly but indirectly through their guilds or livery companies. They hoped to relieve crowding in the metropolis by sending Londoners over to Ulster, and to gain financially by the exploitation of certain territory, notably Derry and its district of four thousand acres and Coleraine with three thousand acres. It should be said that this enterprise was not at the initiative of the merchants but was inspired by the government of the day, so as more readily to hold Ireland in obedience and to propagate the Protestant faith. At any rate, the subscribers put out a lot of money and received no dividends for thirteen years.

Joint-Stock Companies in Centers of Dominance.—The formation of joint-stock companies gave an enormous impetus to metropolitan development. Enterprises, not otherwise to be undertaken, were possible, sometimes to explore, sometimes to colonize, and sometimes just to carry on trade. Of course, they were used for mining and manufacturing, but with these we are not now concerned. The known world of commerce was divided up; one company was to develop the Baltic Trade, others the Russian, the Levant, the East Indian, the West Indian, and so on. The merchants of Paris as well as of London were organized into joint-stock companies. When success came to these companies, it meant an enormous inflow of materials from all parts of the world and a corresponding outgo of goods not needed at home. In other words, it provided for concentration of commerce never before contemplated. Of course, the ambitious metropolis was hard put to it to find capital for such investments. But the fact that shares could be issued enabled it to succeed, for the capital not only of merchants but of orphans and widows, clergymen, gentlemen, and others not able to engage directly in trade, could be invested in stock. And the people of a wide area, the nobles at first, and later others, could be enlisted to give aid to such gainful enterprises. Where the companies were carefully and conservatively managed (usually where the merchants were in charge), the companies were successful because the people would have confidence enough to invest, and the ventures would bring in returns. London was the outstanding illustration of success, Paris of failure.

It was by means of such trading companies that the metropolitan centers, such as Amsterdam, London, and Paris secured new markets and strengthened old ones. Two different kinds of trade were involved, which we may call the "extended" and the "local" or "hinterland." The hinterland trade takes place inside the area: it is intrametropolitan. The extended trade lies outside the area: it takes place between the metropolitan unit and the great beyond. Extended trade between two metropolitan centers may be called intermetropolitan. The hinterland trade is the wheel of the machine; the extended trade the belt connecting the wheels.

The World's Trade Center.—Probably from the first the town had carried on an extended trade with distant towns, whether in the same country or in foreign lands. As early as 1200, Bruges received wares from almost all the known lands of Europe, North Africa, and Asia Minor. The metropolis merely multiplied the connections. The discovery of America and the opening up of the South Seas offered unprecedented opportunities. More distant markets were available, and commodities were brought direct, such as spices and cloth, which had formerly come overland at high cost and in small amounts. Soon they were coming by ship at low cost and in large quantities, so that there arose that phenomenon of modern trade, the glut. The phrase, "a drug on the market," perhaps originally signifying something hard to take or not wanted, might in the 16th century be thought of as taking on a new meaning when oriental drugs and spices reached the European Atlantic ports, not in a single ship but often in a whole fleet of ships. And we must not forget the products of the Americas: Peruvian gold and silver, West Indian sugar, Virginia tobacco, Carolinian indigo and rice, New York furs and New England lumber.

Of course, this is but one side of the trade, for these wares had to be paid for in goods (ordinarily manufactures), except in the case of Spain which secured much of its supplies by forced labor and not by trade. As Britain's empire grew, many of the individual planters and the colonies also appointed agents resident in London to look after their affairs, in the case of the planters to sell their raw products and purchase manufactures.

The counterpart of this extended trade was hinterland trade. Although London might pay Boston (Mass.) for its lumber or fish by sending tea from Ceylon or spices from the East Indies, it was also obliged to send a large amount of hinterland products, woolens, hardware, books, and many luxuries. As the extended trade increased, it was necessary to widen the hinterland market to provide an ample base for further expansion.

The local or home market of the town had been an area having a radius of a score or more of miles. But the growing metropolis was compelled to extend its district more and more, until in the case of London it included substantially all of England. Later, when other cities developed in England to share the foreign trade, London lost some of its home base, notably the territory around about Manchester-Liverpool, which we may regard as functionally one center. Such division of local or home marketing territory does not mean loss of extended trade, because the area that remains may be more intensively developed, and because the metropolis may stress its entrepôt trade.

This is just what London did, it became more and more a port at which distant wares were assembled, and from which they were sent, being stored there for assortment before being shipped elsewhere.

SECOND PHASE: INDUSTRIAL DEVELOPMENT

Although the foundation of metropolitan economy was laid in the general organization of the market, much remained to be done. Further progress lay in the development of manufactures. One of the pillars on which the metropolitan structure rests is the possession of a variety of wares, a full store of all commodities which are available and in demand. These may be secured in extended trade or may be produced within the metropolitan marketing area, either in the metropolis itself or in the hinterland.

Manufacturing in the Metropolis.—It is inevitable that a metropolis, like any other large city, should have manufactures. The existence of a considerable demand right in the place itself invites industries. The manufacturer has small transportation charges on his finished goods and he can keep in close touch with the tastes of the consuming public in the metropolis. Any surplus can readily be disposed of elsewhere by means of the metropolitan marketing organization. The tastes of those outside the metropolis generally follow metropolitan fashions, so that it will not matter if the manufacturer does send his left-overs into the provinces a season or so late. The manufacture of articles of fine clothing and luxuries thrives in the metropolis, women's clothing in Paris and New York, men's in London and Chicago. When knitted hosiery and fine coaches were introduced into England, they were first made in London. These are but a few of the many examples.

To the metropolis went raw products from all parts. From the standpoint of the manufacturer it was advantageous to be close to the focusing point of his supplies. A notable example of this is found in sugar refining in London, meat packing in Chicago, and flour milling in Minneapolis and Kansas City. If no countervailing influences were at work, the advantages of raw materials and a consuming market would make the metropolis as important for its industry as for its trade.

But many of the new industries that have been set up in the metropolis move out into the towns and villages of the hinterland. And from time to time industries are started afresh in the tributary area, avoiding the metropolis entirely. Accordingly, we are justified in stressing the industrial development of the district more than that of the metropolitan center.

Although the movement of industry from the metropolis to the villages and later to towns was a common phenomenon, and one of great importance, we must let the illustrations already given suffice.

The reason why industries leave the metropolis, or why they flourish more in the hinterland than in the center, is that production costs are lower in the former than in the latter. It is cheaper to manufacture cutlery and other hardware in Sheffield and Birmingham because these towns are nearer to the sources of raw material and fuel, and transportation costs are accordingly less.

We find a similar illustration in America. The lumber mills have left Minneapolis for northern towns, or rather, have developed in the north at Bemidji, Virginia, and International Falls, because by cutting the logs in the district where they are grown and by shipping only boards, freight is saved on the waste timber. Because of the high cost of living in larger cities, wages tend to be high in a metropolis. Only strong countervailing advantages will keep an industry in a community where wages are high and where for that reason production costs are excessive. High wages may be due to the high cost of food or to the scarcity of laborers. Labor difficulties likewise increase the cost of production in so far as they force employers to pay higher wages, and often cause strikes and lockouts, as costly to management as to labor. Often taxes are so high in a metropolis that manufacturers seek relief by going either into a country village or a manufacturing town, where the standard and cost of living are low and where tax rates are moderate and the assessment only nominal because there are no expensive public utilities to be maintained. We can see how real the differences in cost were in the case of the shipbuilding industry. Because it cost more per ton to build ships in London than in the western part of England or on the Clydeside in Scotland, it was inevitable that shipbuilding would move from London.

Factories Move to Hinterland.—One way in which the metropolis became commercial and the hinterland industrial, then, is by a movement of the industry from the center to the outlying parts. But the outlying parts developed industries of their own, industries that were never specially identified with the metropolis. The textile manufacturers well illustrate this. Early in the career of metropolitan London, woolen cloth was being made in the villages and towns for sale in London. The industry developed from local skill and models but was organized by clothiers having the needs of the London market in mind. At a later date the cotton industry sprang up in the northern part of England, selling its products through London at first, and later also through Manchester-Liverpool. The iron and steel plants of the north made hardware that was finished in London and machine parts that were put together there, whence they were, of course, sent to all parts of the world.

The Center of Transportation.—At this point we may briefly review the transportation phase of London's metropolitan development. The period we may place roughly at about 1830-1890. Although there had been earlier efforts at highway regeneration, and although the post office had been established, first for government service and later for public use, in both cases centering in London, although stage coaches ran from London to all the important towns, and although there had been real improvement in transportation by means of canals and better constructed highways, nevertheless the real beginning of the third phase came with the railroad era. At first built in the north, the railroads really supplemented the trade with the metropolis in so far as they connected inland points with the coast trade centering in London. Soon practically all the important railroad lines focused on the metropolis. This meant that the hinterland was truly bound to the metropolis by bands of steel, the rails of the new roads.

Contemporaneous with railroad construction came the building up of over-sea traffic on a new and regular basis by means of the steamer. We may say roughly that what was done for London's hinterland trade by the railroad was done for its extended trade by the steamship. The two, of course, are but parts of the same mechanism. With Sheffield cutlery, Lancashire cottons, and Yorkshire woolens, London could buy American tobacco, Canadian furs, East Indian spices, and China tea. By means of the post office, telegraph, telephone and cable, London has been linked with its hinterland and has kept in close touch with much of the rest of the world.

Center of Information and Finance.—We may visualize the fully developed metropolis very crudely in this way: the retail section is the survival (and extension) of the trade of town economy and the wholesale district represents the first phase of metropolitan economy. The industrial suburb is all that the metropolis has (ultimately) to show of the second phase of its development. The great terminals for railroads and steamships are the generally ugly memorials of the third phase. And the financial district stands for the fourth phase. In London it is Lombard Street, not the street itself but the section with financial institutions. In Boston it is State Street, in New York, Wall Street, and Chicago, La Salle Street. Here in these districts are the banks, brokers' offices, stock exchanges, and insurance offices. Here is the most sensitive spot in the metropolitan nerve center.

Center of Centers.—Thus London became a great center of population with the most specialized financial institutions in the world. New utility and luxury goods were produced to meet the needs of the metropolis. It became the center of art, of fashion, and of amusement. Writers, artists, scientists, and musicians flocked to London. As the center of cultural growth and change, this great city's influence was transmitted outward along the axial lines of transportation and communication. Competitive but subsidiary cities were links in the chain that connected its life with that of all other regions. Each, in turn, was the center of its own particular hinterland and found its equilibrium by serving the interests of that hinterland in a specialized way. In Sheffield it is cutlery; Detroit, automobiles; the Twin Cities, flour; Pittsburgh, the steel industry; Shanghai, the center of foreign commerce in China; Cairo and New Orleans, cotton; Paris, Latin culture and fashion; Chicago, meat packing and the center of American railways; New York, a center of finance, and, due to this, the successor to London as the center of dominance for the world.

Changes in London's English Hinterland.—At the beginning of the last century, England had not yet emerged from a system of domestic industry scattered throughout the towns, villages, and countryside. One after another of the national industries—shipbuilding, the textiles, steel products—became concentrated in the centers of a few districts. Glasgow on the Clyde, the center of the shipbuilding industry, and Lancashire, as a textile center, may be cited as examples of this process of specialized concentration. This redistribution of industry, slow in the earlier stages, gained in speed. Towns mushroomed along the arteries connected with London, each housing its special primary and secondary industries and drawing to it the appropriate population types from English, Irish, and Scotch villages and countrysides. Prejudice against the factory system and against the breaking of social ties left countless numbers without an occupation when cotton and other industries concentrated in urban centers. These people preferred to work for lower wages at the backward and parasitic industries that remained dispersed. The young and the unskilled migrated much more freely to the factory centers.

In time, the industrial concentration in England became so extensive that the island was, in a very real sense, the world's factory, having the greatest factory population and the most highly urbanized region on the face of the earth. The relocation and increase of population in urban centers had far-reaching effects on rural social institutions, but the migrants from rural areas and villages had to

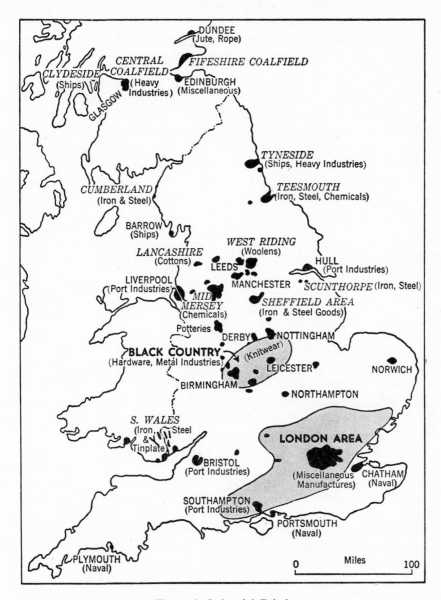

Figure 6. Industrial Britain

From G. T. Renner (Ed.), *Global Geography*, New York, Thomas Y. Crowell Co., 1945, p. 531. By permission.

accommodate their institutions to urban conditions. New schools, clubs, associations, new social classes with their institutions mark out, in part, the changed institutional pattern in England. Similar changes were in process in other parts of the world.

The questions and bibliography for Chapters 7 and 8 will be found at the end of Chapter 8, pages 181-184.

Chapter 8

SELECTIVE DISTRIBUTION OF PEOPLE AND CULTURES
(Continued)

The Social Effects of Ecological Reorganization.—The nature of the ecological reorganization of outlying regions in relation to centers of dominance in the industrialized western world has been indicated in the preceding chapter. Such regions have been drawn into new divisions of labor in producing for a world market. New devices of transportation and communication have emerged which, together with newer techniques in production and trade, have caused the shift of many inhabitants from small to large centers and from old to new occupations. But even where people have remained in their original communities, the latter have been so closely linked with other and larger communities that new ideas and modes of life have come to them. Thus, social change has resulted from sheer increase of social contacts within their own culture. To this type of change there has been added the diffusion of culture from outside which has taken place either indirectly because lines of communication led to world centers, or directly through the movements of business representatives, officials, missionaries, and even extended migration of outsiders to the region.

The Penetrativeness of Ecological Organization.—The frontier region is first penetrated by the impersonal factors involved in ecological reorganization. Commodities of the market place, due to their impersonal and unemotional nature, usually create the initial situation which brings together persons with divergent social backgrounds. The benefits to be derived from the exchange of commodities are immediately apparent to the population of the region and outweigh any emotional attachment to traditional products and tools. However, once contact has been established, tensions arise concerning ceremonial and ideational differences between the two groups. Only gradually, as adjustments are made within the culture to the new commodities, is the way paved for the exchange of ideas and ceremonies which are deeply embedded in the emotional life of the people.

The isolation of a people living far back from the main trade routes of the world passes when the commercial world discovers that the regions they inhabit contain some product which can be exchanged in the world market with material advantage to the producer and consumer. Hawaii was first a watering and provisioning point in the Pacific. The discovery of its potentialities for the production of sugar and other commodities came later. Egypt could produce cotton. The Orient possessed, among other things, great quantities of rice and silk. Other areas possessed gold, diamonds, ivory, and varied agricultural products. All these areas with products to market were, in turn, potential consumers of products from elsewhere. The organization of a production and commodity exchange system involves a series of ecological changes which automatically create new social situations involving tension and readjustment.

THE DEMOGRAPHIC REVOLUTION

The extension of the areas of competition between the regions of the world has been one of the notable results of the Industrial Revolution.

The history of the past two hundred years is most effectively told in terms of the unification of the area of human competition until during this century there has emerged the clear cut lines of a single world ecological system. Competition between neighbours has always existed side by side with their feeling of belonging together among people on the opposite sides of the globe, or on opposite sides of most national boundary lines exists even today only in indistinct form. As has been made clear, competition requires little or no knowledge of our competitors. They may speak a different language, share none of our concepts and none of our values, and yet through the production of goods in what has become a single market, we are in continuous contact with them. It is in this market that the wealth and fate of nations are determined.[1]

Against this background, the demographic revolution of modern times can be understood.

Sociology begins its study of population by considering population distribution. Soils, ores, and other regional resources and their accessibility, as well as the technology affecting productive efficiency, are taken into consideration. If some group is in sole possession of certain resources, its value system determines the use to which such resources are put. The circumstances which bring any given resource into use are: first, the level of technical skill which makes its

---

[1] Nathan Keyfitz, *The Demographic Revolution*, unpublished manuscript, 1948.

use possible and, secondly, culture values which extend the consumption of the resource. For example, had Canada's nickel been discovered by the Algonquin Indians, the technical mining skill which they possessed was wholly insufficient to enable a societal use of it. Nor would the nickel have been any more useful to the earlier white harbingers of western culture. It was only when our culture had developed sufficiently to be able to make efficient use of nickel that a market was created, and the nickel, when discovered, began to be mined. This resource today provides the livelihood of large numbers of Canadians. In the future there may be further shifts in technology which will make unimportant the demand for nickel and many other now-used resources. The population occupied at present in the production of these resources may move to new areas to be employed in other ways. Population changes are frequently related to shifts in the use of resources.

The first effect of the reorganization of the world's productive system, plus the related social changes, was a marked stimulus to population growth.

In the first phase, the application of the increased wealth and knowledge of the Industrial Revolution brought about the lengthening of life. Sanitary organization was an important part of the complex which achieved this. Because birth rates did not decline immediately, there was an unprecedented increase of population. This was in contrast to the greater part of history in which the human race has been decreasing almost as often as it had been increasing. A graph over most periods of one thousand years—if the figures were available—would show no perceptible trend. A single couple doubling every hundred years (which is slower than the rate at which Canada increased in 1931-1941, the slowest decade in its history) starting in the time of Homer, would now have progeny equal to the entire population of the world. With a doubling every twenty-five years, the rate suggested by American data which Malthus used in his illustrations, descendants of a single couple who lived in the time of William the Conqueror would now equal the world's population. Malthus lived at the beginning of this rapid increase, when births were far in excess of deaths and when it seemed reasonable to ask, with some alarm, what would be the outcome of such unprecedented multiplication.[2]

It seemed that the enormous expansion of western European population would press beyond cultural controls to the limit of resources and, hence, eventual famine. In more recent times, Asiatic population expansion has caused concern. Between 1931 and 1941, India showed an increase of fifty millions,[3] due partly to initial,

2 *Ibid.*
3 *Census of India,* 1941, Vol. 1, Part I, Tables I and II, p. 62.

though still limited, shifts to mass production methods, together with the diffusion of techniques for reducing mortality rates. England trebled her population during the period 1801 to 1901 when she was at a similar demographic stage. India, it is felt, has far less room with which to meet the population crisis which its leaders now face. It would appear, also, that cultural inflexibility in the East is a much greater barrier to falling birth rates than it is in the West. The period within which new controls can emerge to meet India's demographic problem will probably be long.[4] However, declining birth rates in Japan suggest that the East may not have to await the slow evolution of demographic controls which occurred in European countries during a corresponding period of growth, but that the direct diffusion of Western controls may bring about the latter stages in demographic adjustments more quickly.[5]

Fears of Race Suicide in the Western World.—After the first stage in the cycle of demographic revolution, new social factors emerged to reduce birth rates and gradually diminish net population increase. Then followed the fears now familiarly sloganized by the phrase "race suicide." These fears operated in situations where the upper classes or the country as a whole showed signs of failure to effect population replacement, due to a rapidly falling birth rate. Industrialized countries in particular have shown a diminishing ratio of births to deaths. For a time, net increases were maintained at a fairly high level. This was the period when the reduction of mortality rates was more slowly matched by the more subtle social factors which restrict the birth rate. The play of these factors affected the upper classes first. This gave rise to the widespread notion that the differential decline in the birth rate, in which the classes on the lower rungs of the economic ladder accounted for most of the country's reproduction, signified that leadership would fall into the hands of "inferior stocks." This "inferior stock" assumption has never been supported by unequivocal evidence. Furthermore, the gradual diffusion of the goals and techniques of the upper classes has tended to pervade all sections of a given society and, as these goals and techniques reached the lower classes, their birth rates also declined.

Falling net reproduction rates are also closely linked with modern urban growth. The city is at the hub of a vast network of transportation which connects it with the surrounding areas which use its services. The city has urbanized not only those who live within its

---

[4] Keyfitz, *The Demographic Revolution.*
[5] Irene B. Taeuber, in *Postwar Problems of Migration,* New York, Milbank Memorial Fund, 1947, p. 26.

boundaries, but also, in varying degrees, those who live in its hinterland. Since urbanization is linked closely with falling net reproduction rates, city growth constitutes an important factor to be considered in studying this phenomenon. The wide distribution of urban centers of more than 200,000 population in modern times shows how extensive such influences are in the world.

TABLE 5

URBAN CENTERS OF MORE THAN 200,000

Major Population Areas	
Western Europe and northern Africa	105
Orient	42
Eastern United States and southeastern Canada	41
Eastern Europe and western Siberia	27
India	20
Minor Population Areas	
Near East-Caucasus Area	11
East Central Coastal South America	10
Western Coastal United States and Canada	8
Coastal Australia and New Zealand	6
Southern Africa	2

Adapted, by permission, from George T. Renner (Ed.), *Global Geography*, New York, Thomas Y. Crowell Co., 1945, p. 412.

The map shown in Figure 1 indicates great concentrations of population in England, Northwestern Europe, the Eastern United States, in Southeastern Asia, and in Western Russia. The cities and most of the population of Soviet Russia (See Figure 7) are concentrated in a broad triangle with its base on a line drawn from Leningrad to the Black Sea and its apex on the east at the Urals, a band in the vicinity of the Caucasus, and a narrow ribbon stretching eastward along the Trans-Siberian Railroad. These areas occupy approximately one fifth of the Soviet Union. Only a few smaller cities lie outside these three areas of urban concentration.

The growth of Russian cities in size and numbers from 1926 to 1939 was unequaled, either in its earlier history or in the urban development of other countries.[6] Most of its cities, large and small, grew very rapidly during this period. Twelve cities of more than 200,000 in 1926 had increased to thirty-nine cities of over 200,000 by 1939. The former twelve cities (Moscow, Leningrad, Kiev, Kharkov, Baku, Gorky, Odessa, Tashkent, Tbilisi, Rostov, Dnepropetrovsk, and Saratov) had 13,557,000 persons in 1939, which was 90 per cent more than their combined populations in 1926. Moscow

6 Harris, "The Cities of the Soviet Union," pp. 107-110.

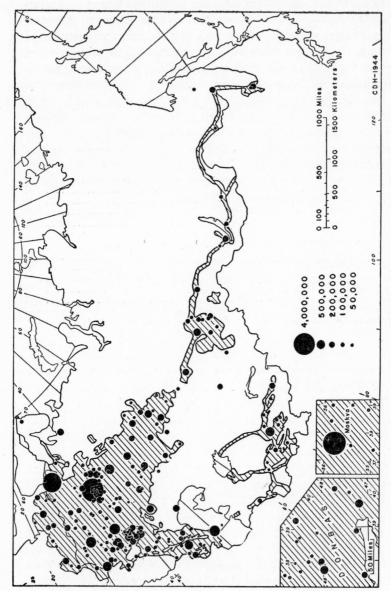

Figure 7. Cities of the U.S.S.R. in Relation to Its Inhabited Area.

From Chauncy D. Harris, "The Cities of the Soviet Union," *The Geographical Review*, Vol. 35, No. 1, January, 1945, p. 109, published by the American Geographical Society of New York. By permission. This map is based on 1939 population statistics. The inhabited area is indicated by shading.

had increased from 2,029,000 inhabitants to 4,137,000 and Leningrad from 1,690,000 to 3,191,000 during this 12-year interval. Three of the original twelve cities had more than doubled their population and one of them, Gorky, had increased 190 per cent. The proportion of urban residents in Soviet Russia rose during this period after 1926 to 32.8 per cent in 1939. Nevertheless, Russia's urban population is proportionately less than that of the United States in 1891.[7] Since 1939 Russia has annexed considerable territory on her western border. The populations of these borderlands include eight cities ranging from over 100,000 to just under 400,000.[8] Russia's industrial revolution has come late, but progress has been rapid. Its industrial and population expansion may be expected to continue at least at an equal pace during the next decade.

TABLE 6

Per Cent of Population, Rural and Urban, for Selected Countries *

Country	Latest Year †		1880	
	Rural ‡	Urban	Rural	Urban
Austria (1934)	54.9	45.1	80.2	19.8
Bulgaria (1934)	76.8	23.2	—	—
Canada (1930)	58.3	41.7	84.1	15.9
England and Wales (1930)	22.7	77.3	32.1	67.9
France (1936)	53.1	46.9	65.2	34.8
Germany (1933)	43.5	56.5	70.9	29.1
Hungary (1930)	45.2	54.8	—	—
Italy (1936)	29.3	70.7	46.2	53.8
Japan (1935)	35.5	64.5	—	—
Sweden (1935)	67.7	32.3	84.9	15.1
Russia (1926)	83.4	16.6	86.5	13.5
United States (1940) §	43.5	56.5	70.5	29.5

* France, Bureau de la statistique générale, *Annuaire statistique de la France, 1938,* Imprimerie Nationale, Paris, 1939, pp. 229-231.
† Date in parentheses is latest.
‡ Includes urban places of under 5,000 population.
§ Figures added from Table 14, Warren S. Thompson, *Population Problems,* 3rd ed., New York, McGraw-Hill Book Co., Inc., 1942, p. 109.

By permission, from *Population Problems,* 3rd ed., p. 112, by W. S. Thompson, copyrighted, 1942, by McGraw-Hill Book Co., Inc.

Rural-Urban Distribution Trends as Affecting Reproduction.— During the period of the great industrial development of the Western World, the trend toward urban residence has continued. From Table 6 it can be noted that the population of England and Wales has become predominantly urban, having an increase of 10 per cent

[7] Frank Lorimer, *The Population of the Soviet Union,* League of Nations Publications, Princeton, Princeton University Press, 1946, pp. 145-150.
[8] Harris, "The Cities of the Soviet Union," *op. cit.,* p. 119.

in city dwellers since 1880. Soviet Russia, on the other hand, was still predominantly rural in 1926. Canada and the United States lay midway between these two in rural-urban distribution of population, but showed the fastest trend toward urbanization, the number of people in their cities having increased 25.8 and 27 per cent, respectively, since 1880. In the United States, the urban development rose spectacularly from 29.5 per cent in 1880 to 39.7 per cent in 1900, to 51.2 per cent in 1920, and to 56.5 per cent in 1940.[9] It is probable that the percentage in 1948 is still higher, as the figures for 1940 do not take into consideration much of the influx into urban areas during the war years. When the United States entered the recent world war, her rural-farm population numbered about 30,000,000, falling to about 25,000,000 by 1945. However, even without the war, the trend toward increasing urbanization of the population was well under way. The war simply accelerated it. Such a trend toward urban concentration is found not only in America, but also in all countries which are becoming rapidly industrialized.

If the pattern of population distribution within a country is predominantly urban, the majority of people live under an urban culture. One of the patterns of urban behavior taken over most readily is that of the small family. An ever-decreasing number have two or more children, many have but one child, and many have no children at all. So small are present-day city families that, on the whole, the population of a city does not even reproduce itself. This is true also for almost all neighborhood areas of a city, except those composed of recent rural or "old country" immigrants. In order to maintain their populations, cities depend upon migration from the rural areas where the birth rate is still comparatively high and where mechanization of agriculture has forced surplus population into the cities for employment. For such rural areas as St. Denis, the creation of a surplus population due to the increased use of machinery on the farms and the high birth rate of the area, and its deflection into the cities, has been well documented.[10]

The tendency toward smaller families in the urban areas is due to a number of factors. Health facilities in the city are much more effective than those found in rural communities and these have facilitated a reduction in urban mortality rates. Urban families call for greater economic and social sacrifices than do rural families. Children in the city are more of a financial liability than in the country where, through their work on the farms, they tend to be an asset.

9 Paul H. Landis, *Population Problems*, New York, American Book Co., 1943, p. 347.
10 Horace Miner, *St. Denis*, Chicago, University of Chicago Press, 1939; see also Ch. 9.

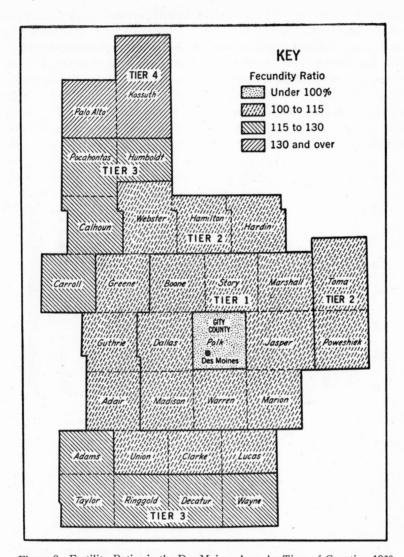

Figure 8. Fertility Ratios in the Des Moines Area, by Tiers of Counties, 1930

By permission, from *Rural Social Trends*, p. 114, by E. de S. Brunner and J. H. Kolb, copyrighted, 1933, by McGraw-Hill Book Co., Inc.

In addition, specific ideological factors operate to influence the birth rate. For example, in the rural areas of French Canada, the value system of the Roman Catholic Church inspires the maintenance of large families. However, such factors seem to be modified in urban areas. Even in Quebec, a province where rural and religious values have combined to keep the reproduction rate high, the size of family has been steadily diminishing under urban influences.[11] However, the reinforcement of rural and religious sentiments temporarily continues to retard the decline in the birth rate.

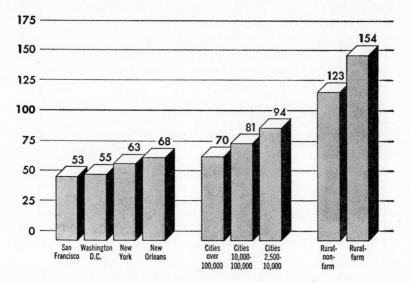

Figure 9. White Replacement Indexes for Selected Communities in the United States, 1940.

In the above indexes a ratio of 429 children aged 0-4 to 1,000 women aged 20-44 = 100, which is exact replacement when age composition and death rates are those in the 1939-41 life tables for the United States. Indexes so calculated give an indication of the way populations are likely to increase (over 100) or decrease (below 100) in a generation, but are not to be regarded as exact predictions. From Warren S. Thompson, *Plenty of People*, New York, The Ronald Press Co., 1948, p. 41.

Other factors in the decline of the urban birth rate are the widespread knowledge of contraceptive measures in the cities as compared with rural areas; the later age of marriage of urban women and the lower proportion of married city women; the greater numbers of childless women in the city, whether due to social or biological reasons being as yet undetermined. As previously indicated, it is the desire

---

[11] Oswald Hall, *Size and Composition of the Canadian Family, with Special Reference to Sample Areas of the Metropolitan Regions in Central Canada*, M. A. thesis, McGill University, Montreal, 1937.

of urban groups to raise their status or at least to maintain for themselves and their children the status they have acquired. In order to do so, family size must be made smaller, not only because of economic reasons, but also in order to conform to the pattern of urban family life. The desire for leisure time by the urban woman is another factor. She wants time to attend clubs, to carve a career, to enter movements, and time to devote to other sharply individualistic goals of self-gratification. Increased status comes to the city woman through her participation in public life, her appearance, and her social activities, rather than because of her home and children as in rural areas. Thus the urban family is kept at a minimum in comparison with the rural.[12]

These downward trends in net reproduction rates have caused great concern to many governments in Europe and elsewhere. As a result, new social and political movements have been initiated in an effort to reverse this trend. However, in no instance have these movements been successful in raising net reproduction rates. Germany seemed to be a possible exception when a short term change occurred. It is thought now, however, that the rise in the German birth rate during the late 1930's can be attributed almost completely to the end of the economic depression and the subsequent increase in the marriage rate. However, social and political controls of population will be treated at length in later chapters.[13]

QUESTIONS

1. Why is the sociologist interested in population and its distribution?
2. Where are the four greatest concentrations of population in the world to be found?
3. What conditions determine the concentrations of populations?
4. Describe the distribution of population in Canada.
5. What factors tend to curtail population mobility?
6. Differentiate between arithmetic and physiological density. From Table 3 evaluate the justification of the claims of Germany, Italy, and Japan that they were overpopulated. What factors should be considered in determining the extent of under- or overpopulation of a country in addition to physiological density?
7. Can you account for the tremendous increase in the world population since the Industrial Revolution?
8. Why is the Industrial Revolution of importance in a discussion of population distribution?

---

12 Thompson, *Population Problems,* pp. 188-213.
13 See Chapter 20.

9. What is meant by an active concentration of population? by a passive concentration of population?
10. What is meant by the concept center of dominance?
11. Sketch the mechanisms involved in London's rise to world dominance.
12. What part do the ecological forces play in the patterning of the world?
13. What factors are responsible for the lowered birth rate in urban areas?
14. Are centers of dominance permanent? Why or why not?
15. What changes did the Industrial Revolution bring about in the distribution of population in England?
16. What are the social effects of ecological reorganization?
17. Commodities penetrate a frontier region more easily than do ideas. Comment.
18. What effect does culture have on the utilization of available resources?
19. What factors influence the declining birth rate of urban areas in the Western World?
20. Can you cite examples other than those given in the text of ideological factors operating in different countries of the world since the first world war to keep the birth rate high?

BIBLIOGRAPHY

ALBIG, W. "The Mobility of Urban Population." *Social Forces,* Vol. 11, March, 1933, pp. 351-367.

ANDERSON, NELS, AND LINDEMAN, E. C. *Urban Sociology.* New York, F. S. Crofts & Co., 1930, Chs. 3 and 10.

BRUNHES, J., AND VALLAUX, C. *Le Geographie de l'histoire.* Paris, Librairie Felix Alcan, 1921.

BURCH, G. I., AND PENDELL, E. *Population Roads to Peace or War.* Washington, Population Reference Bureau, 1945.

CARR-SAUNDERS, A. M. *World Population: Past Growth and Present Trends.* New York, Oxford University Press, 1936.

CHARLES, ENID. "Differential Fertility in Canada." *Canadian J. Pol. Sci. and Ec.,* Vol. 9, May, 1943, pp. 175-218.

COTTRELL, W. F. "Cultural Growth of Internationalism." *Am. Sociol. Rev.,* Vol. 10, No. 5, October, 1945, pp. 586-595.

DAVIE, MAURICE. *World Immigration.* New York, The Macmillan Co., 1936.

DAVIE, MAURICE. *What Shall We Do about Immigration.* New York, Public Affairs Committee, Inc., 1946.

DAVIS, D. H. *The Earth and Man.* New York, The Macmillan Co., 1943.

DAVIS, K. "Human Fertility in India." *Am. J. Sociol.,* Vol. 52, No. 3, November, 1946, pp. 243-255.

DAWSON, C. A. (Ed.) *The New Northwest.* Toronto, University of Toronto Press, 1947.

ENGEL-FRISCH, GLADYS. "Some Neglected Temporal Aspects of Human Ecology." *Social Forces,* Vol. 22, October, 1943, pp. 43-47.

FAIRCHILD, H. P. *People, The Quantity and Quality of Population.* New York, Henry Holt & Co., Inc., 1939.

FINCH, VERNOR C., AND TREWARTHA, GLENN T. *Elements of Geography.* New York, McGraw-Hill Book Co., Inc., 1942.

FORDE, C. DARYLL. *Habitat, Economy and Society.* New York, Harcourt, Brace & Co., Inc., 1937.

GILLETTE, J. M. "Some Population Shifts in United States." *Am. Sociol. Rev.,* Vol. 6, No. 5, October, 1941, pp. 619-629.

GRAS, N. S. B. *An Introduction to Economic History.* New York, Harper & Bros., 1922.

HALL, OSWALD. *Size and Composition of the Canadian Family, With Special Reference to Sample Areas of the Metropolitan Regions in Central Canada.* M. A. Thesis, McGill University, Montreal, 1937.

HARRIS, CHAUNCY D. "The Cities of the Soviet Union." *The Geographical Review,* Vol. 35, No. 1, January, 1945, pp. 107-121.

HERTZLER, J. O. "Sociological Postulates Underlying World Organization and Peace." *Social Forces,* Vol. 22, December, 1943, pp. 125-130.

KEYFITZ, NATHAN. *The Demographic Revolution.* (Unpublished), 1948.

KIRK, DUDLEY. *Europe's Population in the Interwar Years.* League of Nations Publication, 1946.

KOLB, J. H., AND BRUNNER, E. DE S. *A Study of Rural Society.* Boston, Houghton, Mifflin Co., 1940.

LANDIS, PAUL H. *Rural Life in Process.* New York, McGraw-Hill Book Co., Inc., 1940.

LANDIS, PAUL H. *Population Problems.* New York, American Book Co., 1943.

LEPAWSKY, ALBERT. "The London Region: A Metropolitan Community in Crisis." *Am. J. Sociol.,* Vol. 46, No. 6, May, 1941, pp. 826-834.

LIVELY, C. E., AND TAEUBER, C. *Rural Migration in United States.* Washington, U. S. Dept. of Agr., Bur. of Agr. Ec., 1939.

LORIMER, F. "Recent Population Trends in the Soviet Union." *Am. Sociol. Rev.,* Vol. 9, No. 3, June, 1944, pp. 219-223.

LORIMER, F. *The Population of the Soviet Union.* New York, Columbia University Press, 1946.

LORIMER, F., AND OSBORN, F. *Dynamics of Population.* New York, The Macmillan Co., 1934.

MATHERLY, WALTER J. "The Emergence of the Metropolitan Community in the South." *Social Forces,* Vol. 14, March, 1936, pp. 311-325.

McKENZIE, R. D. "The Scope of Human Ecology." *Am. J. Sociol.,* Vol. 32, No. 1, July, 1926, pp. 141-154.

MINER, HORACE. *St. Denis.* Chicago, University of Chicago Press, 1939.

MUKERJEE, R. "The Regional Balance of Man." *Am. J. Sociol.,* Vol. 36, No. 3, November, 1930, p. 455ff.

MUKERJEE, R. "Population Theory and Politics." *Am. Sociol. Rev.,* Vol. 6, No. 6, December, 1941, pp. 784-793.

MUNTZ, E. E. *Urban Sociology.* New York, The Macmillan Co., 1938.

MYRDAL, GUNNAR. *Population: A Problem for Democracy.* Cambridge, Harvard University Press, 1940.

PARK, R. E. "Migration and the Marginal Man." *Pubs. of the Am. Sociol. Soc.,* Vol. 22, 1928.

PARTON, M., AND REEVES, R. "Size and Composition of American Families." *Am. Sociol. Rev.,* Vol. 2, No. 5, October, 1937, pp. 638-649.

PEARL, R. *The Natural History of Population.* New York, Oxford University Press, 1939.

PLATT, R. S. "Environmentalism versus Geography." *Am. J. Sociol.,* Vol. 52, No. 5, March, 1948, pp. 351-359.

Postwar Problems of Migration. Milbank Memorial Fund, 1947.

PRESIDENT'S RESEARCH COMMITTEE ON SOCIAL TRENDS. *Recent Social Trends in the United States.* New York, McGraw-Hill Book Co., Inc., 1933.

QUINN, J. A. "The Nature of Human Ecology, Re-Examination and Redefinition." *Social Forces,* Vol. 17, December, 1939, pp. 161-168.

QUINN, J. A. "Topical Summary of Current Literature on Human Ecology." *Am. J. Sociol.*, Vol. 46, No. 2, September, 1940, pp. 191-226.

QUINN, J. A. "Culture and Ecological Phenomena." *Sociol. and Soc. Research*, Vol. 25, March, 1941, pp. 313-320.

RENNER, GEORGE T. (Ed.) *Global Geography*. New York, Thomas Y. Crowell Co., 1945.

REUTER, E. B. *Population Problems*. New York, J. B. Lippincott Co., 1937.

ROTERUS, VICTOR. "Effects of Population Growth and Non-Growth on the Well Being of Cities." *Am. Sociol. Rev.*, Vol. 11, No. 1, February, 1946, pp. 90-98.

SOROKIN, P. A. *Social Mobility*. New York, Harper & Bros., 1927.

STEINER, J. F. "Populational Trends in Japan." *Am. Sociol. Rev.*, Vol. 9, No. 1, February, 1944, pp. 36-41.

TAFT, D. R. *Human Migration*. New York, The Ronald Press Co., 1936.

TAYLOR, G. R. *Satellite Cities*. New York, National Municipal League, 1915.

THOMPSON, W. S. "Movements of Population." *Am. J. Sociol.*, Vol. 40, No. 6, May, 1935, pp. 713-719.

THOMPSON, W. S. *Population Problems*. New York, McGraw-Hill Book Co., Inc., 1942.

THOMPSON, W. S. *Plenty of People*. Rev. ed., New York, The Ronald Press Co., 1948.

THOMPSON, W. S. *Population and Peace in the Pacific*. Chicago, University of Chicago Press, 1946.

ULLMAN, E. "A Theory of Location for Cities." *Am. J. Sociol.*, Vol. 46, No. 6, May, 1941, pp. 853-864.

Chapter 9

SELECTIVE DISTRIBUTION OF PEOPLE AND CULTURES
(Continued)

Case Studies of Ecological Penetration and Social Change.— While the chapters on culture precede those on ecology, the cultural data can be understood more fully after reading the ecological material, for all these cultures have been affected to some degree by the diffusion of alien culture traits set in motion by traders, missionaries, and imperial functionaries. Invasions and successions of out-group peoples and modes of life have taken place, and illustrations of these processes can be found throughout the text.

An extended treatment of the reorganization of the productive, marketing, transportation, and communication systems is to be found in the preceding chapters. Focal points in these revolutionary changes were the world's great cities, such as London. In the present chapter, attention is focused on four widely spaced case studies which show the changes taking place in the lives of people far removed from the great centers of manufacturing and commerce but still affected by their activities.

The first of these studies is of St. Denis, a small community in the county of Kamouraska in an old, settled area on the south shore of the St. Lawrence River below Quebec City in Canada. The forefathers of the French-Canadians who inhabit St. Denis settled there in the seventeenth century, having come from northern France in the mass of emigration which followed the discovery of the New World. For several centuries their manner of life lay largely outside the technical and social changes taking place in such industrialized areas as the immediate hinterlands of London and New York. More recently, St. Denis has been drawn from its isolated, agricultural way of life into the outside markets to sell its material products and the labor services of an increasing number of its population. St. Denis has not only landless descendants elsewhere in the world but has also developed a small landless local population. Increasingly, the roots of St. Denis are to be found in a system of production, marketing, and occupational mobility which parallels the invasion of part-time residents from outside, new agricultural techniques, city-oriented educational procedures, and different standards of living.

In the space of one generation, the population of the Kunming Lake district of southwestern China has changed greatly from a homogeneous rural people whose way of life was based almost exclusively on agriculture. Such regions, homogeneous as to race, religion, and family life, had a social solidarity which had prevailed for many centuries. Power machinery and new manufacturing techniques have invaded the Kunming Lake region, largely due to the capture of the Chinese coastal manufacturing areas by the Japanese in 1937 and 1938. Diverse occupations have been taken up by workers from within and beyond this area. As in many other sections of China, new forms of production and marketing have come to succeed age-old modes of living. Gradually, changes in family organization and a new world outlook have also come about. These changes have been stimulated, not only by an acquisitive manner of living which has come from outside, but also by the upheavals caused by alien military invasion and civil war. Areas most readily available to waterways and railways were the first to be transformed economically and socially. These spearheaded a new way of life for ancient China.

Much more spectacular have been the changes which resulted from the invasion of alien peoples with modern techniques for the production of agricultural, mineral, and other resources, as in Hawaii and South Africa. The old economy of Hawaii, based on agriculture and fishing, partly succumbed to demands for supplies by the captains of early sailing ships. Next came a series of extractive industries, and eventually the present plantation system emerged as the dominant economy. In such situations of invasion and succession, the lives and institutions of the original natives suffered prolonged disorganization. After enduring so much for so long, they have reached a new equilibrium in occupations and a semblance of solidarity in their reorganized social life. Many other types of invasion reached Hawaii. One racial group after another was brought in to be the work force on the plantations. As each group showed greater independence and aimed at advanced occupational goals, another was brought in to succeed it. In the end, this has resulted in a polyglot population and an unstable social life. The drawing of this section of the world into the larger world market, and its new-found divisions of labor along regional and occupational lines, set the stage for successive cultural and institutional changes, as this case study reveals.

South Africa was invaded by the Dutch and the English as a phase of the expanding pattern of the Industrial Revolution. The

Dutch brought in western agricultural techniques, drove the natives from much of their land, and employed them as agricultural workers and domestic servants. The English mining entrepreneurs speeded up the process of alienating the Kaffir population from its old self-sufficiency on the land. The land base of the native people shrank and various laws pushed them in the direction of having to earn their living by mining and urban occupations. Native peoples found themselves relatively landless, and partially urbanized. As a result, their tribal life disintegrated. All this was described by Lord Olivier in his book [1] from which this case study was obtained in part. What happens when "free enterprise" enters a region in which a primitive folk culture predominates is very fully demonstrated. South Africa is an excellent laboratory example of entrepreneur planning for profits, with relatively little or nothing in directive social controls conserving the interests of others, especially the native population. Perhaps a knowledge of sociology and anthropology will lead to ways of utilizing the resources of such regions with a minimum of social disorganization in the future.

St. Denis.—On the south shore of the St. Lawrence River, about eighty miles downstream from Quebec City, lies the parish of St. Denis. Natural physical boundaries separate it from the other parishes to the east and west and make it a natural unit by itself. Its northeast boundary is the St. Lawrence River, paralleled by a long, low ridge known as the Coteau, which cuts off the river from the sight of the parishioners. At the east end, the Coteau ends in a high, rocky ridge known as Cap au Diable, jutting out into the river. South from the Cap, on the east, runs a long sweep of uncultivated lowland which is difficult to cross in the winter due to the large snowdrifts which accumulate there. This lowland forms a barrier, cutting St. Denis off from Kamouraska, the parish to the east. On the west is the Grande Plaine which runs south from the Coteau. It is an extensive peat bog, also impassable in the winter due to snow-drifts which often reach a depth of ten feet. Thus, St. Denis is cut off from its western neighbor, Rivière Ouelle. Finally, on the south, three miles back from the river and one mile from the edge of the parish of St. Denis, the Appalachian Mountains begin.

The land of the parish is laid out in the traditional French-Canadian pattern which has persisted since seigneurial times. Two "rangs," that is, strips of land about a mile and a half in width, parallel the St. Lawrence River and are separated roughly from one another

---

[1] Lord Olivier, *The Anatomy of African Misery*, London, L. & V. Woolf, 1927.

by a stream known as Des Bras. A road runs the length of each rang, one road stopping in a dead end at the Grande Plaine and the other continuing through to Levis and Quebec from Gaspé. The houses of the habitant farmers have been built along these roads, about 400 feet apart. Behind the houses stretch the farmlands. The land owned by a habitant is customarily about 400 feet wide and the width of the rang in length, or about one and a half miles. The farms are divided into fields which are also long and narrow as the habitant traditionally divides his land lengthwise.

Along the road which runs through each rang there is a strong feeling of social unity. The people who live along one road have frequent contact with one another, while they may visit the families on another road only once or twice a year. These roads along the rangs are known as "chemins," in contrast to "routes," the name given to roads which connect the rangs and which have no houses along them. The one "route" which is an exception roughly divides the parish into quarters, and intersects the "chemin" of the first rang. At this point the village of St. Denis has grown up, containing the institutions which are of service to the community—the church, and the specialized craftsmen.

The parish quarters are also units of social solidarity, even more fully developed than the units along the "chemins." The center of each quarter is marked by a wooden cross which is replaced as a symbol of their faith every generation by the people who live in that quarter of the community. The erection of the cross is made possible by popular subscription and a ceremony is held which reinforces the feeling of unity and the identification of the people with their quarter.

The culture of St. Denis is typical of the rural culture of French Canada. Its history is the story of the selection of strongly Roman Catholic French people to a new environment, to which they adapted the patterns of the old world. The homogeneity of tradition and religious beliefs has persisted to the present day. Adjustments made by the early settlers to the new world have also lasted, for example, large family groups and the system of land tenure. The early antagonism to the English, dating back to 1690 and 1759 when the French-Canadians defended themselves against the invaders, has also persisted. In 1837 an abortive uprising among the French-Canadians brought severe reprisals from the dominant English group, which further added to the feeling of separateness of the habitants, and gave rise to a lasting interest in politics, and the alignment of the Roman Catholic Church with them against English Protestant encroachments.

The culture of St. Denis is a blend of the sacred and the secular which cannot be separated. The round of life, daily and yearly, is dictated by tradition. The behavior of the people is governed by the folkways and mores of their ancestors. The Church gives them guidance according to century-old beliefs. Even in such areas of activity as farming and political participation which in many societies could be termed secular, tradition prevails side by side with scientific methods and popular discussion.

The farming of the community is secular in that methods are open to discussion and experimentation and outside influences such as that of the "agronome," the government agricultural expert. However, the methods of agriculture are, in many ways, still strongly sacred. Tradition, superstition, and religious belief dictate many farming methods, such as the type of fields, the kind of crops, and the time of planting and harvesting. The means of controlling nature are also a blend of modern scientific knowledge and folk beliefs. Along with crop rotation and modern machinery goes the blessing of seeds by the priest and the religious fêtes to ensure good crops and harvests.

The political interest of St. Denis is secular in that it also permits discussion, questioning, and objective thinking. Although the Church is not supposed to exercise its influence in these matters, its covert participation is strongly felt. Party affiliations follow family lines and traditional clique antagonisms. Political activity is traditionally a male prerogative, being considered "too dirty" for women who are expected to confine their interests to the home. Although the Church is not supposed to show any interest in politics, the curé gives indirect support to one candidate through the pulpit. In addition, the church newspaper, L'Action Catholique, tends to give its readers a strong bias in favor of one party.

The main cultural themes of St. Denis center around religion and the land. All life in the community is intricately bound up with these two dominant interests and is lived in terms of them.

The economy of the community was, until recently, based on agricultural self-sufficiency. Even the villagers are closely tied in with rural life. Although they do not own land, they live by supplying special services to the farmers of the parish. The problems of the land, therefore, are the problems of all.

The system of land tenure in St. Denis has given rise to large family groups. Sons are needed to help with the farm labor and daughters to feed and clothe the men. The large family group has become traditional and is strongly backed by church sanctions which prohibit any steps which might be taken to limit its size. The people accept the judgments of their clergy uncritically and thus no effort is made to control family size, even though a smaller family group would be able to survive more easily under present conditions.

The large family group is the basic social unit of French Canada. A person is known to outsiders by his parish and his family name, this information being sufficient to call up all the appropriate attitudes in the person whom he has just met. Social contacts within and without the parish are governed by family ties. For example, a distant parish would never be visited unless a relative resided there.

"The family" consists of all those who live under one roof, but all collateral relations to third cousins are included as "relatives." Much stress is placed upon the family's geneological tree, the knowledge of which is passed down from generation to generation. Pictures of deceased members hang in the "salon" and even the smallest child comes to know about them as persons who are constantly referred to by the living. The masses which are said for the souls of the dead for some time after their demise also tend to keep alive their memory in the family.

Family ties formed by marriage are very important and frequently two families will be linked three and four times within a generation, as when brothers marry cousins or sisters. The marriage is usually decided upon by the two people involved, but requires family consent, a dowry, and a marriage contract before the vows can be taken. The families of the two persons are thereby concerned with the success of the marriage and the raising of the children.

Marriages frequently take place within the kinship group. The Church has adjusted to this situation by making dispensations easy to acquire. The curé takes other considerations than relatedness into account when making his decision, such as age, health, compatibility, and the likelihood of their finding other mates.

The family in St. Denis is the main institution for the transmission of the cultural heritage to the children. The younger generations are taught the sacred-secular ways of their parents as the only correct patterns of behavior. As the culture of the community is homogeneous, the cultural heritage transmitted is the same for all and, with no one of a divergent heritage around with whom to make comparisons, the traditional ways are unconditionally accepted. The Church and the school also add their support to the family teachings.

The habitant's life is bound up with his religion from birth to death. The first notification of a birth to the community is the ringing of the church bells after the child has been christened. As the community is small and all know what family expects a child, no further notification is required. Each stage in the life of the person is recognized by a religious service, and the person acquires new religious and social prerogatives as a result. "Petite communion" marks the beginning of participation in church activities. Until that time the person's family has taught him the main tenets of religion and to pray, but, except for special children's services, he has not attended church. Nor has he had any status in the social life of the community or family. He has played only with relatives and has eaten with the other very young children apart from the rest of the family. Coinciding with "petite communion" the horizons of the child broaden to include church and school attendance and eating with his family. His duties and obligations also increase and the carefree play-days are left behind. His first communion, taken when he has mastered the catechism, marks the transition from baby to school child. "Grande communion," at about fifteen years of age, usually coincides with graduation from the local school and marks the entrance of the child into adulthood. With marriage, also a church ceremony, the person becomes a fully participating member of the community and of the society. The final "rite de passage" is death. Here, again, a church ceremony takes place, which breaks the ties of the deceased person with his society.

The system of land inheritance in the French-Canadian family also ensured the continuation of the society in past centuries. The father was responsible for the establishment of his sons upon the land, one son inheriting the farm of his father when the latter was ready to retire and when most of the children had been established away from the parental home. The same type of society then continued generation after generation. In addition, it gave the father a strong control over the behavior of his children who were dependent upon his good will for their future success.

It was from this pattern of inheritance that the present threat to the solidarity of French-Canadian culture arose. Until recently, the surplus population of French Canada has been absorbed by a country thirsty for settlers.[2] With little good farming land available on the frontiers of Canada, there was no longer an agricultural outlet for the French-Canadian population. The habitants were forced to make other provisions for the future of their children. The industries of the larger cities afforded outlets for some of their sons; to others

---

[2] E. C. Hughes, "The Study of Ethnic Relations," *Dalhousie Rev.*, Vol. 27, No. 4, January, 1948, pp. 477-482.

the habitants provided further education. However, whether the sons went to the cities as laborers or furthered their education, the habitant culture found itself drawn into the markets of the Dominion and of the world. From this point onward, change followed change. The institutions of this community, as of all others, were so closely interrelated that a dislocation in one meant dislocation in all.

The necessity of finding a new means of settling children brought an end to the self-sufficiency of St. Denis. In order to compete in the outside market, changes in farming methods, in mechanization, and in the types of crops were needed. These changes, once established, upset the old division of labor. There was no longer any need for the family as a whole to participate in harvesting and threshing, and this lack of common activity began to weaken the family bonds. Mechanization also displaced many of the farm laborers.

With the access to markets, a demand was created in St. Denis for manufactured products which replaced the home-craft goods of previous centuries. Cloth is no longer woven to any great extent; baking and many other home crafts are speedily fading out. Attempts have been made in county and parish fairs to stimulate these crafts again, but these efforts have met with very little success.

With the increase of mechanization in farming, some of the non-landed sons of the habitants moved to the crossroads, where a village emerged. Here they catered to special needs of the farmers which had hitherto been handled by the farmers themselves. These specialists formed a new class in the community, the non-landed. Owning no land, they were not as intricately bound up with the social order, and many of the folkways and mores lost their control upon this group.

The emigration of many young males from the community left a large surplus of unmarried women for whom the society had to make provision. Most of the girls began to take longer and longer periods of education in order to enhance their marriageability. Some go into the church as nuns, while others become schoolteachers. A few also emigrate to work in the factories of the metropolitan areas. However, a great number are left single, and their dissatisfaction with their lot is a disturbing influence in the community. Many have tried to compensate by taking over behavior which the men consider solely their own, such as political activity. The higher literacy of the women, the emergence of a group of women who think for themselves, the fact that the established way of life no longer offers satisfactory rewards, have tended to weaken the control of the traditional folkways and mores upon their behavior.

The close kinship structure has also suffered as a result of the emigration of youth. Parents no longer know their daughters-in-law or their families. Marriage contracts are becoming more a formality than a tie which binds families of like interest together. The constant contact with the kinship group has been broken and, consequently, the passing down of the family heritage has been disrupted.

As the majority of St. Denis youths now look forward to going to the city for work when they have finished school, they are avid to learn city ways. Despite the disapproval of the curé, some formed friendships with the members of an English summer colony and began to pick up their language and some of their habits. This contact with an outside group also provided an opportunity for testing the efficacy of French-Canadian mores and has tended to break their control upon the individual. Other "city ways" are picked up from the visiting St. Denis emigrées, upon the behavior of whom St. Denis mores have lost their hold. The emulating of a way of life disapproved by the parish, but approved in the world to which these young people plan to go, has proved disruptive to the culture of the community. The family, which could have controlled their children in the past, now have no rewards to withhold and their attempts at discipline go unheeded.

It has become increasingly apparent that the education given to St. Denis youth, at home, at school, and at church, no longer fits them for the life they are to lead. Up until recently, these institutions trained the youth of the community for life in that community. The main emphasis was on farming and religion with a strong ethnocentrism. The child was taught very little of skills to be used in city employment. His knowledge of mathematics was limited; his history had a strong religious and anti-English bias; his geography was of no use other than to locate church dioceses; he had no knowledge of science and only a very limited knowledge of the English language. Such an education does not fit the person for competition and a satisfactory life in the city, nor does it give the youth anything on which to base a sense of security equivalent to that which he left behind in St. Denis. The old rules of behavior no longer hold and the discrepancies between city and country life take their toll in maladjusted personalities.

Among the people who still live on the land, the old mores and the Church continue to exercise control. However, further changes have taken place also in their way of life. Medicine, for example, is losing its folk qualities and is becoming increasingly scientific. The "remancheur"—or bonesetter—the midwife, and the donors of traditional and superstitious "cures" are being steadily replaced by the doctor and the public health nurse. But change for the groups who are still on the land is slow, and their institutions are able to keep pace without too severe maladjustments in the culture.

The French-Canadian society of today, as seen in St. Denis, is still a folk society in that it lives in terms of common understandings which have become rooted in tradition and formed into an organized way of life. The community's common beliefs are expressed in its institutions, rituals, and daily life. The conduct of the members of the community is supported by strongly sacred rules and all share and act by the same definitions of "right" and "wrong" behavior. There is a strong kinship group which regulates the activities of its members and determines the role they shall play in community life, and is, at one and the same time, responsible for the actions of its members and accountable to them for its own behavior. The kinship group is clearly delineated and closely connected with all the other institutions of the society. It is the main mechanism for the transmission of the cultural heritage to the next generation and for the inheritance of property.

On the other hand, the habitant culture is related to modern civilization in that it lives by a money economy, produces for an outside market, and is part of a larger political system in which the parishioner is interested and in which he participates. Certain individuals in the community, such as the curé and the local senator, link the parish to the outside world. The habitant and the city man form a single society organized in terms of status. Each recognizes the other and allows a place for him in his world of social relationships. The nature of the present economy of St. Denis brings it into contact with the larger community and permits diffusion of the outside culture of the city to the parish. Radios, newspapers, roads, the political system, and the parish emigrées link the community with the wider society.[3]

China and Western Technology.—The history of China's industrial development is a story of the resistance of a sacred culture, thousands of years old, to the invasion of the secular industrial techniques of the comparatively young western world. In the last half century, and particularly since the beginning of the recent Japanese-Chinese War, it has become apparent that China could not survive in the modern world without industrialization.

---

[3] Adapted from Horace Miner, *St. Denis*, Chicago, University of Chicago Press, 1939.

The influences of western culture were felt in the coastal areas of China as early as the seventeenth century, when European powers acquired trade agreements with the government. By the end of the nineteenth century, European countries had obtained Treaty Ports. Contacts with western people and western capital prepared the coastal regions for the acceptance of industrialization which commenced in the late nineteenth and early twentieth centuries. Until the Japanese-Chinese War, however, westernized industry remained on the coast and along the Yangtze River, where transportation and communication facilities were near by and inexpensive. When the Japanese army seized these industrial coastal centers in 1937 and 1938, the government of China was forced to move industry into the country's interior. One large group of factories was established in the Kunming Lake district of southwestern China. Due to the isolation of the district, the changes wrought by industrialization in the sacred agricultural culture of China were observed under conditions closely resembling those of a laboratory.

Before the war, the Kunming Lake district was typical of the interior of China. Inhabited by a predominantly rural people, it suffered from overpopulation. In China, the word "overpopulation" has the usual connotation of insufficient resources for the subsistence of the people, but it also means that there are too many people for the available jobs. However, in communities where everyone's livelihood was assured by a strong family system and its extensions, the labor surplus did not show up in unemployment so much as in the fact that the Chinese peasant wasted half his time in idleness. The great excess of labor pressing on limited resources had made human power extremely cheap. The technology of the farmer remained at an almost primitive level, unchanged for thousands of years, with human beings doing the work of animals. Where labor was so plentiful and so inexpensive, labor-saving devices were not only unheard of but would have made no sense to the peasant. Even the plow was rarely used until the ground had been broken, and there was no machine labor and very little animal labor. The Chinese peasant did a tremendous amount of work for very small and steadily diminishing returns.

Handicrafts were carried on by men and women as a part of the rural economy. Many of the peasants did this type of work in off-agricultural seasons and bartered their products in the villages and towns. Other craftsmen were organized in guilds with an apprenticeship system. Whichever was the case, the people so occupied remained an integral part of the rural way of life and a part of its system of social relationships which gave them their status and security.

The family constituted and, in the main, still constitutes the primary unit in the traditional economic system of China. The intimacy of family life provided strong ties between members and developed the sense of belonging to a group. When economic activities could not be confined to the family group, non-family members were brought in. The larger organization was still oriented toward and functioned along family lines, the various employees and members calling one another by terms of relationship and acting as if they were, in reality, closely related. Similarly, the authority structure in such an extended family group resembled the traditional pattern. Authority was exercised by virtue of age and position in the family. The Chinese community was little more than an extended family and the same group identification was retained by all who lived within its boundaries. The individual person in such a system had a sense of responsibility for and to the common mutually dependent system of a closely integrated society. His obligations and rights under such a system were clearly defined and unambiguous. The mores and folkways of the group were clearly delineated. Within this milieu, the individual found—and still finds—meaning for his existence and his behavior. His goals were group goals and his behavior was that which would be approved by the group.

The integration of peasant society in China was enhanced by the contentment of the people. This contentment was the concomitant of a non-expanding and non-escapable society. There was no outlet for the malcontent. Personal initiative was minimized because new ways led nowhere and old ways functioned adequately. Gradually, a feeling of contentment emerged and, on the basis of this contentment with the old ways, a system of ethics had been raised. Part of this contentment showed itself in a disinterest on the part of the peasant in novelty. He was disinterested in new ways of doing things. Nor would he consider moving from his traditional place on the land or in his community to advance his standard of living. Western incentives were completely without attraction for him. He stuck closely to what he knew, no matter how bad, and moved from the known only to avoid trouble.

The social stratification in the Kunming Lake district was according to traditional lines and maintained the age-old distinction between men who work with their minds and men who work with their hands. The former group ruled and the latter were ruled. The former group was entitled to service from other groups and the latter group felt obligated to serve. The highest rank was afforded to officials and scholars, and, more recently, to professional men. Merchants and craftsmen occupied an intermediate position, followed by factory hands and artisans and farmers. Last on the social ladder ranked the laborers, who possessed no skill and owned no land. Within each of these broad categories, there were further rankings. For example, the farmers with the highest status owned land but did not till it themselves; the next rank was held by those who owned and tilled their own land; the next rank was composed of those who worked the land, owning some and renting the rest; the next rank was made up of tenant farmers, and the last by farm laborers.

The result of such social stratification was the development of a leisure class which regarded with pride its emancipation from toil. They benefited from a land system which permitted the land owner to demand as much as half the tenant's crops as rent. The limited land resources left 17.6 per cent of the farmers in the Kunming area with no land of their own and another 39.4 per cent with only a part of their land owned by themselves. Under such circumstances, the leisure class could dictate almost any terms to the peasants who, having no other outlets of work available, were forced to accept them.

The leisure class also had prestige because it was well learned in the classics which dealt with Chinese traditions and moral teachings. In a society ruled by tradition, further prestige was given to those who had access to this knowledge.

Ecologically, the Kunming Lake area was made up of many small villages, a few towns, and a very small number of cities, the largest of which, Kunming, had about 75,000 inhabitants. The villages were the trading centers for the farmers and craftsmen who came there to barter their goods at the fairs and by peddling. In such centers were the institutions which catered to the farmers, as for example, the teahouses. Transportation to these centers was almost entirely by foot on poor roads which connected farms, villages, and towns. The only contact with the rest of the world was a railway and a highway which linked the province to the rest of China and to Burma on the southwest.

The establishment of nine factories in the Kunming Lake district in 1938 by the Chinese Government marked the beginning of the industrialization of the area. With the cutting off of foreign capital to give Chinese industries support, the government was forced to take over the running of these industries itself. The tendency to recruit the personnel for the management of these factories from the middle classes, who had a civil service tradition rather than a commercial outlook, enhanced the idea in the Chinese mind that industry should be government controlled. Very few factories were owned by private capital.

Almost as soon as industry had moved into the area, the effects of industrialization began to be felt. Kunming, which had had a population of approximately 75,000, added 100,000 immigrants, 40,912 of whom came from urban and industrialized coastal areas. Most of these were skilled workmen who had escaped the Japanese occupation of the coastal regions and were attracted to Kunming city by its industrial opportunities. The remainder of the increase in population was accounted for by unskilled labor from the province who came to the city for a wide variety of reasons. Surprisingly, perhaps, only a very small percentage came to work in the factories for economic reasons, although the pay scale was fairly generous. Most of the workers did not send money home and a small percentage received money from their families. Draft deferment was the motive of the majority. A smaller group hoped to raise their status because they confused a government-owned factory with the traditional pattern of the civil service. Still others—and this was especially true of women workers—came to the factories to escape unpleasant home conditions. Partly due to the reasons which motivated those seeking employment, the labor turnover was very high. When the draft danger was over, or the difficult home situation had been remedied, the laborers tended to return to their homes. This trend was enhanced by the fact that the factory worker of the interior of China had no status in his own community and the family looked upon factory work as something of a blot on its good name.

The effects of industrialization were apparent in other areas of life also. The ecological structure of the district changed. Kunming city became the center of dominance of the area, and the smaller towns declined. Commercial institutions began to replace the traditional markets and peddling of wares. A demand was created for manufactured articles and the crafts lost some of their economic strength. Most of the craftsmen, however, preferred to be satisfied with a smaller income than to go into the factories and thereby give up the prestige their craft afforded them. In the city itself, slums developed. People became more individualistic, and the strong family ties were weakened when families became smaller in size and composed of only parents and children.

Along with the large number of immigrants to the district came their folkways and mores, which were foreign to the native population. However, as these immigrants were gradually accepted, many of their ways were taken over. Under this leavening influence, many hitherto sacred mores were subjected to evaluation and began to lose their hold upon the people. The former provincialism gave way to a rising nationalism. New industrial techniques and traditions were introduced, as the immigrants were mainly of a skilled class. Educational methods in the area were changed by immigrant scholars who taught secular ideas and encouraged the individual to think for himself.

Industry necessitated many changes in the customary personal habits of the people. The traditional two meals a day were replaced by three. In addition, industry required a changed outlook in the people who were employed. The unskilled laborer had no tradition of mechanical knowledge, and tools other than agricultural ones of a very rudimentary sort were entirely foreign to him. He found it difficult to master even the most elementary tools of his new, industrialized environment. Before the coming of the factories, the family pattern had predominated in any industry in which the peasant had been engaged, usually at the craft level. The new factory also deviated from tradition in that the worker never learned the whole task, or even his relation to the whole task. This being so, the worker who had been schooled in the craft system found it hard to retain an interest in his work. Those workers who had come to the factory for other than economic reasons were unwilling to learn techniques which would increase their earning power simply because they felt the industry had served its purpose when it helped them escape an undesirable situation. The laborer was not used to regular hours. Nor was he accustomed to his superiors being impersonal strangers.

Industry caused a large toll in personal maladjustment. The peasant who had come to the factory was accustomed to having status in a community, and accustomed to knowing his relationship with all others in the community. The authority structure in his social world had been well defined. His contacts had all been with people with whom he was intimately acquainted. By his movement into the city he had broken from the traditional way of life. He no longer knew his status in relation to the strangers with whom he was forced to live. He no longer had any conception of what his group responsibilities were or even what constituted his group. The result was that he felt lost. The change had been too abrupt. Without the

traditional controls upon his behavior, he frequently became dissatisfied, disorganized, and highly mobile.

In the rural areas, the old mores ceased to have as strong control
over behavior and much of the traditional contentment began to
disappear. The malcontents now had an outlet, a frontier, in the
factory where they could escape all those things which they did not
find to their liking in the rural community. In addition, the industrialization of the district deprived many farmers of earnings which
had hitherto been made from the sale of handicrafts. Thus their income was threatened and many began to lose control of their farms,
sliding down the social scale from part-owners to tenants, and finally
drifting into the cities for employment. Once the peasant had lost his
land, he did not tend to try to return to it but became one of the
masses moving toward urbanization.

All these changes have occurred within eight years. As Kuo-heng
Shih pointed out, industrial change in China has meant a repudiation
of their history and extensive readjustment, although the people
find themselves still a part of an ancient tradition.

Ecological Succession in Hawaii.—Less than two hundred years
ago, the Hawaiian Islands were isolated and undiscovered, inhabited
by some 300,000 natives of Polynesian stock whose culture had not
yet emerged from the Stone Age. Today Hawaii is an integral part
of the world's economy, a center of commerce, and a strategic outpost
of the United States in the mid-Pacific. It is one of the world's
greatest racial "melting pots" and has an Occidental, scientifically
minded culture based on a stable plantation economy. In its development over the last two centuries, Hawaii has followed the pattern
of other insular regions located in the tropics, which were already occupied by a primitive culture and which possessed open
resources.

Before Captain Cook discovered the islands in 1779, the Hawaiians lived under a self-sufficient economy based on fish and taro
root. The occupation of the soil, its cultivation, division, and tenure, the orientation of the ceremonial and religious life of the people,
and the feudal nature of the social organization, were closely interrelated. Proximity to arable land and good fishing grounds determined the arrangement and location of the villages. Hawaiian
villages were usually built near the sea, with paths leading back to

---

4 Adapted from Kuo-Heng Shih, *China Enters the Machine Age*, Cambridge, Harvard
University Press, 1944; Ta Chen, "Population in Modern China," *Am. J. Sociol.*, Vol. 52,
No. 2, July, 1946; Lin Yueh-Hwa, *The Golden Wing*, New York, International Secretariat,
Institute of Pacific Relations, 1944. (Mimeographed.)

orderly, well-irrigated inland fields of bananas, sweet potatoes, and taro, and with excellent roads leading further inland to their fields of dry cultivation where dry-taro, yams, breadfruit, and sugarcane were grown. The division of labor was simple and highly sacred. There was some indication of specialization in that the fishermen belonged to a separate group with their elaborate and efficient equipment, their own taboos, and their own gods.

The units of land held by the chiefs were usually natural regions bounded by physical barriers. The chiefs had absolute power over the lives, lands, and belongings of all their subjects. In addition, the person of the chief was surrounded with elaborate and highly sacred taboos. The feudal nature of the social organization did not prove to be too onerous, however, before the coming of the white man. The sanctity of the chief and his absolute control over the lives of his subjects and their property discouraged rebellion by individuals. Nor did the chief tend to exercise his prerogatives too rigidly, as he needed the support of the people in the almost constant wars. As the pre-European Hawaiian culture placed no value on things unless they were of immediate use, the chief never seized more of the property of his people than he wanted to use at that time. Under such conditions, life was stable and satisfactory for the islands' inhabitants.

When Captain Cook discovered Hawaii, the natives regarded him as a god. His visit had far-reaching implications and set into motion forces which were to change Hawaii within the next two centuries. Within a very few years, Hawaii became a port of call for Pacific vessels needing fresh water and food. Unfortunately, their captains and crews soon dispelled the "white-god" illusion by their misuse of the islands' hospitality. Captain Cook had introduced the idea of trade, hitherto unknown, to the natives. A demand for Western products (especially for iron, and later for textiles and implements) was created and surplus goods which had not had any value up till that time became highly important for the acquisition of the products which the traders brought. The earlier hospitality of the natives now took on a secular meaning and became a calculated exchange of goods. Value having been given to surplus goods, the chiefs began to exercise their powers over the natives by diverting their land and labor into the production of the supplies needed for the ships of the Northwest explorers, fur traders, and whalers which called in port. The burdens on the common people became more and more difficult as their chiefs seized goods for their own self-aggrandizement. The introduction of iron enabled more land to be cleared, plowed, and brought under cultivation, thus introducing many changes in land use and the technology of the people. Cotton cloth began to replace the Hawaiian tapa cloth as a clothing fabric. Western firearms turned the pre-European type of warfare into a serious encounter. Almost as soon as the first ships had sailed away it became evident that the sailors had also left behind venereal diseases and other illnesses such as measles and scarlet fever, which would be considered mild in the Western countries, but which took a huge toll of Hawaiian lives.

About 1800, with the discovery of sandalwood, for which a huge demand existed in the Orient, Hawaii became permanently drawn into the world economy. The islands ceased to be merely a supply station for ships and became a regular port of call for traders, a few of whom settled on the islands. Gradually the chiefs concentrated their energies on satisfying the needs of the invading traders for sandalwood and neglected their land and fishing. The burdens they placed upon their subjects became most severe. Men, women, and children were sent, without proper clothing, into the cold mountains to secure sandalwood, work for which they had no preparation and to which they were unaccustomed. The toll of lives taken by this occupation, and the starvation which resulted from the neglect of the land and sea, were tremendous. Agricultural lands and fishing were abandoned; local economic self-sufficiency declined; native consumption of foreign commodities displaced local manufacturers; population began to concentrate in the emerging seaport towns and a widespread social disorganization ensued. About this time, there were reports of the great apathy and depression felt by the natives who seemed to die in great numbers for no apparent cause.

With the coming of resident traders and the growth of towns, the pioneer economy emerged. This era was initiated by a lengthy period of experimentation and transitory secondary contacts. Relationships with the natives were casual, highly speculative, short-lived, and only for purposes of trade. The settled foreign population was meagre, predominantly young males of uncertain origin and status. These men frequently married native women and thus began the crossbreeding of races which is still a feature of Hawaiian culture. The native population and resources were regarded by the foreigners as raw materials to be exploited as rapidly and as extensively as possible. It was at this period that the invading economy began to make serious inroads on the native culture and established certain economic claims which have persisted and have been expanded to the present day.

About 1820, the first missionaries came to Hawaii and brought an aura of respectability to the emerging towns. The foreign population in these centers began to bring their wives and children to the communities and a considerable foreign resident group grew up. Cattle were brought to the islands at this time and for a short time a Hawaiian equivalent of the American homestead system enjoyed a precarious existence. When the first experiments at plantations proved highly successful the homestead system was pushed further and further out toward marginal lands and eventually succumbed altogether to the plantation system.

For a time the native culture continued to compete with the new western economy. The chiefs defended their claims to the land by legal action, rather than by war. However, the burden on the people had become so heavy that many deserted their chiefs in favor of the less difficult employment offered by white cultivators. The missionaries tended to align themselves with the Hawaiians against the traders and plantation owners, and compelled the foreign group to modify their exploitation of the natives. However, in indirect ways, the missionary did his part to bring in western values and prepare the way for the capitalistic domination of the area. The moral values which the missionary taught were in keeping with western culture. Ultimately they had to join forces with the trader, for without changes in the natives' idea of decency and tenure of property, conversion to Christianity could not occur.

The emergence of the town as the organizing center for the new regime brought about many other changes and is indicative of the dominance of the pioneer economy and of the shifts in Hawaii's position in relation to the world at this time (1830-1860). Trade became more stable and less exploitive in nature. Foreign capital began to move into the towns. Specialization of function, the division of labor, and the integration of the life of the islands through improved means of transportation and communication of the center of dominance with outlying districts, were the indices of the emerging western economy.

With the discovery of gold in California, the Hawaiian plantation system finally succeeded the homestead and trading economy. Up until that time, the plantation system had been competing with other types of economy but was not noticeably dominant due to meagre land, lack of funds, inadequate tools, and an insufficient foreign market, for which it had to compete with other Asiatic countries. With the creation of a foreign market in California and later, during the Civil War, with other areas of America, the planta-

tions boomed. Later, protective tariffs assured a market for the
Hawaiian products in the United States. As a result, more and
more land was diverted to the production of one crop for export, and
diversification of agriculture became a thing of the past. The ups
and downs of the plantation economy, due largely to the fluctuating
demands of world markets, required greater efficiency in plantation
management, and tended to eliminate the less successful plantations.
Hawaii had now become oriented to world markets and eventually
came to epitomize, in its most advanced form, the scientific and technological achievement of the western world.

The early owners of the plantations lived on the land. As the
plantations were passed down from one generation to the next, with
intermarriage between the owning families, it was necessary that the
land be run for the good of the people as well as for the financial gain
of the owners if the system was to endure. Owners and workers
in the plantation system were interdependent. The tendency of the
owners to work on their plantations helped to keep the stereotyped
landlord from developing, as the workers and the owners were able
to recognize one another as individuals.

As plantations grew too large for one man to manage alone,
specialization of function began to occur. A managerial class
emerged with technical skill and increased efficiency. Also, within
the towns, factors emerged and broadened their scope to handle the
acquisition of foreign markets and other financial, legal, insurance,
transportation, and communication problems of the plantation owners.
In addition, due to the shortage of labor, and later, of available land,
scientific advice was sought to increase further the efficiency and
productiveness of the land. Ultimately a huge capital investment
was made to establish and maintain an experimental organization
for agricultural research.

The increased specialization taking place on the plantations, and
especially the emergence of the factors, made Honolulu the dominant
city on the islands. It became the center for all transportation and
communication. In Honolulu, professional, financial, government,
technical, and information services were located, utilizing the best
brains of the country. From this city, communication lines went
out to all parts of the islands and to the rest of the world. Outside
conditions also played a part in the rise of Honolulu to dominance.
It has the best harbor in the islands, and since Hawaii became an
important strategic point for American militarists, the city has
emerged as a naval base of importance, with its foreign population
greatly enlarged by military and civilian personnel.

Correlative to and implicit in the economic succession briefly sketched above, has been a series of ethnic labor invasions and occupational displacements in Hawaii. The more dramatic and significant of these movements were initiated and controlled by the plantation system. As the social order of the natives broke down, these people moved into plantation work. However, the long hours, the difficult work, and the monotony discouraged the natives from working consistently and they tended to move from one plantation to another, ultimately drifting into the towns. In 1852 the shortage of reliable labor had become so acute that two hundred Chinese workers were recruited. Thus began a long term trend of importing labor, exploiting it for a few years, only to have it move away from the plantation and into the towns as other occupational opportunities presented themselves. Japanese, Portuguese, Koreans, Puerto Ricans, Spaniards, and Filipinos flowed into the plantations and out into the towns. These new immigrants, freed from the controls of the mores of their homeland, competed for status in the new country.

That relatively few difficulties arose and that racial prejudice did not develop to the same extent in Hawaii that it has in other regions, is due in large measure to the relatively small number of immigrants arriving at one time and to the fact that these immigrants were brought in to fill occupations where there was little or no competition. Labor was imported only when the preceding plantation workers had left the plantation for other occupations. The group which left became semi-skilled and replaced the group ahead of them, which now entered the skilled class or trade. As long as the Hawaiian economy continued to expand, groups of immigrants were able to establish themselves in occupations whose former occupants were moving upward in the social scale. The relation of each immigrant group with others was symbiotic rather than competitive. It was only when the higher levels in the occupational ladder were reached that competition was really felt and some race prejudice noted. Even here, however, the prejudice was limited to informal understandings within the professional and similar groups. It was not likely to be successful in stopping the invasion of immigrants into those occupations because there was no public sanction of race prejudice and no dogma of racial inequality to support such understandings.

One of the main reasons why such racial dogmas did not develop in Hawaii was the almost complete absence of a "poor white" group. Hence the dominant white group did not feel its position threatened by competition until recently, and then only in a few occupations. The position of the white group as financial rulers of the country is unlikely to be questioned for some time to come. In addition, dogmas of racial inequality were difficult to formulate for the second generation because members of all ethnic groups acquired the same culture. All went to English-speaking schools and learned an American way of life and American-Hawaiian traditions. This common background was further enhanced by the American-dominated economic interests and by the American radio, newspapers, and motion pictures. In addition, Hawaiian culture permits intermarriage between races, this being both cause and effect of the lack of racial dogma.

Hawaii has now passed to the last stage of the economic cycle. The normal processes of production have led to the creation within recent years of a surplus of both capital and potential labor which the system, under its present organization, cannot assimilate. The dominant industries have reached a stage where they cannot profitably absorb additional units of capital investment comparable in size to their profit-seeking reinvestment. The foreign market for this surplus capital, of course, constitutes a potential competitor to the Hawaiian system. The surplus man power built up cannot find within the closed economic system of Hawaii a field for investment. Foreign fields for absorbing the Hawaiian surplus are even more difficult to find in the case of labor than of capital. The impasse, which Hawaii is now reaching in the disposition of its financial profits and labor by-products, is undoubtedly a forecast of the dilemma which other regions will face as the world rapidly becomes a closed economic system.[5]

South Africa.—When the Boers, the first white settlers, came to South Africa, they settled on land suitable for agriculture and cattle raising. The Kaffirs and Bantus, who had dwelt in the regions appropriated by the Boers, remained as squatters on the land, or were forced to accept servile positions on Boer farms, in Boer towns, or in Boer households. The Boers were severe masters, but they were not cruel. Their attitude and behavior toward the native were patriarchal rather than commercial and exploiting. They used the native labor, but relations between the farmer and his natives were rarely intolerable.

The Boers made little or no attempt to interfere with the culture of the natives. They wanted them for labor, but otherwise they paid little heed to what their servants did. The latter retained their tribal loyalties and customs, gradually modifying their culture as

[5] Adapted from A. W. Lind, *An Island Community: Ecological Succession in Hawaii,* Chicago, University of Chicago Press, 1938, and Clarence Glick, "The Relation Between Position and Status in the Assimilation of Chinese in Hawaii," *Am. J. Sociol.,* Vol. 47, No. 5, March, 1942, pp. 667-679.

contacts between the Boers and themselves became more numerous. The natives could be selective concerning which aspects of Boer culture they accepted. Consequently, they tended to take over only those patterns of behavior which did not interfere too much with their own cultural patterns.

Although it is probable that the culture of the native population underwent the most change, that of the Boers did not go untouched. Wherever two groups live in such close proximity that they can see patterns of behavior expressed, it is inevitable that changes will occur in both groups. The Kaffir and the Bantu did domestic work for the Boers. During their period of employment they picked up many Boer cultural traits, frequently taking over only that part of the trait which was expressed in action, because their cultural background left them unable to understand the ideas behind the trait. At the same time, the children of the Boers were tended by natives and from them learned many of their ways. The adults, too, took over many of the Kaffir and Bantu patterns of behavior, and came to know about many others which they did not adopt. The accepted native patterns became part of the Boer culture. Among the natives, also, there were many who were trained in Boer occupational skills such as building. However, the changes which took place in native culture came about slowly and without the imposition of force. As a consequence, their culture was gradually adjusted to the changes over a period of time and, thus, no marked cultural disorganization occurred at this time.

As time went on, a clear-cut division of labor emerged between the two peoples. There was the white man's type of work and the Negro's type of work. The white man performed the more responsible jobs, while the Negro worked as a laborer and accorded the white man respect. Even in the event that the white man and the Negro performed the same tasks, the Negro was much more lowly paid, approximately one tenth of the white man's wage. Yet, despite these factors, relations between the two were unstrained, easy-going, and friendly. The Negro would walk amicably alongside the white man, the Negro in the street and the white man on the sidewalk. Both Negro and white believed in the superiority of the white man. There was never a question of competition for jobs in either of their minds. A satisfactory accommodation and division of labor had been effected.

All might have gone well, had the natives been left sufficient land for their own tribal and domestic requirements. However the varied assets of South Africa attracted more and more immigrants who came to settle on the land or move into the towns. Gradually the white man succeeded the Negro on the land and the culture of the latter began to crumble. With the invasion of the area by new immigrants, capital was attracted to the area to open up new resources, one of which was the mining industry. With the opening of the latter, from 1873 onward, the country was drawn into world markets and competition and the accommodation which the native and the white man had built up was seriously disturbed. Disorganization of the native culture was greatly accelerated, as the men of the tribes were forced into labor in the mines and cut off completely from their families for long periods of time.

The white immigrants came into South Africa to work on the land or in the mines, and promptly absorbed the myth of the superiority of the white man into their way of thinking. Men take over most easily those culture traits which fill basic needs more efficiently than the traits already in operation in their own culture. The white European discarded his European traditions of equality among men, and accepted the South African tradition of white racial superiority. By so doing, he satisfied his basic need for a satisfactory status, without effort, but merely by virtue of his color.

The white man drew the Negro into the new economy of the mining district. Although he regarded the Negro as an inferior being to be kept in a submissive position, he nevertheless taught him to stope, to work machine drills, to sharpen tools, and to do all the jobs of the mine. The white man only took contracts for labor, which the black man did under his direction—at Kaffir wages. This, however, was still in keeping with the accommodation which had been reached between the Negro and the white. The white man was still supervising the Negro's labor and gathering the rewards. The trouble began when mine managers discovered that the Negro could do the same work as the white man and just as efficiently. To the mine manager there were no such divisions as white men and black men; to him there were only grades of labor. It is a technique of his training to try to reduce his labor costs to the most economical blending of expensive and cheap grades. Consequently, mine managers took efficient Kaffirs out of their traditional place and used them to cut costs in the mines by replacing white men, thus drawing natives into economic competition with the whites.

The racial tradition and trade unionism in South Africa revolted at the idea of giving the Kaffir an opportunity to improve his status. They interpreted his competition as a definite threat to their own positions. A conventional color bar was established by collective bargaining in the mines and a demand made in 1926 that it be sanctioned by law. The government was also pressed by the white people, the only group who held the right of franchise, to apply the color bar to the public services. This move greatly increased the cost of public work to the taxpayers, who were also white, but this decision was their own.

The demands for a legal color bar by the South African Labour Party in 1926 appeared to most people of European civilization to be outrageous, and to critical economists and sociologists insanely shortsighted. The Economic Commission, appointed by the South African government in 1925, flatly condemned the policy, and urged that skilled natives should be unionized and paid minimum wages fixed under the Wages Regulation Law. Unfortunately, however, the South African people were too involved in the situation to be able to regard it objectively, or in terms of long-range goals. Excuses and explanations for the color bar were easy to formulate. The rationalizations of the white worker would run somewhat as follows:

We are not making the native's position worse than South African social convention and State policy have decreed that it should be. You assert that he cannot be made a citizen, you enforce his obedience to his employer by legal sanctions, you keep him off the pavements and tramcars, you forbid him to go abroad without a pass, you—South African Europeans—have prescribed for him the permanent status of an underpaid, unskilled, service laborer. We did not introduce this mining industry, and the South African native community might be in a much healthier state if it had never been set up. We don't mind how high you pay the native for the unskilled manual work you assign as his prerogative, but we observe that you do in fact take care to pay him only the wages of a sweated worker. We have made it possible for you to employ him profitably in your mines, and we are doing him no wrong if we limit the number of natives you employ and import so that the native shall not, in this gigantic imposthume of capitalized industry, be employed upon such skilled jobs as will enable you to grind down the imported European worker into a Poor White.

The mines had also brought about the collapse of the native culture. Not only were the accommodative mechanisms between white and black broken down when the Negro became the white man's competitor, but also the social controls of his own group were eliminated with the collapse of his culture. The men of the tribe were forced into the cities to work in the mines. Here they were made to live in totally male compounds, isolated completely from their families. As culture can be transmitted to the next generation only through the imitation of the behavior patterns of adults, the male patterns were almost completely lost to the children of the culture. In addition, the marriage pattern was unable to function. With the males removed from the tribes, the functionaries in government and religion were gone, as well as the means of providing for the women and children economically. The economic structure was upset through the receiving of wages for labor, rather than produce. As all parts of culture are closely interrelated, the repercussions were felt in every sphere of native life. The change had been abrupt and under force, and the native culture was not given time to adapt itself. Social controls collapsed and the native became unsure of his patterns of behavior, and ultimately disorganized.

The disorganization of native culture and the breakdown of social controls upon the average Negro worker made its repercussions felt in the white culture also. Both groups suffered considerably, both economically and socially. A new accommodation was difficult and took a long time to effect. However, in their actions, the white people were following a tendency shared by most groups, that is, they put into effect the behavior pattern which seemed to be most profitable at that particular time. They were unable to visualize the far-reaching effects that this economic adjustment would have upon every institution within the society.[6]

Questions

1. What factors operated to bring St. Denis into world markets? What effects were felt in the community as a result?
2. What were the central themes of the French Canadian society as illustrated by St. Denis? Show how these themes acted as integrating forces in the society.
3. What is meant by saying that the culture of St. Denis was a blend of the sacred and the secular? Give examples.
4. Discuss the importance of the family in St. Denis to the maintenance of a stable culture until the end of the last century. Discuss the role it played in enhancing the trend toward inclusion in outside markets.
5. The necessity of making an adjustment to one new circumstance frequently brings about a long chain of social changes in a society. Discuss and illustrate.
6. The culture of St. Denis does not equip its young people for city living. Discuss.
7. What factors determined the movement of industry to Kunming Province in China?

[6] Adapted from Maurice S. Evans, *Black and White in Southeast Africa*, New York, Longmans, Green & Co., Inc., 1916, and Lord Olivier, *The Anatomy of African Misery*, London, L. and V. Woolf, 1927, pp. 40-45.

8. Describe the culture of Kunming Province prior to industrialization.
9. What effects does Chinese culture in Kunming Province show as a result of industrialization? What are some of the factors in the Chinese culture which retard modern technical innovations?
10. Industrialization of Kunming Province gave rise to much personal maladjustment. Discuss.
11. Hawaii is an example of invasion and succession in respect to ethnic groups, land use, and occupations. Explain and illustrate.
12. Discuss the culture of the Polynesians in Hawaii prior to the coming of the white man. What changes were brought about by the conversion of the Hawaiian agricultural and fishing economy to a trading economy?
13. Describe the Hawaiian pioneer economy. How was it modified by the advent of the missionaries?
14. "The emergence of the town as the organizing center for the new regime brought about many other changes and is indicative of the dominance of the pioneer economy and of the shifts in Hawaii's position in relation to the world at that time." Discuss.
15. Why did racial dogmas fail to develop in Hawaii?
16. Discuss the position of the native in South Africa under the Boer regime. Under the English regime.
17. Why was the policy of the South African Government short-sighted regarding the natives?
18. When advanced civilizations penetrate areas inhabited by more primitive peoples, what methods are used to secure cheap labor? Contrast Hawaii with South Africa in this respect; account for the differences.

BIBLIOGRAPHY

CHENG CH'ENG-K'UN. "Regionalism in China's Postwar Reconstruction." *Social Forces,* October, 1943, pp. 1-20.

CRALLE, W. O. "Social Change and Isolation in the Ozark Mountain Region of Missouri." *Am. J. Sociol.,* Vol. 41, No. 4, January, 1936, pp. 435-447.

CRAWFORD, D. L. *Paradox in Hawaii.* Boston, Stratford Co., 1933.

DAWSON, C. A., MACKINTOSH, W. A., JOERG, W. L. G. (Eds.) *Canadian Frontiers of Settlement.* Toronto, The Macmillan Co. of Canada, Ltd., 1934.

EVANS, MAURICE S. *Black and White in Southeast Africa.* New York, Longmans, Green & Co., Inc., 1916.

FERENCZ, A. *The Impact of Urbanization on French-Canadian Medical Attitudes.* M. A. Thesis, McGill University, 1945.

GILLIN, JOHN. *The Ways of Men.* New York, Appleton-Century-Crofts, Inc., 1948.

GLICK, CLARENCE. "The Relation between Position and Status in the Assimilation of the Chinese in Hawaii." *Am. J. Sociol.,* Vol. 47, No. 5, March, 1942, pp. 667-679.

HAYNER, N. S. "Ecological Succession in the San Juan Islands." *Pubs. of the American Sociological Society,* Vol. 23, 1929, pp. 81-92.

HEMON, LOUIS. *Maria Chapdelaine.* Toronto, The Macmillan Co. of Canada, Ltd., 1940.

HSIAO-TUNG FEI. *Peasant Life in China.* New York, E. P. Dutton & Co., Inc., 1939.

HSIAO-TUNG FEI, AND CHANG, CHIH-I. *Earthbound China.* Chicago, University of Chicago Press, 1945.

HSIAO-TUNG FEI. "Peasant and Gentry: An Interpretation of Chinese Social Structure, and Its Changes." *Am. J. Sociol.,* Vol. 52, No. 1, July, 1946, pp. 1-18.

HUGHES, E. C. *French Canada in Transition.* Chicago, University of Chicago Press, 1943.

HUGHES, E. C. "The Study of Ethnic Relations." *Dalhousie Review,* Vol. 27, No. 4, January, 1948, pp. 477-482.

KOLLMORGEN, W. M. "The Agricultural Stability of the Old-Order Amish and the Old-Order Mennonites of Lancaster County, Pa." *Am. J. Sociol.,* Vol. 49, No. 3, November, 1943, pp. 233-242.

KUO-HENG SHIH. *China Enters the Machine Age.* Cambridge, Harvard University Press, 1944.

LILIENTHAL, DAVID E. *TVA: Democracy on the March.* New York, Harper & Bros., 1944.

LIN YUEH-HWA. *The Golden Wing.* New York, Institute of Pacific Relations, 1944. (Mimeographed.)

LIND, A. W. "Occupational Trends in Hawaii." *Social Forces,* Vol. 7, December, 1928, pp. 290-299.

LIND, A. W. *An Island Community: Ecological Succession in Hawaii.* Chicago, University of Chicago Press, 1938.

LINTON, RALPH. *The Study of Man.* New York, Appleton-Century-Crofts, Inc., 1936.

LINTON, RALPH. "Present Conditions in Cultural Perspective," in Ralph Linton (Ed.), *The Science of Man in the World Crisis.* New York, Columbia University Press, 1945.

MINER, HORACE. *St. Denis.* Chicago, University of Chicago Press, 1939.

MUKERJEE, R. "The Concepts of Distribution and Succession in Social Ecology." *Social Forces,* Vol. 11, October, 1932, pp. 1-7.

MUMFORD, L. *Technics and Civilization.* New York, Harcourt, Brace & Co., Inc., 1934.

MYRDAL, GUNNAR. *An American Dilemma.* New York, Harper & Bros., 1944.

NIEBOER, H. J. *Slavery and the Industrial System.* The Hague, Martinus Nijhoff, 1910.

OLIVIER, SIDNEY OLIVIER, 1st LORD. *The Anatomy of African Misery.* London, L. and V. Woolf, 1927.

PARK, R. E. "Succession: An Ecological Concept." *Am. Sociol. Rev.,* Vol. 1, No. 2, April, 1936, pp. 171-179.

PELTZER, E. "Industrialization of Young Countries and the Change in the International Division of Labor." *Social Research,* Vol. 7, September, 1940, pp. 298-325.

QUINN, J. A. "Ecological and Social Interaction." *Sociol. and Soc. Res.,* Vol. 18, July and August, 1934, pp. 565-570.

QUINN, J. A. "Human Ecology and Interaction Ecology." *Am. Sociol. Rev.,* Vol. 5, No. 5, October, 1940, pp. 713-722.

REDFIELD, R. *The Folk Culture of Yucatan.* Chicago, University of Chicago Press, 1941.

STERN, B. J. "Resistance to the Adoption of Technological Innovations." *Technological Trends and National Policy,* Part IV, Washington, National Resources Committee, 1937.

TA CHEN. "Population in Modern China." *Am. J. Sociol.,* Vol. 52, No. 2, July, 1946.

THOMPSON, E. T. "Mines and Plantations and the Movements of Peoples." *Am. J. Sociol.,* Vol. 37, No. 4, January, 1932, pp. 603-611.

Chapter 10

THE COMMUNITY

Competition and the Ecological Forces

Everywhere in nature, of which man is a part, there is a constant struggle for existence. This involves competition, that is, a struggle between those forms of life whose survival depends upon the satisfaction of similar or identical needs. Between members of a similar species, competition is most severe, as for example, between man and man. Between those forms of life whose needs for space and sustenance are entirely dissimilar, as for example, land and sea animals, competition can hardly be said to exist.

Competition is a constant, impersonal, and unself-conscious type of interaction with others. The application of this definition to plants and animals is obvious. Two species of meat-eating animals in the same location compete for food within a given area, without any conscious recognition of each other as competitors. Among men, it is not so easy to see how the definition of competition applies. Yet, in this field, too, competitors do not recognize each other as such. They are aware that their abilities to compete and survive are being tested severely by others, even though they cannot name and locate them. When men come to recognize their competitors, the struggle loses its impersonal and unself-conscious nature and changes into rivalry or conflict. The fact that competition is forever merging into something different in the human world is an indication that the struggle of man against man for place and sustenance is limited by agreements and social understandings.

While in plant communities competition exists in its purest form, it nevertheless plays a fundamental part in human communities. In the struggle of men and institutions for a place in which to live, there are phases which are as impersonal as anything found in the plant world. This may be clearly seen in the emergence of the city's configuration. Men do their work in connection with institutions, and these institutions come to occupy positions and perform functions which were largely, if not entirely, unforeseen. Cities are the products of natural processes of growth in which men and institutions are selectively distributed to their positions in the course of a competitive struggle. As such is the case, cities can be planned only in a minor sense.

Human Ecology.—It has been observed that a community, whether plant or human, develops a characteristic pattern of distribution as a result of the competitive struggle of its units. The concept of ecology has been developed—first for plant and animal, and now for the human community—to explain how this pattern emerges and changes. The idea of competition is basic in human ecology and the human ecologist proceeds to study the human community in the impersonal manner pursued by the plant ecologist. *Human ecology,* then, explains how human beings and their institutions assume their characteristic patterns of distribution in space at a given time. It pays particular attention also to the organic relations of the distributed units. The latter constitute a symbiotic [1] unity, based on mutual dependence. In the plant community the tree gives shade to the plants which grow at its base while the plants conserve moisture for the tree. Equally unintentional symbiotic relationships obtain between the various regional, institutional, and occupational divisions of labor in the human community. There are areas of the city which are given over to specialized functions such as the financial, wholesale, or shopping districts; other areas are used almost completely for the performance of manufacturing or residential functions. But each city area is dependent upon the functions performed by every other area. The same symbiotic dependence is readily seen within and between the many occupations and professions. Because of the active side of human adjustment, through man's inventiveness, divisions of labor are more dynamic and changing than are the symbiotic conditions under which plants and animals live.

To symbiotic dependence in human communities is added the interdependence which results from communication and mutual understanding. Furthermore, the ecological pattern in the human community is modified by the diffusion of knowledge in regard to community patterns which prevail in a given region. This accounts, in part, for the remarkable similarity in the physical structure of the towns in the Prairie region of North America. Ecological units are communities, regions, and natural subdivisions of both.

---

[1] The possession of a habitat by different species of plants whereby the survival of each species is facilitated by the presence of the other is known as *symbiosis*. This purely impersonal aspect of human communities is called *division of labor*.

The Ecological Processes.—The processes of human ecology are specialized forms of the competitive process with particular reference to the spatial patterns which arise from the operation of the latter. Competitors may survive through migration to a new physical location in the city or region, or through specialization of function. This is one of the main reasons for varied areas and manifold divisions of labor in the highly competitive life of urban communities. Specialization of areas, institutions, and occupations reduces direct competition but increases symbiotic dependence. If each unit performs fewer functions, it must rely more fully upon supplementary functions performed by others. This is illustrated by the concentration of closely allied special agencies in a financial or shopping district. The same idea holds for the institutional network of the city as a whole, for community interdependence in a region, and for regional interdependence in so far as the means of transportation and communication have brought them into relationship with each other.

CONCENTRATION. Concentration is the tendency toward marked population density in certain geographic areas.[2] In the Western World, concentration has resulted mainly from the development of machinery and its application to production, transportation, and communication. This inventiveness of man has also been applied to the organization of great corporate industrial enterprises. It was soon observed that, when located at strategic points of transportation and communication by water and land, these enterprises had special advantages in the competitive struggle. Industry passed from the English countryside to the cities, and the village populations followed them there. These city concentrations increased according to the particular advantages in geographic position in the age of power-driven machinery. For example, London and New York are cities which enjoy great advantages in relation to transportation by water, and later by land and air as well. In addition, the application of power machinery to agricultural production has released an increasing number of persons who must find their occupational niches in expanding cities. This modern tendency toward urban concentration is due mainly to the competitive advantage of the city and especially the great city over small and dispersed productive units, although, under special circumstances, a few of the latter have survived.

Concentration not only characterizes cities within a region, but one region in comparison with another, and is linked with regional

2 See Chapter 7.

specialization in production. England, because of its advantage of position and resources, specialized in manufactured products. Other regions, such as Australia until recently, specialized in agriculture or some extractive industry and their population density remained relatively low.

CENTRALIZATION. While concentration deals with density of populations and social institutions in a given area, *centralization* denotes the tendency of basic types of institutional services to locate at focal points of transportation and communication. The community's most intense activity and interest is associated with these focal points. They attract persons from an area of participation, the extent of which depends upon the competitive strength of their institutions, their degree of specialization, and their transportation facilities. In reference to such central points of activity, the whole diversified physical structure of the community takes form. It is in this sense that centralization may be called the community-forming process. In terms of their specialized functions such centers bring under their control—unself-consciously to be sure—the tributary areas from which their participants come. A city is studded with centers specializing in trade, finance, manufacture, and many other interests. Specialization of service within each of these main center types is very extensive in great cities. All these centralized services have overlapping areas of participation.

These centers of activity within the city vary as to their competitive and attractive power. The focal point of greatest competitive strength in a modern city, and the one most potent in determining its physical structure, is the retail shopping center. It occupies the point of highest land values and its clientele is drawn, not only from the city as a whole, but from relatively remote smaller cities and towns. All traffic and communication lines within the city and those connecting it with outlying cities come to focus in the retail shopping district. Near by is the financial district which is the center of finance, not only for the city within which it is located, but also for all the cities and towns within a very wide radius. In close proximity to the city's central retail and financial districts are the central offices for the administration of business enterprises and other institutional activities within and far beyond the boundaries of the city.

In addition, there are other centers of work, play, business, and education which are somewhat removed from the downtown area. This tendency to develop centers out toward the periphery of the city, which attract a small number of participants, may be called *subcentralization*. Heavy manufacturing requires much space and obtains this at a relatively low cost at some distance from the city's central business district, where its head offices are maintained. This same tendency to locate near the outskirts of the city is noticeable in connection with recreational activities requiring extended space. Then, too, sub-business centers stud the intersecting lines of traffic at regular intervals until the circumference of the city is reached. At these points are found branch banks, chain stores, cinema theatres, and other services whose subcentralization has been made possible through the standardization of goods and services. Subcentralization stimulates and is stimulated by the movement of population to less congested areas and suburbs. Nevertheless, the people who live in these outlying areas, like those far beyond the confines of the city, are compelled to go downtown for specialized services. Thus the subcentralization of standard services and population movements toward the periphery of the city make for wider areas of participation and greater centralization of highly specialized services in finance, administration, and in all the other main fields of human interest. The downtown business, financial and office districts link all outlying centers, not only with themselves, but also with each other.

It now seems feasible to state somewhat more clearly how centralization gives form to the community. The most central point in the city's physical structure is the downtown shopping district, and its attractive power is enhanced by associated financial and other districts. The sub-business and other centers (such as the grouping of industrial plants) which comprise the entire constellation are distributed radially out from this main center as far as population permits. Spread out from each of these centers are the types of houses and neighborhood institutions which give physical form to the widely varied residential areas of the city. To these districts are selected the appropriate population elements with reference to age, sex, race, and class. This physical patterning of the city's expansion makes essential some shifts in the location of centers from time to time. Most stable of all centers is the financial district, such as Wall Street, because its tributary area extends far beyond the local city. The main retail shopping center moves slowly in the direction of those residential areas which have the greatest purchasing power. Work centers, as we have seen, move toward the outskirts of the city. This is particularly true of basic types of manufacturing. Leisure-time centers not associated with trade centers are comparatively shifting and unstable.

Taken as units, cities, towns, and villages are centers when looked at from the point of view of the dispersed population of a region. In each instance, of course, "Main Street" is the focus of attention. Thus the ecological patterning of a region involves a constellation of centers. Under modern conditions of transportation, even the smallest of these illustrate the marked tendency toward centralization. It is quite apparent that, with the advent of the railroad and, more recently, the motor car and hard-surfaced roads, the large village has become increasingly the center for banks, stores, medical services, schools, churches, and amusements patronized by the tributary countryside. Proceeding from village to large town and city, centralization becomes more marked and is accompanied by constantly greater specialization until it reaches its peak in the region's major city.

SEGREGATION. That phase of the selective process which reveals the tendency of like units to form a cluster is called *segregation*. Such units tend to be identical in economic strength and make a similar use of the land. Industrial areas, automobile rows, radio-towns, and financial districts are some examples of industrial and commercial segregation. However, the term segregation is used chiefly with reference to the clustering of well-defined population types. This diversification of an area into a great variety of residential districts is a world-wide phenomenon, but it is seen in its extreme form in the great metropolis, where the forces of competitive selection are most active. Families and individuals may be eliminated from certain communities by adverse selection, and drift into communities of their own type where the pace is to their liking and where the order of life gives a fuller expression to their wishes. The slum is an area of segregation for the unsuccessful and the unadjusted. Into such districts of the city come the immigrants who segregate into colonies with the same language and same cultural background. The only element they share in common with the slum-dweller is a minimum economic choice. In time, the members of the immigrant colony who can escape from this area move to other residential areas more in keeping with their ambitions.

The opposite extreme in the segregation of population types is to be found in neighborhoods occupied by the "Four Hundred," that is, the social elite. In such neighborhoods, there is a great cultural homogeneity as compared with the slum. Instead of being compelled to live beside those with divergent tastes, the residents live by choice in proximity to those with like tastes and similarity of cultural background. Between those two extremes, the whole city breaks up into a diversified patchwork of areas, each with its own physical individuality, its own pattern of social institutions, its class of people, and its appropriate groupings of age and sex. Some of these neighborhoods are occupied by a single sex; others are neighborhoods of "the companionate," that is, adults without children living with them; still others throng with children. There are industrial suburbs where work and residential quarters are side by side; there are "bedroom suburbs" far removed from the city noise and smoke; there are Greenwich Villages and hobohemias; there are areas of furnished rooms, of apartments, of flats, of single dwellings. There are other innumerable segregations of population, which have come about in the selective growth of the metropolis as a whole.

INVASION. The process by which new types of institutions or population groups gradually penetrate an area already occupied and displace its institutions or population groups is termed *invasion*. The units of one area of segregation encroach upon another, usually an adjoining area. It is the lower economic or cultural group which usually invades and displaces higher groups, but frequently the latter invade and displace the former. For example, western industry has invaded the Orient and partially displaced domestic industry. On the other hand, classes with lower standards of living tend to penetrate more exclusive areas and displace their inhabitants. French-Canadians in Montreal, who occupy the lower positions in the occupational ladder, are displacing the English-speaking occupants higher up. There are many indications that they may completely take over the skilled positions in local industry. This occupational invasion also involves spatial movement into residential areas occupied by the English-speaking groups, who are being pushed out into other areas. Segregated areas may be protected from invasion by physical or cultural barriers but, when new transportation lines or industrial enterprises invade such areas, population elements soon join the invasion. Modern devices of transportation and communication have made human groups excessively mobile. They are on the move from country to country, from region to region, and from one section of the community to another.

SUCCESSION. The major effect of invasion is a breakup of the existing population group or use of the land. If invasion results in complete displacement, *succession* has occurred, for succession means a complete change in population type or use of the land. While closely related to the process of invasion, succession may be conceived as a natural sequence of types of occupants or land use which follow each other in predictable fashion. Each stage in the series makes the next inevitable. Invasion of light industry, together with physical deterioration of buildings, brings in successive lower-rental groups until the area passes over from residence to business or, when the time is opportune, to entirely new types of residence and population as, for instance, the transformation of a portion of New York's East Side slum into a skyscraper apartment area.

THE ECOLOGICAL FORCES AND THE COMMUNITY

The ecological forces outlined above will be discussed in this chapter in terms of the metropolitan community. Although they apply equally well to the patterning of the smaller community, of regions, and of the world, it is in the metropolitan city of the western industrial world that they can be seen most readily. In the more simple and primitive communities, the operation of these forces often is not so apparent as in the more secularized industrial communities, with their high rates of vertical and horizontal mobility and their highly specialized division of labor.

By *community* is meant a unit of territory within which is distributed a population which possesses the basic institutions (in their simpler or more specialized forms) by means of which a common life is made possible. The community differs from the *region* in that the latter is a much larger territorial unit, containing within its boundaries a multiplication of communities or territorial units. An area of scattered farmsteads will not ordinarily constitute a community unless to these is added the village center, whose institutions serve these farmsteads regularly. A great metropolis is a community, when taken as a whole, because its subsidiary areas are so specialized that they cater—in a very elaborate way to be sure—to but one or two basic fields of interest. So elaborate are the institutional services of the metropolis that in certain fields such as medicine, finance, and education, remote communities utilize them to supplement their own more rudimentary institutions. It is by means of the specialization which accompanies size and wealth that certain centers come to occupy dominant positions in their respective regions.

Natural Areas.—The concept of *natural area* is used by sociologists to designate areas which have their own particular kinds of buildings, whether used for housing or other purposes, their own institutional adjustments, and natural selection of population elements. Each area may be set off clearly from the other areas by barriers such as rivers, canals, hills, railroads, parks, vacant frontage, industrial and commercial frontage, or by racial differences. But, where no obvious physical barriers exist, natural areas may be delineated in terms of land values; the point of highest land value represents the center (not necessarily the geographic center) of the area, while the points of lowest land value indicate its periphery. Each of these areas tends to have some specialization of function, physical differentiation, and social distinctiveness, yet it is a symbiotic unit of the city as a whole. Such areas are the natural and inevitable products of the ecological processes analyzed above. Natural areas are distinguished from administrative areas such as wards and school districts whose boundaries are drawn artificially. More recently, there have been attempts to make administrative boundaries coincide with natural boundaries. Examples of such natural areas in the metropolitan community are the central business district, including the financial, retail, and wholesale districts; the rooming house areas; "hobohemia"; the slum; residential areas and suburban areas.

The Ecological Patterning in Montreal and New York.—The two documents which follow illustrate the ecological patterning in actual cities. The first shows typical subsidiary areas which have become clearly differentiated from each other. These areas are organically related and are the natural and inevitable products of the forces of metropolitan expansion. In this document also, an attempt has been made to show how, through zoning, the natural boundaries of areas can be made to coincide with administrative areas. In the second document the spatial shifts of certain establishments from one district to another are shown. The spatial shifts have come about in response to the intense competitive struggle for advantageous location.

Modern devices in transportation and communication have stimulated city building. In New York and at similar points of great natural advantage are to be found the most intensive concentrations of population on the earth's surface. New York, expanding from the lower tip of Manhattan Island, has spread itself like a colossus across river and harbor and over the land surface of the surrounding hinterland. The metropolitan district, including tributary areas in New Jersey and Connecticut, occupies some 1,174 square miles and has a population of approximately eight millions. But numerous other centers of population lying outside the metropolitan district are closely dependent upon the metropolis and come under the sway of its life. The two documents that follow illustrate the intense and never-ceasing competition for space and the patterns of distribution that result therefrom.

Montreal, the City as a Growing, Changing Whole.—Within the boundaries of Greater Montreal are to be found the smaller municipalities of Westmount, Lachine, Outremont, and all the others which may be conceived as natural subdivisions in the web of economic and social life of the metropolis of Montreal. While Westmount, for instance, is a separate entity for certain administrative purposes, Westmounters know right well that, in addition to their occupations, their lives are bound up in a daily routine that takes them outside the boundaries of historic Westmount. Indeed, the growth of the special institutional functions which Westmount performs cannot be understood apart from the colossus known as Greater Montreal. While much more autonomous, as more peripherally placed industrial suburbs are bound to be, Lachine's growth and functions are also a natural outcome of the expansion and differentiation of Montreal. In countless ways, its daily routine, population growth, and mode of life are not segmental, but are organic aspects of the metropolis. Residents are becoming increasingly conscious that fire hazards, police protection, health and educational facilities, and religious organization—to mention a few items—are most significantly metropolitan.

The focal point of Greater Montreal is the central business district extending from the Waterfront to Sherbrooke Street, and, approximately, from St. Lawrence Boulevard to Guy Street. Within this area are to be found the headquarters of the transportation and communication systems. Here too are the head offices of the major institutions of Greater Montreal. This is the focal point, too, for the specialized functions which Montreal performs for its immediate hinterland in the St. Lawrence Valley and for the more remote regions of Canada.

As a city grows, more space is required for centrally located financial, commercial, and industrial institutions, some of which invade the residential districts to be found on the outer border of the central business district. However, in Montreal, there is no precisely determined line of demarcation between the central business and surrounding residential areas, since the latter are constantly subject to encroachment by light industry and various types of commercial services. Such invaded districts, especially where zoning is either spotty or non-existent, become dilapidated, unsanitary, and unattractive for better residential purposes. Such areas become congested low-rental areas from which the strongest economic elements in their population tend to move. In brief, this is a central fact in the making of slums in all cities. The term "slum" is an epithet applied to problem areas surrounding central business districts. In slums are to be found the greatest concentration of poverty, disease, delinquency, crime, and vice. To a lesser degree the same phenomena prevail in areas surrounding the outlying larger sub-business centers and industrial constellations. Thus, sections of Rosemount and Notre Dame de Grace which adjoin business and industrial establishments are subject to invasion and dilapidation, which make them in some measure socially unadjusted areas. Where areas of industry, commerce, and residence are not more precisely defined and protected, the slum-making process comes most clearly to view.

Beyond the area of transition and disorganization which surrounds the central business district in Montreal and all other North American cities lies a succession of areas of residence or areas of residence and industry combined. These may be called *sectors,* which in Greater Montreal extend from the borders of the central slum to the outer periphery. One of these sectors is the industrial belt including its subdivisions. Here reference is made to the concentration of industry along the railways and waterways. One section of the industrial belt extends westward along the railways and Lachine canal to Lachine. Another section extends eastward along the railway and river front to Montreal East. This section of the industrial belt has a vertical subdivision northward to the Angus Shops and continues in a half-circle around Montreal's central mountain. In the vicinity of these far-flung segments of the industrial belt are to be found the largest proportion of the houses of wage earners. Obviously, such areas are marked by meagre housing standards. Industrial workers must have low rentals and they must be close to their work on account of long hours and short purses. Housing conditions improve as some of the newer, outlying sections of the industrial belt are approached, but an industry's location at the city's periphery is not by any means a guarantee of satisfactory housing in its vicinity.

Extending outward from near the central business district is a non-industrial better residential sector, pie-piece in shape. Its western extension lies north of Sherbrooke Street and extends to Montreal West. Its northward extension includes Outremont and the city of Mount Royal. In contrast to the industrial belt which lies astride the routes of heavy, slow-moving transportation, the non-industrial sector follows the routes of rapid transportation. This latter sector is occupied by people seeking more extensive residences which have a scenic location and are surrounded by what their occupants term congenial conditions.

Figure 10. Land Us

Prepared by the City Plannir

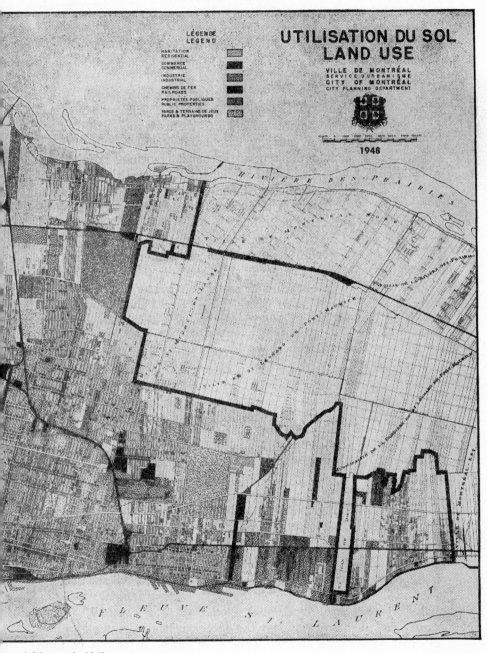

ap of Montreal, 1948

pt., City of Montreal, 1948

A third pie-piece-shaped sector with two main divisions lies between the industrial belt and the sector of high-cost residences. This represents an expansion of the residential territory for members of the lower middle class. The extended use of the bus and automobile supplementing the tram-car has been instrumental in filling this intermediary territory and also pushing farther outward this part of the city's periphery. The septic tank, the prefabricated house, and many other modern devices have led to the expansion of this sector deep into the open country, where low-priced building sites are numerous. Sectors of this type are occupied by members of the lower middle class whose standard of living falls between those who live close to the industrial belt and those who live on Montreal's scenic upper shelves. In other cities are to be found sites which have similar social and scenic desirability.

These sectors may be further broken down into a series of natural subdivisions, each with its particular selection of population and institutions. It should be emphasized strongly that these areas are natural subdivisions of the major sectors of Greater Montreal. Their boundaries do not coincide with those of wards and separate political municipalities that comprise the metropolis. Here and there certain administrative units may have boundaries which coincide in part or in their entirety with natural boundaries formed by such barriers as canals, railroad embankments, and large tracts of vacant land. Sometimes racial and ethnic concentrations act as natural lines of demarcation between these natural subdivisions of the city. Such areas are the product of the inevitable play of forces which select and sift urban population groups to a great variety of areas with their own particular functions and statuses. Each has its own age and sex distribution, its own slants on life, types of housing, and formal as well as informal arrangements through which its groups get on in some tolerable fashion with the main business of living together. In a sense these areas present the class structure of the metropolis, with some overlapping, spread out on its map. In preparing a perspective of the further growth and differentiation of the city into other naturally bounded parts with their own divisions of labor, most intensive research must be undertaken. All such specific uses of the land, together with the particular requirements and attitudes of the population element selected to them can and must be clearly defined if any plans for the development of Greater Montreal are to be acceptable and workable over extended periods of time. When these areas become known, by means of research, they indicate precisely the diversified natural structure of this or any other city.

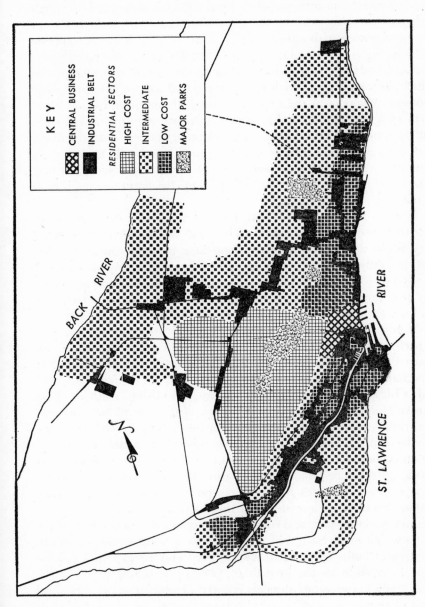

Figure 11. Commercial, Industrial, and Residential Sections of Greater Montreal. Drawn by Professor John Bland, School of Architecture, McGill University, 1948.

In large measure the structure of each of these natural areas of the city has not come into existence by design. Nor will this intrinsic structure cease to exist by the efforts of those who seek to change it in accordance with either sinister forms of exploitation or current fashions in city planning. There is a play of forces, resulting in certain trends of change which we can know and in accordance with which we can work. Much blueprinting and talk of bringing about profound changes in the ongoing life of Montreal and other cities seem to ignore the natural-area factors which are emphasized here. But to ignore them is to make city planning a sort of daydreaming that on the morrow brings disillusionment to the dreamers. City planners have accomplished something of permanent value when they have developed their plans in keeping with the natural organization of the city.

It may be emphasized that the main natural subdivisions of Montreal are now established. The land will continue to be used very much as at present. Only long-time changes can be effected and then only in keeping with the natural lines of development already in sight or to become evident at some future date. It is necessary for any planning board to be constantly on the alert for new trends in land use and function in all parts of the basic differentiated structure of Montreal. The central business area, for instance, will continue to perform its present basic role in the life of Greater Montreal. Increased concentration and specialization of certain functions can be expected. These have emerged in much larger cities like New York and Chicago. Notable changes in merchandising methods have caused Montreal's wholesale subdivision of the central business area to shrink. In this vicinity, certain changes in obsolescent structures may be planned, making way for other services more able to compete for an economic use of space in such a position. The process of the relocation of office buildings in relation to the expansion of central transportation facilities and changes on St. Catherine Street continues. Sections of low standard dwellings have given way to the need for parking space and room for economically powerful establishments which require central locations. The gradual elimination from the area of both light and heavy industry may be expected to continue in relation to the growth of Greater Montreal until, in the main, only those establishments closely dependent upon this focal point of rapid transportation and communication may be expected to remain permanently. The stabilization of the main features of the central area may be facilitated by a city plan which proceeds on an understanding of the natural functions of the central business areas everywhere and of the special exigencies which are intrinsic to any given city.

Furthermore, Montreal's pattern of major industrial establishments has been stabilized in the factory belt sector of the city. Certain tendencies of industry, especially of smaller secondary industrial and commercial establishments, to invade and disorganize residential areas is in evidence in all cities. Such establishments may come under zoning regulations which seek to stabilize the functions of a given area over a long period of time, yet remain sufficiently flexible to permit changes when the need for such is obvious. Guiding industrial establishments into more compact natural locations will cause the elimination of cruder forms of experimentalism in industrial location. In the long run, however, this makes for greater industrial efficiency. In addition, such regulation gives a much greater security to residential sections of the city and makes possible the long-term development of social amenities which are usually native to stable residential districts. City planning regulations can greatly reduce the disturbance to residential functions which takes place in the territory which becomes the central slum, and can reduce, in a lesser way, the disturbance in the vicinity of belts of heavy industry and the outlying sub-business centers.

Competition for Space in New York City.—Despite the fact that progress and change have altered the face of the New York he writes about, Haig's discussion of ecological processes is rewarding reading.

LAND UTILIZATION. At first glance, land utilization in an urban area such as New York and its environs appears to be without rhyme or reason, a confused and baffling welter of anomalies and paradoxes. The land is being used, most of it, very intensively indeed. Nine million people eat and sleep, work and play in the area. But the assignment of the land to the various uses seems to the superficial observer to have been made by the Mad Hatter at Alice's tea party. Some of the poorest people live in conveniently located slums on high-priced land. On patrician Fifth Avenue, Tiffany and Woolworth, cheek by jowl, offer jewels and jimcracks from substantially identical sites. Childs' restaurants thrive and multiply where Delmonico's withered and died. A stone's throw away from the stock exchange, the air is filled with the aroma of roasting coffee; a few hundred feet from Times Square, with the stench of the slaughter-houses. In the very heart of this "commercial" city, on Manhattan Island south of 59th Street, the inspectors in 1922 found nearly 420,000 workers employed in factories. Such a situation outrages one's sense of order. Everything seems misplaced. One yearns to rearrange the hodgepodge and to put things where they belong. The confusion, of course, is more apparent than real. The deeper one delves into the reasons underlying the present layout, the more distrustful he becomes of sweeping indictments

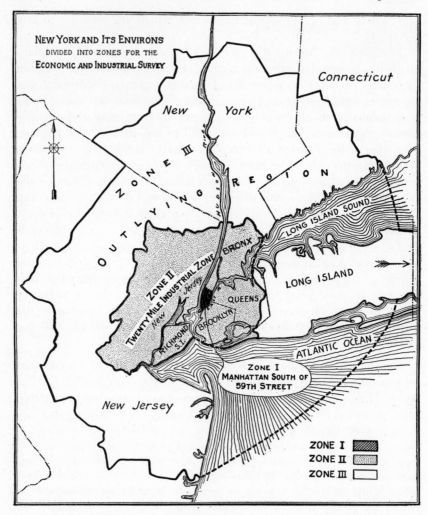

Figure 12. New York and Its Environs, Divided into Zones for
Economic and Industrial Survey

Courtesy of the Regional Plan of New York and Its Environs.

of its soundness and efficiency. Most of the apparent anomalies and paradoxes dissolve into commonplaces when subjected to serious study and detailed examination. . . .

FACTORY POPULATION IN ZONE IS CHANGING. When the city planners speak of decentralization, they usually have prominently in mind the decentralization of factories. Manufacturing seems to them one thing which certainly does not "belong" in the center of the metropolis. . . . Zone I, Manhattan south of 59th Street, consists roughly of the southern third of the island, the heart of the city. The other two zones, together, stretch approximately to the commuting limits of the metropolis.

In the first place, while many more people worked in factories in the center of the city in 1922 than in 1900, fewer worked there than in 1917. The rate of increase in the center, when one compares 1900 and 1922, was 44.8 per cent. For the rest of New York and its environs, the increase was 114 per cent. The population of the entire area increased, between 1900 and 1920, 66.8 per cent. These figures appear to furnish grounds for the belief that the peak of manufacturing in the center of the city was reached about ten years ago and that a process of decentralization is already under way. . . .

Between 1900 and 1912, the wood-products group was the only group in Zone I which actually declined in numbers. Between 1912 and 1917, metals, textiles and tobacco also went into decline. Between 1917 and 1922, the textile group gained slightly; but the chemical, the men's and women's clothing, and the food groups joined the ranks of those that were losing their hold in the center of the city. Printing is the only group showing a consistent record of gain in the central zone throughout the twenty-two-year period.

As the result of these developments, the industrial complexion of the center of the city has changed. In 1900 a representative group of 100 factory hands employed in the center of the city would have contained 33 clothing workers; in 1912 and 1917 the group would have contained 43 clothing workers, and in 1922, 40.

Moreover, in spite of their relative strength in the center of the city, both the men's and women's clothing groups have grown more rapidly in Zone II than in Zone I. As a result while approximately two-thirds of the men's-clothing workers were in the center in 1900, only one-half were there in 1922. Even with women's clothing, in 1900, only about one-seventh of the workers were employed outside the center, whereas in 1922 one-fifth were outside.

These general figures seem to indicate, then, that, on the whole, manufacturing is certainly not more than holding its own in the center of the city and has probably already begun to be crowded out. Moreover, the figures give evidence of considerable variability in the degree of persistence with which the different industries cling to the choice central locations.

When the industries are broken still further into smaller sub-groups, . . . for the years 1900 and 1922 in the center of the city, it is found that the aggregate figures conceal marked variations in the growth and decay of branches of the various industries. While the aggregate figures for the printing industry, for example, show a strong and steady growth in Zone I, amounting to about 50 per cent in the 22 years, the more detailed figures for the sub-groups show that photo-engraving quadrupled in this area, newspaper printing nearly trebled, book-and-job-printing increased approximately the normal 50 per cent, lithography was practically static, and bookbinding

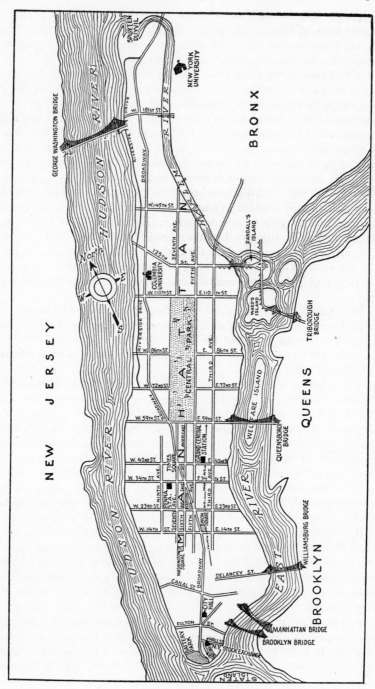

Figure 13. Central New York and Adjacent Areas

declined 20 per cent. Again, while in the aggregate women's clothing about doubled in this central area, one branch, dresses and waists, trebled, and yet another branch, neckwear, lost more than half its employees. In the aggregate, the metal-products industry almost stood still in Zone I; but one branch, technical instruments, more than doubled, and another branch, heavy machinery, declined to less than half its former size. Equally striking statements can be made for practically all other industries.

Turning from manufacturing to the other activities that are competing for choice central sites, serious difficulties are encountered because of scanty statistical data. The space-demands of housing may, however, be roughly gauged by using the census figures of population. In 1900, 1,149,226 people were reported as living south of 59th Street. This number increased to 1,252,893 in 1910, but dropped to 1,063,962 in 1920, a decline of 188,931. Moreover, it is the very poor who are abandoning the center as a place to live. A study of 58 sanitary districts south of 14th Street shows that in the 27 districts which may be fairly classed as slums, there was a decrease in population between 1910 and 1920 of 158,632, a loss nearly large enough in itself to account for the entire population decline in Zone I. Apparently the well-to-do are not being crowded out; they may be doing some of the crowding.

DECENTRALIZATION OF CERTAIN FUNCTIONS. When one begins to seek the reasons for growth and decline in the center, he is immediately impressed by the inadequacy of the terminology, ordinarily used in discussing the problem. Broad terms such as "industry," "manufacture," "commerce," and "trade," are not well adapted to the task in hand. If, for example, a silk mill, formerly located on Manhattan, moves to Pennsylvania but keeps its head office and salesroom in New York, it is not accurate to say that this "industry" has left New York. What has actually happened is that there has been a territorial subdivision of functions which were formerly united in the same place, certain activities being sent to Pennsylvania and certain others kept in the metropolis. Fabrication and certain other functions have gone, but selling and many of the other functions remain. Fourth Avenue is full of establishments bearing the names of manufacturing plants, but no fabrication is in evidence. Though it is the center of the silk industry, not a loom is to be found there. Nor is the situation changed fundamentally if the establishment, instead of retaining its New York office, delegates its selling to a jobber or agent operating in New York under his own name. The significant thing is the amount and the character of the activity which leaves, and the amount and the character of the activity which remains. If a Fifth Avenue merchant sends his buyer to open an office in Paris, transfers his reserve stocks to a warehouse on the waterfront, and places his alteration shop in Long Island City, it is misleading to say merely that the "merchant" is located on Fifth Avenue. He has scattered his activities in many places. If the fact that his sign still graces the Avenue is accepted as the sole test of his location significant facts will be entirely overlooked. Every business is a packet of functions, and within limits these functions can be separated and located at different places.

The pressure for space in the center of New York has stimulated a great deal of relocation of functions which is difficult to catch in any statistical net. A Fifth Avenue merchant testifies that he has found it profitable in recent years to rent extensive accommodation in bonded warehouses instead of storing his imported goods in his own establishment, as was formerly his practice. Many Wall Street lawyers, finding their office space too expensive at four dollars per square foot to use for storage purposes, have sent their old files to Brooklyn, where special facilities have been established to perform this function at relatively low cost. The New York Telephone Company has tried the plan of reducing its commercial offices to mere counterspace and sending its clerical staff to low-rent quarters. A large silk manufacturer, who now uses most of his large building on Fourth Avenue as a stock-room, states that upon the completion of the new vehicular tunnel his New York building will become strictly a sample-room and his stock-room will be in New Jersey. Even in Newark, one of New York's Jersey satellites, the pressure for space in the shopping center has caused one large department store to establish a "service station" on cheap land, where the orders are assembled and the deliveries routed.

The extent to which a business may profitably separate physically certain of its functions from the others varies greatly. In some cases the packet of functions is loosely tied and in others is tied tightly. Obviously the difficulties of coordination and control increase as the disintegration progresses. The scale of the business is a factor of importance in this connection. In a very small business the option of moving part of the functions simply may not exist. It may be a case of moving all or none. A little cigar factory may market its entire output over a small counter in the front of the room and fabricate it with a force of a half-dozen workers in the rear. The proprietor in such a case supervises the entire process and does much of the work. He buys the materials, "bosses" the men, makes cigars, and conducts sales. To separate the functions of fabrication and selling in such a case would increase the costs of management more than would be saved by using the back of the store for some other purpose than for the making of cigars. The little factory must, therefore, stand or fall in competition with the big factory, which can separate its functions at a small increase in costs of management on the basis of some special advantage. In most cases this advantage is found in specializing the product so as to meet the demands of a particular clientele. Perhaps the persistence with which clothing fabrication clings to Manhattan is to be partly explained by the fact that the small size of the shop prevents the physical separation of functions. There is a tendency, then, finding its root in increased costs of management, to resist the separation of functions which derive advantages from close physical proximity. But, as, in a game of chess, a pawn is sacrificed to gain a king, management costs are increased when by so doing site rentals can be decreased by a larger amount.

SPECIALIZED DISTRICTS AND THEIR EFFICIENCIES. Certain advantages also flow from a cohesion of functions in a given district, and the result is a number of specialized centers with definite unities of interest rather than a single diversified center. The shoppers gain real advantages from a consolidated area of shops. Broadly speaking, the financial district contains only such shops as minister to the immediate convenience of the workers in that district. The students at Columbia University do not go to Wall Street to buy their hats or their cigarettes. In the shopping districts, on the other hand, are found only such banks and brokers' offices as minister to the immediate convenience of the shops and their customers. The same factor operates to bring the wholesale silk houses into a fairly well-defined cluster. With factories also there are often material advantages in placing like with like.

A functional analysis of the various branches of the printing industry may serve to test the principle still further. It has already been suggested that the extremely high rate of growth in photo-engraving may be explained, in part at least, by the fact that it is a new industry. But it is also a service industry; that is, its product is used by the printers and convenient access to the printers is of great importance. The time which is saved by its being in a readily accessible location is worth the cost. Newspaper printing, another branch of the printing industry with a high rate of growth in Zone I, occupies the most expensive land of any of the branches. It clings to choice central locations, because, for at least one of its functions, time is all-important. The printing process itself does not gain by being performed on a high-priced site. But a central location is convenient from the point of view of the assembly of the news. Moreover, there must be the closest possible contact between the copy desk and the mechanical department. Finally, and perhaps most important, the papers must be made available to the readers with the least possible loss of time. Time saved is also the explanation for the persistence of job printing in the center. The work that can wait tends to go to outside shops. Work that is "rush" is done down-town. In periodical printing also there is a direct correlation between central location and the time-limits within which the work must be done. In a sample of twenty-two periodicals, edited in New York, with a margin of four days or less between the time of closing the last form and release, eighteen were printed in Manhattan itself and only two were printed on sites more than two hours distant from Manhattan. As the time-margin increases, the per cent printed outside increases. In the case of book-binding, where time is less important, the trade is rapidly abandoning central locations. In the printing industry then, fabrication by itself ranks low in competitive power to command choice sites, but the other functions tied up in the printing packet rank high.

A similar analysis of the other industries would merely reinforce the explanation outlined in the cases of clothing and printing. Fabrication as a function by itself gains nothing from being located on high-priced land. But in the industrial packet there are other functions in varying proportions, which do gain materially because of the contacts afforded by the central sites.

The industries that are leaving Manhattan are those in whose packets these other functions are relatively unimportant. . . .

Wholesalers of groceries and meat have a serious problem of storage, because of the bulky character of the products handled. If, however, the function of price establishment is present to an important extent, as in the case of the fruit and produce markets, they tend to remain clustered in the center. Warehouses offering space to rent were formerly grouped for the most part in a belt along the Manhattan waterfront. The new warehouses now being built are largely in a new belt along the shoreline opposite Manhattan.

The highest land values in the city are in the Wall Street and the 42nd Street sections. The Wall Street district, filled with high buildings, is dedicated to "finance." The 42nd Street section is primarily a retail merchandising section, although it has recently developed considerable importance as a miscellaneous office center. "Finance," as here used, includes the exchanges, the banks, the insurance offices, as well as various professional groups, such as lawyers and accountants. Largely through the control of loanable funds, there is centralized here the function of coordinating the business activities of a very wide area.

POSITION, INFORMATION, DIRECTING CONTROL. The exercise of this managerial function of coordination and control is at first glance singularly independent of transportation. It does not require the transfer of huge quantities of materials. It deals almost exclusively with information. What is all-important is transportation of intelligence. The mail, the cable, the telegraph, and the telephone bring in its raw material and carry out its finished product. Internally easy contact of man with man is essential. The telephone is prodigally used, of course, but the personal conference remains, after all, the method by which most of the important work is done. Conferences with corporation officers, with bankers, with lawyers and accountants, with partners, with fellow directors, fill the day. The work is facilitated when the time of the men whose time is most valuable is conserved. The district must be conveniently accessible and must be at the heart of the system of communication. It must be arranged so as to give the greatest possible ease of contact among men whose presence is desired in arriving at decisions. The financial district is in effect one big structure; the streets, practically cleared of all except pedestrian traffic, are little more than corridors and air-shafts. The corner of Wall and Broad on a busy morning is much more quiet than many a suburban business corner. The geometrical proposition that the contents of two spheres are to each other as the cubes of their diameters has sent skyscrapers up into the air. This was the economical way to produce accessibility in the center.

The closely interrelated and interdependent group in Wall Street find their functions sufficiently facilitated by a central location to make it worth their while to outbid all others for the spot they want. It may be observed that this group of activities in the financial district is concerned, for the most part, with matters of great import, not with petty transactions. A decision as to whether the Kingdom of Norway shall be loaned $25,000,000 of American capital and whether the rate shall be five or six per cent, is obviously more important than a decision as to whether a neighbourhood haberdasher shall be granted a loan of $250 and at what interest rate. One transaction may require no more physical space than the other and about the same amount of time, but the Norway decision will be made by a man whose time may be worth more per hour than the branch-bank manager earns in a month. A change to a more convenient location, which would save the large banker one hour per day, might justify an increase in site rental of $30,000 per year (300 hours at $100 per hour). A similar change in the case of the branch-bank manager would justify an additional site rental of only $300 (300 hours at $1 per hour). . . . .

The number of investment bankers (firms and individuals) in New York City increased from 204 in 1902 to 372 in 1922, or 58 per cent.

The number of insurance brokers south of 59th Street increased from 3,474 in 1912 to 6,613 in 1923, or 90 per cent.

The number of accounting firms south of 59th Street increased from 43 in 1900 to 726 in 1922, or 1,588 per cent.

The number of corporations listed in Moody's Manual as having offices in New York south of 59th Street increased from 69 in 1912 to 570 in 1922, or 726 per cent.

The number of custom brokers and forwarding agents south of Fulton Street increased from 110 in 1900 to 370 in 1922, or 236 per cent.

The number of lawyers south of 59th Street increased from 6,135 in 1900 to 12,769 in 1922 or 108 per cent.

The floor space occupied by the large department stores south of 60th Street increased from 4,101,000 square feet in 1902 to 7,083,000 square feet in 1922, an increase of 73 per cent. In 1912 the corresponding figure was 7,272,000 square feet, there being a marked decline between 1912 and 1916.

The number of middlemen (including commission merchants, converters, brokers, jobbers, selling agents, factors, New York buyers for out-of-town jobbers, New York sales offices of out-of-town manufacturers, etc.) in the wholesale cotton, silk and knit-goods markets south of 59th Street increased from 733 in 1900 to 3,924 in 1922, or 435 per cent.

The number of jewelry jobbers and wholesalers south of 59th Street increased from 387 in 1900 to 1,025 in 1923, or 165 per cent.

Selling in the 42nd Street area is for the most part of two kinds. One type is the trade of quality—the sale of the rare, the exclusive, the unstandardized: rich jewels, rare paintings, fashionable clothing, articles beyond the reach of the masses of men. The limited number of potential customers in the United States of America is at present most easily accessible in the neighbourhood of Fifth Avenue and 42nd Street, near the hotels and the choicest residential district. These are people who can and will pay to have their time saved and their convenience served. The saving in the aggregate is sufficiently large to make it possible for these shops to outbid competing activities for the sites.

THOSE WHO CAN PAY FOR SPACE. The second type may be called the trade of selection, the sale of the required assortment of miscellaneous goods. The modern department store, catering not to the extremely wealthy, but to those of moderate and low incomes, is here the typical agency, although a conveniently grouped assortment of specialty shops under independent ownership sometimes performs the same function. The peculiar function of the great store is to provide an assortment. A woman may more conveniently buy a yard of blue taffeta in the little store on the main street of her suburban home town. But if she wishes to make her selection from twenty shades of a single quality of an identical fabric, she must go to the central shopping district, to the department store, or to several department stores. Much more must she go there if during the same morning she must buy, after a certain amount of prayerful consideration and comparison, a new hat, a pair of silk stockings to match the blue taffeta, and a new set of dishes. Her time is not worth $100 an hour. She need not be greeted by a dozen wonderfully gowned saleswomen in a cathedral-like edifice; but she appreciates fairly prompt and efficient service, and must catch the 11:50 train back to Yonkers. The convenience of the thousands of such persons is sufficient to offset the convenience of the hundreds of de luxe shoppers, with the result that the department store can compete for Fifth Avenue sites on practically even terms with the exclusive shop.

FACTORS IN BAD LOCATION. It has already been pointed out that the small scale of some businesses tends to prevent the division and separate location of functions. There are many other special circumstances which also operate to distort the outlines of the ideal urban layout or to retard conformity to it. Ignorance, inertia, chance and personal idiosyncrasies all play a part. The physical characteristics of the terrain and the peculiarities of the transportation system are important factors influencing a pattern. Conditions of land tenure may retard or facilitate conformity to it. Similarly, the absence of competitive pressure is responsible for much bad location. Several of the most striking cases of misplaced plants in New York are factories making patented articles. Nor is it necessary that the monopoly be complete for an effect to be felt. In some cases, the low competitive pressure is traceable simply to the relative insignificance of the factor of site rentals, as compared with the other factors of cost. Perhaps most important of all the distorting factors is the obsolete building. A surprisingly large number of concerns are the beneficiaries of bargains in rent offered by owners of rundown real estate.[3]

Population Selection in Urban Communities.—Each natural area subdivision of the urban community draws to it the elements of population appropriate to its function. The age and sex distribution of an area are in keeping with its basic social and economic character. For example, in Chicago, Seattle, and many other cities, the outlying

---

[3] R. M. Haig, "Toward an Understanding of the Metropolis," *Quart. J. Econom.*, Vol. 40, No. 3, 1925-1926, pp. 403-430.

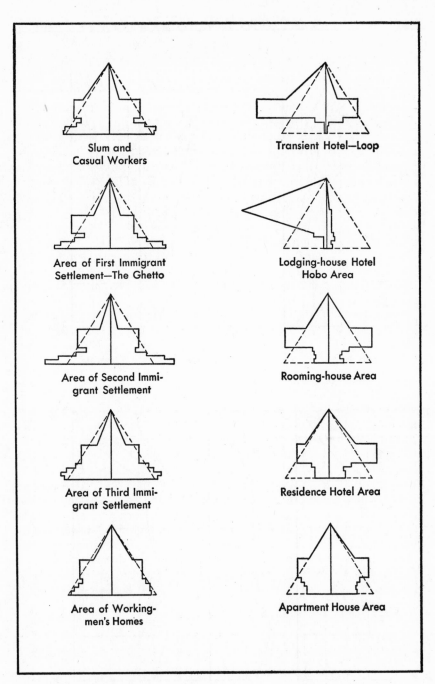

Figure 14. Populations of Selected Census Tracts in Chicago, 1920,
Representing Types of Age and Sex Distribution in the "City"

Redrawn from Charles Newcomb, "Graphic Presentation of Age and Sex Distribution of
Population in the City," p. 93. Undated pamphlet.

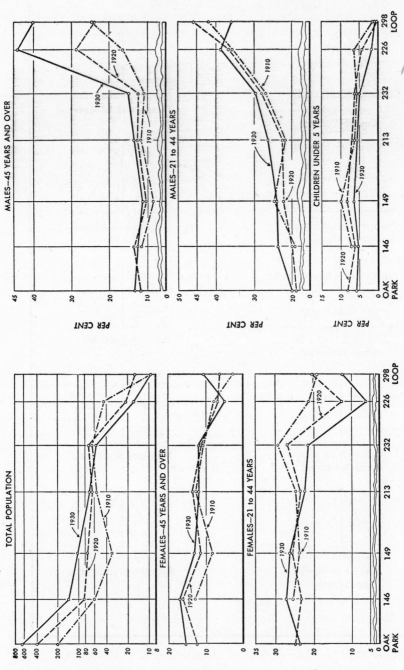

Figure 15. Changes in Total Population and in the Proportion of Selected Age-Sex Groups for Seven Census Tracts for Chicago, 1910-1930.

Tract numbers apply to all six elements of the graph. Each area is shown in true geographic position and relative distance from State and Madison streets. Redrawn from Charles Newcomb, "Graphic Presentation of Age and Sex Distribution of Population in the City," p. 83. Undated pamphlet.

areas are populated predominantly by married couples with children. These areas are, for the most part, female in composition, in contrast to the areas nearest the central business district which are predominantly composed of males over twenty years of age.

Figure 14 shows graphically variations in age and sex structure for a few areas of Chicago. It should be noted that a theoretical age and sex distribution pyramid for certain classifications is delineated by dotted lines. The left side of each diagram shows the male age structure, the youngest age group being at the base, while the right side gives the same information for females. Figure 15 shows the population changes which twenty years brought to the long stretch of Chicago's Madison Street, from the intersection of State and Madison, in the Loop, westward to the Madison Street-Oak Park Avenue intersection on the city's edge. (Tract numbers have been substituted for the intervening street intersections.) The curves show that the Loop lost population and the Oak Park Avenue tract gained in population—a trend which was true for the city as a whole.

ECOLOGICAL FACTORS AND SOCIAL CONTROL

In discussing the distribution of people and their institutions within the metropolitan area, social controls must be taken into consideration along with the ecological factors. The ecological forces are the impersonal factors in a city's growth, whereas the social controls are based on the sentiments and tradition of the area, supplemented by more rational controls including legal regulations. Such controls influence the stabilization of urban areas through their aid in the rejection of inimical population elements and land use.

The main assumption of human ecologists has been that the forces of selective distribution occur at the subsocial level:

Ecological interaction occurs upon different levels from those of . . . social interaction. Social interaction involves consensus. . . . Ecological interaction, in contrast, involves only an indirect and impersonal form of mutual modification by which . . . man influences others.[4]

However, the social factors, involving consensus, are found to be determinants in selective distribution where areas have become organized to maintain their character.

The ecological forces of competitive selection place men and their institutions in locations which afford at least a minimum of opportunity for survival. For a period of time an equilibrium is reached

---

[4] James A. Quinn, "Human Ecology and Interactional Ecology," *Am. Sociol. Rev.*, Vol. 5, No. 5, October, 1940, p. 722.

and these areas are stabilized. The areas of the city which provide
the most stable equilibrium in competitive selection are, first, the
financial districts, such as Threadneedle Street in London, Wall
Street in New York, St. James Street in Montreal, and secondly,
the central business district with its department stores and interdependent businesses, both areas being located at vantage points of transportation and communication. Such areas permit the competitive
forces of selection to operate more freely than do other urban areas.

Even in the financial and central business districts, however, the
impersonal ecological forces operate within cultural controls. Such
cultural inventions as steel construction and elevators made high
buildings possible, which permitted even more economical use of the
land in these areas. However, these inventions which permitted
buildings to rise to phenomenal heights brought about legal control
with respect to height. The invention of the set-back building was
a means of advancing these developments without contravening the
conventional legal requirements and thus brought high buildings
under acceptable social control. Material inventions, legal enactments, and informal status demands operate within the impersonal
ecological factors. Frequently it is when these impersonal ecological
factors are isolated and their results recognized that they come under
the control of the mores and legal enactments carrying penalties.
However, as the full force of the competitive factors is known only
after they have reached an equilibrium, the great problem is to catch
up effectively with the impersonal selectivity in time to impose social
controls.

Turning to the more sacred social factors which play a part in the
distribution of men and their institutions, Professor Firey has focused
his attention upon those natural areas of the city which resist the
invasion of alien elements. Such resistance has been perennially in
evidence.

In the course of time, every sector and quarter of the city takes on something of the quality and character of its inhabitants. Every separate part of
the city is . . . stained with the peculiar sentiments of the population.[5]

The social status of the area repels or attracts population elements,
be that area the slum or the residential districts of the city's elite.

In certain areas in Boston, in which selective factors have reached
an equilibrium, certain social controls [6] based on consensus among the

---

[5] R. E. Park and E. W. Burgess, *The City*, Chicago, University of Chicago Press,
1925, p. 6.
[6] So-called "sentimental variables," as Professor Firey terms them, may be thought of as
a phase of social controls.

residents were brought into play to maintain the status quo. Examples of such areas are Beacon Hill and the Boston Common.

Beacon Hill, which began its existence as an upper-class residential district about 1800, retains its power to attract and hold the "right" families. To have been born on the Hill, or at least to live there, is a source of pride and an assurance of upper-class status in the eyes of the community. The area has been "stained" with the prides and prejudices of persons whose names are featured recurrently in the Boston *Social Register*. Beacon Hill has become characterized by a unity of class sentiment, combined with a consciousness of geographic exclusiveness, out of which matrix the protective social controls have arisen. These social controls have managed to impede the operation of the impersonal ecological factors, at least for the time being.

Located but five minutes distant from the central areas of the city, Beacon Hill is in a position which is very desirable for economic uses. The area has been threatened by the invasion of business and an alien type of residence—the apartment-hotel. In 1922, the residents saw the threat to their district and organized to keep "undesirable business and living conditions from affecting the hill area." [7] The sacred nature of the feelings of the residents about Beacon Hill was and is frequently verbalized. Behind these sentiments are the historical traditions which have become associated with the area, as well as the strong familial ties which keep generation after generation in the same houses. The Beacon Hill Association, composed of persons who maintain such sentiments, managed to influence zoning authorities in Boston to limit the height of buildings, to confine business to a limited area, and to exclude a projected four million dollar apartment-hotel. The residents also collaborated in a building program which consisted of purchasing and remodeling old houses in order to maintain "the quaint charm" of the Hill. They thereby reinforced their sentimental attachments to the area through keeping its appearance stately, old, and steeped in tradition, a reflection of their conception of the area.

The residents of Beacon Hill, through their prestige and wealth, had the ability to maintain their exclusive social sanctuary, regardless of cost. Almost any other population element would have been unable to do so. If business had encroached on the district and land values risen, the population of the district would have found it impossible to hold it as a residential area. As it was, some of the

[7] Walter Firey, "Sentiment and Symbolism as Ecological Variables," *Am. Sociol. Rev.,* Vol. 10, No. 2, April, 1945, p. 143.

upper-class families in Beacon Hill were forced to leave their homes for other less expensive areas, mainly during the depression years when the value of their securities fell.

However, many additional factors, other than cost, operated at the impersonal ecological level to raise legal and social resistance to invasion. In most cities, as business encroaches upon a residential area, the people move away and property is permitted to fall into disrepair. In Beacon Hill, however, an aggressive attack was made which warded off obsolescence. Because of this, Beacon Hill has not shared the fate of such other upper-class districts as Back Bay and Jamaica Plain, which gave way in the face of the competition of newer suburban residential districts.

Beacon Hill seems to have reached a stable equilibrium, which it may be able to maintain, but there is always the possibility that other factors, such as deaths in families, childless families, changes in transportation methods, and other factors as yet obscure, may become cumulative and break down the old "pride of place." Without the sentimental and sacred feeling of the residents about their district, the consensus necessary to the enforcement of social controls would break down and allow free play to the impersonal ecological factors.

The Boston Common is a 48-acre tract of land, wedged into the heart of Boston's business district. For three centuries this city has grown up around the Common, which is protected by city and state sentiment and legal enactments as a symbol of Boston's role in American history. Business has had to go around it and confine itself to an extremely limited space which is markedly inadequate to the needs of a city the size of Boston. Large business establishments have been forced to extend their floor space by devious use of rear and adjoining buildings. Traffic problems in downtown Boston, as a result of the Common, have become acute. Trucking is expensive and much valuable time is lost for citizens, as law and sentiment permit no roads across the Common. Thus, the maintenance of the Common has forced a central business district formation on the city which is very expensive for merchants and customers and inconvenient for all who must pass through it.

The sentiments and legal enactments which surround the Boston Common are more insistent even than those of Beacon Hill. Some expressions of these sentiments are as follows:

> "Here, in short, are our accumulated memories, intimate, public and private."

"Boston Common was, is, and ever will be a source of
tradition and inspiration from which the New Englanders
may revive their faith, recover their moral force, and
strengthen their ability to grow and achieve." [8]

Boston Common has been maintained despite impersonal ecological
forces which demand its use for more utilitarian purposes. However,
for the majority of people in the city and state whose sentiments keep
the Common intact, the maximum use is being made of land, and its
sacred symbolic value enables it to compete successfully with the
secular forces at work in the area.

THE FUNCTION OF ECOLOGICAL ORGANIZATION

The ecological order, operating through the ecological processes,
is a mechanism of competitive selection. The process of location
takes place in accordance with the ecological order in existence when
any individual or social institution begins its life cycle. Each is
subject to the main trends of growth and change going on within
this order.

Individuals locate themselves in areas where the means of subsistence are sufficient to ensure a livelihood and where the population
characteristics are such as to permit the individual to compete with
them successfully for this livelihood. Institutions emerge in those
areas where there is a need for their services and compete with the
existent institutions until those best suited to the needs of people in
the area are dominant or are the only institutions which survive.
Those centers which contain the most adequate institutional services
grow, while other centers become smaller or lose their functions to the
dominant area, whose dominance is due to position, resources, or cultural organization. The centers which are best able to compete in not
only their own regions, but the world, become dominant. Within
a city, the same processes are at work and people and their institutions locate in districts where they are best able to survive.

All human units run the gamut of selective distribution. The
ultimate position of a unit is determined, on the one hand, by the
main features of the ecological pattern of distribution already existing, and by the nature and resources of the given unit, on the other
hand. These units attain a position of equilibrium in relation to each
other, but that equilibrium is much more unstable in the city than in
the country. In the large urban areas, the shifting process is much

---

[8] *Ibid.*, p. 144.

more severe. Certain urban sections of the city are areas of human siftings. No one argues that this impersonal mechanism of selection operates wisely or well. In many ways it is crude. At a given period in the selective processes, certain types are eliminated as failures which the social order might find indispensable at some future date. The equilibrium reached, even when relatively stable, retains this stability only until some new factor enters in, such as an improvement in transportation and communication methods, new inventions, or new resources.

Ecological position is of sociological importance because of its bearing on social contacts and social interaction. The ecological pattern of distribution marks out physical distances between units and determines the direction of social contacts. It is the framework on which the social order is woven.

Questions

1. Distinguish between competition and rivalry.
2. Explain symbiosis and distinguish between plant and human forms.
3. The various ecological processes involve the basic idea of competition. Explain.
4. What is meant by the spatially fixed aspects of human existence?
5. Specialization of areas, institutions, and occupations reduces direct competition but increases symbiotic dependence. Discuss.
6. What is meant by concentration? How does it operate to determine the distribution of people and their institutions?
7. Define centralization. What is its function in the patterning of the city? Give examples of centralization in your own community.
8. What is meant by segregation? What are some of its social effects?
9. Discuss invasion and succession with relation to their importance in altering the pattern of the city. Give examples of invasion and succession in your own community. How were the areas involved affected by this change?
10. Define community, region, natural area. Give examples.
11. How would you go about determining the boundaries of a community? A natural area?
12. How did the ecological processes operate to pattern Montreal and New York?
13. How do social factors operate to determine selective distribution within a community? Give examples of social controls which operate to halt ecological change in your own community.
14. How did the residents of Beacon Hill resist invasion by undesirable people and institutions?
15. What social controls operated to retain the Boston Common despite its detrimental effects to the central business district?

16. The ecological order operating through the ecological processes is a mechanism of competitive selection. Discuss.
17. What is the sociological importance of ecological position?

BIBLIOGRAPHY

ANDERSON, NELS, AND LINDEMAN, E. C. *Urban Sociology.* New York, F. S. Crofts & Co., 1930.

ARENSBERG, C. M., AND KIMBALL, S. T. *Family and Community in Ireland.* Cambridge, Harvard University Press, 1940.

BERNARD, L. L. (Ed.) *Fields and Methods of Sociology.* New York, Farrar & Rinehart, Inc., 1934, pp. 52-64, 288-312.

BLUMENTHAL, A. *Small Town Stuff.* Chicago, University of Chicago Press, 1932.

BURGESS, E. W. *The Urban Community.* Chicago, University of Chicago Press, 1926.

CARPENTER, N. *The Sociology of City Life.* New York, Longmans, Green & Co., Inc., 1931.

COUSENEAU, AIMÉ. *Planning for Montreal.* Dept. of City Planning, City of Montreal, 1944.

DANHOFF, R. H. "New Zuider Zee Lands: Planned Settlement in the Netherlands." *Am. Sociol. Rev.,* Vol. 4, No. 4, August, 1939, pp. 493-506.

DAVIE, M. R. *Problems of City Life.* New York, John Wiley & Sons, Inc., 1932.

DAWSON, C. A. "City Planning and Our North American Social Heritage," in *Housing and Community Planning.* Montreal, McGill University, 1944, pp. 148-155.

DOUGLAS, H. P. *The Church in the Changing City.* New York, George H. Doran Co., 1927.

DURANT, RUTH. *Watling: A Survey of Social Life on a New Housing Estate.* London, P. S. King & Son, 1939.

ENGEL-FRISCH, GLADYS. "Some Temporal Aspects of Human Ecology." *Social Forces,* Vol. 22, October, 1943, pp. 43-47.

FIREY, WALTER. *Land Use in Central Boston.* Cambridge, Harvard University Press, 1947.

FIREY, WALTER. "Sentiment and Symbolism as Ecological Variables." *Am. Sociol. Rev.,* Vol. 10, No. 2, April, 1945, pp. 140-148.

GIBBARD, HAROLD A. "The Status Factor in Residential Succession." *Am. J. Sociol.,* Vol. 46, No. 6, May, 1941, pp. 835-842.

GIST, NOEL P., AND HALBERT, L. A. *Urban Society.* New York, Thomas Y. Crowell Co., 1945.

HAIG, R. M. "Toward an Understanding of the Metropolis." *Quart. J. Econom.,* Vol. 40, No. 3, 1925-1926, pp. 403-430.

HAIG, R. M., AND McRAE, R. C. *Committee on Plan of New York and Its Environs,* Vol. 1, New York, 1927.

HAYNER, N. S. "Mexico City: Its Growth and Configuration." *Am. J. Sociol.,* Vol. 50, No. 4, January, 1945, pp. 295-305.

HAYNER, N. S. *Hotel Life.* Chapel Hill, University of North Carolina Press, 1936.

HILLER, E. T. "The Community as a Social Group." *Am. Sociol. Rev.,* Vol. 6, No. 2, April, 1941, pp. 189ff.

HOLLINGSHEAD, AUGUST B. "Community Research: Development and Present Condition," and discussion. *Am. Sociol. Rev.,* Vol. 13, No. 2, April, 1948, pp. 136-152.

HOYT, HOMER. "Forces of Urban Centralization and Decentralization." *Am. J. Sociol.,* Vol. 47, No. 6, May, 1941, pp. 843-852.

JONES, D. C. (Ed.) *The Social Survey of Merseyside.* Liverpool, University Press of Liverpool, 1934.

LUNDBERG, G. A., KOMAROVSKY, MIRRA, AND MCINERY, MARY. *Suburban Study.* New York, Columbia University Press, 1934.

MACIVER, R. M. *Society, Its Structure and Changes.* New York, R. Long and R. R. Smith, Inc., 1931.

MCKENZIE, R. D. "The Ecological Approach to the Study of the Human Community." *Am. J. Sociol.,* Vol. 30, No. 3, November, 1924, pp. 287-301.

MCKENZIE, R. D. *The Metropolitan Community.* New York, McGraw-Hill Book Co., Inc., 1937.

MUNTZ, E. E. *Urban Sociology.* New York, The Macmillan Co., 1938.

NEWCOMB, CHARLES. "Graphic Presentation of Age and Sex Distribution of Population in the City." Undated pamphlet.

O'BRIEN, R. W. "Beale Street, Memphis: A Study in Ecological Succession." *Sociol. and Soc. Res.,* Vol. 26, May, 1942, pp. 430-436.

OGBURN, W. F., AND COOMBS, L. C. "An Economic Interpretation of the Social Characteristics of Cities." *Am. J. Sociol.,* Vol. 46, No. 3, November, 1940, pp. 305-315.

OSBORNE, L. D., AND NEUMEYER, M. H. *The Community and Society.* New York, American Book Co., 1933.

PARK, R. E. (Ed.) *Outline of the Principles of Sociology.* New York, Barnes and Noble, Inc., 1939, Chs. IX-XIV.

PARK, R. E., AND BURGESS, E. W. *The City.* Chicago, University of Chicago Press, 1925.

PARK, R. E., AND BURGESS, E. W. *Introduction to the Science of Sociology,* Chicago, University of Chicago Press, 1921.

QUEEN, S. A., AND THOMAS, L. F. *The City.* New York, McGraw-Hill Book Co., Inc., 1939.

QUINN, J. A. "Ecological and Social Interaction." *Sociol. and Soc. Res.,* Vol. 18, July and August, 1934, pp. 565-570.

QUINN, J. A. "The Nature of Human Ecology, Re-examination and Redefinition." *Social Forces,* Vol. 17, December, 1939, pp. 161-168.

QUINN, J. A. "The Burgess Zonal Hypothesis and Its Critics." *Am. Sociol. Rev.,* Vol. 5, No. 2, April, 1940, pp. 210-218.

QUINN, J. A. "Topical Survey of Current Literature on Human Ecology." *Am. J. Sociol.,* Vol. 46, No. 2, September, 1940, pp. 191-226.

QUINN, J. A. "Human Ecology and Interactional Ecology." *Am. Sociol. Rev.,* Vol. 5, No. 5, October, 1940, pp. 713-722.

SANDERSON, D. *The Rural Community.* Boston, Ginn & Co., 1932.

SANDERSON, D. "Community Organization for War and Peace." *Social Forces,* Vol. 21, October, 1942, pp. 1-7.

SANDERSON, D., AND POLSON, R. A. *Rural Community Organization.* New York, John Wiley & Sons, Inc., 1930.

SHAW, CLIFFORD. *Delinquency Areas.* Chicago, University of Chicago Press, 1929.

SIMS, N. L. *The Rural Community.* New York, Charles Scribners' Sons, 1920.

UNITED STATES NATIONAL RESOURCES COUNCIL. *Our Cities: Their Role in the National Economy.* Washington, Research Committee on Urbanism, 1937.

WARE, C. F. *Greenwich Village.* Boston, Houghton Mifflin Co., 1935.

WARNER, W. L., AND LUNT, P. S. *The Social Life of a Modern Community.* New Haven, Yale University Press, 1941.

WHYTE, WILLIAM FOOTE. *Street Corner Society.* Chicago, University of Chicago Press, 1943.

WILLIAMS, J. M. *Our Rural Heritage.* New York, Alfred A. Knopf, 1925.

WIRTH, L. "Human Ecology." *Am. J. Sociol.,* Vol. 50, No. 6, May, 1945, pp. 483-488.

ZIMMERMAN, C. C. *The Changing Community.* New York, Harper & Bros., 1938.

Chapter 11

SOCIAL INSTITUTIONS

The preceding chapters have dealt with the concept of role as a means of describing the conduct of individuals. The established roles which are linked in systems of social expectations are called *social institutions*. Of the institutional forms of human association, the following things may be said: first, each institution can be located in a spatial arrangement; second, each institution provides for a minimum of the biological and/or psychological needs of a certain proportion of its members; third, in each institution, the interaction of individuals produces consensus as to goals and the means of achieving those goals which are expressed in the folkways, mores, ritual, and more formal organization; fourth, each institution provides well defined and socially sanctioned roles for its members, those roles being mutually adjusted so that persons engaged in the institutional behavior can best contribute to the functioning of the institution as a whole; and, fifth, the institutionalized patterns of behavior are interrelated with those of other institutions in the social system of the society so as to ensure the adequate functioning of the society as a whole.

All social institutions are cultural in that they arise from the culture of the society and act in accordance with it. As changes come about in the culture, the institutions of the society are forced to redefine their goals and functions in accordance with those changes and thus they reflect what is happening in the culture of a society.[1] Usually a social institution has a life span longer than the life span of any of its members.[2]

Although individual persons participate with others in institutions on a region-wide, nation-wide, and even a world-wide basis, the community is the largest local social world to which they belong. In the analysis of institutions which follows, the urban community constitutes the main focus of attention and other types of communities will be dealt with only for comparative purposes.[3]

---

[1] Talcott Parsons, "The Position of Sociological Theory," and discussion, *Am. Sociol. Rev.*, Vol. 13, No. 2, April, 1948, pp. 156-171.

[2] E. C. Hughes, *The Growth of an Institution: The Chicago Real Estate Board*, Chicago, The Society for Social Research of the University of Chicago, 1931, pp. 7-8.

[3] This method of dealing with the subject of social institutions does not imply that units other than the urban community would have been unsatisfactory. Institutions could be studied

Symbiotic Aspects of Social Institutions.—In the preceding chapter, it was pointed out that ecological forces operate to develop institutions in areas where they will be able to compete most effectively. Certain types of institutions grow up in a given location and make the advent and continuity of a community possible. As they are the basic institutions of such communities they have a marked degree of stability and permanence. For example, the basic institutions which developed such port cities as New York and Montreal, are those related to water transportation. It was the emergence of these transportation institutions which spurred the growth of these cities and, as these institutions grew, so did the cities. New York, Montreal, Houston, and Seattle are located at the end of rail traffic and at the beginning of a sea route; this has made them cities of importance in world trade. Chicago, due to geographic factors, is the center of railroad transportation for the United States. Similar advantages, with variations peculiar to their particular region and geographic position, have made Rio de Janeiro, London, Moscow, Bombay, Paris, and a host of other cities each the center of its particular sphere of dominance.

Other institutions, dependent on the basic transportation institutions, have arisen within these communities as they increased in size. Ecological factors also operate to develop institutions in the community locations where they are best able to compete. For example, all the above-mentioned cities, but especially New York, London, and Moscow, have streets in which are concentrated the financial institutions essential to such centers. These streets are symbolized by Wall Street in New York, with its Stock Exchange, banking, legal, and other institutions. As the financial institutions are closely linked with national and international business, they tend to be relatively permanent. In location, they remain close to the import and export agencies which they serve, although they are much less dependent upon local facilities of transportation and communication than the latter.

When considered in terms of permanence and stability, the institutions of the financial street rank highest. Next in line are those located at the focal point of the transportation and communication system of the city. Elaborate and specialized commercial institutions cluster at this point to form the central business area, in which

---

in units of territory ranging in size from the neighborhood to the world. The urban community has been chosen as the frame of reference because it is a relatively small unit of territority and yet one which is large enough for most types of institutions to be found within its boundaries.

location are to be found the best opportunities for their survival and expansion. Near the central business district are those institutions which, in part, are temporal successors of shops. These institutions extend their services far into the night. Theatres, restaurants, night clubs, bars, and other institutions of this type take advantage of the central location in respect to transportation facilities and the social anonymity which this district affords. All these factors, and others, contribute to the appeal of the institutions of the central business area. Somewhat akin to the central business area are the subcenters which grow up at lesser foci of transportation and communication in the residential subdivisions of the metropolis. To these subcenters and "chain streets" are attracted commercial and amusement institutions to serve the particular district in which they are located.

Households and their associated neighborhood institutions are to be found in all residential areas of the metropolis, whether these residential areas are located at the center of the city or on the periphery. The more independent outlying districts may be classified as residential, industrial, institutional, or mixed suburbs. The neighborhood institutions of residential areas are schools, churches, and their prototypes. Such institutions as the church and school, which concentrate on nonprofit functions, tend to be close to the clusters of households which they serve, and removed from the main arteries of traffic. Such neighborhood institutions and homes seem to thrive best in stable areas within the urban community, that is, in areas where mobility is at a minimum. Unlike the institutions of the central business area, they do not depend on pecuniary power in order to compete for space, but rather on values which gain strength from sentiment, class prerogatives, and other cultural supports which are prevalent to the greatest degree in stable residential areas.

Profit and nonprofit institutions tend to be at opposite poles in the urban selective pattern. Informal social controls are at their peak in the locations to which the nonprofit institutions are selected. These controls depend mainly upon philosophies of life which are founded on the traditions of home, school, church, and closely related institutions. The profit institutions also are subject to social expectations based on sentiment, but, in their case, social expectations have become more calculable and formalized in their contracts.

The institutions of a community come to take on a characteristic pattern of distribution. In this respect, there is a certain parallel between human and plant communities, which can be designated by the word "symbiosis." [4] In the plant community the tree gives shade to the plants which grow at its base while the plants conserve moisture for the tree. Equally unintentional symbiotic relationships obtain between occupations, institutions, and regions. There are areas of the city which are given over to specialized functions such as financial, wholesale, or shopping districts; other areas are used almost completely for the performance of manufacturing or residential functions. But each is dependent upon the functions performed by every other area. However, because of inventiveness and the active side of human adjustment, divisions of labor are more dynamic and changing than are the symbiotic conditions under which plants live.

Institutional Services.—A distinction can with some validity be drawn between basic and service institutions. [5] Basic institutions furnish the economic base while service institutions provide "cultural services and consumption goods." Nevertheless, all community institutions can be studied from the point of view of their service functions. Basic institutions such as those in the fields of steel, rubber, oil, transportation, textiles, farming, and lumbering may provide the means of livelihood for a large number of families. Although their local functions may be limited to the employment they provide and the influential role of their officials in the community, such institutions, through the exporting of their products, link the community with regional or world markets. Utility corporations in the fields of transportation, electricity, and communication also provide jobs and local leadership but their services are used by the community at large. The former type of institutional service depends very little, or not at all, on the relationship which exists between its employees (or functionaries) and the consumers of its products. The latter type of institution, as exemplified by the utility corporation, although its services are of the "push button" type, indirect and impersonal, does seek to maintain attitudes of good will on the part of its customers.

In contrast, the functionaries of other institutions render a more direct and personal type of service, for example, teachers, ministers, doctors, lawyers, ward politicians, undertakers, insurance agents, realtors, labor leaders, social workers, and secretaries. In the situations in which these functionaries operate, they must keep in mind the roles of others in action, be ready and capable of ingratiating, placating, befriending, understanding, advising, and consulting. They

---

[4] See Chapter 10.
[5] E. C. Hughes, in A. M. Lee (Ed.), *New Outlines of the Principles of Sociology,* New York, Barnes & Noble, Inc., 1946, p. 250.

must know just what their statuses involve, their duties and prerogatives, and, on the basis of these, keep their own counsel, revere, or
ignore.

In the rural community, the basic institutions are the farmsteads
while service institutions such as stores, shipping facilities, banking
services, schools, churches, medical facilities, printing, and telephone
services, tend to cluster in town and village centers located at focal
points of transportation. In North America, the primary schools of
rural areas tend to follow the same tendency as their urban equivalents
and be scattered throughout neighborhoods. In some rural areas all
the main services are scattered in single units or in clusters.

Regardless of whether institutions are scattered or concentrated
in towns and villages, the principle of delineating the outer boundaries
of the community is the same. The institutions which most regularly serve the needs of a group of people, who use similar services
in other localities only occasionally, belong within the boundaries of
the community. Such institutions form part of the daily routine
requirements of some members of the majority of the families which
use them.

The concept *institutional complement* is useful in determining the
periphery within which a community lies. This concept includes all
the institutional services without which the community could not
function efficiently as a self-contained unit. It is true, however, that
some communities are able to get along without some of the services
indicated above. Their inhabitants tolerate such a paucity because
the specialized services of a larger community are available to them.

The concept of institutional complement may also be applied to
the natural subdivisions of a city. The residents of such districts
go to institutions in other parts of the city to work, to be amused,
and to worship, to mention the means of solving just a few of man's
vital requirements. The city, through its compactness and its elaborate transportation system, offers to its inhabitants vastly more expanded and specialized satisfactions than does the small community
which contains the bare minimum of service institutions.

Social Systems and Their Institutional Cores.—In approaching
the subject of institutional structure, a review of what has been said
about social systems earlier in this text would be useful.[6] A social
system is a system of social action involving a plurality of interacting individuals which has either certain characteristics which
differentiate it from other social systems or from non-social situa-

---

[6] See Chapter 1.

tions, or in which there is discernible a relatively definite pattern of change. Emerging from and developing in keeping with the culture of the society of which it is a part, a social system is composed of a relatively stable pattern of actor relationships around which action is organized. If the pattern of actor relationships is sufficiently stable, it constitutes the structure of an institutionalized social system, or, in other words, an institution.[7]

The individual person as the actor of roles is the basic unit of an institutionalized social system and occupies the focus of attention as he strives for "desirable goals," assumes responsibilities, and exercises prerogatives in current "actor-situations." [8] Although the actor is the basic unit of a social system, he acts in conjunction with others, each of whom plays different but complementary roles within a given system of social relationships. In playing any role, the person as an actor uses, as it were, one segment of his personality which is called forth by his position and function in the system and according to the expectations of others as to how he should act.

The roles which a person plays vary from one social system to another and even within any social system. In laying a cornerstone for a new post office, the Postmaster General plays a role which calls for one segment of his personality. This is one aspect of a social system centering around the status of Postmaster General. Within the same social system, he is required to play a completely different role which reveals another aspect of his personality when he acts as Postmaster General at a Cabinet meeting. When he returns home at night, he participates in another system of social relationships which requires roles in keeping with his status as husband and father. The "sectors" of personality shown in the latter roles may have little in common with those aspects of his personality displayed while playing the roles of Postmaster General.

For each of the situations in which the Postmaster General participates, there is a system of patterned expectations of how he should act and how others in the situation should act toward him. If he is to retain his position as Postmaster General, his role must be in accordance with this system of social expectations. Similarly, if he is to be a good father and husband, he must anticipate how a family and society expect a husband and father to act, with individual variations caused by his own personality and his interpretation of the role which other members of his social group as well as those who par-

---

[7] Parsons, "The Position of Sociological Theory," *op. cit.*, pp. 156-164.

[8] Talcott Parsons, "The Present Position and Prospects of Systematic Theory in Sociology," in George Gurvitch and Wilbert E. Moore (Eds.), *Twentieth Century Sociology*, New York, Philosophical Library, Inc., 1945, p. 59.

ticipate in any particular pattern expect of a Postmaster General, a husband, and father. Similarly, each member of a society plays roles and interprets his functions in accordance with systems of patterned expectations and shows a segment of his personality in each.

From this point of view, the essential aspect of social structure lies in a system of patterned expectations defining the *proper* behavior of persons playing certain roles, enforced by the incumbent's own positive motives for conformity and by the sanction of others. Such systems of patterned expectations, seen in the perspective of their place in a total social system and sufficiently thoroughly established in action to be taken for granted as legitimate, are conveniently called "institutions." The fundamental, structurally stable, element of social systems then, which, according to the present argument, must play a crucial role in the theoretical analysis, is their structure of institutional patterns defining the roles of their constituent actors.[9]

An institution, then, is the established "core" of a social system. The integration of these interdependent social systems makes up the social system of a society. Each of the many social systems has a character of its own which differentiates it from others as a unit of investigation. The functional interdependence of each social system with others in a given society cannot be overemphasized.

The institution is the important social unit in the organization of individual careers and in the attainment of individual goals. The functional differentiation of social systems and their institutional "cores" allows great flexibility and makes for efficiency both in the creation of needs for individuals and in the satisfaction of these needs.

Institutions and Individual Orientation.—Institutions initiate the person into an orderly routine which acquaints him with the patterns of behavior and the attitudes which will be expected of him in the great variety of life's situations. They define the roles he is expected to play, the goals for which he can strive; and they organize his motivation.

It is through institutions that statuses are ascribed to individuals, long before they comprehend their significance. By status is meant an integration of rights and duties which form part of a social system and which find expression through the persons who hold them.[10] As a child, the person holds the status, with its associated rights and obligations, which belongs to this period of immaturity. His status

---

9 *Ibid.,* pp. 61-62.
10 Ralph Linton, *The Study of Man,* New York, Appleton-Century-Crofts, Inc., 1936, p. 113.

springs primarily from within the institutions of the family, the church, and the school. Implicit in this status are protective controls which limit not only his participation in other institutions, but also the obligations which even the family and the school may put upon him. In addition, his status as a child defines what he is expected to do as well as what he is permitted to do. In other words, it controls his behavior and the behavior of others towards him, that is, it defines his rights and duties at this period of his life.

Institutions ascribe a different status to boys as compared with girls. They ascribe a difference in status with reference to race, religion, nationality, and occupation. For each status ascribed there are sanctioned ways and social pressures to ensure that the person plays his role, and that others act toward him in accordance with the patterns of behavior implicit in the status. While these statuses are subject to modification in rapidly changing social systems, under conditions making for social stability, they tend to change in form very slightly from generation to generation.

Many of the above-mentioned statuses afford little or no choice to the person who fills them. Nor can he choose which aspects of his status to express, as each status has obligations as well as privileges attached to it. He cannot choose his family and he often finds it difficult to break the emotional ties which hold him to it. He is born into a national state which makes increasing demands on his loyalty and fruitfulness. In time of national danger, the state may mobilize all its resources to keep secure the values which he and other citizens live by. Moreover, in such times of crisis the state may require him to bear arms or contribute financially to the struggle for the continuance of those values.

In modern complex social systems the individual must spend a large part of his childhood and adolescence in school. Before he can exercise free choice of statuses, he must fulfil certain requirements. After school, whether he completes his courses or not, he has more freedom in that he may choose to take a job in a factory or office or continue his studies in order to enter one of the professions. His decision, however, is usually in keeping with the ambitions of his family, the attitudes of his class, and the influence of the functionaries of the institutions he wishes to enter. Even in his selection of his vocation, a few institutions outline career possibilities and prescribe the ways in which these may be achieved most readily. He may also find it advantageous to enlist the aid of other institutions such as influential clubs and associations which may enable him to achieve his ambitions.

In the western world with its rapidly developing technology and commercial organization and its highly specialized divisions of labor with respect to regions, occupations, and institutions, there is an almost endless choice of institutions in which the mature person may participate. However, even if a person is a chronic "joiner" he finds that his institutional participation is limited. He is excluded from some institutions because of his sex, others because of the status of his race, his social class, his nationality, his educational attainments, or his religion. Some exclusive clubs, for example, admit only those who have already acquired wealth, prestige, and fame. Despite barriers which may frustrate him in some direction, there still remains a wide range of institutional choice.

In each institution in which he participates the person plays relatively few roles and responds with a part of his personality only, whether he acts as a father, a lawyer, a garage attendant, a labor leader, a board member, or one who holds no distinguishing office. There are, however, a few institutions in which the person responds with the greater part of himself while with others his relations and responses may be casual in varying degrees.

Institutions and Office.—The concept of role and role playing is important in many aspects of sociology. In this particular context it is useful in explaining the reciprocal relationships of institutions and persons.

All institutions prepare their new recruits for playing roles which fit in with the institution's requirements and which contribute to the carrying out of its functions. The roles which the member plays in any institutional structure must also give expression to and further his own personal aims, if he is to retain his connections with the institution. The institution brings out those possibilities of behavior which fit the needs and tolerances of that particular patterned structure by rewarding acceptable behavior. On the other hand, inappropriate behavior is by-passed or repressed.[11] The patterned structure must also fulfil the motivations of its functionaries. This motivation includes conformity to existing social expectations. "Above all, both the disinterested motives associated with 'conscience' and 'ideals' and the self-interested ones must be mobilized in the interest of the same direction of behavior." [12]

In any specific situation, the actor responds with a somewhat specialized part of himself, as, for example, the church warden. The

---

11 Parsons, "The Present Position of Systematic Theory in Sociology," *op. cit.*, p. 62.
12 *Ibid.*

aspects of his personality which are shown in the situation are those which are defined by the group as being appropriate and necessary to the adequate performance of his role. These traditional expectations of the group guide him, sometimes consciously and sometimes unconsciously, in his behavior in that situation. The extent of the group's approval of how he conceives and performs his role spurs his performance and he modifies his role in keeping with their expectations. Theorists have frequently overemphasized the segmentation of personality from this point of view. There are, for example, some situations in which the whole of the person's personality may be brought into play. A person may also be faced with a new situation which can be solved only from the vantage ground of the whole of his accumulated experience. However, even in this situation it would be necessary for him to reinterpret that experience in terms of specialized institutional roles.

Those leading actors who bear special responsibilities in institutional activities are known as functionaries. They act in an *office*, in connection with which their actual roles become defined.

An institutional office consists of a defined set of rights and duties vested in a person, but capable of being transferred to another person in some accepted way. This does not mean that a father, for instance, can be replaced in his family easily or completely, for personal attachment becomes too great. But when one becomes a father there is a pattern of expected conduct lying in wait for him. . . . An office is impersonal in two respects. First, it is older than the individual incumbent and is expected to outlive him. Second, each incumbent is expected to behave within limits, as have his predecessors. Ritual offices are the most impersonal, for in them the incumbent speaks in set phrases which he is not free to alter. The person in an office is judged by the expectations of the office. So long as he meets them, he is free from personal criticism. The office sets the limits of his responsibilities.[13]

The functionary may play his role precisely according to traditional expectations or he may add something to it. The most successful functionary is the one who can catch the spirit of his role and act out those aspects of it which are implicit, as well as explicit. In some measure all functionaries modify their roles to fit in with their own perspectives and abilities. In addition, all functionaries are allowed some flexibility—although this varies in extent—in meeting unforeseen situations which confront institutions. These crises disrupt the customary pattern of group behavior and it is the duty of the functionary to reestablish orderly procedure. At such times, the self-consciousness of the functionary is intensified. He is called upon to

---

[13] E. C. Hughes, in *New Outlines of the Principles of Sociology*, pp. 258 ff.

take the initiative and make decisions and these must be in keeping with the expectations of the group concerning his rights and duties and the spirit of his status and the institution. The self-consciousness of the functionary is further enhanced in that he knows he is being compared with previous leaders or other contemporary leaders in his behavior and in the results he achieves. The group's judgment of the adequacy of his role-playing crystalizes expectations of the functionary's role and, in this way, other attributes may be added to the traditional role. For the functionary himself, the heightened self-consciousness makes the role a living and integral part of his personality.

All institutions have multiple "offices," which are graded in importance and closely integrated. "The relation of offices to one another and to the various classes of people who participate in the institution are its 'working constitution.' "[14] Hall illuminates this point of view:

The doctors of a given department, the various departments of the hospital, and the range of hospitals in the community form a hierarchy in each case. The doctors in a specific department are arranged in strata, such as intern, extern, staff member, staff association member, and the like. Within these strata, there are fine gradations. For example, the staff members (those doctors who have full access to the facilities of the hospital) may be organized into many distinct levels which indicate clearly the prerogatives and prestige of the men concerned. Such a hierarchical pattern provides an exceedingly large number of steps for the new member of the profession. His progress through them symbolizes achievement in his personal career. For the administrator the hospital is a finely articulated status structure; the various positions represent a wide range of rewards to be conferred on doctors attached to the hospital. The number and variety of these rewards function to keep a large staff reasonably satisfied by providing neat packages of advancement at relatively short intervals.

Within the departments competition goes on among the doctors. This competition is tempered by the established set of authority relations and the code of ethics which discourages individualistic striving for position. Between departments there is practically no competition because of the rigid nature of the specialization concerned. There is, however, a jealous struggle for prestige between different lines of specialization.[15]

Status, Role, and the Class Structure.—The selection of institutional functionaries bears directly on the social stratification of the community. High status offices such as membership on the Board

[14] *Ibid.*
[15] Oswald Hall, "The Stages of a Medical Career," *Am. J. Sociol.*, Vol. 53, No. 5, March, 1948, p. 329.

of Governors of a university or hospital offer no financial rewards. Indeed, the opposite is usually true. Governors often contribute large sums of money along with notable personal services to the institution with which they are connected. To be chosen for such a position is a recognition of their status in the community. Such persons tend to be chosen from the upper rungs of the social ladder. This upper-class position came to them, either through being born into families with wealth, fame, or exceptional prestige, or through mounting to wealth, fame, or distinction through their own efforts. Regardless of how they attained their upper-class position, they are chosen for such high positions because they have "arrived." Although the success of doctors is dependent to a large extent on the ability they show in medical institutions, they tend to be drawn from families of professional workers who know the criteria and means to success and can nurture and aid their ambitions.[16] The professional social workers also, with a few exceptions, tend to come from social classes which are one or two ranks above the clients they serve.

The donors rarely become professional workers or clients; the clients almost never become professional workers or members of boards . . . a somewhat similar pattern is found in all institutions supported by philanthropic giving.[17]

Quite apart from considerations of class, there is a careful screening of those who are selected to be institutional functionaries. This is especially true of those at the career level. In business institutions, although men take their positions on the basis of the abilities they have shown, few are promoted without the intervention of good friends or the support of those whose motives are not quite in keeping with the professed aims of "free enterprise." The long climb to preferred positions in such professions as medicine and law involves the considerations just mentioned. The candidates go through a careful screening in high school, college, professional school, and in hospitals as interns. Finally, as persons who can give good account of themselves to their medical sponsors, they approach the goal of acceptable medical practitioners. In preparation for the priesthood, the screening process remains constant for the neophyte who has received a "call." Even in the last years of his clerical preparation he is expected to be able to surmount his doubts and become fully convinced of the validity of his faith. If he shows signs of faltering, he may be advised to seek some other career.

---

16 *Ibid.*, p. 328.
17 E. C. Hughes, in *New Outlines of the Principles of Sociology*, p. 262.

Dissentients in Institutional Offices.—Not every functionary is satisfied with the rules of his office, whether these rules be implicit or explicit. Despite the screening which he has had to survive while preparing to assume such responsibilities and enjoy the accompanying benefits, he may still be restless. He may reveal an urge to make drastic reforms, to be the prophet of a new Utopia-like era, or to otherwise diverge from the "working constitution" of his institution. For example, St. Francis of Assisi, a functionary in the medieval Roman Catholic Church, diverged from his expected role and led a new religious movement which was only later recognized by the original institution from which it grew. Another instance is Martin Luther, who, in attempting drastic reforms, was cut off from the original institution of which he was a functionary and became the founder of the Protestant Reformation. Similar restlessness in the functionaries of other institutions has given rise to new political parties, to new systems of education, and to new national policies.

In a society in which the broadening of institutional responsibilities is a common occurrence, the demand for new divisions of labor with respect to institutional offices is now expected procedure. The clerical leader is likely to receive a great deal of secular advice and even have pressed upon him the aid of a permanent lay functionary to manage the financial aspects of the institution and parish. The larger universities have a division of labor between academic leadership and business administration. The Canadian Pacific Railway has come to the conclusion that two heads are better than one and employs both a president of the railroad and a chairman of the board. These are just a few of the numerous examples which could be cited to document these tendencies toward divisions of labor.

Not only are traditional offices affected by new divisions of labor but, even where the office remains undivided, it has changed in character along with the development of the institution. Mark Hopkins at the end of a log with a student at the other is now no more a symbol of the university and its functionaries than is the hoe a symbol of American agriculture and the farmer. A comparison of the founding fathers and their associates in any area of institutional life with their present-day successors shows clearly how susceptible to modification by changing circumstances are the prerogatives and duties of office.

Chapter 12

SOCIAL INSTITUTIONS (Continued)

Specific social institutions will now be analyzed in four classifications based on their functions: (1) institutions concerned with transmitting the social heritage, (2) instrumental institutions, (3) regulative institutions, and (4) integrative institutions. Although this represents a classification of social institutions, it should be remembered that no rigid categorization of institutions is possible. To some degree, all institutions have all four functions. Even with the highly specialized divisions of labor in Western civilization, institutional overlapping is pronounced. Each institution can be fully understood only by keeping in mind that it is a phase of the total social system. With this limitation in mind, groups of institutions will be analyzed in that category in which their primary functions may be analyzed most readily.

Transmission of the Social Heritage

Under this heading, the family, the school, and the church in its teaching activity, will be studied. Since other sections of this text have carried references to primitive forms of family life, this section will direct attention chiefly to the modern family. Nevertheless, those characteristics which are common to family life everywhere will be discussed.

The Family Group.—The *larger family group* includes grandparents, parents, and their children, in fact all those living who, by birth, marriage, and adoption, bear the family name. More tentatively, those long dead and those yet to bear its name may also be reckoned as belonging to it. The *smaller family group* includes parents and their unmarried children and is the family institutional unit in our mobile civilization. On it falls the responsibility for child care and other functions which are commonly associated with family life. With us the larger kinship group is not formally organized to perform specific functions as was the *undivided household* of ancient Russia and the organized kinship groups of other peoples.

However, in our less mobile rural sections, a close relationship exists between the larger kinship group and the institutional unit. The main effect of this proximity to kin is to keep the smaller family group more effectively under the control of family tradition and thus enhance its solidarity.

Biological Basis of Family Behavior.—First, there is the sex differentiation of the parents. Secondly, with the advent of children, there are divisions of age, denoting on the one hand the strength and stability of adult life and on the other the dependence and plasticity of childhood. Thirdly, there are the individual differences (other than sex) which condition still further the divisions of labor within the family circle. Fourthly, there are the inherited impulses which enter dynamically into the general attitude of sensitivity to the presence and behavior of other persons. The interdependence of these factors gives to the family group the semblance of a biological organism. However, family unity is very indirectly dependent on the interaction of purely physical factors, for the latter become socially conditioned from the outset. More specifically then, family unity results from the interaction of persons within a well-defined social heritage.

By *social heritage* is meant the whole complex of ideas and practices which have accumulated in the past and which are, in turn, transmitted to the present generation. In a broad sense the family heritage represents the accumulated experiences of family groups living under every known social system, ancient and modern. But the family heritage which has taken its form in western civilization affects our family groups far more dynamically than do those ideas about the family life of peoples living under life conditions vastly different from our own. One aspect of the general family heritage is the form of *marriage,* which Westermarck has defined "as a relation of one or more men to one or more women which is recognized by custom or law and involves certain rights and duties both in the case of the parties entering the union and in the case of the children born into it." [1] This definition is broad enough to represent the world-wide family heritage. Within it are included widely different forms of marriage such as monogamy and three forms of polygamy. These forms of marriage have reference primarily to the number of mates which men and women may have at one time as prescribed by custom and law.

---

[1] Edward Westermarck, *Short History of Marriage,* New York, The Macmillan Co., 1926, p. 1.

MONOGAMY. Monogamy is the type of marriage which unites one male and one female. It may co-exist in certain societies with other types of marriage, for polygamy may be only for those who have the necessary status. Monogamy may be modified by the custom of concubinage, whereby children are born to those within the family group who have not a status of wifehood. In no society have sexual relationships been confined within the marriage institution. While the conventional mores of western civilization show a prevalence in such a direction, there is connivance with prostitution and prematrimonial sex experiments. Monogamy as a form of marriage is monopolized by no single stage of cultural development. It is the most common form of the marriage relationship ranging from modern western civilization to the most primitive cultures.[2] The Bushmen, the Andamanese, and the Veddahs are strictly monogamous, and this type of family has never been completely supplanted in any human society.

POLYGAMY. Polygamy is the general term for the marriage of either a man or a woman with more than one mate. The term applied to the marriage of one man to several women is polygyny, and polyandry describes the situation when one woman has several husbands. Lowie adds a third polygamous custom, commonly known as group marriage.[3] Group marriage is a form of polygamous marriage in which a group of men and women share husbands and wives in common. It is also known by the name of sexual communism. This form of marriage has been closely associated with the notions of a primitive state of promiscuity advanced by Lubbock, Morgan, and other writers of the evolutionary school but successfully challenged by Westermarck and his school. There is no bona fide evidence of a primitive state of promiscuity; incest rules are in operation in all types of society, and, in the so-called group marriage, marital rights and duties are defined in the folkways and mores.

Selection of Mates and the Marriage Contract.—Another phase of the family heritage comprises rules for the selection of mates and some form of marriage agreement. These factors are associated with all forms of marriage, but, like the latter, they vary from one civilization to another. The policy of marrying outside one's own family and closely related kinship group, known as *exogamy,* is everywhere in evidence. Among primitive groups, marriage does not take place within the clan (or sib); that is, the group bearing the kinship name. Thus, the clan is the mechanism for defining what

---

[2] A. M. Tozzer, *Social Origins and Social Continuities*, New York, The Macmillan Co., 1925, p. 146.
[3] Robert H. Lowie, *Primitive Society*, New York, Boni & Liveright, 1920, p. 40.

relationships are exogamous. With us, marriage is not usually con-
tracted between persons who are more closely related than second
cousins.

Then, there are the practices in vogue for obtaining a bride such
as *bride capture, bride price,* or *romantic love.* While among some
primitive peoples there is fragmentary evidence of the practice of
bride capture, it was and is a relatively rare method of securing a
wife. Obtaining a wife by purchase, service, or the exchange of gifts
is much more prevalent. *Lobolo* among the Nkuma is an example
of bride price. With the Kamilaroi of New South Wales, brides are
simply exchanged between marrying groups. The story of Jacob illustrates the practice of serving the bride's family for a stipulated
period; among the Yukaghir of Siberia there is an exchange of gifts
between the contracting parties. The practice of giving a dowry
prevails among many peoples, in all stages of culture. While individual choice on the basis of romantic love prevails with us, considerations of money and status are not entirely absent.

The marriage agreement, verbal or written, may mention a few
details such as the transference of property and the names of the
contracting parties. More obviously, the marriage agreement and
the associated ritual which leads up to and concludes a marriage are
representative symbols of the more detailed obligations assumed in
connection with the status of marriage. These obligations in respect
to wife support, care of dependent children, the inheritance of property, and many other matters are defined in the customary practices
and ideas which the family group and community possess as a social
heritage. Certain kinsmen, matchmakers, and other community functionaries act in conjunction with the marrying persons in arranging
for and concluding the act of marriage. But on husband and wife,
particularly in the modern family, falls the permanent obligation
of making the family heritage a going concern. Up to this point
the analysis has dealt with the general family heritage which is a
phase of any civilization.

Within the more inclusive body of family practices and ideas,
which all members of the community share, is the distinctive heritage
of each of the contracting parties. This particular complex of family
experience is the accumulation of a series of lineally descended
families bearing a given name. It touches very closely the life of
the small family group. Rothenbuecher [4] states that a particular

---

[4] This subject of particular family heritages has been discussed at length by Rothenbuecher, *Ueber das Wesen des Geschichtlichen und die Gesellschaftlichen Gebilde,* Tübingen,
1926, pp. 11-18. This section was translated by E. C. Hughes and appeared in Dawson
and Gettys, *An Introduction to Sociology,* The Ronald Press Co., 1929, pp. 62-66.

family history had its beginning with a stern father; that is, with
the man who was distinguished by some special circumstance such
as bringing his family to a certain country or from a lower to a higher
class. Thus, the family begins with a wanderer; it comes to an end
with the death of the last male who bears the name. After that its
distinguishing heritages are soon broken up. The heritage which
distinguishes a given family line includes such elements as their status
in one of the major class divisions of the community, their leanings
toward and achievements in certain occupations or callings, their
manner of participation in religious, educational, political, and other
social institutions, and their material possessions and family ritual.
It also includes an appreciation of the fame, honor, and rank of the
more distinguished members of their family line. On its more subjective side the family background includes the position and treatment of the various members within the series of small family groups
and the feeling that, for better or worse, they belong together. These
inherited social traits are less uniform and stable in young families.

The Process of Organization in the Small Family Group.—The
formally organized family group of parents and their children (actual
or potential) is the family institution in western civilization. It is
the actual unit in community organization which is socially and
legally responsible for the performance of specific family functions.
Supplementary institutions, however, may take over part or all of
its functions if it becomes disorganized. Its organization is not
complete with the act of marriage registration. Aided by the initial
resources of romantic attachment and community expectation, the
members of the family group proceed to define their objectives and
develop administrative organization in accordance with the family
heritage. The achievement of stability in family life requires many
years, although the time element is just one aspect of this whole
process.

The process of family organization is complicated by many factors.
In the first place, the new family unit represents the merging of two
family lines, each of which has its own sayings, ambitions, ritual,
personages, prides, prejudices, and notions about the routine of life.
These lines of cleavage may be further accentuated by differences in
class, in race, and in religion, though in the great majority of marriages these latter barriers are not crossed. Thus, family adjustments within the family circle are facilitated by a measure of
endogamy; one marries outside his own family and nearly related
kinsmen, but ordinarily not outside his own kind. This is important

in our civilization where the contracting parties, though forming a separate family unit bearing the name of the husband, continue bilaterally their connections with the families of the husband and wife. Frequently members of one or both families live temporarily or permanently in the new household. In any case, distinctive family backgrounds are not merged in a new family unit without a struggle.

Secondly, the social nurture of husband and wife in their own families, particularly if these families were unstable, may have pronounced personality defects and bizarre social points of view which turn out to be disturbing elements in the new family situation. Even when their upbringing has been effective and wholesome there are differences in attitudes toward life which, when allied with divergent family traditions, intensify the difficulties of family organization. Then, too, all families must face crises caused by sickness, occupational failure, financial loss, conflicts with other family groups, and various social disappointments. Such crises test to the limit the family's resourcefulness and stability.

Thirdly, the organization essential for the realization of appropriate family objectives allows for a reasonably satisfactory status on the part of each member of the family circle. Each person tends to play the role determined by his own traditions and made to harmonize with the expectations of his neighbors. But these traditional roles are modified to fit the aptitudes and struggle for status of persons in a new family situation. There is bound to be repression and frustration on the part of parents and children, and if such conditions become chronic they may, through their cumulative effects, produce personal and family instability which may be imposed on unborn generations. In the great majority of families, however, the members achieve a status in keeping with their position as functionaries and in accordance with the necessities of their social nature.

Fourthly, the process of family organization is only partially subject to the will and wit of its members. Much more than most of us realize, family organization is a natural and tentative growth stimulated in certain directions by neighborhood conditions and also responding unself-consciously to the unobtrusive changes taking place in community institutions. Then, too, there is a deep undercurrent of family feeling in most families which sweeps aside the cool calculations of the administrative mind and determines unintended trends in family organization. Nevertheless, family life in our civilization demands much forethought.

In the fifth place, one functionary must bear the chief responsibility for keeping the family a going concern. He plans for future contingencies, senses what is involved in a crisis, keeps attention and affection from centering too obviously on one member of the family, is alert to the problem of overdirection in child care, keeps to the fore the emotional dependence of the family members, and makes sure that authority exists though kept in the background. This chief functionary in administering family affairs in most civilizations is the husband. Even with our tendencies toward an equalitarian family, something of the older patriarchal authority is still vested in the husband by tradition and contingency. Frequently, the major responsibility in family administration falls on the wife's shoulders, but usually the chief authority in respect to administrative strategy reposes in the husband, and the wife is the chief social technician. The husband's authoritative role (though moderate) is in a large measure due to his importance as the main breadwinner. Family stability is closely linked with the fact that the husband has a permanent and reasonably remunerative occupation in the local community. When the family's economic means remain at or near the subsistence level, its stability, resting on a sense of community status and social perspective, is reduced to a minimum.

Most families achieve a stable organization. They are going concerns, possessing common objectives even though defined and realized with difficulty. Each has common feeling and at times a very vivid sense of belonging together. Its members mutually share a sense of the family's worth in comparison with other families. Furthermore, the family can perform functions in the development of personality which no other institution can accomplish except in very special cases. Indeed, a family must be very ineffective when a foster home is called upon to take over the care of its children. In most families, some person, whether it is the husband, wife, son, or daughter, possesses the administrative sense which enables those families to survive their crises.

Functions of the Family.—The family, as institutionalized in custom and law, is the socially sanctioned mechanism controlling the reproduction of children and assuring racial continuity. Not all children are born within the socially sanctioned family, as our illegitimacy figures clearly show. The presence of prostitution and clandestine sexual satisfactions reveal the fact that sexual life has not been completely regulated within the marriage tie, although this is an authentic social ideal.[5]

---

[5] See: A. C. Kinsey, W. B. Pomeroy, and C. E. Martin, *Sexual Behavior in the Human Male*, Philadelphia, W. B. Saunders Co., 1948.

The family is the chief agency for the development of personality and at the same time is the chief agency for the transmission of the cultural heritages from the older to the younger generation. Burgess has emphasized the point that these two processes are one. "It is, indeed, in the circumstances of this cultural transmission and in the interaction of the family and its members with the environing community that modifications and conditionings of the personalities of all the members of the family take place." [6] The long period of infancy and childhood, during which the human being is dependent upon the family, emphasizes the importance of this function, even though this phase of family responsibility is being shared more and more by the school, playground, church, and other types of social organization. This socializing and humanizing of the child within this small and intimate social unit makes the family a vantage ground for his membership in the larger society that surrounds the family. Closely connected with the personal development of the child is his emotional dependence upon other persons. The chief satisfaction of the need of the human being for response from others takes place within the family circle. Furthermore, the child not only discovers his own status in respect to other members of the family group, but through the family, in large measure, obtains his status in the community in which it is a unit of social organization.

The family is also a mechanism for the inheritance of property. In fact, the earning of a livelihood and the bequeathal of property have been very important factors in the development of the family institution. We have a long record of marriages taking place because a wife could accomplish important tasks in the household and, incidentally, add to the prestige of the family and kinship group which she had entered by contract. This economic unity has, at least until the present, been an important factor in the social unity of the family.

Family Disorganization.—Family life does not always achieve stable organization. Divorce, separation, and desertion statistics (especially in North America) are indicative of extensive family disorganization, particularly in urban areas. Family disorganization is no doubt a far more widespread phenomenon than such statistics indicate for they deal only with those cases where the process is practically complete. Nor do such statistics measure the extent of disorganization in areas where divorce or legal separation are not

---

[6] E. W. Burgess, "The Family and the Person," *Proc. Am. Sociol. Soc.*, Vol. 22, 1927, p. 134.

socially favored means of dealing with deep-rooted family antagonisms. It is apparent from observation that very many husbands and wives from legally dissolved families have established stable families in their second matrimonial ventures. It has not yet been established by systematic research how extensive is the stability of the families of previously divorced persons. The startling publicity given to a small number of repeaters who have passed through the divorce courts several times has left a distorted picture in the public mind.

Increase in marriage in recent decades, particularly in the lower-age groups, indicates marked continuity of interest in the family institution. This is further supported by the fact that the great majority of first marriages are relatively stable and satisfying. This may perhaps be true also of the marriages of many of the previously divorced.

Family instability seems, in the main, to be a function of the general social disorganization of highly urbanized areas.[7] In areas of extreme mobilization of persons and ideas from widely different regions of the world, the general social heritage is in a state of flux. Consequently, ideas associated with family life are in a state of collision and redefinition. Sacred beliefs vie with secular ideas and the latter with each other. Members of family groups are confused in the conceptions of their roles; the community's expectation in regard to these roles is equally uncertain. Under such conditions, a marked individualization of the aims and interests of the person ensues. That the definition and administration of family objectives frequently break down under such conditions is not astonishing; it is remarkable that disorganization is not more extensive. This individualization of life has been going on for centuries, particularly since the Reformation, and with added tempo since the Industrial Revolution. Its peak is in industrialized sections of North America. Two trends are likely to become increasingly evident: first, it is probable that, with mass immigration at an end for this continent and its main frontiers peopled, a stabilization of community life will take place; secondly, the development of forms of family organization will be in keeping with the needs of an individualistic age.

However, even with the possible disappearance of much of the strain placed upon the family by present community instability, family disorganization will be lessened but it will not disappear. In fact, some measure of family disorganization is present in every type of

---

[7] Yet within the city there are sections in which little family disorganization is apparent.

society and all peoples have their divorce arrangements. Where there are life and growth there is always some disorganization, but it is relative to organization. *Family disorganization* is either a failure to define and to achieve fully those family objectives which satisfy the wishes of its members, or it is the dissolution of those objectives which had been defined. In the latter, disorganization is a process involving a series of tensions associated with major life interests. The conflict manifested in these tension situations becomes increasingly chronic and its forms, rather than the performance of customary functions, absorb family attention. All this is a matter of degree. A family may be said to be seriously disorganized when some of its members, or functionaries from supplementary institutions, reach the decision that it is not a going concern with respect to one or more of its main functions. Such decisions are often arbitrary and fictional, but they reflect the fact that status within the family and the latter's status in the community are very uncertain.

To know the nature of the process of family disorganization is a step toward its solution. A body of knowledge dealing with family life is being assembled. It will be utilized by the professions which deal with families which are maladjusted. It will also be of use in planning prevention. Much of this knowledge, when fully tested, will find its way through the channels of education and publicity into the mental equipment of persons in general who, so equipped, will be in a better position to solve their own family problems.

Educational Institutions.—The school is closely allied with the family in transmitting the social heritage and in developing the personality. Indeed, the teacher acts in the capacity of a substitute parent to the child throughout the greater part of the day, exercising authority, supervising activities, and transmitting certain aspects of the cultural heritage. In the case of boarding schools, the substitute parent responsibilities of the teacher are even more pronounced. The school and the family are also allied in their work because the parents of the child usually take an active part in his education, cooperating with the teacher, tutoring him at home in his studies, and interpreting his school experiences to him.

Although the child in our society spends many of his waking hours in acquiring a systematically organized and standardized education, among many other peoples this is not the case. In other parts of the world where education is not compulsory or the general rule, the child takes over the social heritage of his parents quite informally by observing adults and older children and by imitating their activities in his play. By the time he reaches adulthood, he is master of the folklore, technology, and the rational explanations of the social order of his society.[8] The dominant theme in primitive education is the inculcation of the proper standards of behavior, or, in other words, a strict adherence to the mores. Included in this is a clear recognition and acceptance of the control exercised by the elders and leaders of his society. In such an educational procedure, the climax comes with the initiation ceremonies which make young men and women members of the adult society. Frequently these initiation ceremonies cover extended periods of time in which the young adults face ordeals and receive detailed instruction in the treasured secrets of their people.

While the forms of education found in the western world have become elaborately organized, they possess something in common with the more primitive types of education. Respect for elders and conformity to the mores are stressed in our schools in many ways. In spite of the emphasis placed on the dissemination of scientific knowledge, our schools spend much of their time in transmitting traditional values and the folklore of the society to the child. and in equipping him to be a satisfactory member of his society. The programs of the schools make for social continuity with the past. New ideas do get taught in the schools but, unless they fit into the underlying social heritage, they meet with bitter opposition. Examples can be found in the teaching of the biological and social sciences. The theory of evolution goes contrary to the teachings of the more fundamentalist religious groups and the theory of the relativity of "right" and "wrong" behavior as put forward by the social sciences finds many opponents in all phases of community life. An adequate indoctrination in ancient wisdom prevents quick acceptance of new ideas.

In literate societies, the schools transmit vast areas of human experience to the young. It is the function of the schools to make available the accumulated and accumulating knowledge of mankind to them. Due to limitations in time and energy and due to the interests of the groups controlling education, the material contained in most school texts is very narrowly selected. Yet the contents of the school books change with time, along with circumstances and educational leadership. Nevertheless, they continue to transmit the more conservative elements of the social heritage. Even though social change is speeded up by the broadening of individual experience through the

---

[8] See Chapter 3.

curricula, the schools are rarely the intentional advocates or promoters of an altered social order.

During his school years, the person's mind is disciplined and organized. He becomes literate, learns to compare, differentiate, select, and integrate ideas. He learns to think systematically. At this time the groundwork is laid for further development in scientific objectivity. Among the illiterate, the rudiments of scientific method are present in varying degrees but it is only with the development and expansion of literacy that they may be expected to flourish.

Since the central function of the school is the transmission of the accumulated experience of mankind in general terms, the professional leaders of the educational institutions are constantly on the defensive against the pressure of groups in the society who wish to install partisan ideas within the curriculum. As the public schools are the representatives of the community, they are expected to be the most successful in keeping the school program out of the hands of doctrinaires.

There is no way of isolating the emotions of the child from the remainder of his mental life. Yet, only too often, teachers lose sight of the former by an overemphasis on intellectualism. The child is growing up under the care of the teacher in the role of substitute parent and the social relations of the child with his teacher and others in the school situation are an inevitable part of his educational process. While it is informal, this phase of education can be used with benefit to add to the teachability of the child by using his immediate social awareness to give him greater knowledge of himself and of the world he lives in.

Religious Institutions in Their Teaching Activities.—In conjunction with the more secularized educational institutions, the teaching activities of the church are carried on as one of the most emphasized functions of that religious institution. The church specializes in rendering intelligible the beliefs, doctrines, and creeds which express its faith. Most great religions have their Bibles in which the main tenets of their beliefs are recorded and these books occupy a central place in the development of their religious ideas. In developing and organizing these ideas in the mind of the child, the church provides Sunday schools, associations, and other educational groups which prepare him for church membership. The functionaries, or teachers, in such religious schools are usually devotees with little or no professional training to prepare them for this task. The clergy, who have spent many years in acquiring education which prepares them for leadership in the church at a professional level, rarely take more than a supervisory part in the child's religious education.[9]

The church attempts to present the idealism and systematic organization of beliefs which support its religion and inspire each new generation. The church seeks to make its beliefs control the behavior of its members, by surrounding man's moral obligations in all phases of his life with deeply felt conviction that the faithful will discover a power stronger than themselves making for righteousness and by holding forth the reward of a future life for those who adhere to its moral code.

INSTRUMENTAL INSTITUTIONS

Although all institutions are instrumental in that they represent an organized means of satisfying some continuing need for those who make use of them, there are institutions which have extremely limited goals and highly rational and impersonal techniques for reaching them. The latter type of institution we term *instrumental*. For example, from the point of view of the doctor, the hospital is an instrument for carrying on his medical career. Without access to it, he would be limited in his treatment of patients and therefore could not advance professionally to any great extent. For this reason an intense struggle goes on among many young medical men to gain an affiliation with a good hospital to which their patients may be admitted under their care. Once this has been accomplished, the young doctor finds the specialist's division of labor, the equipment, techniques, and administrative organization which enable him to provide treatment in an assembly-line fashion.

Another such instrumental institution is the hotel, which provides the traveling public with a room, services, and sometimes food, in return for cash payment. The temporary possession of a room permits the isolation of a hermit on the loose. As long as the traveler pays his bill and causes no bother to his fellow hotel dwellers, he is accorded civil treatment. Hotels, like other institutions, are selective of their clientele. This selection on the basis of social class and race maintains their drawing power.

Factories are also instrumental institutions. Their goal is to produce articles which can be sold profitably. They maintain only such labor as will keep the assembly line in motion. If a new

---

[9] This is especially true of Protestant churches.

machine is invented which can be used more profitably than man-power, the men are displaced by it. Management may attempt to cut down the restlessness of its workers by providing working conditions beyond the standard legal requirements. (Nevertheless, there are no substitutes for adequate wages, job security, the recognition of the worth of the individual worker, and the collective power of the workmen.)

Similarly, department stores give goods and services for which they are paid. The personality and behavior of the clerk make little difference to a transaction and it is only his ability to supply goods quickly and efficiently which is important to the customer and to the management of the store. The consumer pays a standardized price, except for a very small group of functionaries who may receive mark-downs or special consideration, due to their positions. Protestations of service in the advertising of the institution may cloud the real nature of its goals. The clerk may express solicitude for the wishes of the buyer, and wear a mask of service, but such disguises are easily broken down when the marketing purpose of the institution is kept in mind and if behavior is closely observed. For example, if the buyer shows untoward delay and indecision in making his purchase, coolness and even hostility may be the response of the clerk to his sales resistance.

Only a few examples of instrumental institutions have been dealt with. Other institutions which come under this heading are banks, public utilities, and a host of others.

REGULATIVE INSTITUTIONS

To some degree, all institutions are regulative. In our society, the family has certain responsibilities respecting the inheritance of property as defined by law. Husbands, wives, and children have rights which are protected by legal regulations. School attendance is controlled by law and supported by the mores. Responding to the school bell, "punching the clock," kneeling or bowing the head for prayer in church, signing into and out of a hotel room, and fitting into all the daily routines of life, are examples of regulation on a formal or informal basis.

However, in this chapter we are mainly concerned with the more formally organized aspects of regulated social behavior. In the com-munity, the municipal government sets up and enforces building codes which determine the height of buildings, their structural materials, and their safety devices. Each home is subject to housing standards enforced by municipal laws. The municipal government constantly observes and supervises the hygienic practices of rooming houses, restaurants, theaters, and hotels and sets forth their responsibilities in law. Street railways, buses, and other public utilities are subject to city, state, or provincial charters.

In addition, it is customary to safeguard the public interest in such matters by a municipal or state commission. No building, however humble, can be built without the permission of municipal authorities. No business can escape submitting to licensing or incorporation procedures. Those citizens who drive cars, or even bicycles, come under a licensing system. Policemen, aided by traffic lights, guide both car drivers and pedestrians at high density points of traffic. One-way streets and parking rules have become familiar to all who drive automobiles in urban areas. The householders of the community are often given mimeographed sheets which instruct them in the use of their garbage containers and where they are to be placed in relation to city streets. Within all urban districts, the web of municipal regulative activities, backed by police power, is steadily spreading out to include new areas of life.

With the popularization of city planning, which has been greatly stimulated by urban traffic problems, cities are being zoned for industry, for commercial establishments, and for various types of housing. While the success of such detailed restrictions of land use depends upon how well they conform to the natural pattern of city growth, they are drawing a tighter net about the planning of individual entrepreneurs and householders. For example, a home built above the "Montrose line," [10] in Westmount, an incorporated city which is a part of Greater Montreal,[11] must be of higher standards in materials and costs than one built below this line. The details involved are precisely stated in Westmount's building code.

An example of a regulative institution which planned the development of a whole region is the Tennessee Valley Authority, which was set up by the United States Government in May, 1933. The region over which it had jurisdiction was the Tennessee River Valley, a geographic, economic, and cultural natural area, cutting across several states. The commissioners of the Tennessee Valley Authority interpreted its aims to be the maximum social and economic development of a retarded region. This included the control of floods and soil erosion through better farming methods, dams,

---

10 The "Montrose line" is delineated by one of the city streets, named Montrose.
11 See discussion of Montreal in Chapter 10.

reforestation, the production of electric power, and the development of all other natural resources to the greatest social benefit.

The Tennessee Valley Authority decided to carry out its plans by democratic means. No development would take place without the voluntary consent and the cooperation of the people concerned, with whom the technicians of the Authority worked closely. In addition, the Authority treated the whole area as an interdependent unit. The control of the river could not be considered apart from the effects of the development on industrial and farming improvements, and vice versa. No development could be considered apart from its effects upon the people. Thus, the powers exercised by the Authority were not drastic because they did not interfere coercively with the lives of the people or with the economy of the valley states. Obviously, building a chain of dams to ease the Tennessee River down its course and protect the valley's inhabitants from seasonal floods did require the inundation of many square miles of inhabited territory. The families who were displaced by the building of these dams were compensated by being transferred, with their consent, to new holdings equal in value to those they had left and where equally good institutional services were provided for them.

In addition, the valley people were encouraged to make use of the cheap fertilizers which the new power development made available. Farmers were advised as to the productive advantages of breaking away from traditional crops and cultivation procedures and adopting new scientific agricultural methods. If they were to have the advantage of cheap fertilizers and competent agricultural advice, they were expected to follow the newer methods of cultivation and crop rotation. They were encouraged to do this but they were left to follow their antiquated agricultural methods if these continued to be precious to them. The more progressive farmers in the valley followed the new techniques and made use of the cheap fertilizer. Soon their farms became models which demonstrated the advantages to their more skeptical neighbors. When the latter saw the increased production and prosperity of the model (or demonstration) farms, the majority of them began to follow the new agricultural methods.

The Tennessee Valley Authority used similar methods for expanding the use of electricity and setting up ports on the river which had been made navigable. Electricity at low rates was made available to the whole region. Voluntary associations were formed to popularize its use. Within the general framework of flood control, the new electrical and navigational resources, the citizens of the Tennessee Valley were left free to accept the improvements offered to them by the Tennessee Valley Authority or to follow their own definition of the North American way of life.[12]

Financial institutions usually come under direct incorporation by state, provincial, or federal governments. Commercial houses are not merely incorporated but are also subject to inspection by state, provincial, or federal authorities. They may be called upon to make reports and exhibit their books to those who are entrusted with their supervision in the interest of public security. When many industrial concerns "folded up" during the world-wide depression of the early nineteen thirties, the excessive losses suffered by investors led to the enforcement of more stringent forms of incorporation.

Certain basic establishments may be taken over entirely by the nation or its constituent states. Long ago the post office ceased to be a privately owned institution. Such common carriers as railroads, steamship lines, and airlines have in many countries become objects of federal ownership and administration. For example, in Canada, the Trans-Canada Airlines and the Canadian National Railways are government-owned and operated.

National constitutions determine which regulative institutions are to be federal and which are to be in the hands of the constituent states or provinces. Education and health institutions have national advisory bodies, but direct jurisdiction over both is divided between state (or provincial) and municipal authorities. In Canada, a provincial department licenses teachers and supervises the schools. The doctors of a province comprise a College of Physicians and Surgeons which acts for the province in supervising the admission of all new doctors to professional status. In Canada and the United States social security is organized on a national basis but the provinces and states have particular responsibilities defined by the federal government. If the individual state or province decides to stay outside the national security program, it is privileged to do so. In Canada, criminal law and the penitentiaries are national rather than provincial responsibilities. Regulations as to immigration and citizenship are on a national basis in both countries. All navigable waterways are regulated by the federal governments.

Most countries have a national army and a national police force, even where they are not to be designated as "police states." There is a much greater centralization of administration in England than in

---

[12] David Lilienthal, *TVA: Democracy on the March*, New York, Harper & Bros., 1944; Herman Finer, *The TVA; Lesson for International Application*, Montreal, The International Labour Office, 1944; Julian Huxley, *TVA: Adventure in Planning*, Cheam, England, Architectural Press, 1943; R. L. Duffus, *The Valley and Its People*, New York, Alfred A. Knopf, 1944.

either the United States or Canada. For example, in England, in-corporation is a function of the Board of Trade, a national institution.

In times of great emergency, the nation may extend its powers over private enterprise and individual choice of employment. If these are not considered to be "in the national interest," they are curtailed until the crisis has passed. For example, during the Second World War, students of the physical sciences were given every encourage-ment to remain in the universities and prepare themselves for duty on a highly technical level. They were given a great degree of leeway as to what they might decide to do after graduation. Not so with potential teachers, for the national emergency could, in a large meas-ure, dispense with their preparation for educational service. At present the physical sciences have not returned from the recent "war front." As a pressure group subsidized by the federal government they have succeeded in extending the period of emergency, both for-mally and informally. Perhaps in the future, as at present, the dis-tinction between war and peace may not be as sharp as it has been in the past. If this is so, we shall have a new definition of "in the national interest," and government control may be extended to new areas of life previously governed by individual choice.

Regulative activities are not limited to the agencies of government. Private clubs determine who can fish, play golf, or associate in many other ways under their entrance regulations. All institutions and associations have rules to which their members must conform. Regulations are so extensive in our civilization that we are always conscious of them. Beyond these formal restrictions are the informal understandings which give a margin of flexibility to all areas of changing human relationships.

INTEGRATIVE INSTITUTIONS

Integration at an Informal Level.—In simpler societies than ours, the individual comprehends the whole range of social life because he participates in most, if not all, of its constituent institutions. With the prevailing complexity of institutions and associations in our society, no one person ever gets an over-all perspective of every aspect of social life. Persons play roles in a wide variety of institutions, for example, the family, labor union, church, and political party. For the majority of individuals, this list can be greatly extended.

Although they may not sense it, all people are intermediaries of culture. They are forced to reconcile the overlapping demands of the institutions to which they owe allegiance of a formal or informal type. In order that the person can retain his own personal integrity, religious ideals must be made consistent with standard business and political practices. As a family man, a person must accept obligations imposed by government such as the payment of school taxes and the provision of educational equipment. His patriotism is given a somber touch by the eligibility of his children for military service.

Membership in institutions tends to overlap. The permutations and combinations of institutional membership which are possible, even within a stable neighborhood, are tremendous. The men work in a wide range of economic institutions; the women have varied club affiliations and shop at different commercial establishments; the children are divided between public, private, and parochial schools; and the families worship at a variety of churches. In each institution in which he takes part, the person finds others whose selection of institutional affiliations differs from his own. Thus men of widely divergent institutional membership can come together in any one specific institution, exchange points of view, and modify one another's perspectives. In time, men come to possess a common understanding which goes far beyond the few institutions and associations to which they give priority.

Without plan or formal organization, the person is given an informal means of integrating his experience and the culture of his society. Each individual is an unofficial ambassador of societal integration. Of course, there are men who formalize these trends by arranging their connections with business firms and associations for the purpose of exploiting them. Some have striven to enter the clubs and associations which seem most useful as a means of furthering their own goals. In our society, to expand calculated contacts seems to be in line with enlightened self-interest.

Informal Integration With Respect to Class.—The institutions, associations, and informal cliques [13] to which a member of our society belongs act as integrating forces in establishing superordinate and subordinate statuses and in expressing prestige. They are also inte-

---

[13] An *association* is "a type of grouping [which] arranges individuals in a structure which does not crosscut the whole society, but characteristically includes some and excludes others. . . . [A] person joins it instead of being born into it. . . . The association may be formally organized with rules of entrance and exit, with additional regulations controlling the behavior of its members. [However,] certain associations may be informal; that is to say, the rules . . . are customary rather than explicitly stated. . . . [T]here is a feeling that the group is 'ours,' that a member should do and not do certain things lest he offend those who belong to his association. There is ordinarily a close identity among the various members and usually a feeling of intimacy among them." W. L. Warner and P. S. Lunt, *The Social Life of a Modern Community*, New Haven, Yale University Press, 1941, p. 32. An example of an association would be a country club or a fraternal order. A *clique* is the immediate social group composed of the close friends and constant companions of an individual.

grative in the sense that they link the social classes together to give the society a loosely knit class structure which permits mobility from one stratum to the next (whether upward or downward) and makes possible a wide range of interclass contact.

In the Western World, three major classes are recognized: the Upper Class, the Middle Class, and the Lower Class. These can be subdivided further. For example, Warner and Lunt,[14] in their study of Yankee City, used the categories of Upper-Upper Class, Lower-Upper Class, Upper-Middle Class, Lower-Middle Class, Upper-Lower Class and Lower-Lower Class. In each they discovered characteristic behavior. For example, in the Upper Class, wealth played a part in determining status, but it was not necessarily more important than a background of generations of white Americans of Upper Class position. Financial and professional achievements were also of importance. Professional reputation, in particular, depended upon opportunity and ability to attain the educational goals prescribed by such bodies as ministerial, legal, and medical associations.

In North America, the differentiation between classes is both obscure and informal. In almost any sizable community, those who preside at meetings and lay cornerstones are persons who are considered to be Upper Class and to have general social prestige. The acquisition of such high status is due to social inheritance, opportunity, ambition, and a knowledge of techniques for manipulating social relationships. Those of lesser prestige expect these few to play their roles well and to add to the status of their communities or even of their nations. These Upper Class people may belong to the status associations which enforce and express their prestige; for example, associations which permit their daughters to become debutantes and their sons to occupy equally obvious social positions. Below them are ranked a long series of lesser statuses, with the least advantaged groups at the bottom. In an analysis of class structure, statistics are of little use. In determining class position, the nebulous and current gradations of social appraisal must be taken into account. Such appraisal has little to do with such tangible factors as the achievement of high ethical standards, for example. Men of good will, good judgment, and personal integrity are not monopolized by any one class.

In our dynamic society, class ideals are considered an important phase of human motivation. If one achieves distinction in war or peace, however lowly his previous estate, he will find it difficult to

---

14 *Ibid.*, p. 88.

resist the blandishments from above. He is invited, "glad-handed," feted, and encouraged to identify his rank with those he had once considered his superiors in rank. When one has unwittingly placed his feet on the lower rungs of this precarious social ladder, he is in a position to enter the cliques and associations on the next rung. A series of overlapping memberships in cliques and associations connect him with others in the class scale. As one goes up the rungs of this ladder, the pressure of ambition and, perhaps, ascription push more insistently upward. This overlapping of associational memberships facilitates interclass contacts. The groups higher up on the ladder look on those below during these social contacts and select for advancement those whom they feel would "fit in" with their way of life, rejecting others who are not up to their standards. The process by which the selection is made is rarely conscious or organized. On this informal basis, all social divisions of a given society afford open channels for integration.

However, class structure does function as a whole. Hughes states:

One must remember that social classes are not merely separate groups of people: they constitute a system of related groups. In the charitable organization the donors and the workers tend to come from one class; the recipients from another. The English Catholics of Cantonville, although a few of them are of the lower middle class ordinarily active in St. Vincent de Paul societies here and elsewhere, have not, like the French of the same class, any web of relationships or any sense of identification with the poor of this community. The poor of Cantonville are not the poor of the English people, Protestant or Catholic.[15]

In conclusion, it may be said that, while classes are not formally organized, the members participate most freely in those institutions and associations which are correlated with socially designated class status. For example, in Yankee City, the Lower-Middle Class took part mainly in men's fraternal organizations and semiauxiliaries. The Upper-Middle Class women had a high participation in social clubs and both sexes took part in charitable and economic associations.[16]

Religious Institutions in an Integrative Role.—Religions vary greatly in their dogmas and rituals but they have this in common: a belief in supernatural support for those who attempt to live the "good life," as defined by their faith; and a belief in something better and

---

[15] Everett C. Hughes, *French Canada in Transition*, Chicago, University of Chicago Press, 1943, p. 125f.
[16] Warner and Lunt, *The Social Life of a Modern Community*, Chs. 20-21.

stronger than themselves. The latter belief is the essence of religion. Many groups and individuals thrill to the notion of being the chosen instruments of a divine purpose. Frequently, sincere devotion or long-drawn-out suffering forms the basis of religious convictions. However, modification of this idealism is widespread. Smugness tends to adulterate religious faith and enables many to think more highly of themselves than their religious achievements warrant. Yet there have always been those who believe, and who live according to their faith. However few these may be statistically, they form the unit core of religious institutions everywhere. Those who exemplify the essence of the integrity of religious institutions cut across all national and ethnic barriers.

The integrative tendency of religion may be shown in its community-wide, nation-wide, and world-wide championship of what religious leaders consider "right" and "good." While Roman Catholics and Protestant churches vary somewhat in the compromises they are willing to make, all, in their mores, are opposed to divorce, to birth control, to a double standard of morals, to exhibitionistic displays of sex in costume and art, to humorous portrayals of the functions of priests, and to political interference. Religious groups resist the present-day tendencies toward secularization. This is particularly emphasized in their struggle to keep religion to the fore in public schools, colleges, and universities.

The growth of science has given religious leaders much concern. They have always had to defend their faith in the face of new explanations which challenged older statements of their faith. In the process, religion has come into the possession of a frontier which seems forever beyond the dictates and knowledge of the natural sciences. Beyond precise science is the world of "make believe" (as in art), the need to believe where we cannot prove, and the will to believe. Religious institutions, in attempting to retain a consistent faith including or in spite of scientific discoveries and new theories, interpret and integrate the relationship between the unknown and the known for their followers.

Everywhere religion is faced with the challenges of secularization and indifference. These facts are not new. They have marked all periods of written history. The extended publicity given to religious problems is a function of our elaborate means of communication. It is now easier to locate the friends and enemies of one's religion. This has given a push toward the alignment of those who strive to support a "good life" with an austerity far beyond the striving of most religious devotees.

Religious institutions have integrative functions which affect the individual. Through the teachings of their faith, they provide a moral code and a faith in a deity which give meaning, orientation, and motivation to personal behavior.

Political Integration.—In our western world, political parties take over the machinery of government and administer national or local governments. To do this effectively, a degree of assent must be gained for their policies and practices. Each party presents its goals to the electorate and seeks its support. Majority approval means that the chief functionaries of government will be members of the victorious party. Even then, the continued allegiance of the electorate is needed by those forming the government established by the victorious party. Its appointees must represent the regional and, in some cases, the ethnic diversities of the nation, its constituent states, and even municipalities. Thus political parties act as integrating forces in a nation. In Canada, for example, French Canadians, who comprise 32 per cent of Canada's population, demand a proportionate membership in the federal cabinet. While the English Catholic group in Canada is not large, it rates at least one cabinet representative. Then there is regional representation from British Columbia, the Prairie Provinces, the central industrial provinces, and the Maritimes. Other powerful groups demanding recognition provide additional incentives to "representative government." Beyond these special interest groups, the loyalty of the common man to parties, whether Liberal, Conservative, Republican, Democratic, or Labor, is perennially sought. Failure to retain dominant public support means defeat for the party in power.

In times when one of the contesting parties has not been able to form a cabinet along strict party lines, the dominant party enters into an arrangement with contesting groups in the establishment of a coalition government. This has been true of France recently, of Great Britain in World War II, and of Canada in World War I. In World War II an effort was made to include in the Cabinet and other administrative offices in the United States those who were at least nominal members of the opposition party, thus ensuring the government of the support of almost all the country's citizens.

This integrative principle extends far beyond the device of coalition government. The leaders of an administration that is strictly Republican or Democratic are under the constant necessity of associating all groups of the nation with its objectives. These goals are defined periodically in order to retain and increase the national following. In part, this definition takes place in the House of Representatives (or the House of Commons). The program of the current administration is criticized by the party in opposition and compromises emerge which are weighted in terms of the power and prestige of the contending parties. Forever edging in and lobbying are all those who seek the fulfilment of special objectives, whether on behalf of the few or the many.

Another integrative function of modern governments is seen in the activities of the civil services, which have been greatly extended. Higher-placed members of the civil services have become familiar with such problems as those of race relations, labor relations, immigration, health, and regional conflicts. They are the technical advisors of government and, although constantly threatened by the purgative powers of new administrators, their influence is widespread. Far more than most people realize, the civil services charter the course of nations and municipalities. They represent a measure of political integration and stability beyond that obtained by temporary political administrations.

Finally, a party long in power aligns itself with all the major institutions in a nation. Each accommodates itself to the other, developing mutual understanding and interdependence. The vested interests of all groups have, in some sense, merged. This has been the case with the extended rule of the Democratic Party in the United States and the Liberal Party in Canada. In the long run, the accumulation of vested interests in such administrative groups works against administrative flexibility and leads to its eventual political defeat.

Integrative Tendencies of Labor Organizations.—The initial objectives of labor organizations were job security and wage rates not too far removed from contemporary costs of living. Those objectives are still present but the labor relations front is much wider and more nebulous than during the earlier struggles between industrial entrepreneurs and the representatives of organized labor. Few individual laborers, except in very small local industries, now attempt to deal with their employers directly. Representatives of organized labor meet the spokesmen of organized capital. These opposing groups struggle for economic gain, power, and prestige.

Labor leaders and industrialists organize battle lines of contending forces. Each group has its staff of legal, economic, and research talent. Each holds press conferences, deals with representatives of government, and seeks to organize on its behalf powerful groups in the nation. Nor is the common man forgotten in these struggles for public support. The strategy is no longer local. Central offices in such centers as Washington and New York are the headquarters of those who direct the nation-wide plans of labor and management.

The mobile character of industrial relations has taken on a new dimension and nature with the organization of workers in vast national unions. The focal point of relationship has been shifted away from the contact between workers and local management to the contact between big union organization and management organization. Although there are exceptions, the usual consequence of the organization of workers on a national basis has been a centralized guidance of labor activities over an industry-wide area. Bargaining is done for the industry as a whole or for large segments of the industry represented by huge corporations. Thus labor relations become increasingly a matter of relationship between gigantic organizations of workers and management, each of which functions through central policy and executive groups. Relations between workers and management in the local plants in the industry tend to lose separate and autonomous character and instead are determined in their basic outlines by the policies, objectives, plans and strategy of the central organizations. Thus to suggest an analogy, workers and management become related and aligned like vast opposing armies, with many outposts and points of contact but with the vast relationship operating along lines set up by the central organizations.[17]

These contending organizations of labor and management are complicated by competitive struggles between industries and the struggle for leadership of rival labor leaders. The labor unions fight not only for the economic security of the wage earners in our society, but also for their own social prestige and political power. The wage earners identify their place in society with the success of their leaders. Some leaders they reject, but they follow with devotion those who touch their imagination and gain for them tangible economic and social advantages. National and local leaders, through the "grapevine" of informal contacts, reach down into the sentiments of the men who compose the membership of the union. This latter is far more potent in reaching union objectives than are the actual formal contracts that give temporary formal stability to union-management relations. This vast hinterland of restlessness and hope kindled by leaders gives to the labor-management frontier the dynamic, undefined nature of a "no-man's land." Thus relations under our economy are essentially unstable. As Blumer says,

All that is needed to set such relations in movement is the initiation of seeking efforts by workers or by management. The conditions which initiate

---

[17] Herbert Blumer, "Sociological Theory in Industrial Relations," *Am. Sociol. Rev.*, Vol. 12, No. 3, June, 1947, pp. 273-274.

such seeking efforts are rife in our society and are likely to remain so. I call attention to only a few of the more conspicuous ones: competition in business with the inevitable effort to achieve efficient, low-cost production and managerial freedom; the effort of management to coup the gains of improved efficiency through technological improvements; the shifting and changing of management personnel with divergent philosophies; the development of new wishes and conceptions of rights on the part of workers; the exercise of pressure by the rank and file, particularly in large democratic unions; the formation of national unions, leading to uniform demands on diversified industrial concerns; the pressure on union leaders to produce increased benefits; the struggle for position on the part of union leaders or those seeking to be leaders; the development of a militant, aggressive psychology on the part of unions; the rivalry between unions for prestige, membership, and the efforts to weaken rival unions; the change in price-wage relationships and the movement of the business cycle; shifts in political power offering either to organized workers or to management the opportunity to actively advance its particular interest; shifts in public opinion which yield the same encouragement; and the appearance of new legislation or new judicial interpretation which opens new vistas of what is permissible. Such conditions—and the list is by no means complete—lead and coerce workers and management into new relations as each party seeks to pursue and to protect its respective interests. In response to such forces, industrial relations in our society become tense, changeable and ever moving.[18]

Twenty-five years ago, the craft unions of the United States and Canada were federated under the general leadership of the American Federation of Labor. This organization had no political party affiliations. Political candidates offering greater advantages to organized labor were supported. Those jeopardizing labor gains were bitterly opposed. Such was the official position. Actually labor leaders have always played "social politics." They and their following sought constantly to obtain public support and social legislation favoring their labor objectives. Obviously, they were the aristocracy of labor, seeking special advantages for the members of their union and themselves. Now all this has been changed.

Industrial unionism (C.I.O.) represents a more recent development in labor organization of workers regardless of skill, cutting across all units of industry, such as coal, steel, automobiles and textiles. This type of unionism competes with the older forms of unionism (A. F. of L.). Jurisdictionally and otherwise, the individual unions seek to bring within their fold all sections of organized labor. In this, they meet strong opposition from the older, vested interests of

---

18 *Ibid.*, p. 273.

organized labor and their public supporters. Industrial unionists are not only "social politicians"; they are also supporters, now, of political parties. In the 1944 federal election, the industrial unions had a special political organization, the Political Action Committee, to support the candidacy of the president, Franklin D. Roosevelt. While the craft unions have not gone this far as yet, their associations with powerful members of the C.I.O. confuse their position and suggest a much more direct party alignment in future elections.

For this current type of unionism manifested by the C.I.O., no area of public life lies outside the search for power and directive leadership. Aggressive leadership jousts not only with industrial magnates but with presidents in office and with the judiciary of the United States. How far this struggle may go in defining new objectives on the part of management, labor, and capital, no one knows at this time.

The contest to extend the interests of wage-earners and redefining the whole frontier of social and economic relationships in North America is now in process. Stability in this dynamic field seems to be far distant. Such is the new front with respect to institutional integration in our time.

Questions

1. Define social institution. What are the main characteristics of social institutions?
2. Of what use would the concept of basic institutions be in a community study?
3. How are the social institutions within a community affected by the ecological processes?
4. What are the characteristics of the institutions to be found on financial streets, focal points of transportation and communication, and residential areas?
5. What is meant by "the symbiotic aspects of institutions"? Give examples.
6. Differentiate between basic and service institutions in a city; in a rural area.
7. What is meant by institutional complement? How is this concept of use in determining the boundaries of a community?
8. Define *a social system*. When does a social system become an institution?
9. Of what importance is the individual in an institution?
10. A person shows segments of his personality in his various institutional roles. Discuss.
11. What part do institutions play in the orientation of the individual?

12. What is the relationship between institutions and persons?
13. What is meant by *institutional office?*
14. Discuss the manner in which a functionary plays the roles connected with his office.
15. "All institutions have multiple offices which are graded in importance and closely integrated." Discuss, using as an example an institution with which you are familiar, other than that cited in the text.
16. What factors are of importance in the selection of functionaries to institutional offices?
17. What factors contribute to changes in institutional offices?
18. "Marriage arises out of the family, rather than the family out of marriage." Explain.
19. Among what peoples are the various marriage systems described in this text practiced? Why are marriage systems so diverse?
20. How are family organization and disorganization related?
21. What are the main factors contributing to marriage stability in North America? to marriage instability?
22. Can the following be termed institutions? Support your opinion.

(a) The Republican Party
(b) Christian Science Church
(c) Polygyny
(d) The 5 and 10¢ store
(e) The Ku Klux Klan

(f) The railways
(g) The Bible
(h) The Telephone Company
(i) Courtship

Classify those which are institutions as those which transmit the cultural heritage, or are instrumental institutions, regulative institutions, or integrative institutions.
23. What part is played in the transmission of the social heritage by the family? the church? the school?
24. Compare education in primitive societies with that of literate societies.
25. What are instrumental institutions? What are their characteristics?
26. The success of the Tennessee Valley Authority points up the possibility of government planning in a democratic, nonpolitical manner. Discuss.
27. Discuss the regulative functions of federal, state (or provincial), and municipal governments.
28. How do institutions help to integrate the society and its class structure on an informal basis?
29. How do religious institutions function as integrating forces in a society? for the individual?
30. Discuss the integrative functions of political parties; of labor organizations.
31. What changes have come about in labor-management relations in recent years?

BIBLIOGRAPHY

ALLPORT, F. H. *Institutional Behavior.* Chapel Hill, University of North Carolina Press, 1933.

ARNOLD, THURMAN. *The Folklore of Capitalism.* New Haven, Yale University Press, 1938.

BALDWIN, J. M. *The Individual and Society.* Boston, R. G. Badger, 1911.

BALLARD, L. V. *Social Institutions.* New York, D. Appleton-Century Co., 1936.

BARNES, H. E. *Social Institutions in an Era of World Upheaval.* New York, Prentice-Hall, Inc., 1943.

BLUMER, HERBERT. "Sociological Theory in Industrial Relations." *Am. Sociol. Rev.,* Vol. 12, No. 3, June, 1947, pp. 271-278.

BOND, H. M. "Education as a Social Process: A Case Study of a Higher Institution as an Incident in the Process of Acculturation." *Am. J. Sociol.,* Vol. 48, No. 6, May, 1943, pp. 710-722.

BURGESS, E. W. "The Family and the Person." *Proc. Am. Sociol. Soc.,* Vol. 22, 1927.

BURGESS, E. W. *Personality and the Social Group.* Chicago, University of Chicago Press, 1929.

BURGESS, E. W., AND COTTRELL, L. S. *Predicting Success or Failure in Marriage.* New York, Prentice-Hall, Inc., 1939.

CARR-SAUNDERS, A. M. *The Professions.* New York, Oxford University Press, 1933.

CARR-SAUNDERS, A. M. *Professions, their Organization and Place in Society.* London, Clarendon Press, 1928.

CHAPIN, F. S. *Contemporary American Institutions.* New York, Harper & Bros., 1935.

COLE, G. D. H. *Social Theory.* New York, 1920.

COMTE, AUGUSTE. *The Fundamental Principles of the Positive Philosophy.* Trans. by H. Martineau. Macmillan & Co., Ltd., London, 1905.

COOLEY, C. H. *Social Organization.* New York, Charles Scribner's Sons, 1909.

COYLE, G. L. *Social Process in Organized Groups.* New York, R. R. Smith, Inc., 1930.

DOUGLAS, H. P. *The Church in the Changing City.* New York, George A. Doran Co., 1927.

ELLIOTT, M. A., AND MERRILL, F. E. *Social Disorganization.* New York, Harper & Bros., 1941.

FINER, HERMAN. *TVA: Lesson for International Application.* Montreal, International Labour Office, 1944.

FRAZIER, E. F. *The Negro Family in the United States.* Chicago, University of Chicago Press, 1939.

FRAZIER, E. F. "The Impact of Urban Civilization Upon Negro Family Life." *Am. Sociol. Rev.,* Vol. 2, April, 1937, pp. 609-618.

HALL, OSWALD. "The Informal Organization of the Medical Profession." *Canadian J. Pol. Sci. and Ec.,* Vol. 12, February, 1946, pp. 30-44.

HALL, OSWALD. "The Stages of a Medical Career." *Am. J. Sociol.,* Vol. 53, No. 5, March, 1948, pp. 327-336.

HAMILTON, W. H. "Institutions," *Encyclopedia of Social Sciences.* New York, The Macmillan Co., 1935, Vol. 4, pp. 84-89.

HAWLEY, A. H. "An Ecological Study of Urban Service Institutions." *Am. Sociol. Rev.,* Vol. 6, No. 5, October, 1941, pp. 629-640.

HERTZLER, J. O. *Social Institutions.* New York, McGraw-Hill Book Co., Inc., 1929.

HOUSE, F. N. *The Development of Sociology.* New York, McGraw-Hill Book Co., Inc., 1936.

HOUSE, F. N. *The Range of Social Theory.* New York, Henry Holt & Co., 1929.

HUGHES, E. C. "The Ecological Aspect of Institutions." *Am. Sociol. Rev.,* Vol. 1, No. 2, April, 1936, pp. 180-189.

HUGHES, E. C. *French Canada in Transition.* Chicago, University of Chicago Press, 1943.

HUGHES, E. C. *The Growth of an Institution: The Chicago Real Estate Board.* Chicago, Chicago University Society for Social Research, Series II, Monograph 1, 1931.

HUGHES, E. C. "Impact of War on American Institutions." *Am. J. Sociol.,* Vol. 48, No. 3, November, 1942, pp. 398-403.

HUGHES, E. C. "Institutional Office and the Person." *Am. J. Sociol.,* Vol. 43, No. 3, November, 1937, pp. 404-413.

HUGHES, E. C. "Position and Status in a Quebec Industrial Town." *Am. Sociol. Rev.,* Vol. 3, No. 5, October, 1938, pp. 709-717.

HUGHES, E. C., "Institutions," in Lee, A. M. (Ed.). *New Outlines of the Principles of Sociology.* New York, Barnes & Noble, Inc., 1946, pp. 225-281.

KINGSBURY, M., AND FAIRCHILD, M. *Factory, Family and Woman in the Soviet Union.* New York, G. P. Putnam's Sons, 1935.

KINSEY, A. C., POMEROY, W. B., AND MARTIN, C. E. *Sexual Behavior in the Human Male.* Philadelphia, W. B. Saunders & Co., 1948.

KIRKPATRICK, C. *Nazi Germany: Its Women and Family Life.* Indianapolis, Bobbs-Merrill Co., 1938.

LERNER, M. *Ideas are Weapons.* New York, The Viking Press, 1939, Essay 16.

LILIENTHAL, D. *TVA: Democracy on the March.* New York, Harper & Bros., 1944.

LINTON, RALPH. *The Study of Man.* New York, Appleton-Century-Crofts, Inc., 1936.

LOWIE, R. *Primitive Society.* New York, Boni & Liveright, 1920.

MacIVER, R. *Society: Its Structure and Changes.* New York, Ray Long & Richard R. Smith, 1931.

MARTIN, R. D. "The Church and Changing Ecological Dominance." *Sociol. and Soc. Res.,* Vol. 25, January, 1941, pp. 246-257.

MEANS, G. C. "Economic Institutions." *Am. J. Sociol.,* Vol. 47, No. 5, May, 1942, pp. 941-958.

OGBURN, W. F. "The Influence of Inventions on American Social Institutions in the Future." *Am. J. Sociol.,* Vol. 43, No. 3, November, 1937, pp. 365-376.

PARK, R. E., AND BURGESS, E. W. *An Introduction to the Science of Sociology.* Chicago, University of Chicago Press, 1921, Chs. 1, 3, 6, 7, 12, 13.

PARSONS, TALCOTT. "The Position of Sociological Theory," and "Discussion." *Am. Sociol. Rev.,* Vol. 13, No. 2, April, 1948, pp. 156-171.

PARSONS, TALCOTT. "The Present Position and Prospects of Systematic Theory in Sociology," in Gurvitch, G., and Moore, W. E. (Eds.), *Twentieth Century Sociology.* New York, Philosophical Society, 1945, pp. 42-69.

PLANT, J. S. *Personality and the Culture Pattern.* New York, The Commonwealth Fund, 1937.

ROETHLISBERGER, W. J., AND DICKSON, W. J. *Management and the Worker.* Cambridge, Harvard University Press, 1947.

ROTHENBUECHER, KARL. *Uber das Wesen des Geschichtlichen und die Gesellschaftlichen Gebilde.* Tübingen, 1926.

SCHANCK, R. L. "A Study of a Community and Its Groups and Institutions Conceived of as Behaviors of Individuals." *Psychol. Monographs,* Vol. 43, No. 2, 1932.

SIMPSON, G. *Émile Durkheim on the Division of Labor in Society.* New York, The Macmillan Co., 1933.

SUMNER, W. G. *Folkways.* Boston, Ginn & Co., 1906.

TAEUSCH, C. F. *Professional and Business Ethics*. New York, Henry Holt & Co., 1926.

TOZZER, A. M. *Social Origins and Social Continuities*. New York, The Macmillan Co., 1925.

WARNER, W. L., AND LUNT, P. S. *The Social Life of a Modern Community*. New Haven, Yale University Press, 1941.

WEBB, B. AND S. *The History of Trade Unionism*. New York, Longmans, Green & Co., Inc., 1920.

WESTERMARCK, EDWARD. *History of Human Marriage*. London, Macmillan & Co., Ltd., 1926.

WHYTE, WILLIAM FOOTE (Ed.). *Industry and Society*. New York, McGraw-Hill Book Co., Inc., 1945.

WILSON, LOGAN. *The Academic Man*. New York, Oxford University Press, 1942.

WRIGHT, C. *A History of Lloyds*. London, Macmillan & Co., Ltd., 1928.

PART III

SOCIAL INTERACTION

INTRODUCTION

THE FOREGOING CHAPTERS have presented the ecological order within which are to be found many and varied societal elements—personal, group, and cultural. The elements are selectively and impersonally distributed by the process of ecological interaction and are arranged in patterned relationships. Such a configuration of interrelated elements is what is meant by ecological organization.

It has become the common practice of sociologists to distinguish between "process" and "organization." Although this is possible for analytical purposes, these two concepts differ only in the degree of the rate of change as measured in terms of different time perspectives. Each is relative to the other. "Process" "emphasizes the dynamic, changing characteristics of social phenomena without any commitment on the normative (progressive) nature of the activities or occurrences. There is also the implication that the goings-on are regular, continuous, and repetitive." [1] Thus process is thought of as action, whereas organization is conceived as form or structure. But process and organization are really the same thing, except that process is viewed as "going on" within a relatively long-time frame of reference, while organization (form or structure) is observed as "existing" or "being" in a relatively short-time or cross-sectional frame of reference. When activity is projected on a time-span of considerable proportions so that the observable events are seen as a continuous series of altered relationships or conditions, then we refer to this as "process." When we see process "stopped" or greatly "slowed down," so that relationships appear to be unchanging we call it organization, form, or structure, as the circumstances warrant. Organization is, then, process "halted" or "slowed down," and process is organization "going on" or "speeded up."

By interaction is meant process in which the action of one entity causes reaction by another. In this action and reaction the course of the original entity is altered as to location, condition, or both. There are several types of interaction, but sociologists are primarily interested in the ecological and the social. Here again we must point out that this duality of types of interaction facilitates description and analysis. If, as we learned in Part II, ecological interaction and

---

[1] Read Bain, "The Concept of Social Process," in *Social Problems and Social Processes*, E. S. Bogardus (Ed.), Chicago, University of Chicago Press, 1933, pp. 103-104.

organization are concerned with the essentially distributive aspects of societary phenomena, we see them as operating to establish a patterned order of persons, groups, institutions and other cultural constructs within which social interaction occurs between the units in contact and communication.

If the process of social interaction is to be fully understood, however, it is necessary to break up the concept into specific and definitive phases, sometimes called the subprocesses of social interaction. Since we have already identified and discussed the competitive phase of interaction as the ecological process *par excellence,* it will be sufficient for our purpose to focus attention on three concepts that have come to be rather generally accepted as designating the major phases of social interaction. They are conflict, accommodation, and assimilation.

Socialization, individualization, social control, social change, and social disorganization refer to products of these major phases of social interaction rather than to distinct phases. There is no fundamental difference in the basic character of what goes on; it is the product that differs, depending upon differences in the interacting elements, in the ecological patterns within which framework the social interaction takes place, in the kind of mechanisms employed, and in the viewpoints of the observers of the phenomena. The same phases are effective in producing a labor union, a gang, or a nation; likewise a delinquent, a politician, or a businessman.

Social interaction means in this context that human beings are affected by the presence of each other. Illiterate or literate, they call out in each other some kind of language gestures indicating common understandings. Social interaction is a process whereby men interpenetrate the minds of each other. This may mean opposition or agreement.

Chapter 13

MAJOR PHASES OF SOCIAL INTERACTION

This chapter introduces certain conceptual tools which are useful in describing social interaction as it occurs in concrete situations. The concepts refer to what are generally regarded as the principal phases of social interaction—conflict, accommodation, and assimilation.

Conflict.—The *conflict* phase is frequently manifested in social interaction through which accumulated tensions become resolved or liquidated. A *tension* is a condition created by the inhibiting of one or more reaction patterns that are pressing for release. Tensions making for a given conflict situation may be single or many and the time sequence needed for their emergence may be brief or long, depending on a number of factors, such as pre-conditioning with respect to matters like race, nationality, language; the presence or absence of such mechanisms of control as tabu, law, moral principles, and traditional attitudes; and such ecological factors as pressure of numbers, segregation, and economic differences. When competitors recognize themselves as such and become aware of their new roles as enemies, that is, as intent upon either eliminating their opponents from the contest entirely or reducing them to a state of subordination and acknowledged defeat, conflict is initiated.

Since contact and communication are necessary to conflict, the idea has been advanced that conflict necessarily is personal, that is, as in some way involving and affecting the status of individual persons. For this to be true does not mean that conflict is dependent on intimate, face-to-face contact nor does it mean that person-to-person vituperative words and gestures are necessarily involved. Nor does conflict always mean that the hostile feelings and pugnacious attitudes are aimed at opposing groups or persons as such, because they may be directed against ideas, policies, or methods.

There is no conflict that does not affect, in some way and to some extent, the inner mental and emotional processes of the individual members of the groups involved. The individual tends to take over in his own person the burden of intergroup conflict, and there the struggle of emotions, memories, and attitudes is just as real and disturbing as it is in the overt forms of warfare, political campaign, or sectarian controversy. Whereas the ecological phases of inter-action are lacking in much emotion, conflict "evokes the deepest emotions and strongest passions and enlists the greatest concentration of attention and effort." [1]

In its higher forms, however, conflict becomes impersonal—a struggle to establish and maintain rules of justice and moral order. In this case the welfare not merely of individual men but of the community is involved. Such are the struggles of political parties and religious sects. Here the issues are not determined by the force and weight of the contestants immediately involved, but to a greater or less extent, by the force and weight of public opinion of the community, and eventually by the judgment of mankind. [2]

In the case of conflict, as with the other phases of social inter-action, behavior occurs according to some socially determined form, with its traditional "rules of the game." These rules vary from cus-tomary practices and regulations, as in the case of factional disputes and lynchings, to such formal devices as the duel and the international rules on the conduct of war. Conflict is manifest in war, in the feud, in litigation by ordeal or trial, in discussion and political campaigns, in strikes and other industrial disputes, in gambling and other forms of fighting play, in race friction, and in sectarian controversy.

Everyday life is full of the situations in which conflicts arise. Each person experiences tensions within himself and in his group relation-ships. These tensions may have their roots in temperamental, eco-nomic, political, cultural, or other differences. No matter what the basic causes may be, the resulting reaction patterns will be displayed in some well known, recognized form. The tensions may be relieved through a process of sublimation; if they are not, conflict ensues.

Overt and Covert Conflict.—Conflict may be overt or it may be covert. Of these two types, Professor Allport writes as follows:

The former is the more primitive; it results from the exercise of pre-potent responses in their full strength and in a manner suited rather to immediate individual satisfaction than to the safeguarding of the social order. Conduct of others which thwarts these activities is countered by struggle responses of a primitive, unsocialized sort. Such overt conflicts occur fre-quently between struggle groups. Nations struggle against one another with methods of warfare designed by each for the destruction of the other's

[1] R. E. Park and E. W. Burgess, *Introduction to the Science of Sociology,* Chicago, University of Chicago Press, 1924, p. 574.
[2] *Ibid.,* pp. 575-576.

material and personal power. Revolutionists, strike rioters, and lynchers carry on an equally unsocialized conflict. In its absence of social modification this behavior resembles the ruthless attack of the angry child, differing from the latter only in a complexity of efferent development productive of more thorough destruction. *Within* the group predatory assertion of desires and the resulting overt conflicts are comparatively rare. Here both the assertion and the struggle against limitation drives are carried on through the socialized agencies of rivalry, competition, and legal political action. . . .

Covert conflict is far more universal than the overt form. It is also more complex and interesting from the psychological standpoint. In covert conflict the forces which represent the two sides of the conflict lie within the individual himself. . . . Because of their concealed nature the full significance of covert conflicts has only recently been discovered. The credit for its discovery belongs chiefly to Freud. Although their main field of study belongs to psycho-pathology, conflicts are also of fundamental importance for the student of social science; for one force in the conflict is usually a socialized drive. Hence the struggle is really *a social conflict compressed into one individual.* Self and *alter* are antagonistic, not between one person and another, but within the person himself.[3]

These types of conflict are two sides of one situation. There is no overt conflict that does not involve at the same time covert conflict in the individual members of the contending groups.

So general is the interest of human beings in conflict and so necessary is an understanding of it for an explanation of many of the most common modes of both individual and group behavior, that some writers have designated it the most fundamental phase of the social process. Certain European sociologists considered the concept so important that they built a whole theory of society about it.[4] It should be noted, however, that these and other writers of the same school were thinking not so much of conflict in the sense in which we understand it as they were concerned with "an eternal and universal struggle for existence." Such a conception of conflict conforms more nearly to our notion of ecological competition. It seems best to confine our use of the term to those conscious, intermittent, emotionalized forms of social interaction between divergent persons, groups, and culture patterns, which serve to lower tensions and release energies, interests, and capabilities for accommodative action.

Accommodation.—Most conflicts have an end. At least the overt expressions of them disappear and the conflicting forces settle down to a more or less even tenor. Smoldering fires of hatred, bitter

[3] From Floyd Allport, *Social Psychology*, Boston, Houghton Mifflin Co., 1924, pp. 336-338.
[4] Gumplowicz's *Der Rassenkampf*, Novicow's *Les Luttes entre sociétés humaines et leur phases successives*, and Ratzenhofer's *Wesen und Zweck der Politik.*

memories of grievances and defeats, and pride in victories won, may linger beneath the superficial calm and order after the noise of battle, the exchange of recriminations, and the clamor for the spoils have ceased. The enemy retreats to prepare for a new assault, or, being decisively beaten, is brought into submission under the white flag, or is pacified and conciliated. The peculiar phase of interaction by which the new equilibrium of forces is effected and maintained, attitudes rationalized, redefined, or transferred following a period of conflict is called *accommodation*.

It is remarked by Reuter and Hart that "accommodation is both a condition and a process. Each may be treated from the point of view of persons and from the point of view of groups." [5] As a condition, accommodation represents an accepted set of relationships and the recognition of a definite status of the person in the group or of the group in the larger social organization. "It is a state of relative mental and social peace, an equilibrium between or among contending forces that is more or less permanent and acceptable because of the existence of a supporting body of habits, sentiments, and institutional organization." [6] Such a condition must not be assumed to represent either a perfect state of harmony or an absolute homogeneity. It is the arrangement, whether temporary or permanent, in which a tolerable status for the group and of the person is secured. It helps to explain why there may be social unity and cooperation despite the diversity of interest and ambition, the presence of hatred and fear, and the divisional alignments of class, race, and nationality, which characterize nearly all societies. Professor Cooley took note of the fact that "the unity of the social mind consists not in agreement but in organization," [7] meaning thereby that all societies are organizations of more or less diverse and sometimes opposing elements which tend to unite according to some pattern of accommodation.

"As a process, accommodation is the sequence of steps by which persons are reconciled to changed conditions of life through the formation of habits and attitudes made necessary by the changed conditions themselves." [8] The term is as applicable to groups as it is to persons. The conditions mentioned refer mainly to the changed status and the new roles established as the outcome of conflict. While accommodation involves inner, psychic changes in the persons affected, it has also a relatively formal and external character as regards

---

[5] E. B. Reuter and C. W. Hart, *Introduction to Sociology*, New York, McGraw-Hill Book Co., Inc., 1933, p. 320.
[6] *Ibid.*
[7] C. H. Cooley, *Social Organization*, New York, Charles Scribner's Sons, 1909, p. 4.
[8] Reuter and Hart, *Introduction to Sociology*, p. 322.

the type of relationship established between or among the culture groups and their members. For the "inner, psychic changes in the persons" affected by social interaction, the psychologists and social psychologists extensively employ the term "adjustment," that is, the formation of attitudes, habit mechanisms, and the alterations of personality through fantasy, delusion, make-believe, and other ways of redefining attitudes, with or without the reordering of social behavior in conformity with social realities. In like manner, the psychologists hold that a person may present all the outward appearance of being socially and psychically adjusted yet be suffering keenly within. It would probably be agreed, however, that satisfactory inner adjustment depends in great measure on satisfactory overt accommodation in social relations. The operation of the process of interaction making for successful and unsuccessful adjustment of personality received our attention in an earlier chapter.[9]

Adaptation.—Another concept that frequently appears in discussions of accommodation is that of *adaptation*. Too often the concepts of adaptation and accommodation are not sharply distinguished from one another. In undertaking to differentiate between them it is hardly sufficient to say that accommodation is the aftermath of conflict and adaptation the natural outcome of ecological competition. Indeed, such a statement is no more accurate than is one to the effect that the latter concept is strictly biological and analogous to accommodation, a social concept. Therefore, it is important to distinguish clearly between the subsocial and the social aspects of the problem before us.

Natural scientists are familiar with processes of change and equilibration going on alternately and yet simultaneously in their fields of study. They are aware of the constant interaction of energies resulting in changes within and without all living organisms, which makes it possible for these organisms to adapt to the peculiar life-conditions in which they find themselves.

Adaptations are of two general types: those occurring within the organism and those occurring between the organism and its physical environment. The first type is divided into three kinds of organic adaptation—structural, functional, and bio-chemical. It is biological and pre-social; the second type, in which we are chiefly interested, may be termed subsocial.

Wherever man has gone throughout the earth, he has been confronted with the problem of adapting his habits and his social or-

---

[9] See Chapter 6.

ganization to the exigencies imposed upon him by the specific kind of physical environment which characterized the area of his settlement. By adding to or subtracting from the amount of his clothing; by utilizing different materials in his clothing; by altering his diet and by reducing or increasing his physical exercise in work and play so as to regulate the physiological processes of digestion, circulation, and respiration, and thus his bodily temperature to the external temperature; by constructing dwellings of suitable materials, size, and structure; by devising and installing heating and cooling systems; and by many other means man has been able, with varying degrees of success, to adapt his life to the vicissitudes of climate. In this adaptation to environment he has been aided by the process of natural selection by which less adaptable individuals have tended to succumb and either move to more favorable environments or perish, leaving the more adaptable ones to carry on under the conditions which their artificial arrangements have made livable for them. We see, then, that acclimatization is very largely a matter of adaptation of the second general type, namely, between the organism and its physical environment.

The interaction between man and the external physical world has always been a complicated process in which the environment stimulates and satisfies man's wishes in certain respects while, until adaptation is complete, it thwarts them in others. Man in his turn has been busy meeting these stimulations either by modifying his environment or by changing his purposes. The story of man's discoveries and inventions, the domestication of animals, the exploration, settlement, and exploitation of the larger part of the earth's land surface, are all indicative of the determination of man to be master of his physical environment. Gradually and by means of a long struggle, man's ingenuity and the accumulation and dissemination of cultures have enabled him to decrease the directness of contacts between most individuals and their natural environment. Thus the action of natural environment upon human behavior has been rendered much more indirect than in the earlier stages of human development. In other words, social environments have come to intervene to a great extent between man and his natural environment, and the process of accommodation has in large measure come to replace adaptation. For example, comparatively few people in western society come in direct contact with the natural resources of food, fuel, building materials, raw fabrics, etc. For the most part, they are in contact with them only indirectly through a series of social contacts, mechanical processes, trade organizations, and financial arrangements.

When a person enters a group for the first time, whether by birth, choice, or compulsion, he is expected to accept a set of attitudes toward the culture traits which characterize the group. If he takes over the new traits and makes them his own, he may be said to be accommodating to the situation. When one adopts the style of dress, the type of dwelling, the dietary practices of a people, he is accommodating himself to existing adaptations rather than making initial adaptations of his own. However, if he were to find himself shipwrecked and stranded on an uninhabited island he would without doubt adapt himself to his surroundings in such matters as food, shelter, protection, and means of escape. If he were the sole survivor, accommodation would be limited to those inner mental adjustments designed to allay his fears, keep up his courage, and revive his hopes of rescue.

Adaptation applies to those changes which tend to equip the organism as such, or provide auxiliary aids for its security and survival, in relation to its physical environment. Accommodation applies to those particular alterations of attitude and value structure which enable persons and groups of divergent types, cultures, and interests to carry on their varied activities together without serious danger to their respective statuses. Adaptation is either biological or subsocial; accommodation is social.

Most discussions of accommodation either explicitly state or imply that it is "an outcome of conflict"; that it "has its origin, directly or indirectly, in a conflict situation." While these statements may be accepted as generally true, they do not tell the whole truth. There are many situations involving differences of opinion, habit, attitude, and interest, wherein the divergencies, once brought into contact with each other, are resolved without perceptible conflict. Two or more persons or groups, faced with a common problem or foe, may gladly forget their differences and decide to unite in a common cause. Two persons of opposite sex may meet, fall in love, marry, and work out their differences without any conflict.

It is equally important to note that all conflict does not end in accommodation. In fact, some conflicts never end. "This is of course true always of a conflict of incompatible impersonal ideals. There is no possibility of a cessation of conflict between a natural and a supernatural interpretation of the universe; between realism and mysticism; between aristocracy and democracy; between capitalism and sovietism. The principles are impersonal and incompatible, and conflict ceases only with the complete eradication of one or the other of the opposing interpretations." [10]   While the adherents of diametrically opposed points of view may cease their overt hostilities, their philosophies may remain live issues indefinitely.

Likewise, conflict does not always disappear when the contending sides accept a set of conditions designed to maintain the status arrived at through conflict. Conflict continues to exist as a kind of latent, under-the-surface opposition. In some cases, conflict may and does appear in subtle and disguised forms within areas of accommodation. Contrariwise, it should be noted that accommodation is possible in situations which are fraught with tension and imminent conflict.[11] This is apt to be true where conflict has been perpetuated year after year, perhaps for generations, until everybody concerned has become habituated to it, as in certain cases of international hatred and warfare, family feud, party strife, and sectarian controversy.

Assimilation.—When once-distinct culture groups come to possess similar sentiments, interests, attitudes, and desires, whether the similarities are mutually recognized or not, the way is open for a sharing and fusing of their culture traits. The simple modification of cultures through contact is called *acculturation,* but when groups having different cultures come to share a common culture, composed of elements contributed by both groups as well as of elements different from either, the groups are said to be assimilated. Becoming culturally identical and indistinguishable is called *assimilation.*

The concept of assimilation suggests the way in which a person or a group becomes an integral part of an inclusive group of which he or it is physically a constituent element, or the way in which two or more culture patterns become merged and blended to constitute a new culture pattern different from any one or all of the component patterns. Many sociological writers have been inclined to restrict the use of the concept to that phase of social interaction by which a person or lesser group is absorbed by and incorporated in a larger and more dominant group. In fact, the term has tended to be limited to the process whereby the immigrant person and group become fully transformed and brought into harmony with the culture complex of their adopted country. Such usage is questionable if it excludes from the process the very real fusion of cultures through the back-and-forth interaction of the cultural elements until one culture pattern

---

[10] Reuter and Hart, *Introduction to Sociology,* p. 329.
[11] See Ralph H. Danhof, "The Accommodation and Integration of Conflicting Cultures in a Newly Established Community," *Am. J. Sociol.,* Vol. 49, No. 1, July, 1943, pp. 14-23.

displaces the other, or a third culture pattern emerges as a blend of the ingredient cultures.

Assimilation is more than the mere borrowing of certain culture traits. It involves changes in the basic structure of culture. As Wilson Wallis points out, "true assimilation has taken place only when the [cultural] feature could persist in the new area if it disappeared from other areas. Its virtual independence and self-sufficiency in the culture is the measure of its assimilation." [12]

This process is one that goes on *within* persons and culture groups. Persons and groups as such are never assimilated to each other or to a common denominator. The more formal alterations of personal and group relations to new cultural patterns and social situations are nothing more than forms of accommodation. Much more fundamental changes in sentiments, attitudes, habitual reactions, and values are essential for assimilation.

Under modern conditions of mobility and change, it is doubtful if assimilation is ever as complete as our definition of the concept would require. Perhaps the nearest approach to complete assimilation, that is, to the point where the person's whole round of life's experience is fully bound up in the standards, ideals, and loyalties of a particular group, is to be found in the sacred, stable groups of relatively simple, isolated, and tradition-bound societies, such as were described in Chapters 3 and 4. Indeed, "this complete assimilation to a given heritage and social group is of course a form of isolation. The provincial person is one habituated to the ways of a particular province and emotionally bound to them." [13] On the other hand, the cosmopolitan person, one who "moves freely in different groups and cultures and is, in general, not sentimentally attached to any group or emotionally dependent upon any particular set of values," [14] is accommodated rather than assimilated.

While accommodation may be made with relative ease and suddenness, assimilation is usually gradual. The adult may find it difficult, if not impossible, to be assimilated to a strange culture. In the case of children and young people, the process may proceed with such celerity as to produce disturbing conflicts between the older and younger generations, and may be so rapid as to be demoralizing. The relative facility with which assimilation may go on is determined by race difference and by differences between individual members

---

[12] Wilson D. Wallis, *An Introduction to Sociology*, New York, Alfred A. Knopf, 1927, p. 377.
[13] Reuter and Hart, *Introduction to Sociology*, p. 358.
[14] *Ibid.*

of the same race. In certain situations the physical marks of race may greatly obstruct assimilation.

With respect to individual differences it is apparent that the extroverted person finds it much easier to change his attachments and loyalties than does the introvert. Sex differences, as such, probably affect the rate of assimilation very little, but where the accommodative process has worked to fix the respective roles of the sexes so as to restrict the mobility and limit the contacts of one sex, usually the female, as compared with the other sex, then the cultural concomitants of sex do tend to determine the relative assimilability of the sexes. Also there may be differences in temperaments which make it easy for some persons and groups to assimilate and difficult for others.

Mention of the relation of amalgamation to assimilation may be made briefly at this point. *Amalgamation* is a biological process and interests us here only because of its sociological implications. The concept refers to the mixing of divergent groups, usually ethnic and nationality groups, by means of interbreeding or intermarriage. In spite of objections and attitudes against it, different racial stocks and cultural groups, when thrown together intimately for any length of time, have tended to mix. Even the Jews, among whom much stress has always been laid upon purity of "race" and culture, have united by intermarriage with alien peoples since as well as during Old Testament times. The extent to which miscegenation between whites and Negroes has gone in the United States does not appear in statistics. That it is considerable is not questioned. To a great degree all of the older foreign elements in the population have amalgamated among themselves and with the native stock. The usual effect of amalgamation is to facilitate assimilation, but that the former is necessary to the latter may be safely denied. On the other hand, it may be said that wherever amalgamation is in process to any appreciable extent it indicates that assimilation has progressed rather far.

The remaining chapters in this part of the book will treat the several phases of social interaction functioning together in a variety of specific socio-cultural situations. The more recognizable forms of social interaction, the more commonly employed mechanisms characteristic of each one, and the most likely effects resulting from social interaction will receive major consideration. It will be shown that the socializing, organizing, disorganizing, and socially controlling principles are integral aspects of social interaction. Throughout the whole march of human events there is a continuous relationship between the past and the present, and an interrelationship between all social phenomena, no matter how unrelated they may appear when superficially considered. These organic and dynamic aspects of social life in concrete situations will be dealt with in the chapters which follow.

QUESTIONS

1. In the Introduction to Part III, what distinction is made between the concepts "process" and "organization"? Why make such distinction?
2. Also in the Introduction, how is "interaction" defined? How are the ecological and social processes of interaction related?
3. What is necessary for an understanding of the full meaning of social interaction?
4. "The same process is effective in producing a labor union, a gang, or a nation; likewise a delinquent, a politician, or a business man." Explain.
5. What is the function of the conflict phase of social interaction? At what juncture in human relations does conflict appear?
6. Explain the personal character of conflict.
7. "Conflict behavior takes the form of certain patterns." Explain.
8. What two types of conflict are discussed by Allport? Distinguish between the two.
9. How are these two types interrelated?
10. What function is served by accommodation?
11. Distinguish between accommodation as a condition and as a phase of on-going interaction.
12. How is adjustment related to the accommodative process and to alterations in personality?
13. Indicate the distinctions between sub-social adaptation and social accommodation.
14. By what means has man made adaptations to his physical environment?
15. Discuss: "Social environments have come to intervene to a great extent between man and his natural environment, and the process of accommodation has in large measure come to replace adaptation."
16. Is accommodation invariably "an outcome of conflict"? Discuss.
17. Can it be said that conflict is possible within areas of accommodation and that accommodation is possible in situations surcharged with conflict? Explain.
18. What is the meaning of assimilation?
19. How do acculturation and assimilation differ from each other?
20. "Assimilation is more than the mere borrowing of certain culture traits." Discuss.
21. Compare assimilation in "relatively isolated, custom-bound societies" and in highly mobile, accessible urban communities.

22. Discuss the roles of age, sex, race, and individual differences with respect to their effects on assimilability.

23. Distinguish between assimilation and amalgamation. How may each influence the other?

Bibliography

ALEXANDER, CHESTER. "Antipathy and Social Behavior." *Am. J. Sociol.*, Vol. 51, No. 4, January, 1946, pp. 288-292.

BAIN, READ. "Cultural Integration and Social Conflict." *Am. J. Sociol.*, Vol. 44, No. 4, January, 1939, pp. 499-509.

BERNARD, L. L. "The Conflict between Primary Group Attitudes and Derivative Group Ideals in Modern Society." *Am. J. Sociol.*, Vol. 41, No. 5, March, 1936, pp. 611-623.

BOGARDUS, EMORY S. (Ed.). *Social Problems and Social Processes.* Chicago, University of Chicago Press, 1933. Part III, "Theories of Social Processes."

BOSSARD, JAMES H. S. "The Law of Family Interaction." *Am. J. Sociol.*, Vol. 50, No. 4, January, 1945, pp. 292-294.

BRYSON, LYMAN, FINKELSTEIN, LOUIS, AND MACIVER, R. M. (Editors). *Conflicts of Power in Modern Culture.* New York, Harper & Bros., 1947.

COOLEY, CHARLES H. *The Social Process.* New York, Charles Scribner's Sons, 1918.

DOLLARD, JOHN F., DOOB, LEONARD W., *et al. Frustration and Aggression.* New Haven, Yale University Press, 1939.

DRASCHLER, JULIUS. *Democracy and Assimilation.* New York, The Macmillan Co., 1920.

DUNCAN, H. G. "A Study in the Process of Assimilation." *Pubs. Am. Sociol. Soc.*, Vol. 23, 1929, pp. 184-187.

EATON, WALTER H. "Alternative Meanings of Adjustment." *Am. Sociol. Rev.*, Vol. 12, No. 1, February, 1947, pp. 75-81.

EUBANK, EARLE E. "Social Processes and Their Accompanying Relationships." *Pubs. Am. Sociol. Soc.*, Vol. 26, 1932, pp. 44-55.

FRANK, LAWRENCE K. "The Management of Tensions." *Am. J. Sociol.*, Vol. 33, No. 5, March, 1928, pp. 705-736.

FRENCH, THOMAS M. "Social Conflict and Psychic Conflict." *Am. J. Sociol.*, Vol. 44, No. 6, May, 1939, pp. 922-931.

GUTHRIE, E. R. *The Psychology of Human Conflict.* New York, Harper & Bros., 1938.

HART, HORNELL. *The Science of Social Relations.* New York, Henry Holt & Co., 1927, Ch. 15, "Solving Conflict by Accommodation."

HOMANS, GEORGE C. "A Conceptual Scheme for the Study of Social Organization." *Am. Sociol. Rev.*, Vol. 12, No. 1, February, 1947, pp. 13-26.

HOUSE, FLOYD N. *The Range of Social Theory.* New York, Henry Holt & Co., 1929, Ch. 22, "Contact and Assimilation."

HOUSE, FLOYD N. "Social Relations and Social Interaction." *Am. J. Sociol.*, Vol. 31, No. 5, March, 1926, pp. 617-633.

HUMPHREY, NORMAN D. "On Assimilation and Acculturation." *Psychiatry*, Vol. 6, November, 1943, pp. 343-345.

JAMESON, SAMUEL HAIG. "Principles of Social Interaction." *Am. Sociol. Rev.*, Vol. 10, No. 1, February, 1945, pp. 6-12.

KELSEY, CARL. *The Physical Basis of Society.* New York, D. Appleton & Co., 1929 edition, Part II, "Man in Control of Nature."

LIGT, BARTHÉLEMY DE. *The Conquest of Violence.* New York, E. P. Dutton & Co., 1938.

MacIver, R. M. (Ed.). *Group Relations and Group Antagonisms.* Institute for Religious Studies, New York, Harper & Bros., 1944.

MacIver, R. M. (Ed.). *Unity and Difference in American Life: A Series of Addresses and Discussions.* New York, Harper & Bros., 1947.

Mayo, Elton. "Routine Interaction and the Problem of Collaboration." *Am. Sociol. Rev.,* Vol. 4, No. 3, June, 1939, pp. 335-340.

Mead, Margaret (Ed.). *Cooperation and Competition among Primitive Peoples.* New York, McGraw-Hill Book Co., Inc., 1937.

Park, Robert E. "Personality and Cultural Conflict." *Pubs. Am. Sociol. Soc.,* Vol. 25, 1931, pp. 95-110.

Park, Robert E. "Social Assimilation." *Encyclopedia of the Social Sciences.* Vol. 2, pp. 281-283.

Park, Robert E., and Burgess, E. W. *Introduction to the Science of Sociology.* Chicago, University of Chicago Press, 1924, Chs. 6, 9, 10, 11.

Queen, S. A., Bodenhafer, W. B., and Harper, E. B. *Social Organization and Disorganization.* New York, T. Y. Crowell Co., 1935, Ch. 19, "Accommodation to Conflict."

Quinn, James A. "Ecological versus Social Interaction." *Sociology and Social Research,* Vol. 18, 1933-1934, pp. 565-571.

Reuter, E. B., and Hart, C. W. *Introduction to Sociology.* New York, McGraw-Hill Book Co., Inc., 1933, Chs. 10, 12, 13, 14.

Sherman, Mandel. *Mental Conflicts and Personality.* New York, Longmans, Green & Co., 1938.

Simmel, Georg. *The Sociology of Conflict.* Translated from the German by Albion W. Small. *Am. J. Sociol.,* Vol. 9, 1903-1904, pp. 490-525, 672-689, 798-811.

Simpson, George. *Conflict and Community: A Study in Social Theory.* New York, T. S. Simpson, 1937.

Sorel, Georges. *Reflections on Violence.* Translated from the French by T. E. Hulme. New York, B. W. Huebsch, 1914.

Spykman, N. J. *The Social Theory of Georg Simmel.* Chicago, University of Chicago Press, 1925, Book II, Ch. II, pp. 112-127, "Opposition."

Williams, Robin M., Jr. *The Reduction of Intergroup Tensions: A Survey of Research on Problems of Ethnic, Racial, and Religious Group Relations.* Social Science Research Council Bulletin 57, New York, Social Science Research Council, 1947.

Wirth, Louis. "Social Interaction: The Problem of the Individual and the Group." *Am. J. Sociol.,* Vol. 44, No. 6, May, 1939, pp. 965-979.

Woolston, Howard. "The Process of Assimilation." *Social Forces,* Vol. 23, May, 1945, pp. 415-424.

Wright, Verne. "Summary of Literature on Social Adjustment." *Am. Sociol. Rev.,* Vol. 7, No. 3, June, 1942, pp. 407-422.

Chapter 14

INTERACTION IN INTERNATIONAL RELATIONS

NATIONALITY AND INTERNATIONAL RELATIONS

There can be no social life without social interaction. As we have noted, social interaction proceeds within the framework of the ecological pattern and in terms laid down by the cultural configuration of the interacting entities. There is an ecology of culture traits and patterns quite as much as there is an ecology of fauna and flora, of slums and high-class residential areas, of tobacco economy and cotton economy, of agricultural villages and industrial cities, of Hollywood bungalows and towering skyscrapers. Moreover, in the world there are also several roughly demarcated but fairly distinct general culture areas: Euro-American, Mohammedan, Chinese, African, American Indian, and Polynesian being among those rather clearly definable.[1] Within these areas characteristic civilizations prevail although with considerable overlapping, as, for example, where the Euro-American civilization has penetrated the Mohammedan, the Polynesian, and other cultural worlds. There are also subareas of culture within the larger, more inclusive areas. For example, the Euro-American culture area may be subdivided into some half dozen subsidiary areas, these in turn being still further divisible. Wissler has also divided the Indian cultures of North and South America into fourteen areas,[2] while Kroeber has divided the same cultures into fifteen areas.[3] Herskovits has identified ten distinct culture areas in native Africa.[4]

Of the great culture areas, the Euro-American comprises what is commonly referred to as Western or Occidental, while the others, with the exception of the African, constitute what is known as Eastern or Oriental civilization. At one time the contacts between these two

---

[1] Several classifications have been made of the great civilizations of the world. The tentative classification presented here is unlike the others, but seems to the writers to be warranted.

[2] Clark Wissler, *The American Indian*, New York, Oxford University Press, 1922.

[3] A. L. Kroeber, *Anthropology*, New York, Harcourt, Brace & Co., 1923, pp. 293-294, 335-339.

[4] M. J. Herskovits, "A Preliminary Consideration of the Culture Areas of Africa," *Am. Anthrop.*, Vol. 26, January-March, 1924, p. 50.

great civilizations were extremely limited. Travelers and traders from the West made intermittent visits to the Far East and occasionally warlike hordes from the East invaded the West. Although the interests of trade made interaction along the cultural border in the Levant or Near East a more frequent occurrence, the farther reaches of these vast culture areas were rarely touched by alien culture contacts.

For centuries the Orient held a strange lure for the adolescent West but remained indifferent to it and uninfluenced by it. The East was satisfied with its culture, one which was already ancient when primitive men roamed the forests of Europe. It remained inscrutable, imperturbable, and aloof. But the West came to the East, bringing with it the more superficial aspects of its cultures, particularly the material objects of culture. All over the East today are to be seen symbols of the mechanical age, which rose and flourished first in the West. These furnish strange combinations and contrasts. Side by side are giant ships and colorful junks, reinforced concrete office buildings and fragile temples, buses, automobiles, and fast-moving electric trains beside rickshaws and plodding ox-carts, western dress with sandals and kimonos.

However, this is simply the veneer of the Occident. Underneath the old life of the Orient remains, changing slowly, appropriating and selectively adopting what it wants. For a long time the West has been well aware of the industrial and trade possibilities in Oriental lands and, in times past, has been inclined to impose its goods and services on peoples regarded as inferior. On the other hand, the Orientals, until recently complacent in the satisfaction of their own superiority, stolidly proceeding on their accustomed course, dealing politely with the representatives of western powers and business concerns, finally asserted themselves. Japan entered the lists of formidable competitors of the United States and other western nations; China, awakening from her cultural inertia of many centuries, showed an increasing resistance to the aggressive approaches of western powers; India grew more defiant of the domination of and more troublesome to the peace of the British Commonwealth; and Turkey, though having assimilated more of western culture than any other eastern nation with the possible exception of Japan, maintained a social distance between herself and the West. As time passed and interaction increased between West and East, certain of the Oriental nations and nationalities became more and more conscious of their inferior status as compared with the leading nations of Europe and America.

As a consequence, they became more assertive in their bids for recognition. Japan, more advanced than the others, aimed at a Japanese hegemony for all of Asia, for the accomplishment of which she initiated a program of military conquest. Initial success in this course of action led to an alliance with the fascist powers of Europe, encouraged her ambitions for power, and caused her to take the offensive against the western democracies in the last war. Thus the cultural exchange between East and West has been alternately promoted and resisted through several centuries in terms of trade, conquest, education, missionary effort, and diplomacy, to be temporarily interrupted by the crashing crescendo of war.

While the cultures of the East and West will probably remain distinct entities for a long time to come, it is possible that in the future there will be more extensive exchange relations in terms of cultural interaction on a basis of greater mutual understanding. Even if the plans for an effective world federation materialize, it is likely that its more formal political and economic aspects will be only partially efficient unless they are supported by a great enhancement of the acculturation of the peoples of the earth. All social interaction, whether between persons, groups, regions, or nations, is largely channelized and directed by culture traits and complexes.

Leaving the subject of interaction between the great, general cultural regions, we will now turn our attention to interaction between nationalized culture areas. Strictly speaking, cultures are not confined by arbitrary lines drawn on the map of the earth. National boundaries and cultural boundaries do not necessarily correspond. However, this does not prevent politically independent units or aspirants for political autonomy from considering themselves as ethnically and culturally distinct from their neighbors. Although the racial identity and the cultural peculiarity of the national group may be largely fiction, if they are treated as realities they are significant for national internal efficiency and loyalty and for international relations.

Nationality and Nation.—The difference between the concepts "nationality" and "nation" is often somewhat confusing to the student. They are alike in that they were originally ethnic or racial concepts used to denote a group which was bound together or believed to be bound together by ties of race or kinship. During the Middle Ages, and continuing through the centuries that followed—particularly the 18th and 19th centuries—there developed a sense of nationality in which notions of racial identity and kinship were lost or were allowed to remain as half truths and half myths. To this sense of nationality was added a consciousness of spiritual and cultural unity. As the result of the unification of principalities, of wars of aggression and conquest, and later through the revolutionary successes of the masses of the people, the national spirit spread rapidly and assumed a political character.[5]

When a nationality group becomes politically organized and an independent state, it is a *nation*. As long as it is merely united in spirit and possessed of common culture traits and fundamental interests which distinguish it from other groups, but lacks independent political organization, it remains a *nationality*. The national spirit, when it exists, usually demands political self-expression and stimulates a restlessness and a striving for recognition as an autonomous national state.[6] Many culturally distinct groups exist as dependencies or subjects of the greater national states without group solidarity and with little or no consciousness of their cultural background and unique characteristics. Indeed, many, if not all, of their distinctive cultural marks are gone. They are not even nationalities. Unless a conscious sentiment of loyalty to their own cultural heritage is aroused in them, they will not become nationalities.

Nationalities are characterized by an internal cohesiveness, a sense of belonging together on the part of the members of the group, and a feeling of being sharers in a common culture and a common way of life. They are also marked by ethnocentrism. When other nationalities are held to be their superiors and when sometimes they are their rulers, then the national self-consciousness takes on something of the nature of an "oppressed nationality psychosis." Even nations, self-governing states as they are, will assume these same nationalistic sentiments if they are threatened, restrained, or forced into positions regarded as dishonorable or inimical to their security or welfare. In time of crisis, either arising within the nation or affecting it from outside its borders, the nation may become extremely nationalistic. This is especially true if the crisis touches its relations with other nations or nationalities. An example of extreme nationalism was that exhibited by Nazi Germany.[7]

[5] See: C. A. Beard, *The Idea of National Interest*, New York, The Macmillan Co., 1934; H. A. Gibbons, *Nationalism and Internationalism*, Philadelphia, F. A. Stokes Co., 1930; C. J. H. Hayes, *Historical Evolution of Modern Nationalism*, New York, Long & Smith, 1931; R. H. Lowie, *The Origin of the State*, New York, Harcourt, Brace & Co., 1937; C. H. McIlwain, *Constitutionalism, Ancient and Modern*, Ithaca, Cornell University Press, 1940; Ramsay Muir, *Nationalism and Internationalism*, Boston, Houghton Mifflin Co., 1917.

[6] See: L. S. Greenberg, *Nationalism in a Changing World*, New York, Greenberg, Publisher, Inc., 1937; Hans Kohn, *The Idea of Nationalism*, New York, The Macmillan Co., 1944; C. H. McIlwain, *Constitutionalism and the Changing World*, New York, The Macmillan Co., 1939; J. H. Rose, *Nationality in Modern History*, New York, The Macmillan Co., 1916.

[7] See: Theodore Abel, *Why Hitler Came to Power*, New York, Prentice-Hall, Inc., 1938; D. J. Dallin, *The Real Soviet Russia*, New Haven, Yale University Press, 1944; M. T.

International relations consist of much more than the interrelations of trade, travel, exchange, and diplomacy, among the national states that exist in the world today, wherein each regards itself as equal, if not superior, to each of the others. The fundamental factors involved are those of human nature and culture, which touch all nationalities, and not merely the relatively few independent nations. The improvement of international intercourse and the amicable settlement of international differences depend more upon an understanding of the human and cultural factors involved than they do upon the more formal aspects of treaty arrangements, the fine technicalities of international law, the official deliberations of the United Nations, or the self-interested negotiations of international bankers, oil companies, or munitions makers. In brief, the chief concern for international relations lies in an understanding and appreciation of the cultural likenesses and differences of the many nationality groups of the world, only relatively few of which have succeeded in establishing and retaining political independence and in being treated as nations. There are numerous organized efforts to seek fuller international acculturation through education, the exchange of professors and students, conferences, literary and scientific reciprocity, and the like.

Since nationalities are distinguished from each other and accorded recognition primarily in terms of their differentiated culture patterns and, in the case of those that have achieved and maintained nationhood, by their political organizations (which are, in fact, culture complexes), it is important that we take account of the ways in which culture tends to determine the interaction between nationalities. Wissler has stated a few principles formulated from our present knowledge of culture. These principles are: (1) the outstanding impressions one people entertain of another are, for the most part, based upon their cultures and only to lesser degrees upon their anatomical characteristics; (2) racial or cultural groups tend to migrate to or to invade areas like their homelands; (3) each true national unit regards itself as superior to all others and holds its culture to be the best; (4) a group tends to regard its culture as synonymous with its life; (5) when a group comes into a new solution to one of its important culture problems, it becomes zealous to spread that idea abroad and is moved to embark upon an era of conquest to force the recognition of its merits; and (6) the setting in a culture area is

Florinsky, *World Revolution and the U.S.S.R.*, New York, The Macmillan Co., 1933; Konrad Heiden, *History of National Socialism*, New York, Alfred A. Knopf, 1935; Adolf Hitler, *Mein Kampf*, New York, Reynal & Hitchcock, 1939; A. Kolnai, *The War Against the West*, New York, The Viking Press, Inc., 1938; F. L. Schuman, *The Nazi Dictatorship*, 2nd ed., New York, Alfred A. Knopf, 1936.

especially favorable to the usurpation of power by one of the tribal or national groups near the center, i.e., the strongest tend to subjugate the weaker groups.[8]

If the above statement of principles is a correct estimate of the role of culture in the interaction between nationalized culture areas, it is easy to see how provocative of tensions international relations may be. Certainly we may conclude that the culture complexes of nationality groups and of nations include many tension-making factors and mechanisms.

PRELUDES TO WAR

A question may be raised as to why emphasis should be placed on war in a discussion of international relations. The reason lies principally in the history of the last decades. At no time in that period have the great national powers of the world been entirely free of war or the tensions that might lead to war.

The War Pattern.—War, like all forms of conflict, follows a fairly well-defined pattern. The pattern begins to take shape in the preparations for war, continues through the war-making behavior of the belligerents, and reaches its dénouement in the final arbitrament of battle, military decision, and peace or armed truce.

War literature, for the most part, contains an unsatisfactory explanation of this particular type of conflict pattern. Little or no account is taken of the natural history of war, of the underlying forces and processes involved in the struggle. It will be the purpose of this chapter, in addition to other phases of international relations, to make an analysis of the interplay of attitudes, motives, and ideals, institutional organizations and mechanisms, which enter into the composition of the war pattern.

Certain significant facts emerge from a study of war. It is evident that war is a social phenomenon growing naturally out of a complex social situation, international in character,[9] in which the element of hostility predominates over every other interest and in which the forces evolve a conflict pattern of behavior by a process of summation. When this process eventuates in concerted group action in the form of armed combat, it is war.

It should not be assumed that all contention between nations is war, or that even all coercion or violence in the relations of nations

---

[8] Adapted from Clark Wissler, *Man and Culture*, New York, T. Y. Crowell Co., 1923, pp. 335-341. See reference for discussion and illustration of the principles stated.

[9] Except in the case of civil war, in which case the two sides usually assume the characteristics of organized states or governments.

is war. It has become very common in recent years to speak quite loosely of "cold war," "psychological warfare," and "war of nerves," just as in the past reference has been made frequently to "trade war," "tariff war," "ideological warfare," and "legal war," the latter meaning any form of legal coercion exercised by one nation against another. Strictly speaking, these are not war. They may or may not be preludes to or accompaniments of actual warfare. Quincy Wright says of these frequently made assumptions that they "render the control of war hopeless. The anarchist striving to eliminate all legal coercion, the isolationist striving to eliminate all intergroup relations, the idealist trying to eliminate all contentions, and the extreme pacifist trying to eliminate all violence are engaged in a hopeless task. On the other hand, it is possible that appropriate modifications of international law and procedure, of national attitudes and ideals, of social and economic conditions, and of the methods by which governments keep themselves in power may prevent the recurrence of war." [10]

The Causes of War.—The problem of the causes of war is most confused. Sorokin says:

The existing literature on war causation reveals the almost hopelessly muddled condition of our knowledge in this field, and in that of causality generally. We find in this literature, first, *an almost unbelievable diversity of causes set forth by different, and sometimes even by the same, investigators.* The causal factors invoked include: sunspots, climate, conjunctions of planets, and other cosmic factors; instincts of pugnacity, of war, of fighting, of herd, and of aggressiveness; overpopulation, underpopulation, high and low birth and mortality rates; universal law of struggle for existence, and other biological factors; fear, fight for freedom, relaxation from inhibitions imposed by civilization, sadism, lust for power, ostentation, vanity, and dozens of other psychological forces; a long list of economic, political, dynastic, religious, aesthetic, educational, and other social factors; diverse cultural conditions like "the true and false culture," *mores,* and the like; philosophical abstractions like Destiny, Providence, and so on; and finally, various "wicked," great- and small-men and groups. This enormous diversity of the causes is sufficient evidence of a lack of a real knowledge of the problem.[11]

Sorokin continues by pointing out the internal inconsistencies of many of the theories offered, the inadequacy of the "single" causal idea, and the defects of the principle of so-called multiple causation. Of the latter, which is very popular at present, he says it is "neither clear, nor unquestionable, nor free from serious logical difficulties."

10 Quincy Wright, "The Causation and Control of War," *Am. Sociol. Rev.,* Vol. 3, No. 4, August, 1938, p. 461.
11 Pitirim A. Sorokin, "A Neglected Factor of War," *Am. Sociol. Rev.,* Vol. 3, No. 4, August, 1938, p. 475.

"Factors which are quite incommensurable and which belong to profoundly different planes of phenomena are put together, and even side by side, under the multiple principle." "Furthermore, even when they are free from this error, the formulae of multiple causation do not give *per se* any criterion for choice of the real causes out of millions of circumstances out of which a war breaks out. . . . the above conglomeration of the factors of our 'multiple causation' is still nothing but enumeration of a few incidental conditions, chosen haphazardly or arbitrarily, mistaken for the causes." [12]

It is obvious that many of these so-called "causes" of war are inconsequential and need not engage our attention. Certain of the theoretically held assumptions, however, are worthy of brief analysis since they are so generally believed and since they bear some marks of plausibility. Whether or not they are causes of war, they are frequently found among the attendant circumstances and conditions of specific war-making patterns. They are tension-contributing factors and, for purpose of discussion, will be treated under three broad headings: ecological, human nature, and socio-cultural.

Ecological Tension-Making Factors.—Upon examination, we find that while many factors making for tension between nation-states lie within the matrices of culture, others are to be found in the ecological order wherein many of the conditions are established and much of the direction of social contacts and social interaction is determined. Since it is within the framework of the ecological pattern that social interaction takes place, we will give attention first to the ecological factors that make for tension in international relations.

ECONOMIC PRESSURES. One of the most significant tensions is economic pressure, which is the inevitable result of the efforts of nations to survive and function as industrial and commercial powers. There was a time, which extended well into the early modern period of history, when the prevailing conception of the right of the nation-state to survive was by aggressive warfare. This was the state's chief function. During this period the industrial and economic activities of its citizens were regarded as forces to be mobilized in support of military activities against other groups.

However, with the speeding-up of trade, communications, transportation, technological processes, and the opening up of new lands with vast mineral, timber, and agricultural resources, the tension of international competition shifted from military provisions and re-

---

12 *Ibid.*, pp. 477-479.

current warfare to an industrial and commercial basis. Military policy became secondary in importance and dependent upon the economic one. The military program became a mechanism of force to prepare the way for commercial and capitalistic penetration and to protect such enterprises when they conflicted with the competitive encroachments of rival groups or when they were opposed by native peoples who were unwilling to be exploited. While the medieval principle of national survival and aggrandizement through warfare, recently revived by certain leading powers, may look as if it were an end in itself, it has a more realistic basis in enhanced economic rivalries, rationalized in terms of racism, manifest destiny, or some other form of ideology.

We see here a struggle for control, for economic power, for prestige. The prizes at stake are foreign markets, the sources of raw materials, or fields for the investment of surplus capital. The contending groups are rivals, each one intent upon eliminating its opponents from the "arenas of friction." The ecological process of invasion and test of fitness prepares the way for a self-conscious contest.[13]

One should not be misled, however, into an acceptance of the foregoing statement of the role of economic considerations in provoking tensions between nations as a form of economic determinism.

Persons or nations are said to act economically when their actions are directed toward obtaining control over goods and services. This naïve conception of economic motives is responsible for a good deal of the confusion which surrounds the problem of the economic causes of war. It is not ordinarily realized that a struggle to obtain control over goods and services may have nothing economic about it—may, as a matter of fact, be quite anti-economic—and that what is generally assumed to be an economic motive may often be but an economic illusion, because a cultural situation insists on finding economic reasons for human behavior. Speaking strictly and accurately, economic motives have nothing to do with the contents of human action but only with the means by which these actions are accomplished. . . .

---

13 Some books dealing with the subject of economic pressure in international relations are the following: Sir Norman Angell, *Raw Materials, Population Pressure and War*, London, H. Hamilton, for the World Peace Foundation, 1936; H. E. Barnes, *The Genesis of the World War*, New York, Alfred A. Knopf, 1926; L. L. Bernard, *War and Its Causes*, New York, Henry Holt & Co., 1944; H. Brinton (Ed.), *Does Capitalism Cause War?*, London, H. & E. R. Brinton, 1935; Editors of *Fortune, Background of War*, New York, Alfred A. Knopf, 1937; Paul Einzig, *Economic Warfare*, New York, The Macmillan Co., 1941; Otto Lehmann-Russbüldt, *War for Profits*, New York, A. H. King, 1930; Richard Lewinsohn, *The Profits of War*, New York, E. P. Dutton & Co., 1937; Horst Mendershausen, *The Economics of War*, New York, Prentice-Hall, Inc., 1940; Frank Munk, *The Economics of Force*, New York, G. W. Stewart, 1940; Philip Noel-Baker, *The Private Manufacture of Armaments*, New York, Oxford University Press, 1937; A. C. Pigou, *The Political Economy of War*, rev. ed., London, Macmillan & Co., Ltd., 1940; Hans Speier and Alfred Kahler (Eds.), *War in Our Time*, New York, W. W. Norton & Co., Inc., 1939; H. W. Spiegel, *The Economics of Total War*, New York, D. Appleton-Century Co., 1942; Quincy Wright, *The Causes of War and the Conditions of Peace*, New York, Longmans, Green & Co., 1935.

It should be apparent by now that all the economic arguments for war are arguments and not motives. There is no evidence in modern times that a nation either plans a war because it feels no other way out of economic distress or because it feels that it is justified in going to war in order to avoid future economic distress. Economic reasons are rationalizations and justifications because a nation needs a justification for its power prestige urges so essential a part of the feeling of solidarity and loyalty. The reason why it needs a justification for war or preparation for war is that our moral system has not as yet provided us with a scheme of values which will enable a nation to obtain the satisfaction of power prestige without war and domination, while at the same time this moral system has outlawed unjustifiable war, violence, and national aggression. Caught in this contradiction, nations must obtain power prestige by conflict and domination, while at the same time they must offer moral or, at any rate, justifiable reasons for such aggression—and economic justifications. Starving millions, factories devoid of necessary raw materials, goods piled high and rotting for lack of markets, capital strangled for lack of investment—all these apocalyptic visions permit us the luxury of hatred, the orgiastic satisfaction in death and destruction, and the tremendous expansion of the personal ego which comes with war, with domination, with patriotic strutting, with a feeling of ruling other peoples—of being great, powerful, and feared. And the more one is dominated at home by a political system which deprives man of personal and civil liberty, the greater the satisfaction obtained by nationalistic tumult and by warlike growling and saber-rattling.[14]

POPULATION PRESSURES. More than a century ago, Malthus perceived the tendency of mankind to increase more rapidly than the means of subsistence.[15] Although somewhat mistaken in some of his conclusions, the correctness of his theory, in its main aspects, has been amply confirmed by others.[16] This tendency of population in certain areas of the world to outrun the means of maintaining itself in comfort has forced men to seek new homes in other parts of the world, has furnished nationality groups with a pretext for extending their boundaries, or for establishing fresh colonies in the less-developed but promising regions of the earth, and has been regarded as a significant cause of international friction. Malthus proposed to control population by means of a check which he called "moral restraint," meaning "a restraint from marriage, from prudential motives, with a conduct strictly moral during the period of restraint." In the case of the failure of this mitigating policy, Malthus declared that alternative

---

[14] Max Handman, "War, Economic Motives, and Economic Symbols," *Am. J. Sociol.*, Vol. 44, No. 5, March, 1939, pp. 629-630, 646-647.

[15] T. R. Malthus, *An Essay on the Principle of Population*, London, 1798, 1803. Reprinted, 1926, by Macmillan & Co., Ltd.

[16] W. S. Thompson, *Population: A Study in Malthusianism*, New York, Columbia University Press, 1915.

checks in the form of war, disease, and famine would operate. In fact, until recently, these latter checks have been the most effective means of meeting the problem of overpopulation.

COUNTRIES OF "TEEMING MILLIONS." The problem of population, so far as size is concerned, may be either one of underpopulation or one of overpopulation. For international relations it is the latter that has provided a rationalization for aggressive tendencies. The contention of the overpopulated nations, however, is largely an expression of the sentiment-attitudes of nationalism and a pretext for imperialistic expansion. The fundamental problem of the countries with "teeming millions" is that of unlimited reproduction, but, in the long run, additional increments of territory and emigration have never served to solve the problem. Unrestrained reproduction does not cease merely because some of the population are forced to move. Their places are soon filled and continue to be filled until the population meets the positive checks of Malthus—disease, plague, famine, and war.[17]

Many nationalistic leaders and writers have seized upon this problem of population pressure to defend the proposition that international warfare is a biologically necessary means to its solution. And yet, by a curious twist of logic, "as soon as this tendency [to check the increase of population] becomes apparent, the same nationalist who invokes the menace of overpopulation as the justification for war, also invokes nationalism to reverse the tendency which would solve the overpopulation problem."[18] Even if the talk of population outlets and access to raw materials is not wholly in line with reality, it must be recognized that it makes a powerful appeal to the masses of

---

[17] Some broad aspects of the subject under discussion are treated in the following: S. Chandrasekhar, *India's Population*, New York, The John Day Co., 1946; W. R. Crocker, *The Japanese Population Problem: The Coming Crisis*, London, G. Allen & Unwin, Ltd., 1931; *Demographic Studies of Selected Areas of Rapid Growth: Proceedings of the Round Table on Population Problems of the 22nd Annual Conference of the Milbank Memorial Fund*, New York, Milbank Memorial Fund, 1944; H. P. Fairchild, *People: The Quantity and Quality of Population*, New York, Henry Holt & Co., 1939; D. V. Glass, *The Struggle for Population*, New York, Oxford University Press, 1936; D. V. Glass, *Population Policies and Movements in Europe*, Oxford, The Clarendon Press, 1940; Ryoichi Ishii, *Population Pressure and Economic Life in Japan*, Chicago, University of Chicago Press, 1937; Dudley Kirk, *Europe's Population in the Interwar Years*, Princeton, Princeton University Press, 1947; Bruno Lasker, *Peoples of Southeast Asia*, New York, Alfred A. Knopf, 1944; W. E. Moore, *Economic Demography of Eastern and Southern Europe*, New York, Columbia University Press, 1945; R. Mukerjee, "Population Theory and Politics," *Am. Sociol. Rev.*, Vol. 6, No. 6, December, 1941, pp. 784-793; Gunnar Myrdal, *Population: A Problem for Democracy*, Cambridge, Harvard University Press, 1940; F. W. Notestein, et al., *The Future Population of Europe and the Soviet Union*, New York, Columbia University Press, 1944; Ta Chen, *Population in Modern China*, Chicago, University of Chicago Press, 1946; W. S. Thompson, *Population and Peace in the Pacific*, Chicago, University of Chicago Press, 1946.

[18] Sir Norman Angell, *The Fruits of Victory*, New York, The Century Co., 1921, p. 89.

the people in crowded lands. Raw materials are sought by all nations and most peoples believe that ownership of resources is a better guarantee than dependence upon the good will of the larger possessing nations.

The problem of surplus population assumed a somewhat different aspect after World War I. The comparative freedom of movement which existed before largely disappeared, and the population pressure argument, while still mainly a rationalization of other and more fundamental motives, carries today a more convincing tone until examined more closely in the light of the economic motivation which it presumes to obey. Population pressure in modern times is simply a function of the state of the industrial arts, the productive efficiency of the community, and unlimited reproduction. Considered from an economic standpoint, the question of whether to engage in war in order to force a reluctant nation with unused land to open its doors to a population without land is a matter of whether the expenditure of men and money needed to prosecute a war (even if success were assured in advance, which, of course, is never the case) will bring larger returns than an equal investment of money in improving the productive equipment of its own economy. However, the policy-makers do not reason in such fashion, for no nation looks upon the pressure of population as a purely economic problem, but as a power problem. Nevertheless, wars of conquest for the sake of adding new areas to the national domain in order to provide outlets for surplus population have been fought and no doubt will be fought again in terms of such rationalization.

Human Nature Factors.—It is sometimes argued that there has always been war because "human nature" demands it; "human nature" does not change, therefore, wars will continue to occur. There are at least two misleading implications in the argument. In the first place, it is very questionable if war has always existed. Most anthropologists hold to the opinion that primitive man, living on the level of savagery, did not engage in organized group fighting. It is more than likely that organized warfare with a conscious purpose did not appear until groups had acquired enough available property to arouse the envy of their neighbors. When this first occurred no one knows. There are, however, human groups, such as the Eskimo, the Barama River Caribs, and numerous other contemporary primitives, who are practically free of the war pattern. Malinowski says that "when two clans or two local groups fight with each other within the framework of the same tribal law, we deal with cases of legal mechanisms, but not with antecedents of war." [19] He states further that before there could be warfare in a strict sense, what he calls the "tribe-state" must have been developed. "The tribe-state has to be defined in terms of political unity, that is, of centralized authoritative power and the corresponding organization of armed force." [20] In this anthropologist's view, then, war is a function of the "tribe-state," or what we have termed the "nation-state." Regardless of when and under what particular circumstances warfare appeared, we know that with the growth of populations and changes in the politico-economic conditions of life, war came to be a fairly common preoccupation of rulers and statesmen. As a consequence, it has become an important part of the culture complexes of all "civilized" peoples.

Secondly, to say that human nature does not change is to deny the facts of human restlessness and development and to anyone who makes such a dogmatic statement it is fair to reply with Hocking, "It is human nature to change itself." [21] The notion that there have always been wars requires more supporting evidence than we have at present, and the assumptions concerning "original nature" are equally undocumented. To assert that "man is a fighting animal" is not to say that he is a "warlike animal." In the first place, we cannot, with validity, characterize animals as warlike, although fighting does exist among them. Man's tendencies and efforts at wish satisfaction may easily take the form of a fighting pattern.

Study has been made in recent years of the nature and function of aggression as a trait of human nature.[22] It seems to the researchers that the impulse which controls aggression is not primary, but derived. "Cultures have patterned aggression in many different ways. The degree to which one individual will fight, attempt to dominate or destroy persons or objects which interfere with his attainment of a goal, is of very great concern in human societies." [23] Moreover, fighting and warmaking are by no means the same. Fighting may be a playful activity, a seeking for new experience, or the fulfillment

---

[19] Bronislaw Malinowski, "An Anthropological Analysis of War," *Am. J. Sociol.*, Vol. 46, No. 4, January, 1941, p. 534.

[20] *Ibid.*, p. 536. Malinowski holds to the opinion that the "tribe-state," a political unit, is a cultural differentiation of the "tribe-nation," a unit of cultural cooperation and the more fundamental cultural type.

[21] W. E. Hocking, *Human Nature and Its Remaking*, New Haven, Yale University Press, 1918, p. 10.

[22] See: E. F. M. Durbin and John Bowlby, *Personal Aggressiveness and War*, London, K. Paul, Trench, Trubner & Co., 1938; Edward Glover, *War, Sadism and Pacifism*, London, G. Allen & Unwin, 1933. These books present inadequate and incorrect analyses of aggressiveness, while the work of John Dollard and associates, *Frustration and Aggression*, New Haven, Institute of Human Relations, Yale University, 1939, offers a more satisfactory interpretation.

[23] Margaret Mead, *And Keep Your Powder Dry*, New York, William Morrow & Co., Inc., 1942, p. 139.

of the wish for recognition, but it may find its satisfaction in numerous ways besides that of war. Man is so constituted that he may be conditioned for either physical combat or social cooperation. If his culture stresses the war-making role, he, being oriented in that culture, will be likely to develop the appropriate patriotic and warlike sentiments and have his habit patterns directed along military lines.[24] On the other hand, if the culture of his group is inclined to emphasize the pursuits of peace and cooperation, his attitudes will be conditioned accordingly. Under these circumstances, if war threatens his nation, the latter will be faced with the problem of defining his capacities for aggressiveness to the end that he will fight.

Socio-Cultural Tension-Making Factors.—Groups tend to develop the kinds of cultures which, in their experience, seem best suited to their needs for survival, security, and well-being. If they find that their surroundings and conditions of life require the development of a fighting class, modern weapons, and a militant spirit, they will be apt to follow the line suggested by the circumstances. To fail to do so may mean their final extinction or submergence. In our world, isolation no longer is sufficient to relieve any sizable politically organized group from the necessity of some sort of war-making attitudes and techniques. The operation of ecological and cultural factors through the centuries has increased the occasions for what we know today as war.[25]

Lying within the field of culture are mechanisms of a social nature that operate to provide tensions between ethnocentric nationality groups. Only a few of these can receive attention here.

NATIONALISM. There is probably no more potent force in creating situations that inevitably arouse antagonisms and stimulate rivalries than the attitude-value complex of *nationalism*. It is this complex which is at the core of the modern national state system. Nationalism

---

[24] See: W. Ackermann, *Are We Civilized?* New York, Covici, Friede, 1936; H. E. Barnes, *History and Social Intelligence*, New York, Alfred A. Knopf, 1926, Ch. 1; Martin Conway, *The Crowd in Peace and War*, New York, Longmans, Green & Co., 1915; D. S. Muzzey, *The Menace of Patriotism*, New York, Ethical Culture Society, 1915; Frederick Palmer, *Our Gallant Madness*, New York, Doubleday, Doran & Co., 1937; C. E. Playne, *The Neuroses of the Nations*, 2 vols., London, G. Allen & Unwin, Ltd., 1925; S. and J. Raushenbush, *War Madness*, Washington, National Home Library, 1937; J. F. Scott, *Patriots in the Making*, New York, D. Appleton & Co., 1916.

[25] See: J. D. Clarkson and T. C. Cochran, *War as a Social Institution*, New York, Columbia University Press, 1941; R. E. Dupuy and G. F. Eliot, *If War Comes*, New York, The Macmillan Co., 1937; G. F. Eliot, *The Defense of the Americas*, New York, Reynal and Hitchcock, 1941; C. H. Hamlin, *The War Myth in American History*, New York, Vanguard Press, Inc., 1927; P. A. Sorokin, *Social and Cultural Dynamics*, 4 vols., New York, American Book Co., 1937, 1941, Vol. III, Part II; Richard Stockton, *Inevitable War*, New York, Perth Co., 1932; Alfred Vagts, *The History of Militarism*, New York, W. W. Norton & Co., Inc., 1937; Willard Waller (Ed.), *War in the Twentieth Century*, New York, The Dryden Press, Inc., 1939.

is a sentiment-attitude embracing the conception of one's own group as a nationality, culturally different from and superior to other similar groups, and embodying notions of national honor, power, and destiny.

Predilection in favor of one's own group, its language, culture, and ideals arises in the process of social interaction by which the nationality group and its cultural values are defined. Around group values the members are emotionally organized for a common sentiment of loyalty. Nationalistic symbols, like language and folk-literature, heroic figures, national anthems, the flag, and national monuments, serve to focus the attention of the people on common objects, which become rallying points for united expression, and tend to stimulate a strong in-group feeling. The youth of the country, especially, are thus conditioned to attitudes of loyalty and pride. The nationality becomes the center of their hopes and aspirations and something to be defended against all others. National historians, poets, and statesmen, together with national ceremonials, military training, and patriotic societies, perform the function of producing collective emotional behavior which intensifies national sentiments.

Moreover, nationalities seek a place of honor in the councils of an organized world, and are rather quick to resent rebuffs or criticism. They may think their "honor" has been affronted and their "rights" violated. This tendency generates the sentiment-attitude of patriotism, a "twin sister" of nationalism. Patriotism is a form of piety. In times of peace, it demands devoted service in the use of the forces and resources of the country to keep it strong and vigorous; in times of international conflict it demands the sacrifices of men, money, and materials to the point of exhaustion if need be.[26]

RECRUDESCENCE OF NATIONALISM. After World War I, which was itself largely the outgrowth of extreme nationalism centered mainly in western and central Europe, there was a recrudescence of nationalism on a large scale. The doctrine of self-determination, which was emphasized in the latter years of the war and at the peace conference, was evidence of the rebirth of numerous minorities and, in some instances, these minorities were elevated to the status of independent states. This achievement of autonomy served to feed rather than to allay nationalistic spirit, with the result that nationalism became a more fruitful source of rivalry and hostility between nations.

---

[26] See: H. W. Baldwin, *United We Stand*, New York, McGraw-Hill Book Co., Inc., 1941; C. A. Beard, *The Idea of National Interest*, New York, The Macmillan Co., 1934; James C. King, "Nationalism," *Am. J. Sociol.*, Vol. 39, No. 6, May, 1934, pp. 818-826; Beverly Nichols, *Cry Havoc*, New York, Doubleday, Doran & Co., 1933; Harry Shapiro, *What Every Young Man Should Know about War*, New York, Knight Pubs., 1937; Walter Sulzbach, *National Consciousness*, New York, American Council on Public Affairs, 1943.

Nationalism was elevated to the status of a religion in Fascist and Nazi states. The ideology of the nation was romanticized, dogmatically expounded, and slavishly followed. Ruptures between sovereign states, instead of being healed, were widened and exaggerated.

The most recent example of emerging nationalism as a threat to world peace is that shown by the anti-capitalistic federation of Soviet states, standing in juxtaposition to the so-called "free enterprise" states. These two cultures are now engaged in a struggle for supremacy. The "free-enterprise" states fortify national ardor and devotion with the slogan "Down with Communism." "The Communist point of view holds that the national spirit is a product of class conflict, an artificial creation of the bourgeoisie used to maintain themselves in power. 'The proleteriat have no fatherland,' has been the Communist slogan. . . . The Communists have emphasized the 'internationalness' of their movement. 'Proletariat of the world, unite!' is the slogan, the Communists think, that ought to sweep away European boundaries and national hatreds, and change nations into federated members of one soviet union." [27] The struggle between these two groups of nation-states began in the years before the Second World War, and although Russia lined up with the "free-enterprise" states on the basis of expediency during the war, the misunderstandings and tensions between them have been revived. Thus nationalism first drove the nations further apart, politically, economically, psychically, and culturally and then plunged them into the most costly and bitter struggle of all time. In this early postwar period, the nationalistic sentiments and symbols which are again being appealed to in preparation for the showdown which may eventually come, are intensifying the tensions between the two groups of nations.

IMPERIALISM. The concept of *imperialism* is but the expansion of the sentiment-attitude of nationalism. It is nationalism which has become conscious of its power and that would extend itself beyond the limits of its territorial boundaries. However, territorial extension is not the only objective of imperialism. Norton designates four expressions of imperialism—predatory, strategic, administrative, and financial.[28] His "predatory" imperialism is that of conquest in order that the conquering nation may exercise power over the lands and peoples of the conquered nations and thus be in a position to exploit their labor and resources for the benefit of the imperial power.

---

[27] William C. White, "Nationalism Darkens World Outlook," *The New York Times Magazine*, January 1, 1933, p. 13.

[28] Henry K. Norton, *Back of War*, New York, Doubleday, Doran & Co., 1928, pp. 100-124.

The excuses of economic or population pressures, or both, are offered for this type of imperialistic action. "Strategic" imperialism is illustrated in the cases of the Panama and Suez canals. That these canals should be built was obviously necessary and, in order that they be built, nations with the capital and engineering ability had to build them. Their strategic connection with world trade and their value in case of war made their construction imperative and tended to justify the means employed to that end. "Administrative" imperialism has sought to justify itself in the demand for law and order in all parts of the world, partly in response to economic considerations and partly on the pretext that the more advanced peoples of the earth had a "duty" to perform in spreading "civilization" among the more backward peoples. So-called "financial" imperialism has tended to follow the extension of commercial and industrial exploitation and capital investment by businessmen, industrialists, and investment bankers in relatively undeveloped but potentially rich lands. As a consequence, whole peoples have been prompted to give patriotic support to these fellow-citizens who were profiting at the expense of others.

Many of the rationalizations of the older imperialism have been supplanted by the justifications of the new order. Mussolini proclaimed the conquest of Ethiopia as a first step toward a restoration of "the imperial glory that was the Roman Empire." Hitler's moves against Germany's neighbors were explained in terms of strategy, not that of building canals, but of "rectifying the grievous wrongs of the Versailles treaty," "repatriation of members of the Greater Reich," who at that time were domiciled outside Germany's borders, and "preparation of strategic frontiers against the intended incursions of enemies of the Fatherland." The militarists of Japan took the view that their invasions of Manchuria and coastal China, and later farther afield, were explainable in terms of "equitable adjustment of frontiers," "establishment of co-prosperity spheres," "setting up of a new order," "taking over the duty of protecting," or simply "coordination."

No great power, even if it would, can avoid affecting international relations; its only choice is of the various ways open to it. The ways fall between national isolation and self-sufficiency; imperialist expansion and aggression; and a policy of economic, political, and cultural cooperation for the advantage of all peoples.

MILITARISM. In a world characterized by nationalism, and acute phases of post-war reaction, even the most peace-loving nation wants to be prepared to uphold its rights and to help restrain aggressive nations. Evidently this policy is being followed in all seriousness by the few remaining major powers today, as is manifested in the spectacle of talk of an even more terrible war to come, of rearmament, and of the resurgence of a defiant militaristic attitude.

Nearly every nation maintains some organization, some body of functionaries, whose business it is to see that some kind of military preparedness is established.   To take care of the necessary details in case of armed conflict with other nations, a military class develops, which is supported by traditional policies and programs.   This military class, with its aims, weapons, and a body of attitudes regarding them and their functions, constitute a military system.   This system is the objectification of the fears of one's neighbors.   So also is it the implement of the national wishes for security and recognition.   Security in war is dependent upon destroying or neutralizing the armed force of the enemy.   It is one force organized to meet another.

When two forces are organized to oppose one another, the chances are more than equal that they will meet sooner or later.   It is this chance of a clash that is responsible, in large measure, for the fears entertained by most national groups.   The extent of the fears depends partly upon the relative strength of the respective military forces and their aggressive policies, but more particularly upon the state of readiness in which the armaments are kept.   Events of the last two wars seem to indicate that mobilization means war.   Mobilization as a preparatory measure merges gradually into military necessity when and if a crisis comes in international relations.   Striking the first blow has great strategic advantage and carries the subject in dispute from the realm of reason to that of emotion, and under such conditions subservience to reason cannot be effectively maintained.

The explanation of militarism lies in the aims and purposes of nations.   To protect those aims and purposes from interference is the excuse for armaments.   While building up of armaments and mobilization for ready use have been denounced as being largely responsible for war, it is not likely that their abolition would guarantee peace.[29] Even if there were complete military disarmament and it were accompanied by "moral disarmament," there would remain the problem of satisfying the necessities and even the ambitions of growing nations.

THE WAR CULT: TRADITION AND RITUAL.   Any movement that has developed a history, a body of traditions, a group of functionaries, and an appropriate set of attitudes has become something of an institution—oftentimes a minor institution, it is true, but capable of be-

---

29 See: John W. Wheeler-Bennett, *The Pipe Dream of Peace*, New York, William Morrow & Co., 1934.

coming a major one. It may become a State or synonymous with a
State. This appears to be the case where militarism becomes institutionalized to the degree that the political organization of the nation-
state is in perfect harmony with it. Such was the case of Italy,
Germany, and Japan before the last war.

Militarism tends to become indoctrinated in sentiment-attitudes,
military training, and preparations for "the war that is sure to come."
These become national fetishes and the people are psychologically
conditioned by impassioned propaganda, "bogies," and alarms. Militarism has its hierarchy, ritual, and liturgy. It has about it all the
emotional tone and fervor of a religion. This is the cult of war—
solemn, serious, doctrinaire. In modern times, the war cult has
become a way of escape from the morbid subjectivism of everyday
life. The people find release and satisfaction in the pomp, splendor,
and pageantry of militarism. There also comes a satisfaction of the
wish for security through military organization.

It is in the war cult that we see the quintessence of a profound faith
in the rightness of the national cause. Herein are summed up in their
fullness the nationalistic ideals, the imperialistic ambitions, and the
militaristic confidence of a people. When these factors reach this
stage in their development, the cause of friendly international relations
is strained to the uttermost. The process of interaction tends to move
swiftly from rivalry toward open conflict.

MOBILIZATION. The part that is played by mobilization in preparation for hostilities has already been mentioned. Modern warfare
calls for the mobilization not only of the armed forces of the nation,
but of the entire population and of all available material resources
essential to the conduct of war. History seems to show that the
winning nation (or group of allied nations) will tend to be the side
which can command the strongest force of manpower and the greatest output of military supplies. If we may depend upon the experience of the last war we may conclude that while aggressor nations
have the first advantage of knowing what they intend to do and may
thus be well prepared in advance of the opening encounter in battle,
their success will depend upon a short, incisive war. Failing in that,
they must be prepared to match their dwindling resources and de-
pleted manpower against the increasing forces and dogged morale
of their adversaries, who will probably win in the long run.

Nothing drives the members of a group together so quickly as a
threat to their security. Seeking a protective unity, they revive group
sentiments of patriotism and nationality, they define their fears—

whether real or imagined—and sow the seeds of hate and the desire for revenge or for aggressive action. Interaction within the group is intensified through the spread of rumors, the repression of divisive interests, the movement of people to centers of military training and industrial activity, and the recruiting and selective impression of men and women for all the many and varied kinds of services called for by preparation for war. These devices serve to stimulate the group self-consciousness.

MECHANISMS OF MOBILIZATION. Conflict and heroic myths spring up and flourish during periods of national uncertainty. These mechanisms of social control have to do with past military achievements and the heroic dead, surprise attacks, disturbances in border areas, the debased status of the enemy's culture, and so on. In times of national danger the myth is effective in arousing and maintaining group fears and suspicions to a degree of intensity bordering on hysteria. Rumors spread and myths become the foci of general attention. Tensions are released and the group gives vent to its hopes and wishes. The group believes myths because it wants to believe them and because they seem to confirm previously held opinions and attitudes. The greater the expectancy and anxiety, the greater the credulity. The predisposition of the members of the social group is the chief element making for the ready acceptance of myths. Myths state for them what they feel must be true of their enemies or about themselves.

Among the symbols or collective representations of patriotic sentiments, one of the most common is the flag.

In situations of great emotional intensity it is natural for the individual to identify himself with the group. In intense moments of patriotism the individual identifies himself with the nation and counts his life as nothing. This identification also extends by psychological association to the symbols and other expressions of national life. The flag for the soldier becomes the embodiment of the spirit of his country and he gladly gives his life to recover it.[30]

The tendency is to identify experiences with the symbol. It represents the collective emotion of the group in conflict in the present and in the past, crystallizing about it a body of common memories that represent the experiences of each and all. "The soldier who dies for his flag dies for his country. He loses sight of the fact that the flag is only a sign . . . it is treated as though it were this reality

---

[30] J. E. Boodin, "The Law of Participation," *Am. J. Sociol.*, Vol. 27, No. 1, July, 1921, pp. 29-30.

[country] itself." [31] It is the objective embodiment of the total vivid reality of life, with its fears and hopes, which are released in a period of emotional excitement such as a national crisis. It is then that the flag is viewed uncritically and becomes a part of one's life and no longer a piece of cloth. The symbol and the complex it represents have come to be objectively undifferentiated.

Closely connected with the flag as symbols of nationality are the national anthems and patriotic songs. Many songs of this type make the flag the focal point of attention and further enhance its appeal. Some hymns and songs embody emotional notes of sadness on account of oppression, suffering, reverses, and losses of territory, or of joy and gaiety because of successes and conquest, and not a few express a feeling of religious ecstasy. It is in the songs of a people that its wish for freedom finds one of its expressions. The French national anthem, the "Marseillaise," is both a battle hymn and a sublimated wish for freedom. One's country is widely sung in national songs as a beautiful and priceless heritage received from the forefathers. England is "precious Albion" and the United States is "the home of the brave and the free." By imagery and the vernacular tongue, the poet touches the heart of the people and wins sympathizers and adherents to the cause of national unity for either defense or offense.

The myth, national anthem, and patriotic song are collective representations that have more definite meaning than the flag because they are embodied in language and get before the group on the printed page and the spoken word. So it is, also, with the slogan. Such patriotic slogans as "United We Stand, Divided We Fall," "Deutschland über Alles," "Britannia Rules the Waves," "Volk ans Gewehr," "My Country Right or Wrong," serve to direct public attention and transform stray sentiments into a fixed collective idea. Such short, pithy sayings, easily learned and readily repeated, enter spontaneously into social experience and, although they may be vague, sometimes fallacious, and often inapplicable in more than theory, yet they succeed in calling out prompt, uncritical emotional responses. They are vague representations that stand as junction points for more specific ideas and interests. In this way they conserve unity.

From what has been said it may be concluded that for a national group to prepare for action against a foe requires a great deal of cultivation of superpatriotic and nationalistic sentiments. It is the function of nationalistic propaganda to originate and spread the myths

---

[31] Émile Durkheim, *Elementary Forms of Religious Life*, New York, The Macmillan Co., 1915. Reprinted by The Free Press, Glencoe, Illinois, 1947, p. 219.

and rumors, slogans, and other collective representations referred to. Propaganda, as a nationalistic measure, is a technique for capitalizing prejudice and is used by each side in international controversy to build up its own morale and to destroy, if possible, that of the other side.

Propaganda is not new in history, but the uses to which it has been put in recent years have multiplied with the utilization of new and improved mechanisms for mass communication. Nations about to undertake a war of aggression and nations that regard themselves as the probable objects of that aggression have been quick to avail themselves of this effective technique for intimidation and persuasion. The media employed for propaganda purposes are many. Newspapers, journals, public speaking, books, motion pictures, and radio broadcasting have all been utilized.

Accommodative Mechanisms of the Prewar Period.—It is hardly likely that the masses of the people of a nation want war, if it can be avoided without too great a sacrifice of national prestige. So much cannot be said, however, of certain interested groups that can be found in every nation. However, as these groups are well aware, war cannot be made until the people, who must do the fighting and producing, are aroused to the fighting mood. One of the chief purposes of the collective symbols and of their propagation, which we have been discussing, is to accomplish this very thing. Until this has been achieved or until such time as some untoward international incident precipitates the issue and creates a crisis in international affairs, certain mechanisms of accommodation are in the ascendency and operate to maintain a *status quo,* or what is called a "balance of power."

The years between the two great wars were hazardous ones for the relations among the large power-states of the world. It was a period during which the foreign policies of the nations assumed two distinctly different directions, with one set of powers—the increasingly arrogant, boastful, and ambitious governments of Germany, Italy and Japan—tending more and more toward an offensive position, and the other powers—the traditionally more pacific, self-satisfied, and isolationist governments of Great Britain, France, and the United States—espousing rather doggedly a strategy of defense. The latter group of states held to the illusion that the defensive is stronger than the offensive, while the former states, eventually joined in an axis alliance, and largely under the tutelage and domination of German diplomatic and military minds, based their strategy upon the real, rather than the imaginary, lessons of World War I. The "balance of power" lay between these two opposed principles, and relations between them were manipulated in accordance with the ideologies implicit in them and the divergent techniques employed to implement them.

Germany, which until 1936 was disarmed and encircled, managed by 1938, to break up the world coalition, to separate Russia from France, to envelop Italy, to invade Austria, to destroy Czechoslovakia, to isolate Poland, to enter into alliance with Japan, and to lull England into appeasement and the United States into a feeling that nothing that happened in Europe or Africa or Asia really mattered, a feeling that coincided fully with American isolationism. England felt safe with her navy, France with her Maginot line, and the United States between the two oceans. Italy strutted her might in Ethiopia and later in Albania and she and Germany together, by "non-intervention," helped to bring about the defeat of the Spanish Republic, while the democracies raised no effective protest. Russia, in the meantime, engaged in carrying out successive "five-year plans" of industrial expansion at home, was not unmindful of what was transpiring to the west and to the east, and, after making a feeble gesture in behalf of the republican cause in Spain, turned to the task of looking after her own frontiers and to the consummation of an alliance with her greatest potential foe at that time, Germany. Japan had long since moved into Manchukuo and northern China and was in process of executing her plans for the establishment of a Greater East Asia Co-Prosperity Sphere with Japan in control.

On the other side, Great Britain, with troubles growing out of the great economic depression and with some of her dominions pulling away from the bonds of empire, was in an appeasing mood at the time of Munich in 1938 and scarcely ready for a showdown with the axis powers when Hitler sent his armies hurtling against Poland in the autumn of 1939. France was no better prepared to face up to the issue. Daladier was with Chamberlain at Munich, the French governments were weak, vacillating, and unstable, her military establishment suffered from dissension and obsolescent equipment and strategy, her economy was depressed and her labor force discontented, but she had the Maginot line. The position of the United States was little different in general, but somewhat more favorable in terms of resources, manpower, and "bargaining" force. Despite powerful minority sentiment for isolation and against "entangling alliances" in Congress and a pledge to neutrality "in the disputes of others," the President, by 1936, began to agitate for an embargo on munitions to the Loyalist government in Spain, and in 1937, called, in effect, for collective action by all the democracies against Germany, Italy, and Japan. His appeal was to "the peace-loving nations" to put a quarantine on aggressors. In the following January, the President called upon Congress for an enormous increase in naval outlays and for a mobilization bill. Successful in securing an extraordinary naval authorization, he next, in January, 1939, spoke of the challenging "storms from abroad" and called for a vast increase in armaments. Thus were the lines drawn between the axis powers, bent on aggression, and the so-called "democracies," which, beginning to sense their danger, were now arousing to take up arms, still in the interests of a defensive policy.

There is never a time when the relations between some of the great powers or among some of the lesser states are not so delicately adjusted that it would take only a small incident to precipitate them into overt conflict in the form of war. This event, the so-called immediate "cause" of war, like the assassination of an archduke and his wife, the sinking of the United States battleship *Maine* in Havana Harbor, or the attack on Pearl Harbor on December 7, 1941, is in reality but an incident in the whole chain of circumstances creating a war situation. It serves merely to release the forces that have up to that time been held in leash by counter forces. It is just at this point that the war-preparing public becomes the war-making crowd.[32] Nationalism, imperialism, and aggressive militarism, utilizing rumors, reports, collective symbols, diplomatic blunders, intrigues, and propagandistic techniques, sweep a nation toward war.[33] Against these factors tending toward conflict the accommodational elements hold out until the "historical moment" or final crisis comes. Occasions of war are many and often trivial; the causes of war are few.[34]

WHEN WAR COMES

Wars do not "just happen"; wars are "made." Some nation, with or without provocation, starts a war. But when can it be said that war has started? Is it when the tensions between two or more national states have reached such a point of antagonism that all hopes of reconciliation or rapprochement are gone and war is so inevitable that it may be said to have started? Is it begun only when the first

---

[32] See Chapter 23, "Social Unrest and Types of Collective Behavior."

[33] See: H. F. Armstrong, *Europe Between Wars.* New York, The Macmillan Co., 1934; V. de Balla, *The New Balance of Power in Europe,* Baltimore, Johns Hopkins Press, 1932; D. P. Heatley, *Diplomacy and the Study of International Relations,* Oxford, The Clarendon Press, 1919; W. L. Langer, *European Alliances and Alignments, 1871-1890,* New York, Alfred A. Knopf, 1939; W. L. Langer, *The Diplomacy of Imperialism,* 1890-1902, New York, Alfred A. Knopf, 1935; Herbert Matthews, *The Fruits of Fascism,* New York, Harcourt, Brace & Co., 1943; Douglas Miller, *You Can't Do Business With Hitler,* Boston, Little, Brown & Co., 1941; Walter Millis, *Road to War, 1914-1917,* Boston, Houghton Mifflin Co., 1935; P. S. Mowrer, *Our Foreign Affairs,* New York, E. P. Dutton & Co., 1924; Francis Neilson, *How Diplomats Make War,* New York, B. W. Huebsch, 1916; F. L. Schuman, *American Policy Toward Russia Since 1917,* New York, International Publishers, 1928; F. L. Schuman, *Europe on the Eve; the Crisis of Diplomacy,* New York, Alfred A. Knopf, 1942; F. L. Schuman, *International Politics: the Western State System in Transition,* New York, McGraw-Hill Book Co., Inc., 1941; F. L. Schuman, *Night Over Europe: The Diplomacy of Nemesis, 1939-1940,* New York, Alfred A. Knopf, 1941; F. L. Schuman, *Soviet Politics, at Home and Abroad,* New York, Alfred A. Knopf, 1946; F. L. Schuman, *War and Diplomacy in the French Republic,* New York, McGraw-Hill Book Co., Inc., 1931; Vincent Sheean, *Not Peace But a Sword,* New York, Doubleday, Doran Co., 1939.

[34] See: L. L. Bernard, *War and Its Causes;* Albert Carr, *America's Last Chance,* New York, T. Y. Crowell Co., 1941; Albert Carr, *Juggernaut, the Path of Dictatorship,* New York, The Viking Press, 1939; Norman Cousins, *Modern Man Is Obsolete,* New York, The Viking Press, 1945; E. M. Earle (Ed.), *Makers of Modern Strategy: Military Thought from Machiavelli to Hitler,* Princeton, Princeton University Press, 1943, 1944; F. L. Schuman, *Design for Power; the Struggle for the World,* New York, Alfred A. Knopf, 1942.

troops, planes, or ships move to the attack? Is it when the first guns
are fired or bombs dropped, or when diplomats are handed their
papers and invited to go home? There was a time when war was
"declared" by means of formal representations of one power to another through the channels of diplomacy; it was then and only then
that the war was started. The last war saw no such prelude to the
opening of hostilities. The aggressor nations set their armies, tanks,
planes, and ships against the "enemy" without formal announcement,
but not without warning. Modern totalitarian states employed techniques of "peaceful" penetration, the tactics of the *fait accompli,* the
"blitzkrieg," the "fifth column," the services of "quislings" inside the
domains of their intended victims, active cells of termitic agents who
bored from within, "the war of nerves" through both subtle and bla-
tant propaganda, and similar mechanisms, without having to fight.
The fighting was started when the other methods failed, when the re-
sistive powers of the opposition had been exhausted, or when, on the
contrary, it looked as if the resistants were about to succeed, either
by themselves or with the aid of allies.

When we say that all wars are "made," we do not mean to suggest
that wars, in general, follow the pattern outlined above, but merely
to suggest that such a pattern has come into use and that it may
conceivably serve as a model for future aggression. If a nation, inclined to take the initiative in making an overt hostile attack, is
equipped with the newest and most efficient weapons, it will be sorely
tempted to employ these first so as to secure an initial strategic advantage over the enemy. Nor does our statement that wars are
"made" necessarily imply that wars are started solely at the order of
and on the initiative of one man or set of men. Not even a dictator
or a military clique can start a war without taking into account the
forces that are present in the situation. Persons are either manipu-
lators of forces or are manipulated by them; in either case they
cannot ignore them. Persons may be able to hasten or delay the
course of events, but they are usually impotent to prevent them, once
the tide of events gets running strongly in a certain direction. Personalities are merely one of many elements that go to make up a
complex of forces and, as such, are mere figures to be used or crushed
by these forces. As often happens, the forces get beyond the control
of any man or group of men.

War-Making Behavior.—The national group, made ready for war
by the factors we have discussed, is now prepared to act. It is no
longer a public—discussing, threatening, and preparing—but an or-

ganized crowd possessed by a dominant mood of hatred for the enemy, and galvanized into a working and fighting unity. At the outset the dominant mood is one of *esprit de corps,* an uncontrolled enthusiasm; but as time goes on and defeats and losses are reported, morale, a dogged determination, a "do-or-die" attitude emerges. All the behavior tendencies of the group are organized in terms of the military aim of crushing the hated foe. In order to justify this behavior to itself and to the world at large the group rationalizes its actions in terms of moral values and the conflict becomes one between the forces of good and evil, of democracy and tyrannical oppression, of Christianity against paganism, instead of the mere struggle of forces of might for supremacy or glory. This latter tendency is a form of accommodation to dissent from within the group and to criticism from without. The group is most intolerant of dissent from its own members, and in its desperate effort to maintain a united front it may deal as summarily with the conscientious objector,[35] the traitor, and the "slacker" as it does with the enemy.

Modern, large-scale warfare requires the active services of all able-bodied citizens. These soon come to be divided into two large categories: the men and women who are inducted into the military organization and those who constitute the non-military civilian force of workers in industry, agriculture, and the numerous voluntary service organizations of civilian defense, first aid, fund raising, and governmental agencies auxiliary to the war effort. All, military and non-military, are subjected to social controls, mostly governmental, which are ordinarily unknown in peace time. For the civilians these include rationing of most consumers' goods, price-fixing, censorship, restricted movements, intensified propaganda, interference with civil rights, and limitations on the powers of employers and employees. Minority groups in the population are likely to be singled out for special surveillance and, if they are racial, ethnic, or political minorities whose loyalty is suspected, they may suffer persecution and confinement.[36] Even the democratic states discover that the conduct of a major war requires a high degree of centralization of functions and authority in the federal government, the impact of which is felt

---

35 See: G. O. Field, *Pacifism and Conscientious Objection,* London, Cambridge University Press, 1945; Harold S. Gray, Edited by Kenneth I. Brown, *Character "Bad,"* New York, Harper & Bros., 1934.
36 See: Earl Brown and George Leighton, *The Negro and the War,* New York, Public Affairs Committee, Inc., 1942; E. Franklin Frazier, "Ethnic and Minority Groups in Wartime, with Special Reference to the Negro," *Am. J. Sociol.,* Vol. 48, No. 3, November, 1942, pp. 369-377; Robert Guerlain, *Those Who Wait,* New York, T. Y. Crowell Co., 1943; Gerhart Saenger, "The Effect of War on Our Minority Groups," *Am. Sociol. Rev.,* Vol. 8, No. 1, February, 1943, pp. 15-22; Dorothy S. Thomas and R. Nishimoto, *The Spoilage,* Berkeley, University of California Press, 1946.

by all the country's communities, institutions, groups, and individuals. In areas overrun and occupied by the enemy, a resistance movement of considerable proportions may develop among civilians who, in many instances, may undertake guerrilla activities of a military nature against the enemy. Thus we see that total war means war brought home to all the people of the contending nations and fought out by many who are not military participants in a real sense.

The military personnel, who prosecute a war on land, sea, and air, are parts of a peculiar type of social organization. Military society is characterized by peculiarities of structure, tradition, behavior, personality roles, status relations, language and other symbols, and, above all, unique function, namely, legalized slaughter and destruction. The limits of space will allow no more than the briefest kind of description of these characteristics. The structure of the military society is highly stratified and hierarchical; the tradition is largely feudal; the behavior is regimented and disciplined and most of it so skilled as to call for lengthy training in the use of weapons and techniques; the personality roles are definitely defined and prescribed; status relations are mostly formal and often strictly impersonal, and are commonly integrated around function as well as class differences; the language is likewise functional and full of "substitute expressions" for objects and activities and of profanities which usually find expression only in single-sex groups in civilian life; and the unique function of taking human life and destroying property with the knowledge that, regardless of one's personal scruples, religious beliefs, and attitude of horror, the individual is absolved of blame because he is integrated into the group which does approve.[37]

Little attention has been paid to the sociology of military operations as such. This is a promising field for research. Military leaders have long dealt with the ecology of war, under such categories as strategy, tactics, and logistics. They know that war is quite as much an ecological phenomenon as it is a geographical, technological, and political one. Ecological factors have always decided where wars are fought, and they may be important factors in determining which side will win. In addition, there are problems of the social organization of the military forces in combat areas, in the rear areas of command and supply, and in the training camps, and the relations of military personnel to the civilian populations with which they come in contact, both at home and in the field.[38]

---

[37] See: *Am. J. Sociol.*, Vol. 51, No. 5, March, 1946. This number of the *Journal* is devoted to articles on human behavior in military society.
[38] *Ibid.*

Effects of War.—When war comes to a world as closely knit as the world is today, and with the warring nations equipped with highly mobile armies, fast fighting surface ships and submarines, long-range bombers and jet-propelled planes, *and* with the atomic bomb, no person, group, or institution that lies within the field of activity or participation is likely to escape feeling its effects. The population undergoes severe dislocations and extensive movements, chiefly in the direction of military establishments and industrial centers, and the whole economy passes through rapid stages of conversion to a wartime basis. Communities organize for civilian defense and for all kinds of war-connected activities; family life is disrupted by separations, the employment of women in out-of-the-home undertakings, and nervous tension; schools, churches, and other community agencies have to adapt themselves to the altered situation; and men and women, and especially young people, are forced to seek adjustment to the abnormal requirements of the times. That many fail in the process is not surprising. War-born neuroses, psychoses, delinquencies, crimes, and maladjusted personalities are among the more tragic civilian products of total war.[39]

WAR IS A RELATIVELY MODERN PHENOMENON. Modern warfare is very different from the so-called warfare of former times. There was a time when picked champions of the two sides fought out their differences in the wager of battle or mercenary armies met on the battlefield and settled the difficulties between war lords, princes, or kings. In such engagements the masses of the people took no part and probably had little interest, for they had little at stake. Today, war engages the interest and support of whole populations. It is an organized attack by a whole community of a species against another community of the same species. Primitive man had more formidable enemies than his own species to fight against, and it was for protection against these that he began to cooperate with his

---

[39] See: Franz Alexander, "The Psychiatric Aspects of War and Peace," *Am. J. Sociol.*, Vol. 46, No. 4, January, 1941, pp. 504-520; *Am. J. Sociol.*, entire number, Vol. 48, No. 3, November, 1942; James H. S. Bossard, "War and the Family," *Am. Sociol. Rev.*, Vol. 6, No. 3, June, 1941, pp. 330-344; Walter Bromberg, "The Effects of War on Crime," *Am. Sociol. Rev.*, Vol. 8, No. 6, December, 1943, pp. 683-691; H. Warren Dunham, "War and Mental Disorders: Some Sociological Considerations," *Social Forces*, Vol. 22, December, 1943, pp. 137-142; E. F. M. Durbin and John Bowlby, *Personal Aggressiveness and War;* Douglas Ensminger, "The Impacts of the War on the Rural Community," *Social Forces*, Vol. 22, October, 1943, pp. 76-80; R. D. Gillespie, *Psychological Effects of War*, New York, W. W. Norton & Co., 1942; Abram Kardiner, *Traumatic Neuroses of the War*, New York, Paul B. Hoeber, Inc., 1941; Edwin M. Lemert, "Social Participation and Totalitarian War," *Am. Sociol. Rev.*, Vol. 8, No. 5, October, 1943, pp. 531-536; Emanuel Miller (Ed.), *The Neurosis of War*, New York, The Macmillan Co., 1940; William F. Ogburn (Ed.), *American Society in Wartime*, Chicago, University of Chicago Press, 1943; Porter Sargent, *War and Education*, Boston, The Author, 1943; R. B. von KleinSmid and C. E. Martin, *War and Society*, Los Angeles, University of Southern California Press, 1940; Willard Waller, *War and the Family*, New York, The Dryden Press, 1940.

fellows and laid the foundations of the State. War was a result and
not a cause of social organization. "Warfare is not coeval with
civilization; it took its intense form at quite a late stage of development; it is, in a way, a by-product of social evolution.[40]

War, then, requires the submission of the individual to the interest
of the group. The dominant sentiments and attitudes of the group
become those of the person. Certain well-defined patterns of conflict behavior have been evolved by the group and made obligatory
upon the individual. When the war-making crowd shouts and waves
the flag, the individual member does likewise; when the prescribed
procedure is to buy war bonds, the individual buys even though it may
mean sacrifice to do so; when the command to "attack" is given, the
soldier obeys. For the individual to stand out against the behavior
of the crowd in wartime is to invite reprisals at the hands of the mob.
From the standpoint of the war-making crowd the exceptional individual is abnormal and will be dealt with as such. No person wages
war alone. He may fight an adversary single-handed, but war is a
group phenomenon and a person participates in it as a group member.

Usually the deciding act of war is battle, and the deciding factors
are the armed forces. This means that the national and imperial
aims—security, prestige, and power—are ordinarily to be obtained
through the complete, partial, or threatened achievement of the military aim, that is to say, through the use of the armed forces in battle
or threat of battle. This is the primary military aim of war. The
accomplishment of the secondary military aim, which "seeks to
weaken the armed forces of the opponent and to strengthen one's own
by impairing or increasing, as the case may be, the material resources
and moral support upon which those forces depend," [41] leads to compromise and an armed truce; whereas the accomplishment of the
primary aim, through the destruction or neutralization of the enemy
armed force, leads to a military decision and overtures for peace.

However, factors other than the armed forces enter in as important
conditioning factors in the decision. These include those already
mentioned—ecological pressures, nationalistic and imperialistic sentiments, obligations incurred by alliances and treaty arrangements, and
the war cult, embracing traditional and well-established conflict patterns. These may be regarded as secondary factors. They may also
include the organization and morale of the civilian population, food
conservation, sale of war bonds, industrial reorganization to meet

---

[40] W. J. Perry, *The Growth of Civilization*, New York, E. P. Dutton & Co., 1923, p. 133.
[41] Adm. Sir Reginald Custance, *A Study of War*, London, Constable & Co., Ltd., 1924,
p. 47.

wartime conditions and demands, and the like. Wartime needs must be met by emergency measures, and the fate of the struggle depends to a large extent on the ability of the civilian population to adapt itself to the situation. Modern warfare is a test of the solidarity and loyalty of the whole group.

THE POSITION OF THE NEUTRAL. The active participants in a war are by no means the only parties interested in the struggle and concerned as to the outcome. Since war is a social phenomenon entailing a whole complex of forces which have their projections in many directions, it may vitally affect all the people of the world, as was the case in each of the recent two world wars. This is so because of the many intercommunity relationships which characterize modern civilization. The role of the non-combatant, or spectator, nation is very important and exceedingly difficult in the modern world. Neutrality is a position which is difficult to maintain. While there may be nations which desire to be regarded as officially neutral, it is likely that the sentiments of their populations are aligned with one side or the other. If the nations are of any considerable commercial importance, they will see in the war an opportunity to advance their own commercial and financial power. The belligerents' loss may become their gain. Moreover, the record of the last war shows that an aggressor nation may not scruple to invade and occupy the territory of an officially neutral state if, by doing so, it may secure a strategic vantage ground from which to carry on the war more effectively.

The position of the onlooker is rendered precarious by the very nature of modern warfare. The mechanisms of war are highly technical, mechanical, and utilized on a grand scale of operations that may cover most of the earth. Operations include blockades, aerial expeditions covering long distances, submarine warfare that may endanger the shipping of neutrals as well as that of the enemy, lethal weapons of terrific force and directed against targets at long range, and of perhaps most importance to the nation that would be neutral, a tendency on the part of one or another of the belligerent powers to disregard the rights of neutrals. Under the circumstances, a spectator group will be almost certain to suffer indignities and losses. Almost certainly, resentments will flare up, old fears and new hatreds will be aroused, and the position of official neutrality will be hard to maintain in the face of public opinion, which may demand the repudiation of neutrality, the severing of relations with the offending belligerent, the mobilization of military forces, and a declaration of war. Generally, at this stage, there is an exchange of notes and diplomatic representations voicing demands by one side for apologies, compensation for losses sustained, pledges to respect the right of neutrality in the future, and expressing sentiments by the other side in accordance with its estimate of the neutral's power to assert itself. These exchanges serve to define the two groups to each other and to clear the atmosphere. On the basis of such definitions, the *status quo* may be preserved or the neutral cease to remain a spectator and become an active combatant. In the latter instance, there results a complete realignment and reorganization of forces. The struggle takes on a new character, and the war proceeds.

When War Ends

In appraising war as a social phenomenon it is important to ask "After war, what?" It is the general consensus that war as it is waged today is wasteful, inordinately costly, and rarely successful in achieving its purported ends.[42] Whatever their motives and ideals for fighting, the people are almost universally left disillusioned and cynical, whereas the contending groups are seldom if ever satisfied with the so-called settlement. The defeated ones nurse their grievances and plot their revenge, while the victors frequently fall out over the spoils, find the burdensome debts impossible to pay, and discover that the business of holding on to what they obtained at so much effort is a major-sized job. World War I was promoted as a "war to end war," but the treaties which followed it left more wounds in international relations than they healed and were not even signed by some of the victorious allied nations. World War II proved to be an even more costly venture and left a world desolate, fearful, and querulous. There is, at the time of this writing, talk of "the next war," which is represented in prospect as more terrible and devastating than the last. If a ledger sheet were to be drawn up on war, it would unquestionably show a debit side weighted down by losses in excess of all the possible gains on the credit side. Against all the wartime advances made in inventions and technology, medical science and practice, the temporary increases in industrial production, the

---

[42] See: Asher Brynes, *Revolution Comes of Age: The Use of War*, New York, Rinehart & Co., 1944; P. F. Douglass, *The Economic Dilemma of Politics, A Study of the Consequences of the Strangulation of Germany*, New York, Europress Co., 1932; Gustav Eckstein, *In Peace Japan Breeds War*, New York, Harper & Bros., 1943; Paul Einzig, *The Economic Foundations of Fascism*, London, Macmillan & Co., Ltd., 1933; Homer Folks, *The Human Costs of the War*, New York, Harper & Bros., 1920; P. Herring, *The Impact of War*, New York, Rinehart & Co., 1941; E. N. LaMotte, *The Backwash of War*, New York, G. P. Putnam's Sons, 1934; L. L. Lorwin, *The Economic Consequences of the Second World War*, New York, Random House, 1942; G. T. Renner, "Natural Resources in the Post-War World," *Am. J. Sociol.*, Vol. 49, No. 5, March, 1944, pp. 430-440; H. Mendershausen, *The Economics of War*, Part IV.

rise in employment and wage-incomes, the ennobling sentiments of self-sacrifice and devotion to country, the enhancement of group unity and accord within the national structure, and so on, must be debited the colossal expenditures of materials and human life, the terrific destruction of property, the heritage of rancor and hate, and a world still divided and preparing to draw the sword again. War has been branded as "cruel, barbarous, economically disastrous and politically atavistic, and generally unconscionable. This recognizes the problem but contributes nothing to its solution. Furthermore, what we have learned about the effects of war, while it has made peace more desirable, has not made war any less inevitable." [43]

There are some writers who discuss war as an institution and conclude from their reasoning that war is, therefore, inescapable. To the contrary, it needs to be pointed out that war occupies an anomalous status in the international social order; that its function has never been clearly defined and agreed upon; that its structure is variable and not fixed in custom and tradition; that its conduct runs to excesses that have so far defied regulation by agreement and international law; and that, unlike a true institution, no one knows what to expect of it. Although all war is ideological, it is more than that. It is, likewise, a struggle for something tangible, like land and living space, and something practical, like power. At one time, war included in its structure a body of usages that tended to be legitimatized and accepted as necessary to its conduct, and which could be counted on to resolve differences by a kind of judicial trial, but as war is now waged, its use as "a policy for adjudicating national differences is utterly discredited." [44] War is, in final analysis, a political process, non-rational and non-institutional in form, by means of which warlike states seek, by aggression and force of arms, to impose upon those with whom they enter conflict a political and economic order which is in the former's interest.

WAR IS DIFFICULT TO EXPLAIN. We do not know what all the forces making for the last two world wars were—nor for any war situation, for that matter—and we may never know all of them. Until we do know them and have techniques for controlling them, war will continue to be a menace and a probability. Most advocates of peace fail to grasp this important fact. There are some pacifists who think that war can be stopped by wishing to have it stopped. To

---

43 R. E. Park, "The Social Function of War: Observations and Notes," *Am. J. Sociol.*, Vol. 46, No. 4, January, 1941, p. 551.

44 G. H. Mead, "National-Mindedness and International-Mindedness," *Int. J. of Ethics*, Vol. 39, July, 1929, p. 400.

make war impossible, such a wish would have to become universal and more powerful than all the combined wishes that make for war. To ignore the interplay of economic and social forces that cause men to hate and fear each other, feel themselves superior and others inferior, make them unwilling to adjust their differences on any other basis than a show of force, is to invite failure in war prevention. As we have undertaken to show, the forces which have to do with war are very complex. They call for much study and research. It may be that the time will come when national states may be able to find satisfaction for their wishes without resort to force of arms in mortal combat. That time has not yet arrived.

New Levels and Bases of Accommodation.—In spite of the difficulties in the prevention of future wars, the fact remains that specific wars do end, and they do so in the form of accommodation. In the course of the conflict and following it in the negotiations for a settlement, the situation gets redefined and the contenders acquire a new status. If and when a final peace accord is made, it is accomplished through that particular mechanism of accommodation known as deliberation.

The true spirit of deliberation is one of suspended judgment. That this spirit characterizes most peace tribunals is doubtful since the victors are usually flushed by the satisfaction of their success and are inclined to drive a hard bargain, while the vanquished smart under the humiliation of their defeat in arms and tend to be bitterly resentful of their disadvantageous position. A recognition of this natural but irrational state of affairs led in the past to a considerable use of arbitration, in which third parties representing neutral states served to mediate the differences. This was especially the case where the conflict had terminated in a draw; it was less true where the outcome of the struggle had been decisive. The two great wars of this century, however, afforded no such role to the neutrals since there were no particularly influential states in that category. Moreover, the wars did not end short of the complete vanquishment of one side by the other. As this is written, three years after the cessation of hostilities in World War II, the situation as regards a settlement and a conclusion of peace is chaotic, with the major victorious powers unable to agree on terms among themselves. Long before the war ended, the heads of these allied governments met, conferred, and entered into agreements pertaining to postwar reparations, division of occupied territory, the disposition of large segments of population, trusteeships over mandated areas, and the like, and did so not in terms of a just and lasting peace, but rather in terms of appeasing each other and particularly in the interest of furthering the united war effort against the still actively belligerent common enemies. These understandings, mostly secretly entered into, have remained to plague the several states involved and to prevent concerted action looking to a judicious, rational, and final settlement of the desperate plight of the defeated nations and of the disturbed relations among the victorious powers. As the world exists today, war remains a final, awful instrument of policy. But what we see at present is a reversal of that logic, namely, policy being made the instrument of war. Along this course may easily lie disaster for the world.

International Adjustment Without Resort to Arms

It should not be concluded from what has been said in this chapter that all international differences eventuate in overt conflict. It would be just as incorrect to assume that international conflict, when it does occur, must take the form of the war pattern. The history of international relations reveals innumerable instances of differences between nationality groups that have been adjudicated without resort to armed force. Competition may go on for years and may even take on the nature of conscious rivalry without the rivals engaging in military maneuvers against one another. Diplomacy, commonly employed as an accommodative mechanism, may and often does have about it the character of sublimated conflict.

It is becoming increasingly apparent that, as the world is constituted at present, national states, with their national ambitions, pride, and power complexes, are not always able to negotiate their differences in a spirit of mutual appreciation and understanding. This condition was recognized at the conclusion of the first World War and the League of Nations was established for the express purpose of furnishing a medium through which international relations might be strengthened and peace maintained in the world. But the League was poorly fashioned for its task and failed to be more than a kind of public forum wherein certain national grievances were aired and from which disgruntled nations withdrew to deal unilaterally regarding their difficulties with other nations. The League was a loose organization of "selfish, corrupt, and warlike states," which, without a radical change of attitude on the part of the constituent governments, could be little more than impotent in the cause of peace. The League's chief weakness was its lack of power to enforce decisions.

At the end of World War II, the League of Nations was disbanded and the United Nations Organization was instituted along similar lines. The principal value of the UN as presently constituted and implemented is, like that of the old League, its function as a deliberative body for the adjustment of differences arising between member states and for the attempts it may make in behalf of better understanding in the interest of peace. But the UN is without the force necessary to the accomplishment of the purpose for which it was created. It, too, will fail unless it is reorganized and granted the powers of a superstate government. Those powers must include, among possible others, the authority to enact and enforce laws, to utilize the facilities of the World Court for the application of international law to the adjudication of differences between nations, and to be equipped with an international police force subject solely to its orders, for the enforcement of its decisions and those of the Court. Such powers should be confined entirely and strictly to matters of concern with international relations and the comity of nations, and should in no wise jeopardize or interfere with the internal affairs of sovereign nations. The present outlook for such reorganization and implementation of the UN is far from being hopeful.

With or without some kind of world government, international disharmonies generally will be accommodated sooner or later. Short of war, the form of accommodation that will be followed in a given international contest will depend to some degree upon the relative strength of the two sides, the nature of their cause and its standing in the estimation of the rest of the world, and the extent to which the war pattern is threatened. The typical forms of accommodation most commonly applied to the adjustment of discordant international relations are compromise, conciliation, superordination and subordination, and possible stratification.

COMPROMISE. *Compromise* is a process of give and take. When groups began to avoid force or, having resorted to it with only partial success, and to effect exchanges in terms of mutual concessions, the way was opened for the development of intergroup cooperation. Compromise is most generally employed where the competing or conflicting nationality groups are approximately equal with respect to their bargaining power. In every case of treaty arrangement by negotiation rather than by dictation, the principle of compromise is present, and when two competing nationality groups find themselves faced by a common foe they are usually ready to compromise their differences in the interest of their mutual security. "By every possible means, force, persuasion, money, and joint interest, social groups have sought aid from other groups in war. . . . On a continent with twenty-eight sovereign states of varying size and multitudinous interests, no one nation would dare rely upon its own unaided resources to maintain its political and economic position. Combination is inescapable, if for no other reason than to forestall hostile combination." [45]

CONCILIATION. According to Simmel, *conciliation* is a subjective method of avoiding or of terminating conflict, in contrast to the objective character of compromise. It is an elementary attitude which, like the disposition to quarrel, has been developed in experience because of its usefulness in certain situations. It emerges on occasion as an unreasonable urge to avoid strife for a time. Curiously enough, this urge may come after full utilization of energy in conflict. Unlike the pacific attitude, which it resembles, conciliation does not seek to avoid conflict or to bring it to an end regardless of cost. Conciliation is a removal of the roots of conflict without reference to what has gone before in the form of struggle or accommodation through surrender or compromise as well as to what may arise later to provoke misunderstanding and possible conflict. [46]

SUPERORDINATION AND SUBORDINATION. Simmel gave considerable attention to this form of accommodation particularly as it pertains to personal relations where the elements of domination and submission enter in, as in the case between the leader and his followers, the superior and the inferior. [47] Similar relationships of superordination-subordination are to be found in the interrelations of many nationality groups. There is no great national power that does not represent the superordinate role in relation to some one or more colonies, dependencies, protectorates, or spheres of influence. The ways in which these minorities have been acquired vary from wars of conquest, in which they or their former possessors were the losers, from mandates or trusteeships delegated by some international body, to purchase, by which they merely changed hands, so to speak, from one dominant power to another. Many of these minority groups have for centuries been pawns of international politics, intrigues, and wars. Sometimes they adopt the submissive attitude and not infrequently are grateful to their superiors. Often, however, they

---

45 From: *Back of War*, by Henry K. Norton. Copyright 1928 by Doubleday & Co., Inc., pp. 170-171.

46 See: Georg Simmel, as translated by A. W. Small, "The Sociology of Conflict," *Am. J. Sociol.*, Vol. 9, No. 6, May, 1904, pp. 805-806.

47 See: Georg Simmel, *Soziologie*, pp. 171-186. Small's translation of this part of Simmel's work appeared in the *Am. J. Sociol.*, Vol. 2, September, 1896, pp. 172-186. An interpretation is also to be found in N. J. Spykman's *The Social Theory of Georg Simmel*, Chicago, University of Chicago Press, 1925, pp. 97-108.

merely adjust themselves to the situation and never relinquish their desire for national autonomy. In the latter case, the control of the dominant power enjoys little prestige; it is simply tolerated. Within the subject group there is apt to be great restlessness, agitation, and even rebellion and the problem of government from the standpoint of the superordinate group is fraught with many difficulties. But this form of accommodation is not confined to the relations between the greater powers and the lesser minorities and subject peoples. The position of Germany after her defeat in World War I is a case in point. The secondary role assigned to her among the great nations of the world was a source of bitter resentment and it is said to have had a great deal to do with the ease with which Hitler came to power, since it was he who promised to restore Germany to her former greatness and to lead her on to world domination. Submission in such an instance does not mean acquiescence, and the subordinate nation, as it becomes increasingly conscious of its strength and potential power in world or regional affairs, may assert itself and demand the recognition it desires.

POSSIBLE STRATIFICATION. Under certain circumstances the superordinate-subordinate relationship shows a tendency to become securely established and rigidly integrated in the culture patterns of the two groups. The most common forms taken by stratification are slavery and caste. Some time before the dawn of history man found that it was more profitable not to kill a conquered enemy, but to disarm him and make him a laborer. Since then slavery has existed in all parts of the world and has disappeared in Europe and America only within the last century. Even today it persists in certain parts of Arabia and Africa. In India the elaborate caste systems were to a great extent built up through conquest and the subjugation of smaller tribal groups. Other forms of stratification also continue to function.

THE POCKETING OF CULTURAL MINORITIES. There are to be found in many parts of the world today numerous cultural minorities that at one time enjoyed the status of independent nationalities, but which now are in practical subjection to dominant groups. Some of them have been almost wholly denationalized and their members have probably forgotten their cultural heritage. Everything that could be done has been done by their superiors, even to the use of force, to weed out any traces of the former culture patterns. Any degree of self-determination for many of them is an impossibility under present arrangements. It has been the fate of many such groups to be bandied about from one power to another, to be divided and sub-divided, without having a voice as to their preference regarding their destinies. As long as a cultural minority is able to struggle against its lot as a pawn of international politics, the process of stratification can hardly be said to be complete, but numbers of them have gone down in the struggle. The first World War liberated several such groups and enabled them to realize their centuries-old wish for independence, only to find themselves a quarter of a century later once more suborned by a single great power as an aftermath of the last war. How long they may have to remain as cultural pockets under the domination of a larger inclusive national group only time will tell.

It is apparent from what has been said that the process of accommodation involves the equilibration of economic, political, cultural, and social differences which issue in the course of competition and conflict. This accommodation of differences explains how it happens that there may be continuous trade, a certain amount of co-operation, and a certain feeling of good will among nations, in spite of a great diversity of interest, aim, and ambition among them, and despite the ever-present factor of national rivalries, competitive armaments, and political intrigues.

Questions

1. Critically evaluate the classification of general culture areas given in this chapter.
2. Explain some of the difficulties that stand in the way of freer interaction between the civilizations of the Occident and the Orient.
3. What have been some of the important culture traits that have passed from the West to the East? from the East to the West?
4. In what respects do the general culture areas mainly differ from each other?
5. What is meant by saying that "cultures are not confined by arbitrary lines drawn on the map of the earth"?
6. Differentiate between "nationality" and "nation."
7. What characterizes the "national spirit"?
8. Of what do international relations consist?
9. According to Wissler, in what ways does culture tend to determine the interaction between nationalities?
10. Why should war figure so largely in a discussion of international relations?
11. What is war? Why is it incorrect to assume that all contention between nations is war?
12. What does Sorokin have to say about the causes of war?

13. What are the ecological factors making for tension in international relations?
14. In what sense are the tensions due to economic pressure factors in "a struggle for control, for prestige"?
15. Why should economic considerations in provoking tensions between nations not be taken as a form of economic determinism?
16. What relation did Malthus see between population pressure and international tension?
17. Is war a biologically necessary means of solving the problem of overpopulation? Why?
18. In what respects did the problem of surplus population take on a somewhat different aspect after World War I?
19. Is man a warlike animal? Discuss.
20. Under what circumstances, according to Malinowski, may the war-making pattern have arisen?
21. Discuss fully the statement that "man is so constituted that he may be conditioned for either physical combat or social cooperation."
22. "War has its roots in culture and not in man's nature except as his nature is a reflection of culture." Discuss.
23. What is the meaning of nationalism and what is its role as a tension-making mechanism?
24. How did the doctrine of self-determination, as applied in practice after World War I, affect international relations between 1919 and 1939?
25. "Imperialism is but an expansion of the sentiment-attitude of nationalism." Explain.
26. What are some tangible evidences of imperialism?
27. How do imperialistic powers and leaders rationalize their ambitions and actions in terms of the so-called "new order"?
28. Discuss the implications of the statement to the effect that "no great power, even if it would, can avoid affecting international relations."
29. In what sense is militarism "an objectification of fears"? Wherein lies its explanation?
30. What are the characteristics of the war cult?
31. What part does mobilization play in the preparation for hostilities?
32. By what means are people psychologically mobilized for war?
33. Explain the respective roles of conflict and heroic myths, the flag, national anthems and patriotic songs, slogans and propaganda in conditioning a people for action against the enemy.
34. What accommodative mechanisms are operative during the prewar period?
35. At what point and under what circumstances does the war-preparing public become the war-making crowd?
36. What is the difference between the causes of war and the occasions for war?
37. Discuss: "Wars do not 'just happen'; wars are 'made.'"

38. Describe war-making behavior.
39. What are the characteristics of "military society"?
40. List some of the factors that characterize the ecology of military operations as such. Do the same for the factors of social organization.
41. What are some principal effects of modern warfare?
42. What do you understand by Perry's statement that war "is, in a way, a by-product of social evolution"?
43. What can be said of the role of the individual in war?
44. Give the primary and secondary factors making for decision in war.
45. Why do the spectators, though not actually participating in a war, invariably take sides? What makes the neutral's position a precarious one?
46. What will a ledger sheet on war be likely to show as regards debits and credits?
47. If war is not an institution, in the complete sense, what is it?
48. Why is it difficult to explain war?
49. Have you reason to think that the war pattern will be less frequent in its occurrence in the future? Why?
50. What is the meaning and function of deliberation in international relations?
51. Compare the League of Nations and the United Nations as to their constitution, functions, and success in strengthening international relations and maintaining peace.
52. What arguments are advanced for and against some type of world government?
53. Characterize and explain the functions of compromise, conciliation, superordination-subordination, and possible stratification in so far as they apply to the accommodation of discordant international relations.
54. Explain the plight of the subordinated cultural minorities.

BIBLIOGRAPHY

American Journal of Sociology, Vol. 51, No. 5, March, 1946. All articles treat of "Human Behavior in Military Society."

ANGUS, H. F. (Ed.). *Canada and Her Great Neighbor: Sociological Surveys of Opinions and Attitudes in Canada Concerning the United States.* Toronto, The Ryerson Press; New Haven, Yale University Press, 1938.

BAIN, READ. "Morale for War and Peace." *Social Forces,* Vol. 21, May, 1943, pp. 418-425.

BERNARD, L. L. *War and Its Causes.* New York, Henry Holt & Co., 1944.

BORNSTEIN, JOSEPH, AND MILTON, PAUL. *Action Against the Enemy's Mind: This Psychological War.* Cornwall, N. Y., Cornwall Press, 1942.

BOSSARD, JAMES H. S. "War and the Family." *Am. Sociol. Rev.,* Vol. 6, No. 3, June, 1941, pp. 330-344.

BRYNES, ASHER. *Revolution Comes of Age: The Use of War.* New York, Rinehart & Co., 1944.

CALLIS, HELMUT G. "The Sociology of International Relations." *Am. Sociol. Rev.,* Vol. 12, No. 3, June, 1947, pp. 323-334.

CHADWICK, H. MUNRO. *The Nationalities of Europe and the Growth of National Ideologies.* New York, The Macmillan Co., 1945.

CHANDLER, ALBERT R.   *Rosenberg's Nazi Myth.*   Ithaca, Cornell University Press, 1945.

CLARK, GROVER.   *The Balance Sheet of Imperialism: Facts and Figures on Colonies.*   New York, Columbia University Press, 1936.

CLARKSON, JESSE D., AND COCHRAN, THOMAS C.   *War as a Social Institution.*   New York, Columbia University Press, 1941.

COOLEY, CHARLES H.   *Human Nature and the Social Order.*   New York, Charles Scribner's Sons, 1902, pp. 232-261, "Hostility."

COTTRELL, W. F.   "Cultural Growth of Internationalism."   *Am. Sociol. Rev.,* Vol. 10, No. 5, October, 1945, pp. 586-595.

DAVIE, MAURICE.   *The Evolution of War.*   New Haven, Yale University Press, 1929.

DEHUSZER, GEORGE B., ET AL.   *New Perspectives on Peace.*   Chicago, University of Chicago Press, 1944.

DETWEILER, FREDERICK G.   "The Anglo-Saxon Myth in the United States."   *Am. Sociol. Rev.,* Vol. 3, No. 2, April, 1938, pp. 183-189.

DURBIN, E. F. M., AND BOWLBY, JOHN.   *Personal Aggressiveness and War.*   New York, Columbia University Press, 1939.

EAGLETON, CLYDE.   *Analysis of the Problem of War.*   New York, The Ronald Press Co., 1937.

EARLE, E. M. (Ed.).   *Makers of Modern Strategy: Military Thought from Machiavelli to Hitler.*   Princeton, Princeton University Press, 1943, 1944.

EDDY, G. S.   *The Abolition of War.*   New York, Geo. H. Doran Co., 1924.

FIELD, G. O.   *Pacifism and Conscientious Objection.*   Cambridge, Cambridge University Press, 1945.

FINER, HERMAN.   *America's Destiny.*   New York, The Macmillan Co., 1948.

GANTENBEIN, JAMES W.   *The Origins of World War II.*   New York, Columbia University Press, 1948.

GISEVIUS, HANS B.   *To the Bitter End.*   Translated from the German by R. and C. Winston.   Cambridge, The Riverside Press, 1947.   Opposition to Hitler inside Germany.

GORER, GEOFFREY.   *The American People: A Study in National Character.*   New York, W. W. Norton Co., Inc., 1948.

GREGG, R. B.   *The Power of Non-Violence.*   Philadelphia, J. B. Lippincott Co., 1934.

GRUENBERG, SIDONIE M. (Ed.).   *The Family in a World at War.*   New York, Harper & Bros., 1942.

HAYES, C. J. H.   *The Historical Evolution of Modern Nationalism.*   New York, Richard R. Smith, 1931.

HERRING, HUBERT.   *And So to War.*   New Haven, Yale University Press, 1938.

HUGHES, E. R.   *The Invasion of China by the Western World.*   New York, The Macmillan Co., 1938.

INGERSOLL, RALPH.   *The Battle Is the Pay-Off.*   New York, Harcourt, Brace & Co., 1943.

JANOWSKY, OSCAR I.   *Nationalities and National Minorities.*   New York, The Macmillan Co., 1945.

KELSEN, HANS.   "International Peace—By Court or Government."   *Am. J. Sociol.,* Vol. 46, No. 4, January, 1941, pp. 571-581.

KOHN, HANS.   *The Idea of Nationalism.*   New York, The Macmillan Co., 1944.

KOHN, HANS.   *Western Civilization in the Near East.*   New York, Columbia University Press, 1936.

KOHN, HANS.   *World Order in Historical Perspective.*   Cambridge, Harvard University Press, 1942.

LANDECKER, WERNER S.   "International Relations as Intergroup Relations."   *Am. Sociol. Rev.,* Vol. 5, No. 3, June, 1940, pp. 335-339.

McVoy, Edgar C. "Wartime Controls in a Democratic Society." *Am. Sociol. Rev.,* Vol. 11, No. 1, February, 1946, pp. 85-89.

May, Mark. *A Social Psychology of War and Peace.* New Haven, Yale University Press, 1943.

Mead, Margaret. *And Keep Your Powder Dry.* New York, William Morrow & Co., 1942.

Meyer, Cord, Jr. *Peace or Anarchy.* Boston, Little, Brown & Co., 1947.

Millis, Walter. *Road to War: America, 1914-1917.* Boston, Houghton Mifflin Co., 1935.

Nicolai, G. F. *The Biology of War.* Translated from the German by Constance and Julian Grande. New York, The Century Co., 1918.

Ogburn, William F. (Ed.). *American Society in Wartime.* Chicago, University of Chicago Press, 1943.

Prebble, John. *The Edge of Night.* New York, William Sloane Associates, 1948. A novel on the hidden origins and scattered effects of war.

Rappard, William E. "Economic Nationalism," in Harvard Tercentenary Publications, *Authority and the Individual.* Cambridge, Harvard University Press, 1937.

Renn, Ludwig. *Warfare: The Relation of War to Society.* New York, Oxford University Press, 1939.

Reves, Emery. *The Anatomy of Peace.* New York, Harper & Bros., 1945.

Rocker, Rudolf. *Nationalism and Culture.* New York, Covici-Friede, 1937.

Salter, Sir Arthur, et al. *The Causes of War: Economic, Industrial, Racial, Religious, Scientific and Political.* New York, The Macmillan Co., 1932.

Shiber, Etta. *Paris-Underground.* New York, Charles Scribner's Sons, 1943.

Social Science Research Council. *Public Reaction to the Atomic Bomb and World Affairs: A Nation-Wide Survey of Attitudes and Information.* Ithaca, Cornell University Press, 1947.

Sorokin, Pitirim A. "The Conditions and Prospects of a World Without War." *American Journal of Sociology,* Vol. 49, No. 5, March, 1944, pp. 441-449.

Sorokin, Pitirim A. "A Neglected Factor of War." *Am. Sociol. Rev.,* Vol. 3, No. 4, August, 1938, pp. 475-486.

Speier, Hans, and Kahler, Alfred. *War in Our Time.* New York, W. W. Norton Co., 1939.

Steiner, Jesse F. *Behind the Japanese Mask.* New York, The Macmillan Co., 1943.

Thomas, Dorothy S., and Nishimoto, Richard. *The Spoilage: Japanese-American Evacuation and Resettlement.* Berkeley, University of California Press, 1946.

Thompson, Warren S. *Population and Peace in the Pacific.* Chicago, University of Chicago Press, 1946.

Waller, Willard. *The Veteran Comes Back.* New York, Dryden Press, 1944.

Waller, Willard. *War and the Family.* New York, Dryden Press, 1940.

Waller, Willard (Ed.). *War in the Twentieth Century.* New York, Dryden Press, 1940.

Weinberg, S. Kirson. "Problems of Adjustment in Army Units." *Am. J. Sociol.,* Vol. 50, No. 4, January, 1945, pp. 271-278.

Winslow, E. M. *The Pattern of Imperialism: A Study in the Theories of Power.* New York, Columbia University Press, 1948.

Wirth, Louis. "Types of Nationalism." *Am. J. Sociol.,* Vol. 41, No. 6, May, 1936, pp. 723-737.

Wiskeman, Elizabeth. *Prologue to War.* New York, Oxford University Press, 1940.

Wright, Quincy. *A Study of War.* 2 vols. Chicago, University of Chicago Press, 1942.

Chapter 15

INTERACTION IN ETHNIC RELATIONS

RACIAL AND CULTURAL DIFFERENCES

Cultures tend to establish and maintain many media, through which their traits and patterns are transmitted. Among the chief carriers of cultural elements are human groups and persons. In the preceding chapter we noted that a nationality is a group which is self-conscious about what it considers the uniqueness of its particular cultural heritage when that is brought into interaction with the culture patterns of other nationality groups. In this chapter we are to consider interaction between ethnic or so-called "racial" groups.

In undertaking to account for what are commonly called "race prejudice," "the race problem," and "race conflict," to analyze their many manifestations, and to understand their effects as seen in social interaction, one is confronted with the difficulties which are involved in biological and ethnological terminology and the popular notions of "race." The conclusion of modern anthropology and genetics is

. . . that the popular and the scientific views of "race" no longer coincide. The word "race" as applied scientifically to human groupings has lost any sharpness of meaning. Today it is hardly definable in scientific terms, except as an abstract concept which may under certain conditions, very different from those now prevalent, have been realized approximately in the past, and might, under certain other but equally different conditions, be again realized in the distant future. . . . It would be highly desirable if we could banish the question-begging term "race" from all discussions of human affairs and substitute the noncommittal phrase "ethnic group." That would be the first step toward rational consideration of the problem at issue.[1]

Race as Defined in Social Experience.—For the purpose of our discussion, we may be somewhat less than scientific in our treatment of "race" as a sociological concept which tends to be defined in social experience in terms of a number of factors, many of which have nothing to do with physical characteristics such as skin color, cephalic

---

[1] Julian Huxley, "The Concept of Race," *Harper's Magazine*, Vol. 170, May, 1935, pp. 697-698.

index, color and texture of hair. In strict usage, the concept of "race" refers to biological and not to cultural phenomena. It is not to be confused with mythical conceptions of race in everyday speech.[2] The distinguishing marks of "race," as "race" is experienced in social interaction, may or may not include the above-mentioned traits. Rather, they are any and all traits that have become associated in thinking and in behavior with what is regarded as "race." These traits commonly include factors of geography, where the people live; of history, what they have done; of ethnology, from what ethnic stocks they have sprung or are supposed to have originated; of culture, what they wear, what they eat, how they talk, and a whole host of similar factors connected with their folkways, mores, and institutions, as well as beliefs about their real or imagined biological differences. Some one of these traits, or several of them in combination, when identified in experience with a group or group member, constitute the criterion of "race" as the term is generally understood and as it enters into ethnocentrism, and into prejudice and antipathy toward the so-called "racial" out-group. When these traits happen to come within the group's experience as defining a person as a member of a particular "race," they easily become attached by association to all members of the "racial" group in question.[3]

Race as Concept Rather Than Fact.—Ellsworth Faris has stated that

race is a difficult word. It is not a fact; it is a concept. If we inquire as to the number of races, we learn that some anthropologists make three races, others five, and so on through a varying number up to nineteen; and the point is that however many or few there may prove to be, they are all made, that is, constructed. The members of the human species vary through a continuous series, and the division into races has always something in it of the arbitrary. It is easy to distinguish the Chinese, the Swedes, and the Bantus from one another, but if we try to divide the whole of mankind into races there remain unsolved problems and peoples that are not fitted into any division. This does

---

[2] See: M. F. Ashley-Montagu, *Man's Most Dangerous Myth: The Fallacy of Race*, New York, Columbia University Press, 1942.

[3] See: B. M. Allen, "The Biology of Race Relations," *Sociol. and Soc. Res.*, Vol. 18, 1933-1934, pp. 340-351; Gunnar Dahlberg, *Race, Reason and Rubbish*, New York, Columbia University Press, 1942; D. G. Haring, *Social Differences and Human Resemblances*, Syracuse, Syracuse University Bookstore, 1947; Otto Klineberg, *Race Differences*, New York, Harper & Bros., 1935; M. H. Krout, "Race and Culture," *Am. J. Sociol.*, Vol. 37, No. 2, September, 1931, pp. 175-189; H. A. Miller, "Changing Conceptions of Race," *Pub. Am. Sociol. Soc.*, Vol. 21, 1927, pp. 106-112; M. R. Neifeld, "The Race Hypothesis," *Am. J. Sociol.*, Vol. 32, No. 3, November, 1926, pp. 423-432; E. B. Reuter, "Racial Theory," *Am. J. Sociol.*, Vol. 50, No. 6, May, 1945, pp. 452-461; H. J. Seligman, *Race Against Man*, New York, G. P. Putnam's Sons, 1939; S. M. Strong, "Human Nature and the Color of Skin," *Prairie Schooner*, University of Nebraska Press, Vol. 20, pp. 3-15; D. Zeleny, "Race and Culture," *Sociol. and Soc. Res.*, Vol. 14, 1929-1930, pp. 438-449.

not mean that there are no races, but it does mean that men who talk glibly about race often do not realize the difficulty of their subject.[4]

Race Prejudice.—Race prejudice is a term commonly applied to a general and complex attitude toward a person or group which places the emphasis upon differences of race (as those differences are currently understood) and of culture. From what has been said above, it would seem that what is commonly designated as "race prejudice" is not necessarily a prejudice aroused by biological differences, but rather is it an attitude stimulated by the interaction of different culture patterns which may or may not be associated with distinguishing physical traits. When physical features like color and hair texture are associated they become visible symbols of divergence which intensify prejudice. Race prejudice, strictly defined, is limited in meaning to those pronounced attitudes directed against or in favor of members of an ethnic group which are based upon preconceptions or prejudgments formed upon the indirect evidence of hearsay and tradition. Prejudice is either negative or positive, depending on whether the object calls out an antithetical attitude or one of predilection. The more fundamental and essentially personal feelings of repulsion felt when the representatives of one race come into face-to-face association or direct competition with members of another race are more properly designated as racial antipathy. This distinction should be kept clearly in mind when these terms are used hereafter.[5]

Both forms of prejudice are so inextricably involved in the interaction of cultures that it is often impossible to separate the biological and the cultural factors. It is for that reason that they must be discussed as belonging together. Not only is race antithesis a product of social interaction that has become imbedded in the culture patterns of all groups which have had irritating contacts with other ethnic groups, but also it acts as a check to social interaction between such

---

[4] Ellsworth Faris, "Remarks on Race Superiority," *Soc. Serv. Rev.*, Vol. 1, March, 1927, p. 39. See also Ralph Linton, *The Study of Man*, New York, D. Appleton-Century Co., Inc., 1936. In his chapter on race, Linton replaces the word "race" by three terms—"breed," "race," and "stock." His "breed" is "a group of individuals, all of whom vary about a particular norm with respect to each of their physical characteristics." A number of these breeds "whose ideal types have a series of characteristics in common" constitute a "race," while "stocks" are groups of similar races. His "breeds" are "genuine biological entities" but the "races" which are made up of "breeds" are abstractions.

[5] See: Chester Alexander, "Antipathy and Social Behavior," *Am. J. Sociol.*, Vol. 51, No. 4, January, 1946, pp. 288-292; O. C. Cox, "Race Prejudice and Intolerance—a Distinction," *Social Forces*, Vol. 24, December, 1945, pp. 216-219; George B. de Huszar, *Anatomy of Racial Intolerance*, New York, H. W. Wilson Co., 1946; F. G. Detweiler, "The Rise of Modern Race Antagonism," *Am. J. Sociol.*, Vol. 37, No. 5, March, 1932, pp. 738-747; Kelly Miller, "Is Race Prejudice Innate or Acquired?" *J. Appl. Sociol.*, Vol. 11, 1926-1927, pp. 516-525; E. F. Young, "What Is Race Prejudice?" *J. Appl. Sociol.*, Vol. 10, 1925-1926, pp. 135-141.

groups and plays an important role in determining the specific forms interaction between them will assume.

Interracial Contacts and Increase in Race Feeling.—Improved means of communication brought the peoples of the earth closer together, competition expanded to world-wide proportions, and primary relationships gave way to increasing secondary contacts, and the people on the earth became concentrated in cities. These trends resulted in an intensification of rivalries between competing ethnic groups and the factors of biological and cultural difference served to reinforce the economic and other tensions between them. At the same time as the *physical distance* that had separated the peoples of the earth, and had made possible the development of more or less distinct ethnic groups, was being surmounted by improved means of transportation and communication, *social distance,* in terms of misunderstanding and suspicion, increased.

Out of His Place.—When we say of a person that "he is out of his place" we do not usually mean that he is occupying a spatial location for which he is not fitted or that he is too near us so far as physical contact is concerned. What we mean is that he is "out of character," that he has abandoned the role in which we are accustomed to find him, that he has assumed a social status which is displeasing to us. The same notion is applied to a group under similar conditions. In the United States, under the system of slavery, the question of the "place" of the Negroes was seldom raised by the white and colored peoples. It was known and generally accepted by both groups. Economically the Negro slave was in a symbiotic position. He worked at his own jobs and did not threaten either the social or economic security of the white man. But as a free man—and especially when he migrated to the North—the Negro came into competition with the native-born whites, just as does the present-day immigrant. The native-born whites in this new situation felt that their jobs and standards of living were threatened. Racial antipathy, the defense-reaction in such situations, was expressed in various ways and extended to all phases of white-Negro relations.

Numbers in Relation to Race Friction.—If we borrow a term from the physical sciences, we may say that as the "pressures" of contacts on the inner precincts of personality and the preserves of group culture become more frequent and persistent the resistance offered will indubitably produce friction. This social attrition tends to vary in direct ratio to the mass, attacking, and interpenetrating qualities of the colliding groups.

There were two young refined Negro men in a northern community who had been well received by the community and with seemingly no prejudice. They were an intimate part of the social life of the community, attended dances, and went to social affairs unrestrictedly. When the wartime migration of Negroes to the north began this community received a quota of common laborers. Simultaneously with the appearance of these low-grade Negroes, the doors of the erstwhile friends of the cultured Negroes were closed to them, much to their surprise and bewilderment.[6]

What was the cause of this sudden reversal of attitude toward the two colored men? Manifestly, it was not due to any change in the men themselves. It was principally a question of *numbers* and all that that implies.[7] Points of contact are multiplied by the sheer weight of numbers, the pressures are felt more directly in personal and group relations in industry, area of residence, and social intercourse, and the abstract quality of racial antipathy—in all probability latent and invisible all the time—is more highly stimulated and is given tangible expression.

Social Ritual and Racial Antipathy.—Along with the fact of increase or decrease in numbers of the antipathetic objects must be considered the manner of approach or of withdrawal, the *qualities of attack or retreat,* the attitude of assertion or of uncertainty. The widely different and changing aspects of the phenomena of race relations are, in these respects, perplexing and difficult to analyze. It is inadvisable to generalize too broadly about such matters because the nature of the behavior on both sides of the racial lines may be just as different in each instance as are the variable impulses and caprices of human nature. For example, consider these two cases:

In the University where I was a student during my Freshman year there were two Mexican girls, who were members of my class. We students were accustomed to having Mexicans all about us for the school is located in a border state in which there are thousands of Mexicans residing. But most of us had known them as farm laborers or as domestic servants and had always heard them called "Greasers." We had most certainly regarded them

---

6 E. F. Young, *Race Prejudice with Particular Reference to the American Negro,* unpublished Ph.D. dissertation, University of Chicago, 1924, p. 149.

7 The census of 1940 gave the Negro population of the United States as approximately 13,000,000, or 9.8 per cent of the total population of 131,669,275. More than 78 per cent of the Negro population lived in the South. Of the 9,904,619 Negroes living in the three southern Census divisions, 45 per cent were classed as rural farm, 19 per cent as rural nonfarm, and 36 per cent as urban. See T. Lynn Smith, "A Demographic Study of the American Negro," *Social Forces,* Vol. 23, March, 1945, pp. 379-387, for a discussion of some of the discrepancies in census data for the Negro population.

as inferiors. When these girls came to the University we were naturally curious about them for they seemed so clean and not at all like the majority of the Mexicans we thought we knew so well. Some of the girls tried to make friends with them but found it hard to draw them out. They went everywhere together and avoided associating with us for a long time. Finally, after several weeks they "loosened up" and would talk with us, walk with us between classes, and so on, but they never attended any school affairs although they were always included in the invitations extended to the Freshmen girls.[8]

Arthur Brown took the referral slip from her hand and hurried to the waterfront. As he entered the big shipyard he could see Negro workers swarming over several huge unfinished hulls—welding, cutting, fitting together heavy pieces of steel plate.

He went into the office confidently. After a short wait the assistant general manager talked to him.

"So they sent you down to get that I.B.M. (International Business Machine) job, huh?" he asked. "Well, son, I can't give you that."

"You mean it's filled already?"

"Nope. But I'm afraid you wouldn't fit into our office. We have five men on those machines. As it happens, they're all white."

"I'll get along with them."

"Well—" The general manager chewed speculatively on a big cigar. "Maybe you would and maybe you wouldn't. My experience says you wouldn't."

"How about letting me try?"

"Nope, couldn't do it. And I'll tell you why. About five or six years ago I took a colored fellow outa' the yard and put him on an office machine. He was no good—just couldn't do the work. The other follows said he balled up the whole department, and I had to take him out. I learned a lesson from that: colored boys are all right for the heavy yard jobs, but they don't work out in an office." [9]

So we see that numbers of persons involved is not always a significant factor in cases of racial contact. One or two individuals of a racial minority who display aggressive behavior may be the cause of unfavorable reactions against them and be in large measure responsible for the formation of adverse judgments against the whole group which they represent. On the other hand, one or two inoffensive persons of the racial minority may, under ordinary circumstances, expect to find themselves the objects of discrimination and rejection, regardless of the attitude they take. In any case, the penetration of

---

8 From a student's paper on "Race Relations in . . ."

9 Edward H. Lawson, "Arthur Brown Applies for a Job," *J. of Social Issues*, February, 1945, p. 13.

a racial group or the attempted entrance of a member of such a group into neighborhoods, occupations, and institutions that are monopolized by others is resented. Such a social invasion arouses hostility.

Direct Contacts.—The reactions that may occur in interracial relations will depend, also, upon the nature of the contacts involved. These contacts, as we have already learned, may be either direct or indirect, or a mixture of the two. The former are the contacts occurring in the more or less intimate experiences of the group or of the person. Frequently, it requires no more than one such experience to produce a favorable or an unfavorable reaction, and later experiences with the same object may either confirm or modify the initial impression. First and single experiences often result in the formation of unjust attitudes because of their inadequacy, the haste with which they occur, and preconceptions already held. On the other hand, the one and only experience may be deceptive in the opposite direction and may lead to altogether too favorable judgments.

As a small child I had no serious dislike for Mexicans. They went to the same school as I did. I played with them and argued with them. I was never afraid of them, in fact they were the same as a white person in my estimation. . . .

However, since I have taken greater notice of Mexicans, their traits, habits, customs, etc., my ideas have become decidedly changed. Living near the border of Arizona and Mexico, I have had good chances to see the Mexicans living their customary life. In their homes, the lower classes are the filthiest, dirtiest, most slovenly people I have ever seen, or hope to see. Naturally, coming from such homes they are horribly displeasing to look upon, and are low mentally and morally as well. Because of this I have developed a fear of them. They are not a race that I trust very much.[10]

Such reactions as the one described are more or less automatic, irrational, and deep-seated. Though they are not always associated with "racial" characteristics, except indirectly, they tend to be applied to the racial or nationality group as a whole. Perhaps a different set of experiences with some refined and educated Mexicans would result in a more favorable attitude. Nevertheless, such intimate associations as those in industry, in school or college, between members of different ethnic groups, where the relations rest largely on a basis of competition and rivalry, are almost certain to result in a clash of prestige motives and the situation almost invariably gets defined in terms

---

[10] Quoted by E. S. Bogardus, "Analyzing Changes in Public Opinion," *J. Appl. Sociol.*, Vol. 9, May-June, 1925, pp. 378-379.

of ethnic or cultural differences rather than in terms of personal qualities and merit.

Indirect Contacts.—Not all attitudes regarding members of races and nationalities differing from one's own are acquired through primary or first-hand experiences. Every person has attitudes that are to be accounted for in some other way. Usually, these come second-hand from such sources as tradition, myth, history, rumor, or report. Once established in the mental habits of the individual, such attitudes are nearly as stubborn and as hard to modify or eradicate as those acquired by direct contacts. In so far as these indirect contacts are effective in forming and fixing the attitudes of the person, they may be called in truth prejudicial factors and the resultant attitudes may be termed "prejudices."

In early childhood the individual tends to get his first impressions of other races and other peoples through what he hears about them from his elders, or from observing and imitating their behavior toward members of the divergent groups in the local community. At what age these impressions are first recorded by the child is not definitely established and, no doubt, varies widely according to the conditions surrounding the child, such as the presence or absence of diverse groups in the community, the general attitude of the public toward those that are there, or the way in which grown-ups and older children discuss racial and nationality differences in the presence of the child.

The influence of talk overheard by children at home, school, and elsewhere in which derisive names are applied is only occasional; that of talk in which cultural efforts are humorously treated may be moderately frequent. Probably few children are often exposed to discussion of other groups that is marked by emotion. More obviously considerable is the influence of the lack of mention of the existence of other groups in the community. The children in American residential neighborhoods are growing up to a large extent with the feeling that, while there are many races, one knows about them only from the pages of textbooks and from the newspapers or industrial contacts in life. In many cases here even the attitude of patronage is not known because the existence of other races does not rise to consciousness in the home or through social contact.[11]

Not only may histories and other books and newspapers convey misleading and sometimes hostile ideas about Negroes and other ethnic groups, but the moving picture and the stage have also made their contribution to unfavorable impressions. Past conceptions and mis-

---

[11] Bruno Lasker, *Race Attitudes of Children*, p. 94. Copyright, 1929, by Henry Holt and Co., Inc.

conceptions tend to persist in some quarters, and are transmitted in the cultural heritage to succeeding generations.

Typical Reaction Patterns.—To the types of social contact we have described, direct and indirect alike, the initial reactions may be either of two types, various combinations of the two, or gradations between the two extremes. The response to the novel and different racial object may be one of curiosity, wonder, or astonishment, one of fear, disgust, or repulsion, or a mixture of two or more of these. A response of the first type is one of approach and the second type of response is one of withdrawal. Generally, curiosity is the initial step in the reaction "which the individuals of one race display when they come in peaceable contact for the first time with members of another group having marked physical characteristics." [12] "Curiosity can exist only so long as the distance to the stimulating object is such as to permit flight or fight when the situation gets defined or out of control." [13]

Sometimes the response is an automatic one in which case curiosity plays a minor or negligible role. In every case the response is to some dominant stimulus which is some one aspect of the situation. The aspect which ultimately dominates will determine the nature of the response. In human beings, for example, the stimulus-response factors are complicated by the preconditioning of the individual, his age, previous experiences, and the presence of imagery. In any case, Young says, "the tendency to approach and incorporate the object with the economy of the individual, is, as it were, counter-balanced by the tendency to destroy or avoid the object as dangerous to the individual. Alternation of attention between various stimulating aspects of an object and the mutual checking of conflicting motor responses may finally produce a complete debacle so that motor disorganization occurs." [14]

Because of these inhibiting tendencies, tensions are set up and a conflict situation is present within the person. These tensions are accompanied by emotions which give a definite feeling tone to the situation and to the response. The emotion of fear is one most commonly present in interracial contacts. "Curiosity turns to fear when the distance to the stimulating object decreases sufficiently to reveal clearly its dangerous aspects and to challenge forcibly the ability of the individual to control the situation." [15] There are varying degrees

---

[12] E. F. Young, *Racial Prejudice, with Particular Reference to the Negro*, p. 79.
[13] *Ibid.*, p. 81.
[14] *Ibid.*
[15] *Ibid.*, p. 106.

of intensity to the fear, ranging from diffidence and uncertain apprehension to terror, consternation, and even loss of consciousness, and death.[16] "Racial contacts have ever involved an element of fear, particularly fear of bodily harm. It ranges in clearness from a vague sense of uncertainty to more or less rational fears depending upon one's ability to make a satisfactory interpretation of the situation." [17]

The conduct of the first natives to whom we were introduced pleased us all. They showed themselves in a very amiable light, sold their corn cheaply and without fuss, behaved themselves decently and with propriety, though their principal men, entertaining very strange ideas of white men, carefully concealed themselves from view, and refused to be tempted to expose themselves within view or hearing of us.

Their doubts of our character were reported to us by a friendly young Arab as follows: "Kassangra, chief of Ruanda, says, 'How can the white men be good when they come for no trade, whose feet one never sees, who also go covered from head to foot with clothes? Do not tell me they are good and friendly. There is something very mysterious about them; perhaps wicked. Probably they are magicians; at any rate, it is better to leave them alone, and to keep close until they are gone.' " [18]

Also, disgust and repulsion are oftentimes reactions to unpleasant sensory stimuli.

The unsophisticated African entertains aversion to white people, and when, on accidentally or unexpectedly meeting a white man he turns or takes to his heels, it is because he feels that he has come upon some unusual or unearthly creature, some hobgoblin, ghost, or sprite; and when he does not look straight in a white man's face, it is because he believes in the "evil eye," and that an aquiline nose, scant lips, and cat-like eyes afflict him. The Yaruba word for a European means a peeled man, and to many an African the white man exudes some rancid odor not agreeable to his olfactory nerves.[19]

Body Odors in Relation to Food Habits.—So far as scientists have been able to discover, body odors are in no way due to *racial* differences, but are rather to be accounted for in terms of differences in food and other habits. Regardless of the cause, it is a fact that

---

[16] See: W. B. Cannon, *Bodily Changes in Pain, Hunger, Fear and Rage*, New York, D. Appleton & Co., Inc., 1915; G. Stanley Hall, "A Study of Fears," *Am. J. Psychol.*, Vol. 8, January, 1897, pp. 149-249; Kurt Riezler, "The Social Psychology of Fear," *Am. J. Sociol.*, Vol. 49, No. 6, May, 1944, pp. 489-498.

[17] Young, *Racial Prejudice with Particular Reference to the Negro*, pp. 109-110.

[18] Mungo Park, as quoted by Edward W. Blyden, *Christianity, Islam, and the Negro Race*, London, P. S. King & Son, 1888, p. 161.

[19] Mojola Agbebi, in G. Spiller (Ed.), *Universal Races Congress, Papers on Interracial Problems*, London, P. S. King & Son, 1911, p. 344.

unpleasant odors have the very definite effect of creating social distances as well as tending to widen spatial distances. White persons have found the body odors of Negroes offensive and may be surprised to learn that they, too, are credited by colored peoples as emitting odors equally offensive.[20] The role of smell in social contacts has been treated very little in scientific literature and is a subject that is not commonly discussed in polite society. This latter fact alone is enough to give some idea of the repulsive nature of the subject for many people.

Traditional Racial Attitudes.—From a consideration of these elemental tendencies to respond emotionally and eruptively to strange and different social objects we proceed to a discussion of racial attitudes, which have the character of social behavior patterns, more or less rationalized in the group and held by the group in accordance with precedent and the established mores. However, the sequence of reaction tendencies through a continuum from (a) sensation to (b) emotion, and finally to (c) sentiment and (d) attitude, is not so definite and regular as might seem to be the case from our discussion where this order has been implied, if not specifically stated. Actually they tend to present a configuration of tendencies rather than a continuum, and the reaction patterns appear in a variety of arrangements and combinations which depend upon a complex of factors in each situation. As we have indicated, attitudes being held in group tradition may be first in the experience of the person before there is any sensory experience whatever, and many times with little or no emotional involvement. It may be discovered, moreover, that the experience with the racial object is quite different from what might have been expected from the nature of the attitude acquired from one's own group tradition or gossip. So we see that there are many possible ways in which reaction tendencies may arise and many forms which they make take.

Positive and Negative Racial Prejudgments.—Following closely upon naïve, simple, and direct reactions, and as soon as the values in the situation become defined, there arise attitudes, either positive or negative, directed toward the objects of curiosity or fear. These attitudes seem to be more or less spontaneous tendencies to maintain

---

[20] It is questionable if body odors alone produce immediate antipathetic reactions. The reactions are probably most generally influenced by ideas about pleasant and unpleasant odors which are held and passed around in the group. Moreover, offensive odors play an important part in social relations within the group as well as between racial groups, as witness much current advertising of soaps, toilet preparations, etc. For a discussion of the role of smell in social contact see W. H. Hudson, *A Hind in Richmond Park*, New York, E. P. Dutton & Co., 1923, pp. 74-91.

social distances. In the case of the positive attitudes there is displayed a tendency to show a predilection or preference for the other racial group, whereas in the case of negative attitudes, the tendency is to manifest antagonism or aversion for the other. In one instance, the other group becomes an object of appreciation; in the other instance, it becomes an object toward which demonstrations of hostility are directed.

The simple facts of interbreeding and intermarriage that have been going on among the diverse racial and cultural groups of the world through a long history seem to indicate that the positive attitudes are not, in all persons, less pronounced than the negative ones. Indeed, attitudes of the positive sort most generally lead to the transformation of the symbiotic relation into a social relation without the usual friction and hostility characteristically generated by the negative attitudes.[21] There is a popular explanation to the effect that prejudice and antithetical attitudes are based on strangeness or difference. This is true to a certain extent, but where people live together there is bound to occur some miscegenation. The mulattoes are proof of this fact; so are the mestizos of Latin America, the blue-eyed Eskimos, the half-caste Eurasians of India, and other mixed bloods.[22]

Racial Stereotypes and Personal Reactions.—Speaking generally, attitudes about race tend to become fixed or stereotyped. This does not mean that there are set rules of conduct binding on the different groups in their relations with each other. It does mean that certain patterns of behavior presented by the groups to their members tend to shape the individual's beliefs and to control his conduct within certain prescribed limits.[23] The individual usually takes on the atti-

---

21 See: W. O. Brown, "Culture Contact and Race Conflict," in *Race and Culture Contacts*, edited by E. B. Reuter, New York, McGraw-Hill Book Co., Inc., 1934, p. 40.

22 See: Romanzo Adams and Committee, *The Peoples of Hawaii*, Honolulu, Institute of Pacific Relations, 1925; Brewton Berry, "The Mestizos of South Carolina," *Am. J. Sociol.*, Vol. 51, No. 1, July, 1945, pp. 34-41; E. Franklin Frazier, *The Negro Family in the United States*, Chicago, University of Chicago Press, 1939, Ch. 11; Gilberto Freyre, *Brazil: An Interpretation*, New York, Alfred A. Knopf, 1945; W. H. Gilbert, Jr., "Memorandum Concerning the Characteristics of the Larger Mixed-Blood Racial Islands of the Eastern United States," *Social Forces*, Vol. 24, May, 1946, pp. 438-447; Marcel Giraud, *Le Métis Canadien: Son rôle dans l'histoire des provinces de l'Ouest*, Paris, Musee d'Ethnologie, 1945; E. L. Hedin, "The Anglo-Indian Community," *Am. J. Sociol.*, Vol. 40, No. 2, September, 1934, pp. 165-179; Gunnar Myrdal, *An American Dilemma*, 2 vols., New York, Harper & Bros., 1944; Vol. I, pp. 123-129; K. W. Porter, "Relations between Negroes and Indians within the Present Limits of the United States," *J. Negro Hist.*, July, 1932, pp. 287-367, and July, 1933, pp. 282-321; Arthur Ramos, "Contact of Races in Brazil," *Social Forces*, Vol. 19, May, 1941, pp. 533-538; E. B. Reuter, *The Mulatto in the United States*, Boston, R. G. Badger, 1918; E. B. Reuter, *Race Mixture*, New York, McGraw-Hill Book Co., Inc., 1931; J. C. Russell, "The Short Dark Folk of England," *Social Forces*, Vol. 24, 1946, pp. 340-347; W. C. Smith, "The Hybrid in Hawaii as a Marginal Man," *Am. J. Sociol.*, Vol. 39, No. 4, January, 1934, pp. 459-468; C. A. Weslager, *Delaware's Forgotten Folk: The Story of the Moors and Nanticokes*, Philadelphia, University of Pennsylvania Press, 1943.

23 See: Bertram W. Doyle, *The Etiquette of Race Relations in the South: A Study in Social Control*, Chicago, University of Chicago Press, 1937; Samuel M. Strong, "Negro-

tudes of the group in which he finds himself. He accommodates his life organization to the social organization and to the superorganic culture. When one's naïve and direct reactions to members of other races do not coincide with the reactions of others in the same or similar situations, or when his reactions are challenged by facts or contrary opinions, then he assumes the role of a defender and becomes the center of conflict. It is then that he endeavors to rationalize his attitudes and this he usually does on moral grounds or in terms of pseudo-scientific arguments.

The Group's Rationalization of Its Own Prejudices.—The final stage in the natural history of racial attitudes is the development of race dogma or philosophy. At the core of these dogmatic attitudes are popular theories of racial inequality.[24] Here is to be found a confusion of myth, tradition, history, and biological misinformation. Each race, no matter what its color or cephalic index, tends to arrogate to itself all those superior qualities which it deems to be essential in any way to its status. Achievement is the criterion by which superiority is invariably determined. In other words, each race supports its claims to superior qualities and status in terms of its cultural accomplishments or its achievements in conquering and subjugating other peoples, the inferiors. It is not our intention to go into the many points of issue raised in the ever-present discussions on this subject, but merely to cite a reference which serves to show that the debate is a more or less purely academic one, without substantial foundation in fact.

THE ROLE OF RACE IN SOCIAL ACHIEVEMENT

The next great revolution in human thought came two thousand years [25] later, with the invention of true machines, the development of mechanical appliances, and the creation of a new scientific method and exact experimental disciplines, whose import it is even now impossible to foretell. Nothing like it had ever happened before, and in retrospect its truest ex-

White Relations as Reflected in Social Types," *Am. J. Sociol.*, Vol. 52, No. 1, July, 1946, pp. 23-30.

[24] The outstanding classic on the subject of racial inequality is J. A. de Gobineau's *The Inequality of Human Races*, New York, G. P. Putnam's Sons, 1853-1855. Other works dealing with the subject from the same viewpoint include: Madison Grant, *The Passing of the Great Race*, New York, Charles Scribner's Sons, 1921, and Lothrop Stoddard, *The Rising Tide of Color*, New York, Charles Scribner's Sons, 1929. Critical of the various theories of racial superiority are the following: J. Barzun, *Race: A Study of Modern Superstition*, New York, Harcourt, Brace & Co., 1937; F. H. Hankins, *The Racial Basis of Civilization: A Critique of the Nordic Doctrine*, New York, Alfred A. Knopf, 1931; F. O. Hertz, *Race and Civilization*, London, Macmillan & Co., Ltd., 1928; Paul Radin, *The Racial Myth*, New York, McGraw-Hill Book Co., Inc., 1934; Seligman, *Race Against Man*; L. L. Snyder, *Race: A History of Modern Ethnic Theories*, New York, Longmans, Green & Co., 1939.

[25] By permission from *The Racial Myth*, by Paul Radin, pp. 69-72. Copyrighted, 1934. New York, McGraw-Hill Book Co., Inc.

planation is to be sought in the hypothesis that the human brain, which, anatomically speaking, is so young, had at last begun to function maturely.

But what people participated in this astounding revolution? Do they belong to a single general physical type, to a circumscribed area, to a specific nationality? And do they speak the same tongue? The facts are before us and not a few have been unearthed by German scholars.

The preliminaries of the scientific renaissance that took definite form in Italy at the end of the fifteenth century are unquestionably to be sought among the Arabs and the Jews. It was they who kept alive the Greek tradition, particularly in medicine; it was they who continued the Greek tradition of mathematics and gave it an entirely new perspective by introducing the Arabic notation and algebra—the two weapons that have made modern mathematics possible and which had come to them from India. To these two we must add the concept of zero which had also come from India. The combination of the three made the work of the Pole Copernicus, the Italian Galileo, the German Kepler, the Englishman Newton, and the Frenchman Descartes possible.

Other factors, too, were instrumental in preparing the condition on which these great men could work and be effective—modern trade and the capitalistic system, the invention of the compass, of movable type, and of rag paper and books. The compass, movable type, and rag paper represent the contributions of China to the western world, and if we add gunpowder our debt to that great civilization is incalculable.

In all these achievements, two distinct races were involved, the Caucasian and the Mongolian. Among the Mongolians we find a mixture even greater than that for the Caucasians. For the Caucasians we have every single variety of that race represented—Mediterranean, Alpine, Nordic—all of them in the most inextricable mixtures and combinations. If we try to associate the achievements of this epoch with specific peoples, we find the following contributions: Trade and the capitalistic system were predominantly the contribution of the Jews, Italians, English, and Spaniards; mathematics that of the Italians, French, English, north Germans, and Jews; physics, until the nineteenth century, that of the Italians, English, French, and Dutch; in the nineteenth century, these same peoples, with the addition of the Germans and the Jews. Chemistry was the creation of the English and French, although it was in the Germany of the nineteenth century that it celebrated some of its greatest triumphs. Modern biology began in Italy in the early eighteenth century and made definite advances in Germany, Holland, and England at the same period. Essentially, however, its greatness rests upon the achievements of the French, English, Germans, and, within recent times, Americans.

Here we have long-heads and round-heads, blonde and brunet, blue-eyed and black-eyed, short and tall, rubbing shoulders in a most unaristocratic manner, and not concerned in the least about the purity of their blood.

It is thus clear that no physical type was correlated with this revolution, that it took place in a circumscribed area only if we regard Europe as a whole, with the possible exception of Spain and the Balkans, as such. Russia must be included because it was there that some of the most distinctive achievements in the chemistry, zoology, and mathematics of the nineteenth century were made.

In other words, we are in the presence of a fairly well-crystallized European culture, a new entity if you will, but one based on a Greek, Arabic, Jewish, Chinese, and even American Indian heritage, for its two primary foodstuffs are potatoes and maize and its fundamental form of pleasure is a mild narcotic that has surely done more to make man more acceptable to himself than any measure known to him for the last five thousand years: tobacco.

And so was the torch of civilization handed down from one generation to another, in many and diverse ways and by many and diverse peoples, all of them criminally oblivious of the racial qualifications they were supposed to possess or of the unpardonable manner in which their carelessness as to the purity of their blood was to affect the German theorists of the nineteenth century.

Looking to its achievements, usually in the realm of culture, the ethnic group tends to ascribe to itself an innate mental capacity superior to that of other ethnic groups. The fact that scientific evidence in support of such an assumption is lacking does not deter the ethnocentric myth-makers.

Another variant of the racial myth is that of "race purity," recently greatly stressed in Germany. "Race purity" serves the demagogue superbly and performs the function of giving a "spiritual" basis for national unity in times of stress and confusion. Racial creeds and dogmas find a ready acceptance in the popular mind and serve to clinch racial attitudes by giving them a semblance of respectability and scientific authority. They not only pertain to notions of mental ability and cultural achievement, but also to morality, criminality, and the like. Where members of different "races" are thrown closely together in a competitive way, "one has need of the spiritual distance created by belief in one's own 'election' and the satanic character of the 'others.' " [26]

Overt Forms of Racial Conflict.—Of the two major types of attitudes discussed in the last section, the negative or antagonistic ones alone result in overt manifestations of hostility, and the extent to which they do so is dependent upon certain factors mentioned previously, namely, the nature of the contacts, numbers and distribution of the provocative objects, and the degree and nature of their penetration. The forms which conflict takes are culturally determined

[26] Erich Voegelin, *Rasse und Staat*, Tübingen, J. C. B. Mohr, 1933, p. 153.

and tend to vary according to the social definition of the situation. These definitions are often bound up in tradition and in the self-consciousness of the group as to its status, and the nature of the threat to its security. Some of the familiar forms of conflict will now receive attention.

Terrorism.—Terrorism is a form of conflict long employed by the whites in the United States in dealing with Negro criminals or suspects. The lynching of Negroes is rare in the North, but race riots, with their reign of terror for both whites and Negroes, are more numerous. Lynching is the mechanism of dealing with the individual, rioting is the mechanism of dealing with the mass. In the South, lynching was for many years a socially accepted and traditional way of dealing with the obstreperous Negro. The true Southerner had the situation socially defined for him and he knew how to act. Evidently, such customary and extra-legal methods of dealing with a situation in which a Negro had committed or was suspected of having committed an offense were designed to serve as factors of control by means of intimidating the other Negroes.[27]

The real explanation of lynching is that it is in the accepted mores of the community. Lynching is, for the lynchers, a moral act. There is no feeling of guilt, no remorse for killing a human being. Members of the mob see themselves as heroes ridding society of someone who has no right to live. On the other hand, with changes taking place in the mores, many Southerners are horrified at the record of lynchings and are turning their attention to the suppression of mob rule that flouts the dignity of the law and the criminal courts. More than five thousand persons (not all objects of race hatred) have been victims of lynching in the United States. The numbers are decreasing through the years.[28] It should not be concluded that the South has any less moral strength than the North simply because there have been more lynchings in that section of the country. If most of the lynching terrors have occurred in the South, most of the race riots have occurred in the North.[29]

---

[27] See: Jessie D. Ames, *The Changing Character of Lynching*, Atlanta, The Commission on Interracial Cooperation, Inc., 1942; Arthur Raper, *The Tragedy of Lynching*, Chapel Hill, University of North Carolina Press, 1933; E. B. Reuter, *The American Race Problem*, New York, T. Y. Crowell Co., 1927, Ch. XV; Frank J. Tannenbaum, *Darker Phases of the South*, New York, G. P. Putnam's Sons, 1924; Walter F. White, *Rope and Faggot*, New York, Alfred A. Knopf, 1929.

[28] Lynchings of Negroes in the United States numbered 90 in 1890, 65 in 1910, 53 in 1920, 20 in 1930, 4 in 1941, 6 in 1942, 3 in 1943, 2 in 1944, and 1 in 1945. The first year of peace, 1946, saw the number increase to 6.

[29] The Chicago Commission on Race Relations, *The Negro in Chicago*, Chicago, University of Chicago Press, 1922; Alfred McClung Lee and N. D. Humphrey, *Race Riot*, New York, The Dryden Press, Inc., 1943; B. F. Robinson, "Sociology of Race Riots," *Phylon*, Vol. 2, 2nd Quarter, 1941, pp. 162-171.

Although the Jewish people do not constitute a "racial" group in a scientific sense, they are generally so regarded in the popular mind and have suffered repeated persecution accordingly. Outbreaks against them occurred in Nazi Germany where they were not only proscribed and boycotted but terrorized and victimized by Nazi mobs. Thousands fled into exile, and many more thousands were confined in prisons and concentration camps, where they were subjected to unspeakable cruelties, torture, horrors of the gas chamber, and pseudo-scientific experimentation, and where hundreds of thousands perished. While such overt hostile acts are commonly regarded as racially inspired, they are more often engendered by cultural differences, economic competition, and nationalistic fanaticism. They represent what has taken place in many parts of the world for centuries in what is a widespread anti-Semitic movement.[30] Wherever strange people exert too great pressure upon the precincts of a racial or national integrity or economic or cultural security, such spontaneous and eruptive outbursts of hatred and open hostilities seem bound to occur and they will almost inevitably be attended by some form of terrifying experience for the minority group.

Discrimination.—Another and more common, but less sanguinous, form of conflict pattern is discrimination. The majority group has found many ways of keeping the minority group in its place. In legislation, before the courts of law, in employment, and in various minor ways the situations are defined differently for the two groups and always to the advantage of the dominant group. If the group discriminated against accepts its inferior status and does not resist, then more coercive and repressive measures are seldom adopted; but if, on the contrary, the racial minority fails to make an accommodation on the basis laid down by the racial majority, the conflict pattern takes on a more violent form.

Many cases could be cited in which there appear to be unmistakable evidences of discrimination in the courts where no explanation can be found other than "race."[31] There is reflected in such cases a con-

[30] See Isacque Graeber and S. H. Britt (Eds.), *Jews in a Gentile World: The Problem of Anti-Semitism*, New York, The Macmillan Co., 1942; Stanley High, "Jews, Anti-Semites, and Tyrants," *Harper's Magazine*, Vol. 185, June, 1942, pp. 22-29; L. J. Levinger, *Anti-Semitism Yesterday and Tomorrow*, New York, Conference on Jewish Relations, 1946; Maurice Samuel, *The Great Hatred*, New York, Alfred A. Knopf, 1940; Maurice Samuel, *Jews on Approval*, New York, Horace Liveright, Inc., 1932; D. S. Strong, *Organized Anti-Semitism in America: The Rise of Group Prejudice During the Decade, 1930-1940*, Washington, American Council on Public Affairs, 1941; Hugo Valentin, *Anti-Semitism, Historically and Critically Examined*, New York, Viking Press, 1936.
[31] See: E. Franklin Frazier, "The Pathology of Race Prejudice," *The Forum*, Vol. 77, June, 1927, pp. 856-862; Guy B. Johnson, "The Negro and Crime," *Annals Am. Acad. Pol.*

dition in society which assumes that members of divergent racial groups are not entitled to the same treatment before the law as that accorded to members of the superordinate group. It can hardly be said that such antipathetic attitudes are purely personal with juries and judges. They are clearly reflected attitudes held in society.

In the matter of employment the situation is not favorable to the person who was born with a different color. Racial orthodoxy seems to demand that the respective statuses of the white and the colored races be maintained as nearly intact as the interests of industry will permit. Negro workers are by all odds the most available in many parts of the United States for personal service positions—"blind alley" jobs—which lead to nothing beyond the merit of long and faithful service. They are the porters, waiters, messengers, elevator boys, chauffeurs, janitors, cooks, maids, and yard "boys." [32]

The present problem of Negro workers is twofold. In industry they have only marginal status as recent comers, with barriers of tradition and prejudice to overcome. And in agriculture, too, they have only marginal status, as a result of the decreasing necessity for workers in this field. Since 1920, there has been an addition of nearly two million southern Negroes to the population of the North, and they are today more urban than rural in their distribution.

Of the four major occupational fields in the South—cotton cultivation, cotton fabrication, tobacco growing and manufacturing, and iron and steel—cotton cultivation holds the largest number of Negroes. There are over 700,000 Negro tenant families, representing about 3,500,000 persons. It never has been possible for these families to earn an adequate living. Studies show the average *annual* earnings before the present war to fall below $200. In 1929, the average income was less than a fourth of the income of farmers in other sections—$186 as compared with $528. For tenants the average annual income was $73, and for sharecroppers $38. The eastern cotton belt, where most of the Negroes live, together with the Appalachian Ozarks, constitute the major economic problem of the South and of the nation.

Prior to the present war, the heaviest concentrations of Negro workers were still in unskilled branches of industry, and in agricultural and domestic and personal service, but there had been a fairly significant penetration into industry and into positions above the unskilled level. . . .

and Soc. Sci., Vol. 217, September, 1941, pp. 93-104; Charles S. Mangum, The Legal Status of the Negro, Chapel Hill, University of North Carolina Press, 1940; Roscoe C. Martin, The Defendant and Criminal Justice, Austin, University of Texas Press, 1934, Ch. II; Thorsten Sellin, "Race Prejudice in the Administration of Justice," Am. J. Sociol., Vol. 41, No. 2, September, 1935, pp. 212-217; G. T. Stephenson, Race Distinction in American Law, New York, D. Appleton & Co., 1910.

32 See: Charles S. Johnson, "Black Workers and the City," Survey, Vol. 53, March 1, 1935, pp. 641-643, 718, 719, 721; Myrdal, An American Dilemma, Vol. 1, Chs. 12-13; Ira deA. Reid, The Urban Negro Worker in the United States, 1925-1936, Vol. 1: Statistics by Regions, Washington, U. S. Gov. Printing Office, 1938; C. R. Weaver, Negro Labor, A National Problem, New York, Harcourt, Brace & Co., 1945.

In the southern urban areas, the average annual wage (white and Negro) is $865 as compared with $1,219 for workers in other sections. However, the Negro earnings represent a differential in the average wages of the South amounting approximately to 30 percent.

In the typical northern industrial city, the average weekly wage for Negro male white collar workers in 1936 was $23; and for female workers, $15.82. The skilled Negro male averaged $18.77 and the skilled female, $13.37. All these figures are considerably below the level necessary for a health-and-decency standard of living.

This economic inadequacy is back of many of the problems of education, health, housing, family life, and general cultural development. It is reflected in high Negro mortality rates from tuberculosis, typhoid, pellagra, influenza, and childbirth, and also in infant mortality. These rates are from two to four times those of whites, and are largely controllable.

It requires a profound crisis to disturb the deepest occupational patterns which regulate our national working habits. The racial stratification of jobs has been one of the national traits. The present war, with its acute demand for industrial manpower, reveals the real strength of the resistance to any change of the pattern of racial stratification in occupations.[33]

True, as Johnson says, it takes a major crisis like a World War to make even a dent in some of the deepest prejudices and traditional behavior patterns known to mankind. Foreign propaganda, immediately before and during the last war, played up race discrimination and conflict in the United States and, in order to minimize the effect of this and to secure the support of the Negro in the war effort, certain concessions to the idea of race equality and some inducements to encourage participation were proffered to Negro workers. Despite official and other attempts to secure fair employment practices in industry, the evidence shows that considerable discrimination in war industries, in army camps, and in the various branches of government continued to be manifested against Negroes and other colored people.[34] If anything, race tension was intensified during the war and there is reason to believe that race relations generally, and not simply white-Negro relations, deteriorated appreciably.[35]

[33] Charles S. Johnson, "Striking the Economic Balance," Survey Graphic, Vol. 31, November, 1942, pp. 496-497.

[34] See: Earl Brown and George Leighton, The Negro and the War, New York, Public Affairs Committee, Inc., 1942; E. Franklin Frazier, "Ethnic and Minority Groups in Wartime, with Special Reference to the Negro," Am. J. Sociol., Vol. 48, No. 3, November, 1942, pp. 369-377; E. T. Hall, Jr., "Race Prejudice and Negro-White Relations in the Army," Am. J. Sociol., Vol. 52, No. 5, March, 1947, pp. 401-409; Charles S. Johnson, Patterns of Negro Segregation, New York, Harper & Bros., 1943; Florence Murray, "The Negro and Civil Liberties during World War II," Social Forces, Vol. 24, December, 1945, pp. 211-216; Myrdal, An American Dilemma, Vol. 1, Ch. 19; Logan Wilson and Harlan Gilmore, "White Employers and Negro Workers," Am. Sociol. Rev., Vol. 8, No. 6, December, 1943, pp. 698-705; Ruth D. Wilson, Jim Crow Joins Up, New York, William J. Clark Press, 1944.

[35] See: Charles S. Johnson, "The Present Status of Race Relations in the South," Social Forces, Vol. 23, October, 1944, pp. 27-32.

Negroes are excluded from many industries and trades. In many trades they are barred from serving apprenticeships and many vocational schools exclude Negro students from some courses. Although the large, powerful labor organizations carry on their books the pledged doctrine that they will not discriminate on a basis of race or color, the labor unions [36] follow a variety of practices and policies, mostly adventitious, on the ground that local autonomy determines union conduct in each district. On the basis of an analysis of the relation of the Negro to organized labor, Northrup draws the following conclusions: environment largely determines union racial policy; the philosophy of the particular union and its leaders greatly influences policy; when there is a labor shortage, egalitarian policy tends to prevail, but when there is a labor surplus, a discriminatory policy returns; national union control of policy as to admission and promotion is likely to benefit Negroes more than will local control; and the policies of rival unions may influence racial policy, depending upon circumstances.[37] As a result of adverse union practice, not less than a quarter-million Negro workers are denied trade union affiliation.[38] Moreover, "the Negro is on the fringe of the warp and woof of our industrial network. In the main, he is the last hired, and the first fired. He suffers not only from unemployment but underemployment and is considered in many instances unemployable." [39]

In addition to the inequality of the conditions of economic advancement of the Negro and the white there are, even after the abolition of legal inequality, numerous other evidences of discrimination against the colored race. In the South the right of suffrage is rather generally denied the Negro citizen,[40] the "Jim Crow" laws and ordinances operate to segregate the races in public places, and in the North many of the same restrictions are being applied to areas of residence, schools, churches, theaters, restaurants, etc., if not by law, at least in practice.[41] Segregation is both an evidence of conflict and a form of accommodation.

[36] Except, of course, the all-colored unions, like that of the Pullman porters. See: B. R. Brazeal, *The Brotherhood of Sleeping Car Porters*, New York, Harper & Bros., 1946. The interracial policy of both the C.I.O. and the Share-Croppers Union is quite liberal.

[37] See: Herbert Northrup, *Organized Labor and the Negro*, New York, Harper & Bros., 1944. See also Horace R. Cayton and George S. Mitchell, *Black Workers and the New Unions*, Chapel Hill, University of North Carolina Press, 1939; S. D. Spero and A. L. Harris, *The Black Worker: The Negro and the Labor Movement*, New York, Columbia University Press, 1931.

[38] See: Ira deA. Reid, *Negro Membership in American Labor Unions*, New York, National Urban League, 1930.

[39] F. C. Covington, "Color: A Factor in Social Mobility," *Sociol. and Soc. Res.*, Vol. 15, 1930-1931, p. 145.

[40] This restriction has been eased in recent years, but still applies in several states to party primaries.

[41] See: Trevor Bowen, *Divine White Right*, New York, Harper & Bros., 1934; H. M. Bond, *The Education of the Negro in the American Social Order*, New York, Prentice-Hall,

Ridicule and Patronage.—Further evidence of racial hostility is to be seen in ridicule and patronage. These are not necessarily related behaviors, although patronage often savors of "making fun," more or less indirectly, of some disliked person or group. As devices for controlling the "inferior" person or group, these two probably have no superiors. Though often disguised as a joke, ridicule has a pungent, stinging quality that seldom misses its mark and drives home the unpleasant fact that the object is held in contempt. The idiosyncrasies of colored people, their speech and mannerisms, the seriousness and dramatic character of their religious behavior, their funerals, weddings, and baptisms may be laughed at and mockingly imitated. Their hopes and ambitions may be intentionally misconstrued and derided. They have long been burlesqued to furnish amusement for their detractors. And yet there frequently runs through this ridicule the element of innocent banter, of good-natured humor that means no harm to anyone. However, it is often hard for the object of the mirth to make a distinction. Ridicule is one of the most powerful mechanisms of social control.

On the side of patronage, the attitude is always one involving a downward gesture. The dominant group finds great satisfaction in condescending to do something for those who are held beneath them, thereby reminding their "inferiors" of "their place." Sincere efforts to improve the position of the minority racial group should not be confused with those affable movements designed to impose obligations upon them. Activities of the latter sort tend to create a form of caste relationship between the two groups; the one becoming the master, the other the slave; the former bestowing largess the better to secure its hold, the latter sinking deeper into the bondage of perpetual indebtedness and obligation.

Inc., 1934; E. W. Burgess, "Residential Segregation in American Cities," *Annals Am. Acad. Pol. and Soc. Sci.*, Vol. 140, No. 229, November, 1928, pp. 105-115; John Dollard, *Caste and Class in a Southern Town*, New Haven, Yale University Press, 1937; E. Franklin Frazier, "Negro Harlem: An Ecological Study," *Am. J. Sociol.*, Vol. 43, No. 1, July, 1937, pp. 72-78; Lester Granger, "Negroes and War Production," *Survey Graphic*, Vol. 31, November, 1942, pp. 469-471, 543-544; Charles S. Johnson, *Growing Up in the Black Belt*, Washington, American Council on Education, 1941; Charles S. Johnson, *Negro Housing*, Washington, The President's Committee on House Building and Home Ownership, 1932; Charles S. Johnson, *The Negro in American Civilization*, New York, Henry Holt & Co., 1930, Chs. 10-21; Charles S. Johnson, *Shadow of the Plantation*, Chicago, University of Chicago Press, 1934; Charles S. Mangum, Jr., *The Legal Status of the Negro;* B. E. Mays and J. W. Nicholson, *The Negro's Church*, New York, Institute of Social and Religious Research, 1933; Hortense Powdermaker, *After Freedom*, New York, The Viking Press, 1939; Robert L. Sutherland, *Color, Class, Personality*, Washington, American Council on Education, 1942; Doxey A. Wilkerson, *Special Problems of Negro Education*, Washington, Advisory Committee on Education, 1939; Carter G. Woodson, *The Mis-Education of the Negro*, Washington, The Associated Publishers, Inc., 1933; Carter G. Woodson, *The Negro Professional Man and the Community*, Washington, The Association for the Study of Negro Life and History, 1934; Thomas J. Woofter, Jr., and Associates, *Negro Problems in Cities*, New York, Doubleday, Doran & Co., 1928.

Race and Nationality.—Mention has been made of the fact that a belief in racial continuity tends to act as a social force, arousing national consciousness. While it is true that continuity of racial descent is chiefly a matter of tradition and not capable of being proved in ethnology, it remains a very definite factor in producing a consciousness of nationality. The traditions and sentiments of a common racial origin and descent, whether founded on fact or on false assumption, constitute a significant force producing and advancing a nationalistic movement. When a people, holding traditional beliefs of racial origin and descent, find themselves the object of prejudice and antipathy because of their racial differences, or supposed racial differences, they tend to be stimulated emotionally thereby. Racial continuity and purity become idealized conceptions and the group feels strengthened if it can be stirred emotionally in its struggle for recognition and national status by an appeal to racial origins as well as to cultural traditions. For this reason, racial conflict frequently gets identified with the struggles of nationality groups, and the former tends to reinforce the latter.

Nazi Germany afforded an excellent example of this identification of national aspirations with the myth of racial purity and superiority. The Jewish Zionist movement for a national home in Palestine, though not inspired by race doctrine in the strict sense, is so interpreted by many people. Among American Negroes there has been a pronounced growth of militant sentiment of racial pride and solidarity in recent years. This movement constitutes one of the significant developments in their racial history. While it differs in degree, it does not differ so much in kind, from so-called nationalistic movements elsewhere. A particularly interesting example of the "nationalistic" attitude of American Negroes was the "back to Africa" movement inaugurated in the early 1920's by Marcus Garvey. This movement was launched auspiciously, but ended in disillusionment for many and financial ruin for others.[42]

Race prejudice and antipathy serve to give all members of the group a common definition of a situation requiring group action. As rallying points around which the nationality-group forces mobilize for aggression or defense, they are unequaled.[43] They have survival

[42] See: Walter A. Daykin, "Nationalism as Expressed in Negro History," *Social Forces*, Vol. 13, December, 1934, pp. 257-264; Amy J. Garvey (Ed.), *Philosophy and Opinions of Marcus Garvey*, Vol. 1, New York, Universal Publishing House, 1923; Guy B. Johnson, "Negro Racial Movements and Leadership in the United States," *Am. J. Sociol.*, Vol. 43, No. 1, July, 1937, pp. 57-71; T. G. Standing, "Nationalism in Negro Leadership," *Am. J. Sociol.*, Vol. 40, No. 2, September, 1934, pp. 180-192.
[43] Hortense Powdermaker, "Channeling of Negro Aggression by the Cultural Process," *Am. J. Sociol.*, Vol. 48, May, 1943, pp. 750-758.

value for the group but there is danger that, if survival is defended to the absolute exclusion of all that is foreign in race and alien in culture, the group may suffer for want of new blood and new cultural values.

Trends of Control in Race Relations.—Many of the forms and mechanisms employed by the dominant white group in its dealing with the "race problem," while undoubtedly viewed by the colored group as forms and mechanisms of conflict, ordinarily have been considered by the white group to be ways of accommodating themselves to a difficult, if not absolutely dangerous, state of affairs. Certainly the difficulties and "problems" have not been those of one side alone. The race-conscious Negro group has had to face handicaps that have seemed to them to be insuperable and have been forced to adopt means of adjustment in such circumstances.

The Negroes were economically and culturally dependent upon the more numerous white group. They were without ancestral pride or family tradition. They had no distinctive language or religion; these, like their folkways and moral customs, were but recently acquired from the whites and furnished no nucleus for a racial unity. The group was without even a tradition of historic unity or of racial achievement. There were no historic names, no great achievements, no body of literature, no artistic productions. The whole record of the race was one of servile or barbarian status apparently without a point about which a sentimental complex could form. The one distinctive fact of the race was a characteristic physical appearance. But color was everywhere associated with servile status and backward culture; it was a fact of which the rising members of the group were ashamed and from which they desired to escape; it was not a fact of which they were proud.[44]

It is with such unpromising racial and cultural heritages that the Negro group in the United States has had to make its adjustments to the superior numbers and culture of the white population. In view of this fact and in the face of widespread prejudice against them, it is remarkable that the Negroes have accomplished so much and improved their status so greatly.

Historically and sociologically, only four possible ways of terminating race friction have been discovered. These ways of resolving differences between racial groups will now receive brief attention.

Elimination.—Expulsion as a means of ridding a population of undesirable elements has been employed in all times and among all peoples to some extent. In this connection mention may be made of the fantastic plan conceived by some white Americans as a solution of

---

[44] E. B. Reuter, *The American Race Problem*, rev. ed., New York, T. Y. Crowell Co., 1939, pp. 396-397.

the race problem, namely, a plan to deport to Africa or elsewhere all persons of Negro descent found in the United States. Others propose to have all Negroes segregated in one or two states, but the states are never definitely indicated.[45] Just how these plans would be put into effect is not known and their proponents never seem quite sure of the details. So far, methods of expulsion as applied to the Negro have consisted mainly of terroristic practices employed in some local communities. These have served to drive large numbers of the racial minority from the communities, or to deter them from entering the communities or taking up residence there. Certain communities are notoriously anti-Negro and in some instances signs warn the Negro that his presence will not be tolerated.

Amalgamation.—Whenever members of different races meet on intimate peaceable terms and on a basis of approximate equality, some interbreeding is bound to occur. Even where the racial differences are originally pronounced, the process tends to go on to some extent and, as the differences become less marked through succeeding generations, the process shows a decided increase until, in many parts of the world today, the distinctive marks of race are practically lost. Not infrequently, the half-breeds and mixed bloods become the object of prejudice of both of the parent groups, a prejudice often more intense than the parent groups hold toward each other, although important differences occur between one situation and another. "In the early phases of intermixture the mixed-blood children are conspicuous merely because they differ from the parents. Theirs is a problem of incomplete social assimilation as well as of incomplete biological amalgamation. As the processes of assimilation and amalgamation continue the status of the mixed bloods changes. They gradually become the preponderant or 'normal' type and then are no longer considered hybrids but a new 'race.' In this way complete racial intermixture in any given region solves the problem which arises from partial intermixture."[46] If the mixed bloods are shown a greater preference by the dominant group, the attitude of the subordinate group tends to change to a more favorable one, also, and the lighter skin and the higher status of the mixed group tend to become symbols and patterns to be emulated. For example, race prejudice against

---

45 See: W. P. Calhoun, *The Caucasian and the Negro in the United States,* Columbia, S. C., Bryan Co., 1902; O. M. Donaldson, *Mexico for the Negro,* New York, Negro National League, 1915; T. W. Evans, *Solution of the Negro Problem,* Dublin, Ga., The Author, 1924; "49th State," *Compass,* March, 1936, p. 17; Walter L. Fleming, *Deportation and Colonization,* New York, Columbia University Press, 1924.

46 Everett V. Stonequist, *The Marginal Man: A Study in Personality and Culture Conflict,* New York, Charles Scribner's Sons, 1937, pp. 10-11. Ch. II, "The Racial Hybrid," is also rewarding.

Negroes creates an attitude on the part of some colored people which forms color lines within the color line. It is almost inevitable that there should grow up among Negroes themselves distinctions based on skin color and hair texture when these symbols bring, almost automatically, denial of opportunity in the community. This discrimination within the colored group affects marriage, business relations, cultural and economic opportunity, and progress always in favor of those having the lighter shades.

On the whole, however, amalgamation indicates that there is a definite tendency for members of both contiguous groups to overcome repugnance and for the appearance of more tolerant attitudes. For example, wherever both groups have some common basis for sympathetic contacts, as happened between the Negroes and the American Indians, intermixture went on with only a minimum of friction. Reuter points out that there is "a pronounced Negro strain in a number of Indian tribes." He goes on to say: "In some cases the Negroes were more numerous than the Indians and the reservations became Negro and mulatto settlements with little more than a tradition of Indian ancestry. The so-called Croatan Indians in North Carolina, the 'Redbones' of South Carolina, the 'Moors' of Delaware, the 'Melungeons' of West Virginia, and other similar groups of the present day are wasted Indian tribes that have been swamped by intermixture with escaped slaves, free Negroes, and mulattoes, and white outlaws and rovers." [47]

The extent to which intermixture of the white and colored populations has occurred is unknown.[48] It was no doubt considerable in the days of slavery, but once the status of the Negro became that of a nominally free people, intermixture declined appreciably, although extramarital relations have continued to some extent since then. Many states forbid intermarriage between the two groups and in most of the other states there is strong sentiment against it.

The sources of the increase of mixed-bloods are the relatively few legal marriages of white and colored partners; concubinage of Negro women with white men, the true extent of which has never been known; promiscuity in sexual relations, probably at one time much more frequent than at present; and the natural increase of the mulattoes themselves, which is shown by the census figures to have been rapid. In 1920, the last census year in which mulattoes were counted separately, the percentage of Negroes of mixed blood was reported

---

[47] Reuter, *The American Race Problem*, pp. 123-124. See also, footnote 22 of this chapter, and M. J. Herskovits, *The American Negro*, New York, Alfred A. Knopf, 1928.
[48] Reuter, *ibid.*, pp. 132-137; Reuter, *The Mulatto in the United States*, pp. 105-165.

as 15.9 as compared with a percentage of 11.2 in 1850, the first time the census enumeration distinguished between mulattoes and full-blood Negroes. It is probable that the actual number of mixed bloods would be in excess of any enumeration figures. Since one may expect a more rapid increase of mulattoes than of full-blood Negroes in the future, there will be an obvious tendency for the colored population to become more and more a mulatto population.

Accommodation.—Accommodation between ethnic groups in contact with each other varies considerably in form and in degree depending on a variety of differential factors in many kinds of situations. However, some kind of accommodation is certain to be reached either with or without prior conflict. Absence of overt friction in race relations is no sure indication of complete accommodation. It may simply mean a temporary truce, a bowing to necessity, while under the surface smoulder the fires of hatred and suspicion which only await an issue to fan them into a conflagration.

The early position of the Negro in the United States was that of the slave. In a stratified society, slavery is one type of ranking which invariably carries with it the evaluation of subordination. Sociologically speaking, it was a form of accommodation. It is a system of involuntary servitude that has been at one time or another operative in practically every part of the world and one that shows a tendency to persist in certain quarters in spite of the attitude of most civilized nations in opposition to it.[49] In its extreme development, it tended to become a caste system, in many cases based on racial lines. This phase of the system never fully matured in the southern United States where it was always possible for Negroes to earn or buy freedom. There was a tendency, however, toward such a caste system on a racial basis. Legislation was passed in some states to prevent the slave from becoming a free, educated Negro. Emancipation put an end to this tendency.

SLAVERY AND THE PLANTATION SYSTEM. The history of slavery goes back long before improved agriculture, but with the development of landholding and land cultivation on a large scale slavery attained its full magnitude as an institution. Negro slaves were first introduced into the American colonies in 1620 and from that time until 1865 they constituted the chief labor force in the agricultural

---

[49] As recently as 1935, Ignatius Phayre, in "Slave Markets of Today," *Current History*, Vol. 42, April, 1935, pp. 42-46, stated that slaves were being bought and sold in fifteen different countries, including several that were members of the League of Nations. During World War II and since, there have been reports of hundreds of thousands of "displaced persons" being held in "slavery" in central and eastern Europe.

areas of the South. Their labor seemed especially suited to the plantation system of economic organization and, though it tended to decline in the North as unprofitable, it persisted in the South until ended by war, although there are many indications that eventually it would have been abolished there without the process of overt conflict in the form of the war pattern.

One important consideration in the plantation system, wherever found, was that which had to do with the attitudes and sentiments which came to characterize the master-slave relationship. Though slavery, generally speaking, is a positional-status arrangement forcibly imposed, it was invariably supported by more or less definite life-philosophies on the part of the master class and of the slave caste.[50]

Manifestly the master-slave relationship was one of accommodation. Since the slaves were chattels, there is no doubt but that, generally, their masters treated them as valuable pieces of property. Most writers on slavery, holding the point of view of the dominant race, have made much of the supposed congeniality of the slave status to the Negro individually, and have ignored the not infrequent manifestations of discontent in the form of escapes and open revolts.[51] Many sought and some secured freedom. While the slave usually made a mental adjustment to his condition of bondage, it is doubtful if it was often one of contentment. It is obviously impossible to prove statistically whether restlessness and rebelliousness, or passivity, docility, and satisfaction, were characteristic of the slave attitude.

CAUSES OF STRATIFICATION. The causes of relatively permanent superior-inferior relationships may be briefly summarized as follows:

Racial and other ethnic differences explain, in part, the stratification of social class positions and statuses.[52] Not that these differences are insurmountable, but they are surrounded by a body of tradition and sentiment that makes it possible for certain racial and cultural groups to maintain unchangeable positions of superordination and other groups to have reciprocal positions of subordination to them. Differences of skin color, speech, religion, and custom tend to make divisions of the population relatively unyielding. The tendency for sentiments and attitudes of ethnic superiority and inferiority, of racial purity and hybridization, to persist is one explanation of this phenomenon. On this point Thouless remarks: "The sentiment of

---

[50] See: B. A. Botkin, *Lay My Burden Down: A Folk History of Slavery*, Chicago, University of Chicago Press, 1945.

[51] Herbert Aptheker, *American Negro Slave Revolts*, New York, Columbia University Press, 1943; J. C. Carroll, *Slave Insurrections in the United States, 1800-1865*, Boston, Chapman & Grimes, 1938.

[52] See Chapter 17.

respect felt by the inferior for the superior remains, and, so far as this sentiment (and the opposite sentiment of the superior to the inferior) underlies such social grouping, the relationship tends to be permanent." [53]

Following their emancipation from slavery the Negroes found themselves possessed of a legal status for which they were unprepared. As a result, they easily fell prey to the corrupting influences of unscrupulous politicians, who not only encouraged them to take immediate advantage of their freedom to assert themselves politically but to seek social equality as well. The inevitable consequence was to bring the Negroes into direct conflict with the white population of the South. Race antipathy, which had been largely covert during the slavery period, now flared up in a most bitter form. The struggle of the southern white population to maintain their supremacy against the freed Negroes and their "carpetbagger" friends is largely responsible for the attitude of the southerners toward the Negroes today. The struggle for status during the period of reconstruction after the Civil War has become a tradition in the South and the superior status established at that time the white group is determined to maintain. The accommodation made was one of superordination for the white group and one of subordination for the colored group and so long as the Negro "keeps his place" the dominant group is satisfied.

There is no doubt that certain advantages inhere in the superordinate-subordinate relationship in some areas of life, as for example, in educational, industrial, and military institutions, where the relationship makes accomplishment more certain and possibly more efficient, but there is a question as to its value in race relations, where it involves holding several millions of people to a more or less perpetual status of inferiority and submission.

This mode of organization works ideally when the inferiors in a social group accept the relationship willingly for the purpose for which the organization is working. This happens when they form sentiments of respect for the superiors of the organization and feel themselves in sympathy with the object of the organization. [54]

But grave social dangers lurk in this type of social relationship when the inferiors feel that the purpose of the arrangement is not to their interest; when they have no reason to form sentiments of respect for the superior group; when, on the contrary, they have reason to feel that their interests are permanently subordinated to those of the

---

53 R. H. Thouless, *Social Psychology*, London, University Tutorial Press, 1925, p. 159.
54 *Ibid.*, p. 161.

superiors; when they continually feel the disrespectful, if not positively hostile gestures of their superordinates; and when they know that their subordinate status is being perpetuated in spite of legal provision to the contrary. It is because an increasing number of Negroes are coming to resent openly the implications and the realities of their subordinate status that this basis of accommodation is becoming more and more unstable, irksome, and intolerable.

RATIONALIZATION, SUBLIMATION, AND IDEALIZATION. For nearly eighty-five years the colored element in the population has had to content itself with working out other forms of accommodation within the more inclusive accommodative process we have just discussed. In part these forms of accommodation have been brought over from the time of slavery; in part, they are new forms which emerged to compensate for the unsatisfactory subordinate pattern of accommodation. Individual Negroes in their contacts with white people have learned the value of compromise and the importance of conciliating the feelings of the white superiors. Though they may rebel within, not many Negroes find it expedient to rebel openly, at least in their personal contacts with members of the other race. Consequently, as individuals and as a group, the Negroes have resorted to many of the subtler forms of accommodation to help them through trying and difficult situations. Rationalization, sublimation, and idealization are common modes of adjustment with them. The former, by which is meant a kind of pseudo-logical reasoning for the purpose of justifying or explaining behavior that has been questioned or that is the subject of conflict, takes the form of finding "excuses" for the inferior status, for the "race problem," and for the prejudice of the white group toward him and of his group toward the white.

Booker Washington's reiterated assertion that if he were to be born again he would choose to be a Negro because the Negro race is the only one which has a great problem—contains a suggestion of this protective philosophy.[55]

Not only did Booker Washington thus give expression to his own personal adjustment in rationalistic terms, but he helped to make articulate a basis of accommodation for his race.

Expressions of sublimated feelings are found in the songs, laughter, and the free and easy manner so characteristic of the Negro. These mechanisms have proved useful to the colored race in that they represent the transference of tendencies away from expressions that

[55] George Vincent, "Rivalry of Social Groups," Am. J. Sociol., Vol. 16, No. 4, January, 1911, p. 475.

would bring them into conflict with the white majority and toward values that are approved by the latter. The "white folks" appreciate and applaud the singing and the "carefree" antics of the Negroes more than any of their "traits" unless it be their docility. The Negro has found in them a means to an achieved status.

Idealization seems to be a universal tendency of oppressed groups. Repressed peoples may make an adjustment to difficult situations by means of an idealized conception either of the past or of the future. This type of accommodation seems to take the form of an abstraction of some aspect of the situation. There is something here in the way of daydreaming, anticipation, and symbolism. This tendency is usually limited to a few sensitive, sentimental persons, but in the case of the colored people it appears to be rather general. This is especially true of their religious behavior where it catches the imagination of the masses and transports them into an expression of ecstatic behavior.[56] In the field of art creations idealization is of two types, positive and negative. The spirituals and folksongs of the American Negroes are illustrations of the first type and their "blues" songs and much of their jazz music illustrate the second type. As people gain more freedom and a larger measure of control over their present life they are not so much concerned with a future world, no matter how vividly it may be conceived. But since there is so little freedom and control by the Negroes over their immediate existence they find in their orgiastic religious expression and in their tempestuous ragtime music the outlet which they crave.[57]

---

[56] The more sophisticated and race-conscious Negroes appear to have little interest in the emotional and orgiastic religious behavior which occupies such a large place in the life of the rural Negroes of the South and to a lesser extent of the proletarian Negro workers of the cities, both South and North. For many of the former group this attitude may be in the nature of a conscious or half-conscious repudiation of primitive religious expression as an index of inferior race status and as a carry-over from slavery days.

[57] For the American Negro's religion, art, and music see: T. D. Ackiss, "Changing Patterns of Religious Thought Among Negroes," *Social Forces*, Vol. 23, December, 1944, pp. 212-215; E. D. Beynon, "The Voodoo Cult Among Negro Migrants in Detroit," *Am. J. Sociol.*, Vol. 43, No. 6, May, 1938, pp. 894-907; F. W. Bond, *The Negro and the Drama*, Washington, Association Publishers, 1940; S. A. Brown, A. P. Davis, and U. G. Lee, *The Negro Caravan*, New York, The Dryden Press, 1941; W. L. Daykin, "Race Consciousness in Negro Poetry," *Sociol. and Soc. Res.*, Vol. 21, September-October, 1936, pp. 45-53; W. L. Daykin, "Social Thought in Negro Novels," *Sociol. and Soc. Res.*, Vol. 19, 1934-1935, pp. 247-252; R. N. Dett, *Religious Folksongs of the Negro*, Hampton, Va., Hampton Institute Press, 1927; A. H. Fauset, *Black Gods of the Metropolis*, Philadelphia, University of Pennsylvania Press, 1944; N. A. Ford, *The Contemporary Negro Novel*, Boston, Meador Pub. Co., 1936; R. H. Gillum, "The Negro Folksong in American Culture," *Journal of Negro Education*, Vol. 12, Spring, 1943, pp. 173-180; John Hoshor, *God in a Rolls Royce*, New York, Hillman, Curl, 1936; G. P. Jackson, *White and Negro Spirituals: Their Life Spans and Kinship*, New York, J. J. Augustin, Inc., 1944; Guy B. Johnson, "The Negro Spiritual," *Am. Anthrop.*, Vol. 33, April-June, 1931, pp. 157-171; J. W. and J. R. Johnson, *The Book of American Negro Spirituals*, New York, The Viking Press, 1940; J. S. Lash, "On Negro Literature," *Phylon*, Vol 6, 3rd Quarter, 1945, pp. 240-247: Alain Locke, *Negro Art*, Washington, Associates in Negro Folk Education, 1936; Alain Locke, *The Negro and His Music*, Washington, Associates in Negro Folk Education, 1936; Alain Locke, *The New Negro*, A. and C. Boni, 1925; B. E. Mays and J. W. Nicholson, *The Negro's Church;* H. W. Odum and G. B. Johnson, *The Negro*

The Negro Seeks to Improve His Status.—An increasing number of Negroes are not content to remain in a half-world of superordinate-subordinate relationships where they must seek the fulfillment of their wishes by cajolery and flattery or in the fantasies of primitive forms of religion or in the whimsicalities of song and dance. Some have thought to improve their status by escaping from what they regarded as the unfriendly and economically unsatisfactory environment of the rural South and by migrating to northern industrial centers where they thought they would find larger opportunities and privileges of work and life. In 1910 there were in the northern states 1,025,674 Negroes. The number was slow to increase until the first Great War served to expand the established industries of the region and thus create a labor shortage, which the Negroes sought to fill. From 1916 to 1920 more than half a million Negroes moved north, and during a later period, 1921 to 1925, an equally large number migrated and settled principally in a few northern cities. Subsequent waves brought many thousands more, until by 1940 it was estimated that in thirty years some 1,750,000 Negroes had moved from the South to the North. With the outbreak of the second World War, another sizable movement set in, with uncounted numbers leaving southern farms and cities for northern and Pacific Coast centers of wartime production.[58] Here the Negroes have been faced with new problems and conditions of employment and living. The pressure of increased numbers has been felt by the northern and western white populations as a competitive force, occasions for friction have multiplied, and the Negroes have found themselves bewildered and helpless, the objects of fresh discriminations, and the centers of conflict.[59]

---

and His Songs, Chapel Hill, University of North Carolina Press, 1925; J. A. Porter, Modern Negro Art, New York, The Dryden Press, 1943; N. N. Puckett, Folkbeliefs of the Southern Negro, Chapel Hill, University of North Carolina Press, 1926; S. C. Watkins, Anthology of American Negro Literature, New York, Modern Library, 1944.

[58] See: A. Bontemps and J. Conroy, They Seek a City, New York, Doubleday, Doran & Co., 1945; L. C. Florant, "Negro Internal Migration," Am. Sociol. Rev., Vol. 7, No. 6, December, 1942, pp. 782-791; Edmund Fuller, A Star Pointed North, New York, Harper & Bros., 1946; C. V. Kiser, Sea Island to City, New York, Columbia University Press, 1932; E. E. Lewis, Mobility of the Negro, New York, Columbia University Press, 1931; S. C. Mayo, "Rural and Urban Residence of Negroes in the United States," Rural Sociology, Vol. 10, March, 1945, pp. 10-16; T. Lynn Smith, "A Demographic Study of the American Negro," op. cit.; R. C. Weaver, "Economic Factors in Negro Migration—Past and Future," Social Forces, Vol. 18, October, 1939, pp. 90-101.

[59] See: St. Clair Drake and H. R. Cayton, Black Metropolis: A Study of Negro Life in a Northern City, New York, Harcourt, Brace & Co., 1945; Dean Dutcher, The Negro in Modern Industrial Society, Lancaster, Pa., Science Press, 1930; E. Franklin Frazier, "The Impact of Urban Civilization upon Negro Family Life," Am. Sociol. Rev., Vol. 2, No. 5, October, 1937, pp. 609-618; E. Franklin Frazier, The Negro Family in Chicago, Chicago, University of Chicago Press, 1932; Claude McKay, Harlem: Negro Metropolis, New York, E. P. Dutton & Co., 1940; National Urban League, Employment Problems of the Negro, revised, New York, National Urban League, 1945; H. R. Northrup, Will Negroes Get Jobs Now?, Washington, Public Affairs Committee, 1945; Lee and Humphrey, Race Riot; B. F. Robinson, "War and Race Conflicts in the United States," Phylon, Vol. 4, 4th Quarter, 1943, pp. 311-327; Richard Sterner, The Negro's Share, New York, Harper & Bros., 1943; R. C. Weaver,

Numerous leaders among the Negroes have preached a doctrine of absolute equality between the races and several have been advocates of militant "nationalism." A more moderate element in the colored group believes that, as the group rises to higher economic, social, and cultural levels, new bases of accommodation will have to be found. Two ways seem open to them. One way is that of voluntary segregation, with the building up of a culture and a social organization paralleling somewhat that of the whites. The other way, and the one which is apparently most favored by the leaders, is that of integration and identification, so far as the American white mores will permit, of the fortunes of the Negro with those of the white group.[60]

BI-RACIAL ORGANIZATION AND INTERRACIAL COOPERATION. Meantime there is the tendency for the Negroes to effect an accommodation on the order of a bi-racial organization in which they are following the first way and constructing a social life and institutions of their own with white patterns serving as models. Moreover, there is a growing tendency for the two ethnic groups to cooperate in dealing with many common problems. While in the past the Negro has looked to the whites to provide him with education, charity, and other emoluments to his welfare, in recent years he has been able to participate more largely in his own education, public health and welfare measures, and self-support.

Participation along bi-racial lines is demonstrated in the formation and functioning of such organizations as the Commission on Interracial Cooperation, Commission on Race Relations of the Federal Council of Churches, the Fellowship of Reconciliation, the National Boards of the Y. M. C. A. and the Y. W. C. A., the National Association for the Advancement of Colored People, the National Urban League, and several others.[61] More and more, members of the two

---

"Defense Industries and the Negro," *Annals Am. Acad. Pol. and Soc. Sci.*, Vol. 223, September, 1942, pp. 60-66; T. J. Woofter, Jr., and Associates, *Negro Problems in Cities*, New York, Doubleday, Doran & Co., 1928.

[60] See: Edwin R. Embree, *Brown Americans: The Story of a Tenth of the Nation*, New York, The Viking Press, 1943; Edwin R. Embree, *Thirteen Against the Odds*, New York, The Viking Press, 1944; M. J. Herskovits, "Some Effects of Social Selection on the American Negro," in *The Urban Community*, E. W. Burgess (Ed.), Chicago, University of Chicago Press, 1926, pp. 91-98; Mozell C. Hill, "Basic Racial Attitudes toward Whites in the Oklahoma All-Negro Community," *Am. J. Sociol.*, Vol. 49, No. 6, May, 1944, pp. 519-523; Mozell C. Hill, "A Comparative Analysis of the Social Organization of the All-Negro Society in Oklahoma," *Social Forces*, Vol. 25, October, 1946, pp. 70-77; Mozell C. Hill and T. D. Ackiss, "Social Classes: A Frame of Reference for the Study of Negro Society," *Social Forces*, Vol. 22, October, 1943, pp. 92-98; Rayford Logan (Ed.), *What the Negro Wants*, Chapel Hill, University of North Carolina Press, 1944; Kelly Miller, "Separate Communities for Negroes," *Current History*, Vol. 25, March, 1927, pp. 827-831; Roi Ottley, *New World A-Coming*, Boston, Houghton Mifflin Co., 1943.

[61] See: Gunnar Myrdal, *An American Dilemma*, Vol. 2, pp. 819-850; Robin M. Williams, *The Reduction of Intergroup Tensions: A Survey of Research on Problems of Ethnic, Racial and Religious Group Relations*, New York, Social Science Research Council, Bull. 57, 1947.

races are showing a disposition to get together for the discussion of their mutual problems, the formulation of programs for better understanding, and actual cooperative participation in attempts to put their programs into effect.

Bi-racial organization alone cannot prevent racial clashes. So long as two racial groups occupy the same territory, the chances of conflict will always be present. Accommodations once established are constantly in danger of being disturbed by social and economic changes, which require new bases of adjustment. Bi-racial organization does serve, however, to lessen the points of contact where friction is most likely to be generated. It sets up a *modus vivendi* which tends to become incorporated in the thinking and mores of both groups with appropriate attitudes to insure a maximum of participation with a minimum of hostility, and it makes possible the continuation of the acculturation process begun in the days of slavery.

Assimilation.—Acculturation has been going on between the white and Negro populations in the United States since the earliest contacts between them as masters and as indentured servants or slaves. With difficulty the Negro has accommodated himself to the civilization of the whites, but accommodate himself he has. But he has done more. He has become a limited or conditioned participant in the white culture, adapting certain elements of it to his needs and circumstances, adopting other traits with little or no modification, and adding certain peculiar elements or adaptations of his own to the dominant culture. It has been charged that the Negro was and still is in contact only with American culture and that he could not escape absorbing some of it. But he is creating also his own folk arts which will enrich his life. Moreover, he has made and continues to make his contribution to the predominant culture of America, which he shares with the white group, though in a lesser measure than they do.[62]

But the Negro in the United States has not been assimilated. Certainly this is true of the group as a whole and it is probably equally

[62] See: Paul E. Baker, *Negro-White Adjustment*, New York, Association Press, 1934; Ruth Benedict, "Recognition of Cultural Diversities in the Post-War World," *Annals Am. Acad. Pol. and Soc. Sci.*, Vol. 228, July, 1943, pp. 101-107; H. M. Bond, *The Education of the Negro in the American Social Order*, New York, Prentice-Hall, Inc., 1934; W. E. B. DuBois, *Black Folk—Then and Now*, New York, Henry Holt & Co., 1939; W. E. B. DuBois, *Dusk of Dawn*, New York, Harcourt, Brace & Co., 1940; Charles S. Johnson, *The Negro in American Civilization*, New York, Henry Holt & Co., 1930; Guy B. Johnson, "Some Factors in the Development of Negro Social Institutions in the United States," *Am. J. Sociol.*, Vol. 40, No. 3, November, 1934, pp. 329-337; Alain Locke, "The Negro's Contribution to American Culture," *J. Negro Ed.*, Vol. 8, July, 1939, pp. 521-529; Sanford Winston, "Cultural Participation and the Negro," *Am. J. Sociol.*, Vol. 40, No. 5, March, 1935, pp. 593-601.

true of the individual. In view of the antithetical attitudes and mechanisms employed by the dominant race to keep the Negro in his "place," it is hardly likely that he ever is able to enter completely and permanently into the full fellowship of the whites. Even the light-skinned mulatto, who succeeds in "passing" into the society of the whites and perhaps even marrying into that group, must inevitably do so with reservations, an ever-present fear of exposure, and a self-consciousness born of the secret he carries and tries constantly to conceal.[63] It is the Negro intellectual who has become most fully acculturated who is usually the most race-conscious and finds within himself and in his attitudes powerful hindrances to assimilation.

The assimilation process is going on simultaneously with that of accommodation and acculturation, but that it soon will reach its ultimate fruition in the case of the Negro in the United States is extremely unlikely. Some time in the future, perhaps, after conditions have changed greatly, the Negro in this country may find between himself and his fellow citizens of the white race no bars to satisfying social interaction, no inhibitions and repressions, but, rather, the way open for free and loyal participation in and enjoyment of his country's institutional and spiritual values on a basis of equality with the whites.[64]

In some countries, where the conditions have worked out differently, the diverse racial elements in the population have been assimilated to a mutually shared social life. Amalgamation has assisted the process, as it may do in the United States in the course of several generations. For example, in England there is the result of a mixture of a prehistoric, long-headed race and the Romans, Normans, and Teutons. Today they are all Englishmen. The Slavs who invaded ancient Greece about the eighth century B. C. have become Hellenes, and the Lombards, who swept into northern Italy in 568 A. D. and established themselves there, have become Italians. To the Balkan populations have been added Finns, Jews, and other peoples; the French, Spaniards, Germans, and other European peoples represent a similar admixture of racial types; while in Brazil and some other

---

[63] John H. Burma, "The Measurement of Negro 'Passing,' " *Am. J. Sociol.*, Vol. 42, No. 1, July, 1946, pp. 18-22; E. W. Eckard, "How Many Negroes 'Pass'?" *Am. J. Sociol.*, Vol. 52, No. 6, May, 1947, pp. 498-500.

[64] See: Clarence I. Chatto and Alice L. Halligan, *The Story of the Springfield Plan*, New York, Barnes & Noble, Inc., 1945; W. E. B. DuBois, "Prospects of a World Without Race Conflict," *Am. J. Sociol.*, Vol. 49, No. 5, March, 1944, pp. 450-456; Ellsworth Faris, "Prospects of a World Without Intolerance," *Am. J. Sociol.*, Vol. 49, No. 5, March, 1944, pp. 457-464; Charles S. Johnson, "The Next Decade in Race Relations," *J. Negro Ed.*, Vol. 11, October, 1942, pp. 465-470; Charles S. Johnson, *Preface to Racial Understanding*, New York, Friendship Press, 1936; Alain Locke, "Whither Race Relations?" *J. Negro Ed.*, Vol. 13, Spring, 1944, pp. 398-406; R. M. MacIver (Ed.), *Unity and Difference in American Life: A Series of Addresses and Discussions*, New York, Harper & Bros., 1947.

Latin-American countries is to be found a like situation with white and colored intermixed.[65] In most of these countries the racial conflicts ceased after the initial conquests were made and the first impacts of antagonistic races and incompatible cultures were over. The usual effect of amalgamation is to facilitate the process of assimilation, but that the former is necessary to the latter may be questioned. However, wherever accommodation, acculturation, and amalgamation are proceeding to any appreciable extent they may confidently be expected to lead to gradual assimilation.

THE MARGINAL POSITION OF THE ORIENTAL. Before we leave the subject of ethnic relations in the United States we must mention the anomalous position of those of Oriental ancestry who are citizens of the country because they were born here but who, because they bear the peculiar marks of their "race," are the victims of race prejudice.[66] For most of them the situation is tragic, as the following document shows:

If it is so hard for us to get into suitable vocations here, why don't we go back to Japan? we are frequently asked. Only a few days ago I was walking across the Quad on our campus with an American classmate, and he turned around to me and said: "Gee! you fellows are lucky! Look at the great advantage you American-educated fellows have over the rest of your people when you go back to the old country." I suppose his attitude reflects that of most Americans. "Well," I should like to ask, "what do you mean by going back to our old country? We've never been there in the first place." Most of us were born here. As to having advantage over the people of Japan, we have the wonderful advantage of being quite unable to speak their language or read their papers, of being totally ignorant of their customs, history, or traditions, of holding different ideals, of thinking in different ways. Yes, we have as much advantage over the people in Japan as a deaf mute has over a man in possession of all his faculties. An American would have an infinitely easier time in Japan than we would, for they would excuse a foreigner

---

[65] Adams, *The Peoples of Hawaii;* Carleton S. Coon, *The Races of Europe,* New York, The Macmillan Co., 1939; Freyre, *Brazil: An Interpretation;* M. J. Herskovits, "The Negro in Bahia, Brazil: A Problem in Method," *Am. Sociol. Rev.,* Vol. 8, No. 4, August, 1943, pp. 394-404; G. M. Morant, *The Races of Central Europe,* New York, W. W. Norton & Co., 1940; Donald Pierson, *Negroes in Brazil: A Study in Race Contact in Bahia,* Chicago, University of Chicago Press, 1942; Arthur Ramos, "Contact of Races in Brazil," *Social Forces,* Vol. 19, May, 1941, pp. 533-538; T. Lynn Smith, *Brazil: People and Institutions,* Baton Rouge, Louisiana State University Press, 1946.

[66] The total Chinese population of the United States was 77,504 in 1940. Of this number nearly 42 per cent were native born. The Japanese population for the same census year was 126,947, a decrease of 11,887, or 8.6 per cent, from the 1930 figure. Of this number well over 62 per cent were native born. Between 1920 and 1940 the number of the native-born Japanese, called Nisei, increased from 29,672 to 79,642, and the number of foreign-born Japanese, known as Issei, decreased from 81,338 to 47,305. The only other sizable Oriental group in the population is that of the Filipinos, numbering 45,563 in 1940, an increase of 355 over 1930. Of course, Chinese, Japanese, and Filipinos are not terms applicable to sub-racial categories, but rather to nationality groups.

if he made mistakes, but we, with our Japanese names and faces, would have to conform to their rigid standards or else be "queer." As for advantage in education, with some of the universities over there like Imperial, Waseda, and others ranking with the leading universities of the world, what chance have we products of the American rah-rah system against their mature scholars? The trouble with us is that we have been too thoroughly Americanized. We have attended American schools, we speak English exclusively, we know practically nothing of Japan except what an average American knows; our ideals, customs, mode of thinking, our whole psychology is American. Although physically we are Japanese, culturally we are Americans. We simply are not capable of fitting into Japanese society, so we are destined to remain here.[67]

This cynical attitude is shared by thousands of American-born yellow-skinned people. These people are as thoroughly accommodated to the culture of their native land as it is possible of them to be under the circumstances, and yet they find themselves without status in any nationality or racial group. Indeed, they are men without a country. The American-born Mexican is in much the same position socially, especially if he carries in his physical features pronounced Indian characteristics.

The Race-Relations Cycle.—In this chapter we have surveyed the phases of social interaction as they are manifested in what has been termed "the race-relations cycle" as it may be observed in the interaction between the majority white group in the United States on the one hand and the American-born minority ethnic groups on the other. The cycle consists of the several recurring stages in the natural history of relations between racial groups conspicuously different from each other in one or more particulars. In the following chapter we will observe the cycle as it is revealed in the relations of Americans to immigrants, and of invading racial groups to the so-called "natives" at the points of invasion.

The race-relations cycle is a kind of ideal-typical conception of race relations which may, but rarely does, follow an invariable order. This means that the "initial contacts of a symbiotic, categoric sort" and the various phases of interaction—conflict, accommodation, and assimilation—assume diverse arrangements, thus constituting in different situations variations from the ideal pattern.[68] Cultural restric-

67 Kazuo Kawai, "Three Roads, and None Easy: An American-Born Japanese Looks at Life," *Survey*, Vol. 56, May 1, 1926, pp. 164-166. Mr. Kawai was born in Japan, but has identified himself with the American-born Japanese group and writes of them in this article.

68 See: E. S. Bogardus, "A Race-Relations Cycle," *Am. J. Sociol.*, Vol. 35, No. 4, January, 1930, pp. 610-617; W. O. Brown, "Culture Contact and Race Conflict," *op. cit.;*

tions and racial barriers may slacken the speed of the interaction; they may perhaps block it altogether for a time; but they cannot stop it indefinitely.

In summarizing the interaction between the whites and the Negroes in the United States in terms of a race-relations cycle we find that the cycle assumes something like the following pattern: The Negroes were first introduced into the country by traders as indentured servants and as slaves. As such they lived symbiotically, that is side by side, with the whites, but in a different social world. Some few among them obtained their freedom and a new status. The status of slavery was not crystallized for fifty years. The initial reactions to the Negroes were mainly those of curiosity and sympathy. From the invention of the cotton gin and the spread of cotton culture the role of the Negro underwent a marked change. Henceforward his role was fixed as that of a slave in the form of a stratified relationship to the white population. Thus the Negroes remained, with the comparatively few exceptions of those who were freed or who escaped, until the time of their emancipation. It was at this time that the race-relations cycle began anew. The Negro entered into competition with the white man, and conflict ensued. There was accommodation as a condition in slavery, and accommodation as a phase of interaction has been proceeding since the freeing of the Negroes, with adjustment made mainly in terms of superordination and subordination. Occasionally, there are reversions to conflict, usually local in character, with subsequent returns to accommodation. Assimilation has proceeded concurrently with accommodation but with the former greatly slowed up by reason of the obstacles of ethnic and cultural differences. When the cycle will be completed, if ever, no one knows.

The combined questions and the bibliographies for Chapters 15 and 16 will be found on pages 409-414.

Jitsuichi Masuoka, "Racial Symbiosis and Cultural Frontiers: A Frame of Reference," *Social Forces*, Vol. 24, March, 1946, pp. 348-353; R. E. Park, "The Nature of Race Relations," in Edgar T. Thompson (Ed.), *Race Relations and the Race Problem*, Durham, N. C., Duke University Press, 1939, Ch. 1; R. E. Park, "Our Racial Frontiers on the Pacific," *Survey*, Vol. 56, May, 1926, pp. 192-196.

Chapter 16

INTERACTION IN ETHNIC RELATIONS (Continued)

When Aliens and Natives Meet

The Problem of Incorporating the Alien.—Every individual who migrates from one country to another is a member of a "race" and of a nationality. As we have seen, the former concept has lost much of its specific significance, but as a stereotyped and idealized conception it still plays an important part in the interaction of persons and groups. Its present importance, like that of the concept of nationality, lies largely in its connotations of cultural differentiation. Therefore, when members of diverse racial groups and nationalities enter a country as immigrants they come as bearers of alien culture traits which must be dealt with in some way by the recipient culture group. How to incorporate these foreign people with their alien cultures has ever been the problem of the countries receiving them.

The processes by which an alien group becomes an integral part of the inclusive group of which it is physically a constituent element will be first to receive our attention. One naturally thinks of the practical problems that have confronted the United States, Canada, and the South American countries which have received large, heterogeneous population groups from other lands. One recalls sight-seeing visits to the crowded, often smelly urban areas which bear the picturesque names of "Little Italy," "Chinatown," "Greek Town," and the like, with their shop signs in unfamiliar characters, their narrow streets and alleys crowded with dark-skinned and dark-eyed children and careworn women. One reads of the problems of crime, dependency, and poor housing conditions which, so the information goes, are greatly complicated and made more alarming by the fact that the country is overrun by "foreigners." One learns that our native standards of living are being lowered and that our most sacred institutions are being jeopardized by people bearing unpronounceable names, savoring of garlic, and reading newspapers that look like sheets of hieroglyphics. One hears of legislative enactments designed to restrict the immigrant invasion and to make the land safe for "one-hundred-per-centers." In this manner the popular mind pictures the immigrant problem.

Immigrants generally come as individuals or in family groups, but when they arrive in numbers sufficiently large to create a "problem" for the native population they are commonly viewed in the mass and treated categorically. Consequently, the group aspects of the problem will receive major emphasis in our discussion.

Reconciliation in Secondary and Impersonal Contacts.—As in so-called race contacts, the alien group is chiefly known through indirect, casual, socially distant contacts made through hearsay, newspaper stories, and propagandistic media. In these and other similar ways the majority group develops popular notions, "stereotypes," as Walter Lippmann calls them, of group traits, physical and cultural, which

. . . are never accurate either in detail or in broad outline. . . . There is, of course, always more than one stereotype applied to American minorities. Thus we have stereotypes of the German, English, or Portuguese Jew at odds with that of the Russian "Kike," mental pictures of fat, beer-drinking Germans and of arrogant Prussians, of Russian Bolshevists, and of Russian aristocrats, of "darkeys" and "bad niggers," of "greasers" and of Latin Americans. . . . Peculiarly enough, where a member of one racial group becomes intimately acquainted with some member of another race, the individual is admitted to be an exception to the accepted stereotype of his group; but, no matter how many such exceptions are discovered, the stereotype is still retained for the rest.[1]

These attitudes will change when the conditions that produced them change, but in the meantime they serve to hinder the development of more intimate and personal contacts. They are cultural barriers to interaction on terms of understanding and mutual respect.

The first contacts of the newcomers with the strange people of their adopted country are of necessity secondary, since a common language is lacking. Nevertheless, fortuitous and opportunistic adjustments are readily made, particularly on the side of obvious culture changes. Immediate needs must be satisfied, such as securing employment, avoiding humiliation, and making oneself understood. Accordingly, changes pertaining to dress, manners, and language are made as advantageous adjustments to the new situation. Many foreigners make no attempt to progress beyond this point, being quite satisfied when they have shed the more visible evidences of foreignness. This is particularly the case with those who have come as adults.

---

[1] Donald Young, *American Minority Peoples: A Study in Racial and Cultural Conflicts in the United States*, New York, Harper & Bros., 1932, pp. 13-14.

Among children the changes come more readily and are deeper and more significant. The superior number and variety of contacts made by young people are responsible in great measure for this situation. Moreover, they are less under the control of the old world heritages and the institutions and associations of the immigrant community.

The nature of the adjustment is at best no more than a practical and material one, a matter of adapting to what is essential. It is not designed to promote a passionate desire on the part of adult aliens to know the new country, to participate actively in its life to the fullest extent, and to regard it as their own.

Reconciliation in Primary and Personal Contacts.—The process of making citizens is a much more complicated and subtle one than that described above. It means more than the opportunistic adoption of cultural values during casual contacts, because of their immediate advantage, and the sampling of random bits of native culture meagerly and grudgingly offered by the natives or forced by them upon the newcomers. Rather, it means participation not only in practical affairs but also in the common ideals of the community. For this to be realized an abundance of contacts of the primary and intimate sort is required. These are the contacts of man to man, group with group, and of each and all with the problems of a common life.

Viewing the problem from one angle, it appears to be one of education. With the aid of public schools, night schools, settlement houses, public libraries, welfare agencies, and members of the professions, the aliens are brought gradually into more intimate contact with their native neighbors. Some of these agencies have small chance to reach the older generation of aliens who are circumscribed by Old World heritages, permanently handicapped by their use of a foreign language, and for the most part worn by toil to the point of physical and mental exhaustion. It is for the younger members and the second generation especially that these agencies offer opportunities to enter into a more complete understanding of the New World culture. Often the teachers of the foreigners are the saloon keeper, the *padrone,* the quack doctor, the labor boss, the ward politician, and the policeman. They are frequently the only natives who establish direct and friendly relations with the aliens. While they may have interests that are subversive to those of the immigrants whom they pretend to help, they manifest a personal interest and that fact elicits a confidence in them that is born of ignorance and desperation.[2]

2 A. M. Rihbany, *A Far Journey,* Boston, Houghton Mifflin Co., 1914, pp. 245-246; Pauline V. Young, *The Pilgrims of Russian-Town,* Chicago, University of Chicago Press, 1932, pp. 125, 127-129.

Many foreigners, earnestly desiring the sympathy and understanding which they believe they would find if they could but meet and know the better elements in the native population, have to wait a long time before the contacts are made if, indeed, they are ever made. Continuing to live with their own people, compelled by their reserve and personal limitations or by the rebuffs they receive to remain in their small circle, change comes slowly and feebly.

Accommodative Mechanisms.—Immigrants display a well-known tendency toward segregation. The elemental conflicts for place and recognition and the struggle for existence are acute and vivid. Mobility and change run at high speed both horizontally and vertically. Such a group is usually composed of a single nationality or language group, and represents a unity based on a common culture. The language of the new land remains practically unused. In most immigrant areas the factor of a common language is the chief characteristic making for a satisfactory life.

Segregated immigrant colonies in the cities of the new world are little more than bits of the Old World transplanted to the soil of the new one. Frequently, there are to be found whole neighborhoods peopled from the same villages or districts of the old country.[3] Most of the newcomers spend their lives within the confines of the segregated foreign area, toiling and dreaming, and not infrequently berating the natives whom they do not know and of whom they are suspicious and fearful and who, in turn, do not understand or sympathize with them.

Segregation of foreigners into residential enclaves is largely spontaneous and makes certain contributions in helping the foreign group make the transition from their transplanted culture to that of the new environment. In other words, the immigrant colony with its transplanted institutions serves as a medium of accommodation between two divergent culture patterns. This is not always an unmixed good, however, since it means that some individuals will be content to remain in their segregated areas without contacts with the native culture. The new immigrants find in those of their own nationality who have preceded them the points of identity with the life they have known which make them feel "at home" until they can get a foothold in their adopted land. This familiar and ready-made society is the nursery which initiates them into the life of the new community.

---

[3] R. E. Park and H. A. Miller, *Old World Traits Transplanted*, New York, Harper & Bros., 1921, pp. 147-158.

Among the agencies devised by aliens in their segregated districts, and commonly first in the experience of new arrivals, are certain institutions organized and operated by their more settled and accommodated predecessors for the mutual benefit of the members of the colony. These institutions render practical services that the natives are not prepared to give. They are adapted to the needs of the foreigner, and are often the only institutions within his reach. Prominent among such agencies are the mutual aid societies, which provide sickness, death, and funeral benefits; the foreign-language newspapers, which, serve to make articulate for their readers the new-felt needs that arise in the new situation and communicate to them essential features of the culture of the new community; religious institutions which include, in addition to the parish church and the synagogue, various clubs, societies, and schools, and which occupy a central position of prestige and influence; and numerous other cultural agencies such as theaters, singing and orchestral organizations, and athletic clubs. In addition, there are the informal meeting-places like coffee houses, cafés, and restaurants, often tucked away in obscure corners of the ghettos, Chinatowns, or little Italys, where men and women gather for food and drink, music, singing, and animated discussion of varied topics in the mother tongue. These social centers tend to become institutionalized, and certain personages, such as poets, artists, and other leaders, become vital parts of the institution: Such places constitute small, compact social worlds with the intimate qualities of primary groups. Here are freedom and amity under the benign influences of which the ego expands, finds release, and expresses itself. Here also the group's ambitions become energized and articulate. Here are to be obtained recognition and response through the kindly criticism or the generous praises which are offered freely by those who really count in the immigrant's world.

Bulking large in the estimation and loyalty of most of the larger foreign-speaking groups is the nationalistic character of many of their organizations. Existing primarily to assist the immigrant to realize his desires for security, recognition, and response in the anomalous and confusing social situations of his new environment, they serve also to keep "alive the patriotic spirit and love of the fatherland." This nationalistic character is usually realized through the more formal combinations of local aid and benefit societies on the basis of city-wide, and eventually nation-wide units. The patriotic citizen is puzzled by these ethnic organizations, and particularly so by the nationalistic societies. It is difficult for him to see how they can exist without endangering the structure and negating the functions of the native institutions that he holds most sacred. This may be true to some extent of some of them, but it is not necessarily true of all.

The several kinds of ethnic institutions cannot be judged indiscriminately and categorically as regards their roles in social interaction. For the most part they serve as steppingstones for the immigrant's passage from one social world to another. Without the guiding and sustaining influence of agencies possessing characteristics that are familiar and real to them, their position would be singularly helpless. Such agencies function to connect the old and tried with the new and untried, the far and the near, the past and the present, and to prepare their members for the future with less fear and possible demoralization than would be the case otherwise. In certain respects these agencies are heritages, but not wholly so. They represent, as well, the efforts of the immigrants to adapt their heritages to the demands of a novel environment. Many of the nationalistic organizations serve as training schools for citizenship. Some of them very definitely encourage their members to participate in the affairs of the larger community. Though their meetings may be conducted in the mother tongue, they frequently instruct their members in civic pride and duty. They often join in the observance of national holidays, they display the national emblem, they conduct their deliberations in an atmosphere of freedom often unknown in the old country. In short, they constitute significant links between the immigrant group and the environing community.[4]

Interaction Between Aliens and the Greater Community.—Up to this point this chapter has treated the problem of immigrant adjustment largely from the standpoint of the arriving immigrants. These immigrants in the new country find those who have preceded them, who have already established their own segregated settlements, and have developed a variety of cultural agencies designed for their mutual benefit and to serve as a means of adjustment. But the early immigrants found no such ethnic areas and agencies awaiting them. Their contacts with the people and culture of the new country were much more direct and immediate than those experienced by later arrivals. As there was little or no segregation at first, social interaction was often disorganizing for the group and demoralizing for the individual. Since most immigrants came in groups, however, their

---

[4] Clarence I. Chatto and Alice L. Halligan, *The Story of the Springfield Plan*, New York, Barnes & Noble, Inc., 1945; Samuel M. Strong, "Observations on the Possibility of Attitude Modifications: A Case of Nationality and Racial Group Inter-Relationships in Wartime," *Social Forces*, Vol. 22, March, 1944, pp. 323-331.

tendency was to remain together, and thus the segregated immigrant colonies, both urban and rural, came into existence. We have just discussed the functions these communities came to serve.

Changing Attitudes of Americans Toward the Immigrant.—In the early days of large-scale immigration into the United States the initial attitudes of the Americans vacillated considerably between the extremes of curiosity and friendly welcome, on the one hand, to those of fear and dislike on the other. Immigrants were wanted because their labor was needed on the farms and in the new industries that were springing up, but in the minds of many Americans there was a sense of impending trouble for the country if reservations and restrictions were not placed upon the inflow of foreigners. The newcomers were prompted by mixed motives to make a trial in a strange world. Some were undoubtedly impelled to come in a spirit of adventure, others came to escape the economic hardships or the religious and political restrictions imposed upon them in the old world, and still others were attracted by the lure of fortunes to be made in the new country.[5]

As the numbers of incoming immigrants increased, the opposition to them began to be organized and to take on a formidable character. The traditional attitude of organized labor toward immigration and immigrants has been one of strong opposition. Patriotic societies and politicians of the chauvinistic variety have been quick to join forces with organized labor in their fight against immigration, particularly that of Orientals and of southern Europeans. These groups stand out conspicuously because of their widely divergent racial and cultural traits. By comparison with them the earlier immigrants are regarded as most praiseworthy and are extolled for their thrift, industry, and abilities. In contrast the newer aliens are considered as lazy, indigent, worthless characters, who, by reason of their numbers, high birth rate, and low standards of living, are greatly disturbing to those of "old, pure (sic) American stock."

Both unorganized and organized exploitation of and discrimination against foreigners have been common practices in the United States.

---

[5] See: Lawrence R. Chenault, *The Puerto Rican Migrant in New York City*, New York, Columbia University Press, 1938; Maurice R. Davie, *Refugees in America: Report of the Committee for the Study of Recent Immigration from Europe*, New York, Harper & Bros., 1947; Maurice R. Davie, *World Immigration*, New York, The Macmillan Co., 1936, Chs. 2-7; Marcus Lee Hansen, *The Atlantic Migration*, Cambridge, Harvard University Press, 1940; Marcus Lee Hansen, *The Immigrant in American History*, Cambridge, Harvard University Press, 1940; Marcus Lee Hansen, *Mingling of the Canadian and American Peoples*, New Haven, Yale University Press, 1940; Milbank Memorial Fund, *Postwar Problems of Migration*, New York, Milbank Memorial Fund, 1947; Donald R. Taft, *Human Migrations: A Study of International Movements*, New York, The Ronald Press Co., 1936, pp. 26-33, 71-81.

Many of the better-adjusted immigrants have also joined in these practices. Ignorance of the language, customs, and laws of the country places the foreigners at the mercy of unscrupulous interpreters, shyster lawyers, unethical employment agents, and unsympathetic police judges and justices of the peace. In matters of occupation, conditions of work, wages, and rental charges, the aliens usually have not been in a position to choose and thus have been grossly exploited.[6]

Restrictive Legislation.—Among the first to be singled out for restrictive legislation were the Orientals, including the Chinese, the Japanese, and East Indians.[7] The Chinese were the earliest of the Orientals to migrate to the United States and first began to reach this country in the pioneer days. At that time there was little race consciousness and they were generally welcomed as a labor force and a definite place was assigned to them in the loose social organization of the time. They were rather favored because of their cleanliness, industry, and unobtrusiveness. Attitudes against them developed, however, as their numbers increased and as their competition began to be felt in the mining camps and agricultural areas of the West. Prejudices directed against all foreigners tended to be intensified against those who were not of the white race. As the tide of national and race consciousness rose and spread, the movement for exclusion of members of the colored races emerged and, so far as Chinese laborers were concerned, culminated in the Exclusion Act of 1882.

Some Japanese had been migrating to the United States before 1885, but it was not until that year that the Japanese government legalized emigration. Following that date these Orientals began to come in increasing numbers to meet the demand for unskilled labor on the West coast, "a demand accentuated by the sudden cessation of Chinese immigration."[8] Anti-Japanese attitudes soon became evident, however, and agitation for their exclusion on economic and cultural as well as racial grounds developed as many of the Japanese prospered and came into direct competition with white Americans.

---

[6] See: Edith Abbott, *Immigration: Select Documents and Case Records*, Chicago, University of Chicago Press, 1924, Part III; Grace Abbott, *The Immigrant and the Community*, New York, The Century Co., 1917; Orvis Collins, "Ethnic Behavior in Industry: Sponsorship and Rejection in a New England Factory," *Am. J. Sociol.*, Vol. 51, No. 4, January, 1941, pp. 293-298; Maurice R. Davie, *World Immigration*, Ch. 12; Pauline R. Kibbe, *Latin Americans in Texas*, Albuquerque, University of New Mexico Press, 1946; Selden C. Menefee, *Mexican Migratory Workers of South Texas*, Washington, U. S. Works Projects Admin., U. S. Govt. Printing Office, 1941; Young, *American Minority Peoples*.

[7] From the standpoint of race the East Indians do not belong in a category with the other Orientals. They are in the main long-headed, dark-skinned Caucasians, not very different from the Mediterranean. However, they have been classed in the non-white group for exclusion purposes.

[8] R. D. McKenzie, "The Oriental Finds a Job," *Survey*, Vol. 56, May 1, 1926, pp. 152-153.

Treaty arrangements permitted Japanese laborers to come until 1911, when a new treaty limited entry to those who came for purposes of trade only. None the less, the tide of immigration continued and much talk of the "yellow peril" was heard on every side. The so-called Gentlemen's Agreement failed to work and the movement for absolute exclusion gained adherents and momentum. Finally, in 1924, the Immigration Act excluded all aliens ineligible for citizenship with the exception of a few special classes.[9]

Legislation for the purpose of regulating and restricting immigration into the United States has not been and is not now confined to non-white aliens. There always comes a time in the history of an immigrant-receiving nation when it resorts to legislation in an effort to control the problem of immigration. Prior to 1882 control in the United States was left to the several states, but in that year the federal government assumed control, following Supreme Court decisions adverse to the state-control policy. At first national legislation dealt primarily with means of individual selection, but finally it culminated in the restrictive legislation of 1921 and 1924. These acts, which established the principle of admitting aliens on a quota basis, were directed against the inflow of all alien immigrants with the exception of those coming from Canada, Newfoundland, Mexico, and the independent countries of Central and South America, which countries were exempted from the provisions of the acts.

The Act of 1924, which inaugurated a permanent policy, classified all aliens into two categories: immigrants and non-immigrants. Practically all of the latter are temporary sojourners, such as government officials, visitors for business or pleasure, aliens in transit through the country, etc., and are not subject to restriction. All other aliens fall into the category of "immigrants," further divided into quota and non-quota immigrants, the former being chargeable against the quotas of their respective countries and the latter immigrants who may enter without reference to quota limitations, such as aliens returning from visits abroad, certain professional persons and their families, students in American institutions, etc. "Quota immigrants" include all other aliens not specified as non-immigrants or as non-quota immigrants.[10]

---

[9] The Filipinos, though Orientals, were not affected by the earlier legislation since the Philippine Islands were, until very recently, a dependency of the United States. According to a ruling of the United States Supreme Court in 1925, Filipinos were not eligible for citizenship unless they had served in the United States Navy for a period of three years. Between 1920 and 1940 the number of Filipinos in the United States increased from 5,603 to 45,563. They are neither aliens nor citizens.

[10] The Act of 1924 established permanently many of the restrictive features of the temporary Act of 1921, and introduced some new features. The Act of 1924 fixed the annual quota of each nationality at 2 per cent of the number of foreign-born individuals of

Canada, another country receiving immigrants in considerable numbers, has for many years given careful attention to its immigration policy. It has been the practice of this country to encourage and assist, so far as possible, immigration from English-speaking countries, including the British Commonwealth and Eire. These people come with not only the language problem solved in advance, but also a background of the history, traditions, and institutions of the English people. These cultural heritages are in harmony with those of the country receiving them and tend to ease the problem of adjustment very materially.

Every nation has the duty of determining so far as it is able in a complex social world the kind of population it needs and wants. When it has accomplished this goal so far as to control the influx of alien elements into its population, it usually comes to display what Bogardus calls "fair-play tendencies" toward its foreign-born groups and to reduce in number and frequency its antagonistic activities.

In spite of certain sporadic, poorly organized, inadequately financed, and oftentimes mismanaged movements favorable to aliens, the acculturation and accommodation of the first-generation immigrants is slow and uncertain. Certain factors act as a hindrance to his complete incorporation into the new life and culture, as, for example, antithetical attitudes held by and legal obstacles raised by the recipient population, coupled with the reserve of the immigrant, his difficulty with the language, his partial isolation within the confines of his segregated communities,[11] and counter attitudes he has adopted as direct reactions to the conditions of life and the opposing attitudes he finds in the new country. Repelling forces tend to destroy the idealized notions nearly all immigrants bring with them, and unless there are other forces in the environment helping to restore confidence, to construct new and suitable ideals, and to develop sentiments of coherence and identification with the larger community, the results are apt to be permanently disorganizing.[12] Hindering attitudes and legal proscriptions prevent large numbers of acculturated immigrants

---

that nationality who were resident in continental United States as determined by the census of 1890. The nationalities most adversely affected by the quota provision were those of south and eastern Europe, since they had supplied most of the immigrants since 1890, the countries of northern Europe having reached the peak of their emigration in the 70's and 80's. See Maurice R. Davie, *World Immigration*, New York, The Macmillan Co., 1936, Ch. 8, for details.

11 It should be noted that the immigrant colony is incorporated as a whole into the life of the larger community. Through various contacts in school, work, and by means of its own papers, the segregated group gradually loses much of its original ethnic distinctiveness. This facilitates migration to successive areas of residence, except in rural communities, in which modes of life are more and more like those of the surrounding community.

12 See: W. I. Thomas and F. Znaniecki, *The Polish Peasant in Europe and America*, New York, Alfred A. Knopf, 1927, Vol. II, pp. 1647-1821.

from enjoying the status which would be satisfying to their wishes and cultural interests. They can never participate fully in the life of the social world around them. Indeed, it is doubtful if first-generation immigrants, particularly if they come as adults, ever complete the cycle of interaction with the cultural and social life of the new world through its final phase—assimilation.

Difficulties of the Second Generation.—Social interaction operates somewhat differently in the case of the descendants of immigrants who are born in the new world, except where racial visibility predominates. Many of the mechanisms employed by the first-generation immigrants, such as segregation in their own ethnic areas, the continuance of the familiar universes of discourse, the perpetuation of the customs and manners that belong to the old-world heritage, and the like, do not appeal to most of the members of the second generation. In fact, these mechanisms frequently become points of friction between the two generations. On the other hand, much of the acculturation which goes on among the older generation is made possible through the children, who many times are the chief contact-makers between the parents and the culture of the larger community.

While the second generation finds social interaction relatively easier to negotiate, many times difficulties are thrown in their paths and their reactions to typical American situations are connected with some misapprehension, and result in maladjustment. With their family ties and their basic culture rooted in the segregated foreign settlements, they go back and forth between home and school, between their isolated ethnic group and the shop or factory, parochial church or synagogue, or motion-picture theater. They seek to imitate the new environment, look for its most pleasurable aspects, and find in their parents and the transplanted old-world neighbors little sympathy and understanding. Since they are without the stabilizing influences of memories and sentiments connected with life in the old country and since they have not yet established a *rapport* with the life and institutions of the native community, they are more or less at loose ends and occupy that difficult, unsettled, half-world position of marginal persons.[13] The mores of their parents and the colony to which they belong are competing for their allegiance against the allurements and uncertain promises of the larger world around them. Within them the conflict for recognition and status goes on.

[13] Everett V. Stonequist, *The Marginal Man: A Study in Personality and Culture Conflict,* New York, Charles Scribner's Sons, 1937. See also Milton M. Goldberg, "A Qualification of the Marginal Man Theory," *Am. Sociol. Rev.,* Vol. 6, No. 1, February, 1941, pp. 52-58; Arnold W. Green, "A Re-Examination of the Marginal Man Concept," *Social Forces,* Vol. 26, December, 1947, pp. 167-171.

Accommodation and Assimilation.—Gradually and almost imperceptibly, though sometimes rapidly and precipitously, accommodation functions to effect a reconciliation between the individual and his environment.[14] Compromises are effected with both the old and the new conditions. Attempts at conciliation, particularly toward one's family, on the one hand, and toward one's teacher or boss, on the other, are often made, and rationalization, especially where the situation seems most hopeless, as in the case of the second-generation Orientals, tends to go on. Idealization in the form of artistic creations and literary efforts furnishes emotional release for the pent-up desires of some, and sublimation transfers the interests and energies of many toward those values or modes of behavior that are believed to be socially acceptable to the Americans. However, when the natural tendencies are suppressed by a hostile environment and a hard life they may find expression in crime, vice, revolutionary and other subversive activities which are familiar expressions of this pattern.[15]

Time and a number of wholesome and satisfying contacts with the members and culture of the new world community will generally serve to complete the accommodation through conversion, and afford opportunities for participation. Conversion is that form of accommodation which functions to carry the person or group over from one culture complex to another, from one loyalty to another. The phenomenon is well known in the field of religion, but it appears quite as often in the transfer from one nationality or cultural group to another. It means the denial of old traditions and customs, of familiar beliefs and standards, and the acceptance of a new set of norms. Since full conversion means the abnegation of that which is past, and the taking on of a new life organization and philosophy, it is doubtful if it is ever possible for one who has built up a complete life structure. For this reason those who migrate as adults seldom if ever make the transition successfully. It is for those of the second and third generations to find a place and status in the new country through conversion.

Along with accommodation, as it affects the American-born descendants of immigrants, goes assimilation. The assimilated person becomes incorporated fully into the new environment. The heritages of family and nationality have been abandoned or reconciled. He

---

[14] Whereas the immigrants tend to face the new world in groups, the members of the second generation are more likely to meet it as individuals.

[15] It has been observed that while immigrants tend to commit their crimes according to the traditional patterns inherited from the Old World, their children and grandchildren choose more American ways of committing crimes. See Young, *American Minority Peoples*, p. 444 and Ch. 7.

comes to share the sentiments and attitudes of those who do not know the race and culture of his father's country. Intermarriage sometimes enters as both cause and effect of the accommodative and assimilative interactions. The individual has recognition and status in terms of which he finds the satisfaction of his wishes and because of which he can enter imaginatively and without undue self-consciousness into the larger social order.

The American-born children of Orientals occupy the anomalous position of being citizens and in many cases fully acculturated to American life without finding acceptance among their fellow Americans. Their position is a desperate one in many respects. This is particularly true in the continental United States. In Hawaii, a possession of the United States, relatively good opportunities and tolerance exist for the racial minorities and the mixed-bloods, but even there numerous barriers are raised against their full acceptance.[16]

So we see the cycle of social interaction working itself out in the case of the American-born citizens of alien parentage, with the exception of the Mexicans and the Orientals. The cycle is usually well advanced in the second generation and is virtually complete in the third.

CONTROLLING "NATIVE" CULTURE PEOPLES

In writing of the direct contacts arising from the migrations of peoples and resulting in the meeting of these peoples and their cultures, E. B. Reuter divides such contacts into two kinds, namely, those contacts resulting from the migration of people from one political area to another, and those which appear "in the areas of contact where representatives of an advanced culture intrude themselves into the territory of a culturally retarded or militaristically impotent people."[17] It is with the first of these two kinds of direct contact that we have been dealing in the preceding division of this chapter. The rest of the chapter will treat of contacts of the second kind.

Contacts Resulting from Invasion.—The interests which move a culturally advanced people to invade the territory occupied by a retarded or weak people may be either economic, or political, or both, or for the purpose of "civilizing the natives." Which interest motivates the invaders and the auspices under which they come will determine to a considerable extent the nature of the initial contacts

---

16 See: Edwin G. Burrows, *Hawaiian Americans: An Account of the Mingling of Japanese, Chinese, Polynesian, and American Culture,* New Haven, Yale University Press, 1947.
17 By permission, from *Race and Culture Contacts* by E. B. Reuter (Ed.). Copyrighted, 1934. New York, McGraw-Hill Book Co., Inc., pp. 4-5.

between them and the native peoples.[18] They may come as mission-aries for the ostensible purpose of converting the "heathen"; they may appear as traders to traffic in goods; they may come as entre-preneurs or factors desirous of exploiting the natural resources of the land and the labor of the natives; or they may come as conquerors either for the purpose of establishing a naval or military base, to take and hold territory for colonization, or to give support to the business enterpriser against the troublesome native population.

The initial contacts between the intruders and the native peoples may be friendly or hostile, depending upon the attitudes generated by the two parties to the situation. Usually the missionary and the trader desire peace and make their approach to the natives accordingly. If the missionary, unwittingly to be sure, comes as an advance agent of the trader, the exploiter, or the conqueror, he undertakes by per-suasion to win over the natives to a receptive frame of mind. If he comes, as he frequently does, in the wake of the others, then his role is that of pacificator and his function, of which he himself is often unaware, is to clinch the hold already taken by his predecessors by furthering the work of detribalization and deculturation. In either case he is the representative of the economic and political forces of the country from which he comes, as well as of special sectarian in-terests.[19]

The trader's entrance into the area of the natives may prove to be mutually beneficial, especially if the natives' culture is already prepared to be of service to the interests of the trader. Illustrative of this point is the history of the early contacts between certain Indian tribes and the fur traders. While the trader's objective was essentially preda-tory, he was not interested in preempting the land of the natives nor in reducing them to a servile position.[20] When, on the contrary, the intruders come to exploit the land and its natural wealth, to settle the area, to establish a government there, or to make other use of the area and its resources, then the contacts between invaders and natives soon result in open hostility.

Where the interests of the invaders and those of the natives co-incide to some extent, that is, where they may be promoted to the

---

[18] See: René Maunier, *Sociologie Coloniale*, Paris, F. Loviton et Cie., 1932, Part II.

[19] See: R. E. Park, "Missions and the Modern World," *Am. J. Sociol.*, Vol. 50, No. 3, November, 1944, pp. 177-183; Maurice T. Price, *Christian Missions and Oriental Civili-zations*, privately printed, Shanghai, China, 1924, and distributed by the University of Chicago Press; Archibald Baker, *Christian Missions and New World Culture*, Chicago, Willett, Clark & Co., 1934.

[20] Exceptions are traders who become definitely attached to a new region and who may not wish to return to their home base, but prefer to remain and establish an impersonal, symbiotic relationship with the natives. See also F. J. Teggart, *The Processes of History*, New Haven, Yale University Press, 1918, pp. 80-84, 144-145.

mutual benefit of both sides, the attitudes tend to be friendly and conciliatory. On the other hand,

. . . the contacts of the native peoples and the intruders may be initially hostile and lead immediately or soon to overt conflict. . . . From the invaders' point of view and for the accomplishment of the ends they have in view, the native population is useless or obstructive and their attitudes indifferent. In the circumstances, a crude display and use of force and power to the destruction or exclusion of the native people is the order of the day. The nature of the resources to be developed or the other needs of the invaders may call for the enslavement of the native population, the exploitation of the vital power as well as of other natural resources. In any such circumstance, the early conflicts, when they do not result in the expulsion of the invaders and do not completely destroy or drive out the native people, presently give way to a type of accommodation in which the natives accept a servile or other subordinate role in territory that was formerly theirs.[21]

Even where the first contacts have been friendly, as in the case of trader-native relationships, the time comes sooner or later when the invaders will covet the land, the resources, and possibly the labor of the natives and, in such circumstances, the conciliatory contacts will give way to antagonistic ones. However, it cannot be said that such change in contacts is always the result of changed intentions and attitudes on the part of the invaders alone. During the period of peaceful interaction transformations go on within the culture patterns and social organizations of the natives which, in the course of time, place the latter in a weakened and more vulnerable position.[22] Clark Wissler summarizes these changes as follows:

1. Any kind of intimate contact between Europeans and primitive tribes tends to break down tribal control.

2. Economic prosperity among native tribes dependent upon the presence of Europeans tends to strengthen the opposition of the younger generation and so to lead to a breakdown.

3. Conflicts in sex patterns respecting property, labor, and social relations are often contributory to the disintegration of tribal control.

4. At all times the proper functioning of native leadership is essential to the preservation of tribal life.[23]

---

21 Reuter, *Race and Culture Contacts*, pp. 5-6. See also Maunier, *Sociologie Coloniale*, Part III.

22 So-called native cultures are themselves probably often the results of accretions of culture patterns brought in and fused by successive groups of immigrants in times past. See: W. H. R. Rivers, *History of Melanesian Society*, 2 vols., New York, G. P. Putnam's Sons, 1915. Our present interest is primarily with the interaction between Euro-American cultures and those of native peoples, however.

23 Clark Wissler, "European and American Indian Cultures in Contact," in *Race and Culture Contacts*, edited by E. B. Reuter, p. 123.

It may be said, then, that the interaction between foreign invaders and native peoples is determined in the final analysis by the objectives of the invaders, on the one hand, and by the relative strength or weakness of the natives on the other hand, irrespective of the nature of the initial contacts. Sooner or later their interests are certain to clash and manifestations of open hostility will appear.[24] Though the numbers of the intruders may be comparatively few, their greater military strength will probably bring the natives into subjection if it does not actually eliminate or expel them.[25] Once the super-ordinate-subordinate relationship has been established, conflicts may recur and the process of controlling the natives may be a continuous one.

Typical Forms of Control.—In certain areas of friction between dominant foreign groups and native populations, depopulation of the native stocks has been the result. When settlement rather than the exploitation of native labor is the objective of the invading group, the elimination of the natives from the scene may be the desired goal, although instances are rare where such a goal led to the deliberate and wholesale slaughter of the native peoples. In Australia, Tasmania, New Zealand, and Africa such methods were resorted to on more than one occasion. Usually such "man hunts" were excused on the ground that they were necessary for the protection of the life and property of the European settlers. In the Americas numerous aboriginal tribes were wantonly destroyed. This destruction was carried on until well into the nineteenth century.[26] The principal factors contributing to the depopulation of the native tribes of Africa have been slavery and warfare.

Other factors leading to the decimation of primitive populations in contact with the white race have varied considerably in their effectiveness in the different areas of contact, but generally fall under the following main considerations: (1) changed habitat, due in most cases to forced migrations or to confinement on reservations; (2) break-up of tribal connections; (3) European clothing, adversely affecting the health of the natives; (4) altered or limited food supply, due in part to the introduction of foreign dietary practices and habits and, in part, to the driving out of game and the destruction of other

---

24 Maunier, *Sociologie Coloniale*, Ch. 9.

25 The facts of history belie the notion that invading white groups have been invariably successful in their incursions into the territory of backward peoples. In several instances climate has been a factor on the side of the natives. For example, some regions in Africa and elsewhere are wholly unsuited to white settlement. In such regions it is practically impossible for the whites to establish a permanent foothold.

26 See: Robert Gessner, *Massacre*, London, Jonathan Cape & Harrison Smith, 1931.

sources of food formerly depended upon by the natives; (5) the recruiting system, which involves the segregating of the sexes on
plantations and in mining centers, and which subjects the natives
to unknown hardships and oftentimes to harsh and brutal treatment;
(6) the "civilizing" of the native to the extent of destroying the
native culture, the attempted superimposition of a different culture,
and the partial or complete eradication of the native communal
and chieftainship systems, with direful physical and psychological
results; [27] (7) the introduction of the white man's vices of alcohol and narcotics; (8) the greater destructiveness of intertribal
wars due to the introduction of the white man's guns and ammuni-
tion; (9) the introduction by the invaders of non-indigenous diseases;
(10) miscegenation between intruders and natives; and (11) declining birth rate and increasing infant mortality rate.[28]

Assuredly not all of the alleged causes of depopulation of native
peoples in contact with white invaders can be ascribed solely to such
contacts, although it is likely that numerous tendencies at work in the
primitive populations and making for their gradual destruction may
have been aggravated by the presence of and the mechanisms of control employed by the dominant whites. For example, the practice of
certain primitive peoples of preventing the rearing of children so that
there might be less competition for the meager food supply of the
region is of long standing. Moreover, harmful narcotics, destructive battles, and other decimating influences were at work among
many native peoples before the coming of the white man. That
the latter has contributed more than his share to the destruction
of native populations and cultures, however, and that he has done
this quite deliberately in numerous instances, is not to be questioned.

THE RITUAL OF RACE RELATIONS. Since the natives constitute
an economically subservient as well as a politically and socially despised group wherever they are brought under the domination of a
more powerful invading group, the tendency is for them to be consigned to specially designated areas of residence. These segregated
areas sometimes form large reserves, as in the case of the remnants
of American Indian tribes and of many of the Bantus of South

---

[27] By no means do all invaders wish to uproot the native cultures. It is believed by
some colonizers and administrators that the retention by the natives of most of their cultural characteristics adds to their contentment and docility and facilitates the task of
governing them.

[28] The above classification of possible contributing causes of depopulation is based
mainly upon an adaptation from G. H. L. Pitt-Rivers, *The Clash of Culture and the Contacts of Races,* London, George Routledge & Sons, Ltd., 1927, Chs. 4-7.

Africa,[29] and sometimes segregated districts in the towns and cities. Such residential segregation is commonly supplemented by segregation in public conveyances, places, and institutions.

Posters daubed "For Europeans only" are a standing affront to us in esplanades, botanical garden seats, parks, promenades, railway sidings, tram shelters, and public conveniences. In seaside resorts we blacks can bathe, as at East London, only in an absurdly small section of the beach where the edge is least desirable, elbowed out by miles of excellent frontage available for the happy white race, there being no resting seats for us although we pay town rates. In public hospitals where there are no Bantu nurses our lot is not always a happy one, and I can confirm this from the experience of one of my children at the hands of an unsympathetic white nurse. In religious circles too the colour obsession is not wanting. . . . In the Civil Service we are confined to junior clerkships, even in our native areas where the Prime Minister promised us an open way to the top. . . . In many cases salesmen in shops delight in keeping us waiting while they gossip with their European friends, and flare out in anger, hurling vituperative epithets, if you dare humbly to interrupt and ask to be served.[30]

The tendency is for the dominant group to attempt by every means within its power to keep the native in his "place." The natives, though frequently exceeding the invaders in numerical strength, are sooner or later almost certain to be reduced to a subordinate position. While they may retain relatively untouched many features of their native cultures, they cannot retain their economic, political, and social independence. For the invaders it is control in these latter considerations that constitutes the "native problem." [31] The conflict is, as Brown points out, rarely one of race; it is one "between an alien power and a native folk." [32]

29 See: Earl E. Muntz, Race Contact, New York, The Century Co., 1927, Ch. 5; I. Schapera, "Present-Day Life in the Native Reserves," in Western Civilization and the Natives of South Africa, I. Schapera (Ed.), London, George Routledge & Sons, Ltd., 1934, Ch. 2.

30 D. D. T. Jabavu, "Bantu Grievances," in I. Schapera (Ed.), Western Civilization and the Natives of South Africa, pp. 298-299. See also Edgar H. Brookes, The Colour Problem of South Africa, Lovedale, C. P., Africa, Lovedale Press, 1933; R. L. Buell, The Native Problem in Africa, 2 vols., New York, The Macmillan Co., 1928; Geoffrey Gorer, Africa Dances, New York, Alfred A. Knopf, 1935; Richard C. Thurnwald, Black and White in East Africa, London, George Routledge & Sons, Ltd., 1935.

31 See: W. O. Brown, "Culture Contact and Race Conflict," pp. 36-37; Buell, The Native Problem in Africa.

32 In South Africa, for example, the "Cape colored question" is the "race question," and refers to a problem quite distinct from that of the so-called "native problem." The former refers to the mixed-bloods resulting from the miscegenation of the early Dutch, French Huguenot, and German settlers (who fused and became known as Boers) with the natives. In late years there have developed pronounced attitudes against such interbreeding, with the result that the colored or mixed-bloods constitute a "problem." See: Maurice S. Evans, Black and White in South East Africa: A Study in Sociology, 2nd ed., New York, Longmans, Green & Co., 1916, Ch. 10; R. E. Park, "Race Relations and Certain Frontiers," in Race and Culture Contacts, E. B. Reuter (Ed.), Ch. 5; R. F. A. Hoernlé, "Race-Mixture and Native Policy in South Africa," in Schapera, Western Civiliza-

The new conflict is one for recognition and status and over questions of interests, rights, and social equality. Playing a subordinate role outside of slavery or caste, and sometimes within them, is distasteful and, as a consequence, is regarded merely as a temporary adjustment and something to be escaped as soon as possible. The only way of escape, barring the eviction, withdrawal, or absorption of the invaders, is to demand the right to penetrate the cultural order and social system of the dominant group on terms of equality. To fail to reach this objective means that the natives remain in a marginal position with respect to the native culture and social system on the one hand, and those of the dominant group on the other. They are dependent upon the latter and are to a considerable extent alienated from the former. Since the native's chief stock in trade with the whites is his labor he is generally eager to sell it where and when it will be to his advantage. While there is still much indentured unskilled labor, particularly on plantations and in mines, the demand for domestic service and for labor of all kinds in the towns and cities attracts the natives to the urban centers even though it may mean subjecting themselves to greater prejudice and discrimination.

Imposition of Alien Law and Government.—Another evidence of native subordination is in the imposition of alien law and government. The favorite method of the past seemed to consist in imposing the mores of the dominant group upon those of the natives and enforcing them until they became a more or less accepted part of the culture of the community. The practices of different governments have varied greatly in this respect and have differed within themselves at different times, due mainly to the wide dissimilarities between them and the native mores on the one hand and between the many divergent native practices on the other. Some governments, disposed to leniency, have tacitly recognized many native customs and established native administrations paralleling their own to some extent, allowing a modicum of self-government or home rule. Often the rules of jurisprudence are modified to suit local custom and tribal belief. On the other hand, many governments have been ruthless in their efforts to stamp out native practices, superstitions, and notions of group vengeance. They have set up rulers and magistrates of their own who would be completely subservient to the dominant group and its laws; they have resorted to force to bring the natives to terms and to protect the inter-

tion and the Natives of South Africa, Ch. 11; William M. Macmillan, The Cape Colour Question, London, Faber & Gwyer, 1927; Daniel Thwaite, The Seething African Pot, London, Constable & Comary, 1936.

ests of the whites against those of the natives. In numbers of instances the principle of extraterritoriality has been established with special courts, and governed by foreign laws.[33] The general tendency has been to weaken the native organization with the result that a reign of anarchy followed which could be controlled only by forceful means. Exceptions are to be found, of course. For example, in Hawaii, "because of his local birth, the Hawaiian has enjoyed, even under American control, a special advantage in the political realm. It seems likely, therefore, that the well-known penchant of the Hawaiian for political campaigning and speech making is derived in part from the social status and economic position which politics provides." [34]

Compensatory Mechanisms.—The native, on his side, though weakened and subordinate in the economic, political, and social phases of life, frequently resorts to the use of certain compensatory mechanisms. Briefly stated, these include such things as "baiting" the invaders, subtle and scarcely noticeable sabotage in employment and in other ways, developing a native press which serves as a medium of protest, starting and supporting nativistic movements of one sort or another, all uniformly devoted to the cause of independence or equal rights, and the widespread development of secret societies, clubs, and esoteric religious cults and orgiastic religious movements. These latter serve as refuges from mundane struggles and failures and lend purpose and dignity to the lives of their adherents.[35]

Assimilation.—Where the processes of detribalization and cultural disintegration have gone on to such an extent that the natives are left in a state of dependency upon the white man's culture and social system and yet are not an integral part of these, the future is dark and precarious for both groups unless the assimilative phase of interaction can have free play. Acculturation will go on where there is not complete isolation, which is impossible today. Amalgamation is certain to occur in the future as it has in the past, in spite of taboos against interbreeding and laws against intermarriage. What remains to complete the cycle of alien-native interaction is assimilation.

It is highly improbable that assimilation to a common, shared life will be possible for many native populations, in the near future. For

---

[33] Shih Shun Liu, *Extraterritoriality, Its Rise and Its Decline*, New York, Columbia University Press, 1925.

[34] A. W. Lind, "Modifications of Hawaiian Character," in *Race and Culture Contacts*, edited by E. B. Reuter, p. 242. See also, A. W. Lind, *Hawaii's Japanese: An Experiment in Democracy*, Princeton, Princeton University Press, 1946. Edwin G. Burrows, in *Hawaiian Americans*, in discussing the adaptations made by the non-native elements in Hawaii, emphasizes the point that the Hawaiians themselves have bought their political advances by positive economic losses.

[35] Lind, "Modifications of Hawaiian Character," *op. cit.*, pp. 239-241.

some groups, however, assimilation is going on already and is almost certain to increase and gradually incorporate more and more members of both groups within its compass. In spite of the sentiment-attitudes of prejudice, racial and cultural superiority, and intolerance, which have so effectively blocked its progress, assimilation is a possible future aid in solving the "native problem" and the "race question."

Questions

1. What are some difficulties faced by the person who would understand "race prejudice"?
2. How does Huxley dispose of the concept "race"?
3. How may "race" be defined sociologically?
4. What does Faris mean when he says race "is not a fact, it is a concept"?
5. Define "race prejudice." How is the term commonly used?
6. Give the meaning and significance of "social distance" in race relations.
7. What is meant by saying a person is "out of his place"?
8. How is the concept "pressure" used in the study of racial contacts?
9. What effect does the fact of "numbers" have in determining racial attitudes?
10. How do "qualities of aggressiveness" affect the situation?
11. To what extent and in what ways are racial attitudes determined by direct contact? By indirect contact?
12. Explain in terms of race relations: "The tendency to approach and incorporate the object with the economy of the individual is, as it were, counterbalanced by the tendency to destroy or avoid the object as dangerous to the individual."
13. What part is played by sensory stimuli in racial contacts?
14. What is meant by saying that reaction tendencies tend to present a configuration rather than a continuum?
15. Give illustrations of both positive and negative racial attitudes.
16. What do the facts of interbreeding and intermarriage between members of different racial groups reveal as to the nature and formation of racial attitudes?
17. "Attitudes about race tend to become fixed or stereotyped." What is meant? Illustrate.
18. Discuss the development of race dogma or philosophy as the final stage in the natural history of racial attitudes.
19. What does Radin say on the subject of racial superiority?
20. What purpose may be served by the "race purity" myth?
21. How do you explain the psychology of lynching and other forms of terrorism?
22. Discuss discrimination as a form of conflict pattern in race relations.

23. What places do ridicule and patronage have in racial conflict?

24. In what ways does race conflict become identified with nationality struggle?

25. What is the social role of race prejudice and antipathy?

26. What is the nature of the racial and cultural heritage of the Negro group in the United States? What part has it played in their adjustments to the dominant numbers and culture of the white population?

27. Discuss the pros and cons of elimination as a solution of the "race problem" in the United States.

28. Why is it said that "racial admixture does not necessarily give evidence to solving the race problem"?

29. Why are statistics on the number of mulattoes regarded as incomplete evidence of the extent of race mixture?

30. To what extent does slavery as a form of accommodation rest upon physical force? Upon mental attitudes?

31. To what causes may stratified relationships be attributed?

32. Defend or criticize the stratification of human relationships.

33. What are the roles of rationalization and sublimation in the area of race relations?

34. What are the meaning and function of idealization? What are some forms of its expression in the accommodation of Negroes?

35. Discuss the proposals of Negro leaders for the solution of the problems of their race.

36. What is meant by and involved in "participation along bi-racial lines"?

37. Why has the Negro in the United States not been assimilated?

38. What barriers stand in the way of the American-born Oriental and prevent him from finding complete acceptance?

39. What is meant by "the race-relations cycle"? What pattern does it present in white-Negro relations in the United States?

40. State the problem of incorporating the alien culture group.

41. Distinguish between reconciliation in secondary contacts. In primary contacts.

42. To what extent and in what ways is reconciliation a matter of education?

43. What are some community agencies assisting the process of accommodation?

44. What do you consider to be the significance of the fact that the segregated ethnic colonies in the new world are "little more than bits of the old world transplanted to the soil of the new one"?

45. How may segregation hinder the process of accommodation? How may it assist the process?

46. What part do the immigrants' own agencies perform for their members in assisting in adjustment?

47. Defend or criticize the nationalistic organizations of the immigrants.

48. What is meant by saying that such agencies "function to connect the old and familiar with the new and untried, the far and the near, the past and the present"?

49. To what extent and in what ways are such agencies "immigrant heritages" and to what extent do they represent adaptations to the new environment?

50. What are some of the motives causing people to emigrate to new and strange lands?

51. How and why did the attitude of the recipient population toward immigrants change as time went on and as the tide of immigration rose?

52. What forms were taken by organized opposition to immigration? Explain.

53. Why have Orientals been singled out for special discrimination?

54. Discuss the history of Oriental immigration and exclusion.

55. What is the character of the present immigration policy and legislation of the United States? of Canada?

56. What attitudes on the side of the recipient population tend to hinder the complete incorporation of the alien in the new life and culture? What ones on the side of the immigrants?

57. In what respect is the second generation involved differently from the first generation in the process of social interaction? Be explicit.

58. Discuss the contacts resulting from the invasion of "representatives of an advanced culture into the territory of a culturally retarded and militaristically impotent people."

59. How does Wissler summarize the changes in the culture patterns and social organization of the natives brought into contact with the culture and social systems of invaders?

60. What, in the last analysis, determines the course of interaction between invaders and native peoples?

61. What factors are invariably involved in the control of native populations by foreign powers and with what effects?

62. Can all of these factors be ascribed to white-native contacts? If not, why not?

63. What are some characteristics of the ritual of race relations?

64. What conditions in the United States are suggested to you by the list of Bantu grievances given by Jabavu?

65. What do you understand by "the native problem"? How does it differ from "the colored question" in South Africa?

66. If the conflict is rarely one of race, as Brown says, what is it? What characterizes the conflict and what is its usual outcome?

67. Discuss the nature and effects of the imposition of alien law and government.

68. What compensatory mechanisms are frequently resorted to by the subordinated natives?

69. Since contact between alien and native peoples is inevitable, what seems to be the most promising solution to their mutual problems?

Bibliography

ADAMIC, LOUIS. *Two Way Passage.* New York, Harper & Bros., 1941.

ADAMIC, LOUIS. *What's Your Name?* New York, Harper & Bros., 1942.

AMERICAN COUNCIL ON RACE RELATIONS. *Studies in the Reduction of Prejudice.* Chicago, American Council on Race Relations, 1947.

ASHLEY-MONTAGU, M. F. *Man's Most Dangerous Myth: The Fallacy of Race.* New York, Columbia University Press, 1942.

BARZUN, JACQUES. *Race, A Study in Modern Superstition.* New York, Harcourt, Brace & Co., 1937.

BENEDICT, RUTH. *Race: Science and Politics.* New York, Modern Age Books, 1940.

BROWN, FRANCIS J., AND ROUCEK, JOSEPH S. (Editors). *One America: The History, Contributions and Present Problems of Our Racial and National Minorities.* New York, Prentice-Hall, Inc., 1945.

BURMA, JOHN H. "Humor as a Technique in Race Conflict." *Am. Sociol. Rev.,* Vol. 11, No. 6, December, 1946, pp. 710-715.

CHILD, IRVIN L. *Italian or American? The Second Generation in Conflict.* New Haven, Institute of Human Relations, Yale University, 1943.

COON, CARLETON S. *The Races of Europe.* New York, The Macmillan Co., 1939.

DAVIE, MAURICE. *What Shall We Do About Immigration?* New York, Public Affairs Committee, 1946.

DAVIE, MAURICE. *World Immigration.* New York, The Macmillan Co., 1936.

DAY, GEORGE M. *The Russians in Hollywood: A Study in Culture Conflict.* Los Angeles, University of Southern California Press, 1934.

DEBO, ANGIE. *And Still the Waters Run.* Princeton, Princeton University Press, 1940.

DETWEILER, FREDERICK G. "The Negro Press Today." *Am. J. Sociol.,* Vol. 44, No. 3, November, 1938, pp. 391-400.

DETWEILER, FREDERICK G. *The Negro Press in the United States.* Chicago, University of Chicago Press, 1922.

DOYLE, BERTRAM W. *The Etiquette of Race Relations in the South.* Chicago, University of Chicago Press, 1937.

DRAKE, ST. CLAIR, AND CAYTON, HORACE R. *Black Metropolis: A Study of Negro Life in a Northern City.* New York, Harcourt, Brace & Co., 1945.

DUBOIS, W. E. B. "Prospect of a World Without Race Conflict." *Am. J. Sociol.,* Vol. 49, No. 5, March, 1944, pp. 450-456.

EMBREE, EDWIN R. *Brown Americans: The Story of a Tenth of the Nation.* New York, The Viking Press, 1943.

FAIRCHILD, HENRY PRATT. *Race and Nationality—As Factors in American Life.* New York, The Ronald Press Co., 1947.

FINOT, JEAN. *Race Prejudice.* Translated by Florence Wade-Evans. New York, E. P. Dutton & Co., 1924.

FLOYD, ARVA C. *White Man-Yellow Man.* Nashville, Abington-Cokesbury Press, 1946.

FRANCIS, E. K. "The Nature of the Ethnic Group." *Am. J. Sociol.,* Vol. 52, No. 5, March, 1947, pp. 393-400.

FRANKLIN, JOHN H. *From Slavery to Freedom*. New York, Alfred A. Knopf, 1947.

FRAZIER, E. FRANKLIN. *The Negro Family in Chicago*. Chicago, University of Chicago Press, 1931.

FRAZIER, E. FRANKLIN. *The Negro Family in the United States*. Rev. ed. New York, The Dryden Press, 1948.

GRAEBER, ISACQUE, AND BRITT, STEUART H. (Editors). *Jews in a Gentile World: The Problem of Anti-Semitism*. New York, The Macmillan Co., 1942.

GREEN, ARNOLD W. "A Re-Examination of the Marginal Man Concept." *Social Forces*, Vol. 26, December, 1947, pp. 167-171.

HALSEY, MARGARET. *Color Blind*. New York, Simon & Schuster, 1946.

HANSEN, MARCUS LEE. *The Immigrant in American History*. Cambridge. Harvard University Press, 1940.

HERSKOVITS, MELVILLE J. *The Myth of the Negro Past*. New York, Harper & Bros., 1941.

JANOWSKY, OSCAR I. (Ed.). *The American Jew: A Composite Portrait*. New York, Harper & Bros., 1942.

JOHNSON, CHARLES S. *Growing Up in the Black Belt*. Washington, American Council on Education, 1941.

JOHNSON, CHARLES S. *Patterns of Negro Segregation*. New York, Harper & Bros., 1943.

JOHNSON, CHARLES S., AND ASSOCIATES. *To Stem This Tide*. Boston, Pilgrim Press, 1943.

KIBBE, PAULINE. *Latin Americans in Texas*. Albuquerque, University of New Mexico Press, 1946.

KLINEBERG, OTTO (Ed.). *Characteristics of the American Negro*. New York, Harper & Bros., 1944.

KLINEBERG, OTTO. *Race Differences*. New York, Harper & Bros., 1935.

KONVITZ, MILTON R. *The Alien and the Asiatic in American Law*. Ithaca, Cornell University Press, 1946.

LASKER, BRUNO. *Race Attitudes of Children*. New York, Henry Holt & Co., 1929.

LAVIOLETTE, FOREST E. *Americans of Japanese Ancestry: A Study of Assimilation in the American Community*. Toronto, Canadian Institute of International Affairs, 1945.

LEE, ALFRED McCLUNG, AND HUMPHREY, NORMAN D. *Race Riot*. New York, The Dryden Press, 1943.

LIND, ANDREW W. *Hawaii's Japanese: An Experiment in Democracy*. Princeton, Princeton University Press, 1946.

LITTLE, K. L. *Negroes in Britain: A Study of Racial Relations in English Society*. London, Kegan Paul, Trench, Trubner & Co., Ltd., 1947.

LOCKE, ALAIN, AND STERN, BERNHARD J. *When People Meet: A Study in Race and Culture Contacts*. Rev. ed. New York, Hinds, Hayden & Eldredge, Inc., 1946.

LOGAN, RAYFORD W. (Ed.). *What the Negro Wants*. Chapel Hill, University of North Carolina Press, 1944.

LONG, HERMAN H., AND JOHNSON, CHARLES S. *People vs. Property: Race Restrictive Covenants in Housing*. Fisk University, Nashville, Race Relations Department, American Missionary Assn., 1948.

MACCRONE, I. D. *Race Attitudes in South Africa: Historical, Experimental and Psychological Studies*. New York, Oxford University Press, 1937.

MANGUM, CHARLES S. *The Legal Status of the Negro*. Chapel Hill, University of North Carolina Press, 1940.

MARCSON, SIMON. "The Control of Ethnic Conflict." *Social Forces*, Vol. 24, December, 1945, pp. 161-165.

McWilliams, Carey. *Brothers Under the Skin*. Boston, Little, Brown & Co., 1943.

Myrdal, Gunnar. *An American Dilemma*. 2 vols. New York, Harper & Bros., 1944.

National Committee on Immigration Policy. *Immigration and Population Policy*. New York, Academy Press, 1947.

Odum, Howard W. *Race and Rumors of Race*. Chapel Hill, University of North Carolina Press, 1943.

Ottley, Roi. *New World A-Coming*. Boston, Houghton Mifflin Co., 1943.

Parkes, James. *An Enemy of the People*. New York, Penguin Books, Inc., 1946.

Pierson, Donald. *Negroes in Brazil: A Study of Race Contact in Bahia*. Chicago, University of Chicago Press, 1942.

Radin, Paul. *The Racial Myth*. New York, McGraw-Hill Book Co., Inc., 1934.

Reuter, Edward B. *The American Race Problem*. Rev. ed. New York, T. Y. Crowell Co., 1939.

Reuter, Edward B. (Ed.). *Race and Culture Contacts*. New York, McGraw-Hill Book Co., Inc., 1934.

Reuter, Edward B. *Race Mixture*. New York, McGraw-Hill Book Co., Inc., 1931.

Reuter, Edward B. "Racial Theory." *Am. J. Sociol.*, Vol. 50, No. 6, May, 1945, pp. 452-461.

Ross, Malcolm. *All Manner of Men*. New York, Reynal & Hitchcock, 1948. Deals with the crisis in race relations.

Smith, William C. *Americans in the Making: The Natural History of the Assimilation of Immigrants*. New York, D. Appleton-Century Co., Inc., 1939.

Smith, William C. *Americans in Process: A Study of Our Citizens of Oriental Ancestry*. Ann Arbor, Mich., Edwards Bros., 1937.

Sterner, Richard. *The Negro's Share*. New York, Harper & Bros., 1943.

Stonequist, Everett V. *The Marginal Man*. New York, Charles Scribner's Sons, 1937.

Strong, Edward K., Jr. *The Second-Generation Japanese Problem*. Stanford University, California, Stanford University Press, 1934.

Tannenbaum, Frank. *Slave and Citizen: The Negro in the Americas*. New York, Alfred A. Knopf, 1947.

Thomas, Dorothy S., and Nishimoto, Richard. *The Spoilage*. Berkeley, University of California Press, 1946.

Thomas, William I., and Znaniecki, Florian. *The Polish Peasant in Europe and America*. 2 vols. New York, Alfred A. Knopf, 1927.

Thompson, Edgar T. (Ed.). *Race Relations and the Race Problem*. Durham, N. C., Duke University Press, 1939.

Tuck, Ruth. *Not With the Fist: Mexican Americans in a Southwestern City*. New York, Harcourt, Brace & Co., 1946.

Warner, W. Lloyd, Junker, Buford H., and Adams, Walter. *Color and Human Nature: Negro Personality Development in a Northern City*. Washington, American Council on Education, 1941.

Warner, W. Lloyd, and Srole, Leo. *The Social Systems of American Ethnic Groups*. New Haven, Yale University Press, 1945.

Weaver, Robert C. *Negro Labor, a National Problem*. New York, Harcourt, Brace & Co., 1945.

Wittke, Carl. *We Who Built America: The Saga of the Immigrant*. New York, Prentice-Hall, Inc., 1939.

Young, Donald. *American Minority Peoples: A Study in Racial and Cultural Conflict*. New York, Harper & Bros., 1932.

Young, Pauline. *The Pilgrims of Russian-Town*. Chicago, University of Chicago Press, 1932.

Chapter 17

INTERACTION INVOLVING CONSIDERATIONS
OF STATUS

CHARACTERISTICS OF STATUS

We are now about to enter upon a discussion of one of the most confused and difficult problems of sociological analysis. It is the problem of social differentiation and the interactional relations that stem from such differentiations. While students of society have long been engaged in describing and analyzing certain recognized inequalities among persons and groups, they have failed to reach agreement of the meanings of the basic concepts necessary to this task: the functions performed by inequalities in affecting interaction among unequal entities, and the relationships that have grown up among the unequal entities.

In his book, *Social Differentiation,* C. C. North presents an analysis of certain significant social differences among members of a group, based upon a fourfold classification of differences of function, differences of rank, differences of culture, and differences of interest.[1] He does not ignore individual differences which are due to biological factors. But, since such differences are regarded as presocial and as having significance solely in terms of their social definitions, North considers them only as they shed light on the social relations of individuals or as they serve as "foundations or bases on which these social differences rest." His classification, then, is essentially a social one.

North's classification may be applied with equal validity to the social differentiation of groups. Groups, like persons, come to be distinguished from one another in terms of function, rank, culture, and interest. In preceding chapters we have discussed social interaction as it operates between groups demarcated mainly by distinctive culture patterns, and by which patterns each is more or less controlled. The three chapters which directly follow this will deal with social interaction between persons and groups not widely different in cul-

---

[1] C. C. North, *Social Differentiation,* Chapel Hill, University of North Carolina Press, 1926, pp. 4-5.

ture—in fact, living together under the same culture patterns—but differing from each other in matters of interest. This chapter will deal with inter-personal and inter-group interactions where the basic culture patterns of the persons and groups involved differ little or not at all from each other, but where differences in sub-culture patterns and in matters of function and rank are important considerations. Certain underlying biological differences, especially those of race, sex, and age, may also enter into the interactions. We will undertake to discover how these differentiating factors enter into the determination of status and how, in turn, different statuses become significant and often primary criteria in interaction and in determining the character of certain types of personal and group relationships, and hence, of the structure of social organization.

Before proceeding, it should be pointed out that the items in North's classification are not mutually exclusive. For example, a single group may display an overlapping between two or more of the classes of difference. Cases may be cited of the military system and of the priestly class, in both of which there is a conjunction of function and rank. Whether the rank is due to specialized function or whether the function comes to be identified with rank is relatively unimportant; the fact is that they tend to go together in these and other similar cases. North's classification is little more than a convenient device for assisting us in analyzing our problem.

Position and Status.—Most students of social differentiation either make no distinction between "position" and "status," or define one in terms of the other. These concepts and others related to our central problem will have to be more sharply and rigorously defined and tested in terms of external and observable phenomena before they can be used in social investigation and analysis.[2] For the purpose of our discussion, we will use "position" as an ecological concept, and "status" as a socio-psychological concept. As applied to individuals and groups, or to any objective datum or unit, or class of data of

---

[2] The following references will serve to show the confused state of conceptualization in this area: Maxwell R. Brooks, "American Class and Caste: An Appraisal," *Social Forces*, Vol. 25, December, 1946, pp. 207-211; Kingsley Davis, "A Conceptual Analysis of Stratification," *Am. Sociol. Rev.*, Vol. 7, June, 1942, pp. 309-321; E. E. Eubank, *The Concepts of Sociology*, Boston, D. C. Heath & Co., 1932, pp. 92, 327-329; H. P. Fairchild (Ed.), *Dictionary of Sociology*, "Position, Ecological," and "Status," New York, Philosophical Library, 1944, pp. 226, 307-308; E. T. Hiller, *Social Relations and Structures*, New York, Harper & Bros., 1947, Ch. 22; Ralph Linton, *The Study of Man*, New York, Appleton-Century-Crofts, Inc., 1936, Chs. 7-8; R. E. Park and E. W. Burgess, *Introduction to the Science of Sociology*, Chicago, University of Chicago Press, 1921, 1924, p. 55; Talcott Parsons, "An Analytical Approach to the Theory of Social Stratification," *Am. J. Sociol.*, Vol. 45, May, 1940, pp. 841-862; Talcott Parsons, *Max Weber: The Theory of Social and Economic Organization*, New York, Oxford University Press, 1947, pp. 428-429; W. Lloyd Warner and P. S. Lunt, *The Social Life of a Modern Community*, New Haven, Yale University Press, 1940, especially Ch. 5.

ecological interaction and organization, *position* refers to the place held by such units on a scale of functionally defined values in an ecologically organized frame of reference. In other words, persons, groups, occupations, and culture traits, as well as communities, geographic areas, and locations in space, get "placed" in positions on a graduated scale of functionally defined values by the operation of the process of ecological interaction.

In such a frame of reference, the position of one unit is always relative to the positions of other units of the same functional order or category, and that of one class of data is relative to the positions of classes of data of different orders or categories. The values involved in the placement of diverse functions, and of the persons, groups, and other objects that possess and express them, in a graduated order of positions, are simply the normative judgments which culture groups apply to a variety of criteria which have significance, and thus functional worth, to the groups. The criteria include such things as sex, age, occupation, education, achievement, possession of wealth, and the like, when they pertain to persons and groups possessing them, or they may include factors of accessibility, transportation and communication routes or channels, territorial size, numbers and composition of population, etc., as they characterize communities, regions, spatial locations, etc. These criteria are actually broken down in practice into sub-criteria, each evaluated according to an accepted scale of values.

For example, the criterion of sex has as its sub-criteria those of maleness and femaleness, with concomitant conceptions of masculinity and femininity, by which, in part, institutionalized functional roles have long been assigned to individuals by every culture group we know anything about. Age, as a criterion for evaluation, is commonly broken down into age levels, each level being defined principally in terms of its functional importance for the social group, and the individual at each level tending to share in the position assigned to that level and the roles held to be proper and necessary to it. Occupation, with its many subdivisions in the more developed societies, represents another functional category of manifold possibilities for evaluation, both within given occupations and as between occupations, with corresponding positions of different degrees of value assigned to them and to their members. Lastly, possession of wealth rates one a higher position than does the absence of such possession in an economic order where "money talks" louder than other criteria, but tends to assume a quite different position on the evaluational scale in a society where money, or its counterpart, has no appreciable function.

The same sort of analysis is applicable to other criteria and their sub-categories.

In every society characterized by mobility and change, "jockeying" for position is always present in some form and to some extent. The process works ceaselessly to distribute selectively persons and groups, culture traits, occupations and businesses, and the like, according to the position on the functional scale where they can best contribute to and fit into the constantly reshaping pattern of ecological organization. The more freely competitive, in some instances, and the more cooperative, in other instances, the process of interaction, the easier it is for persons, groups, institutional agencies, and even whole communities, to alter or to have altered their functional positions, with corresponding alterations in the status norms associated with and considered appropriate to the relative positions.

While many positions seem to be established and fixed, as indeed they are to a great extent in most societies, there are many situations in which positions are created or changed by the deliberate effort of somebody or some group. Functional positions of whatever sort are not usually altogether the outcomes of chance or the consequences of some inexorable "law" of economics or of nature. Rather, they are the result of more or less deliberate choices of people seeking to adapt certain features of their social environments to their purposes or to adjust themselves to the as yet uncontrollable aspects of their social environments.

The individual may come into a given position at a particular period in his life-cycle in a variety of ways, depending upon the degree to which he possesses and expresses the functional qualities that are appreciated and valued by his culture group at the time. His precise position will depend upon the definition of the specific function or class of function and on his performance as a bearer or active agent of that function. He may be born to his position, if it is one that passes from generation to generation by tradition, or is one that is determined by sex, age, race, and the like. He may have a certain position thrust upon him, so to speak, by the exigencies of a situation that compels him to function in a definite fashion as, for example, loss of one's means of livelihood, one's wealth, etc. Or he may achieve his position by his own efforts, the degree of flexibility of the social order permitting. The first two ways are largely beyond the control of the individual; one is by ascription, the other by accident. The third way depends upon range of opportunity and choice and upon one's ability and willingness to put forth effort to gain the position and to hold it once it has been achieved. In all three ways, the cultural norms play an important part by defining and evaluating the functions, setting the criteria considered basic to their performance, and establishing status systems in terms of which positions are rendered attractive or un-attractive, rewarding or non-rewarding.

Position, being a functionally defined and evaluated conception, has been characterized as follows:

To characterize a position, we say that it is subjective in the sense of ex-isting in the minds as well as in the behavior of the societal members; yet it is objective in the sense of being common to many minds and therefore in-dependent of any one mentality; it is also reciprocal in the sense of implying rights and obligations which the incumbent of the position has with respect to the incumbents of other positions; and it is functional and purposive in the sense of serving both a function (or functions) and a purpose (or pur-poses) with regard to the rest of the structure.[3]

Every individual has one or more positions simultaneously, and will normally move through a series of positions during a lifetime. Even the infant, physically helpless and dependent upon others for nourishment and care, is not without a function in the family system. The anomalous position of the beggar, who may be regarded as "use-less and good for nothing," is functional from the standpoint of the philanthropist. The hereditary ruler may be tyrannical and thus abhorrent to his subjects, but it by no means follows that he is with-out function and the position that goes with that function. Every culture group provides for the training and preparation of the young for positions which they may be expected to assume in later life. The educative process, particularly in western cultures, is designed to equip the young group members for a variety of positions in adult life, what specific positions they will be depending, in part, upon the mem-bers' aptitudes, interests, and ambitions, and also upon the number of positions available and the statuses associated with them and their incumbents. While it is sometimes difficult to discern a purpose be-hind a given position, it may be assumed to be there. If it were not there, the position would not exist in the social structure.

Positions, in that they have an objective character as well as a subjective one, are theoretically amenable to statistical enumeration. Practically, however, there are many positions that defy enumeration and exact classification. In this respect, institutional positions are easier to identify than those of an association, let us say. One reason why this is so is to be found in the nature of functioning in institu-tions as compared with functioning in primary and in non-primary,

---

3 Davis, "A Conceptual Analysis of Stratification," *op. cit.*, p. 309.

but non-institutional, groups. As Faris has said, "It is in the institution that we find the essential opposite of the primary group, where the forms are fixed, the rules prescribed, the offices laid down, and the duties set forth with definite clarity and relative inflexibility. The person is no longer acting freely but is acting in an office, performing a definite institutional function." [4]

Not all functionaries in institutional patterns and structures hold offices, but they do have positions therein. "The more specialized activities of an institution are carried on by functionaries who fulfill offices. An institutional office consists of a defined set of rights and duties vested in a person, but capable of being transferred to another person in some accepted way." [5] Actually, non-officeholding functionaries in an institutional organization have rights and duties, but these are not transferable in the same way and to the same extent as are those of the officeholder. Presumably, the institutional claims upon them are less than they are upon those selected to hold office. Just as the institutional claims upon them are less binding, so are their positions in the institution likely to be less rewarding in terms of status and other compensations and remunerations.

This brings us now to a consideration of *status,* which has been mentioned several times. We have implied that a position may carry with it a certain status, and that status may help one to acquire a position. This is particularly true of an office, which may have a definite status attached to it. But while status may be associated with position, it is not to be identified with position. Status refers to "institutionalized conduct between prearranged positions. Accordingly, we should not, as is sometimes done, use this word to express the idea of favorable or unfavorable reputation. For this idea we use more specific terms, such as rank, rating, honor, and prestige. To be sure, these are included in the general concept of status which, in addition, comprises utilitarian reciprocities and even power-relations." [6] Thus we see that status is a matter of accepted social usages that have been developed rather than deliberately created, and have become established in the folkways, mores, and institutional practices of societies. These usages, however, do not apply equally to all persons and to all groups within the containing social structure. Persons and groups have different statuses and those of each status have their own special rights and duties, sanctioned by the inclusive society.

---

[4] Ellsworth Faris, "The Primary Group: Essence and Accident," *Am. J. Sociol.,* Vol. 38, No. 1, July, 1932, p. 50.
[5] E. C. Hughes, in A. M. Lee (Ed.), *New Outline of the Principles of Sociology,* New York, Barnes & Noble, Inc., 1946, p. 258.
[6] Hiller, *Social Relations and Structures,* pp. 333-334.

DETERMINANTS OF STATUS

Status is generally determined by the different ways in which persons and groups customarily regard and treat one another. Conversely, persons and groups tend to interact with others in terms of prescribed and understood notions concerning their own and the others' prestige, honor, privileges and immunities, responsibilities and obligations, violabilities and inviolabilities. Also, as previously mentioned, the status factor in interaction may depend on the respective positions of the interacting parties, including considerations of rank, degree of specialization, authority or power inherent in the positions, and the accomplishments of the incumbents. "If or when a person's claims are norm-supported, they are his rights; and when his obligations are so prescribed, they are his duties. In addition each may be granted privileges which he can exercise if he so chooses. Such paired advantages and disadvantages are not necessarily equal." [7]

Statuses, like positions, rest on inequalities. This is so whether the statuses are ascribed, assumed, or achieved.[8] The determinants of status include, at least, those of class, the life-cycle, ethnic or racial factors, sex differentials, and uniquely personal and situational factors. Of these five sets of determining factors, all may be wholly or only partly assigned by ascription, assumption, and achievement. On the face of it, this statement seems insupportable, especially with respect to such factors as race, sex, and age, since these identifying characteristics would seem to preclude all possibility of assumption or achievement. However, instances can be cited where individuals of, let us say, the Negro race have overcome a prescribed inferior status either by "passing" or by accomplishments out of the ordinary for members of their race. Age-status and sex-status have likewise been surmounted often enough to warrant using them as exceptions to the rule. Nevertheless, most inequalities of status are so well established and so rigidly directed that most persons and groups are unable or unwilling to master the difficulties of altering their statuses. This is so even in a comparatively free and idealistic society. Unique personal and peculiar situational factors, though they may be initially ascribed, are often the easiest to overcome by choice or effort. Class status, again initially ascribed, may be altered by option and achievement in a society of so-called "open classes." As we have remarked, there are cases where ascribed statuses inherent in sex, age, and race

---

[7] *Ibid.*, p. 332.
[8] *Ibid.*, pp. 335-337.

differences have been altered by assumption and achievement, although manifestly they have been changed with great difficulty.

Class as a Determiner of Status.—*Class* is another term that is loosely used to identify differentiated groups in the social structure. Consequently, most of its uses are misleading and render the concept difficult to manipulate in sociological analysis. About the only common element in its many definitions and usages is that class is a stratum in a hierarchical arrangement of positions wherein concepts and observances of rank rest on corresponding notions and practices of inequality. Within each class there is an assumed equality of rights, privileges, and duties. These, together with attitudes regarding relations with members of other strata, constitute the class status. Indicative of the tendency of students of the subject and others to make "class" a kind of omnibus concept are such designations as upper, middle, and lower classes, the "working class," the "white collar class," the "intellectual class," the "professional class," the "leisure class," the "bureaucratic class," the "managerial class," the "capitalist class," the "bourgeois class," the "propertied class," the "merchant class," and so on almost *ad infinitum*. Some writers assign Negroes, women, children, the aged, etc., to separate classes, or castes. Also, such generic terms as social, non-social, pseudo-social, and anti-social are given as class designations.

Manifestly, such a proliferation of class names cannot accurately and adequately serve taxonomic purposes, let alone the requirements of analysis and generalization. There are those who hold that the essence of class differentiation lies in a subjective element, like "class-consciousness" or "feelings" of class difference; others hold that, on the contrary, class is an objective, empirical reality with tangible behavioral manifestations; while still others contend that class combines something of both subjective feeling states and objective attributes.[9] On this last point, we read by way of clarification, "The idea of class sentiment as essential to analyses of class differentiation implies that individuals are not in a class unless they feel that they are. If this were so, the criteria for class differentiation as a scientific term capable of being used in research, would lie in the *feelings of class differentiation* and wherever those feelings did not occur, there would be no class differentiation." [10]

In addition, we find some social scientists who deny the existence of social classes, at least in modern society and in the sense in which

---

[9] George Simpson, "Class Analysis: What Class Is Not," *Am. Sociol. Rev.*, Vol. 4, No. 6, December, 1939, pp. 827-835.

[10] *Ibid.*

we are using the term. For example, Cox says: "In other words there are, in capitalist society, no social classes amenable to objective circumscription. . . . There is, moreover, no class consciousness among social classes, for social classes are merely heuristic constructs." [11]   In this respect, Cox seems to agree with Carr-Saunders and D. C. Jones, whom he quotes as saying that, in their study of the social structure of England and Wales, no social classes could be found.[12] Again, we read that W. Sombart, while recognizing that "fairly definable large groups, estate and class," do exist, there are no social strata in our society.[13]

When social classes, as "social strata" in society, are not admitted to have existence, other analyzable divisions of society are identified, albeit by different names. For example, in labeling "social classes" as mere "heuristic constructs," Cox appears to be satisfied with a broad two-fold division of population into "estates" and "political classes," the former a category borrowed from Sombart and meaning "large unions based upon a community of living, and organically integrated in a community," [14] and further characterized by Cox as "social status strata, which ordinarily develop in relatively static social orders," and which "may be correctly employed to mean status, degree of rank, position in the world, state, public, property, profession, social class, and so on." [15] Thus estate, though not found (so it is said) "in modern, capitalist society," is just another ambiguous term, a kind of catchall concept, capable of including, among other categories, "social class," which had previously been denied existence. The term "political class," for which Cox says "the designation economic class might have been used," turns out not to be a "class" at all, but "a power group which tends to be organized for conflict," and "is always class conscious." This so-called "class" is by definition a "party," an action body, which may or may not be identified with social class, though it has often been given some such designation as "ruling class" or "revolutionary class." [16]

If further definition of class and sub-classes is needed, perhaps that given by Davis will suffice: *Class* is *"a type of stratum in which the positions are acquired at birth by succession from the parents but*

---

[11] Oliver C. Cox, "Estates, Social Classes, and Political Classes," *Am. Sociol. Rev.*, Vol. 10, No. 4, August, 1945, p. 467.
[12] A. M. Carr-Saunders and D. C. Jones, *A Survey of the Social Structure of England and Wales*, London, Oxford University Press, 1927.
[13] Cox, "Estates, Social Classes, and Political Classes," *op. cit.*, pp. 466-467.
[14] Werner Sombart, *Der Modern Kapitalismus*, London, T. F. Unwin, 1913, Vol. 2, p. 1091.
[15] Cox, "Estates, Social Classes, and Political Classes," *op. cit.*, p. 467.
[16] For our treatment of "party," see the next chapter.

may be altered later by achievement or lack of it. The child acquires, by virtue of his parents' class position, certain advantages or disadvantages in the competition for specific statuses." [17] The last sentence, by referring to how the individual's chances in the competitive struggle for different statuses are conditioned by his acquisition—or probably more accurately speaking, by ascription to him—of an initial status through a definite position inherited from his parents, shows one way in which class position affects status. In other words, one is born into a class—that of his family—and to the status which that class has had accorded to it by the defining society. If one is to change his class status he must perforce change his class position.

Types of Classes.—If the concept of class has reference to a mass phenomenon rather than to an organized, associational, or communal grouping, "it must denote a particular state of affairs objectively ascertainable as well as connoting attributes of the state of affairs it denotes," [18] and it should be possible to identify demonstrable characteristics of classes and to construct a typology of classes therefrom. In other words, if classes exist as objective phenomena, they should be capable of differentiation into types according to recognized indices or characteristic features. As remarked earlier, the criteria by which "classes" have been demarcated have been subjective as well as objective. They have been speculative as well as factual, and particularistic rather than universal in their applicability.

Since class is one kind of stratum in a hierarchy of socially stratified positions, we may expect to find the criteria of differentiation in the body of "moral sentiments" which normally govern exchange and authoritarian-power relations, and which reside in the institutional pattern of the social system. By "moral sentiments" is meant those evaluational judgments which a society makes and tends to enforce with respect to socially approved and desired functions and which, being evaluative and thus discriminating, constitute a normative pattern which Parsons calls "the scale of stratification." [19] How functions and how corresponding functional positions and performances will be "ranked" on a given scale of stratification will depend on which functions and positions will be "rated" higher and which lower than others at any time in a given society. Different societies and a given society at different periods in its life history will have differing scales of stratification.

---

[17] Davis, "A Conceptual Analysis of Stratification," *op. cit.*, p. 321. The italics are by the present authors.

[18] Simpson, "Class Analysis: What Class Is Not," *op. cit.*, p. 834.

[19] Talcott Parsons, "An Analytical Approach to the Theory of Social Stratification," *Am. J. Sociol.*, Vol. 45, No. 6, May, 1940, p. 844.

Since classes are not organic entities like families, associations, etc., their distinguishing marks will have to be sought in the behavior of persons and groups as they interact with each other in terms of the above-mentioned moral sentiments and by the symbols of class status as these are defined and held in a particular social system. Leaving the subject of so-called "class behavior" for treatment in the next section, we will give attention briefly to the symbols that are generally emphasized as indices of class status.

One fairly clear mark of position, and corresponding class status, is "level of living." According to this criterion, one's level of living more or less automatically "places" in the same class other individuals and the groups of individuals who display similar behavior and who employ similar level-of-living symbols. Classes may, then, be typed by the different levels of living manifested by their members. This measure of class distinction is so largely economic in nature that classes so differentiated are commonly referred to as "economic classes." Some students of class, such as Karl Marx and his disciples, regard economic differentials as the chief, if not the only, marks of class. Max Weber distinguished the following types of classes in economic terms:

(a) A class is a "property class" when class status for its members is primarily determined by the differentiation of property holdings; (b) a class is an "acquisition class" when the class situation of its members is primarily determined by their opportunity for the exploitation of services on the market; (c) the "social class" structure is composed of the plurality of class statuses between which an interchange of individuals on a personal basis or in the course of generations is readily possible and typically observable. . . . The concepts of class and class status as such designate only the fact of identity or similarity in the typical situation in which a given individual and many others find their interests defined. In principle control over different combinations of consumers goods, means of production, investments, capital funds or marketable abilities constitute class statuses which are different with each variation and combination. Only persons who are completely unskilled, without property and dependent on employment without regular occupation, are in a strictly identical class status. Transitions from one class status to another vary greatly in fluidity and in the ease with which an individual can enter the class. Hence the unity of "social" classes is highly relative and variable.[20]

It is probably not so much the acquisition and possession of wealth and the display of the symbols of wealth that make for class distinc-

---

[20] From *Max Weber: The Theory of Social and Economic Organization*, edited by Talcott Parsons, pp. 424-425. Copyright 1947 by Oxford University Press, New York.

tions as it is the concentration of these into the hands of a relatively few people, who, because of their possessions, come to regard themselves as superior to the non-possessors. This feeling of superiority, with correlative feelings of inferiority on the part of non-possessors, often gives the possessors a sense of power over the non-possessors and thus establishes a basis for inequality in their respective statuses. Moreover, it is only in cultures that accord prestige to ownership and to the things that ownership can provide that class differences can generate and thrive, and these differences confer unequal statuses on owners and non-owners. To be sure, it is a fine question as to which is cause and which effect—the situation or the defining culture. In all probability the condition arose and was followed by modification of culture, which, in turn, tended to become dominated by the higher status groups who molded it to suit themselves and thereby intrenched themselves within it. The society that has the ideal of equality strives at least sporadically to modify the inequalities upon which class statuses rest.

Economic position is a factor of varying importance, however, in determining class status. To attempt to analyze classes under the two-fold classification of bourgeois and proletariat is to oversimplify the matter. To classify economic groups as either owners or non-owners, employers or wage-earners, etc., is to overlook such categories as independent enterprisers who employ no labor, office and white-collar workers, and employed professional people who may or may not identify themselves with the wage-earning groups. It also includes employees and government officials, the unemployed, whose interests may be identical with or may run counter to those of the proletariat, the agricultural owner-operators, who have rarely joined forces with the business interests of the urban centers, and agricultural tenants, who know little of and probably care less about the interests of the industrial workers. Such divisions, based on economic existence, do not tell the whole story of how and why people behave as they do in their interaction for status. Considerations other than economic will receive attention in other parts of this chapter.

The So-called "Class Struggle."—When individuals or groups act according to what they think are the norms of their class they are generally acting in their own self-interest. They are interested primarily in maintaining their status in their class or in attaining to a status of a higher order in a class above them. This is the objective of most of their economic behavior. As means to that end they may seek prestige and recognition through whatever seems to be required, such as conspicuous use of leisure, conspicuous consumption,[21] philanthropic gestures, "playing the social game," and their counterparts, as defined in the class structure. These are the symbolic devices utilized to the end of enhancing or retaining class status.[22]

But the "class struggle," as represented in the literature on the subject, is very different from individual and group striving for status. In fact, we are prepared to assert that economic classes, as such, do not struggle, for the simple reason that, as we have said, classes do not exist as closed, organic systems,[23] and therefore lack the group consciousness, organization, unity of purpose, and the other prerequisites for effective conflict. It was due principally to the writings of Karl Marx and Friedrich Engels, in the middle of the last century, that the notion of the struggle of classes for supremacy was promulgated and furnished the ideology for present-day Communism. They said:

The history of all hitherto existing society is the history of class struggle. Freeman and slave, patrician and plebeian, lord and serf, guild-master and journeyman, oppressor and oppressed, stood in constant opposition to one another, carried on an uninterrupted, now hidden, now open fight, a fight that each time ended either in a revolution, reconstitution of society at large, or in common ruin of the contending classes. . . . The modern bourgeois society that has sprouted from the ruins of feudal society has not done away with class antagonisms. It has but established new classes, new conditions of oppression, new forms of struggle in place of old ones. Our epoch, the epoch of the bourgeoisie, possesses, however, this distinctive feature: it has simplified the class antagonisms. Society as a whole is more and more splitting up into two great battle camps, into two great classes directly facing each other: Bourgeoisie and Proletariat.[24]

According to the doctrinaire Marxian ideology, a clear dichotomy exists between the exploiters and the exploited of the world and it is held to be the mission of the latter "class" to wage an unremitting fight against the former "class" to the end that a "classless" social order may be established. The instrument chosen as the means to this goal is worldwide revolution. Among the many criticisms that can

---

[21] See: Thorstein Veblen, *The Theory of the Leisure Class,* New York, The Viking Press (B. W. Huebsch), 1922.

[22] Numerous scales that attempt to measure socio-economic status have been devised. For bibliography, see F. Stuart Chapin, *Experimental Designs in Sociological Research,* New York, Harper & Bros., 1947, pp. 152-153.

[23] The only exceptions to this statement are castes, slavery, and a feudal type of economic organization, and these forms do not exist in Western civilization. Moreover, it seems to be characteristic of these structures that, where and when they do exist, their members are accommodated to their positions and "struggle" little or not at all.

[24] *Communist Manifesto,* Chicago, Chas. H. Kerr & Co., 1917, pp. 12-13. See also Karl Marx, *Capital* (English translation), Chicago, Chas. H. Kerr Co., 1906-1909.

be made against this principle, a very important one for us to consider is that of the underlying misconception of the nature and function of classes. That classes exist, we are agreed, but that they are capable of carrying on a conflict as entities, we must deny. What actually happens is that not classes, per se, but ideological groups, in the form of parties, cliques, sects, associations, unions, and the like, organize and interact with each other, competitively and in conflict, as representatives of what is called the "class struggle." [25] Thus, we read:

Consequently, each social class tends to stimulate many conflict groups each of which appeals to the same class comrades and claims to be the only and true representative of the real "class interest." This necessitates a choice between rival conflict groups, creates uncertainty and indifference in the minds of many, and leads to intensified campaigning for the sympathy and allegiance of everyone, even those not belonging to the same social class. Yet, the co-existence of conflict groups prevents any of them from becoming identical with a social class. First, lower classes provide followers for conflict groups of the upper classes, whereas individuals of upper classes join conflict groups of the lower or middle classes, mostly as leaders or financiers. Second, indifference to the functions of the conflict groups, reluctance to accept the obligations and sacrifices of conflict organizations, or disappointment with the slow development of the movement, its policies or leaders, prevents the full identification of all class fellows with a conflict group. Third, the power of conflict groups or the economic dependence of the lower and middle classes leads to a varying degree of intimidation, creating passive followers. Fourth, other social groups, not originated by the class structure, limit the feeling of class unity and reduce participation in conflict groups. Finally, persons whose class interest is divided because they live not in but at the outer fringe of a class, or between two classes, may be unable to define their class position and thus refrain from any affiliation. In spite of these variations between social classes and conflict groups, each purposive group recruits the majority of its followers from one social class. Both are inseparably interrelated, thrive and fall together, as long as the growth of conflict groups is not suppressed by the state.[26]

Because inequalities between classes are largely those due to inequities in the distribution of wealth and of bargaining power, they mean corresponding inequalities of educational opportunity, of availability of medical services, of legal protection, of recreation, and of employment and access to the means of livelihood. Many of the conditions productive of these inequalities are preventable. In order to

[25] Arthur Schweitzer, "Ideological Groups," *Am. Sociol. Rev.*, Vol. 9, No. 4, August, 1944, pp. 415-426.
[26] *Ibid.*

continue, a society which tolerates such diversities of life and labor will be dominated by violent contrasts. Its culture will be effete and futile for it will not have its roots in a common life participated in by everybody. It will be subject to divisive invidious comparisons and antagonisms. Though classes have been termed accommodation mechanisms, they, like most accommodated population elements, easily may and frequently do furnish the rationale for and the participants in conflict.

Since the so-called "class struggle" is a struggle for status, by which is meant a struggle for the achievement and exercise of the rights, privileges, prestige, and power that are supposed to inhere in a given class structure, and since the classes themselves are not equipped for waging the struggle, the contest is drawn between groups that are initiated for the purpose. In view of the fact that the members of the lower-class segments of the population are usually the most disadvantaged, it is generally the champions of the interests of the "common man," "the workers," "the forgotten people," who enter the lists in their behalf and oppose the so-called "plutocrats," "the capitalists," "the exploiters," "the oppressors." The interaction that ensues may assume any one of several forms of conflict, ranging from the boycott and the strike, on the one hand, to revolution, on the other. Space will allow for only a brief consideration of one such pattern of conflict.

Industrial Conflict.—Industrial-group alignments have their genesis in the selective process of competition. They are mainly organized around economic interests and sentiments connected with occupation. On the one side is the capitalistic, employing, or entrepreneur group and on the other side a sizable group of organized workers and a great mass of unorganized, mostly unskilled, workers. The first two groups have organized in order to deal with each other more advantageously, whereas the third group remains a relatively inarticulate, but by no means insignificant, factor in the industrial order. Between the organized and the unorganized labor groups there is suspicion and covert antagonism, with occasional outbursts of open hostility, especially when the latter group interferes with the bargaining between employers and the organized labor unions. Both organized groups are organized and equipped for conflict. In fact, they are primarily conflict groups and the interaction between them is one of almost constant strife.[27]

---

27 For information on the organizations of employers and workers consult the following references: E. Wight Bakke, *Mutual Survival: The Goal of Unions and Management*, New

Economic dissatisfactions naturally promote organizations of labor for the purpose of correcting them. This fact projects the whole movement into the larger social situation with its prejudices and antipathies, its disputes and settlements, and its changes in status and control. Sometimes labor and employers can get together and build up social machinery to effect an adjustment of differences and thereby reduce unrest. It is in labor organizations, however, under conditions generally prevailing in the industrial field, that the fighting pattern is developed. Organizations like the American Federation of Labor, the Congress of Industrial Organizations, and the Canadian Trades and Labor Council are conflict groups whose main function is bargaining. By employing the devices of obstruction and forced unemployment they exert pressure on the employers to gain their ends. Battles lost, restraining court injunctions and decisions, adverse legislation, and the like, become traditions and are carried in the memories of labor group members, feeding their fears, restlessness, and resentment. They enter into the thinking of the whole labor organization and become foci of attention and the centers of collective sentiments and attitudes. Group consciousness is intensified through agitation and fresh outbreaks of hostilities. Rankling under the sting of numerous defeats and ever-sensitive about its inferior status, labor continues to rely upon the traditional means of combat as the basis of its behavior pattern.

Face to face with a crisis, organized workers fall back upon their traditional mechanisms for fighting employers. Of these, the strike is the one most commonly used. It is one of the "old habits of the unions." The strike is a collective and temporary quitting of work during normal work-time to coerce employers or others who are regarded as blocking the wishes of the organized workers.[28] It is in

---

Haven, Yale University Press, 1946; C. E. Bonnett, *Employers' Associations in the United States*, New York, The Macmillan Co., 1922; R. S. Brookings, *Industrial Ownership*, New York, The Macmillan Co., 1925; J. G. Brooks, *Labor's Challenge to the Social Order*, New York, The Macmillan Co., 1923; L. J. Ducoff and M. J. Hagood, *Labor Force Definition and Measurement*, New York, Social Science Research Council, 1947; W. Z. Foster, *American Trade Unionism*, New York, International Publishers, 1947; H. Harris, *American Labor*, New Haven, Yale University Press, 1939; E. Levinson, *Labor on the March*, New York, Harper & Bros., 1938; H. A. Logan, *The History of Trade-Union Organization in Canada*, Chicago, University of Chicago Press, 1928; H. A. Millis and R. E. Montgomery, *Economics of Labor*, Vol. 3, *Organized Labor*, New York, McGraw-Hill Book Co., Inc., 1939; S. H. Patterson, *Social Aspects of Industry*, New York, McGraw-Hill Book Co., Inc., 3rd ed., 1943, Chs. 13-14; T. Veblen, *The Engineers and the Price System*, New York, The Viking Press, 1933, Chs. 2-3; T. Veblen, *The Theory of Business Enterprise*, New York, Charles Scribner's Sons, 1936, especially Ch. 6; T. Veblen, *The Vested Interests and the State of the Industrial Arts*, New York, The Viking Press (B. W. Huebsch), 1919, Sec. 5; T. Veblen, *Absentee Ownership and Business Enterprise in Recent Times*, New York, The Viking Press (B. W. Huebsch), 1923, Chs. 6, 8, 9.

[28] Strikes may be aimed at (1) employers, (2) non-union workers, (3) rival unions, (4) objectionable foremen, (5) non-union materials, (6) jurisdictional disputes, or (7) in

the working-group mores. Usually, when the conditions are ripe and the forces are lined up ready for an outbreak of hostilities, the strike pattern becomes operative almost automatically. It represents an outburst of inhibited feelings through familiar channels of expression. As a rule, the behavior is injudicious and irrational, spends itself in resentful and sometimes violent reactions, and more often than not ends in futility, defeat, and despair.

As a weapon of offense, the strike is used as a means to an end, the end being the securing of better conditions of life and labor. As a weapon of defense, it is an attempt to display labor's power and to give expression to its defiance. A strike is not simply a method of bargaining. It is a mass phenomenon controlled by basic human desires and intentions which will emerge in action even though the union may know in advance that no great gain in bargaining power will accrue from it. The strike is a frame of mind.[29]

For a long time the public has stood in a precarious position when there was an economic struggle in process. Though not a combatant, it has often been the chief sufferer and has recently taken more than a passive interest in the oft-repeated conflicts. The force of public opinion is often the deciding factor in the settlement of an industrial dispute. Recognizing this fact, it is part of the technique of each side to discredit the other in the court of public opinion as well as to strive to win moral support for its own cause. Propaganda, therefore, is directed as much to arousing the fears and prejudices of the public as it is to waging direct attacks upon the opponent's position. Epithets, conflict myths, and subversive propaganda that tend to discredit the opposition are counted on to be as decisive in the conflict as are those more direct mechanisms in the nature of threats of violence, hostile demonstrations, employment of strike-breakers and spies, the use of the boycott and the black list, the injunction,[30] and

sympathy with other striking union workers. Varying reasons are given by unions for calling a strike. They represent rationalizations, for the most part, rather than real reasons.

[29] See E. T. Hiller, *The Strike*, Chicago, University of Chicago Press, 1928. This is the best sociological treatment of the strike. See also S. Crowther, *Why Men Strike*, New York, Doubleday, Doran & Co., 1920; J. I. Griffin, *Strikes*, New York, Columbia University Press, 1939; G. W. Hartmann and T. Newcomb, *Industrial Conflict: A Psychological Interpretation*, New York, The Cordon Co., 1939; Almont Lindsey, *The Pullman Strike*, Chicago, University of Chicago Press, 1942; M. Olds, *The High Cost of Strikes*, New York, G. P. Putnam's Sons, 1921; Patterson, *Social Aspects of Industry*, Chapter 16; Samuel Yellen, *American Labor Struggles*, New York, Harcourt, Brace & Co., 1936.

[30] See Clinch Calkins, *Spy Overhead: The Story of Industrial Espionage*, New York, Harcourt, Brace & Co., 1937; F. Frankfurter and N. Greene, *The Labor Injunction*, New York, The Macmillan Co., 1930; Leo Huberman, *The Labor Spy Racket*, New York, Modern Age Books, 1937; R. Hunter, *Violence and the Labor Movement*, New York, The Macmillan Co., 1914; H. W. Laidler, *Boycotts and the Labor Struggle*, New York, John Lane Co., 1914; J. F. Scott and G. Homans, "Reflections on the Wildcat Strikes," *Am. Sociol. Rev.*, Vol. 12, No. 3, June, 1947, pp. 278-287; A. G. Taylor, *Labor Problems and Labor Law*, New York, Prentice-Hall, Inc., 1938; Leo Wolman, *The Boycott in American Trade Unions*, Baltimore, Johns Hopkins University Press, 1916.

revolution. Frequently, the latter devices react unfavorably on the side making use of them.

Governmental action is at least one point in economic conflict at which the public, as "the party of the third part," enters as an active participant in the struggle. A government, however, usually lines up with the employers against the striking employees. While governments are ostensibly committed to safeguarding the life, liberty, and property of all their citizens, in practice they usually protect only property, especially the property of employers. The assumption is that the greatest public interest is served by such an alignment.

Labor unions have tried various methods of enlisting the public on the side of the workers but without much success. Two of these methods are the boycott and the union label.[31] There is a social boycott as well as an economic one and both sides in the conflict make use of it. There may be a boycott of a company's plant, of non-union tools, of social institutions such as the church and the press, of merchants who handle non-union-made goods, of welfare activities of the companies, and of persons in the community thought to be unfriendly to labor. The workers' use of the boycott is more overt and direct than the employers', but in both cases it may be a powerful force.

The union label has been regarded as an ideal weapon—an ideal far from realization in effectiveness. The label is a mark placed upon goods manufactured by organized labor under union standards of production. It implies living wages, acceptable working conditions, satisfactory hours, and an absence of sweated or juvenile labor. Its potential effectiveness rests largely on the publicity given to the insignia so that workers, their families, and the public may become acquainted with the weapon. Another technique of striking workmen is what is called "picketing." Primarily directed against the employer, it aims to prevent strike-breakers from entering the picketed establishment and thereby giving aid to the employer. It is used also to impress the public with labor's plight and to acquaint the public with their cause.[32] Though these mechanisms of collective force may be peaceful in plan and execution, they are fraught with the danger of violence. The methods of both sides are intended to serve the double purpose of winning the struggle by embarrassing or by damaging the opposition, and of enlisting the sympathy and support of the public.

---

[31] A. T. Helbing, *The Departments of the American Federation of Labor*, Baltimore, Johns Hopkins University Press, 1931, Ch. 3.
[32] John A. Fitch, *The Causes of Industrial Unrest*, New York, Harper & Bros., pp. 220-221; Hiller, *Social Relations and Structures*, pp. 115-122.

The Effects of Industrial Conflict.—The cessation of hostilities and the resumption of industrial production after a strike does not mean that the conflict between employers and employees is at an end. It usually means that the strikers have been forced by loss of morale, depletion of strike funds, or the pressure of public opinion or governmental interference, to withdraw for the time being and to accept the terms laid down. Very rarely does a strike end with better feeling on the two sides and a real desire of both elements in the conflict to let bygones be bygones and to get down to business on a basis of good will and cooperation.[33] Each defeat is a body blow to labor morale, resulting in another period of depression of spirit, agitation, and restlessness, and the revival of group-consciousness and the anger pattern before the stage of overt hostilities emerges once more. Then the vicious cycle is repeated.[34] However, numerous companies have made a successful *rapprochement* with their labor forces by recognizing their unions and by other means that have been accepted by both sides as satisfactory.

Through their unions, organized workers have gained better conditions of work, reasonable hours, and more satisfactory wages. These and other values come to have a group significance, and trade-union attitudes are constructed with reference to them. The conflict between the ideals of the unions and the interests of employers is incidental to bargaining. The unions are organized primarily as business organizations and throughout their history have fought to compel employers to recognize them as business and bargaining entities. They have developed a technique of group action.

This struggle for recognition has developed a group-consciousness on the part of labor with respect to status and to control in industry. This means, of course, that the personality of the individual worker is invariably bound up with the interests of his union, that he tends to identify the group struggle with his own status and personal objectives. His standing as a person, as the head of a family, and as a citizen of the community, depends upon the outcome of the labor-group conflict. This is not only a matter of security and recognition in the specific job, which might conceivably be left to the operation of the largely impersonal competitive process, but is also a question of deciding who shall control industry, what interests shall dominate, and how the outcome of all this shall affect the status of the workers, individually and collectively, in the larger inclusive society.

---

[33] Hiller, *Social Relations and Structures*, Ch. 17.
[34] *Ibid.*, pp. 5-11, 216-217; Alvin H. Hansen, "Cycle of Strikes," *Am. Ec. Rev.*, Vol. 11, December, 1921, pp. 616-621.

As to the effects on the job itself, the struggle has tended to slow up production because of restrictions on output imposed by the unions, time lost through strikes and lockouts, wastes of production and distribution due to lack of coordination between management and labor, duplication of services in response to union demands, and the waste of manpower incident thereto.[35] Moreover, as a result of the pressure brought to bear upon industry by organized labor through the use of the strike and other bargaining methods, and by unorganized labor through the practice of rapid labor turnover, the job, for all that it implies in the way of wages, hours, and conditions of employment, has ceased largely to be something to be fought for; the job has become more than just a source of livelihood; it has become a means by which the workers may share in the control of industry.

The effects of industrial conflict divide themselves into those that affect the community and those that affect the workers in their relation to the community. In a general way industrial conflicts leave their marks on the communities in which the overt expression of conflict occurs. Community forces tend to be divided into factions and the struggle is likely to affect every phase of community life for a long time afterward. Racial and nationality-group antipathies, religious prejudices, and political differences tend to be identified with the struggle going on in industry. Sometimes veritable civil war ensues. Many scars of battle remain, and the wounds to personal and group prestige are slow to heal. The effects of these battles upon the workers in their relation to the community are varied, depending upon such factors as their numerical strength, their racial composition, and their prior status in the community. Even though many people have a theory of industrial relations which holds to the principle of labor's rights, equality of opportunity, equal pay for equal work, and participation in industry, when it comes to undergoing the inconveniences, they follow the line of least resistance to let their more personal interests overshadow their social ideals. This usually means that, aside from a few intellectuals who stand with labor not only in theory but in practice, the labor group may find itself in opposition to the majority of its fellow citizens.

Accommodation in Industrial Relations.—As we have seen, interaction in industrial relations involves the interests and activities of three groups: the owners of the means of production and of distribution, represented by the shareholders, the bondholders, managers, etc.;

---

[35] Stuart Chase, *The Tragedy of Waste*, New York, The Macmillan Co., 1925; Marshall Olds, *The High Cost of Strikes*, New York, G. P. Putnam's Sons, 1921.

the industrial workers, represented by the wage earners, organized and unorganized, and the labor surplus; and "the public." In the resolution of the differences among them, the aims of these groups must be realized in some measure if there is not to be economic chaos. To the end that there be some semblance of order, efficiency, and stability in industry, various forms of accommodation of differences have been evolved. Some have been reasonably successful in effecting temporary surcease of animosity and overt conflict to troubled industries, but none of them has succeeded in effecting complete and lasting assimilation of interests, ambitions, and requirements of the three major groups concerned. Since neither side, unless it be "the public," seems disposed to be conciliatory, except possibly in emergencies such as war, there seem to be but four principal ways of accommodation of differences open. These are compromise, deliberation, superordination-subordination, and participation.

Compromise is the usual form of accommodation proposed by "the public" in its organized capacity, the State. With the passing of small competing industries and the appearance of collective bargaining between organized employers and organized labor, the traditional governmental policy of *laissez faire* was no longer feasible. This meant that modern governments have come to exercise some supervision over the activities of industry and the relations between employers and employees.

The chief mechanisms used for the adjustment of industrial differences are "trade agreements and arbitration within industry and also mediation, arbitration, and investigation on the part of the state and Federal governments. In industrial, as well as international, relations, the prevention rather than the settlement of conflicts is receiving more attention." [36] Recent federal legislation in the United States has made compulsory investigation and arbitration practically obligatory upon industry and labor alike. While at one time these compulsory mechanisms were looked upon as means of last resort, they are now largely mandatory. Their necessity is argued on the grounds that strikes, lockouts, and other methods of conflict are wasteful, costly, and, most important, injurious to public interest. Experience since the last war has made the public, through the agency of government, exceedingly short-tempered with recurrent disputes and work stoppages in key industries like coal, steel, and transportation, held to be essential to national security. If voluntary negotiation, arbitration, and compromise were not to be depended upon, then compulsion had

---

[36] Patterson, *Social Aspects of Industry*, p. 431.

to be resorted to. Although certain benefits inhere in these mechanisms, both voluntary and compulsory, they usually do little more than
bring temporary relief of industrial tensions. Decisions arrived at
through the voluntary employment of arbitration or mediation are of
the nature of compromises and may be acceptable, for the time being,
to the two sides. If a compulsory decision follows the judicious weigh-
ing of all the facts it, too, may be in the form of a compromise, albeit
a forced one, but such compromise may be expected to do little to allay
the feelings of the contending parties; it may effect a truce and nothing more. On the other hand, if a decision gives to one side all that
it demands and compels the other side to capitulate, it does not represent a compromise; it merely redefines the already existing superordinate-subordinate relationship.

What has been said about mediation and voluntary arbitration
applies to the use of deliberation as a means of achieving accommodation. Sometimes the disputants come together, with or without outside mediation, for the purpose of deliberating upon and settling their
differences in their own way and in a spirit of mutual respect. Mediation is neither compulsory nor judicial; it is simply friendly advice.
In the case of industrial arbitration, however, there is a board, person,
or court for the purpose of making an investigation and submitting a
decision which, in voluntary arbitration, may be accepted or not by
the contending parties. In either case the accommodation, if one is
made, grows out of deliberation, or negotiation.

It has been pointed out that many strikes end in failure. This
usually means that the defeated workers must accept the terms dictated by the employers or by an intervening governmental agency. If
the dispute is settled by compulsory methods and the decision is
against labor and its demands, the result is the same. The former
superordinate-subordinate relations of employer to employees remain
as before, or perhaps to the greater disadvantage of the defeated party.
Short of a successful revolution or general strike the respective positions of the two groups in industry generally are not permanently
affected by temporary readjustments. As long as employers control
the means of production and are so commonly supported by the laws,
as also by courts and other governmental agencies, there is little likelihood that the superordinate-subordinate form of accommodation will
be permanently affected in the industrial field in its entirety. The
great hope of the workers of escaping finally from their unsatisfactory
subordinate position in industry lies, for the majority, through participation, and for a minority through revolution and the seizure of
control.

Participation is the final form of the process of accommodation. It involves a working arrangement between employers and employees, each allowed to retain his distinctive vocational position and to perform his particular function, but with mutual tolerance and understanding, and with each fulfilling his role as partner and co-operator in a common enterprise. It is a new definition of the division of labor based on the principle of democracy. Before this is possible, both sides in the industrial relation must recognize that the other side is made up of human beings and that neither side has a monopoly on virtue or idealism. When this common definition of the situation has been reached, and only then, is the way open for mutual good will and for the adoption of a policy of joint ownership and management. Where participation has been tried in the form of shop committees, employees' representation, stock ownership, profit sharing, etc., it has had different degrees of success. Opinions differ as to the value of such schemes, although the general plan of promoting participation has gained headway among employers in the United States in the last several decades.[37] Wherever the scheme is being experimented with it is indicative of a movement in the direction of greater democracy in industry. When we have gone as far in intergroup interaction as to work out a plan whereby the differences tend to fade into insignificance and, in the light of understanding and a desire for fair dealing, the members of the divergent groups come to share in mutual responsibilities and in the enjoyment of common satisfactions, we discover that we have gone about as far as we can in the direction of settling differences and solving conflicts without getting over into something different, namely, revolution.[38]

Other Areas of Economic Conflict and Accommodation.—Economic conflict and accommodation are not confined to the area of interests we have been discussing. Not only is conflict waged and resolved in accommodation between employers and employees, but also between organized and unorganized workers, landlords and tenants, farmers and vested interests, producers, consumers, and middlemen, and between all of these and what is usually referred to as

---

[37] See: C. C. Balderston, *Profit Sharing for Wage Earners*, New York, Industrial Relations Counselors, 1937; Chester I. Barnard, *The Functions of the Executive*, Cambridge, Harvard University Press, 1938, Chs. 5, 11; Ralph C. Davis, *Industrial Organization and Management*, New York, Harper & Bros., 1940, Ch. 26; Burleigh B. Gardner, *Human Relations in Industry*, Chicago, Richard D. Irwin, 1945; W. E. Moore, *Industrial Relations and the Social Order*, New York, The Macmillan Co., 1946, Chs. 9-10; S. Howard Patterson, *Social Aspects of Industry*, New York, McGraw-Hill Book Co., Inc., 1943, Chs. 18-19; F. J. Roethlisberger and W. J. Dickson, *Management and the Worker*, Cambridge, Harvard University Press, 1939, Parts II, III, V; W. C. Teagle, *Employee Representation and Collective Bargaining*, New York, American Management Association, 1935.

[38] See Chapter 25 for a discussion of the revolutionary type of social movement.

"the general public." Among these groups conflict goes on unceasingly—much of the time covertly, some of the time overtly. In all these situations the fundamental motive forces and behavior patterns are much the same. The public, as "consumer," has been persuaded to organize consumers' leagues, cooperatives, and other societies for the sake of self-defense against profiteering, especially in the necessities of life. All parties have at one time or another sought protection in legislation and the courts, but almost invariably these latter have favored the interests representing the largest capital investments and hence the greatest power.

Since groups with special class interests and statuses to maintain have been thought of, ordinarily, as accommodated groups, it may be well to consider briefly some of the other typical forms of the accommodative process and the mechanisms employed to establish and to maintain accommodated relationships. To some extent the ecological process of segregation serves the purpose of establishing distance between the groups, but, since spatial distance is difficult to maintain in a mobile, changing society, the factor of social distance becomes one of great significance. "Expressions like 'upper and lower classes,' 'social promotion,' 'N. N. is a climber,' 'his social position is very high,' 'right and left party,' 'there is a great social distance,' and so on, are quite commonly used in conversation, as well as in economic, political, and sociological works. All these expressions indicate that there is something which could be styled 'social space.' " [39] They also indicate that a person's or group's position, status, rank, and so on, are matters of social distance and that their standing and integrity, as representative of class membership, are likewise determined largely by the social distance intervening between them and others, especially others of a different stratum. Not infrequently class-conscious persons and groups adopt some one or more symbolic mechanisms for the purpose of creating and fortifying the lines between them and others. These mechanisms may be the immaterial ones of *hauteur,* snobbishness, titles of rank, specialization in certain forms of etiquette, salutation, speech, and the like, or they may be visible marks of differentiation in the form of uniforms, insignia, crests, exclusive societies and clubs, high church and low church, and the like. These and other evidences of "class difference" serve to "show a person his place" and to see that he stays there.

The existence of classes means, as we have said, a gradation of social levels in terms of position and status. Of necessity, this involves

---

[39] P. A. Sorokin, *Social Mobility,* New York, Harper & Bros., 1927, p. 3.

the superordination of some and the subordination of others. How this has come about we have already seen. In conversation one frequently hears the expression "rank and file," which, in military parlance, means the leaders and the led, those who order and those who obey. In all societies such divisions are to be found between those who exercise authority and those who do obeisance to that authority. The expression does not mean that "the file" has no rank, no status; it simply means that the file is of a lower order, that of the subordinate. Other mechanisms devised for maintaining the superordinate-subordinate division include rules and regulations, theories of divine right and of hereditary rule, the practice of charity and the establishment of hospitals, schools, and other philanthropies by one "class" for the benefit of the "lower classes," the perpetuation of the notion that equal opportunities exist for all who will exert themselves, the diversion of attention away from the "class struggle" to conflicts in the political, racial, national, or sectarian spheres, and the idealization of a future world of equality, fraternity, and universal brotherhood.

The Weakening of Class Barriers.—There are societies in which the class lines are drawn with considerable exactness and across which it is practically impossible for members to move. Though the caste system in India seems to be weakening at certain points, and though much has been done in the last half century to eliminate the religious observance of caste distinctions and to liberalize Hinduism and encourage social reform, the caste system remains today, after many centuries of turbulent history, deeply imbedded in the mores of millions of people. Also, wherever ruling aristocracies and aristocracies of wealth have developed they tend to constitute closed groups between which and other groups intermarriage and social intercourse are practically prohibited. Under such conditions, if a member of an inferior group succeeds in raising himself to the cultural level of the superior group, he is likely to find the social recognition of the superordinate group withheld from him.[40]

With the fall of the Bastille in the French Revolution, there fell a social order which had been based on privilege and tyranny. To replace it, there arose a new social class based on greater equalization of opportunity, the so-called "middle class." Though the achievements of the French Revolution have since been seriously jeopardized

---

[40] See: S. Sighele, *Psychologie des Sectes*, Paris, M. Giard et Cie., 1898, pp. 42-51. A translated portion of this citation is to be found in R. E. Park and E. W. Burgess, *Introduction to the Science of Sociology*, Chicago, University of Chicago Press, 1921, 1924, pp. 202-207.

by the rise of a new order of privilege and power based on ownership and control of capital wealth and the centralization of economic domination, nevertheless many of the gains of that historic event have not been lost, for there exists today, in most western societies, a large middle class—more properly middle classes—which serves, according to democratic ideology, as the open sesame for those of ambition and energy in the lower classes, and acts in many ways as a buffer between the aristocracy of wealth, on the one side, and the proletariat on the other side. To a great extent this middle class, regarded as being numerically strong, but actually unmeasurable statistically and considerably divided within itself, holds the balance of power between the upper and lower classes. To it the submerged classes look, more or less in vain, for support in their collective struggles against the intrenched position of the rich, and to it the masters of wealth and power hold out inducements, largely political in nature, in order to keep it pacified and "in line." Since large numbers of the middle-class society hope to succeed in penetrating, at some time, the exclusive precincts of *la haute société,* they pay much attention to imitating the ways and manners of life of that society, including "conspicuous consumption," the cultivation of snobbish exclusiveness, and the pursuit of higher education for the sake of future aggrandizement rather than for learning.

All along the line of differentiated classes, from the bottom to next to the top, there is a struggle to rise from one level to a higher one. In the more democratic societies the way is nominally open for such vertical mobility.[41] It is the belief that anyone may climb this "social ladder" that makes endurable for so many persons the conditions of economic insecurity, political uncertainty, legal inequality, and social disorganization in which they live. But, in the last analysis, the criterion by which to judge the accommodation of class differences will be the extent to which all members of a society, high and low, rich and poor, officials and ruled, etc., participate in and contribute to the common good. No society can exist at a dead level. While it is the professed aim of the communist and other radical groups to establish a classless society,[42] this may be regarded as a myth.

The Life-Cycle in the Determination of Status.—In addition to a positional status which he shares, consciously or unconsciously, with others of his class, an individual's position and status within the framework of the institutional structure and cultural norms of his

---

[41] See: Sorokin, *Social Mobility,* Chs. 16-19.
[42] See: Marx and Engels, *Communist Manifesto,* p. 42.

group are also partially determined by his age at any given time during his entire life cycle. It must be pointed out at once, however, that when we speak of one's age as another significant determinant of status, we do not mean simply his biological or chronological age. Although physiological marks and possible psychological factors constitute the chief tangible or functional criteria of differentiation between individuals living in different age levels, it is with the divergent culture patterns, their nature and the results of their interaction, that we are primarily interested. In other words, we postulate the existence of what Linton calls "age-sex sub-cultures" [43] upon which to base an analysis of age differences as determiners of status differences. In the next division of this chapter, we will do the same for the factor of sex.

The principal problem involved here is the stratification of societies along age-sex lines. This stratification is not a matter of chance, but is determined in what Ruth Benedict calls the "cultural configuration." [44] More particularly, what Hiller refers to as the adult "characteristic or key status" [45] is incorporated in the cultural configuration. All other age-sex statuses are derived from and with reference to it. In most cultures the key status is that of the adult male, and the various personal statuses of other family members, of both sexes and of all ages, are derived therefrom until such time as other male members are allowed by the culture norms to acquire independent key statuses of their own. Since key statuses are ordinarily sex-linked, it is to such key statuses and the structuralization of derivative statuses in terms of them that we must look to find certain criteria for status determination where sex and age are the variables.

As we have suggested, different cultural configurations display different forms of status stratification by age levels. This may be seen clearly in some of the type cases of anthropology and sociology, such as that of the Comanche warrior, where "a man who has become too old for active participation in war was expected to surrender his 'medicines' and after this was eligible for the post of Peace Chief," [46] whereas, according to Granet, in the classical aristocratic Chinese family, the key status position does not begin until the biological period of late maturity, following the final rituals for the deceased father. [47] It is also obvious that other statuses, such as that of boy

[43] Ralph Linton, "Age and Sex Categories," *Am. Sociol. Rev.*, Vol. 7, No. 5, October, 1942, pp. 589-603.
[44] Ruth Benedict, *Patterns of Culture*, Boston, Houghton Mifflin Co., 1934, Chs. 1, 7.
[45] Hiller, *Social Relations and Structures*, pp. 339-340.
[46] Linton, "Age and Sex Categories," *op. cit.*, p. 599.
[47] Marcel Granet, *Chinese Civilization*, New York, Alfred A. Knopf, 1930.

or youth in the Comanche, and the eldest son in Chinese culture, are oriented to these key statuses. In some cultural groups the whole social order rests upon a basis of age classification. This was true of the ancient Incas.[48] Generally speaking, western societies resort to rather simple classifications, such as infancy, childhood, youth or adolescence, middle age, and old age, with variations on these designations. Linton says that "whatever the system of age classification employed by a particular society it will be found that the categories which it establishes are ranked in a prestige series. The term prestige is here taken to mean social influence, not the degree of care or attention received." [49] Moreover, "within single sex series it seems to be an almost universal rule that the prestige order of the age categories below the adult level corresponds to this order in the individual life cycle. The most important variations between systems are those which occur in the relative ratings of adults and aged. There are certain societies in which adult status is, theoretically as well as actually, the high point in the life cycle, loss of physical powers being attended by immediate loss of prestige. In others the prestige of the individual theoretically increases steadily with age. . . . In a few ancestor worshipping societies this trend is carried to its logical conclusion. The aged eventually become spirits, wielding more power over their descendants than they had when alive." [50] In western societies the prestige of age has been considerably diminished by the decline of older religious ideas, by the increase in the competitive character of modern economic activity, by alterations in the functions of the family, and by the growth of individualism and of democratic ideas. It is readily seen that these changes in the prestige relationships among the different age groups have disturbed the older forms of accommodation. In our society the members of the different age groups have entered into more direct competition with each other, thus inaugurating a new cycle of social interaction among them.

Even so, the cultural processes of the United States are not markedly different from the processes of cultures wherein status determination is in terms of age levels. Their outstanding difference from the folk societies is a more complicated system of determination, which is associated with the decline of extended kinship and the rise of specialized occupations and their accompanying "class" differentiations and groupings as status determiners. The key status in American culture is, as Parsons points out, that of the male adult

---

[48] A. M. Tozzer, *Social Origins and Social Continuities*, New York, The Macmillan Co., 1925, p. 208.
[49] Linton, "Age and Sex Categories," *op. cit.*, p. 596.
[50] *Ibid.*, p. 597.

breadwinner's status, and, "generally speaking, his occupational status is the primary source of the income and class status of his wife and children." [51]

Specific Key and Derivative Statuses.—In keeping with what has been said we will hereafter employ the term "status of orientation" to refer to the culturally determined key status of a given life cycle.[52] "The status preceding it will be termed the status of 'annunciation,' and that following it, the status of 'renunciation.' This system of terminology aims at a higher degree of abstraction than is conventional in characterizing age-sex groups. Its purpose is to free sociological analysis from some of the connotations of the western cultural terms of childhood, adolescence, adulthood, and old age, and to emphasize the relativity of a given age-sex terminology to a given cultural configuration." [53] Thus "the individual passes through a system of statuses forming part of a moral universe designated by his culture. One of the designated statuses will be the one in which he will attain the maximum of integration with the major institutional systems of the culture (i.e., orientation), and, typologically, he must pass through a status of preparation for (i.e., annunciation), and one of withdrawal from (i.e., renunciation of), this major integrated status." [54] Chronological time periods that correspond roughly with the three status universes are determined differently by different cultures.

In view of the fact that all cultures tend to differentiate between the sub-cultures or statuses of different age levels, and since these differentiated cultures and sub-cultures present such a variety of forms of ascription and proscription, compatibility and incompatibility, violability and inviolability, implicit and explicit valuations and norms, reciprocity and obligation, etc., it is impossible to generalize about them except in the most tentative terms. A comparative study of the age statuses in different culture groups can be illuminating, as indicated by the following illustrations.

During the twentieth century, two significant changes have taken place in the ritual of the debut, and these run parallel to two changes in modern American life: (a) a liberalized attitude toward young girls, their rights and their activities; and (b) a modifying of upper social class barriers.

---

51 Talcott Parsons, "Age and Sex in the Social Structure of the United States," *Am. Sociol. Rev.,* Vol. 7, No. 5, October, 1942, p. 608. This whole article may be read with profit in connection with this topic and that dealt with in the next division of this chapter.

52 The terminology used in this and the next few paragraphs has been drawn from a paper by I. C. Belknap and H. J. Friedsam, "Trends in the Theory of Mental Disorders of Later Maturity," and read before the Southwestern Sociological Society, March 26, 1948. (To be published.)

53 *Ibid.*

54 *Ibid.* See also, Hiller, *Social Relations and Structures,* Chs. 22-25.

A result is that the conscious dominating role of the parent generation during the debutante season has diminished. One aspect of this is that the season has become less of a period during which the girl is looked upon by the parent generation to see how she has "learned her lessons" and where she will fit into the restricted social circle, since the social aptitudes of the modern girl are already relatively visible before she becomes a debutante. Another aspect is that these "experienced" girls are considered more capable of making their own rules and arrangements, their own decisions as to their choices of friends, mates, and careers. The season, thus, becomes a period of time during which the members of the younger set are permitted to put their aptitudes to use freely and intensively with each other, with relatively little interference from the older group, although always according to procedures established by them and under their formal supervision. . . .

A second change in the introduction into society that has come about recently is its extension to include members of social divisions formerly excluded. Even after the first World War, the debutante list was almost completely composed of girls from "Assembly" families. In terms of American class structure, this means families of the upper-upper class, or "old families." But before that time, many families in America began to adopt habits of living approximating those of the Assembly members. The initial stimulus was the acquisition of enough income to live in a certain way, to frequent certain places, to send their children to private schools, and to train them for the more socially approved professions. The accumulating of wealth, in itself, was no entrée into debutante circles. But what the wealth could buy, in terms of a way of living, modified the class barriers as one generation followed another. Children of the early twentieth century who, because of their parents' increased income, gained private schooling, professional training, a cultivated and leisurely atmosphere in the home, and possibly a sizable inheritance, now have grown children of their own who have been accustomed all their lives to this atmosphere.

Although the training of a pre-debutante is no longer a conscious discipline of learning the skills of ladyhood from governess, tutor, dancing master, and Mademoiselle, the ceremony of the debut is nevertheless a rite which involves long preparation according to a fairly well-defined system. It is not an "event" which parents suddenly decide to "give." The preparation for the introduction into society is a way of living and begins almost with the birth of the child. The pre-debutante must grow up in a debutante-producing environment.

. . . being a debutante means being a *functioning* member of a special social group. Failure is heartbreak, for it is very public, and it has occurred. Therefore, the parents of a girl who is not fairly sure of minimum acceptance must weigh the risks.

Family background is of prime importance, both as to family history and occupation. Financial standing has great significance. Conduct and character are factors also. But all of these values are weighted and dependent upon each other. . . . Obviously, then, *any* girl cannot become a debutante in the full meaning of the term. The girls who gain entrée to this guarded social circle must know the prerequisites and fulfill them, just as definitely as does a pledgee of a Greek Letter Fraternity or a petitioning member of a restricted club.

During the spring vacation from school in the senior year, the first formal ceremony of separation occurs for the girls about to become debutantes. This is the Junior Bal Masque, given each year for charity, the symbol that a new season has begun. Tickets are issued by invitation only, thus restricting participation to the debutantes of the new season, to those of the two past seasons, and to young men congenial to these girls. . . . Thus, they are officially set apart as a new group: an age and social class separation. The second ceremony, one that marks the separation from their childhood situation, is an individual ceremony, the formal introduction party.

The introduction ceremony formerly consisted of two parties: a tea, at which the girl's parents presented her to their friends, and a dance or dinner dance for presentation to the girl's contemporaries. This form is still kept when advisable. . . . Though the introduction party is the greatest single event for the individual girl, it is but a part of her debutante career. A whole year is given to her for her season.[55]

Adolescent adjustment in our society was conceived to be a four-fold process intermediate to childhood and adulthood wherein the individual is oriented toward four predominant status demands or goals. These are: (1) emancipation from the parental family, (2) the establishment of intimate cross-sex relationships, (3) achievement of economic independence, and (4) achievement of peer group acceptance and participation. . . . [Perhaps most important for successful adolescent adjustment to the norms of that level and for preparation for adult life, the writer develops the hypothesis that] extensive and intimate participation in the informal groups of one's peers at adolescence is necessary for the successful adaptation to adolescent status demands generally as well as to adult status demands. It would seem that the niceties of social adjustment learned in the informal group life of adolescents are in many ways more directly relevant to subsequent adult adjustment, and are less easily dispensed with, than many of the abstractions and Utopian ideals of the class-room and textbook. . . . Also, by participating in the variety of closely knit peer groups (fraternities, clubs, teams, and random associations) the adolescent finds himself in a familiar and meaningful universe made up of similarly situated people from whom he may derive motivation and sympathetic support for his inevitable conflicts with the parent generation.[56]

A system of age-grades apparently prevailed among the Tasmanians. Promotion from one grade to the next was determined by age and merits recognized by the tribe. Secret ceremonies accompanied initiation into each,

[55] From James H. S. Bossard and Eleanor S. Boll, "Rite of Passage—A Contemporary Study," *Social Forces*, Vol. 26, No. 3, March, 1948, pp. 248-252.

[56] N. J. Demerath, "Adolescent Status Demands and the Student Experiences of Twenty Schizophrenics," *Am. Sociol. Rev.*, Vol. 8, No. 5, October, 1943, pp. 513, 518. See also L. S. Cottrell, Jr., "The Adjustment of the Individual to His Age and Sex Roles," *Am. Sociol. Rev.*, Vol. 7, No. 5, October, 1942, pp. 617-620.

but an unusual degree of mystery centered about admission to the third and highest grade, the members of which possessed certain regulatory powers. When a man was of age to marry, he usually seized a woman by stealth or force from another tribe. In other words, marriage was exogamous and by capture. . . . With advancing age the lot of the Tasmanian was not an enviable one. To be sure, the old men enjoyed a certain prestige on account of their wisdom and experience, their plurality of wives, and their knowledge of the mysteries of the highest age-grade, and the old women possessed a similar measure of authority within their own sex. But the exigencies of a wandering life made it impossible to care for the sick and the infirm. So the aged, when they had grown feeble, were provided by their fellows with a little food and left behind to die.[57]

The lure of a title creates among the young men [of Samoa] an atmosphere of competition lacking in the opposite sex. A man rarely secures his first title, usually a low one, before the age of thirty, often not before forty. He must, therefore, demonstrate his worthiness over a long period of years. He seeks to excel his companions in economic pursuits—not so markedly, however, as to arouse envy and hatred. He strives to cultivate propriety in deportment, facility in oratory, proficiency in ceremonial, and qualities of leadership. He may apprentice himself to a master in some specialized profession, such as carpentry, or he may cultivate special skill as a wood carver, barber, tool maker, or the like. Demonstrated merit finds its logical reward in a title and a place in the village assembly.[58]

For it is this way with old people in every country in the modern world; they are often poor and unhappy, but they are not unhappy solely because they are poor. They are also unhappy because they are old. For age in the world we have created and accepted is the ultimate tragedy, the most devastating experience of life. That fact meant little nationally when age was in an extreme minority among our people, but it means much today and will mean more tomorrow. . . .

It is our tradition, our necessity, and our instinct (sic!) to care for the aged; but there is a very great difference between the practical operation of that instinct between, say, 1850 when the life expectancy was 35 years, and today when it is 60 and going higher. In 1850, in a world teeming with aggressive youth, old age was a distinction and not a problem. Today it is a problem and not a distinction.

The spirit of youth is a fine thing, but far less humane and potentially joyous than the spirit of maturity, which has no American reputation at all, save in routine business and the more solemn professions. That blind spot in our thinking and feeling is a powerfully aging factor in modern life. Youth is conventional, largely unoriginal, indeed, almost exclusively imitative, and has to be. Glorify that and one glorifies whatever is the moment's fashion, whether communism, fascism, pacifism, or militarism. Youth follows.

---

[57] G. P. Murdock, *Our Primitive Contemporaries*, New York, The Macmillan Co., 1934, pp. 9-10.
[58] *Ibid.*, p. 76.

It rarely leads. Youth's imitations of maturity are the source of its daring and its occasional enterprise.

. . . Something is saying into the ear of every man and woman over forty in the civilized world, unless that person is mounting on a rising tide of success, "You are older. You are getting old. You are not so good as you used to be."

Though that saying begins with a truth and ends with a lie, it steals into the unconscious on the pass word of its first specious truth, and stays there and festers. And our superstitious and lagging social thought approves the formula. By that process a man passes almost immediately from a state in which all of his delinquencies are blamed upon youth and inexperience to one in which they are assigned to the infirmities of advancing years.[59]

The above selections have been introduced to bring out some of the sharp contrasts between age-status levels as they are defined in primitive and in present-day cultures and to show how these status definitions determine, in large measure, the process of interaction both within and between the different sub-cultures to which the definitions refer. It should be apparent, also, that since as many as three, and sometimes four generations, live together simultaneously, they inter-act in ways to serve as checks and balances, the one upon each and all of the others, not as the dead and the living, as in some societies, but as competing and conflicting contemporaries. Other points to notice are: (a) that certain outstanding differences between the life cycles lie in the extended annunciation status in some cultures, in contrast to its foreshortened character in others, (b) the tendency to a greatly abridged status of renunciation in upper and middle-class American society, thus prolonging the status of orientation, as compared with the very late achievement of orientation status in the classical Chinese family, and (c) a corresponding lengthening of the period of annunciation and shortening of that of renunciation. Moreover, the elements of stress and strain, as they affect adjustment to status and to inter-status relations, seem to fall chiefly upon different age levels in the different cultures. For example, it appears that the old-age status, that of renunciation, in American culture is one of considerable strain from anxiety, futility, and rejection, whereas similar psychological involvements seem to be lacking in certain primitive cultures where one's later years are filled with honors, respectability, and authority.

Further analysis of age (and sex) statuses in American culture seems to indicate that they vary among the lower, middle, and upper

---

[59] Roy Helton, "Old People: A Rising National Problem," *Harpers Magazine*, Vol. 179, October, 1939, pp. 451-453.

classes.[60] "On the basis of empirical material now available it is possible to say, at least tentatively, that the forms of disjunction between the life-cycle statuses for the lower class differ from those of the middle class since the former place greater emphasis on kinship ties. On the other hand, vertical mobility appears to be more important to the middle class, and that class tends to assign stronger status determining functions to the role of the adult male breadwinner than does the lower class. One of the concomitants of this, as Parsons has indicated, is a fundamental asymmetry in the roles of the middle class male and female." [61]

Until recent years in western societies, and even now in primitive societies, the primary and basic training of the child and his nurture through the period of annunciation status was a function of the family, augmented by the play group and the neighborhood. For some time, however, the tendency has been for the educational function to be more largely delegated to the school and other outside agencies. None the less, the family remains the chief cultural group wherein may be observed the interaction between the age-status groups. This is seen most clearly in the parent-child relationship.

Conflict Between Parents and Children.—It can scarcely be said that there is economic competition between parents and their *young* children. Interaction between them, however, frequently takes the form of conflict. Nimkoff names four elements in family life— intimacy, continuity, duration or contact, and parental dominance— which offer a setting especially conducive to conflict.[62] All of these factors of family life are natural and inevitable and it is to be presumed that, even under the best of circumstances, the development and rearing of children will be attended by certain tensions. However, as Nimkoff indicates, the usual causes of tension in the interaction between parent and child are either parental detachment, due either to indifference or to ignorance, or misuse by the parent of his dominant status. The misuse of dominance, he says, may be due to temperament or faulty training, compensation for the sense of inferior-

[60] See: W. A. Davis and J. Dollard, *Children of Bondage*, Washington, American Council on Education, 1940; Talcott Parsons, "An Analytical Approach to the Theory of Social Stratification," *Am. J. Sociol.*, Vol. 45, No. 6, May, 1940, pp. 841-862; Talcott Parsons, "Age and Sex in the Social Structure of the United States," *Am. Sociol. Rev.*, Vol. 7, No. 5, October, 1942, pp. 604-616; W. L. Warner and P. S. Lunt, *The Social Life of a Modern Community*, New Haven, Yale University Press, 1946.

[61] Belknap and Friedsam, "Trends in the Theory of Mental Disorders of Later Maturity."

[62] M. F. Nimkoff, "Emotional Tensions Due to Family Relationships: The Relation of Parental Dominance to Parent-Child Conflict," *Social Forces*, June, 1931, Vol. 9, pp. 559-563. See also, M. F. Nimkoff, *The Child*, Philadelphia, J. B. Lippincott Co., 1934, pp. 155-165.

ity on the part of the parent, or undue identification, by which he means "excessive and unintelligent affection."

Conflict between parents and children, in age anywhere from infancy to adulthood, may take many different patterns and may center around any number of specific causes of tension.[63] Conflicts involving young children or adolescents may produce in them serious personality difficulties, inner tensions, feelings of difference from others, and other marks of personal disorganization.

Among the areas of conflict between age-status groups outside the family are those of politics, religion, education, and economic activity. In the latter area, the struggle seems to be getting more acute as modern industry is tending to replace older workers by younger ones. Specialization and speed are required these days and the older, less adaptable workers are no longer wanted.[64] This raises the serious question of old-age security which has become a very live issue in the last few years, including as it does the question of old-age pensions.[65] While there is no doubt that the financial difficulties of the older people are in a large proportion of the cases real, and since old-age pensions do not contribute adequately to the support of the aged, it is suggested that the very real fact of social isolation, a symbol of denial of secure status, is a more important contributant to the old-age problem.

Sex in the Determination of Status.—In entering upon a discussion involving sex differences it is necessary at the outset to differentiate between certain concepts of sex in culture and certain facts of sex in nature. That these concepts are in many respects fictional is an important consideration, as we shall see later. Sex in culture involves a complexity of notions dealing with the conventional roles of the sexes, their relations to each other as conditioned by the mores, the ramifications of sex in art, literature, popular psychology, etc. Sex

---

63 See: Jessie Bernard, *American Family Behavior*, New York, Harper & Bros., 1942, pp. 280-293; E. W. Burgess and H. J. Locke, *The Family*, New York, American Book Co., 1945, pp. 538-543; Kingsley Davis, "The Sociology of Parent-Child Conflict," *Am. Sociol. Rev.*, Vol. 5, No. 5, August, 1940, pp. 523-535; R. M. Dinkel, "Parent-Child Conflict in Minnesota Families," *Am. Sociol. Rev.*, Vol. 8, No. 5, August, 1943, pp. 412-419; E. B. Reuter and Jessie R. Runner, *The Family*, New York, McGraw-Hill Book Co., Inc., 1931, Ch. 12.

64 See: Stuart Chase, "Laid Off at Forty," *Harpers Magazine*, Vol. 159, August, 1929, pp. 340-347; Abraham Epstein, *Facing Old Age, A Study of Old Age Dependency in the United States and Old Age Pensions*, New York, Alfred A. Knopf, 1922, Chs. 1-2; A. J. Todd, *Industry and Society*, New York, Henry Holt & Co., 1933, pp. 320-322.

65 See: Abraham Epstein, *Insecurity—A Challenge to America*, New York, Random House, Inc., 1933; I. M. Rubinow (Ed.), *The Care of the Aged*, Chicago, University of Chicago Press, 1931; I. M. Rubinow, *The Quest for Security*, New York, Henry Holt & Co., 1934, pp. 219-288; I. M. Rubinow, *Social Insurance*, New York, Henry Holt & Co., 1913, Chs. 19-23.

in nature implies a consideration of its character and functioning apart from civilization. Our interest here is confined primarily to sex behaviour as the result of cultural conditioning.

From a naturalistic point of view, the primary reason for the dichotomy of sex is reproduction. Nature has endowed the two sexes with the requisite physiological and psychological mechanisms for their functioning in their respective roles. However, reproduction is but the beginning of a long process, which, among human beings as well as other higher animal forms, involves a prolonged period of intimate union between parent—particularly the mother— and offspring. The tie binding the male to his mate gradually brings him too under the domination of the developing child. "The life career of the male, already greatly modified for the seeking of the female, becomes further changed toward retaining possession of her; toward feeding her and protecting her while she is carrying and guarding the young." [66] Thus the roles of the two sexes become still further differentiated. Here we may witness the beginning of the economic dependence of the female.

Along with the evolution of sexual differentiation goes a growing interdependence between the sexes. Differentiated though they are by nature as to their "life careers," their extended association through the long period of their offspring's infancy tends to develop manifold psychological attachments, such as habits, sentiments, mutual interests, and the like, which contribute to the permanency of their union. The basis for the family institution is probably found in the need of the human infant for care and protection over a long period of time and in the sharing of that responsibility by the two parents. It is conceivable that the careers of the two sexes, their seeking and mating, the reproducing of their kind, and the natural family would have remained little changed from what they presumably were in a "state of nature" if it had not been for certain developments in the superorganic culture patterns. These, altered by changing economic conditions of life, affected the careers and relations of the sexes, and divided male and female into "masculine" and "feminine" categories and assigned to them conventional social roles.

Masculine and Feminine Social Roles.—Modern science is gradually accumulating a body of evidence on sex differences which shows rather conclusively: (a) that "sex as a determinant of the position

---

[66] H. S. Jennings, "From Amoeba Up," *Survey Graphic,* Vol. 12, December, 1927, p. 273.

of an adult in the community is based largely on tradition, and (b) that apart from the reproductive functions there are no differences between the sexes that can be traced to fundamental hereditary behavior patterns." [67] To be sure, certain contrasts in gross anatomical structure, in physical strength, height and weight, color-blindness and hemophilia, metabolism, and glandular functioning, have been noted by researchers in the field of sex differences. Then there are various notions about sex differences in intelligence, learning ability, achievemental capacity, peculiar personality traits, etc. "The error of ascribing the reviewed differences to a sex constitution lies in the supposition that because two facts occur together, one must be the cause of the other, and that inasmuch as the physical differences are present at birth, they must be the cause of any subsequent differences between the sexes. This error is dispelled by a comparative study of the facts in various societies and even in different classes and generations of any one society." [68] In other words, many of the differences popularly ascribed to biological inheritance are due to cultural definitions.

The history of the controlling influence of sex on culture patterns is a long one, and it may take many more years of scientific research into its many complexities before it will be fully understood. However, a few simple facts seem to stand out rather clearly from the investigations of the past which are worthy of mention. These are: (a) the early recognition by the male of the economic value of woman; (b) the emergence of a division of labor between the sexes as the natural consequence of physiology and habit; (c) the training of the two sexes for their respective social roles by the older generation and thus perpetuating the dichotomy of the social roles in custom and tradition; (d) the sex life of primitive peoples was and is no more unconventional and free of social controls than is that of the so-called civilized peoples; (e) and practically universal subordinate status of women in political affairs and in the wider community controls in spite of the questionable suppositions about a primitive matriarchate; and (f) the development of rationalizations in all societies concerning the assumed inherent incapacity—physical and intellectual—of women to cope with men on a basis of equality in order to give credence and support to the traditional divergent sex mores. [69]

---

[67] Mark A. May, "The Adult in the Community," in *Foundations of Experimental Psychology*, Carl Murchison (Ed.), Worcester, Clark University Press, 1929, p. 754.

[68] Hiller, *Social Relations and Structures*, p. 403.

[69] For discussions of these and other culturally defined and culturally held sex mores see Havelock Ellis, "Sex in Relation to Society," *Studies in the Psychology of Sex*, Philadelphia, F. A. Davis Co., rev. ed., 1929, Vol. 6, 1913; J. K. Folsom, *The Family and Democratic Society*, New York, John Wiley & Sons, Inc., 1943, pp. 624-629; Margaret Mead, *Coming of Age in Samoa*, New York, William Morrow & Co., 1928; Margaret Mead,

The Institutionalization of Sex Statuses.—The necessity for some socially sanctioned regulation of the interaction between the sexes probably grew out of the need for assuring to the offspring resulting from sexual union the lasting care and protection which their long period of infancy required and for carrying out the several functions which came to characterize the family.[70] "Thus it appears that marriage has its source in the family, rather than the family in marriage." [71] What effect the establishment of marriage had on the interaction of the sexes is difficult to say other than to express the belief that, beyond the fact of giving to their union a greater degree of permanency under the social control of custom or of law, it may have served to impress them with a larger measure of responsibility to each other, to their offspring, and to society. Moreover, its relatively long duration may have tended to impress upon the partners the necessity for finding enduring and satisfactory bases of accommodation through conciliation, compromise, superordination-subordination, and, in some societies, a greater measure of participation for the wife in the common affairs of the family and community.

It is evident that we have to deal here with four different, but interrelated, sets of facts: maleness, femaleness, masculine roles, and feminine roles. Since conceptions concerning all of these elements enter into status determination, there is bound to be confusion, and no attempt to institutionalize them in the form of differentiated statuses has ever proved to be unfailingly successful. Since the roles, and hence the statuses, of females are by cultural definition more completely sex-linked than are those of the males, and since it appears from the evidence at hand that men have had a greater part than women in shaping and insisting upon the institutional patterns for the regulation of interaction between the sexes, it is easy to understand why, throughout history, women have been less well adjusted to and satisfied with the roles and statuses assigned to them.

In some cultures the sex roles are clearly and rather inflexibly separated and hence come very little or not at all into competition with each other. But in most modern western cultures this situation does not prevail to an extent sufficient to remove grounds for friction, discontent, and frustration, particularly for many women who tend

Sex and Temperament in Three Primitive Societies, New York, William Morrow & Co., 1935; North, Social Differentiation, Ch. 7; M. Vaerting and Mathias Vaerting, The Dominant Sex: A Study in the Sociology of Sex Differentiation, New York, Doubleday, Doran & Co., 1923; Edward Westermarck, Early Beliefs and Their Social Influence, New York, The Macmillan Co., 1932, Ch. 10.
    [70] See above, pp. 268-269.
    [71] Willystine Goodsell, The Family as a Social and Educational Institution, New York, The Macmillan Co., 1919, p. 8.

to feel the inequities more keenly than do the men. The only alternative condition would be that of no differentiation of roles and statuses related to sex differences. This seems to be the objective of the feminist movement, which, incidentally, has met with considerable difficulty, the reason being that there are apparently enough women who find the present partial separation of roles and statuses, while perhaps not wholly satisfactory, at least somewhat compensated for by feminine qualities and achievements as significant symbols of family status and as important parts of its "standard of living" which reflect credit on it.[72]

Certain facts bearing on the subject and borne out by current anthropological and sociological data seem to confirm the hypothesis that varieties of family life and intersexual relations are in close relationship to woman's status in society and often to her place in the hierarchy of economic positions. Also, "that the social and economic position of women is fundamental in determining their status as a group in society generally, and in particular their place in marital and family relationships."[73] In middle-class America, the economic position of women is, generically speaking, more anomalous than assured, especially outside of marriage. Nevertheless, and partly as a result of this position, their role in the family is, on the whole, dominant. But their domestic status, with its dominance, must function in a social situation which, in terms of tradition and the conventional mores, makes little or no provision for dominance as a socially sanctioned role. Thus, their dominance becomes extra-legal and they exercise their desires to dominate as a license and not as a right. The situation is one, therefore, wherein there is a "combination of character structure which demands the chance to dominate, a social situation in which the characters have freedom to dominate, and institutional forms which do not adequately recognize, dignify, circumscribe, and safeguard such a maternal role."[74]

If key statuses are not absolutely prescribed, as they are in some cultures, they tend to be more narrowly limited for female members of the society than for the males. The age-status period of annunciation is commonly given over to preparation for the later assumption of these key roles. During the early years of this period, differentiated sex categories are not emphasized, but as the individuals

---

[72] See: Talcott Parsons, "An Analytical Approach to the Theory of Social Stratification," *Am. J. Sociol.*, Vol. 45, No. 6, May, 1940, pp. 853-854.

[73] Marvin K. Opler, "Woman's Social Status and the Forms of Marriage," *Am. J. Sociol.*, Vol. 49, No. 2, September, 1943, p. 146.

[74] Margaret Mead, "On the Institutional Role of Women and Character Formation," *Zeitschrift für Sozialforschung*, Vol. 5, p. 75.

approach or reach puberty their conduct becomes more clearly differentiated and obligatory for the two sexes. Writing of age-sex categories in primitive societies, Linton says that "cultural factors are least important in connection with the infant category, which is established primarily by the infant's helplessness and complete dependence upon adults. Sex differences are of little importance at this stage, a fact reflected in most age-sex terminologies. Nearly all languages seem to have a single asexual term for infant, corresponding to our 'baby.' " [75]

Numerous primitive societies do not recognize a period of adolescence and they make no provision for it in their social structure. In such societies, "the child status with its patterns of submission and dependence may be extended upward to include the adolescent period, or the adult status with its multitude of social obligations may be extended downward to include it." [76] Where this condition prevails, there is likewise no clear-cut differentiation of sex status until the status of orientation, the key status for the average adult, is assumed. In some cultures, the assumption of this status is attended by more or less elaborate ceremonial and initiatory ritual; in others, only by informal acceptance of the adult roles. Accordingly, we find that the sharpest delineation between the statuses of the two sexes comes, more often than not, during late adolescence and the reaching of maturity, with the assumption of the status of orientation, although most cultures make some preparation for this transition by the ways in which they take care of the annunciation statuses of the sexes.

In all cultures each of the major status universes—annunciation, orientation, and renunciation—are broken down into sub-statuses, which become increasingly differentiated for the two sexes as passage is contemplated and then made from annunciation to orientation. Commonly, the sub-statuses of the orientation-status universe are those of family, occupation, and community relations. Typically, in our culture, the adult male sub-statuses are those of husband, father, provider, and participant in outside community affairs, whereas those of the adult female are wife, mother, housekeeper, and to a much lesser but increasing degree, extra-familial occupational and community-participation roles. For the average adult male, especially of the lower and middle classes, the sub-status roles are quite well-established in the respective class sub-cultures, while those for adult females

---

[75] Ralph Linton, "Age and Sex Categories," *Am. Sociol. Rev.*, Vol. 7, No. 5, October, 1942, p. 593.
[76] *Ibid.*, p. 596.

have shown a tendency to expand in variety and flexibility in recent years, thus affording to American women, particularly of the middle-class position, larger freedom than formerly in choice of vocational, community, and political roles outside of marriage, or in conjunction with marriage. Thus, changed economic and social conditions have contributed to the redefinition of roles in the status sub-categories, particularly for adult females.[77] Due, in the main, to forces quite outside the feminist movement, these gains in status for women have been made. First came coeducation; then new and larger opportunities for independence and self-support in industry, business, and the professions; next the right of suffrage and the right to hold political office. These advances, great though they have been, fall short of affording equal status to American women in all matters of employment, wages, legal and civil rights, etc. As might be expected, such alterations in the relative statuses of the sexes forced the interaction between them into new patterns. After many centuries, during which conflict between the sexes was largely covert, there has now developed a period of partial equality, which means competition and rivalry, essentially economic, with prospects for renewal of conflict, this time as overt behavior.

Racial and Ethnic Factors Affecting Status.—Some of the ways in which racial and ethnic characteristics influence the statuses of persons and groups have already been dealt with in the two preceding chapters. They will receive only summary mention at this point.

Ethnic qualities become partial determiners of status according to the definitions of them in different cultural configurations. The ethnic factors invariably tend to contribute to a conception of statuses in a stratified order. Ordinarily, this means that the numerically larger and culturally "superior" group allocates to itself a higher position on the status scale than that accorded to minority and presumed "inferior" groups. Thus, status ethnically derived gets defined in terms analogous to class status, with some students inclined to designate such status as that of "caste." [78] For example, the United States is said to be structured along caste lines, with the Negro population, among other minority groups, occupying a subordinate caste position

---

[77] See: Martha C. Ericson, "Child-Rearing and Social Status," *Am. J. Sociol.*, Vol. 52, No. 3, November, 1946, pp. 190-192; Mirra Komarovsky, "Cultural Contradictions and Sex Roles," *Am. J. Sociol.*, Vol. 52, No. 3, November, 1946, pp. 184-189; Elizabeth K. Nottingham, "Toward an Analysis of the Effects of Two World Wars on the Role and Status of Middle-Class Women in the English-Speaking World," *Am. Sociol. Rev.*, Vol. 12, No. 6, December, 1947, pp. 666-675.

[78] See: W. Lloyd Warner, "American Caste and Class," *Am. J. Sociol.*, Vol. 42, No. 2, September, 1936, pp. 234-237.

and hence having the status of a low caste group.[79] There was considerable opposition to the idea.[80] According to the principle of caste, as applied to the United States, "the two dominant racial groups represent castes, the membership of which is dictated by accident of birth (supposedly, but not uniformly, racial characteristics). There is very little interchange of membership from one of these castes to the other. In addition, each has a class system within its population and there is both rising and falling in the rating-levels within each caste." [81] As Davis states,

Caste in the Deep South integrates into one system all aspects of white-Negro behavior: social, sexual, economic, political, educational, religious, legal, associational, and recreational. The basic subsystem—caste—is a rigid stratification, maintained by physical, social, and psychological punishments and rewards. Everywhere in the South, caste establishes and maintains an endogamous and socially separate system of white-Negro relationship in which by birth the Negroes are all of lower, and the whites all of higher, status. This social caste system is more rigid than that described in the classic literature on Hindu castes.[82]

The principal arguments advanced against the so-called "caste school" include the contentions that (a) "it is impossible for a person to become a member of any given race other than by birth; but, although the membership of castes is ordinarily limited by birth, it is quite possible for two or more castes to merge if they so will it—consequences notwithstanding. An individual may be initiated into a caste but clearly not into a race"; (b) "the structures of race and of caste relationship are incommensurable. Caste has reference to the

[79] So prolific have been some social anthropologists and sociologists in writing in this vein that it is impossible to cite more than a few references. See: W. A. Davis and John Dollard, *Children of Bondage;* W. A. Davis, B. B. Gardner, M. R. Gardner, and W. L. Warner, *Deep South,* Chicago, University of Chicago Press, 1941; John Dollard, *Caste and Class in a Southern Town,* New Haven, Yale University Press, 1937; Kingsley Davis, "Intermarriage in Caste Societies," *Am. Anthropol.,* Vol. 43, July-September, 1941, pp. 376-395; Gunnar Myrdal, *An American Dilemma,* New York, Harper & Bros., 1944, p. 667; Richard Sterner, *The Negro's Share,* New York, Harper & Bros., 1943; W. L. Warner, "Social Anthropology and the American Community," *Am. J. Sociol.,* Vol. 46, No. 6, May, 1941, pp. 785-796; W. L. Warner and W. A. Davis, "A Comparative Study of American Caste," in E. T. Thompson (Ed.), *Race Relations and the Race Problem,* Durham, N. C., Duke University Press, 1939, pp. 219-240; W. L. Warner, B. B. Junker, and W. A. Adams, *Color and Human Nature,* Washington, American Council on Education, 1941.

[80] See: Maxwell R. Brooks, "American Class and Caste: An Appraisal," *Social Forces,* Vol. 25, December, 1946, pp. 207-211; O. C. Cox, "Class and Caste: A Definition and Distinction," *J. Negro Ed.,* Vol. 13, Spring, 1944, pp. 139-149; O. C. Cox, "The Modern Caste School of Race Relations," *Social Forces,* Vol. 21, December, 1942, pp. 218-226; O. C. Cox, "Race and Caste: A Distinction," *Am. J. Sociol.,* Vol. 50, No. 5, March, 1945, pp. 360-368.

[81] E. T. Hiller, *Social Relations and Structures,* New York, Harper & Bros., 1947, p. 618 and Ch. 37.

[82] Allison Davis, "Caste, Economy and Violence," *Am. J. Sociol.,* Vol. 51, No. 1, July, 1945, p. 7. See also C. L. Golightly, "Race, Values, and Guilt," *Social Forces,* Vol. 26, December, 1947, pp. 125-139; W. E. Moore and R. M. Williams, "Stratification in the Ante-Bellum South," *Am. Sociol. Rev.,* Vol. 7, No. 3, June, 1942, pp. 343-351.

internal social order of a society; race suggests a whole people, wherever found about the globe"; (c) "race sentiment and interest tend to be universal; while caste sentiment and interest tend to be circumscribed and localized"; (d) "races are not status-bearing entities in the sense that castes are"; (e) "unlike caste in India, Negroes in America have been seeking to increase their participation and integration in the dominant culture. The absence of such striving is an inseparable feature of the caste system"; (f) "endogamy is of different significance in caste and race relations. The caste is socially and contentedly locked within its immediate marital circle; the race, on the other hand, is opportunistic and will intermarry or refuse to do so as its interest and cultural strategy demand"; (g) "the world view of the caste is turned inward, and its force is centripetal; that of Negroes is turned outward, and its force is centrifugal." [83]

It is not our purpose to disprove or to support any of these arguments. We merely suggest that the presence of "race" in a system of status relationships does not, by itself, establish the basis for a caste system. Simply because "race" is a constant among many variables does not, *ipso facto,* provide the criterion upon which to base an impregnable system of stratification. Caste, as a generic term, has been variously used,[84] but is not universally recognized or employed as a designation of ethnic status.

Unique Personal and Peculiar Situational Factors in Status Determination.—While statuses determined primarily by age, sex, and race differences have physical and physiological components as well as cultural ones, and, as a result, may be somewhat more rigidly delimited in institutional forms than are the statuses associated with class distinctions, nevertheless, in many culture groups such as our own there will often be possibilities for refinement, amelioration, and change of status through personal endeavor or by reason of peculiar circumstances in given situations. To attempt to discuss the many implications of this statement would require more space than we have at our disposal. Therefore, mention will be made only of a few exceptions to the standardizing effect of status upon social relations.

It is well known that in an open class system, some individuals are passing up or down the rating scale all of the time. It may have been

---

[83] O. C. Cox, "Race and Caste: A Distinction," *Am. J. Sociol.,* Vol. 50, No. 5, March, 1945, pp. 362-368.

[84] Among other applications, "caste" has been used to denominate the stratified positions of women, children, soldiers, the professions, the élite, criminals, etc., as well as of "races." See Herman Keyserling, "Caste in America," *Forum,* Vol. 53, July, 1928, pp. 103-106; S. Sighele, *Psychologie des Sectes,* as quoted in Park and Burgess, *Introduction to the Science of Sociology,* Chicago, University of Chicago Press, 1924, pp. 205-206.

noticed, also, how personal relations frequently deviate from and cut across the norms prescribed by status. The democratic tradition holds out hope to all who wish to advance themselves by whatever means—wealth, learning, ability, political "pull," specialization, etc.— that they may succeed in reaching the highest pinnacle of "success," which means social recognition and elevated rank. Moreover, the conditions and requirements of modern living afford to specially qualified persons the opportunity to achieve high status rating in functionally unique positions, "there being no other positions that can perform the same function satisfactorily." [85] When and where there is freedom of mobility there is always the possibility of migrating from a situation having a status system that some persons find inhibiting and frustrating to one offering new status opportunities. There are likewise areas or communities within a larger culture region wherein the amount and type of stratification differs from the average, as, for example, between new and old communities, between those having high economic differentiation and those that are more economically homogeneous, or between a settled, prestige-conscious group and a frontier community. [86] Finally, all persons of both sexes, all ages, and of whatever economic class or ethnic stock, come at one time or another into situations characterized by non-status categories of relationship. The child starting to school for the first time enters an unstructured and undefined (for him) situation. The entrance upon any new and unfamiliar situation, such as marriage, the birth · of the first child, the first employment, meeting a stranger, and the like, though generally provided for in the institutional norms, represents for the individual an experience for which he is not wholly prepared. If categoric behavior patterns fail to meet the situation, others may be tried or new ones improvised.

Structured Systems in Interaction

So far our discussion in this chapter has been centered on two systems involved in social interaction: position and status, with implications of a third system, that of action. These three interrelated systems together constitute the culturally determined and institutionally structured framework which conditions, motivates, limits, and supports all social interaction.

[85] Kingsley Davis and W. E. Moore, "Some Principles of Stratification," *Am. Sociol. Rev.*, Vol. 10, No. 2, April, 1945, p. 244, footnote 3.

[86] See: William H. Form, "Status Stratification in a Planned Community," *Am. Sociol. Rev.*, Vol. 10, No. 5, October, 1945, pp. 605-613; E. T. Hiller, *Social Relations and Structures*, Ch. 38.

We have undertaken to show how individuals and groups, as entities, stand in relation to one another in terms of prearranged positions of a stratified order, and how these positions assume, achieve, or have ascribed to them reciprocal statuses which serve to establish institutional norms of conduct according to degree of rank, prestige, honor, and power or authority presumed to inhere in such human and social distinctions as class membership, age, sex, ethnic identity, and peculiar personal and situational characteristics. Oriented to these scales of stratification are comparable social systems of action. Since, as we have learned, "the content of the scale, the specific standards and criteria by which individuals are ranked, is not uniform for all social systems but varies within a wide range," [87] it follows that action systems will vary correspondingly.

The Nature of Action Systems.—Parsons [88] observes that

It has already been stated that the smallest elementary unit of human action which is still relevant to the action schema is what has been called the unit act. These unit acts may be conceived of as combined to constitute more and more complex concrete systems of action. These systems are organic in the sense that they have structurally and analytically important emergent properties which disappear when the breakdown of the systems into units or parts is carried far enough. Neither economic rationality nor value integration is a property of unit acts apart from their organic relations to other acts in the same action system. But allowing for this organic character the action schema may, descriptively, be carried out to the highest conceivable degree of complexity of concrete action systems.

. . . the acts and action systems of different individuals, in so far as they are mutually oriented to one another, constitute social relationships. In so far as this *inter*action of the action systems of individuals is continuous and regular these relationships acquire certain identifiable, relatively constant properties or descriptive aspects. One of them is the structural. Another is involved in the relative priority of *Gemeinschaft* and *Gesellschaft*.

What is said here concerning the action systems of individuals is equally applicable to groups. While it is true that the individual person is the unit of composition of group structure, it is also true that his whole personality is not involved in any one group, although there are, of course, limitations on the compatibility of different group memberships. Nevertheless, it is in the interaction of individuals as group members, and of groups as concrete units, that individual per-

---

[87] Talcott Parsons, "An Analytical Approach to the Theory of Social Stratification," *Am. J. Sociol.*, Vol. 45, No. 6, May, 1940, p. 847.

[88] By permission from *The Structure of Social Action* by Talcott Parsons. Copyrighted, 1937. McGraw-Hill Book Co., Inc., pp. 743-744.

sonal and group properties emerge and get reduced to properties of systems of action. Hence there is no analytical theory of personalities or of groups which is not translatable into terms of the properties or characteristics of action. Because of the organic wholeness of social action systems, unit acts of individuals or of groups, structuralized as they are by the prearranged nature of systems of position and by the stratified constitution of systems of status, cannot be adequately described, analyzed, or understood apart from the particular concrete action system within which they occur. By way of illustrating these points, let us consider certain action systems as they are reflected in the unit acts of individual members of a solidary kinship unit.

Basic to all kinship structure are birth and sexual union. The individual becomes a member of such a group either by birth in one or by entering into a socially legitimized sexual union, a marriage. Marriage, as used in this context, is a unit act by which two persons, man and woman, unite and establish thereby a new kinship group. Kinship groups

are always to a certain extent "solidary" not only in the sense of mutual aid and support but also in the sense that they form units in the system of stratification of the society; their members are in certain respects treated as "equals" regardless of the fact that by definition they must differ in sex and age, and very generally do in other qualities, and in achievements, authority, and possessions. . . . Groups of equals must, under a caste system, in the nature of the case be rigidly endogamous, for husband and wife are necessarily of the same class status. But in a system not resembling the caste type husband and wife need not be rigidly equal by birth, although they become so by marriage, and a married couple and their children, even though equals at birth, may change their class status during their lifetimes.[89]

In the final analysis, persons and unitary groups of persons, both cultural sub-systems, and the relations that come to exist between them in terms of their stratification according to systems of ecological positions and systems of institutional statuses, are organized social actions. "A systematic survey of social actions is a necessary prerequisite for all social studies. Without knowing what the various ways are in which men deal actively with other men and how those ways have evolved, we cannot understand their efforts to regulate normatively their mutual activities . . . or the positions they individually occupy and the functions they perform in their communities, or the organized groups which they create, maintain and destroy." [90]

---

[89] Parsons, "An Analytical Approach to the Theory of Social Stratification," *op. cit.*, pp. 850-851.
[90] Florian Znaniecki, *Social Actions*, New York, Rinehart & Co., Inc., 1936, p. ix.

Questions

1. Upon what factors does North base his classification of social differences? What is the meaning given to each of these factors?
2. How are the concepts "position" and "status" defined and differentiated in the text?
3. What are some of the ways by which the individual may come into a given position at a particular period in his life-cycle?
4. What is meant by saying that "Every individual has a position or more than one simultaneously, and will normally move through a series of positions during a lifetime"? Discuss.
5. What makes an institutional position easier to identify than one that is not institutional?
6. In what respects are official and non-official positions alike and in what respects are they different from each other?
7. At this point, give a more refined definition of "status" than that heretofore presented.
8. Speaking generally, how is status determined?
9. What are the five sets of coordinate determinants of status? What are some ways by which status may be altered at the will of the individual?
10. What are the essential and what are some non-essential elements involved in the analysis of class differentiation?
11. What disposition are you prepared to make of the arguments to the effect that there are no social classes in modern society?
12. Wherein may we expect to find the criteria of class differentiation?
13. Discuss "level of living" as one fairly clear mark of position and of corresponding class status.
14. What may be deduced from the statement: "It is probably not so much the acquisition and possession of wealth and the display of the symbols of wealth that make for class distinctions as it is the concentration of these into the hands of a relatively few people"?
15. Explain: "Economic position is a factor of varying importance in determining class status."
16. What is the end-object of most economic behavior? What are some means employed to that end?
17. Why may it be said that economic classes, as such, "do not struggle"?
18. Criticize the doctrinaire Marxian ideology of "class struggle."
19. Through what media or agencies is the so-called "class struggle" carried on?
20. What are some concomitants of the inequities in the distribution of wealth and of bargaining power?
21. What are the characteristics of industrial conflict?
22. What role does tradition play in industrial conflict?
23. What relation does "the public" have to industrial conflict?

24. What mechanisms are utilized by both sides in the conflict to influence public opinion?

25. What are the effects of industrial strife on the worker in relation to his job? On the job itself? On the community? On the relation of the worker to the community?

26. What are the chief mechanisms used for the accommodation of industrial differences? Discuss each of these mechanisms in terms of their nature and value as accommodative devices.

27. What is meant by participation as a form of accommodation? What evidences can you give to show that this form of accommodation is increasing in favor in industrial relations?

28. What are some areas of economic conflict outside the industrial field?

29. What are some other typical forms of the accommodative process and mechanisms employed to establish and maintain accommodated relationships?

30. Discuss the implications for social interaction of the divisions in society between those who exercise authority and those who obey that authority.

31. What are some evidences that class barriers are weakening?

32. Discuss the rise of the middle classes and their function.

33. What, in the last analysis, is the criterion by which to judge the accommodation of class differences?

34. What factors, besides biological or chronological age, tend to determine the status and functioning of persons of different ages in all societies?

35. What parts are played by "cultural configuration" and "key status" in the stratification of societies along age-sex lines?

36. Discuss the differences between the social positions and statuses of the different age groups in primitive societies and in modern western society.

37. What are meant by age-statuses of "annunciation," "orientation," and "renunciation"? Which one of these is found ordinarily to hold the "key status"?

38. What ideas concerning typical "key and derived statuses" do you get from the comparative study of the age statuses of different culture groups?

39. What is the significance for social interaction of the fact that as many as three, and sometimes four generations, live together simultaneously?

40. What does the analysis of age statuses by lower, middle, and upper class levels reveal?

41. What elements in family life are especially conducive to parent-child conflict? Explain.

42. How are we to account for some of the conflict between age-status groups outside the family?

43. What are the significant facts about "sex in nature" that affect the interaction between the sexes?
44. Account for masculine and feminine social roles.
45. What is apparently the history of sex under the controlling influence of culture patterns?
46. Discuss the institutionalization of sex statuses.
47. What confusion exists because of the failure to satisfactorily institutionalize the factors of maleness, femaleness, masculinity, and femininity?
48. Discuss some of the implications for family life and intersexual relations of the economic position and functional status of women in middle-class America.
49. Compare men and women as to the prescription of their respective key statuses.
50. Discuss the sub-universes of the major statuses as they are differentiated for men and women.
51. What part do racial and ethnic factors play in the determination of status?
52. What evidence does the so-called "caste school" offer in support of its ideas? What arguments have been advanced against the contentions of this group of social scientists?
53. How do unique personal and peculiar situational factors enter into the determination of status?
54. What three interrelated systems constitute "the culturally determined and institutionally structured framework which conditions, motivates, limits, and supports all social interaction"?
55. Of what do action systems consist?
56. How are the properties or characteristics of action related to the analyses of personality and group organization?
57. Why is it said that "a systematic survey of social actions is a necessary prerequisite for all social studies"?

BIBLIOGRAPHY

Adamic, Louis. Dynamite: The Story of Class Violence in America. Rev. ed. New York, The Viking Press, 1934.

Angell, Robert Cooley. The Integration of American Society. New York, McGraw-Hill Book Co., Inc., 1941.

Arlett, Ada H. The Adolescent. New York, McGraw-Hill Book Co., Inc., 1936.

Bakke, E. Wight. Mutual Survival: The Goal of Unions and Management. New Haven, Labor and Management Center, Yale University, 1946.

Bakke, E. Wight. Obstacles to Labor and Management Peace. New Wilmington, Pa., The Economic Business Foundation, 1947.

Benoit-Smullyan, Emile. "Status, Status Types, and Status Interrelations." Am. Sociol. Rev., Vol. 9, No. 2, April, 1944, pp. 151-161.

Bossard, James H. S. The Sociology of Child Development. New York, Harper & Bros., 1948. Part IV, "Class and Status Differentials"; Part VI, "Child Development and Non-Family Groups"; Part VII, "The Changing Status of Childhood."

BOSSARD, JAMES H. S., AND BOLL, ELEANOR S. "Rite of Passage—A Contemporary Study," *Social Forces,* Vol. 26, March, 1948, pp. 247-255.

BOTKIN, B. A. *Lay My Burden Down: A Folk History of Slavery.* Chicago, University of Chicago Press, 1945.

BROOKS, ROBERT R. *When Labor Organizes.* New Haven, Yale University Press, 1937, Chs. 4 and 5.

BURGESS, ERNEST W., AND LOCKE, HARVEY J. *The Family from Institution to Companionship.* New York, American Book Co., 1945, Ch. 9, "Expectations and Roles."

COX, OLIVER C. *Caste, Class, and Race: A Study in Social Dynamics.* New York, Doubleday & Co., Inc., 1948.

DAVIS, W. ALLISON. "American Status Systems and the Socialization of the Child." *Am. Sociol. Rev.,* Vol. 6, No. 3, June, 1941, pp. 345-354.

DAVIS, W. ALLISON, AND DOLLARD, JOHN. *Children of Bondage.* Washington, American Council on Education, 1940.

DAVIS, W. ALLISON, GARDNER, BURLEIGH, B., AND GARDNER, MARY R. *Deep South: A Social Anthropological Study of Caste and Class.* Chicago, University of Chicago Press, 1941.

DAVIS, KINGSLEY. "A Conceptual Analysis of Stratification." *Am. Sociol. Rev.,* Vol. 7, No. 3, June, 1942, pp. 309-321.

DAVIS, KINGSLEY. "The Sociology of Parent-Child Conflict." *Am. Sociol. Rev.* Vol. 5, No. 4, August, 1940, pp. 523-535.

DAVIS, KINGSLEY, AND MOORE, WILBERT E. "Some Principles of Stratification." *Am. Sociol. Rev.,* Vol. 10, No. 2, April, 1945, pp. 242-249.

DEGRÉ, GERARD. "Freedom and Social Structure." *Am. Sociol. Rev.,* Vol. 11, No. 5, October, 1946, pp. 529-536.

DOLLARD, JOHN. *Caste and Class in a Southern Town.* New Haven, Yale University Press, 1937.

EMBREE, EDWIN R. *Thirteen Against the Odds.* New York, The Viking Press, 1944.

FARIS, ROBERT E. L. "Interaction of Generations and Family Stability." *Am. Sociol. Rev.,* Vol. 12, No. 2, April, 1947, pp. 159-164.

FELDMAN, HERMAN. *Problems in Labor Relations.* New York, The Macmillan Co., 1937.

FRAZIER, E. FRANKLIN. *The Negro Family in the United States.* Rev. ed. New York, The Dryden Press, 1948, Parts II, III, V.

FRAZIER, E. FRANKLIN. *Negro Youth at the Crossways.* Washington, American Council on Education, 1940.

FRAZIER, E. FRANKLIN. "Occupational Classes among Negroes in Cities." *Am. J. Sociol.,* Vol. 35, No. 5, March, 1930, pp. 718-738.

FREYRE, GILBERTO. *The Masters and the Slaves: A Study in the Development of Brazilian Civilization.* New York, Alfred A. Knopf, 1946.

FRIEDRICH, CARL J. "The Role and the Position of the Common Man." *Am. J. Sociol.,* Vol. 49, No. 5, March, 1944, pp. 421-429.

GARDNER, BURLEIGH B. *Human Relations in Industry.* Chicago, Richard D. Irwin, 1945.

GOLDEN, CLINTON S., AND RUTTENBERG, HAROLD J. *The Dynamics of Industrial Democracy.* New York, Harper & Bros., 1942.

GOLDHAMER, HERBERT, AND SKILO, EDWARD A. "Types of Power and Status." *Am. J. Sociol.,* Vol. 45, No. 2, September, 1939, pp. 171-183.

GREEN, ARNOLD W. "The Middle-Class Male Child and Neurosis." *Am. Sociol. Rev.,* Vol. 11, No. 1, February, 1946, pp. 31-41.

HARBISON, FREDERICK H. "The Basis of Industrial Conflict." Ch. 9 in William Foote Whyte (Ed.), *Industry and Society*. New York, McGraw-Hill Book Co., Inc., 1946.

HARTMANN, GEORGE W., AND NEWCOMB, THEODORE (Eds.). *Industrial Conflict: A Psychological Interpretation*. New York, The Cordon Co., 1940.

HATT, PAUL. "Class and Ethnic Attitudes." *Am. Sociol. Rev.*, Vol. 13, No. 1, February, 1948, pp. 36-43.

HILL, MOZELL C., AND ACKISS, THELMA. "Social Classes: A Frame of Reference for the Study of Negro Society." *Social Forces*, Vol. 22, October, 1943, pp. 92-98.

HILLER, E. T. *Social Relations and Structures*. New York, Harper & Bros., 1947, Part VI.

HSIAO-TUNG, FEI. "Peasantry and Gentry: An Interpretation of Chinese Social Structure and Its Changes." *Am. J. Sociol.*, Vol. 52, No. 1, July, 1946, pp. 1-17.

HSU, FRANCIS L. K. *Under the Ancestors' Shadow: Chinese Culture and Personality*. New York, Columbia University Press, 1948.

HUGHES, EVERETT C. "Dilemmas and Contradictions of Status." *Am. J. Sociol.*, Vol. 50, No. 5, March, 1945, pp. 353-359.

HUTTON, J. H. *Caste in India: Its Nature, Function and Origins*. Cambridge, England, Cambridge University Press, 1946.

KOOS, EARL LOMON. *The Middle Class Family*. New York, Columbia University Press, 1948.

LANDIS, PAUL H. *Adolescence and Youth*. New York, McGraw-Hill Book Co., Inc., 1945.

LANDTMAN, GUNNAR. *The Origin of the Inequality of the Social Classes*. Chicago, University of Chicago Press, 1938.

LAWTON, GEORGE. "The Study of Senescence: Psychiatric and Sociological Aspects." *Am. J. Sociol.*, Vol. 44, No. 2, September, 1938, pp. 280-281.

LESTER, RICHARD A., AND SHISTER, JOSEPH (Eds.). *Insights into Labor Issues*. New York, The Macmillan Co., 1948.

LEWIS, RALPH. "Officer-Enlisted Men's Relationships." *Am. J. Sociol.*, Vol. 52, No. 5, March, 1947, pp. 410-419.

LEVY, DAVID M. *Maternal Overprotection*. New York, Columbia University Press, 1943.

LINTON, RALPH. "A Neglected Aspect of Social Organization." *Am. J. Sociol.*, Vol. 45, No. 6, May, 1940, pp. 870-886.

LUNDBERG, F., AND FARNHAM, M. F. *Modern Woman: The Lost Sex*. New York, Harper & Bros., 1947.

MACIVER, R. M. *The Web of Government*. New York, The Macmillan Co., 1947, Ch. 6, "Property and Status."

MEADOWS, PAUL. "The Worker: Archetype of Industrial Man." *Social Forces*, Vol. 25, May, 1947, pp. 441-445.

MERTON, ROBERT K. "Social Structure and Anomie." *Am. Sociol. Rev.*, Vol. 3, No. 5, October, 1938, pp. 672-682.

MILLIS, HARRY A. (Ed.). *How Collective Bargaining Works*. New York, Twentieth Century Fund, 1942.

MILLS, C. WRIGHT. "The Middle Classes in Middle Sized Cities." *Am. Sociol. Rev.*, Vol. 11, No. 5, October, 1946, pp. 520-529.

MINER, HORACE. "The French-Canadian Family Cycle." *Am. Sociol. Rev.*, Vol. 3, No. 5, October, 1938, pp. 700-708.

MOORE, WILBERT E. *Industrial Relations and the Social Order*. New York, The Macmillan Co., 1946, Chs. 1, 11-24.

MOSCA, GAETANO. *The Ruling Class*. Translated by Hannah D. Kahn. New York, McGraw-Hill Book Co., Inc., 1939.

MYERS, RICHARD R. "Myth and Status Systems in Industry." *Social Forces,* Vol. 26, March, 1948, pp. 331-337.

NIMKOFF, MEYER F. *Parent-Child Relations.* Los Angeles, University of Southern California Press, 1935.

NORTH, CECIL C. *Social Differentiation.* Chapel Hill, University of North Carolina Press, 1926.

PAGE, CHARLES HUNT. *Class and American Sociology.* New York, The Dial Press, 1940.

PALM, FRANKLIN C. *The Middle Classes Then and Now.* New York, The Macmillan Co., 1936.

PARSONS, TALCOTT. "An Analytical Approach to the Theory of Social Stratification." *Am. J. Sociol.,* Vol. 45, No. 6, May, 1940, pp. 841-862.

PARSONS, TALCOTT. *Max Weber: The Theory of Social and Economic Organization.* New York, Oxford University Press, 1947, especially pp. 218-254, 324-386, 424-429.

POLLAK, OTTO. "Conservatism in Later Maturity and Old Age." *Am. Sociol. Rev.,* Vol. 8, No. 2, April, 1943, pp. 175-179.

POPE, LISTON. *Millhands and Preachers.* New Haven, Yale University Press, 1942.

RAPER, ARTHUR F. *Preface to Peasantry: A Tale of Two Black Belt Counties.* Chapel Hill, University of North Carolina Press, 1936.

RUNNER, JESSIE R. "Social Distance in Adolescent Relationships." *Am. J. Sociol.,* Vol. 43, No. 3, November, 1937, pp. 428-439.

SCHNEIDER, JOSEPH. "Social Class, Historical Circumstances and Fame." *Am. J. Sociol.,* Vol. 43, No. 1, July, 1937, pp. 37-56.

SHEPPARD, MURIEL E. *Cloud by Day: A Story of Coal and Coke and People.* Chapel Hill, University of North Carolina Press, 1947.

SHERIF, MUZAFER. *An Outline of Social Psychology.* New York, Harper & Bros., 1948, Ch. 13, "Adolescent Attitudes and Identification."

SIMMONS, LEO. *The Role of the Aged in Primitive Society.* New Haven, Yale University Press, 1945.

SOROKIN, PITIRIM A. *Social Mobility.* New York, Harper & Bros., 1927.

STRECKER, EDWARD A. *Their Mother's Sons.* Philadelphia, J. B. Lippincott Co., 1946.

SUTHERLAND, ROBERT L. *Color, Class and Personality.* Washington, American Council on Education, 1942.

SYMONDS, PERCIVAL M. *The Psychology of Parent-Child Relationships.* New York, D. Appleton-Century Co., 1939.

VAN GENNEP, A. *Les Rites de Passage.* Paris, Noury, 1909.

WARNER, W. LLOYD, AND LOW, J. O. *The Social System of the Modern Factory— The Strike: A Social Analysis.* New Haven, Yale University Press, 1947.

WARNER, W. LLOYD, AND LUNT, PAUL S. *The Social Life of a Modern Community.* New Haven, Yale University Press, 1941.

WARNER, W. LLOYD, AND LUNT, PAUL S. *The Status System of a Modern Community.* New Haven, Yale University Press, 1942.

WARNER, W. LLOYD, AND SROLE, LEO. *The Social Systems of American Ethnic Groups.* New Haven, Yale University Press, 1945, Ch. 8.

WEST, JAMES (pseudonym for Carl Withers). *Plainville, U. S. A.* New York, Columbia University Press, 1945, Part 3, "Social Structure: The Class System."

YELLEN, SAMUEL. *American Labor Struggles.* New York, Harcourt, Brace & Co., 1936.

ZNANIECKI, FLORIAN. *Social Actions.* New York, Farrar & Rinehart, 1936.

Chapter 18

INTERACTION IN POLITICAL AND SECTARIAN RELATIONS

—

PARTIES IN INTERACTION

The last chapter dealt with certain features of the interactive relationships of classes and status groups, which remain relatively unorganized. When the members of such a group reach the point of having a collective consciousness, even though vague and only partially rational, they may seek ways and means of realizing their desires through organized action bodies either of their own creation or from among those already existent in the social order. These corporate associations, instituted and perpetuated for definite action, we may call *parties*.

The term "party" will be employed to designate an associative type of social relationship, membership in which rests on formally free recruitment. The end to which its activity is devoted is to secure power within a corporate group for its leaders in order to attain ideal or material advantages for its active members. These advantages may consist in the realization of certain objective policies or the attainment of personal advantages or both. Parties may have an ephemeral character or may be organized with a view to permanent activity. They may appear in all types of corporate groups and may themselves be organized in any one of a large variety of forms. They may consist of the following of a charismatic leader,[1] of traditional retainers, or of rational adherents, that is, persons adhering from motives of expediency or of attachment to absolute values. They may be oriented primarily to personal interests or to objective policies. In practice, they may be officially or merely in fact solely concerned with the attainment of power for their leaders and with securing positions in the administrative staff for their own members. They may, on the other hand, predominantly and consciously act in the interests of a social group or a class or of certain objective policies or of abstract principles. The attainment of positions in the administrative staff for their members is, however, almost always a secondary aim and objective pro-

---

[1] "Charismatic," as applied to leadership, is a term that means prestige or authority that rests on the sacred, heroic, or exemplary character of the leader himself.

grammes are not infrequently merely a means of persuading outsiders to participate.[2]

This analysis of the party leads to the conclusion that the concept may have a broader meaning than that ordinarily given to it. While parties are primarily categories of the political order, their activities are not confined to governmental entities, such as municipality, state, and nation. Their activity is oriented towards the attainment and exercise of power or authority, that is, influence on social structure and functions regardless of their content or objectives. Parties may take the form of those associations we commonly call "parties," or, equally appropriate, those known as labor unions, manufacturers' associations, federations of labor, and even religious sects, if such bodies function in the manner of "parties" as described above.

Since party organization assumes a variety of forms, we shall discuss a few concrete examples in terms of their historical appearance, their principal areas of operation, their general objectives, and their effects on the social order.

When we come into the arena of politics, in the narrow sense of that term, we discover a division of forces into rival parties. Since politics are chiefly concerned with government, we find that parties are divided according to the one that happens to be "in" power or in control of the government at the time and those that are "out" of control of the situation but would like to get into power. The "ins" are generally well united, at least at those times when they must meet the opposition at the polls, whereas the "outs" may be composed of one or several dissident groups that never get together. Usually one or two of the latter will have a sufficient following to constitute minorities of various proportions but usually at no time possessing enough power to affect the political scene very materially.

The Natural History of Political Parties.—Modern political parties are of comparatively recent origin and not for a long time after they had been established did they receive legal and constitutional recognition. It is probable that in some way parties originated in primitive secret societies, from which they emerged as the political functions of these early organizations became more openly defined in response to public wants.

Secrecy is a common but varying characteristic of such groups. In general, there are matters of more or less importance, usually pretended at least to be important, the knowledge of which is carefully restricted to

---

[2] From *Max Weber: The Theory of Social and Economic Organization,* edited by Talcott Parsons, p. 407. Copyright 1947 by Oxford University Press, New York.

members of the group. Meetings of the group are in general exclusive, although certain meetings may be held to which the general public is admitted.

Membership in such societies is customarily bestowed through ritualistic *initiation* ceremonies. In these ceremonies, and as marks of their fulfilment, some savages mutilate the candidate by knocking out or filing the teeth, by slashing the skin in certain ways, by tattooing, etc. Mutilations and disfigurements in initiations into "civilized" secret societies are not unknown, and frequently, where actual mutilation is not practiced, it is the custom to "treat the candidate rough." Badges of membership other than mutilations or set styles of hairdressing are commonly employed, such badges as bracelets, ear and nose rings, watch chains, brooches, etc.

Membership is frequently, but not always, attained by *degrees*. The accepted candidate is, by ritual process, admitted to the lowest degree of membership; then after a certain time, he is admitted, if found "worthy," to the next degree; and so on up. Admission to a higher degree is determined sometimes by choice of those already members in that degree; sometimes by the payment of a fee, which may increase in magnitude with the elevation of the degree; sometimes by the ability of the candidate to "stand on examination" or go through the ritual or certain set feats of endurance to the satisfaction of the group, sometimes by the combination of two or all of these methods. The fees for the higher degrees in some savage lodges are relatively high, so that only the very wealthy can attain to them.

The standing and influence of the member within the society increases with his elevation through the degrees, and his power outside of the group may increase likewise, through the influence of the society in the tribe. The men in the highest degrees of some savage lodges virtually dominate the community, although they may not constitute the legal political authority.

In some savage and civilized secret societies, however, there are no degrees, admission to the society being complete and full in one initiation.[3]

In civilized secret societies the political function is more obscure, and in most cases where it exists its presence is not openly admitted. The Ku Klux Klan, however, is an example of one such secret order in which the political function is openly avowed in both declaration and activity. Every university student who has experienced an election for student offices or other political procedure on a modern university campus knows the power of the fraternities to swing things their way. The "barbs" always recognize this power and usually organize to meet it.

It is not a far cry from the secret society of both savage and civilized men to the gang. The gang is a type of secret society. For some time the gang has been recognized as a political force of no

---

[3] Knight Dunlap, *Social Psychology*, Baltimore, Williams & Wilkins Co., 1925, pp. 149-150.

mean significance, particularly in the American city, and the way in which it emerges from the gang stage to that of the local political organization has been the subject of considerable study and a matter of some concern to many who deplore its activities in municipal politics. William F. Whyte has described this evolutionary process among the "street corner boys" of "Eastern City" as follows:

A Cornerville man can get ahead either in Republican or in Democratic politics. The nature of his activity will depend upon which route he chooses, for there is a fundamental difference between the two careers.

The Republican politician gets ahead by drawing himself to the attention of the upper-class people who control the party in the state, and, in so doing, he draws himself away from Cornerville. The career of Judge Gennelli provides an outstanding example of such behavior. He was born in Cornerville of a poor Italian family. He sold papers and shined shoes when he was a boy. He put himself through law school, became active in Republican politics, and won a minor judiciary appointment. Becoming more successful in his law business, he set up offices in the center of the Eastern City business district and hired girls of native American background as secretaries. Some time later he was given a better appointment on the bench. Quite early in his career he had moved out of Cornerville to a fashionable suburb. He won his party's nomination for attorney-general and waged a vigorous campaign to win the Italian vote. In this he failed. The Republicans lost and Gennelli ran behind his ticket. He fared little better in Cornerville than the other Republican candidates. Upper-class people looked upon him as an excellent judge and felt that his career testified to the vitality of American democracy. Cornerville people looked upon him as a high-class lawyer who was not concerned with helping them out of trouble. However, his inability to swing the Italian vote did not prevent Gennelli from rising. A later Republican administration promoted him to the highest court in the state.

The Democratic politician gains his strength from the support of Cornerville people. His success depends upon his ability to deal with groups of people inside his district. Therefore, in order to understand his career, it is necessary to have some general knowledge of the nature of these groupings.

Corner gangs, such as the Nortons, or corner boys' clubs, such as the Cornerville S. and A., are to be found throughout the district. They function as independent units, and at the same time some of the smaller ones fit in as parts of larger organizations.

In Cornerville there are a number of political clubs, each one started by a politician and built around him. Such a club is organized for the purpose of electing its boss (or one selected by him) to public office and of providing him with the voting strength necessary in order to make good political connections. In return, the boss is expected to advance the interests of the members. The members are pledged to support all candidates indorsed by the club. In practice, the boss decides which candidates are to be indorsed. When the club boss runs for office, he can generally count on the active support of most of his members; but often the club is united only nominally in other contests. The political club is made up of a number of corner gangs. (The boss and some members may be above the corner-boy level, but the bulk of the members consider themselves corner boys and are so looked upon by others.) The boss's own clique, with which he started his club, can be relied upon to support his decisions, but the other cliques maintain their informal associations and a considerable independence of action. Unless the boss takes pains to tie the cliques in closely with the nucleus of the club through consulting their leaders on matters of policy and giving recognition to the informal clique organization in prestige and favors, the club may break up.

A man who is part of a large family and can "swing" its vote to one candidate or another becomes thereby a political figure of some consequence. Such a man will probably be a leader or close to the top in his informal group associations, in which case the groupings will all support the same politician. It is the man who is not a leader in one or both groups who faces a possible conflict. If his family supports one group and "the boys" support another, he must choose between his loyalties. That situation accounts for the defection of many men from either the family policy or the policy of the informal group.

Another break in the united group front results when the group is committed to Politician A but one of its members is committed to Politician B because he has received some specific favor. In this case the other members will recognize that this man is "doing the right thing" in discharging his obligations, and they will not put pressure on him to support Politician A.

The politician does not build his organization out of an undifferentiated mass of people. He grows up in a society which is complexly organized. To be successful in his career, he must be familiar with its ramifications and know how to win the support of the groups which make it up.

No politician in Cornerville can be successful without the support of corner boys, and many corner-boy leaders enter politics. The corner-boy leader performs some of the politician's functions for his followers. He looks after their interests and speaks for them in contacts with outsiders. Yet there are a number of things he cannot do. He cannot get them political jobs or favors unless he subordinates himself and his group to some politician. It frequently· occurs to him and his followers to ask themselves why the leader should have to subordinate himself. He feels that the politicians have neglected the people's interests. His friends try to persuade him to enter the contest. If he has any capacity for public speaking, their urgings will be hard to resist. He will begin to extend his contacts so that he moves in wider and more influential circles.[4]

The training received in gang organizations fits in nicely with the plans of local politicians, and the political machine of the modern American city may be built up largely in the way described above.

---

[4] William Foote Whyte, *Street Corner Society*, Chicago, University of Chicago Press, 1943, pp. 205-209.

The fundamental character of the secret society and of the gang is the same in relation to politics. Both lend themselves to political manipulation and utilization through their ability to trade some advantage in the way of influence, votes, or money, with the political bosses in return for protection, favors, and the like. Two types of organization have grown up in the American city to take care of the mobilization of individual voters, namely, the civic association and the political machine.[5] It is to the latter type of organization that the gang lends itself.[6]

Historically, the political party is a substitute for revolution.[7] Being crude, costly, disturbing, and, at best, only a partial remedy for the evil it would seek to correct, revolution gave way to a procedure by which a durable organization of citizens might appeal for the right to govern the state. This same idea is developed by Sir H. S. Maine, where he says:

Party is probably nothing more than a survival and a consequence of the primitive combativeness of mankind. It is war without the city transmuted into war within the city, but mitigated in the process. The best historical justification which can be offered for it is that it has often enabled portions of the nation, who would otherwise be armed enemies, to be only factions.[8]

Parties arose to give a semblance of order and organization to intergroup conflicts over questions of civic policy and authority. As a substitute for internecine warfare and revolutionary measures, parties were organized and the contrary forces were mobilized by them for strife without physical combat. Just how and when the secret societies first entered the more peaceful and orderly process is not clear but it may be that they, being already in existence, served as nuclei around which the early parties were organized, or they may have been drawn into the political arena at a later time because their power and efficiencies were important to party leaders. Just as the "bosses" and "party machine" may use the parties for power and patronage of office, so may they also make use of the secret societies and gangs for the same reasons. Thus political parties, secret societies, and gangs belong together in any general consideration of political conflict.

---

[5] See: Nels Anderson and Eduard C. Lindeman, *Urban Sociology*, New York, Alfred A. Knopf, 1928, pp. 295-296; Noel P. Gist and L. A. Halbert, *Urban Society*, New York, T. Y. Crowell Co., 1941, pp. 448-466; C. E. Merriam, *Chicago: A More Intimate View of Urban Politics*, New York, The Macmillan Co., 1929; R. E. Park et al., *The City*, Chicago, University of Chicago Press, 1924, p. 35.

[6] See: F. M. Thrasher, *The Gang*, Chicago, University of Chicago Press, 1927, pp. 452-486.

[7] See: A. D. Morse, *Parties and Party Leaders*, Boston, Marshall Jones and Co., 1923. An "Amherst Book."

[8] H. S. Maine, *Popular Government*, London, J. Murray, 1886, p. 101.

The Political Function of Parties.—The political party may be thought of as political activity in institutionalized form. It maintains its authority by adapting itself to changing social and economic conditions. Failure to do so will eventually lead to defeat. To resist change is a mark of strength in an institution, but the ability to make needful adjustments to change is necessary for its survival. This applies to political parties as well as to other institutional agencies.

The party developed out of alignments previously held and drawn according to conflicting class or other interests. It arose to advance the cause of one group or another and tended to gain power and recognition and finally, legal acceptance, as it sought to dominate the government and direct legislation.

The chief function of the dissenting groups, the reform and protest groups, that constitute the "third parties" and "fourth parties," is to furnish the chief contending parties with issues. In the early days of party government in the United States, for example, the old parties never lacked for dominant issues for fighting purposes, but in more recent years what issues there are have cut across party lines. The issues of the trusts, the gold standard, and the like, have gone down in history as practically settled, so far as the two great parties are concerned. In the campaign of 1948 in the United States, such issues as foreign policy, civil rights, and domestic economy cut across party lines. Third parties form around issues and leaders. They must have affirmative programs of their own and not merely assorted discontents. Their issues tend to be taken over by the major parties in due course of time and the leaders generally desert them at a critical time or, if defeated, usually lose the following they may once have possessed.[9]

The class struggle has been carried into the arena of politics. In fact, it is there constantly in some one or several of its phases. "Special privilege," "the pork barrel," "graft," "boodle," "log rolling," and other devices, are almost continuously employed to benefit the interests of some class or classes in the community at the expense of some other class or classes. Political parties have been organized to carry on the class fight more effectively, as, for instance, the Labor Party in England, the Non-Partisan League in the United States, the Socialist parties of various complexions in different countries,

---

[9] See: Pendleton Herring, *The Politics of Democracy: American Parties in Action,* New York, W. W. Norton & Co., Inc., 1940; Arthur N. Holcombe, *Political Parties of Today,* New York, Harper & Bros., 1924; Charles E. Merriam, *American Political Ideas,* New York, The Macmillan Co., 1920; Charles E. Merriam, *New Aspects of Politics,* Chicago, University of Chicago Press, 1925; Edward McC. Sait, *American Parties and Elections,* New York, The Century Co., 1927.

and the Communists in Soviet Russia. Conservative political parties can usually be counted upon to represent and support the class of wealth and aristocracy; the liberal parties, whether liberal by name or not, generally espouse the cause of the bourgeoisie, the middle-class landowners, and the small businessman; while the radical parties, by whatever designation they are known, are the active exponents of the cause of the proletariat, the workers, and the peasants. Thus we see that political party alignment is frequently along class lines. This is much more true in European countries than it is in the United States and Canada.[10]

As we have said before, parties may seek the achievement of objective aims; that is, to advance the cause of the group or that of the nation. Other parties, however, may seek to secure the personal advantage of their leader or leaders. Robert Michels has referred to the parties built around the personalities of their leaders as "charismatic," particularly if the leader's influence is by virtue of qualities so striking as to seem supernatural.[11] Such a party will be identified with the leader. Examples are furnished by the Nazi party in Germany, with Hitler as Der Fuehrer, and by the Fascist party in Italy with Mussolini as leader. Michels indicates that such parties are generally young, ardent, doctrinaire. Usually charismatic leaders start parties of their own, but sometimes they appear after the party is active. In times of general social unrest the charismatic type of party is most likely to appear and is most likely to succeed.

Party Strife: Its Forms and Mechanisms.—Political parties are not mere aggregates of people drawn by the attraction of a set of principles, ideals, or aims to which they subscribe collectively. Parties, to be effective, must have organization and leaders as well as objectives. Actually they have what are termed, in popular parlance, "machines" and "bosses." The machine represents the permanent working organization of functionaries, committees, campaign funds, and party propaganda organs. The boss is the titular and usually the real head of the party machine. There may be one boss, or several bosses with divided territory and functions. The boss runs the machine by suffrance or by the choice and with the support of the other

---

10 See: Charles A. Beard, *The Economic Basis of Politics*, New York, Alfred A. Knopf, 1922; H. L. Childs, *Labor and Capital in Politics*, Columbus, Ohio State University Press, 1930; Seba Eldridge, *Political Action*, Philadelphia, J. B. Lippincott Co., 1924; Nathan Fine, *Labor and Farmer Parties in the United States*, New York, Rand School Press, 1928; A. N. Holcombe, *The Middle Classes in American Politics*, Cambridge, Harvard University Press, 1940; Robert Hunter, *Labor in Politics*, New York, The Socialist Party, 1915.
11 Robert Michels, "Some Reflections on the Sociological Character of Political Parties," *Am. Pol. Sci. Rev.*, Vol. 21, November, 1927, pp. 752-772.

party leaders and their henchmen, unless he is a charismatic leader, who may assume the role of dictator. However, if they would succeed, even dictators must be mindful of certain forces with which they have to deal and to which they must respond. The party often pays more attention to the leader than it does to its objectives. If the leader is weak, the objectives must be strong; otherwise the party disintegrates.[12] If the boss is strong he tends to use the party machinery to serve his own ends. Pronouncements of objectives become little more than catch phrases to attract attention away from the leader and his self-aggrandizing machinations.

Often the boss is classed as a corrupt professional politician. This he frequently is. Whether he is in charge of the party machinery in a precinct, a ward, a district, or a state, he occupies a favored position to levy tribute and to receive graft, both "honest" and dishonest.[13] On the other hand, the boss may be regarded as filling a useful and necessary place in party politics, particularly in the local community. Though he may be the recipient of favors and graft, he does look after the interests of the party and takes care of his constituents. In many ways he acts as a benefactor and humanitarian. The poor and distressed members of his constituency are his special charges. While his chief responsibility is the building up and maintenance of a strong political organization, he may consider that this can best be accomplished through the loyalty and allegiance of grateful citizens who have been the recipients of his benefactions. That these benefactions are made possible from the spoils acquired from other sources seems to the boss to be perfectly legitimate.[14] In spite of all that may be said for the boss, however, his name has long been linked with the most vicious and disreputable elements and activities in city life. From these he derives most of his strength and to them he extends his protection. It is this linkage between party politics, represented by the city boss and his machine, and the corrupt influence of the underworld that has given to the former its unsavory reputation and has made

---

12 See: Robert Michels, "Über die Kriterion und Entwicklung politischer Parteien," *Schmollers Jarbuch*, Vol. 51, August, 1927, pp. 1-23.

13 See: C. H. Garrigues, *You're Paying for It: A Guide to Graft*, New York, Funk & Wagnalls, 1936; W. I. Riordon, *Plunkitt of Tammany Hall*, New York, McClure, Phillips & Co., 1905.

14 See: Matthew Josephson, *The Robber Barons*, New York, Harcourt, Brace & Co., 1935; Matthew Josephson, *The President-Makers*, New York, Harcourt, Brace & Co., 1940; Ferdinand Lundberg, *America's Sixty Families*, New York, Vanguard Press, Inc., 1937; Twila E. Neely, "The Sources of Political Power: A Contribution to the Sociology of Leadership," *Am. J. Sociol.*, Vol. 33, No. 4, March, 1928, pp. 769-783; W. B. and J. B. Northrop, *The Insolence of Office*, New York, G. P. Putnam's Sons, 1932; J. T. Salter, *The Pattern of Politics*, New York, The Macmillan Co., 1940; J. H. Wallis, *The Politician*, Philadelphia, F. A. Stokes Co., 1935; M. R. Werner, *Privileged Characters*, New York, Robert M. McBride & Co., 1935.

"bossism" "synonymous with community disorganization of the most extreme sort." [15]

Among the other mechanisms of party politics are the party convention and the party platform. The convention is a rallying process designed to revive interest, to define the issues where they exist, and to create issues where none exist, to select the standard bearers, and to condition the party followers emotionally for the coming campaign. The party convention has been termed "the great American rite," for after a century it is now firmly rooted in the political life of the country. James Truslow Adams says of it: "The two chief functions of the convention are as simple as they are important. It is clear that a Parliamentary or Congressional form of government must be worked by means of parties. Parties must have programs and candidates, and in the United States these are supplied by the convention. . . . In the century of its existence, however, serious defects have become apparent in what seemed so simple and adequate a method. In trying to analyze these we find that the evils may be divided into those which spring from certain rules and those which are inherent in the system." [16] The evils growing out of the rules might be corrected by changing the rules, but the evils that are inherent in the system may be corrected only by abandoning the convention system. Adams points out that the chief evil in the system lies in the fact that "the series of lower conventions on which the delegate system of the national one rests extends not to the individual citizen but to the control of the local bosses." [17] So we see that the convention tends to be dominated by the bosses through their control over the delegates to the convention. The bosses control their followers by patronage of one sort or another; the delegates control the convention; therefore, the stake the bosses play for in a convention is a high one. In fact, it involves the control of the party and party government. The convention becomes a great game, with moves and counter-moves of political strategists, whose purpose is either to

15 See: J. F. Dineen, *Ward Eight*, New York, Harper & Bros., 1936; F. Dobyns, *The Underworld of American Politics*, New York, The Author, 1932; Mabel A. Elliott and Francis E. Merrill, *Social Disorganization*, New York, Harper & Bros., 1944, Ch. 32; H. F. Gosnell, *Boss Platt and His New York Machine*, Chicago, University of Chicago Press, 1924; H. D. Lasswell, "Chicago's Old First Ward; a Case Study in Political Behavior," *National Municipal Review*, March, 1923, pp. 127-131; S. P. Orth, *The Boss and the Machine*, New Haven, Yale University Press, 1919; Harold Zink, *City Bosses in the United States*, Durham, Duke University Press, 1930. For discussion of "boss rule" in states, see Isaac R. Pennypacker, "Quay of Pennsylvania," *American Mercury*, Vol. 9, November, 1926, pp. 357-364; Lane W. Lancaster, "The Background of a State 'Boss' System," *Am. J. Sociol.*, Vol. 35, No. 5, March, 1930, pp. 783-798.
16 James Truslow Adams, "The Convention: A Great American Rite," *The New York Times Magazine*, May 8, 1932, p. 4.
17 *Ibid.*

bring about the nomination of a candidate of their choice or to defeat the candidate of their rivals.

As a rule the party platform, adopted in convention, is a meaningless assortment of phrases designed to beguile and disarm the people "back home." Ostensibly it is supposed to set forth the particular aspects of the issues for which the party stands and for which it will work if successful in the campaign. Actually, it commits the party leaders to nothing. Platitudinous statements fill its paragraphs and these furnish much of the material for the speeches of the candidates in the ensuing campaign. Pledges of adherence to the party's program as set forth in the platform are not infrequently forgotten by the successful candidate after election. Consequently, the platform becomes merely another of the traditional rites of the American political party game. The convention and the platform serve mainly as mechanisms to arouse conflict attitudes and to give a new zest to the humdrum of political life.

On such occasions, and during the campaigns which follow, the party leaders play upon the minor chords of fear and traditional sentiment-attitudes. The old familiar shibboleths are revived and redefined in terms of present fears and hopes. The conservative elements fan the distrust of change into the fear of revolution. *"Fear of change is the corollary of the desire to conserve the present and, consequently (where there has been no violent breach), the past. It is, therefore, to the advantage of the Conservative to stimulate alarmism about the vague grisliness of the unknown."* [18] On the other hand, the liberal and radical forces picture the corruption of the present order, breathe discontent, and stir up emotional reactions in favor of remote and vague theories of a Utopian social order. Loyalty to the group leaders and standards are urged and vows of allegiance are reaffirmed with religious solemnity. "Following the leader" is a trait common enough in politics and ensures political action with a minimum of critical thought.

Party campaigns build up a mood of expectancy and antagonism. Strenuous efforts are put forth to get out the vote. Speech-making and propaganda campaigns through the press and other mediums of communication tend to blind the citizens to the real issues by high-pressure methods, "steam-roller" tactics, and through deliberate distortion and misrepresentation of facts. The way is open for corruption and "log rolling," bribery, and graft, through the collection

---

[18] G. E. G. Catlin, "Doctrine of Power and Party Conflict," *Am. Pol. Sci. Rev.*, Vol. 19, November, 1925, p. 728.

and expenditure of enormous campaign funds, the promise of favors, and special privilege. Through such attempts to "swing the vote," the will of the voters is thwarted, their confidence is forfeited, and their sense of obligation to government is impaired. Such conditions help to explain the growing apathy and indifference to political questions and political action by increasing numbers of citizens.

The average citizen has a rather vague and general conception of government. He is inclined to think of it as an entity in itself and divorced from the interests and actions of individuals. Governmental policies at any given time are thought of as the policies of the party that happens to be in power. The citizen cannot make articulate his desires and demands, in most cases, because of the machinery interposed between him and the governing body. As Lippmann says, "the government consists of a body of officials, some elected, some appointed, who handle professionally, and in the first instance, problems which come to public opinion spasmodically and on appeal." [19] The voters lend their assistance to one party machine or another to retain power already held or to gain control of the government.

In a sense, then, voting is "an act of enlistment, an alignment for and against, a mobilization." This is the idea of voting held by Morse, Maine, and Lippmann. An election is, therefore, "historically and practically a sublimated and denatured civil war, a paper mobilization without physical violence." [20] Though originally it was an alignment of physical forces ready to engage in mortal combat, it has been transmuted into an alignment of moral, economic and social forces. Even now, in some communities, it retains much of its historical, physical, and military character.

Typical Forms of Accommodation.—So usual is it for contending political factions, parties, and leaders to compromise their differences, that the terms "compromise" and "politic" have come to mean much the same thing. As we have said, politics is like a game. By the same token, politicians are something of gamblers, playing for stakes, taking risks, and being governed by a code in which strategy and compromise occupy a large place. The prize at stake is the control of government with all its appurtenances of patronage and power. Since in politics, as in many other things, a part is better than nothing, politicians seek to secure for themselves what they can even though it may mean making concessions and effecting a division of

19 From Walter Lippmann, *The Phantom Public.* Copyright, 1925, by Walter Lippmann. Used by permission of The Macmillan Co., publishers, New York, p. 72.
    20 *Ibid.,* p. 58.

the spoils. Consequently, the game of politics is characterized by "log rolling," "trimming," trading, and bargaining. Favors are passed around in return for other favors. Rivals forget their differences and become friends in the face of opposition. Frequently, differences between parties tend to fade out, if not to disappear altogether. In fact, any genuine line of cleavage between the two major parties in the United States has largely disappeared and, though the lines are clearly drawn between Tory and Labor in Britain, the field of the middle way, the area of compromise and of coalition government, is extending year by year.

It is the classic tradition of democratic governments that the majority shall rule. This is supposed to make government rest on a basis of accommodation in the form of superordination-subordination. As a popular ideal it is supported by numerous rationalizations. *Vox populi, vox Dei* is its motto. On this point, Walter Lippmann remarks:

> The attempt has been made to ascribe some intrinsic moral and intellectual virtue to majority rule. It was said often in the nineteenth century that there was a deep wisdom in majorities which was the voice of God. Sometimes this flattery was a sincere mysticism, sometimes it was the self-deception which always accompanies the idealization of power. In substance it was nothing but a transfer to the new sovereign of the divine attributes of kings. Yet the inherent absurdity of making virtue and wisdom dependent on 51 per cent of any collection of men has always been apparent. The practical realization that the claim was absurd has resulted in a whole code of civil rights to protect minorities and in all sorts of elaborate methods of subsidizing the arts and sciences and other human interests so they might be independent of the operation of majority rule.
>
> The justification of majority rule in politics is not to be found in its ethical superiority. It is to be found in the sheer necessity of finding a place in civilized society for the force which resides in the weight of numbers.[21]

Georg Simmel gives a sociological analysis of this same phenomenon where he says:

> A peculiar form of subordination to a number of individuals is determination by vote of a majority. The presumption of majority rule is that there is a collection of elements originally possessing equal rights. In the process of voting the individual places himself in subordination to a power of which he is a part, but in this way, that it is left to his own volition whether he will belong to the superior or the inferior, i.e., the outvoted party. We are not now interested in cases of this complex problem in which the superiority is entirely formal, as, for example, in resolves of scientific congresses, but only with

---

[21] *Ibid.*, pp. 57-58.

those in which the individual is constrained to an action by the will of the party outvoting him, that is, in which he must practically subordinate himself to the majority. This dominance of numbers through the fact that others, though only equal in right, have another opinion, is by no means the matter of course which it seems to us today in our time of determinations by masses. . . .

When majority rule exists, two modes of subordination of the minority are possible, and discrimination between them is of the highest sociological significance. Control of the minority may, in the first place, arise from the fact that the many are more powerful than the few. Although, or rather because, the individuals participating in a vote are supposed to be equals, the majority have the physical power to coerce the minority. The taking of a vote and the subjection of the minority serves the purpose of avoiding such actual measurement of strength, but accomplishes practically the same result through the count of votes, since the minority is convinced of the futility of such resort to force. There exists in the group two parties in opposition as though they were two groups, between which relative strength, represented by the vote, is to decide.

Quite another principle is in force, however, in the second place, where the group as a unity predominates over all individuals and so proceeds that the passing of votes shall *merely give expression to the unitary group will.* In the transition from the former to this second principle the enormously important step is taken from a unity made up merely of the sum of the individuals to recognition and operation of an abstract objective group unity. . . . In case the group is a self-existent structure—whether consciously or merely in point of fact—in case the group organization effected by union of the individuals remains along with and in spite of the individual changes, this self-existent unity—state, community, association for a distinctive purpose—must surely will and act in a definite manner. Since, however, only one or two contradictory opinions can ultimately prevail, it is assumed as more probable that the majority knows or represents this will better than the minority. According to the presumptive principle involved the minority is, in this case, not excluded but included. The subordination of the minority is thus in this stage of sociological development quite different from that in case the majority simply represents the stronger power. In the case in hand the majority does not speak in its own name but in that of the ideal unity and totality. It is only to this unity, which speaks by the mouth of the majority, that the minority subordinates itself. This is the immanent principle of our parliamentary decisions.[22]

The theory of majority rule is practically impossible of realization in a large modern state. Though the full complement of qualified electors should participate in an election, which never happens, their

_____

[22] From the translation of Simmel's *Soziologie* by A. W. Small, *Am. J. Sociol.*, Vol. 2, 1896-1897, pp. 181-183.

votes would be so divided among the several parties that a minority would be more than likely to elect. This has often happened in the elections of presidents of the United States. To be sure, one party or another may secure a majority of the seats in the national congress or parliament and thus control the legislative program of the government. It not infrequently happens, however, that the only majority to rule is a coalition of two or more parties, because no one party can muster a majority. It is in this latter type of case that we observe much of the "log rolling" and compromise previously mentioned.

The great hope of democratic government lies in the free discussion of issues and candidates. Walter Bagehot well established the advantages of government by discussion when he wrote:

A government by discussion, if it can be borne, at once breaks down the yoke of fixed custom. The idea of the two is inconsistent. As far as it goes, the mere putting up of a subject to discussion, with the object of being guided by that discussion, is a clear admission that that subject is in no degree settled by established rule, and that men are free to choose in it. It is an admission, too, that there is no sacred authority—no one transcendent and divinely appointed man whom in that matter the community is bound to obey. And if a single subject or group of subjects be once admitted to discussion, ere long the habit of discussion comes to be established, the sacred charm of use and wont to be dissolved. "Democracy," it has been said in modern times, "is like the grave; it takes, but it does not give." The same is true of "discussion." Once effectually submit a subject to that ordeal, and you can never withdraw it again; you can never again clothe it with mystery, or fence it by consecration; it remains forever open to free choice, and exposed to profane deliberation.

Discussion, too, has incentives to progress peculiar to itself. It gives a premium to intelligence. To set out the arguments required to determine political action with such force and effect that they really should determine it, is a high and great exertion of intellect. Of course, all such arguments are produced under conditions; the argument abstractedly best is not necessarily the winning argument. Political discussion must move those who have to act; it must be framed in the ideas, and be consonant with the precedent, of its time, just as it must speak its language. But within these marked conditions good discussion is better than bad; no people can bear a government of discussion for a day, which does not, within the boundaries of its prejudices and its ideas, prefer good reasoning to bad reasoning, sound argument to unsound. A prize for the argumentative mind is given in free states, to which no other states have anything to compare.

Tolerance, too, is learned in discussion, and, as history shows, is only so learned. In all customary societies bigotry is the ruling principle. In rude places to this day, anyone who says anything new is looked on with suspicion, and is persecuted by opinion if not injured by penalty. One of the greatest pains to human nature is the pain of a new idea. It is, as common people say, so "upsetting," it makes you think that, after all, your favorite notions may be wrong, your firmest beliefs ill founded; it is certain that till now there was no place allotted in your mind to the new and startling inhabitant, and now that it has conquered an entrance, you do not at once see which of your old ideas it will or will not turn out, with which of them it can be reconciled, and with which it is at essential enmity. Naturally, therefore, common men hate a new idea, and are disposed more or less to ill-treat the original man who brings it. Even nations with long habits of discussion are intolerant enough. In England, where there is on the whole probably a freer discussion of a greater number of subjects than ever was before in the world, we know how much power bigotry retains. But discussion, to be successful, requires toler- ance. It fails wherever, as in a French political assembly, anyone who hears anything which he dislikes tries to howl it down. If we know that a nation is capable of enduring continuous discussion, we know that it is capable of practising with equanimity continuous tolerance.

The power of a government by discussion as an instrument of elevation plainly depends—other things being equal—on the greatness or littleness of the things to be discussed. There are periods when great ideas are "in the air," and when, from some cause or other, even common persons seem to par- take of an unusual elevation. The age of Elizabeth in England was con- spicuously such a time. The new idea of the Reformation in religion, and the enlargement of the *maenia mundi* by the discovery of new and singular lands, taken together, gave an impulse to thought which few, if any, ages can equal. The discussion, though not wholly free, was yet far freer than in the average of ages and countries. Accordingly every pursuit seemed to start for- ward. . . .

In this manner, all the great movements of thought in ancient and modern times have been nearly connected in time with government by discussion. Athens, Rome, the Italian republics of the Middle Ages, the communes and states-general of feudal Europe, have all had a special and peculiar quickening influence which they owed to their freedom, and which states without that freedom have never communicated. And it has been at the time of great epochs of thought—at the Peloponnesian War, at the fall of the Roman Republic, at the Reformation, at the French Revolution—that such liberty of speaking and thinking have produced their full effect.[23]

Partly as results of the development of freedom of discussion, new lines of participation in democratic government have emerged. No longer is the voter under the necessity of getting his information on

[23] Walter Bagehot, *Physics and Politics; or, Thoughts on the Application of the Prin- ciples of "Natural Selection" and "Inheritance" to Political Society.* Copyright, 1884, by D. Appleton & Co., pp. 161-166. By permission of Appleton-Century-Crofts, Inc., New York.

issues and candidates from the candidates themselves or from their spellbinding advocates at political rallies. He now has access to this information through the newspapers, journals of opinion, radio, and, in late years, television. If he is intelligent and interested he is no longer dependent on one side for his information nor is he content with anything less than an opportunity to hear and weigh all sides. As a result, an increasing segment of the electorate is coming to question and to deliberate on political matters. Moreover, a growing number are tending to break traditional party lines and to act independently. This increasing insurgency and independence is beginning to effect a redefinition of political action by elevating the character and tone of campaigns, by requiring party leaders and candidates to improve their techniques, and by demanding a clearer and more honest statement of party policies. There is also being manifested a growing power of organized minorities. While these may represent subversive interests, they more frequently represent civic-minded citizens who know what they want and have found at last a means of becoming articulate and of making their power felt at the seats of government.[24]

In contrast to this picture of comparative freedom of choice and action on the part of citizens living under democracy, is that of many millions of the world's population living today under a one-party system of government. Totalitarianism, under whatever rubric it may be designated, has ever been a challenge to democracy. In recent decades this challenge has been met and fought out but the issue is still drawn between the ideologies of democracy and autarchy and the end of the struggle of each for domination is not in sight.[25]

CLASS AND STATUS FACTORS IN PARTY POLITICS

Mention has been made previously of the tendency of the interests of classes and other status groups to be transmuted into political terms and, in specific situations, to be translated into political action. Apart from the development of what Weber has termed "expediential asso-

24 See: V. O. Key, *Politics, Parties and Pressure Groups*, New York, T. Y. Crowell Co., 1942; Peter Odegard, *Pressure Politics*, New York, Columbia University Press, 1928; E. M. Sait, *American Parties and Elections*, New York, D. Appleton-Century Co., 1939.
25 See: R. A. A. Anshen (Ed.), *Freedom: Its Meaning*, New York, Harcourt, Brace & Co., 1940; M. J. Bonn, *The Crisis of European Democracy*, New Haven, Yale University Press, 1925; R. C. Brooks, *Deliver Us from Dictators*, Philadelphia, University of Pennsylvania Press, 1935; C. D. Bruns, *Challenge to Democracy*, New York, W. W. Norton & Co., Inc., 1935; E. H. Carr, *The Soviet Impact on the World*, New York, The Macmillan Co., 1947; R. G. Swing, *Forerunners of American Fascism*, New York, Julian Messner, Inc., 1935.

ciations," classes and status groups have no agencies or corporate means of their own of interacting advantageously with other class or status groups or with other forces inherent in the social order. Hence, either directly or indirectly, they turn to political parties and governmental sources for support. Long before the disadvantaged classes and status groups recognized the potency of political methods as possible mechanisms for their advancement to power and improved status, the classes of property and wealth had already seized upon these instruments and by one means or another had used them in their own behalf. The latter groups were as quick, however, to resist what they regarded as governmental interference in and control of business as they were willing to accept the protection of their interests by government. To this end they employed their financial and other resources to back one or another and sometimes both political parties in their bid for power, hired and maintained lobbies at the seats of government, and otherwise exerted pressures on the political and governmental processes wherever and whenever it was deemed expedient and profitable to do so.

Several factors contributed to the entrance of certain of the less favored classes and status groups into the political arena, either through their own party organizations or by strategically using their strength in support of whichever one of the existing parties promised to be most helpful to their interests. Among the factors were those just recited: that is, as a countermove to the increasing political influence of industrial and financial capitalism or whatever source of influence it was necessary to checkmate in the struggle for power. Other factors operating to lead class groups to turn to politics for redress of grievances as well as for enhancement of status include the decline of the *laissez-faire* doctrine and expanding economic and other functions of government. To these can be added the rise of organized labor, the trend toward emancipation of women, growth of public education and literacy of the masses, increase in the use of media of mass communication, the resurgence of popular democracy, recurrent economic depressions and increase in criticism of the capitalistic system, a social conception of private property, and the spread of reformism. The New Deal in the United States served as an encouragement to the "forgotten man," and the rise to power of socialistic parties in Europe particularly added weight to the movement of the so-called "common people" to assert themselves politically. It is not strange, then, that organized workers, women, ethnic and racial minorities, the aged, and reformists like the prohibitionists, the single-taxers, and the agrarians, should constitute pressure groups and either set up their own parties for political action, or seek to achieve their ends through established party channels.[26]

It may be well to point out here what are some of the present consequences of this continual struggle for politico-economic power. Those who still accept the symbols and values of ideological democracy will have to re-examine their postulates and strive for the reimplementation of their beliefs in a new setting. This necessity has been dramatically emphasized by the recent rise of the totalitarian ideologies of Nazism, Fascism, and Communism. The *laissez-faire* method of dealing with the politico-economic problems of the nineteenth century is now dead. An increase in social controls with respect to economic activity is readily seen. This is in keeping with traditional conceptions of representative government. We are moving toward a type of organization in which the state leaves economic enterprise and initiative in private hands as far as possible but intervenes at strategic points to remove maladjustments and injustices, to promote stability, and to provide social security for all. It is within some such framework of economic, political, and social structures and value systems that all groups may find their place and function.[27]

Interaction Involving Divergent Religious Faiths

The Nature of the Sect and Its Mission.—In the field of religious belief, practice, and administration, there has always been a tendency for groups to separate themselves from the main body of the larger religious group, to set themselves off from others, and to constitute distinctive bodies emphasizing peculiarities of doctrine, different modes of worship or forms of ecclesiastical authority, and defense reactions toward outsiders. Such separations arise out of conflict with the parent group and with other separatist groups. As a consequence, the new group is self-conscious and usually antagonistic, and

---

26 See: H. Agar, *The People's Choice,* Boston, Houghton Mifflin Co., 1937; C. A. Anderson, "Agrarianism in Politics," Ch. 10 in J. S. Roucek, *Twentieth Century Political Thought,* New York, Philosophical Library, Inc., 1946; William Beard, *Government and Technology,* New York, The Macmillan Co., 1934; C. L. Becker, *New Liberties for Old,* New Haven, Yale University Press, 1941; J. R. Commons, *Legal Foundations of Capitalism,* New York, The Macmillan Co., 1924; G. S. Counts, *The Schools Can Teach Democracy,* New York, John Day, 1941; F. J. Goodnow, *Social Reform and the Constitution,* New York, The Macmillan Co., 1911; H. Laski, *The Rise of Liberalism; The Philosophy of a Business Civilization,* New York, Harper & Bros., 1936; F. M. Marx, *Public Management in the New Democracy,* New York, Harper & Bros., 1940; F. C. Palm, *The Middle Classes Then and Now,* New York, The Macmillan Co., 1936; F. D. Roosevelt, *On Our Way,* New York, John Day, 1934; H. M. Stout, *Public Service in Great Britain,* Chapel Hill, University of North Carolina Press, 1938; O. Tead and H. C. Metcalf, *Labor Relations Under the Recovery Act,* New York, McGraw-Hill Book Co., Inc., 1933; L. D. White and T. V. Smith, *Politics and Public Service,* New York, Harper & Bros., 1939.

27 See: Walter Lippmann, *The Method of Freedom,* New York, The Macmillan Co., 1934.

sets up frontiers that cut off one area of life and interest from another. Such a voluntary association, which, however, admits only persons with specific religious qualifications, is known as a *sect*. By this group the conflict out of which it arose is carried on.[28]

Sectarian controversy manifests itself in a variety of forms. Differences on doctrinal points, ceremonial practices, authority, and similar subjects furnish the matters over which the controversy may be waged. The document quoted below illustrates the conflict character of sects and the schisms that arise within sectarian bodies, resulting in the multiplication of minor sects.

All these facts represent a serious, a formidable, persecution, directed against men who, whatever may have been their faults, were at least actuated by motives of the purest philanthropy. It is not difficult, however, to discover the causes of the antipathy they aroused. To the great majority of the clergy, whose parishes were invaded, and who were often themselves abusively attacked by ignorant lay preachers, they were naturally extremely obnoxious, and the "Weekly Miscellany," which was the organ of clerical opinion, was steadily hostile to the Methodist movement. Bitter, but not unprovoked, denunciations from the pulpit were the origin of the riots at Wednesbury and of nearly all the savage outbursts in Cornwall; and not a few of those in other districts were directly instigated by Anglican clergymen. The example of the bishops encouraged the assaults. Gibson, indeed, wrote against the Methodists like a Christian and a gentleman, but Warburton and Lavington assailed them with the coarsest and most scurrilous invective. . . . Usually the Methodists were denounced as Dissenters, but their leaders steadily repudiated the designation, and in England at least they met with little sympathy from the real Dissenters. The fierce fervor of Methodist devotion was as uncongenial to the spirit then prevailing in Dissent as it was to the spirit of the Established Church; and the Dissenters were at this time negotiating with a view to obtain full political privileges, and were therefore peculiarly indisposed to ally themselves with so unpopular a body as the Methodists. Watts, it is true, showed some courtesy to Whitefield, and Doddridge once admitted him to his pulpit, and preached himself once in Whitefield's tabernacle, but his conduct was severely and authoritatively censured by the leaders of his sect. On one occasion Wesley mentions three Dissenting ministers who formally excluded from the sacrament all who consented to hear him.

Another very common charge was that of Popery. This accusation arose from the fact that Catholicism was of all forms of religion the most hated, and, at a time when Jacobitism was still formidable, the most dreaded by Englishmen; and it derived some consistency from the fasts and other ascetic practices of the first Methodists, from the real resemblance which their style

---

28 Some sects are nominally pacific in that they seek to avoid controversy and other conflict patterns, as witness the Society of Friends (Quakers), the Mennonites, the Amish, etc.

of preaching bore to that of the Missioner friars, and their outbursts of
fanaticism and credulity to those recorded in the Lives of the Saints, and from
the indulgent language in which Wesley sometimes spoke of Catholic books
of devotion. . . . Considering the immense doctrinal chasm between the
Catholics and the Methodists, the pertinacity with which the charge of Popery
was repeated against the latter is very remarkable. . . . Cries of "Popery,
Popery!" interrupted the Methodist preachers. It was reported that Wesley
was born and educated in Rome, and in 1744, when all Catholics were ordered
to leave London, Wesley thought it advisable to delay his intended departure
from the metropolis lest it should countenance the charge. . . .

The movement was also marred by its full share of personal and sectarian
antipathies. Whatever calumny, whatever injustice, whatever violence of
language was displayed by the enemies of Methodism, they never equalled the
ferocity exhibited by the saints in their internal quarrels. It was in 1770 that
Wesley, alarmed at the progress of Antinomianism, and connecting it with
the fatalism of the Calvinists, caused some minutes to be published reflecting
on Calvinism, and censuring the general depreciation of good works. He was
accused of teaching justification by works, and his speedy and emphatic dis-
claimer was not sufficient to prevent a schism between the Arminian and
Calvinist Methodists. . . . The Calvinistic party acknowledged Lady Huntingdon as their leader, and she excluded all Arminians from her chapels, and
removed Fletcher of Madeley from his position at the head of her college of
Trevecca. Soon after, the leaders of her party began an attack upon Wesley,
which in its outrageous scurrility has never been surpassed. Berridge of
Everton satirized him in doggerel verse as a fox,

> The most perfect and holy and sly,
> That e'er turned a coat or could pilfer and lie,

while Toplady and Rowland Hill assailed him in the most abusive prose. . . .
"I much question," wrote Toplady, "whether a man that dies an Arminian
can go to heaven." He pronounced his great opponent to be "without honour,
veracity, or justice"; to be "the most rancorous hater of the gospel system
that ever appeared in this land"; to be "a low and puny tadpole in divinity,"
actuated by "Satanic shamelessness and Satanic guilt." . . . Of the language
of Rowland Hill a very short specimen will be sufficient. In a pamphlet of
not more than forty pages he calls Wesley, among other names, "a designing
wolf," "a dealer in stolen wares," "as unprincipled as a rook, and as silly as a
jackdaw," "a grey-headed enemy of all righteousness," "a wretch," guilty of
"wilful, gross, and abominable untruth," "a venal profligate," "a wicked
slanderer," and "an apostate miscreant." He dwells with much more than the
zest of Lavington upon the alleged impurity of the "Perfectionists," describes
the followers of Wesley as "a ragged legion of preaching barbers, cobblers,
tinkers, scavengers, draymen, and chimney-sweepers"; and declares that
"the sum and substance of John's whole preaching is I, I, I, and my brother,
my brother and I have done all the work of God that has been done in these

nations." This pious production is in the form of a letter and the author concludes it in his usual sanctimonious fashion, "Yours sincerely for Christ's sake."

On the other side, it must be admitted that the tone adopted was very different. Wesley himself wrote but little in the controversy, and that little was written with great moderation. The task of supporting the Arminian side was chiefly thrown upon Fletcher, Vicar of Madeley, a Swiss naturalized in England. He was a man of singularly sweet and gentle disposition, and his many writings against the Calvinists, though not a little tedious to a secular reader, are at least perfect models of controversial amenity maintained under extreme provocation.[29]

Professor Faris has described lucidly the role of conflict in the development of the sect:

The conflict unites the sect, creates *esprit de corps,* and heightens morale. Usually, but not always, if the conflict be too severe so that confidence is lessened, dissensions may arise and factions appear. Conflict united the German people for four years, but when they began to feel that the cause was lost the conflict broke up the unity of the nation. In the sect, however, a conflict can be with the "world," which is a subjective image, and it is possible for a sect to survive great disasters since they are so certain of ultimate success. The sect therefore has always some degree of isolation and is more apt to have a high morale when they succeed in securing a location shut off from the rest of the world. There are, however, devices of cultural isolation which overcome lack of physical separation, as can be observed in the present state of the Christian Science church. In this case isolation depends upon a separate vocabulary and particularly upon the admonition not to argue or discuss the matter with outsiders. The Masons, and to some extent the Mormons, achieve isolation by secrecy.

In this conflict period of the life of the sect the tendency is toward exclusiveness wherever feasible. Certain economic relations with the "world" are necessary, but the cultural life is protected. There is always a tendency to be an endogenous tribe. Sometimes to marry an outsider is to forfeit membership in the group. . . . Intermarriage never becomes general until disintegration has set in, and it is always a destructive influence, for queens make good foreign missionaries and no child can easily despise the religion of his mother.

A highly interesting aspect of the development of a sect is found in the tendency to divide and become two sects, typically more bitter toward each other than toward the "world" which they formerly united in opposing. . . . But whether the group divides or not, a period arrives when the isolation begins to disappear and the customs of the outside world with its beliefs and

29 W. E. H. Lecky, *A History of England in the Eighteenth Century.* Copyright, 1882, by D. Appleton & Co., Vol. 2, pp. 630-633, 650-652. By permission of Appleton-Century-Crofts, Inc., New York.

practices, even its ideals and doctrines, begin gradually to penetrate the group.[30]

Although a sect is nearly always part of a larger group it never-theless thinks of itself as different and apart. Thus, all Protestant sects are parts of Christianity, but each and every one of them con-siders itself distinct from all the rest. And, indeed, they are. Yet, ideally, the sect includes the whole group. It sets up standards for everybody and conceives itself to be as broad as humanity. All should be brought into its peculiar kind of fold. In order to fulfil its mission of saving the world and winning converts to itself, it attacks the forces, including the other sects, that oppose it or in any way hinder its purpose. It criticizes, threatens, and condemns; it hurls epithets and invectives; it holds out promises and rewards; it punishes and perse-cutes; it subtly spreads its propaganda by teaching and by ingratiating itself with those it seeks to attract to itself. These are familiar means of social control and are self-protective as well as aggressive measures.

The social consequences of the aggressive attitude of sectarianism are not hard to find. As has been suggested, this attitude usually leads to exclusiveness, disparagement and denunciation of those of other faiths, painful personal discords, acrimonious verbal assaults through the press and from the pulpit, the blocking of community enterprises that do not fit neatly into the sectarian scheme, the hinder-ing of international and interracial relations on a basis of good will and mutual benefit, the interfering with normal and wholesome mar-riages because of obstacles thrown up in response to ecclesiastical authority, the meddling in affairs of state and tampering with the laws and courts through pressure tactics, attempts to dominate in the educational field so as to propagate and perpetuate particularistic ideas, dictation to individuals and groups as to the performance of their private and social duties and in some times and places the foster-ing of warfare.

If the group achieves a territorial isolation and succeeds in attract-ing numerous adherents, it may become the dominant power in the region. As such, it may control the government, the press, and the schools, and be able to propagandize its peculiar tenets at will. Thus a new stage in the evolution of the sect may be achieved and the group transformed into a political "party" or into a nationality. Throughout much of sectarian controversy there is evident an almost complete lack of knowledge on each side of the values held by the

---

30 Ellsworth Faris, "The Sect and the Sectarian," *Pubs. Am. Sociol. Soc.*, Vol. 22, 1928, pp. 150-152.

opposition. Ecclesiastical jealousies, racial antipathies, the economic struggle itself, social cleavages, the baser appeals of politicians unable to find any real and worthy issues for their campaigns, each and all contribute in some measure to the war among religious groups.

Typical Forms of Accommodation.—In spite of their differences, sects and sectarians do succeed in accommodating themselves to each other and to the secular world around them. In fact, much of the conflict that goes on among them and between them and the outside world is due to a resistance against the secular trend; but, since sects are human groups, they feel the pull of human needs in the direction of the "fortunes of the world" and, though resisting and rationalizing, they tend to respond to secularization.[31] It is in connection with the need for and the difficulties of accommodation to present-day conditions that many of the most serious problems of institutionalized religion emerge. For organized religious groups to surrender their distinguishing features and their proselyting techniques may mean the sacrifice of more than their identity; it may mean the loss of what they conceive to be their special function and mission in the world. However, if they abandon their narrow, doctrinaire sectarianism, they may save themselves for the larger task of fostering and preserving a measure of idealism, tolerance, and the "experience of inspiration" in a troubled world. We shall now proceed to examine some of the forms typically taken by the accommodation of sects and sectarians.

The phenomenon of conversion is well known in the field of religious belief and practice. The controversies of antipathetic sects are often allayed and the mental conflicts of individual members of the antagonistic sects likewise solved by means of conversion. As in the case of nationalism, so in religion, conversion serves the function of transporting the group or the person over from one group loyalty to another, from one center of allegiance to another that is regarded as affording a greater body of satisfactions. It means the denial of old traditions and customs, of familiar beliefs and moral standards, and an acceptance of a new set of norms.

A change of religion would be a momentous rupture with the carefully guarded tradition, unless one at the same time attached himself to the people whose religion he adopted; in that case one would enter into the traditions of that people, would be under obligation to venerate its institutions, would

---

[31] See: H. Richard Niebuhr, *The Social Sources of Denominationalism,* New York, Henry Holt & Co., Inc., 1929.

accept its protecting deities as his own, and would thereby be protected against the wrath of his own national gods, that is, his ancestors. A change of religion is like the fate of a slave who changes his master. The new master into whose family and tribe he enters undertakes to protect him. But everything in the heathen resists such a step.[32]

The Nature of Conversion.—Conversion is a rapid overturning of one's whole life organization, a turning of one's back on a way of life long cherished. There is grave danger that the break-up of the personality may leave it without attachments at both ends. If the elements that made for personal organization and balance are suddenly destroyed, and no new and satisfying standards and ideals are found to replace them, we have a case of unadjustment to any social norm. The process of conversion is incomplete. However, as the process of conversion is experienced by most people, stabilizing ideals are realized imaginatively if not always practically in the new group.

To be complete, conversion involves turning back on one's former way of life. It would seem as though this would be out of the question for one who has built up a complete life organization. Adolescence seems to be the age at which conversions occur most successfully.[33]

Ordinarily the process of conversion involves some compromise. Discriminating converts accept those parts of the new culture that satisfy certain wishes and reject what would entail too great a rupture with the past. Sometimes the members of a sect will divide on the conditions of compromise, the more secularized members accepting them and the more orthodox ones preferring to suffer persecution for their faith or migrating to new regions where they hope to be left in peace. Such was the case with the Mennonites, the Mormons, and the Dukhobors.

The great diversity of faiths and outlooks existing in the western world today usually leads to the adoption of one of two attitudes on the part of those who still maintain an active interest in religion. The first attitude is that of latitudinarianism, or easy tolerance. According to this, one religion is as good as another. This type of thinking has tended to penetrate most of the evangelical churches to some extent, and while some may find its temper admirable, others

---

[32] Johan Warneck, *Living Forces of the Gospel*, translated by Neil Buchanan from the 3rd German edition, Edinburgh, Oliphant, Anderson and Ferrier, n. d., pp. 138-139.
[33] See: G. Stanley Hall, *Adolescence*, New York, D. Appleton & Co., 1916, Vol. 2, p. 294; E. D. Starbuck, *The Psychology of Religion*, New York, Charles Scribner's Sons, 1901, pp. 28-45; William James, *The Varieties of Religious Experience*, New York, Longmans, Green & Co., Inc., 1903, pp. 189-258.

criticize it as weak on the intellectual side, impotent to meet the great moral questions of the time, and easily giving place to complete indifference to religion of any kind. The other widespread attitude is that of intolerance. This is the typical sectarian attitude which leads to exclusiveness, antagonism, and overt hostility between religious bodies.

Even if it is not possible or desirable to bring the divergent religious groups together in the bonds of an ecclesiastical unity, nor to discover the highest common factor in their respective creeds upon which a new religion can be based, it has been found possible, in some instances, to bring them together purely for the sake of obtaining a better understanding of the issues which separate them, and for the consequent agreement as to certain common objectives. This is the way of accommodation through deliberation.

As in the areas of interracial, international, and industrial relations the value of informal meetings and conferences of representatives of the different groups has been found helpful in creating a better understanding of the backgrounds of their respective problems and positions, so, too, religious sects are finding such deliberations valuable. Notable though many such conferences of recent years have been, they usually have found it advantageous to overlook the very questions of tradition and difference which must be thoroughly investigated before real understanding can be attained. Frequently they have concerned themselves with only those social problems which are a challenge to all persons, religious and irreligious, alike. None the less, probably the most promising means to understanding and cooperation lie along the way of frank and sincere deliberation. Deliberation in the spirit of conciliation may lead to tolerance, which is the next step in transmuting the sect into a denomination, that is, into an accommodated group.

When denominational status, the tolerant attitude, and the desire for cooperation have been attained, then the way is open for accommodation to proceed another step toward participation, which implies unity with diversity. It means common effort toward the realization of certain goals without organic unity. Organic unity—the merging of religious groups—has been achieved in numbers of instances, as among several denominations in Canada and among a few in the United States, but such unity usually means that the uniting groups divide within themselves, some members choosing to remain outside the united bodies and to retain their distinctive features. Thus, the number of sects may be increased and the number of sectarians remain relatively the same.

The Newer Sectarian Lines.—In the United States and Canada the sectarian spirit has tended to wane somewhat in recent years although, even now, it flares up in certain quarters. Certain leaders keep animosities alive and frequently hurl verbal broadsides against those they choose to regard as the foes of Christianity, or Protestantism, or what not, but the bulk of the laity are not easily aroused. A generation and more ago the atmosphere was surcharged with vitriolic accusations and counter-accusations. Sectarian champions debated throughout the country and evangelistic fervor was at a white heat. Those were the halcyon days of sectarianism in the United States.

Today the battle lines are drawn across sectarian lines, as sectarian lines were known in the last century. In fact, what amounts to new sectarian divisions are to be seen in the conflict being waged between Fundamentalism and Modernism, between High Church and Low Church, Conservatism and Radicalism, traditional Christianity and newer cults, some of them spiritistic as Spiritualism, therapeutic as Christian Science, and syncretistic as Theosophy. Although some of the diversity of religious opinion and practice has been imported, much of it is homemade. Moreover, in America today, all the churches and faiths are faced with an increasing indifference to all forms of organized religion. With this fact confronting them it has behooved the intelligent leaders of all phases of religious belief to modify their bellicose activities among themselves and to give their attention to the great problem looming before them all, namely, how to save what they have that is worth saving. Many of the sects have been accommodated to each other in denominations. They define the situation as a struggle between religion and secularism.

QUESTIONS

1. What are the nature and functions of "parties"?
2. What is the theory about the relation between primitive secret societies and political action?
3. Discuss the role of the gang as to its political activities.
4. What is meant by saying that "Historically, the political party is a substitute for revolution"?
5. "The political party may be thought of, then, as political activity in institutionalized form." Explain.
6. What functions are served by reform and protest groups or "third parties"?
7. Discuss the connection between the class struggle and politics.
8. Characterize "charismatic" parties and "charismatic" leaders.

9. What functions are served by the party "machine" and the party "boss"?

10. Discuss the respective functions of the party convention and the party platform. What can you say about their present usefulness?

11. Discuss the changing character of political campaigns in terms of functions, techniques, and changed socio-economic conditions.

12. Voting is "an act of enlistment, an alignment for and against, a mobilization." What is the significance of such military terms as applied to voting?

13. What is the place of compromise in the accommodation of political differences?

14. Discuss Simmel's analysis of the principle of majority rule.

15. What is the significance of Bagehot's treatise on government by discussion? What is the connection between tolerance and government by discussion?

16. What evidences, other than those mentioned in the text, do you see of the development of new lines of participation in politics? Discuss the role of the independent voter.

17. What factors contributed to the entrance of less-favored classes and status groups into politics?

18. What are some of the consequences of the continual struggle for politico-economic power?

19. What characteristics are generally found in a sect?

20. Of what does "sectarianism" consist?

21. Discuss the different phases of social interaction and the different mechanisms employed by sects in their struggle for status and control.

22. What are some of the social consequences of sectarianism?

23. Discuss the significance of the statement to the effect that "though resisting and rationalizing, sects tend to be drawn toward the 'fortunes of the world.'"

24. How do you characterize and explain conversion, compromise, deliberation, and participation as they affect sectarian relations?

25. What effects grow out of the latitudinarian and the intolerant attitudes?

26. Explain: "Participation implies unity with diversity."

27. What implications are to be seen in "the newer sectarian lines"?

BIBLIOGRAPHY

ARMBRUSTER, GORDON H. "An Analysis of Ideologies in the Context of Discussion." *Am. J. Sociol.*, Vol. 50, No. 2, September, 1944, pp. 123-133.

BEARD, CHARLES A. *The American Party Battle.* New York, The Macmillan Co., 1928.

BEARD, CHARLES A. *The Economic Basis of Politics.* New York, Alfred A. Knopf, 1932.

BOGARDUS, EMORY S. *Democracy by Discussion.* Washington, American Council on Public Affairs, 1942.

BONE, HUGH A. *"Smear" Politics: An Analysis of the 1940 Campaign Literature.* Washington, American Council on Public Affairs, 1941.

BRADEN, CHARLES S. *Modern Tendencies in World Religions.* New York, The Macmillan Co., 1935.

CALVERTON, V. F. *The Passing of the Gods.* New York, Charles Scribner's Sons, 1934.

CHILDS, HARWOOD L. *Labor and Capital in National Politics.* Columbus, Ohio State University Press, 1930.

COLE, G. D. H., AND COLE, MARGARET. *A Guide to Modern Politics.* New York, Alfred A. Knopf, 1934.

COLE, STEWART G. *History of Fundamentalism.* New York, Richard R. Smith, 1931.

DINNEEN, J. F. *Ward Eight.* New York, Harper & Bros., 1936.

DOBYNS, FLETCHER. *The Underworld in American Politics.* New York, The Author, 1932.

DOUGLASS, H. PAUL. *Protestant Co-operation in American Churches.* New York, Institute for Social and Religious Research, 1930.

ELLIOTT, MABEL A., AND MERRILL, FRANCIS E. *Social Disorganization.* New York, Harper & Bros., 1941, Ch. 32.

FERGUSON, CHARLES W. *The Confusion of Tongues.* New York, Doubleday, Doran & Co., Inc., 1928.

FERGUSON, HARVEY. *People and Power: A Study of Political Behavior in America.* New York, William Morrow Co., 1947.

FLYNN, EDWARD J. *You're the Boss.* New York, The Viking Press, 1947.

FURFEY, PAUL H. *The Gang Age.* New York, The Macmillan Co., 1926.

GIST, NOEL P. *Secret Societies: A Cultural Study of Fraternalism in the United States.* Columbia, University of Missouri Studies, Vol. 15, No. 4, October 1, 1940.

GOSNELL, HAROLD F. *Machine Politics: Chicago Model.* Chicago, University of Chicago Press, 1937.

HECKSCHER, AUGUST. *A Pattern of Politics.* New York, Reynal & Hitchcock, 1947.

HERRING, PENDLETON. *The Politics of Democracy: American Parties in Action.* New York, W. W. Norton & Co., Inc., 1940.

HOLCOMBE, ARTHUR N. *The Middle Classes in American Politics.* Cambridge, Harvard University Press, 1940.

HOLCOMBE, ARTHUR N. *The New Party Politics.* New York, W. W. Norton & Co., Inc., 1933.

HOLCOMBE, ARTHUR N. *Political Parties of Today.* New York, Harper & Bros., 1924.

HUTCHINSON, PAUL. *The Ordeal of Western Religion.* Boston, Houghton Mifflin Co., 1933.

KENT, FRANK R. *The Great Game of Politics.* New York, Doubleday, Doran & Co., 1924.

KENT, FRANK R. *Political Behavior: The Heretofore Unwritten Laws, Customs and Principles of Politics as Practiced in the United States.* New York, William Morrow & Co., 1928.

KEY, V. O., JR. *Politics, Parties and Pressure Groups.* New York, T. Y. Crowell Co., 1942.

LUNDBERG, FERDINAND. *America's Sixty Families.* New York, The Vanguard Press, 1937.

MACFARLAND, CHARLES S. *Christian Unity in Practice and Prophecy.* New York, The Macmillan Co., 1933.

MACIVER, R. M. *Leviathan and the People.* Baton Rouge, La., University of Louisiana Press, 1939.

MACIVER, R. M. *The More Perfect Union.* New York, The Macmillan Co., 1948.

MacIver, R. M. *The Web of Government.* New York, The Macmillan Co., 1947, Chs. 7-8.

MacLeod, W. C. *The Origin and History of Politics.* New York, John Wiley & Sons, Inc., 1931.

McKean, Dayton D. *The Boss: Machine Politics in Action.* Boston, Houghton Mifflin Co., 1940.

McWilliams, Carey. *A Mask for Privilege: Anti-Semitism in America.* Boston, Little, Brown & Co., 1947, 1948.

Mecklin, John M. *The Story of American Dissent.* New York, Harcourt, Brace & Co., 1934.

Merriam, Charles E. *The American Party System.* New York, The Macmillan Co., 1940.

Michels, Robert. *Political Parties: A Sociological Study of the Oligarchical Tendencies of Modern Democracy.* New York, Hearst's International Library, 1915.

Mims, Edwin, Jr. *The Majority of the People: A Grammar of Democracy.* New York, Modern Age Books, 1941.

Moscow, Warren. *Politics in the Empire State.* New York, Alfred A. Knopf, 1948.

Odegard, P. H., and Helms, E. A. *American Politics.* New York, Harper & Bros., 1938.

Sait, E. M. *American Parties and Elections.* New York, D. Appleton-Century Co., 1939.

Salter, J. T. *Boss Rule.* New York, McGraw-Hill Book Co., 1935.

Salter, J. T. *The Pattern of Politics.* New York, The Macmillan Co., 1940.

Shipley, Maynard. *The War on Modern Science: A Short History of the Fundamentalist Attack on Evolution and Modernism.* New York, Alfred A. Knopf, 1927.

Silcox, Claris E., and Fisher, Galen M. *Catholics, Jews and Protestants.* New York, Harper & Bros. for the Institute of Social and Religious Research, 1934.

Stroup, Herbert H. *The Jehovah's Witnesses.* New York, Columbia University Press, 1945.

Thrasher, Frederic M. *The Gang.* 2nd rev. ed. Chicago, University of Chicago Press, 1936.

Wallis, J. H. *The Politician.* New York, F. A. Stokes Co., 1935.

Webster, Hutton. *Primitive Secret Societies.* Rev. ed. New York, The Macmillan Co., 1931.

Wright, J. F. C. *Slava Bohu: The Story of the Dukhobors.* New York, Farrar & Rinehart, 1940.

Chapter 19

INTERACTION INVOLVING INTER- AND INTRA-COMMUNITY RELATIONS

Urban-Rural Interactions

The community is not merely an organized group of people occupying a locality and carrying on certain activities; it is a cultural area as well. Robert E. Park said of the neighborhood that it has "sentiments, traditions, and a history of its own." [1] The same may be said of a community. Sharers though cities are in the more inclusive culture of their region, nevertheless each one comes to possess a cultural character and tone peculiar to itself which tends to distinguish it somewhat from other communities. Not only, then, do communities differ from one another in ecological pattern, but they tend to be unlike in the matter of folkways, mores, and bodies of sentiment, which get carried along in the traditions of the social unit and contribute to the community's "esprit de corps."

Along with their differences, communities possess many similarities, particularly communities which are about the same size and located within the same region. Some observers are of the opinion that communities are coming to be more alike as they come under the influence of the dominant cultural centers. None the less, variations do exist and these constitute the distinguishing marks of varied types of communities and make possible the classification of communities according to a variety of criteria. Communities have been classified as to size; in terms of location and characteristic features, such as rural, urban, suburban, and "rurban"; [2] with reference to function, as centers of production, centers of trade and commerce, political centers, health or recreation resorts, cultural centers, and those with diversified functions; and with respect to special cultural and sentimental characteristics, such as ethnic communities and religious or idealistic communities.

---

[1] R. E. Park, "The City," *Am. J. Sociol.*, Vol. 20, No. 5, March, 1915, p. 579.
[2] C. J. Galpin applied the term "rurban" to scattered farmsteads in which the farmers made use of nearby villages and towns for trade and other purposes. See his *Rural Life*, New York, The Century Co., 1918, pp. 90-96.

Each community of whatever size or character, unless completely isolated, is in interaction with other communities of the same class, as well as with communities of other classes. Communities of one class, especially if they are located in the same ecological or cultural region, compete with one another for trade, outlets for their products, clientele, and additions to their populations.[3] Each strives to excel its fellow communities and to rise to a higher status, perhaps in a different class. Competing communities may become rivals and rival communities may declare open hostilities against each other if the struggle for recognition, status, and power tends to be prolonged and bitter.[4] When rival or hostile communities are about evenly matched in terms of size, wealth, leadership, background resources, and sentiments of community loyalty, the conflict is likely to be long drawn out and probably will end in a draw or die out through declining interest or the passing of the leaders. On the other hand, interaction between communities almost certainly will end in the eventual domination by the one with the greater resources and more advantageous location. This appears to be what is taking place in the interaction between urban communities on the one hand and rural communities on the other. Since it is impossible for us to consider the many ramifications and implications of inter-community interaction as it involves the several different types of communities listed, we shall content ourselves with a discussion of interaction between urban and rural communities.

Differential Characteristics of Urban and Rural Cultures.—The distinctions between urban and rural are no longer clear-cut, but they have significance in all those countries where areas and cultures formerly rural are rapidly becoming urbanized.[5] Apart from the arbitrary distinctions made for purposes of the Census Bureau (which assigns all population centers of twenty-five hundred and over to the urban class) the two concepts are relative to each other; that is, the rural tends to shade off into the urban. This was not always so, however, and it is not the case now in some parts of the world.

3 See: Niles Carpenter, *The Sociology of City Life*, New York, Longmans, Green & Co., 1931, pp. 401-402; N. P. Gist and L. A. Halbert, *Urban Society*, New York, rev. ed., T. Y. Crowell Co., 1941, pp. 108-111; R. D. McKenzie, *The Metropolitan Community*, New York, McGraw-Hill Book Co., Inc., 1933, Part III, especially Ch. 12.

4 See: Jesse F. Steiner, *The American Community in Action*, New York, Henry Holt & Co., 1928, Ch. 11.

5 See: Gist and Halbert, *Urban Society*, pp. 3-4; R. E. Park in *The City* by Park and E. W. Burgess, et al., Chicago, University of Chicago Press, 1925, pp. 1-2; S. A. Queen, W. B. Bodenhafer, and E. B. Harper, *Social Organization and Disorganization*, New York, T. Y. Crowell Co., 1935, pp. 194-196, 229-230; Dwight L. Sanderson, *The Rural Community*, Boston, Ginn & Co., 1932, pp. 6-11; P. A. Sorokin and C. C. Zimmerman, *Principles of Rural-Urban Sociology*, New York, Henry Holt & Co., 1929, Ch. 2; Jesse F. Steiner, *Community Organization*, rev. ed., New York, The Century Co., 1930, pp. 18-21.

The chief differences between urban and rural cannot be measured in terms of the size of population aggregates. Urban and rural are different ways of life characterized by differences in social organization. Of the nature of the city Park says:

> The city, from the point of view of this paper, is something more than a congeries of individual men and of social conveniences—streets, buildings, electric lights, tramways, and telephones, etc.; something more, also, than a mere constellation of institutions and administrative devices—courts, hospitals, schools, police, and civil functionaries of various sorts. The city is, rather, a state of mind, a body of customs and traditions, and of the organized attitudes and sentiments that inhere in these customs and are transmitted with this tradition. The city is not, in other words, merely a physical mechanism and an artificial construction. It is involved in the vital processes of the people who compose it; it is a product of nature, and particularly of human nature.[6]

From the standpoint of its culture the city is urbane, sophisticated, cosmopolitan. The urban community partakes of that type of generalized culture we have previously referred to as secular as distinguished from the simpler, more naïve, and sacred type of culture. But just as the urban community tends to have a peculiar culture of its own, so does the distinctly rural community. What Parks says of the city could be said with equal truth of the rural hamlet if a different list of physical traits—one including barns, granaries, silos, general stores, a village green—were substituted. For the rural community also has "a body of customs and traditions, and of organized attitudes and sentiments that inhere in these customs" and that are transmitted with the rural heritage. The real differences lie not merely in different artifacts, but rather in divergent philosophies of life. The typical rural dweller recognizes that he holds ideas and opinions that differ from those held by the urbanite. His reactions to his environment are those called out by the peculiarities and necessities of that environment.[7]

> The modern rural community is one of separate farmsteads and usually a village center. This dispersion of the farms arose in the settlement of free or cheap land or was due to physiographic conditions, and its permanence was made possible by the relatively new system of direct inheritance which preserved the integrity of a farmstead of sufficient size to form an efficient agricultural unit. . . .
>
> The life of the community was at first largely in neighborhood groups; but as population increased and transportation improved, centralization of the

---

6 Park and Burgess, *The City*, p. 1.

7 See: H. Coudenhove-Kalergi, "The New Nobility," *The Century Magazine*, Vol. 109, November, 1924, pp. 3-6; Sorokin and Zimmerman, *Principles of Rural-Urban Sociology*, Ch. 13.

economic, religious, educational, and political life of the community in the village came about through the principle of social economy.[8] As its institutions and organizations become stronger, their interdependence becomes more obvious and their better integration a necessity; the common interests of the community and the concept of the community receive recognition. . . .

The social life, which also in the early days was largely confined to the neighborhood, becomes centralized in the village, at first in connection with voluntary associations and community institutions; and the provision of facilities for recreation and sociability finally becomes an object of community activity as a means of social defense against the superior social attractiveness of urban life. . . .

Another feature of the rural community which distinguishes it sharply from that of the village community is the institutional form of its organization, with the entire separation of the political, economic, religious, and educational functions in discrete institutions, leaving only its sociability under customary control and with a definite tendency toward its institutionalization. . . .

Social control was made difficult by the prevailing doctrines of liberty, independence, equality, and political rights, which were particularly acceptable in a new country. The primary sanctions recognized were those of the law rather than those of custom. The rural community has evolved in an age of individualism and competition. Individualism was fostered by the most rapid increase in means of communication, while the collective mind, which ever moves more slowly than the individual, was unable to evolve a mechanism for maintaining social control. Community solidarity and *esprit de corps* are much weaker than in the village community, but morale becomes stronger on account of the ease and celerity with which public opinion can be formed, because of more and better leadership, and through the fact that it is increasingly due to voluntary loyalty from intelligent personal conviction. . . .

Arising as a group of individuals seeking personal advantage, whose individualism sought expression in associations and in the formal organization of institutions, the rural community has gradually centralized its activities in the village center as a means of social economy, and the integration of its special-interest groups is demanded as a means of self-preservation. So arises a new type of local social organization, with a physical basis because it is a locality group, but held together by psychological relations which are voluntary rather than customary. It is becoming integrated as a means of adapting the life of the local group so that it may maintain a satisfactory culture and have its place in the control of a world-wide economy resulting from free communication.[9]

---

[8] See: R. M. MacIver, *The Community*, New York, The Macmillan Co., 1928, pp. 334ff.
[9] Dwight Sanderson, *The Rural Community*, pp. 556-560. See also A. W. Hayes, *Rural Sociology*, New York, Longmans, Green & Co., 1929, Ch. 13; Charles R. Hoffer, *Introduction to Rural Sociology*, rev. ed., New York, Farrar & Rinehart, 1934, Ch. 18; Roy H. Holmes, *Rural Sociology*, New York, McGraw-Hill Book Co., Inc., 1932, Ch. 12; G. A. Lundquist and Thomas N. Carver, *Principles of Rural Sociology*, Boston, Ginn & Co., 1927, Ch. 9; Dwight L. Sanderson, *The Farmer and His Community*, New York, Harcourt, Brace & Co., 1922, Ch. 1; Dwight L. Sanderson, *Rural Sociology and Rural Social Organiza-

This description of the rural community emphasizes the roles of voluntary associations and institutions, but also indicates something of the character of the relations of rural people to each other and to their culture. Mention is made of adaptations in the social life of the rural community as "a means of social defense against the superior social attractiveness of urban life." This latter point is very significant in that it reveals the modern rural community in contact with urban centers and that interaction is operative between them, with the result that the rural community is on the defensive.

Interaction Between Urban and Rural Communities.—The cities and towns have drawn the major part of their subsistence from the open country, rural hamlets, and villages. They have attracted a large share of the nation's ability, energy, and ambition through attracting its young men and women. That this was necessary for the development of the towns and cities is not questioned, but that it imposed a penalty upon the country is also a fact. Not only is it quality of manhood of which the town robs the country; it is of mass of manhood as well.

During the first half of this century interaction between urban and rural communities in the Western World has increased mainly because of the tremendous improvements in the system of communication. An appreciation of this change is difficult for the present generation, who have always known automobiles, surfaced highways, telephones, city newspapers, the airplane, and the radio.[10] Many of the changes have been subtle and pervasive and have left their impression on practically all phases of city and rural life. One general effect is the tendency to bring the city to the country.

Ecological Interaction.—Reference has already been made to the movement of population from country to town, from town to city.[11] This trend continued fairly evenly until 1927. For that year and for the two following years it showed a decided decline over preceding

tion, New York, John Wiley & Sons, Inc., 1942, Chs. 12-13; Dwight L. Sanderson and R. A. Polson, *Rural Community Organization*, New York, John Wiley & Sons, Inc., 1939, pp. 46-54; N. L. Sims, *Elements of Rural Sociology*, rev. ed., New York, T. Y. Crowell Co., 1934, Ch. 4; N. L. Sims, *The Rural Community*, New York, Charles Scribner's Sons, 1920, Part II; T. Lynn Smith, *The Sociology of Rural Life*, rev. ed., New York, Harper & Bros., 1947, pp. 336-342; Carl C. Taylor, *Rural Sociology*, rev. ed., New York, Harper & Bros., 1933, Chs. 23-24.

10 See: M. M. Willey and S. A. Rice, *Communication Agencies and Social Life*, Recent Social Trends in the United States Monograph, New York, McGraw-Hill Book Co., Inc., 1933, pp. 1-5.

11 Many thousands of "rural" dwellers are added to the populations of cities every year by the process of extending the boundaries of municipalities and incorporating them within the corporate limits of the cities. In other words, they become "urban" dwellers without changing their location.

TABLE 7

ESTIMATES OF THE FARM POPULATION, BIRTHS AND DEATHS OCCURRING IN THE FARM POPULATION, AND NUMBER OF PERSONS MOVING TO AND FROM FARMS, UNITED STATES, 1940-47 *

Year	Farm Population on Jan. 1	Change Through Natural Increase			Change Through Migration						
		Total	Births	Deaths	Total†	Civilian Migration			Military Migration		
						Total†	To Farms	From Farms†	Total	To Armed Forces	From Armed Forces
	(000)	(000)	(000)	(000)	(000)	(000)	(000)	(000)	(000)	(000)	(000)
1947	27,550	419	674	— 255	281	— 266	1,077	—1,343	547	— 159	706
1946	26,850	354	604	— 250	1,306	603	1,684	—1,081	703	— 191	894
1945	25,190	345	591	— 246	— 676	— 476	817	—1,293	— 200	— 300	100
1944	25,521	355	610	— 255	—1,493	— 988	994	—1,982	— 505	— 605	100
1943	26,659	390	660	— 270	—2,779	—1,920	819	—2,739	— 859	— 859	—
1940	29,048	417	702	— 285	—1,357	—1,146	814	—1,960	— 211	— 211	—
1941	29,988	400	696	— 296	— 681	— 606	690	—1,296	— 75	— 75	—
1942	30,269										

† Including persons who have not moved but who are no longer in the farm population because agricultural operations have ceased on the place where they are living.

* Press release of the Bureau of Agricultural Economics, United States Dept. of Agriculture, Washington, August, 1947.

years. After 1929 and during the economic depression of the 1930's it was reversed, to be resumed during World War II.

Estimated recent losses and gains in farm population in the United States, as shown in Table 7, give a fair impression of this movement during the war years. Most of the increase noted in the last two years was due to migration to farms, although for 1946 the natural increase of 419,000 greatly exceeded the in-migration of 281,000. Evidently the increase of farm population due to migration reached its peak in 1945, with the demobilization of some 703,000 young farm dwellers from the armed forces to civilian life. However, it is probable that not all of these remained on the farms for long.

The high birth rate on the farms in 1946, the highest since 1929, was partially a result of demobilization. Least important of the sources of increase was civilian migration. The net balance of moves to and from farms by civilians gave an increase of 337,000 to the farm population in the two-year period. Actually the net civilian migration to farms was larger than this in 1945, but a small net migration from farms in 1946 offset the 1945 migration gain to some extent. As in former years, the total number of persons moving to and from farms was much greater than the net migration. More than a million people moved in each direction in 1945, and again in 1946. The net gain in farm population through civilian migration in the year 1945 offset only 12 per cent of the 5.1 million net loss that occurred between 1940 and 1945 through civilian migration. Whether the shift in migration is temporary or permanent is relatively unimportant for the purpose of this discussion. The significant thing is that the movement from farms to towns and cities and from cities and towns to the farms is largely the result of changes in economic factors affecting life in both city and country.[12]

A great number of persons classified as "rural" by the Census Bureau do not live on farms. According to the 1940 census, 22.9 per cent of the total population of the United States were classed as rural farm and 20.5 per cent of the total population as rural non-farm.

---

[12] For discussions of migration between farm and city and city and farm, see: C. J. Galpin, "Analysis of Population Movements to and from Farms," Washington, United States Dept. of Agriculture, October, 1927; Wilson Gee and Dewees Runk, "Selection in Cityward Migration," *Am. J. Sociol.*, Vol. 37, No. 2, September, 1931, pp. 254-265; Rudolph Heberle, "The Causes of Rural Urban Migration: A Survey of German Theories," *Am. J. Sociol.*, Vol. 43, No. 6, May, 1938, pp. 932-950; Hoffer, *Introduction to Rural Sociology*, pp. 61-69; Holmes, *Rural Sociology*, Ch. 9; Paul H. Landis, "Internal Migration by Subsidy," *Social Forces*, Vol. 22, December, 1943, pp. 183-187; Paul H. Landis, *Rural Life in Process*, New York, McGraw-Hill Book Co., Inc., 1948, Chs. 13-17; W. P. Mauldin, "Selective Migration from Small Towns," *Am. Sociol. Rev.*, Vol. 5, No. 5, October, 1940, pp. 748-758; Dwight L. Sanderson, *Rural Sociology and Rural Social Organization*, New York, John Wiley & Sons, 1942, pp. 79-94; T. Lynn Smith, *The Sociology of Rural Life*, Ch. 9; Sorokin and Zimmerman, *Principles of Rural-Urban Sociology*, Part V; A. S. Whiteley, "The Peopling of the Prairie Provinces of Canada," *Am. J. Sociol.*, Vol. 35, No. 2, September, 1929, pp. 240-253.

In addition, urban centers in 1940 contained a farm population of 330,723, making a total farm population of 30,546,911.[13] The catch-all category of "rural non-farm" includes all except the population living inside the corporate limits of urban centers and the so-called farming population. To be sure, some attempts have been made to identify these remnants with the village population, i.e., the inhabitants of incorporated centers of less than 2,500 people.[14]

Recent years have witnessed a rapid development of rurban fringes around large urban centers. In these country-city fringes,

farmers find themselves confronted by new neighbors who are more interested in discussing wage rates, layoffs, and collective bargaining than in such earthy topics as crop rotation, dairy herd improvement, or the merits of hybrid seed corn. And suburbanites find their new farmer friends are not always sympathetic to their desire for water and sewage facilities, bigger schools, and other such city conveniences—all of which cost money and add to the farmers' taxes. Yet more and more of these very same farmers are looking to the cities for seasonal wage employment, recreation, schooling, and worship. Likewise more and more suburbanites are turning to the soil in quest of a more wholesome and more secure way of life than they have known in the cities. The farmer is becoming citified and the suburbanite is becoming countrified.[15]

Besides the challenge of the land use problems resulting from this new type of settlement, Firey described the fringe area as a problem one for several reasons:

(1) It removes land from agricultural productivity; (2) platting becomes unguided, uncoordinated, and generally in excess of effective demand, thus creating vast tracts of idle land, irregular settlement patterns, and tax-delinquent holdings; (3) taxes must increase in order to maintain services . . . but such taxes commonly exceed the tax-paying capacity of both farmers and

---

[13] See: Smith, *The Sociology of Rural Life*, p. 46. Elsewhere (p. 16) Smith says: " 'Rural non-farm,' one of the United States Census categories, is almost a contradiction in terms; in addition to the residents of villages and hamlets it includes a hodgepodge of everything urban—from roadhouses, night clubs, and tourist camps, to boarding schools, summer resorts, and canning factories—which is to be found outside the corporation limits of towns and cities."

[14] *Ibid.*, p. 47. See: J. H. Kolb and E. deS. Brunner, *A Study of Rural Society*, Boston, Houghton Mifflin Co., 1935, pp. 11, 81-83, 229-247.

[15] Walter Firey, *Social Aspects of Land Use Planning in the Country-City Fringe: The Case of Flint, Michigan*, Spec. Bull. 339, Michigan State College Agr. Exp. Sta., June, 1946, p. 5. See also R. B. Andrews, "Elements in the Urban Fringe Pattern," *J. Land and Pub. Utility Ec.*, Vol. 18, May, 1942, pp. 169-183; J. Allan Beegle, "Characteristics of Michigan's Fringe Population," *Rural Sociology*, Vol. 12, No. 3, September, 1947, pp. 254-263; Walter Firey, "Ecological Considerations in Planning for Rurban Fringes," *Am. Sociol. Rev.*, Vol. 11, No. 4, August, 1946, pp. 411-423; W. R. Gordon and G. S. Meldrum, *Land, People and Farming in a Rurban Zone*, Bull. 285, Rhode Island Agr. Exp. Sta. and Bur. of Agr. Ec., Dept. of Agriculture cooperating, 1942; R. R. Myers and J. Allan Beegle, "Delineation and Analysis of the Rural-Urban Fringe," *Applied Anthrop.*, Vol. 6, Spring, 1947, pp. 14-22; Myles W. Rodehaver, "Fringe Settlement as a Two-Dimensional Movement," *Rural Sociology*, Vol. 12, March, 1947, pp. 49-57; J. F. Thaden, *The Lansing Region and Its Tributary Town-Country Communities*, Spec. Bull. 302, Michigan State College Agr. Exp. Sta., March, 1940; George S. Wehrwein, "The Rural-Urban Fringe," *Ec. Geog.*, Vol. 18, July, 1942, pp. 217-228.

shop workers; (4) unregulated platting frequently permits tracts to be subdivided with no deed restrictions, thereby ruining adjacent subdivisions that
may have started under high deed restrictions; (5) fringe dwellers are
frequently unprepared and ill informed about buying land, getting implements,
and cultivating gardens; (6) the fringe area boosts land values to the point
at which it no longer pays to continue agricultural operations.[16]

While many problems of integration and coordination inhere in
the fringe areas between city and country, this particular form of the
process of rurbanization is likely to increase. Equally significant are
certain other ecological and social tendencies at work to effect interaction between urban and rural population, factors which profoundly
influence the modes of living and culture patterns of the two types of
communities.[17]

Among the principal urban social patterns that are invading the
rural communities and tending to alter the economy of rural life are
commercialism, capitalism, specialization, and organization. Traditionally, the life of the city has been its trade. The city evolved from
the market place. For obvious reasons, the city finds its chief activity
in commerce or in the production of goods for exchange. On the
other hand, agriculture has been relatively free from trade. "Production was mainly for immediate consumption, not for exchange. Farming was self-sustaining, having little need even for a money medium.
But industry altered all this by creating wants to be supplied by the
city and by requiring raw stuffs of the farms. Thus trading has been
induced and that through the medium of money until the country
produces for the market, for money, for profit; and the farmer becomes as dependent upon selling and buying as is the townsman.
The completeness of this dependence measures the extent of commercialization, hence the degree of urban domination." [18]

Interaction is further illustrated by the spread of capitalism, a concomitant of industrialization and urbanization, from the city to the
country. Land is of particular importance to agriculture because it
is the only natural resource that is basic to this industry. Therefore,
the farmer is vitally interested in the potentialities of the land he
works and is greatly concerned with the possibilities of its ownership.[19] But modern farming for the market and for profit requires

---

[16] Firey, *Social Aspects of Land Use Planning in the Country-City Fringe: The Case of
Flint, Michigan, op. cit.,* p. 3.
[17] See: E. T. Hiller, "Extension of Urban Characteristics into Rural Areas," *Rural
Sociology,* Vol. 6, September, 1941, pp. 242-257; T. C. McCormick, "Major Trends in Rural
Life in the United States," *Am. J. Sociol.* Vol. 36, No. 5, March, 1931, pp. 721-734; N. L.
Sims, "The Social Process and Rural Civilization," *Pubs. Am. Sociol. Soc.,* Vol. 26, August,
1932, pp. 62-67. Sims' article is the principal source of data for the rest of this section.
[18] Sims, "The Social Process and Rural Civilization," *op. cit.,* p. 63.
[19] See: Taylor, *Rural Sociology,* Ch. 6.

more than land. In order to work it profitably, machinery, labor, and credit are needed in greater proportion. Because it is more difficult for operators to get both the land and capital needed, the amount of farm debt, mortgages, and the number of farm tenants tend to be increased.[20]

But it is not alone in the use of larger amounts of capital that farming is taking on the urban pattern; it is also in its development of a wage-earning class. Just as the extensive employment of capital in manufacturing enterprises created an owning class and a proletarian mass who were devoid of property rights in the instruments of production, so is the use of much capital in agriculture creating a few owners and many tenants. In fact, the consequences of capitalization are much the same in agriculture as in industry. Mass production which has come to the farms gives further evidence in point. The result of this is crop yield far in excess of the consumptive power of the population, even as overcapitalization in industry has brought a capacity for manufacturing way beyond any market demand. With the means of mass production on the farms go heavy fixed charges, leading to a scramble for profits in the country as in the city. So capitalistic farming prevails and mode-of-living agriculture is pushed to the wall. Thus, in another way, urbanism overrides and supplants rural culture.[21]

Specialization has also come to the farms from the industrialized cities. Until a generation ago the average farmer and his family in the United States and Canada were not only engaged in the craft of husbandry, but in many other arts and crafts as well.[22] This included the creative arts and crafts such as carpentry, woodcutting, blacksmithing, painting, sewing, baking, and the like. Today, little is left to farm dwellers in contact with urban shops and emporia but the craft of husbandry and even that, in late years, has tended to develop along special lines. The one crop, and that a money-crop, has appeared and become extensively developed. This has increased rural dependency and subordination.

---

20 *Ibid.*, Ch. 11 and Bibliography.
21 Sims, "The Social Process and Rural Civilization," *op. cit.*, p. 64. See also W. B. Bizzell, *The Green Rising*, New York, The Macmillan Co., 1926, Chs. 2, 3, 4, 6; J. M. Gillette, *Rural Sociology*, New York, The Macmillan Co., 1922, Chs. 11, 14, 15; E. A. Goldenweiser and L. E. Truesdell, "Farm Tenancy in the United States," Census Monographs IV, Washington, Govt. Printing Office, 1924; C. Horace Hamilton, "Social Effects of Recent Trends in the Mechanization of Agriculture," *Rural Sociology*, Vol. 4, March, 1939, pp. 3-19; Hayes, *Rural Sociology*, Ch. 5; Hoffer, *Introduction to Rural Sociology*, Chs. 2 and 9; H. W. Laidler, *Concentration in American Industry*, New York, T. Y. Crowell Co., 1931, Ch. 20; J. K. MacKinsie, "The Combined Reaper-Thresher in Western Canada," *Pamphlet No. 83*, Ottawa, Dominion of Canada, Dept. of Agriculture, New Series, 1929; L. E. Matthael, "More Mechanization in Farming," *Int. Labor Review*, Geneva, Vol. 23, No. 3, March, 1931, pp. 324-368; T. Lynn Smith, *The Sociology of Rural Life*, Ch. 15; C. C. Zimmerman, *The Changing Community*, New York, Harper & Bros., 1938, Ch. 6; C. J. Zintheo, "Machinery in Relation to Farming," in L. H. Bailey (Ed.), *Cycl. Am. Agr.*, New York, The Macmillan Co., 1912, Vol. 1, pp. 208-209.
22 See: Sorokin and Zimmerman, *Principles of Rural-Urban Sociology*, pp. 285-290.

Sims attempts to evaluate the results of urban dominance.

Profits they must make if they are to live, for no other choice remains when once mode-of-living agriculture has been abandoned. But few, it appears, have learned how to make profits; and some are questioning whether the system will really permit many to do it. Endeavoring as best they can to succeed, the farmers have been compelled to adopt still more of the urban complex; they have organized. The co-operative movement is the result. This shows them resorting to other methods of industry to secure profits, as, for instance, to standardization and controlled production, to regularized marketing, to monopoly, to price fixing, to processing and to various other devices employed by urban corporations. Perhaps organization will avail to make business farming successful. Be that as it may, it is a question whether any considerable part of the country population can long resist complete submission to business farming. In other words, can any nation's culture remain half modern and half mediaeval in its subsistence mores? It is doubtful if it can. It is also a question whether mode-of-living and profit-seeking agriculture can operate side by side in a city-made civilization.[23]

The Process of Urbanization.—The "urbanization" of the rural community signifies that urban and rural cultures are fusing, with the result that there will be eventually but one general culture pattern for the whole country. All this means more than the capitalization, organization, commercialization, mechanization, and specialization of the agricultural economy. The rural community is being brought in contact with urban life through the spectacular series of developments in transportation and communication. Urban areas are expanding, city services are being extended, and the mobility of both urban and rural people is increasing. Rural communities are dominated by urban centers because in the latter is centralized the control of capital, credit, the markets, prices, labor and manufacture, and trade. Their non-pecuniary institutions, mode of life and social attitudes are also being patterned after those of the city through its fashion centers, newspaper offices, "radio cities," schools and universities.

Rural Social Changes as One Observer Sees Them.—Sims says:

Rural grouping as represented by the neighborhood, primary association and local trade centers is being supplanted by the city mode. Larger social areas, wider contacts, broader interests and newer forms of association are not only being made possible and easy by new methods of communication, but, what is more significant, they are being forced by the new economy. Localism is yielding to the influence of metropolitanism. The megalopolis is gathering

---

[23] Sims, "The Social Process and Rural Civilization," *op. cit.*, pp. 64-65.

to itself the little towns and country neighborhoods as a hen gathereth her chicks under her wing. Wide districts have been thus affected. As the city proper is largely devoid of primary community life, so the regions of conurbation tend to become wholes without distinct parts. In other words, they become decommunalized. Some idea of the extent of this is indicated by data from the last census which showed in the United States ninety-three cities of 100,000 or more population. In them and the environs defined by a twenty-five mile radius dwelt nearly half of the nation's people. In these areas the community form is undergoing the type of urbanization indicated. Beyond them in the far-flung reaches, out of touch of the megalopolises, where live the most rural half of the nation, there are lesser cities, exerting in a small way something of the same influence also.[24]

The conflict that once characterized urban-rural relations in most quarters no longer exists to any great extent. The supposed differences between rural and urban dwellers, with respect to religious beliefs, aesthetic interests, and conduct, have been exaggerated in the past.[25] When two peoples occupy contiguous territory, but live in different social worlds, ambiguous notions are almost certain to arise and influence their contacts and retard their interaction.

Conflict patterns appear in such situations and, if blows are not struck, at least each side attempts to discredit the other by use of disparaging gossip, invidious comparisons, and epithets. The economically dominant group, in this case the urban dwellers, tends to subordinate the rural folk. The latter, relatively self-sufficient for so long, avoided contacts with the superior city group as much as possible and thus minimized the overt expression of antagonism. As changes in the ease and celerity of movement led to the invasion of the rural districts by travelers, summer boarders, salesmen, and sightseers from the cities, resistance to city ways gave ground. Each group began to see the other's divergent cultures in a new light.

Discontent pervaded the rural population, particularly the more susceptible young people. These became more urbanized in their tastes and wants, more critical of their elders and more exacting in their demands, more independent and difficult to hold in the rural environment. Disorganization in the rural neighborhood, family, and other institutions, was followed by attempts at reorganization according to the urban pattern. While this reorganization is by no means complete, it has proceeded far in the United States and certain other western countries.

---

[24] *Ibid.*, p. 66. The census referred to is that of 1930.
[25] E. de S. Brunner and I. Lorge, *Rural Trends in Depression Years*, New York, Columbia University Press, 1937, pp. 300-328; P. A. Sorokin, "Rural-Urban Differences in Religious Culture, Beliefs, and Behavior," *Pubs. Am. Sociol. Soc.*, Vol. 23, 1929, pp. 223-238; Sorokin and Zimmerman, *Principles of Rural-Urban Society*, Part IV.

We have mentioned the movement of farm products and of rural population. A large proportion of the young, and of females in particular, move to the cities. Like all migrants, they carry with them a certain amount of mental baggage, so to speak, as well as their worldly goods. Thus rural attitudes and habits, rural interests and ideas, are transplanted by them to the cities, thereby creating in the urban environment rural culture areas. Not only has this been true of immigrant peasant groups from the old world and of Negro migrants from the agricultural South, but it applies to other rural invaders of urban centers. As a consequence, cultural conflicts inevitably arise. Elements of accommodation, however, are present and gradually the majority of the newcomers adjust themselves to the urban mores. Thus social interaction operates in two directions between the urban and the rural communities.

INTRA-COMMUNITY INTERACTION

In some of the preceding chapters and in some of those which follow, some treatment is given to the ways in which population centers, particularly urban centers, tend to react to the influx of new population and cultural elements from outside, and also to some of the ways in which these fresh increments of population and culture interact with the indigenous people and culture patterns of the cities. In this section we shall undertake to view the processes of interaction as they function within those local communities which are apparently on the losing end of the urban-rural interactional process.

"Littletown" in a Changing Order.—In the United States and Canada there are many agricultural and industrial villages and small towns which have witnessed the decline of their populations, the loss of much of their business to nearby cities, and the weakening if not actual disappearance of many of their institutions and communal functions. This was especially true of the decade from 1920 to 1930. The years since 1930, marked by depression and war, have seen a subsiding of these tendencies.[26]

---

[26] See: Brunner and Lorge, *Rural Trends in Depression Years*, Ch. 3; Douglas Ensminger, "The Impacts of the War on the Rural Community," *Social Forces*, Vol. 22, October, 1943, pp. 76-80; J. H. Kolb, "Agricultural and Rural Life," *Am. J. Sociol.*, Vol. 39, No. 6, May, 1934, pp. 787-799; R. K. Lamb, "Mobilization of Human Resources," *Am. J. Sociol.*, Vol. 48, No. 3, November, 1942, pp. 323-330; T. B. Manny, "The Conditions of Rural Life," *Am. J. Sociol.*, Vol. 40, No. 6, May, 1935, pp. 720-728; William F. Ogburn (Ed.), *American Society in Wartime*, Chicago, University of Chicago Press, 1943, pp. 1-16, "Population," by William F. Ogburn; pp. 40-62, "The American Town," by W. Lloyd Warner; pp. 63-81, "The Urban Community," by Louis Wirth; and pp. 82-104, "Farms and Farming Communities," by Lowry Nelson.

While some small centers have disappeared, others have appeared. Studies indicate that the disappearance and reappearance of small trade centers is due to the mobility of the open country population rather than to the growth of major trading and industrial towns. The small centers are not losing out in numbers, on the whole. They remain to perform vital, if changed, functions for their rural constituencies.

What has been happening to many small towns and villages and how these communities have been meeting the situation is revealed in the case of "Littletown," a "cozy village in a hollow of the beautiful, surprisingly abrupt hills of southwestern New York. Nearly a century and a half old, 'Littletown' grew slowly but was regarded as a coming town." First, it became something of a commercial center in the days of canal transportation in New York state, and then came very nearly being in the heart of the first oil development in the country, but was passed by in favor of a location a few miles away. Finally, it had ambitions to become a manufacturing town.

LITTLETOWN SPEAKS FOR ITSELF

In the first decade of the present century, Littletown made its bid as a manufacturing center. A knife factory, a pulley works, a cheese-box factory, and a novelty concern erected buildings and began operations. Perhaps a hundred men were employed, with two dozen others in the two older mills that had been long established for the grinding of feed and flour and the sawing of lumber. An enterprising citizen with little taste put up a whole street of somber houses, all alternately alike, on the edge of town. We had our factories and our slums. We were on the way to becoming a big town.

The knife factory died first and one of the banks took it over. The novelty firm moved on. The pulley works went under two years ago. The box factory merged with the saw mill.

The buildings still stand there, sagging, empty, and the Chamber of Commerce is busy dangling bait before the eyes of small city businesses, hoping to entice them here. A year or so ago some of the younger business men became impatient and from somewhere managed to raise two thousand dollars, which they gave, together with an old barnlike structure, to a man with an idea for an airplane. The plane almost flew, at that.

Commerce, oil, manufacturing—they have all paid us but fleeting visits. They roused our hopes, they made us dream. Yet on the hillsides the sleek cows still graze, the milk trucks roll through town in the early morning, and the only mills that stood the test of time are the feed and flour mills, grinding out food for the cows. Even the saw mill is owned by the same men that own the feed mill. And it makes cheese-boxes. We have not wanted to be rural, but it seems that we cannot help it.

Although Littletown is small, it does not lack facilities for trade. There are three chain groceries in town, hated like poison by the proprietors of the locally owned groceries, of which there are also three. The local stores are forever urging us to keep our dollars at home, to support home industries, to remember old friends; but so far only one of them has cleaned up his place of business, painted the front an attractive color, enamelled the shelves, and removed the cat from the warm show window. He gets some of the business that the bright, neat chains get, but the other two have their troubles.

We did have two bakeries, one of them half a grocery also. The bakery has gone bankrupt; the combination hangs on. Bread trucks come in daily from Oleander with fresh rolls and bread and pastry, attractively done up in boxes or transparent paper with no flies inside, and most of our housewives prefer to buy their baked goods that way.

If you wish to buy a pair of shoes in our town, you have many opportunities. When the last census was taken, there were only two thousand eight hundred and forty-four feet in the village, but there are six places in which to buy shoes. There are two men's clothing stores, one pool room, one men's and women's clothing store, and two dry goods stores—all selling shoes. Of course, no one of them has a large assortment of either sizes or styles, but you may find what you want if you are lucky.

There are two meat markets, one run by the man who also manages the moving picture theater. But two of the chain groceries also carry meat, and so one of the markets has put in a line of bread and rolls, cakes and canned goods. He is new to town and swears that if the competition extends to other stores he will put in dresses and cameras and a soda fountain.

There is the ever present ice cream parlor, whose owner, in partnership with his brother, also runs an ice cream factory. They make very good ice cream, putting real cream from the local dairies into it; thus it costs more to make than do the frozen puddings turned out by the Buffalo factories, and so their business remains small. The drugstore on the opposite corner from the ice cream parlor carries the Buffalo brand.

There are two drug stores and they both sell drugs in addition to watches, alarm clocks, cameras, radios, candles, wall paper, candy, mirrors, pictures, greeting cards, toys, and what not. And there are two pool rooms, two hardware stores, two electric stores, the proprietor of one of which doubles as a funeral director, three restaurants, two gift shops with jewelers' counters, two hotels, four garages.

Yes, we have the facilities for doing business. Two of everything at least, including two banks to handle the inevitable bankruptcies that come more frequently in recent years. If Prosperity ever dared walk down our main street it would be plucked raw before it had gone half a block.

We used to have business too. The farmers' teams crowded the streets, and their children the stores, and everyone was happy. They used to give you a bag of candy when you paid your bill. But business is drifting to Oleander now, with its ten-cent stores and its larger stocks of suits and dresses and furniture, only twenty-five minutes away over a good paved road that we were mighty pleased with when it was first laid down.

Sometimes we look back on the paving of that road and grin crookedly. We were as proud as Punch when the job was finished. There were editorials in the paper, photographs of leading citizens, and all that. We came within an inch of having one of those celebrations with a symbolic wedding. If our storekeepers could have seen how much of their business was going to roll over that road to Oleander, they would have worked for a symbolic funeral instead.

But they didn't see it and went right on doing business as they had done it for years before, when we had to buy from them or go without. But now, if we don't like what they have or the price that they set upon it, we can try in Oleander without much trouble. A lot of small-town business men are making that same mistake; they do not seem to realize that the swamps and hills that cut their customers off from the rest of the world are being filled and levelled now, and that their business is in competition with every other store of the same line within forty miles. Even Oleander, now with nearly twenty thousand people, complains that some of the trade is going off to Buffalo, seventy miles to the northeast; and Oleander has some large stores.

One of the things that keeps business poor is the fact that there just aren't as many people to buy goods as there used to be. Our village declined 11.7 per cent in population between the last two federal censuses. As for the countryside round us, a drive over the dirt roads in any direction will show what is happening there, as house after house stands empty with its shutters banging in the wind. It does no good to call those dirt roads "side" roads; they were main roads when our village was growing and our present number of stores were founded, and the people who traded with us came over them to market.

Modern methods of agriculture have made it possible for one farmer to handle more stock and more land than several farmers could in the former days, and the surplus farmers have moved away. The poorer land is going out of cultivation, as not worth a man's time, and the better land is being tilled more cheaply and better. The population of the old canal and post road days is not needed any more. Men do not go down the meadows four and six abreast, swinging their scythes, at harvest time; one man rides round on a mower. One man sitting on a tractor turns two or three furrows at once. One man milks two cows at once while leaning against a post and watching the machine suck and blow. Farming is a business now, and the sheriff sells out the man who cannot run his farm in a business way.

The people that live in Littletown are nice. The Legion and the Ku Klux would accept them all. We have very few foreign families—you could count them on one hand—and still fewer colored. There are the usual number of faithful elderly spinsters waiting to join Ma and Dad, who died and left them without the job that had been husband and children to them; the usual number of widows and widowers living alone with their memories in rambling, solitary houses; the usual number of retired farmers sniffing the wind wistfully in the morning; the usual number of children playing in the yards of the smaller houses on the side streets. There are not many young people, though; the population takes a running jump over the twenties, and the few that are left keep asking, "What's doing in the city? Are jobs opening up there yet?"

It makes it rather hard on the young folks in high school. They are determined not to be like Mother and Dad, but there are few in between to copy after. So they read the magazines and go to the movies and get their styles of dressing and acting from there. A little too much lipstick, talk rather coarse and loud, clothes just a bit extreme, and a faraway look of cities over the horizon when the school bell has rung for the last time, tell their story.

A year or two ago one of the men from the college of agriculture gave the young folks in our high school a questionnaire about their choice of a vocation. Only 16.5 per cent of them said they were planning to do work similar to their father's, and only 13.8 per cent were intending to stay in town. Their dreams will change, of course, and disappointment will also come; but that does not change the present situation much. Our young folks do not like us and see no future for themselves with us.

On Sunday morning the bells in five steeples ring the call to worship, and the doors of five churches open for the crowds of worshippers who will not come. All of our churches have a seating capacity far in excess of their resident membership. Yet we are a fairly religious town; for a census that the churches took one year showed that over half of our population belonged to some church, and the average for the United States is less than that.

Our churches are costly affairs. In 1930 we spent, one of' the ministers estimated, $17,507 for the four Protestant churches alone. Thirty years before that the records show that the cost of these same churches, with more members, was only $7,089. I do not attribute this rise to extravagance but to the upward tendency of our necessities; thirty years ago we did not feel that a college education was necessary for our ministers; but we do now, for so many of us are college educated that we abhor scientific blunders in the pulpit. And college men cost us more than illiterate, or semi-so, ministers. The same is true of our pipe organs, our redecorated buildings, our robed choirs. Those things are part of our modern culture.

Our extravagance comes, however, in our insistence that each small church group must have those things for itself. The Methodists, with only ninety-four members, must have those things just as do the Baptists, with two and one-half times as many people over whom to spread the cost. Some people I know have actually declined to join one of our churches, not because they did not feel spiritually ready, but because they knew they could not stand the financial pressure that is put upon its members. The gospel is far from free in our town.

Some efforts have been made toward interchurch cooperation. Union services are held on summer evenings, and even the smallest building is adequate to hold the combined audiences. The young people of three of the churches began a joint society, but the older folks of one church withdrew their young people after a few weeks, saying that they were having too good a time with the others and feared they might be "weaned away" from their own church. Two of the churches have had a joint men's class for a few years, and the men got along with one another there as well as they did in the lodges or the business men's clubs; but when talk began of union of the two churches at a time when one of them was without a minister some of the women said things that put a stop to it.

Although we are losing population, our school is becoming more crowded every year. The classrooms are full of seats. It seems that out in the country districts, as the little schools lose students until only a few are left and the cost per pupil becomes high, the schools are closed and those few children are taken in to our school by buses. Also, more young people above the age at which they are legally required to go to school are wanting to continue on through the high school; they feel the need of higher education in this day. We shall have to build a new building for them eventually and yet we hesitate at the cost and keep putting it off. A large part of our tax-paying townsmen are retired farmers whose income is small and limited, whose children are already educated and gone, but whose influence is great.

Last year the farmers took a step that disgusted the business men. They organized a cooperative feed store in one of the empty buildings, to handle feed and flour and the like, buy seeds and fertilizer, and ship some produce as well. The business men regard it as very ungrateful of them, especially in the midst of this business depression. If they had only taken some stock in the knife factory or the airplane industry now, the farmers would have been showing real cooperation. But this event proves to them that the farmers do not understand civic needs.

And the storekeepers agitate home trade, dangle decaying buildings before decaying industries as an attraction to come to Littletown and die. Just between the main highways of travel, just on the edge of the oil field, not big enough to be a city, not small enough to be a hamlet—wanting things, almost getting things, too alive to die and too dead to grow, what shall become of us?

We have the poor comfort of knowing that our lot is not solitary. There are many villages like ours today, facing what we face. We hear talk of the decentralization of industry, of the putting of great factories into small units scattered over many towns, but we know that salvation for us does not lie in the scheme. It may be done, but we know that it will be the villages nearer the great cities than we are that will profit. And the extent of their profit is doubtful; industry began in small towns once and left them; we had factories once, and they are gone, nor have the prodigals shed many tears of penitence as yet. Many villages like us are waiting for either factories or farmers to come back; for over one hundred thousand acres of farm land have been abandoned in our county alone, many times that in the state, and millions in the whole country.

Of this, I think we are certain; that the process of shrinking will go on until there are just enough farmers left outside our village to supply the milk that the market demands. And when that point is reached there will also be just enough stores left in Littletown to supply the needs of these farmers. The churches will either die or merge the one with the other until there are just enough churches to accommodate us all, villagers and farmers, in our worship. The little district schools will probably draw together in consolidation until our youth can find in the minimum number of good schools the maximum preparation for life.

These things will not happen easily. They will be accompanied by struggle and pain. Littletown is not going to die. Littletown is going to start over again, this time with its eyes open, its goal more real.[27]

Changing Community Functions and Activities.—The inhabitants of every community, large or small, have long taken for granted the performance of certain functions by the community and its institutions. These functions have tended to become standardized. As community life becomes more complex these functions tend to be expanded.[28] However, as communities find their population dwindling, their trade declining, their hopes of future greatness vanishing, they find it necessary to abandon certain secondary functions for lack of funds, leadership, or interest, and to place their reliance in the basic institutions. Many of the fads of institutional organization will be given up. For some time, one proposition and then another will be suggested for the revival of business, for holding the young people, for making the community more citified, and many of these will be tried out; but most, if not all of them, are foredoomed to failure.

The prospering community attracts to itself wealth, potential leaders, and human material. The towns and villages like Littletown see their sources of wealth disappearing, their young and ambitious members departing for new fields of opportunity. Such periods are marked by the growth of individualism, a weakening adherence to custom and local mores, personal and group maladjustments, and abortive schemes for reorganization.[29] Maintenance, leisure-time, aesthetic, business, religious, intellectual, political, and other sets of mores will continue to find their expression through institutional

27 William G. Mather, Jr., "Littletown: The Story of an American Village," *Harper's Magazine*, Vol. 170, January, 1935, pp. 199-208.

28 See: Walter Burr, *Small Towns: An Estimate of Their Trade and Culture*, New York, The Macmillan Co., 1929, Chs. 8, 9, 13; E. C. Lindeman, *The Community*, New York, Association Press, 1921, Chs. 3, 7, 8; R. M. MacIver, *Community: A Sociological Study*, New York, The Macmillan Co., 1917, Book II, Chs. 2, 4.

29 See: James M. Williams, *The Expansion of Rural Life*, New York, Alfred A. Knopf, 1926, Part I; Zimmerman, *The Changing Community*.

forms. Some of these will be found in the local community; others will find their fruition in more dominant centers, but will continue to serve the needs of the surrounding hinterland by means of extended communication facilities. Old barriers between farmers and townsmen, among several struggling religious denominations, among the surviving business men, and even between the little town and the larger and more thriving communities will probably disappear. Instead there will come a greater amount of cooperation, a more inclusive social world.[30]

Community Organization.—Depression and war are not new experiences for a multitude of communities. Nevertheless, these crises have put community resources, ingenuity, and facilities to a most severe test. As a consequence, "there has been a notable shift of interest from the traditional programs of community organization to more fundamental problems of social and economic security which demand state and federal, rather than local community, action." [31] No doubt the methods of administrating federal relief and rehabilitation projects by federal and state authorities during the depression years and the many federally centralized controls of wartime tended to weaken the feeling of local responsibility. The region and the nation, rather than the local community, became the units in terms of which planning and rehabilitation programs were formulated. Centralization of administration and functions detracted interest and support away from the community.

Intragroup Interaction

Undercurrents of Group Life.—Beneath the surface of group life and organization the interplay of forces striving for recognition, status, and response within the boundaries of the group may be observed. In the course of this interaction, issues emerge and over these the forces contend for place and preferment. Upon the outcome

[30] See: Walter Firey, "The Optimum Rural-Urban Population Balance," *Rural Sociology,* Vol. 12, June, 1947, pp. 118-127; Jesse F. Steiner, *The American Community in Action,* New York, Henry Holt & Co., 1928, Ch. 9.

[31] Jesse F. Steiner, "Community Organization," *Am. J. Sociol.,* Vol. 40, No. 6, May, 1935, p. 788. See also Frank D. Alexander, "Constructive Measures for Southern Rural Communities," *Social Forces,* Vol. 24, December, 1945, pp. 181-185; F. Stuart Chapin, Jr., "A Plan for Citizen Participation in Community Development," *Social Forces,* Vol. 25, March, 1947, pp. 313-320; Wayland J. Hayes, *The Small Community Looks Ahead,* New York, Harcourt, Brace & Co., 1947; H. F. Infield, *Cooperative Communities at Work,* New York, The Dryden Press, Inc., 1945; R. F. Leonard, "Community Adjustments in Reservoir Affected Communities," *Social Forces,* Vol. 21, December, 1942, pp. 199-203; T. Lynn Smith, "Trends in Community Organization and Life," *Am. Sociol. Rev.,* Vol. 5, No. 3, June, 1940, pp. 325-334; L. B. Tate, "The Role of Informal Activities in Community Life," *Am. Sociol. Rev.,* Vol. 10, No. 2, April, 1945, pp. 158-160.

in each instance do the unity and stability of the group depend, and upon this group unity the effectiveness and status of the smaller group in the larger community rests.

Elsewhere we have had occasion to consider the interaction of groups and to point out the significance of the tensions which emerge as a result of the intergroup relationships. Many of the tensions of family life, of labor unions, of sects, of political parties and of educational institutions, are merely the intragroup reflections of intergroup tensions. When considered as units of interaction, groups tend to take over the intergroup tensions and, within the minds of their members, fight out the disturbing issues. For the groups involved, this may be organizing or disorganizing.

Factional Rallying Points.—In the inner precincts of group life alignments are formed in terms of compatibility of interests, similarities of temperament, likenesses of taste, etc., It is when crises or issues arise in the affairs of the group that these alignments show up most distinctly. It is then that such intragroup divisions take on the character of factions. The following document reveals the points of difference around which factions typically tend to rally in the local neighborhood, the community center, the school, and similar groups.

Neighborhood Gossip.—Neighborhoods are always storm centers of factions and frictions, hatreds and loves, treasons, stratagems, and spoils. People do not need to be taught to work together. They know how. They do need leadership, . . . for the factional spirit, undirected, works in its own contentious way. Half an hour's clothesline gossip can spoil more organization plans than a dozen national conferences can devise in a year. The factional spirit works on people's emotions, while reformers are wasting time trying to reach their common sense. Folks live with friends and enemies, not ideas; their neighborhood standing depends upon whom they know, not what they think. The worker who sees beneath the surface of these controversies finds that they reveal many hidden currents of neighborhood life— currents which will undermine his own plans if he does not take them into account.

One of the most spectacular of New York's community centers broke down recently for just this reason. If mere brains could have settled the matter, this center would have guided the destiny of the city. A voting majority of its controlling board were economists and social philosophers of national standing; it represented millions of wealth; the amount of preliminary conference that went into its organization could have created the Sugar Trust.

But when the organizer started his machinery going, it seemed to grind out nothing but thin air; no spirit of civic improvement, no adult education, no recreation, no anything. Nobody knew just why. The people got together in the center all right, but they seemed to put in most of their time hating each other while the Machinery for Community Expression clattered over their unconscious heads until it ran down by itself.

The trouble was simple: It was the Neighbor with the Loose-tongued Wife. He was a man with political ambitions, who created a following through his personal magnetism; the wife subdued his enemies through her dreadful instinct (sic!) for scandal. Thus they built up a personal faction. They saw in the center a possible source of personal power. Some of their enemies saw in it a chance to get back at them. When the center opened, it became an absorbing battleground for two rival factions. After each scrimmage the wounded limped off bearing a number of friends with them, vowing to darken the center's doors no more.

This kind of thing bewildered the director. He knew all there was to know about organized recreations, and how a community organization ought to work if people would let it alone. But the people wouldn't let it alone. He therefore ceased trying to make the place a center, and it became merely another organized recreation attended by docile boys and girls who would do as they were told—at least when the police did the telling.

Work-Caste and Other Factions.—While they may have a thousand different manifestations, these factions classify themselves into a few origins. One of the most immovable and persistent is the work-caste, always present among women and, to a less degree, among men. In our neighborhood the stenographers will not associate with the saleswomen, who in turn snub the factory workers, while they all make outcasts of the housemaids. I have seen a body of men carefully choosing a committee to head a neighborhood civic festival; they picked their chairman not primarily for ability, experience, political power, natural leadership, or religious affiliations, but because he was foreman in a factory whose employment gave neighborhood prestige.

In this case the factory itself made a line of cleavage which cut through all other factional interests, religious, political and even personal. No one could tell just why; the factory was an old one, and the workers had always been clannish by custom, the people had endowed them with neighborhood leadership until tradition had given them a power dangerous to tamper with.

This particular example of work-caste had in it an element of tradition which is itself a strong factional power. There are certain churches, certain families, certain clubs that are always factional rallying points. The initiative of any of these groups automatically arouses opposition from others who have traditionally fought them; right or wrong has little to do with the matter.

A Janitor as Factional Leader.— . . . Another New England school center was nearly wrecked in the launching by an old janitor with a large local following who worked openly to discredit everything it did. He stood in the hallways and insulted the patrons; he locked schoolrooms and refused to open them even when ordered to do so by authority; and on the occasion of the first big neighborhood gathering, he locked up the stereopticon and hid the cables, nearly breaking up the meeting. He boasted that the school authorities would not dare to discipline him because he had too many friends in the neighborhood, and he was right. When the authorities threatened to try him under civil service rules, several prominent neighborhood leaders made a counter-threat to boycott the center. Personal loyalty was stronger than public spirit.

The difficulty was solved for a time by the appointment, as supervisor, of a woman who had even a stronger neighborhood hold than the janitor. She knew her people and she bided her time. One day when she had the troublemaker conspicuously at a disadvantage she suddenly turned on him with a tongue-lashing that left him wild-eyed and speechless; when he turned to the neighborhood for sympathy, he found most of the sympathy already aligned on the other side. But a year later the supervisor married. Her successor knew nothing of the neighborhood line-up; the janitor easily worsted him and disrupted the center again.

Manipulating the Neighborhood Line-Up.—The most impressive example I know of the devastating effect that can be produced by one who knows the neighborhood line-up and how to use it occurred in this same city when what we may call the Hetty Green Community Center was launched. It was in a neighborhood about equally divided between a group of well-to-do brokers, factory officials and petty professional men, and a group of factory operatives and day laborers. A group of the well-to-do, having conservatively considered the matter, formed a committee among themselves to promote a neighborhood organization in the Hetty Green School. Just then a number of their less laundered neighbors petitioned the school committee independently, but with the same idea. The school authorities called a neighborhood mass meeting to see if a common basis could be found, and for a time it looked as if these two elements, for once agreed upon a common need, might be coaxed together.

But here the school principal stepped in. She didn't want the community organization in her school at all. She knew every phase of every factional discord in her neighborhood. Systematically she combined the different prejudices and conflicts, as an organist manipulates her stops. By the date of the mass meeting she had brought into white-hot conflict every factional element in her part of the town, contriving to give each separate clique the idea that its own pet enemies were planning to capture the organization.

That mass meeting will always remain a neighborhood classic. Amenities began when a collarless citizen announced to the crowded hall that he was against wasting the taxpayers' money to allow a "bunch of bums"—this with a venomous glance at a glowering group across the hall—to use the schoolhouse as a loafing place. Six of the be-bummed rose hotly to explain what must come to pass before they would allow the collarless one "or the likes of him," to run the affairs of the neighborhood. Then a laundered neighbor in the rear arose to point out what would happen if any of the great unwashed were allowed to contaminate the building where his children went to school. This brought up the unwashed in a clamorous body and the mêlée went merrily on.

A few sane citizens tried to call attention to the issues the neighbors had met to discuss, but the principal was too alert to let the factional spirit be sidetracked. With adroit rhetoric she managed to convey to all the warring elements that each could be saved from the other only by voting the project down. Meantime, the majority of the gathering sat silent, noses aloft. They had come for one object—to vote with their friends, and the tumult was to them as the braying of a band on election night. And so they voted the organization down and went their ways, ready for the next opportunity to thwart their neighborhood enemies.[32]

Factional Quarrels.—Factional disputes appear to be quarrels fought out within the group, such as the neighborhood, the family, the trade union, or the political party, and waged over issues which arise quite naturally in group life. Issues are defined on matters such as policy and programs, each issue enlisting the support of a number of partisans who see in the triumph of their issue the satisfaction of their own special interests.

Traditional fears and hatreds play a definite role in determining the nature and course of many factional disputes. It is not uncommon for the positions of leadership to repose by tradition upon certain persons, families, and classes. In addition, the disputes often continue long after the original issues have ceased to be known to the participants. Factions, representing as they do split-offs or divisions of a larger, inclusive group, have the nature of a "public." They represent opinions which are not shared by the rest of the containing group. These differences of opinion lead to extended discussion, the taking of sides, and perhaps the permanent disruption of the larger group. Occasionally the dispute passes over into physical combat, blows are struck, the lives of the disputants are threatened, and sometimes partisans meet death in the course of the fray.

Factional quarrels may be spread beyond the confines of the group or social circle initially involved and thus become divisive factors in the community. This is especially likely to happen in the small town where gossip is more pervasive than in larger centers, and where the variety of interests of the inhabitants is at a minimum. Steiner, in speaking of the disturbing influence of cliques and factions in the life of a community, expresses the opinion that such hostile groups function most conspicuously in the higher social classes. He says:

---

32 E. M. Barrows, "Backyard Battlefields," *The Survey*, Vol. 51, October 15, 1923, pp. 67-69.

Here we find few clear-cut social divisions, but many cliques, each striving to gain precedence over the others. Since it is usually in this stratum of society that the leaders are found, it becomes a very difficult matter to build up a community organization in which all factions will be properly represented and offense given to none. In some communities this balance of power between rival social factions is so carefully adjusted that the inauguration of new enterprises disturbs the status quo and produces difficulties that can hardly be overcome. Perhaps it is the very lack of permanent status of social classes that intensifies the factional spirit and jealousies so detrimental to unity of action in community affairs.[33]

Factions and Litigation.—The dispute may be carried over into the field of judicial procedure, and the conflict assumes the character of litigation.

The judicial conflict is, therefore, absolute conflict insofar as nothing enters the whole action which does not properly belong in the conflict and which does not serve the ends of conflict; whereas, otherwise, even in the most savage struggles, something objective, some pure freak of fortune, some sort of interposition from a third side, is at least possible. In the legal struggle everything of the kind is excluded by the matter-of-factness with which the contention, and absolutely nothing outside the contention, is kept in view. This exclusion from the judicial controversy of everything which is not material to the conflict may, to be sure, lead to a formalism of the struggle which may come to have an independent character in contrast with the content itself. This occurs, on the one hand, when real elements are not weighed against each other. On the other hand, the controversy is often shifted to elements which have no relation whatever to the subject which is to be decided by the struggle. Where legal controversies, accordingly, in higher civilization are fought out by attorneys, the device serves to abstract the controversy from all personal associations which are essentially irrelevant. If, on the other hand, Otto the Great ordains that a legal controversy shall be settled by judicial duel between professional fighters, there remains of the whole struggle of interests only the bare form, namely, that there shall be struggle and victory.

This latter case portrays, in the exaggeration of caricature, the reduction of the judicial conflict to the mere struggle element. But precisely through its pure objectivity because it stands quite beyond the subjective antithesis of pity and cruelty, this unpitying type of struggle, as a whole, rests on the presupposition of a unity and a community of the parties never elsewhere so severely and constantly maintained. The common subordination to the law, the reciprocal recognition that the decision can be made only according to the objective weight of the evidence, the observance of forms which are held to be inviolable by both parties, the consciousness throughout the whole procedure of being encompassed by a social power and order which are the

---

[33] Steiner, *The American Community in Action*, p. 32.

means of giving to the procedure its significance and security—all this makes the legal controversy rest upon a broad basis of community and consensus between the opponents. It is really a unity of a lesser degree which is constituted by the parties to a compact or to a commercial transaction, a presupposition of which is the recognition, along with the antithesis of interests, that they are subject to certain common, constraining, and obligatory rules. The common presuppositions, which exclude everything that is merely personal from the legal controversy, have that character of pure objectivity to which, on its side, the sharpness, the inexorableness, and the absoluteness of the species of the struggle correspond.[34]

Self-Interest.—In factional quarrels, Simmel writes that "the whole obstinacy and uncompromising persistence with which parties in such struggles often maintain the controversy to their own hurt has, even in the case of the aggressive party, scarcely the character of an attack in the proper sense, but rather of a defense in a deeper significance. The point at issue is the self-preservation of the personality which so identifies itself with its possessions and its rights that any invasion of them seems to be a destruction of the personality; and the struggle to protect them at the risk of the whole existence is thoroughly consistent. This individualistic impulse, and not the sociological motive of struggle, will consequently characterize such cases." [35]   This seems to have been the case with the old janitor and the school principal in the document cited above.

Neither personal self-interest nor factional alignments are as disruptive in community life as might be thought. Usually, factions lack permanence. They generally lose whatever force they might normally have when the group or the community or the larger containing social order faces a crisis. Emergencies serve to rally all factions to a common cause. Nevertheless, whether for good or for ill, many social groups and most institutional structures and communities are likely to have factions as inevitable aspects of their composition.[36]

The Feud.—Very similar to the factional dispute is the feud in which hatred is toward an inner enemy of the group. The object of each feuding group is to rid the community of the other. Hatred is not due, therefore, to personal motives primarily, but to the fact that the object of hatred threatens the unity and very existence of the

34 From a translation of Georg Simmel's *Soziologie* by A. W. Small, "The Sociology of Conflict," *Am. J. Sociol.*, Vol. 9, 1903-1904, pp. 508-510.

35 *Ibid.*, p. 508.

36 See: Mabel A. Elliott and F. E. Merrill, *Social Disorganization*, New York, Harper & Bros., 1934, pp. 610-611; Gist and Halbert, *Urban Society*, pp. 362-363; Lowry Nelson, *Rural Sociology*, New York, American Book Co., 1948, pp. 159-165, 172-184; Sanderson, *Rural Sociology and Rural Social Organization*, pp. 552-554.

group. This is what Simmel calls "the peculiar phenomenon of social hatred." This form of conflict behavior is seen in the blood feuds of the Southern highlanders, amongst criminal gangs in large cities, and in the Corsican *vendetta,* the Sicilian *mafia,* and the Neapolitan *camorra.*

[THE RIHBANY CLAN]

When I first came into this world the Rihbany clan experienced the usual rejoicing which comes to a Syrian clan when a man child is born to one of its families. My kindred rejoiced at my advent, not merely because I was a son instead of a daughter, important as that was, but because I was an asset of the clan, a possible reinforcement to their fighting strength, which they had to use often against another powerful clan in the town, called Jirdak. In the Jirdak camp, however, a correspondingly great sorrow was felt. On the same night on which I was born they lost by death one of their most valiant fighters. . . . As clans, we lived in accordance with the precept, "Eye for eye, tooth for tooth, burning for burning, wound for wound," and no favor. . . .

Clannish life has its decidedly romantic side. Provided one is able and willing to forget the larger interests of civilization and the nobler visions of nationalism and human brotherhood, and make the rule of his social life the faulty maxim, "My clan, right or wrong," I know of no more delightful social state than that which clannish life affords. As I write, the past rises before me like a bewitching dream. I am carried back to the time when the hearts of all my kinsmen throbbed, beat for beat, with my heart; when every one of their homes was as much mine as my own fireside, when we lived in life's shifting lights and shadows, "all for each and each for all." The fact that we dwelt among antagonistic clans served only to heighten our heroism, strengthen our clannish cohesion, and intensify the delightfulness of our kinship.[37]

Feud Areas.—While the feud has ceased to be a pattern of conflict in the southern mountains, because of the breakdown of isolation, the peaceful penetration of educational and cultural influences, and a more intelligent administration of the law, something akin to it has found new adherents among the underworld gangs of gamblers, criminals, and bootleggers in the cities. This is gang "warfare." This revival of the conflict pattern in the urban community and in the industrial centers is only another evidence of the general increase of lawlessness which has accompanied the breakdown of primary controls in the secondary relationships of city life. Criminal gangs have increased with this growing disregard for law and order and rivalry has become

---

[37] A. M. Rihbany, *A Far Journey: The Autobiography of a Syrian Immigrant,* Boston, Houghton Mifflin Co., 1914, p. 3.

more intense, hatred more bitter, until, by a process of summation, the rivalry breaks out in mortal combat. With the killing of one gangster the vicious circle of murder and blood revenge is set in motion and, unless brought in check by the full force of public opinion backing the strong force of the police and the courts, will continue until one side or the other is exterminated.

Not only do gangs make war on each other and thereby confine their hostilities within the boundaries of "gangland," but they are usually in one common cause against the larger society. By a psychological process built around the repressive activities of the forces of law and order in the community, these forces come to stand for the thwarted purposes and balked desires of the gangsters.

The Feud and the Unity of the Larger Group.—While revenge is the law which governs the conduct of most feuding groups, it is their status in the larger containing community that is most involved. The prestige and honor of the group are defended at all costs. The spirit and tradition of the *mafia, camorra,* and *vendetta,* heritages brought here by Italian immigrants from the old country, were adapted to the American environment by the so-called "Black Hand" societies. These "societies" are in reality secret gangs, which have as their chief functions "blackmail, private vengeance, and domination of the Italian-American community by intimidation and violence." [38] The blind passion and antithetical sentiments that are directed toward outsiders are in marked contrast to the sentiments of loyalty which prevail among the members of the in-group. Rival gangs in the new world display these same characteristic sentiments of retaliation and "blood-lust." They are evidences of the pronounced ethnocentrism of small, detached primary groups.

In common with most forms of interaction, the feud is governed by a fairly definite and strict code. Though perhaps not so formal and highly conventional as the code which regulates the fighting of a duel, yet among feudists there are certain well-recognized demands of fairness and honor which usually act as controls upon the situation.

Conflict Inevitable in Certain Situations.—It has been said that "through its conflicts a neighborhood finds its strength; also its greatest needs." Such struggles in the community as those that have been described and analyzed here reveal the interaction of social forces that are inherent in the line-up of nearly every community. These forces are bound to clash in the natural course of events. Conflicts

---

[38] F. M. Thrasher, *The Gang: A Study of 1313 Gangs in Chicago,* Chicago, University of Chicago Press, 1927, pp. 203-204.

arise out of a disorganized or unorganized social situation, a restlessness and discontent, a desire for the expression of suppressed emotions and unfulfilled wishes. Ambitions, natural and normal in
themselves, run at cross-purposes and, failing to find satisfaction in
wholesome activities, emerge at the crossroads of community life,
ready to struggle for an outlet. To reveal these forces as they engage
in conflict has been the aim of this section. It is not our purpose to
condemn them nor to suggest corrective action. Bases and mechanisms
of accommodation have been discussed in this and earlier chapters so
that it is hardly necessary to treat them here. Suffice it to say that
much of the conflict that goes on in these more primary, face-to-face
situations tends to be sublimated sooner or later and the struggle of
antagonistic persons and factions is subordinated to the best interests
of the group and of the greater society.

When conflict passes from the lower levels of brute force, and rises
to higher social planes, enemies become rivals and the conflict situation
is redefined in terms of some larger group to which the contesting
parties belong. Boy gangs may be converted into boys' clubs or boy
scout troops and thus seek to surpass each other in effective service.
Neighborhood rivalries may be sublimated under the stimulus of civic
improvement programs. The sublimation rather than the elimination
of conflict may very well be the aim of the social engineer. Society
would be very different from what it is if it were not for the differences, antipathies, rivalries, and hostilities between individuals and
groups. It is through divergence as well as like-mindedness that a
solidarity comes to characterize groups and institutions.

QUESTIONS

1. According to what different criteria may communities be classified?
2. In what respects and on what bases may communities interact with
   one another?
3. Discuss the differentiating characteristics of urban and rural cultures.
4. In what respects has interaction between urban and rural communities changed in the last half century?
5. What changes have taken place in the movement of population
   between city and country? How do you account for the changes?
6. Who are included in the census category of "rural non-farm" population? What does Smith think of the term?
7. What are the characteristic features of the recently-developed "rurban
   fringes" around large urban centers? According to Firey, what
   problems inhere in these areas?
8. Discuss the trend of commercialism in essentially rural areas.

9. Do the same for the spread of capitalism, specialization, and organization.
10. What other indications of the spread of urbanization can you give? Discuss.
11. Discuss the conflict between urban and rural communities and show why and how it is being lessened at present.
12. What is meant by "rural urbanization"? Explain.
13. Give a detailed analysis of what has been happening to "Littletown" and its prototypes throughout the country in recent years.
14. What changes are occurring in community organization, activities, and functions? Why are these taking place?
15. How are factional disputes and feuds alike? How are they different from each other?
16. What is the role of tradition in factional disputes?
17. Discuss the features and advantages of the legalistic pattern of conflict as outlined by Simmel.
18. What is the significance of the personal element in factions and disputes between factions?
19. What does Simmel mean by "the peculiar phenomenon of social hatred"?
20. Why has the feud largely ceased to be a pattern of behavior in the mountains but shown a tendency to revive in certain urban communities?
21. How may we account for the inevitableness of conflict in certain types of community situation?
22. Why may the sublimation rather than the elimination of conflict well be the hope and aim of the social engineer?

BIBLIOGRAPHY

ARENSBERG, C. M., AND KIMBALL, S. T. *Family and Community in Ireland.* Cambridge, Harvard University Press, 1940.

BECKER, HOWARD, AND USEEM, RUTH HILL. "Sociological Analysis of the Dyad." *Am. Sociol. Rev.,* Vol. 7, No. 1, February, 1942, pp. 13-26.

BLUMENTHAL, ALBERT. *Small-Town Stuff.* Chicago, University of Chicago Press, 1932.

BOSSARD, JAMES H. S. "Family Table Talk—An Area for Sociological Study." *Am. Sociol. Rev.,* Vol. 8, No. 3, June, 1943, pp. 295-301.

BOSSARD, JAMES H. S. "The Law of Family Interaction." *Am. J. Sociol.,* Vol. 50, No. 4, January, 1945, pp. 292-294.

BOSSARD, JAMES H. S. *The Sociology of Child Development.* New York, Harper & Bros., 1948, Part II, "The Child and His Family Setting"; Part III, "Facets of Family Life"; Part V, "Some Problem Families."

BRUNNER, EDMUND deS., AND KOLB, J. H. *Rural Social Trends.* New York, McGraw-Hill Book Co., Inc., 1933.

BURGESS, ERNEST W. (Ed.). *The Urban Community.* Chicago, University of Chicago Press, 1926.

CANNON, LEGRAND. *Look to the Mountain.* New York, Henry Holt & Co., 1942. A novel about the creation of a new community.

CHAPIN, F. STUART, JR. "A Plan for Citizen Participation in Community Development." *Social Forces,* Vol. 25, No. 3, March, 1947, pp. 313-320.

DAWSON, C. A., AND YOUNG, EVA R. *Pioneering in the Prairie Provinces.* Toronto, The Macmillan Co. of Canada, Ltd., 1940.

DEBO, ANGIE. *Prairie City.* New York, Alfred A. Knopf, 1944.

ELLIOTT, MABEL A., AND MERRILL, FRANCIS E. *Social Disorganization.* New York, Harper & Bros., 1941, Ch. 30, "The Small Town."

FARIS, JOHN T. *The Romance of Forgotten Towns.* New York, Harper & Bros., 1924.

FAUGHT, MILLARD C. *Falmouth, Massachusetts.* New York, Columbia University Press, 1945.

FIREY, WALTER. "Informal Organization and the Theory of Schism." *Am. Sociol. Rev.,* Vol. 13, No. 1, February, 1948, pp. 15-24.

GIST, NOEL P., AND HALBERT, L. A. *Urban Society.* Rev. ed. New York, T. Y. Crowell Co., 1941, Parts IV-VI.

GREENE, JOSIAH E. *A Bridge to Branfield.* New York, The Macmillan Co., 1948. A novel about a typical failing rural community.

HAYES, WAYLAND J. *The Small Community Looks Ahead.* New York, Harcourt, Brace & Co., 1947.

HAYNER, NORMAN S. *Hotel Life.* Chapel Hill, University of North Carolina Press, 1936.

HILLER, E. T. "The Community as a Social Group." *Am. Sociol. Rev.,* Vol. 6, No. 2, April, 1941, pp. 189-202.

HILLER, E. T. *Houseboat and River Bottom.* Urbana, University of Illinois Press, 1939.

INFIELD, HENRIK F. *Cooperative Communities at Work.* New York, The Dryden Press, 1945.

JONES, VIRGIL CARRINGTON. *The Hatfields and the McCoys.* Chapel Hill, University of North Carolina Press, 1948. The story of a famous feud.

KINNEMAN, JOHN A. *The Community in American Society.* New York, F. S. Crofts & Co., 1947.

LANDIS, PAUL H. *Rural Life in Process.* Rev. ed. New York, McGraw-Hill Book Co., Inc., 1948.

LINDSTROM, DAVID EDGAR. *American Rural Life.* New York, The Ronald Press Co., 1948.

LYND, ROBERT S., AND LYND, HELEN M. *Middletown.* New York, Harcourt, Brace & Co., 1929.

LYND, ROBERT S., AND LYND, HELEN M. *Middletown in Transition: A Study in Cultural Conflicts.* New York, Harcourt, Brace & Co., 1937.

MCKENZIE, RODERICK D. *The Metropolitan Community.* New York, McGraw-Hill Book Co., Inc., 1933.

MORGAN, ARTHUR E. *The Small Community.* New York, Harper & Bros., 1942.

MUMFORD, LEWIS. *The Culture of Cities.* New York, Harcourt, Brace & Co., 1938.

NELSON, LOWRY. *Rural Sociology.* New York, American Book Co., 1948, Part IV, "Social Interaction in the Rural Environment."

QUEEN, STUART A., AND THOMAS, L. F. *The City: A Study of Urbanism in the United States.* New York, McGraw-Hill Book Co., Inc., 1939, Part III, "Distributive and Selective Aspects of the City."

SANDERSON, DWIGHT L. *The Rural Community: The Natural History of a Sociological Group.* Boston, Ginn & Co., 1932.

SANDERSON, DWIGHT L. *Rural Sociology and Rural Social Organization.* New York, John Wiley & Sons, Inc., 1942.

SANDERSON, DWIGHT L., AND POLSON, ROBERT A. *Rural Community Organization.* New York, John Wiley & Sons, Inc., 1939.

SMITH, T. LYNN. *The Sociology of Rural Life.* Rev. ed. New York, Harper & Bros., 1947, Ch. 9, and Parts III-IV.

SOROKIN, PITIRIM A., AND ZIMMERMAN, CARLE C. *Principles of Rural-Urban Sociology.* New York, Henry Holt & Co., 1929.

SOROKIN, PITIRIM A., ZIMMERMAN, CARLE C., AND GALPIN, C. J. *Systematic Source Book in Rural Sociology.* Minneapolis, University of Minnesota Press, 1930, Vol. 1, Part I, Ch. 3, "Origin of Rural-Urban Differentiation"; Ch. 4, "Fundamental Differences between the Rural and Urban Worlds."

STEINER, JESSE F. *The American Community in Action.* New York, Henry Holt & Co., 1928.

SUMNER, W. G. *Folkways.* Boston, Ginn & Co., 1906, Ch. 13, "Kinship, Blood Revenge, Primitive Justice, Peace Unions."

THOMAS, WILLIAM I., AND ZNANIECKI, FLORIAN. *The Polish Peasant in Europe and America.* New York, Alfred A. Knopf, 1927, Vol. 2, Ch. 3, "Disorganization of the Community."

VON RHODE, CARL. "The Suburban Mind." *Harper's Magazine,* Vol. 192, April, 1946, pp. 289-299.

WARNER, W. LLOYD. *A Black Civilization.* New York, Harper & Bros., 1937. Detailed account of conflict between Murngin clans which have some of the characteristics of primitive factions.

WEST, JAMES (pseudonym for Carl Withers). *Plainville, U. S. A.* New York, Columbia University Press, 1945.

WHYTE, WILLIAM FOOTE. *Street Corner Society: The Social Structure of an Italian Slum.* Chicago, University of Chicago Press, 1943.

WIRTH, LOUIS. "Urbanism as a Way of Life." *Am. J. Sociol.,* Vol. 44, No. 1, July, 1938, pp. 1-24.

WOODS, ARTHUR E. *Community Problems.* New York, The Century Co., 1928.

WOOLSTON, HOWARD. *Metropolis: A Study of Urban Communities.* New York, D. Appleton-Century Co., 1938, Introduction and Chs. 3, 4, 14.

YANG, MARTIN C. *A Chinese Village: Taiton, Shantung Province.* New York, Columbia University Press, 1945.

YOUNG, KIMBALL. *Social Attitudes.* New York, Henry Holt & Co., 1931, Ch. 9, "Conflict Situations between Clients and Case Workers," by Stuart A. Queen; Ch. 11, "Group Crises Produced by Voluntary Undertakings," by Florian Znaniecki.

ZIMMERMAN, CARLE C. *The Changing Community.* New York, Harper & Bros., 1938.

Chapter 20

INTERACTION INVOLVING INTELLECTUAL AND MORAL VALUES

———

Intellectual Values and Group Interests

We have already learned that attitudes are one's socially conditioned preparedness to react to persons, ideas, institutions, or other objects. Correlative with attitudes are what Thomas and Znaniecki have termed *social values*, that is, the objects and activities which have common meanings for the members of a particular group or society.[1] Thus we see that attitudes and values belong together; they are inseparable. An attitude emerges directly or indirectly out of social situations and is an organization of the person's experience subjectively considered. A value is the objective counterpart of the attitude, and possesses qualities that elicit the common interest of group members.[2]

Single attitudes and values may be paired, but most values are not simple or single, and the corresponding attitudes toward them tend to be complex. For example, religious attitudes, concerned as they are with a whole system of values in the form of persons, ideas, ideals, and rituals, are complex attitudes. These paired complex attitudes and complex values constitute what may be called attitude-value complexes. They cover all the fields of human interest and experience. But not all groups and not all persons within given groups of the same general culture show the same interest in what appear to the observer to be like values. Accordingly, since they hold somewhat different attitudes toward them, it may be concluded that personal and group differences signify different definitions of objects.[3]

Anything that has "value," that is, anything that is capable of being appreciated, tends to become an object of group interest. Through-

---

[1] See: W. I. Thomas and F. Znaniecki, *The Polish Peasant in Europe and America,* New York, Alfred A. Knopf, 1927, Vol. I, pp. 21-22. The same reference applies to the 1917 edition published in five volumes by R. G. Badger, Boston.

[2] *Ibid.,* pp. 22-30. Robert E. Park had previously used the term "attitude" in a pamphlet, *Principles of Human Behavior,* privately published in 1915.

[3] The acquisition and integration of attitudes in the life-organization of the person have been treated in Chs. 5 and 6.

out this book we have, by implication if not explicitly, indicated what are some of the more common values that serve as centers of group interest and as factors in motivating the behavior of persons and groups in typical ways. In this chapter we will treat two particular value-complexes which differ fundamentally from most of the others referred to in their relatively generalized, idealized, and formalized character, as contrasted with the more pragmatic, utilitarian, and adaptive character of other value-complexes. These are the intellectual and moral values.

Certain groups have particular interest in intellectual values. Indeed, vested interests develop where some special privilege or prestige is accorded to the intellectual role and to achievement in that role. So differentiated do certain persons become in terms of their intellectual roles and attached status in certain societies at certain times that they assume the character of a special class. They constitute an aristocracy of learning, of ideas, to be respected and obeyed. In other societies they are anathema to the masses and are assailed by the popular leaders.

It must not be supposed, however, that either intellectual capacity or intellectual accomplishment are in themselves passports to high estate. The opportunities afforded to the latter depend in large measure upon the group's goals at any given time. The influence of the leader is at best a precarious one; he may be honored today and despised tomorrow. When the security of the group is thought to depend upon the control of the unseen or the supernatural, the services of the seer, the worker in magic, or the priest are in demand. When the dependence is upon a show of strength and skill at arms, the warrior chief and the military class have prestige; when the end sought is success in the fabrication of goods and in trade, the craftsmanship of the artisan, the organizing ability of the entrepreneur, and the skill of the merchandiser are required. When other practical necessities of the group have to be met they may call for minds trained to deal with the problems of the laboratory, the classroom, the halls of state, and the forum; and when the leisure-time interests of the group are ascendant, then it may look for its satisfactions to the artist,[4] "scientist for the sake of science," and the litterateur.[5]

---

[4] See: Alexander Goldenweiser, *Robots or Gods: An Essay on Craft and Mind*, New York, Alfred A. Knopf, 1931. Goldenweiser differentiates between the "craft mind" and the "intuitive mind." These are represented as being in contrast and as "two fundamental principles in conflict."

[5] See: Lewis Leopold, *Prestige: A Psychological Study of Estimates*, London, T. Fisher Unwin, 1913, pp. 16-62; W. D. Wallis, *Culture and Progress*, New York, McGraw-Hill Book Co., Inc., 1930, pp. 196-197, wherein are discussed "cycles of authority."

The social functioning of several of the above-mentioned types has been treated in preceding portions of this book. All are presumed to have the intelligence, knowledge, and skill requisite to the performance of their respective roles, but only certain of them can lay claim to being intellectual in the sense that they are "individuals who specialize in cultivating knowledge and are therefore called 'scientists' " and who thus "perform social roles of a definite class." [6] Znaniecki employs the term "scientist" broadly and as synonymous with the man of knowledge, as well as scientist in the ordinary sense of the term. They are all specialists in knowledge.

Intelligence, considered as innate mental ability, is not a monopoly of any class or set of men, but the claims to intellectual achievement may be so conceived by certain groups, who hope to benefit thereby. There are also, says Znaniecki,

social circles to whom knowledge in general or systematic knowledge in particular appears to be positively valuable. Participants in these circles must be convinced that they need the cooperation of "scientists" to realize certain tendencies connected with this valuable knowledge. In order to be qualified as a scientist whom his circle needs, a person must be regarded as a "self" endowed with certain desirable characteristics and lacking certain undesirable characteristics. Social status must be granted to a person who is thus needed and qualified as a scientist. And this person must perform social functions which will satisfy the needs of his circle in the matter of knowledge; in other words, he must cultivate knowledge for the benefit of those who grant him social status.[7]

Znaniecki sets up a four-fold classification of the types of social roles of men of knowledge which he discusses. Class A includes *technological experts* and *technological leaders,* the former being "the diagnostician who defines the relevant data in the situation, their essential components and interrelations and the theoretic foundations for planned collective tasks; he performs the 'staff' or advisory function"; the latter is "the executive-director who devises the plan and selects the instrumentalities for its execution on the basis of a complex of practically-oriented, heterogeneous knowledge." [8] In Class B, Znaniecki places *sages,* a group of men of knowledge who "provide intellectual justification of the collective tendencies of their party, sect, stratum." They fall into two categories: the *conservative* and the

---

[6] Florian Znaniecki, *The Social Role of the Man of Knowledge,* New York, Columbia University Press, 1940, p. 21.

[7] *Ibid.*

[8] For this statement and what follows of Znaniecki's typology of scientists' roles, we have drawn on R. K. Merton's review of *The Social Role of the Man of Knowledge,* which appeared in the *Am. Sociol. Rev.,* Vol. 6, No. 1, February, 1941, pp. 111-115.

novationist. Each of these has its "apologists for existing tendencies" and "idealists with norms not contained in the existing order or in the opposition-party." Conservative apologists are "standpatters" and conservative idealists are meliorists; novationist apologists are opportunists and novationist idealists are revolutionary.

A third class, C. *scholars* (i.e., schoolmen), are either sacred or secular. The *sacred scholar* "perpetuates sacred truths through exact and faithful reproduction of their symbolic expressions; he is charged with the maintenance of a self-contained, stable, unchallengeable, sacred system of unchanging truths." Of the *secular scholar* there are presented five sub-types: (a) the *discoverer of truth,* who "initiates a 'school of thought' with a claim to 'absolute truth' validated by the certainty of rational evidence"; (b) the *systematizer,* who "tests and organizes the total existing knowledge in certain fields into a coherent system by means of deduction from the self-evident first principles established by the discoverer"; (c) the *contributor,* who "furnishes new findings which are implicitly or explicitly expected to furnish new proof that experience accords with the master's system; revises 'unsatisfactory' inductive evidence until it is so integrated or is 'justifiably' rejected"; (d) the *fighter for truth,* who "ensures the logical victory of one school over another by convincing scholars in a polemical situation that his school has a truth-claim validated by rationalistic evidence. (Differs from tendentious partisan sage by confining polemics to a closed arena accessible only to those who hold truth as a dominant value.)"; and (e) the *disseminator of knowledge,* of whom there are two subdivisions, (1) the *popularizer,* who "cultivates amateur interests among adults, thus aiding popular support of learning, especially in democratized society," and (2) the *educating teacher,* who "imparts theoretic knowledge to youth as part of their non-occupational education."

To the fourth type, D, belong the *creators* or *explorers of knowledge.* Of these, there are two sub-types: 1, the *discoverer of facts,* or *fact-finder,* who "discovers hitherto unknown and unanticipated empirical data, largely as a basis for modification of existing systems of knowledge," and 2, *discoverer of problems,* or the *inductive theorist,* who "discovers new and unforeseen theoretic problems which are to be solved by new theoretical constructions."

By this classification Znaniecki represents what he considers are the composition and structure of the social roles of various types of scientists. It should be remembered that individual men of knowledge may embody more than one of these distinguishable roles. This he may conceivably do concurrently or by a series of transformations from one role to another, depending upon the interaction of the component elements in the situation in which the "scientist" finds himself at a given time. These elements include the individual's personal characteristics and qualifications, an effective audience or circle, the status accorded him and his profession of knowledge, and the specific kind of knowledge wanted in a given social situation.

Needless to say, intellectuals constitute a decided minority in any population and frequently occupy the subordinate place generally accorded to a minority. If there is a powerful aristocracy, either of wealth or of rule, it may afford to the intellectual minority its chief protection against the intolerance and damaging action of the masses. Professor Ross points out that "nowhere are the ignorant so free to harry the learned as in a political democracy in which they are used to being flattered by stump orators, 'spell-binders,' candidates for public office, and other seekers of popular favor." [9] Thus the status of intellectuals is relative, and varies from one society to another, and from one time to another in the same society. All classes of intellectuals are frequently lumped together by their detractors, the citizenry at large. Nevertheless, certain segments thereof do tend to differentiate between the particular kinds of knowledge and skill which are appreciated and valued, and those kinds which are feared and sometimes detested. For example, certain social structures exert pressures for the adoption of attitudes toward new and unanticipated empirical data. Likewise, certain leaders in one field of knowledge may resent innovations that impinge upon their vested interests. "The technological leader regards genuinely new facts with suspicion, for they may destroy belief in the rationality of his established plans, or show the inefficiency of his plans, or disclose undesirable consequences of his program." [10] Similarly, "the technological expert, under the control of the leader, is circumscribed in new fact-finding lest he discover facts which are unwelcome to the powers that be, as for example, new but 'unwanted' inventions." [11] Illustrative of the same principle is the recent censure by the Russian government of some of its writers and artists who were alleged to be guilty of "departing from Communist ideology" in the manner in which they developed their ideas and themes.

Perhaps the status and functioning of intellectuals can be understood more clearly if we adopt a different classification from that given and contrast the roles of three intellectual types—artist, phi-

9 E. A. Ross, *Principles of Sociology*, rev. ed., New York, The Century Co., 1930, p. 245. By permission of Appleton-Century-Crofts, Inc., owners of the copyright.
10 Merton, review of *The Social Role of the Man of Knowledge, op. cit.*, p. 114.
11 *Ibid.*

losopher, and scientist—with those of the so-called "men of action."
The intellectual types mentioned are not alike, to be sure, but they
resemble each other in that they are all observers and interpreters.
Of these types, O. L. Schwarz says: "The technical and the artistic
genius have a maximum power of observation and of constructive
imagination built thereupon; the philosophical genius has a maximum power of interpretation; in the scientific genius the two abilities
are balanced." [12]   Indeed, so divergent are these types of intellectuals
in their points of view, their objectives, their methodologies, their
conclusions, that they frequently disagree and, on occasion, join in
conflict against each other.   They and their disciples tend to form
schools of philosophic thought, technical or artistic systems, and
espouse particular scientific theories.   Within their respective fields
they often form divisive groups that react antipathetically to each
other.   It is only when they are all compared with the man of action
that their likenesses appear in greater relief.   In contrast, the man of
action does not stand high in intellect, though he is likely to be an
intellectual pretender.   In his class belong the professional leaders
of the masses—the politicians, the statesmen, the "go-getting" business executives, and the social reformers.   Though these persons are
largely dependent upon the guiding ideas formulated by the intellectuals, they are the ones who, in most times and places, receive the
rewards, praise, and honor bestowed by the worshipful masses.[13]
Moreover, they are often the chief instigators of the attacks of the
unlearned against the learned.

On the whole the attitudes of the learned and of the unlearned are
incompatible.   The former is apt to be as intolerant of the ignorance
and superstitions of the untutored as the latter is of the ideas and
innovations promulgated by the former.   Ross points out that

. . . it is childish to imagine that the ignorant tend to be humble in their
ignorance and defer respectfully to men of great knowledge. The fact is the
ignorant, unless from childhood they have been taught to look up to the
learned, feel envy and jealousy of those of so much greater influence than
themselves and welcome an excuse for bringing them low. This is why in
the early civilizations the learned, if they stood outside the charmed circle
of the priesthood, *cultivated a paternal relation* to those they taught so that
it should be a sacred lifelong obligation of the pupils to succor and protect
their teachers. In old China the scholars built up such a prestige for themselves among the people that it was quite "the thing" to wear spectacles and
affect the scholar's stoop.[14]

12 O. L. Schwarz, *General Types of Superior Men,* Boston, R. G. Badger, 1916, p. 114.
13 *Ibid.,* pp. 134-138.
14 Ross, *Principles of Sociology,* p. 244. New York, The Century Co., 1930. By permission of Appleton-Century-Crofts, Inc.

As we have suggested before, however, the unlearned are often encouraged in their attacks upon men of learning by persons who appeal to prejudice for the sake of furthering their personal, class, or party interests. Preachers of the more militant sects, "jackleg" lawyers, unscrupulous politicians, demagogues, quacks, and charlatans find in the untutored minds of large numbers of people the soil ready for sowing the seeds of discontent, discord, and violence. Material improvements, which can be seen and which may be regarded as "practical," are usually more readily accepted by the masses than are innovations in the realm of ideas. This helps to explain why the inventor, the scientist in applied science, the technician, and even the creative artist are more respected than are the scholar and theoretical scientist, particularly in North America.

Varied are the areas of conflict between the learned and the unlearned, the theorist and the practical-minded, the "man of thought" and the "man of action." Two areas will serve as illustrations: education and the press.

Since the American people are generally committed to the idea of public education and since most of the schools, lower and higher, in the United States and Canada, are public agencies, the schools have tended to become the battleground of political, religious, and class interests. To control the educative processes through control of the educational system is to control largely the attitudes and interests of the future citizens. Therefore, the control of education, particularly of teachers, subject matter, and methods, is the objective of numerous special-interest groups other than the educators.[15]

The conscientious teacher and school administrator who wish to uphold high standards in their work find themselves hampered by particularistic interests in the community. Not infrequently they are between two fires for "the impartial pursuit of truth involves a conflict with any group that has already reached a decision in regard to any particular truth. And the more groups that have reached absolute decisions regarding any one subject, the more certain is conflict.

---

[15] See: C. E. Arnett, *Social Beliefs and Attitudes of American School Board Members,* Emporia, Kansas, 1932; Howard K. Beale, *Are American Teachers Free? An Analysis of Restraints upon the Freedom of Teaching in American Schools,* New York, Charles Scribner's Sons, 1936; H. P. Beck, *Men Who Control Our Universities,* New York, King's Crown Press, 1947; D. E. Bunting, *Liberty and Learning,* Washington, American Council on Public Affairs, 1942; F. Stuart Chapin, *Contemporary American Institutions,* New York, Harper & Bros., 1935, Ch. 10; Bella V. Dodd, "The Conspiracy Against the Schools," Committee for the Defense of Public Education, New York City, 1941; W. Gellermann, *The American Legion as Educator,* New York, Columbia University Press, 1938; Florence Greenhoe, *Community Contacts and Participation of Teachers: An Analysis of the Community Relationships of 9,122 Public School Teachers Selected as a National Sample,* Washington, American Council on Public Affairs, 1941; John Ise, "Shackles on Professors," *Social Frontier,* Vol. 3, May, 1937; Bruce Raup, *Education and Organized Interests in America,* New York, G. P. Putnam's Sons, 1936.

How is history, for instance, to be taught so as to please the D. A. R. *and* the English Speaking Union, the Chamber of Commerce *and* the A. F. of L., the League of Nations Club *and* the American Legion?" [16] Under such circumstances, every educator who seeks to impart the truth as it is revealed through research and in the long history of human experience, and to inculcate in the developing person the selected and tested elements of the culture heritage is "bound to come sooner or later into conflict with . . . all dogma, and the sum of human prejudices." [17]

The problem of freedom of teaching and of learning is always present. Such freedom is one of the first to disappear in a society that is taken over by a totalitarian regime. However, there is no absolute guarantee of academic freedom in the United States. It is axiomatic that in a class-structured society, whatever its nominal form of government, public education will conform very nearly to the ideals and interests of the controlling class. Since ours is a society with a pronounced middle-class bias, it follows that the formulation of educational standards and content reflect the canons of bourgeois ideology.

Education in the United States and Canada is in the middle of a crisis today. Never entirely adequate to its task, it is less so now in the face of greatly increased pupil enrollment, teacher shortage, and mounting costs. Mass education is an expression of the widely held belief that it is the open sesame to economic and social success. Humanitarian influences have led to the restriction of child labor, thus freeing large numbers of children for school attendance, which has been made compulsory in most states. In general, free tuition, free textbooks, and free transportation are provided. The deficiency in the supply of qualified and certified teachers is partly an outgrowth of the recent war, when many teachers abandoned teaching to enter military service or industry. Many of these former teachers have not returned to the classrooms and the recruiting of new teachers has been difficult due to more attractive vocational opportunities elsewhere and to the unsatisfying conditions which so often surround the teaching function in the average American community: poor salaries, insecure tenure, overwork, interference with the teacher's personal life, and low status position. To help alleviate some of these conditions, the employed teachers in many communities have organized to influence public opinion and to secure favorable legislation,

---

[16] Bergen Evans, "College Courses in 'Indecent' Literature," *Scribner's Magazine*, Vol. 97, April, 1935, p. 243.
[17] *Ibid.*

especially affecting tenure. Recently, unions of teachers in several communities have resorted to the strike as a means of focusing attention on their plight. Such tactics are no doubt regarded as unprofessional by many thoughtful educators, but extreme measures may be justified if they are required to deal with special interests and public lethargy.

In the area of newspaper publication, the battle for "the freedom of the press" goes on. A "free press" is an ideal held by most journalists and publishers. When the newspapers broke away from the domination of political machines, the move was heralded as a stroke in the direction of independence. Of course, many newspapers were never able to shake off political-party control completely and most of them, as Professor Park points out, soon came under the sway of "a new political power," the power "embodied in the news and the reporter," and in the growing number of readers.[18] Since the modern city newspaper is a kind of common carrier and since its function is to inform and to entertain, it is a powerful medium through which to reach large masses of people with all sorts of ideas and impressions. Naturally, such a medium is much sought after as a channel for the dissemination of political, religious, educational, scientific, and other notions.

Though most newspapers may be independently owned, it must be remembered that the publishing of newspapers is also a business for the owners, managers, and editors. As a business it must be made to pay and the ability to pay depends upon the willingness of the readers to buy and, what is more important for most newspapers, of the advertisers to advertise.[19]

The line between advertising and news is often hard to draw, because the "news value" of events which are of public significance is frequently accompanied by "advertising value" for particular persons or groups. It is to the advantage of innumerable individuals and interests to obtain newspaper mention in such a manner as to serve their ends. In selecting the daily grist of events which they will record or discuss, newspaper publishers and editors are compelled to balance these two sets of values against each other. Their judgments are affected by all of the influences of suggestion and maneuvering by others to which human beings are subject. In this situation there is provided a setting for the activities of those individuals whose function it is to create favorable attitudes or responses on the part of the public toward

---

18 "The Natural History of the Newspaper," in R. E. Park, E. W. Burgess, and R. D. McKenzie, *The City*, Chicago, University of Chicago Press, 1925, pp. 80-98.
19 See: H. L. Ickes (Ed.), *Freedom of the Press Today*, New York, Vanguard Press, Inc., 1941; A. M. Lee, *The Daily Newspaper in America*, New York, The Macmillan Co., 1937; O. W. Riegel, *Mobilizing for Chaos*, New Haven, Yale Univ. Press, 1934; M. M. Willey and R. D. Casey (Eds.), "The Press in the Contemporary Scene," *Annals Am. Acad. Pol. and Soc. Sci.*, Vol. 219, January, 1942.

their clients or their clients' goods or services. They influence, when they can, the process of news selection. The press agent and publicity manager are known from the past; more recently has appeared the public relations counsel. The objective of these specialists in general, is the conjoining of news values with the interests of clients (who may or may not also be buying advertising space) by projecting the latter into news situations. . . . Techniques for accomplishing the general objective are varied and constantly changing. Reiteration is important. The purpose is always the same: to induce attitudes and behavior by the public in accordance with predetermined calculations of private interest. This is best effected when the reader unsuspectingly accepts as impartial or disinterested news or magazine matter which has been charged with publicity values.[20]

If there is conflict here, it is confined largely to that between the professed ideal of a "free press" and the demand for an enlightened and unbiased public opinion on the one hand, and the practical business considerations of publishers and editors on the other. In so far as the press is trammeled or guided in its practices by subservience to the interests of persons or special groups, it falls short of being as great a benefactor and intellectual emancipator of humanity as it sometimes claims to be.

In view of the shortcomings of the press, the school, the pulpit, and other media committed to the spread of knowledge and the creation of enlightened attitudes, it would seem that for the accommodation of conflict between the learned and the unlearned a greater reliance must be placed upon the perfection of scientific techniques employed in the accumulation and diffusion of knowledge. The raising of the literacy rate in the general population and the training and encouragement of individual and scientific thinking would be a step in the same direction. Bringing education up to date with new information and scientific discoveries would be another.[21] Greater attention on the part of men of learning to the spread of their ideas and scientific data, in language that can be understood by nonspecialists, and restraint on the part of these same learned specialists in discoursing authoritatively on matters outside their fields of inter-

---

[20] By permission from *Communication Agencies and Social Life,* Recent Social Trends in the United States monograph, by M. M. Willey and S. A. Rice, pp. 176-177. Copyrighted 1933, McGraw-Hill Book Co., Inc.

[21] Chapin, *Contemporary American Institutions,* Ch. 9; M. E. Curti, *The Social Ideals of American Education,* New York, Chas. Scribner's Sons, 1935; L. H. Gulick, *Education for American Life,* New York, McGraw-Hill Book Co., Inc., 1938; Gove Hambidge, *New Aims in Education,* New York, McGraw-Hill Book Co., Inc., 1940; E. C. Lindeman, *Social Education,* New York, New Republic Press, 1933; E. J. McGrath (Ed.), *Toward General Education,* New York, The Macmillan Co., 1947; A. F. Myers and C. O. Williams, *Education in a Democracy,* New York, Prentice-Hall, Inc., 1942; J. H. Newlon, *Education for Democracy in Our Time,* New York, McGraw-Hill Book Co., Inc., 1939; T. L. Norton, *Education for Work,* New York, McGraw-Hill Book Co., Inc., 1938; Thomas Woody, *New Minds, New Men,* New York, The Macmillan Co., 1932.

est and about which they probably know less than others, would add to their prestige and usefulness. Moreover, a saving sense of humor which implies sympathy with the foibles and weaknesses of fellow beings should not be ignored.

INTERACTION INVOLVING MORAL PRINCIPLES

According to W. G. Sumner, "the word 'moral' means what belongs or appertains to the mores." [22] He holds that the mores of a group at any time seem true and right, and all members of the group are expected to comport themselves in accordance with these indigenous elements in the group's life. Since the mores declare that which is right and proper, so do they also declare that which is bad and wrong. To go contrary to the mores of the time and place is, then, to do that which is wrong or to fail to do that which is right. Nearly all students of the problem since Sumner have been inclined to follow him in this reasoning. However, there have been those who have ignored or rejected Sumner's not very precise theory and have substituted something else in its place. Alfred M. Lee is one writer who has not abandoned the notion of the mores as a useful concept, but who has undertaken to formulate a more definitive generalization about the relation of the mores to moral principles. Lee says, by way of introducing his discussion: "By not distinguishing between a conception that might well be denominated morals or moral principles and the one that he called mores, Sumner permitted his employment of mores to fall heir to some of the vagaries associated with the other word." [23] He says further:

This identification of the morals with the mores overlooks their chief characteristic: They are on a different level of generalization from the folkways and mores. As is indicated below, the conventions and morals may well be regarded as societal conceptions, and the folkways and mores as more precise and compulsive group constructs. Consequences to this theory of the fact that groups vary widely in size—from the dyad to something very large—are taken up below.

In this formulation, it is suggested that culture consists of three levels of social generalization from behavioral phenomena. These are: (1) *the individual level,* which may be defined culturally in terms of a continuum of patterns that range from practices to habits; (2) *the group level,* defined in terms of a similar continuum that extends from folkways to mores; and (3)

---

[22] W. G. Sumner, *Folkways*, Boston, Ginn & Co., 1906, p. 37.
[23] Alfred M. Lee, "Levels of Culture as Levels of Social Generalization," *Am. Sociol. Rev.*, Vol. 10, No. 4, August, 1945, p. 487.

the societal level, defined in terms of another continuum that may be thought of as running from conventions to morals or moral principles. If it were not for the aura of absolutism some are now attempting to gather about "values," there would be no objection to that term as a synonym for morals.[24]

Thus the two bothersome concepts, mores and moral principles, have been assigned to two different levels of culture, the former to the level of group constructs of behavior patterns and the latter to the category of societal concepts of behavior patterns. Pursuing Lee's analysis, we read:

Mores are practical, expedient, and compulsive; their contrast with society's morals is a measure of what is popularly labeled as group hypocrisy. Mores and other folkways are so inclusive that an adult member of several groups finds himself equipped to handle most problems involving social relationships in terms of the folkways of the groups to which he belongs rather than through reference to more rational procedures. . . . These patterns, which in a professional field conflict sharply with the textbook idealisms dictated by societal expectations (conventions-morals), are the practical and expedient understandings and techniques, the customary ways of exercising power, cutting corners on the morals, handling aggressiveness, exploiting submissiveness, and making the best of public relations and industrial relations situations.

Conventions are societal generalizations of the folkways of constituent groups over long periods of time, characterized by being sufficiently glittering and general, even though dogmatic, to permit rationalistic avoidances of apparent contradiction. The morals are conventions derived over long periods from the mores of historical and contemporary groups and from traditional human aspirations, frustrations, and ascetic tendencies. . . .

Morals represent crystallizations of a society's traditional aspirations as vaguely defined, somewhat colored by dominant group or class mores. They are chiefly significant in shaping the superegos of the young and in providing the main staples for propagandists—glittering generalities and name-calling symbols, righteous justifications and condemnations, suitably and variously interpreted, for certain social institutions, functionaries, and courses of action. Morals have no necessary congruity with the mores of a society's constituent groups or with the habit patterns of individuals. . . . Such subjects as theology, ethics, and traditional—but not scientific—"social science" concern themselves to a great measure with working out rationalizations between morals and group mores.[25]

As ideally conceived societal expectations, one can readily understand how moral principles may become the focal points of tension

---

[24] *Ibid.,* p. 488.
[25] *Ibid.,* pp. 492-494.

in social interaction. It is obvious from the above that moral values and moral rules of conduct are social realities and that they have a place in every culture. Like all cultural elements, they arise out of the life experiences of societies and may become endowed with the characteristics of truth and uprightness. As such, they and their symbolic representations become instruments in the hands of persons and groups for the purpose of guiding, intimidating, disciplining, and counseling others. Everywhere, however, there are persons and groups who believe that they are divinely appointed possessors and protectors of morality. Acting on that belief, they set themselves up as the revealers of moral truth and the arbiters of moral conduct. Though morality is relative to time and place, and to degree of responsibility by reason of age, intelligence, or other status,[26] these purists would have it unequivocal and absolute.

The "professional" moralists are not the only persons interested in the subject of morality. Every society is concerned with the problem of group and personal conduct; every society tends to develop and attempts to maintain certain standards of "right" conduct; every society seeks to secure individual and collective conformity to its standards as far as possible and, in doing so, contrives mechanisms of social control.[27] The tendency for societies, particularly the more complex and secularized ones, is to rely upon certain agencies in the enforcement of moral ideals. Non-conformity is an offense in any society—more serious in some than in others—to which a defensive or a repressive attitude will most likely be taken. If the official censors and enforcement agencies are lax in the performance of their duties, then the moral tone of the community is likely to be lowered and social control to break down. This is what happens when the mores of certain groups in a society or the habits of individuals are decidedly at variance with the society's moral definitions.

The fact that, in general, group folkways and mores are not wholly congruous with the major moral premises of the society helps to explain, also, the conflict that frequently arises between groups. For example, the teen-age groups often adopt behavior patterns that seem to them eminently right and proper, but which cause surprise or distress among their elders. Conversely, the insistence of the elders on compliance of the younger generation to their more conservative definitions may result in disobedience and alienation of

---

26 See: Alfred L. Hall-Quest, *It's Not Our Fault (Why We Can't Be Good)*, New York, Horace Liveright, 1929; Freda Kirchway (Ed.), *Our Changing Morality*, New York, A. & C. Boni, 1924; Walter Lippmann, *A Preface to Morals*, New York, The Macmillan Co., 1929; A. L. Lowell, *Conflicts of Principle*, Cambridge, Harvard University Press, 1932; Edward Westermarck, *Ethical Relativity*, New York, Harcourt, Brace & Co., 1932.
27 See Chapter 24.

the young. In other typical situations, involving the clash of mores of groups and the behaviors of individuals with each other, the self-appointed or delegated moral custodians seize the opportunity to inveigh against corruption, to censor the theater, the movies, the press, and literature,[28] and to agitate for reforms. Out of this clash of divergent mores a readjustment of standards may emerge.

Although groups are made up of persons, persons do not always choose to conform to the standards of the group. When the person digresses widely from the group mores, he is subject to group pressure and possibly punished. However, a member of a modern social group is aware of the fact that what applies to men does not always apply to women. Certain professions have codes of their own. What is applicable in the bohemian atmosphere of Montmartre would be out of place on Main Street. What the law of his state forbids may not be a matter of legal definition in another state. He may think that a certain course of action is proper and reasonable, but may be made to feel that such action, if carried out, would not harmonize with what the neighbors, or his family, or his church, or his business associates may think is right and sound conduct.

Whether A pays his debts, helps B who is in trouble, drives his car recklessly, is or is not faithful to his wife—these are matters of personal morals. If, however, we consider whether business reputation demands prompt payment of debts, whether kindness to neighbor is esteemed in A's community, whether an automobile club condemns reckless driving, whether A's social set frowns on sex relations outside of wedlock, we have crossed into the field of social morality. . . . Standards of personal or individual morals are very largely determined by the mores of the several groups through which the youth passes and to which the adult belongs.[29]

None the less, there is always the possibility of criticism or revolt on the part of the individual. If he does not like the requirements of one group, he may align himself with another group in which the standards are more to his tastes. He may defy the group and take a chance of escaping its wrath. He may attempt to argue it out with the group and to change the group mores from within. What we see here is not, however, a conflict between the concerns of the

---

28 See: H. I. Brock, *Meddlers:Uplifting Moral Uplifters*, New York, Ives Washburn, Inc., 1930; H. Broun and M. Leech, *Anthony Comstock, Roundsman of the Lord*, New York, A. & C. Boni, 1927; M. W. Dennett, *Who's Obscene?* New York, Vanguard Press, 1930; M. L. Ernst and A. Lindey, *Hold Your Tongue: Adventures in Libel and Slander*, New York, William Morrow & Co., 1932; M. L. Ernst and A. Lindey, *The Censor Marches On*, New York, Doubleday, Doran & Co., 1940; M. L. Ernst and Pare Lorentz, *Censored: The Private Life of the Movie*, London, Cape & Smith, 1930; M. L. Ernst and Wm. Seagle, *To the Pure; a Study in Obscenity and the Censor*, New York, Viking Press, Inc., 1928; E. J. Young, *Looking Behind the Censorships*, Philadelphia, J. B. Lippincott Co., 1938.

29 J. H. Tufts, *America's Social Morality*, pp. 3-4. Copyright, 1933, by Henry Holt and Co., Inc.

individual and the compulsions of the group. Rather it is the clashing of the mores of two or more groups within the individual's personality. Personalities emerge and find their expression in the life of some group or groups.

In discussions in previous chapters of the interaction between nationalities, races, ethnic groups, classes, the sexes, and sects, the sundry conflicting elements in each type of situation received attention. In every case there were some elements that involved questions of "right" and "wrong" attitudes and practices. Among the many elements discussed were the attitudes of the strong toward the weak, the rich toward the poor, the demands of the ego versus those of group welfare, repression versus expression, materialistic values over against spiritual ones, emotional behavior versus rational behavior, the profit motive against public interest, liberty versus restraint, loyalty as opposed to disloyalty, the ethics of slavery and caste in contrast to the norms of open classes, and the relative merits of might and of right. In every sphere of life the person and the group are faced with some such dilemmas as these. There is nearly always a tendency to seek a solution in line with individual or group self-interest. But the answer is not simple. For members of the more sacred, custom-regulated societies, like the Kwakiutl and the Zuñi, the answer is relatively uninvolved for it is to be found in the traditional patterns handed down from the ancestors. In fact, simple societies face few dilemmas, for with them conduct involves mainly their own inner circle and for such conduct the controls, implicit or explicit, are binding on all alike, except where there are definite permissive exclusions from the categorical compulsives. When we consider, however, the more secularized societies and groupings of the western world, where the horizons of culture and social interaction are broader and more subject to the impact of outside forces, where distinctions have made their appearance within the group itself, moral standards lose much of their rigidity. They change in some areas of life and lag in others and are felt with uneven force and are applied with uncertain pressure at different points and times. In many respects present-day group mores and societal morals represent incomplete secularization. In some areas of life the old magico-religious taboos still dominate to a great extent, whereas in other phases of life, as in moving pictures and on the stage, there is displayed an ultra-sophistication that is amazing to many people and a plague to the professional moralist. It is largely because of this disparity in the different aspects of modern morality that there are moral dilemmas.

For the absolutist on the subject of morals there is no compromise. So far as he is concerned, all doors to accommodation and personal adjustment are closed except on the terms which he stipulates. That means the way of conversion, a complete right-about-face, a surrender to the absolute standards that were presumably established once and for all time by some law-giver in the remote past.

Conventionalization has always afforded a means of accommodation that has seemed to satisfy all but the most confirmed purist. This means suiting the action to the occasion. Nudism is still under the ban in most communities, but near-nudism is being tolerated at bathing beaches, on the stage, and to a somewhat lesser extent in the ballroom. The sculpture or painting that would offend because of its portrayal of the undraped human figure becomes a work of art and generally acceptable under the saving influence of convention. What may pass on the stage would probably be barred from the moving-picture screen. Books alluding to sex that may be classified as classic or as "good literature" may pass the censor, although some of the same contents in paper cover, bought from the newsstands, would be confiscated as "trash." Conventionalization eases tensions, "saves faces" and reputations, and makes "right" those things that would be "wrong" under other circumstances. Conventions "permit rationalistic avoidances of apparent contradiction." That which is allowed by convention at one time may be incorporated in the mores of a later time.[30]

Rationalization is a familiar escape-mechanism in the field of morals. It is a form of personal accommodation. James Harvey Robinson says that "most of our so-called reasoning consists in finding arguments for going on believing as we already do." [31]

One of the most important aspects of the process of "rationalization" of action is the substitution for the unthinking acceptance of ancient custom, of deliberate adaptation to situations in terms of self-interest. To be sure, this process by no means exhausts the concept of rationalization of action. For in addition this can proceed in a variety of other directions; positively in that of a conscious rationalization of ultimate values; or negatively, at the expense not only of custom, but of emotional values; and, finally, in favour of a morally sceptical type of rationality, at the expense of any belief in absolute values.[32]

Two rather broad types of situation afford the individual possible bases for resorting to the rationalizing process by way of justifying his behavior both to himself and to others. One type of situation is

30 Thomas H. Grafton, "The Sociology of Right and Wrong," *Am. Sociol. Rev.*, Vol. 12, No. 1, February, 1947, pp. 86-95.
31 J. H. Robinson, *The Mind in the Making*, New York, Harper & Bros., 1921, p. 41.
32 From *Max Weber: The Theory of Social and Economic Organization*, edited by Talcott Parsons, p. 123. Copyright 1947 by Oxford University Press, Inc., New York.

that in which behavior, although in accord with the mores of a group to which the person belongs, is challenged or called into question. On such an occasion, the individual may rise to defend and justify the behavior pattern by what seems to him to be a reasonable motive. Often he does not know the real reasons for his beliefs and actions, since many of his ideas and behavior patterns have been adopted unconsciously. Attitudes on matters of "right" and "wrong," religious faiths and observances, political issues, international questions, race relations, and other matters important to his group, are generally taken over without any clear knowledge of whence they came or why they are as they are. For the purpose of offering what seems to be a rational motive, those aspects of the situation that are compatible with the wishes of the person or of the group which he represents arise into consciousness and suggest reasons that make the attitude and behavior seem "right" and even necessary.

The other type of situation that may lead to rationalization is one in which the individual, although acting within a given cultural context, hits upon a way of meeting a new and unfamiliar condition or a new way of meeting an old condition. Such random acts, if they bring satisfaction and prove to be expedient, are reinforced through the release of tension and tend to become habitual with the individual.[33] These habitual response tendencies of individuals, or "individual peculiarities," as Linton has called them,[34] may constitute no infringement on the group mores and thus excite no adverse reaction from the group. If they commend themselves to the group as being efficient, they may, in time, be incorporated in the folkways and, possibly, in the mores of the group. In the first instance, they must successfully pass the test of group approval. If they do not, they must be explained and vindicated. In other words, they invite rationalization. Of these we read:

modern Western civilization has thrown emphasis on direct and indirect adaptations of individuals to a swiftly changing technology. Since modern technology creates a constant pressure for new and more rapid adaptations to it, Habit-ways seldom persist long enough to develop into Folkways or to acquire the moral sanction necessary to the development of Mores.

Habit-ways are at the root of much personal and social maladjustment. Under the pressure of technological expediency, Habit-ways tend to displace old Folkways and to detach the moral sanction from Mores as their customary overt behavior is displaced. Moral values, having no longer a relation to

---

[33] See: William J. Cousins and Paul Oren, Jr., "Habit-Ways: A Footnote to Sumner," *Social Forces*, Vol. 25, May, 1947, pp. 416-418.

[34] Ralph Linton, *The Study of Man*, New York, Appleton-Century-Crofts, Inc., 1936, pp. 274-275.

actual behavior, persist in the minds of the members of our society. Individuals go on believing that certain types of behavior are "right"; however, they consistently act in ways diametrically opposed to these "spoken" values. From such personal and cultural dilemmas stem much social disorganization.[35]

Another way of accommodating moral dilemmas is that of idealization. Instead of resisting, persons very often choose to transmute their prejudices, hatreds, and fears into idealized conceptions of their foes, be they human or non-human. Obstacles, such as temptations, that have to be met, are translated through idealization into ways of salvation, molders of character, and sources of inspiration. The hostile forces become touchstones in the realization of ideal goals.

Compromise is frequently resorted to in effecting accommodation between divergent moral principles. "Rightness" is not very likely to be found at either extreme of opposing moral issues. At any rate, it is often found to be expedient and probably more nearly "right" to adopt a course of action near the middle way. While it may be admirable, now and then, to take a stand on an issue and maintain it, regardless of consequences, such procedure does not necessarily mean that the stand taken is the correct one. It may merely mean that one is stupid or has the courage of his convictions. If the latter virtue is the greater good, then there can be no great objection to it. But if it represents obstinacy only and if it serves to impede progress, thwart justice, prolong conflict, or create an impasse, then it may prove to be the lesser good.

Since moral principles, as well as group mores, are evolving variables, they are of necessity responsive to the changing social life of which in part they are the product. Their observance by societal members and their enforcement upon those who would digress widely from them are essential to the preservation of social organization and group solidarity.[36]

QUESTIONS

1. Discuss the relation between attitudes and values.
2. How are intellectual values involved with group interests?
3. How does Znaniecki characterize the "man of knowledge" and define his social role?
4. What are the four principal classes, with their subdivisions, of the types of social roles of men of knowledge as presented by Znaniecki?
5. How does the fourfold classificatory framework fit individual cases?

---

[35] Cousins and Oren, "Habit-Ways," *op. cit.*, p. 418.
[36] For a more extended treatment of the mechanisms of social control see Chapter 24.

6. "Nowhere are the ignorant so free to harry the learned as in a political democracy." Explain and illustrate.
7. Compare the "man of thought" with the "man of action" as to their respective characteristics and social roles.
8. When and under what circumstances do the ignorant feel humble in their ignorance and when not?
9. Discuss "freedom of teaching" and "freedom of the press" in the light of the discussion in the text. What can you add to what is said there?
10. What proposals are made for the more general avoidance of conflict between the learned and the unlearned?
11. What are the respective positions of Sumner and Lee on the subject of the relation of the mores to morals?
12. Show how moral principles may become matters of special-group interest.
13. What do you understand by "moral relativity"?
14. Are there differences between social morality and personal morality? If so, what are they?
15. What are some of the "moral dilemmas" confronted by persons and groups today? Compare folk societies and secular societies with respect to these dilemmas.
16. Discuss: "In many respects present-day group mores and societal morals represent incomplete secularization."
17. Discuss conversion, conventionalization, rationalization, idealization, and compromise as forms of accommodation in the realm of moral principles and behavior.
18. What are the implications for social interaction of the idea that moral principles, as well as group mores, are "evolving variables, responsive to the changing social world of which they are in part the product"?

BIBLIOGRAPHY

BARNES, HARRY E. *Intellectual and Cultural History of the Western World.* New York, Reynal & Hitchcock, 1941.

BEALE, HOWARD K. *Are American Teachers Free? An Analysis of Restraints upon the Freedom of Teaching in American Schools.* New York, Charles Scribner's Sons, 1936.

BECK, HUBERT P. *Men Who Control Our Universities.* New York, King's Crown Press, 1947.

BELL, ERIC T. *The Search for Truth.* New York, Reynal & Hitchcock, 1934.

BOUGLÉ, C. CÉLÉSTIN. *The Evolution of Values.* New York, Henry Holt & Co., 1926.

BUNTING, DAVID E. *Liberty and Learning: The Activities of the American Civil Liberties Union in Behalf of Freedom of Education.* Washington, American Council on Public Affairs, 1942.

CASE, CLARENCE M. *Essays in Social Values.* Los Angeles, University of Southern California Press, 1944.

COMMITTEE ON THE FREEDOM OF THE PRESS. *A Free and Responsible Press.* Chicago, University of Chicago Press, 1947.

DESMOND, ROBERT W. *The Press and World Affairs.* New York, D. Appleton-Century Co., 1937.

DRAKE, DURANT. *The New Morality.* New York, The Macmillan Co., 1928.

ERNST, MORRIS L., AND SEAGLE, WILLIAM. *To the Pure: A Study of Obscenity and the Censor.* New York, The Viking Press, 1928.

GOLDENWEISER, ALEXANDER. *Robots or Gods: An Essay on Craft and Mind.* New York, Alfred A. Knopf, 1931.

GRAFTON, THOMAS H. "The Sociology of Right and Wrong." *Am. Sociol. Rev.,* Vol. 12, No. 1, February, 1947, pp. 86-95.

GREENHOE, FLORENCE. *Community Contacts and Participation of Teachers.* Washington, American Council on Public Affairs, 1941.

HOBHOUSE, LEONARD T. *Morals in Evolution.* 5th ed. New York, Henry Holt & Co., 1928.

HOLMES, HENRY W. (Ed.). *Fundamental Education: Common Ground for All Peoples.* Report of a Special Committee to the Preparatory Commission of the United Nations Educational, Scientific and Cultural Organization, Paris, 1946. New York, The Macmillan Co., 1947.

HUTCHINS, ROBERT M. "Ideals in Education." *Am. J. Sociol.,* Vol. 43, No. 1, July, 1937, pp. 1-15.

JOHNSON, CHARLES S. "Education and the Cultural Process." *Am. J. Sociol.,* Vol. 48, No. 6, May, 1943, pp. 629-632.

JOHNSON, GERALD K. "Freedom of the Newspaper Press." *Annals Am. Acad. Pol. and Soc. Sci.,* Vol. 200, November, 1938, pp. 60-75.

KINGSBURY, SUSAN M., HART, HORNELL, AND ASSOCIATES. *Newspapers and the News: An Objective Measurement of Ethical and Unethical Behavior by Representative Newspapers.* New York, G. P. Putnam's Sons, 1937.

KIRCHWEY, FREDA (Ed.). *Our Changing Morality.* New York, Boni, 1924.

KOBRE, SIDNEY. *Backgrounding the News: The Newspaper and the Social Sciences.* New York, Twentieth Century Fund, 1939.

KOLB, WILLIAM L. "Sociologically Established Family Norms and Democratic Values." *Social Forces,* Vol. 26, May, 1948, pp. 451-456.

LANGDON-DAVIES, JOHN. *Man Comes of Age.* New York, Harper & Bros., 1932.

LAZARSFELD, PAUL. *Radio and the Printed Page: An Introduction to the Study of Radio and Its Role in the Communication of Ideas.* New York, Duell, Sloan & Pearce, 1943.

LIPPMANN, WALTER. *A Preface to Morals.* New York, The Macmillan Co., 1929.

LIPPMANN, WALTER. *Liberty and the News.* New York, Harcourt, Brace & Co., 1920.

LYND, ROBERT S. *Knowledge for What?* Princeton, N. J., Princeton University Press, 1939.

MARKUN, LEO. *Mrs. Grundy: A History of Four Centuries of Morals Intended to Illuminate Present Problems in Great Britain and the United States.* New York, D. Appleton-Century Co., 1930.

MENCKEN, H. L. *Treatise on Right and Wrong.* New York, Alfred A. Knopf, 1934.

NIEBUHR, REINHOLD. *Moral Man and Immoral Society.* New York, Charles Scribner's Sons, 1932.

PARK, ROBERT E. "Education and the Cultural Crisis." *Am. J. Sociol.,* Vol. 48, No. 6, May, 1943, pp. 728-736.

PEPPER, STEPHEN C. *A Digest of Purposive Values.* Berkeley, University of California Press, 1947.

RANULF, SVEND. *The Jealousy of the Gods and Criminal Law at Athens. A Contribution to the Sociology of Moral Indignation.* 2 vols. London, Williams & Norgate, 1933, 1934.

RAUP, BRUCE. *Education and Organized Interests in America.* New York, G. P. Putnam's Sons, 1936.

RUSSELL, BERTRAND. "The Role of the Intellectual in the Modern World." *Am. J. Sociol.,* Vol. 44, No. 4, January, 1939, pp. 491-498.

SALMON, LUCY M. *The Newspaper and Authority.* New York, Oxford University Press, 1924.

SHERIF, MUZAFER. *The Psychology of Social Norms.* New York, Harper & Bros., 1936, Ch. 7, "Social Values."

SUMMERS, H. B. (Ed.). *Radio Censorship.* New York, H. W. Wilson Co., 1939.

SWIFT, EDGAR JAMES. *The Jungle of the Mind.* New York, Charles Scribner's Sons, 1931.

TUFTS, JAMES H. *America's Social Morality. Dilemmas of the Changing Mores.* New York, Henry Holt & Co., 1933.

WESTERMARCK, EDWARD. *The Origin and Development of Moral Ideas.* 2 vols. London, Macmillan & Co., Ltd., 1906.

WHITE, LLEWELLYN, AND LEIGH, ROBERT D. *Peoples Speaking to Peoples.* A Report of the Commission on Freedom on the Press. Chicago, University of Chicago Press, 1946.

WILSON, LOGAN. *The Academic Man: A Study in the Sociology of a Profession.* New York, Oxford University Press, 1942.

YOUNG, KIMBALL (Ed.). *Social Attitudes.* New York, Henry Holt & Co., 1931. Ch. 1, "The Concept of Social Attitudes," by Ellsworth Faris; Ch. 2, "Human Nature, Attitudes, and the Mores," by Robert E. Park; Ch. 3, "Attitudes and the Redirection of Behavior," by L. L. Bernard.

ZNANIECKI, FLORIAN. "Education and Self-Education in Modern Societies." *Am. J. Sociol.,* Vol. 36, No. 3, November, 1930, pp. 371-386.

ZNANIECKI, FLORIAN. *The Social Role of the Man of Knowledge.* New York, Columbia University Press, 1940.

PART IV
SOCIAL CHANGE

INTRODUCTION

AT VARIOUS POINTS in the preceding chapters the relation of social interaction to social change has been touched upon. In fact, the course of social change has been traced throughout the whole of this volume. Wherever and whenever physical, cultural, and social elements act and react upon each other in the ecological and social processes there is change. Activity and change are ever-present, universal facts.

Scientists do not regard the data of their respective fields of investigation as fixed and unchanging entities. It was not always thus in man's thinking about his world. In Galileo's time most things on earth were held to be fixed. In fact, the earth itself was thought of as fixed and flat and as resting on pillars or a foundation. Similarly, heaven was regarded as fixed; hell was fixed; the statuses of men and women, masters and servants, rulers and ruled were fixed; practically all things were fixed. But Galileo discovered that the earth moves and thus introduced a new conception of the universe into the thinking of men. The different species of biological organisms were generally considered fixed until Darwin made his discoveries and promulgated his theories of the origin of species, natural selection, and the survival of the fittest. These men served to revolutionize the previously held notions about physical and organic nature. Despite the advances made in scientific knowledge there are many persons who continue to hold antiquated and unscientific beliefs because they have closed minds or are outside the sphere of contact with the findings of science.

The delusive traps of superstition, magic, and metaphysics enmeshed men's minds until the middle of the 16th century, with a few exceptions like Roger Bacon, who lived in the early part of the 13th century, and who was outstanding in his advocacy and practice of the scientific method. It remained for Francis Bacon, Galileo, Copernicus, Bruno, Bodin, Kepler, and Newton to initiate an era of scientific enlightenment. With the application of the method of verified observation and experimentation, certain basic facts of intelligence have emerged. Among these are the facts that order exists and that it is discoverable; that things show a general tendency to develop in an orderly sequence of changes; that these changes represent an unfolding from within outward, in accordance with inherent tendencies or indigenous patterns and in response to and in accordance with their respective environments; and that observing, measuring, and recording comparable data lead to the formulation of generalizations which serve as basic assumptions and hypotheses for further investigation.

The facts of social change are observable and can be described. Our present techniques of investigation make it possible to measure and explain at least some of these facts, with approximate accuracy. The personnel of society changes from moment to moment. Manners and customs change with varying degrees of rapidity and ease. The rich may become poor and the poor may prosper. Technological improvements may provoke accelerated production and increased consumption of goods or they may eventuate in industrial depression and widespread unemployment and distress. When changes occur in human relationships, the structure and codes imposed upon the individual, and the processes by which the individual is inducted into his place as a person, then we face social change in the strict sense.

If social change is an observable phenomenon, how may it be recognized? What are some of its indices? An index is an easily observable phenomenon which has been found to accompany a less observable but more fundamental process. For instance, the physical movement of individuals and families is of itself relatively inconsequential, but the fact that where there is movement family life and control tend to weaken is of importance. Movement is easily and readily observed; it is an index. Indices appear to fall into two general categories—those that give evidence of social change in the direction of social disorganization and those which are manifestations of change toward social reorganization. Actually, such a clear-cut dichotomy does not exist. Often the appearance is greater than the reality for not infrequently what appears to be disorganization is really an incidental, or sometimes important, factor in reorganization.

On every hand in modern competitive society are to be seen indications of social disorganization. The increase in numbers of what Simmel significantly called "the inner enemies"—the dependents, the defectives, and the delinquents—supplies tangible evidence that the social order is breaking down at certain points. Other indices are the many conflict situations cited in previous chapters, the manifold expressions of unrest and discontent in persons and in social groups, and neighborhood deterioration and community chaos. On the other hand, observable indices of social efforts toward a more satisfactory social order are by no means lacking. Advances in culture trait-complexes and culture types, increases in leisure time and its social uses, community planning and reorganization, more scientific attitudes toward defectives and delinquents, improvements in social work techniques and practices, forward developments in medical knowledge and public health service, gains in intergroup understanding and cooperation, and similar developments show unmistakable tendencies in the direction of social reorganization. These forms of social change follow one another invariably and uninterruptedly in successive cycles throughout the entire on-going of social interaction.

There is no separate and distinct process of social change. Social interaction *is* the process of social change. The two things are inseparable and coincident. Where there is interaction there will be change. The competitive and conflict phases of social interaction are often considered as disorganizing, while the accommodative and assimilative phases are commonly thought to be reorganizing. But such impressions are misleading. Since the former phases of interaction are more or less necessary to the latter phases, it is possible for one to conceive of competition and conflict as indirect factors in effecting social reorganization. If emphasis is placed on social change as a result or an effect of social interaction it merely represents a shift in point of view and amounts to the same thing as regarding accommodation as a condition or a state, or as regarding assimilation as an accomplished fact.

It will be the function of Part IV to focus attention on a number of factors that affect and determine the nature and rate of social change. The following chapter will deal with the ecological and demographic dynamics of social change and the next chapter will discuss social change in terms of its cultural dynamics. Subsequent chapters will deal, respectively, with some of the unorganized and more or less ephemeral response tendencies in social change, the mechanisms employed in social control, and the role of organized social movements as effecting more significant and enduring social reorganization.

Chapter 21

ECOLOGICAL DYNAMICS OF SOCIAL CHANGE

Trends in Population Growth and Distribution

The process of ecological interaction described in Part II serves, among other things, to distribute individuals and population groups spatially, temporally, and vocationally.[1] It is in connection with this process that we observe changes in location and position. In so far as these changes in spatial, temporal, and functional distribution affect the structure and interactivity of groups, they may be said to be factors in social change.

It appears that man, in common with all life-forms, is engaged in establishing and maintaining a state of equilibrium between himself, collectively as well as individually, and the conditions of his physical environment. This primary search for balance and order proceeds endlessly in many areas of human experience. Elsewhere in this book we have treated this universal activity in such areas as institutional behavior, group relations, personality adjustment, and cultural change. Our present concern is with the problem of the equilibrium of "resources" and numbers of people.[2] The factor of "numbers" in relation to "resources" is a matter of population growth and distribution in terms of all kinds of human and cultural resources, as well as those called "natural" of a given time and place.[3] Unlike the subhuman life-forms, where numbers depend almost entirely on the "land" and on the outcome of a ruthless struggle for existence among competing life-forms, human populations, while also definitely involved in the "man-land ratio," have developed cultures which

---

[1] See especially Chapters 7, 9, and 17.

[2] There are no resources *sui generis* existent in "nature"; there are only potential resources which become actual resources when defined and treated as such. When we speak of "natural resources" we mean the "land" and all that the term implies in the way of soil and its fertility, water, minerals, etc. We also speak of "human resources," which, together with the so-called "natural resources," are primary. "For their development these depend upon the building up of technological resources, institutional resources, and capital resources."—Rupert B. Vance, "Human Resources and Public Policy: An Essay toward Regional-National Planning," *Social Forces*, Vol. 22, October, 1943, p. 20.

[3] Paul Meadows, "Balance and Imbalance in Human Social Adjustment," *Social Forces*, Vol. 22, May, 1944, pp. 415-419.

serve to some extent as intervening and mitigating forces in the interactional process.[4]

Population Growth.—At one time, populations grew almost entirely through an excess of births over deaths. This growth was regarded as natural and healthy. The low rate of mobility enabled populations to maintain a fairly high degree of homogeneity. The children born into the community were easily absorbed into its way of life and problems of social adjustment were negligible.

In primitive culture groups, the problems of population were questions of number and of quality, primarily the former. The question of number "may present a practical problem either because of paucity or because of an excess of numbers."[5] Of the importance of population size, Smith[6] says:

The level of living of a population—one of the most widely accepted indexes of national achievement—is influenced by its size. In the main a small population results in a higher level of living than a large one. This general relationship is reflected in the high level of living characteristic of such relatively sparsely settled countries as Australia, New Zealand, Canada, and the United States. In comparison, the densely populated countries of India, China, and Japan have low standards of living. The contrast between the levels of living prevailing in these two groups of countries is at least in part due to differences in the numbers of people included in their respective populations.

. . . Other factors conditioning level of living include natural resources, technological skills, and social organization. The direction and magnitude of the effect on level of living, of changes in these factors, as well as in the size of population are obvious. The level of living actually realized by a people results from the interrelation of all these conditions.

Viewed from a political and military standpoint, the number of persons in a population assumes a more tangible and meaningful role. The military strength of a nation in wartime and consequently its bargaining power in peacetime are to a considerable extent tied up with the magnitude of the forces that it can marshal for both the production line and the battle line. The size of the labor and fighting forces is also largely dependent upon the size of the population from which they are drawn. A large population as a rule means a powerful nation, whereas a small population results in a relatively weak nation. It should be noted, however, that as was the case with respect to level of living, size of population is not the sole factor determining military capacity.

---

[4] *Ibid.*, pp. 416-417. See also T. Lynn Smith, *Population Analysis*, New York, McGraw-Hill Book Co., Inc., 1948, Ch. 1 and pp. 388-389. Smith believes that the concept "optimum population" is "of dubious validity and slight utility."

[5] E. B. Reuter, *Population Problems*, Philadelphia, J. B. Lippincott Co., 1923, p. 6.

[6] By permission from *Population Analysis* by T. Lynn Smith. Copyrighted, 1948. New York, McGraw-Hill Book Co., Inc., pp. 3-5.

The number of people in a population may increase or decline during the course of time. This fact accounts for one important dynamic in population analysis; the other fact is that of population mobility, which will receive attention in the next section of this chapter.

In situations characterized by overpopulation or by underpopulation, the practices considered necessary either for decrease or increase of population numbers become imbedded in the respective cultures and traditions of the people. Suicide, infanticide, and killing of the old have long been and still are socially approved practices among peoples who constantly feel the pressure of overpopulation on their sources of livelihood. Also, abortion practices to counteract the effects of excessive fecundity, and social inducements and compulsions to impel women to bear and rear children, have been utilized in different societies in order that increase or decrease of population might be regulated. Other practices frequently followed by overpopulated nations are those of attempted territorial expansion through the seizure of land, colonization, and assisted emigration. Meadows, in criticizing these practices, remarks that "A 'numbers' policy or a 'land' policy has dominated the 'arts' policy in the achievement of balance. Fascist imperialism in the 1930's has been the most recent example of the futility and wastefulness of this technique of balance." [7] Rejecting the principle of utilizing the "numbers policy" and the "land policy" to the practical exclusion of revolutionizing the "arts policy" in the interest of effecting a better balance, he says:

Human economies are, in a sense, cultural configurations built up around an arts policy. Few economies change their arts policy; those which do, change very slowly. Most of the associations of men have worked within the economy as given, fearful of the modification of the economic arts. Instead, they choose to alter the other factors in the man-land ratio: birth rates, death rates, size of the land, level of living. Only modern industrial economies have achieved a conscious, telic control of their arts policy.[8]

The quality aspect of the population problem, while for most groups more significant than the question of quantity, is less directly connected with ecological factors and processes.[9] Nevertheless, whatever enters into the scheme of human relations to determine vocational position and economic standing, urban growth and rural decline, migrations and relocations of peoples, may have bearing on quality. That selective distribution affects fecundity, and therefore numbers,

---

[7] Meadows, "Balance and Imbalance in Human Social Adjustment," *op. cit.,* p. 417.
[8] *Ibid.,* p. 418.
[9] See: Henry P. Fairchild, *People: The Quantity and Quality of Population,* New York, Henry Holt & Co., 1939; Reuter, *Population Problems,* Chs. 13-15, 20-21; Warren S. Thompson, *Population Problems,* New York, McGraw-Hill Book Co., Inc., 1942, Chs. 21-22.

is fairly well established, but that such selection works to the disadvantage of the more intelligent and socially superior is not conclusively shown by any available data.[10] It would seem, rather, that the differential birth rate in favor of the economically disadvantaged and physically and mentally less fit groups is due principally to culture patterns and social attitudes that place economic ease and social pleasure above child-bearing among the socially and economically favored groups, together with the persistence of attitudes and religious principles that protect the weak and retarded at the expense of the ambitious and able. Care should be exercised, however, not to confuse poverty with inferiority. Poverty itself is not to be taken as evidence of inferior native endowment because poverty is produced by many causes, which may or may not include native inferiority.

From the varied standpoints of racial survival, national welfare, and individual well-being, the questions of a population's size and quality are of social importance. There is the problem of determining and maintaining the most desirable ratio between the number of people and the area and resources of the land and of the technological and industrial arts, in order to secure the general welfare, an adequate working force, and national defense in case of need. It is also necessary to determine the needs for and to obtain the required population types so as to have available at all times competent leadership, capable professional services, and an intelligent citizenry. In fact, these problems are rather generally recognized. Efforts to control population growth range from folkways and techniques of uncertain value to official promulgations and practices of great variety. However, relatively few of the conscious and formal efforts have been completely successful; at least, not as intended.[11] A comprehensive population policy, obviously so desirable from the viewpoint of na-

---

[10] See: A. M. Carr-Saunders, *World Population*, Oxford, Clarendon Press, 1936, Chs. 7 and 8; Wilson H. Grabill, "Effect of the War on the Birth Rate and Postwar Fertility Prospects," *Am. J. Sociol.*, Vol. 50, No. 2, September, 1944, pp. 107-111; Philip M. Hauser, "Population and Vital Phenomena," *Am. J. Sociol.*, Vol. 48, No. 3, November, 1942, pp. 309-320; Clyde V. Kiser, *Group Differentials in Urban Fertility*, Baltimore, The Williams and Wilkins Co., 1942; Paul H. Landis, *Population Problems*, New York, American Book Co., 1943, Chs. 6-9; Alva Myrdal, *Nation and Family*, New York, Harper & Bros., 1941, Ch. 6; National Resources Planning Board, *The Problems of a Changing Population*, Washington, Government Printing Office, 1938, Chs. 5 and 6; Frank Notestein, "The Differential Rate of Increase among the Social Classes of the American Population," *Social Forces*, Vol. 12, October, 1933, pp. 17-33; Raymond Pearl, *The Natural History of Population*, London, Oxford University Press, 1939, Chs. 4 and 5; W. B. Reddaway, *The Economics of a Declining Population*, New York, The Macmillan Co., 1939; E. B. Reuter, *Population Problems*, Philadelphia, J. B. Lippincott Co., 2nd ed., 1937, Ch. 17; Smith, *Population Analysis*, Ch. 11; Thompson, *Population Problems*, Chs. 11-13; Rupert B. Vance, "The Regional Approach to the Study of High Fertility," *The Milbank Memorial Fund Quarterly*, Vol. 19, pp. 356-374; Sanford B. Winston, "The Relation of Certain Social Factors to Fertility," *Am. J. Sociol.*, Vol. 35, No. 5, March, 1930, pp. 753-764.

[11] See: Carr-Saunders, *World Population*, Chs. 9, 16, 17; D. V. Glass, *Population Policies and Movements in Europe*, Oxford, The Clarendon Press, 1940; D. V. Glass, *The Struggle for*

tional welfare and social stability, has been lacking. Any nationally-planned program of social change in the direction of better conditions of life and labor, national security and prosperity, and human welfare generally, will perforce have to deal intelligently and scientifically with the trend of population growth.[12]

Population Mobility.—It is with population mobility and its influences on social change, and not with the more inclusive social mobility, that we have to deal at this point. Our interest here is with the movement of people in space and its so-called "vertical mobility up and down the socio-economic ladder" of ecological positions, and not with "all responses or adjustments to the manifold suggestions and stimulations provided through the medium of communication." [13]

Social change is unthinkable without man's desire to move about in space and from one socio-economic level to another. Mere stability of position of man and his institutions, continuity and rigidity of form or structure, cannot account for personal growth and functioning. Permanence of residence contributes to group unity, to the preservation of institutional organization, and to communal living.

The land is in the nature of an underlying material bond that holds the group together in space. It brings the people into physical proximity and, as they become attached by work or residence to certain areas, keeps them in proximity. Each group feels the need of habitat or a meeting place, not merely as a refuge but as a kind of tangible and material symbol of group identity and purpose. The family has a home, the sect a church or meeting place, the fraternal order its lodge or grotto or temple, the gang its rendezvous. In the absence of a common habitat, one is projected as an ideal or objective: the Jews have a Zion.[14]

Population, New York, Oxford University Press, 1936; Rudolf Heberle, "Social Factors in Birth Control," *Am. Sociol. Rev.*, Vol. 6, No. 6, December, 1941, pp. 794-805; Landis, *Population Problems*, Ch. 10; Frank Lorimer, Ellen Winston, and Louise K. Kiser, *Foundations of American Population Policy*, New York, Harper & Bros., 1940; Alva Myrdal, *Nation and Family;* Gunnar Myrdal, *Population: A Problem for Democracy*, Cambridge, Harvard University Press, 1940; Frederick Osborne, *Preface to Eugenics*, New York, Harper & Bros., 1940; Joseph J. Spengler, *France Faces Depopulation*, Durham, N. C., Duke University Press, 1938; Warren S. Thompson, *Plenty of People*, New York, The Ronald Press Co., 1948; Warren S. Thompson, *Population and Peace in the Pacific*, Chicago, University of Chicago Press, 1946; Thompson, *Population Problems*, Chs. 25-26.

[12] Landis, *Population Problems*, Ch. 25.

[13] A. W. Lind, *A Study of Mobility of Population of Seattle*, Seattle, University of Washington, 1925, p. 8. The word "mobility" will be used throughout this discussion as it is generally used in ecological and sociological writings, that is, to mean movement of any kind, the act of moving or of being moved. This is done because the term is so used in all the literature even though the authors would prefer the simple term "movement," leaving the concept "mobility" for a more exact reference to "capacity for and freedom of movement, whether the movement is self-induced or externally initiated or assisted." "Mobility" thus becomes one of the two basic postulates of ecological interaction, the other postulate being "contact," the former being a prerequisite to the latter.

[14] By permission from *Introduction to Sociology* by E. B. Reuter and C. W. Hart. Copyrighted, 1933, McGraw-Hill Book Co., Inc., pp. 258-259.

The physical movement of people through space takes many different forms, ranging from the daily movements of many thousands of persons between place of residence and place of work,[15] in the performance of the round of work activities, in the search for recreation and entertainment, in "tourism," in pilgrimages and visits, in vagabondage and other forms of more or less aimless wandering, to the migration of peoples from land to land and from one part of a country to another in search of a place of settlement and the possibility of achieving a new and improved status. All such movements, except those of a most local vicinal character, are relatively new experiences in the history of man. Geographic explorations and discoveries, travel in the interest of trade, and developments in the means of communication tend to stimulate man's wish to see new places, to meet new people, and to try his hand at living in a new habitat, and improvements in transportation facilities bring to him the easier realization of his desire. Thus man's increased mobility and consequent movement have promoted fresh advances in culture.[16] These statements refer to historic rather than to prehistoric population movements.

The great mobility of the modern world also contributes to social change in the direction of social disorganization. The historic unity and continuity of the social group tends to be destroyed when man is divorced from the land and the possession of the tools of his trade. Changes in industrial and business enterprises have tended to concentrate migration in the direction of centers of dominance, with resultant urbanization of large numbers of people and secularization of most institutions. Urban residence and mode of living are likewise relatively new experiences for the masses and have resulted in much social confusion and personal demoralization. The system of employment in competitive industries and businesses over which the individual exercises little or no control, and the conditions of living in multiple dwellings and rooming houses so characteristic of modern cities, foster and often compel excessive movement with its attendant break in the intimate relationships so conducive to personal stability and social organization.

Nearly all institutions have been changed in the course of adapting to the impacts attending ecological movement. Some, like the country store, the blacksmith shop, the one-room rural school, and the old-fashioned neighborhood, have found it impossible to adapt them-

---

15 See: Kate K. Liepman, *The Journey to Work*, New York, Oxford University Press, 1944.
16 Carl Bücher, *Industrial Evolution*, trans. by S. M. Wickett, New York, Henry Holt & Co., 1901, p. 347.

selves and have practically disappeared. Others either have moved with the movement of their constituents, have altered their basic structures, or have modified their functions.[17]

No other institution, save possibly among those directly connected with industry, transportation, and communication, has been so fundamentally affected as has the family. The decline of the kinship group, with the emergence of the marriage group, is one of the first noticeable effects resulting, in large measure, from mobility.

Old ties begin to break when young people hire out to work, especially when they seek employment at a distance from the old home. When they marry and settle far away, contacts tend to grow fewer and less intimate; the next generation is likely to have rather vague ideas of the relatives "in the old country" or "back East." Not only is there detachment from kinsmen; there are contacts with strangers. Sons and daughters marry persons whom their parents have never seen and who frequently belong to different religious, economic, and nationality groups.[18]

The larger freedom of mobility of work- and pleasure-seeking of the members of the modern family has tended to release them to a considerable extent from the jurisdiction of the primary-group controls that once inhered in family life. The chief consequence of this tendency is a growth of individualism. From their studies of the large family group of the Polish peasant, Thomas and Znaniecki reached the following conclusions which they "hypothetically propose as sociological laws":

The real cause of all phenomena of family disorganization is to be sought in the influence of certain new values—new for the subject—such as: new sources of hedonistic satisfaction, new vanity values, new (individualistic) types of economic organization, new forms of sexual appeal. This influence presupposes, of course, not only a contact between the individual and the outside world but also the existence in the individual's personality of certain attitudes which make him respond to these new values—hedonistic aspirations, desire for social recognition, desire for economic security and advance, sexual instinct (sic). The specific phenomenon of family disorganization consists in a definite modification of those pre-existing attitudes under the influence of the new values, resulting in the appearance of new, more or less different attitudes. The nature of this modification can be generally characterized in such a way that, while the attitudes which existed under the family system were essentially "we"-attitudes (the individual did not dissociate his hedonistic tendencies, his desires for recognition or economic security, his sexual needs from the tendencies and aspirations of his family group), the

---

17 See pp. 250-253, 270, 515-516.
18 S. A. Queen, W. B. Bodenhafer, and E. B. Harper, *Social Organization and Disorganization*, New York, Thomas Y. Crowell Co., 1935, p. 79.

new attitudes, produced by the new values acting upon those old attitudes, are essentially "I"-attitudes—the individual's wishes are separated in his consciousness from those of other members of his family. Such an evolution implies that the new values with which the individual gets in touch are individualistic in their meaning, appeal to the individual, not to the group as a whole; and this is precisely the character of most modern hedonistic, sexual, economic, vanity-values. Disorganization of the family as primary group is thus an unavoidable consequence of modern civilization.[19]

Thus we see that the contact-producing movement of the family members, as individuals and not as a collective unity, leads to the supplanting of group-consciousness by egoistic-consciousness. Familial attitudes are lost in favor of individual wish-fulfillment. Factors contributing to these changes in attitudes are undoubtedly numerous, but conspicuous among them is that of ecological movement. However, it should be noted that "contact between the individual and the outside world" is much more dependent on the means of communication than on physical movement.

MIGRATION. A major form of population mobility is migration. It is a special kind of movement of people in that it commonly involves a single linear movement from one habitation to another, and involves, to a considerable extent, the breaking of personal, communal, and cultural ties. It is a change of location, intentionally permanent, and implies a change of position in the ecological order and of status in the social order. Migration has sometimes been used as applicable only to the movements of groups of people, such as family units or numbers of such units, perhaps whole villages or large masses of people moving toward new habitats under the impulsion of adverse or perilous conditions where they are, or because of the attractions of another location. Hollingshead gives the conditions underlying migrations under two broad categories: "(1) *changes in the physical environment,* such as cataclysms in nature; and (2) *changes in the socio-cultural environment.*" [20] He goes on to say: "Under primitive conditions most migrations were probably caused by a combination of both. Most modern migrations, however, have been conditioned by *changes in the socio-cultural environment.*" [21]

Migration is not confined to groups, however. There are individual migrants, who are subject to the same motivating factors as

19 W. I. Thomas, and F. Znaniecki, *The Polish Peasant in Europe and America,* New York, Alfred A. Knopf, 1927, Vol. 2, pp. 1167-1168.
20 A. B. Hollingshead, in A. M. Lee (Ed.), *New Outline of the Principles of Sociology,* New York, Barnes & Noble, Inc., 1946, p. 107.
21 *Ibid.*

group members. Hollingshead and others seem to consider modern migrations, in the main, as individual and family movements, compared with earlier migrations which tended to assume the character of mass movements.

Perhaps the best example of true migration is that type of movement of people leading to settlement. The settler is one who moves with the idea of making the change of habitation permanent; by intent or otherwise he tends, generally speaking, to sever "home ties." His position may be affected by the move and it is usually his desire that it shall be improved. While he and his descendants, to the second and third generation, may retain many of the traits of the culture from which he has migrated, the true settler will endeavor to accommodate himself to his new environment and to become assimilated. The settler puts down roots, as it were, in the new habitat; he welcomes fresh contacts and seeks identification with his surroundings.[22]

On the other hand, migration does not always entail movement from one country to another or the crossing of administrative boundary lines, as from one state to another within the same country. Mere movement from one place to another, such as change of residence from one apartment or house to another in the same city, cannot be called migration. Nor can the movements of seasonal workers as they follow the crops and the harvests, with their usual return to their starting places at the end of the season, be termed migration, although such workers are commonly referred to as "migratory." But there is internal migration as well as international migration, as witness the trek of the Mormons, starting in 1838 from Missouri to Illinois, and later resumed in 1844 when they migrated westward to the place of final settlement in what is now Utah; the recurrent movements of the Mennonites in search of a permanent resting place; the migrations of thousands of Negroes from the rural South to the industrial northern and Pacific Coast cities; the almost continuous flow of rural-farm and rural-village population cityward; and other similar move-

22 On the subject of migration and settlement, see Louis Adamic, *Two-Way Passage*, New York, Harper & Bros., 1941; Nels Anderson, *Desert Saints: The Mormon Frontier in Utah*, Chicago, University of Chicago Press, 1942; Maurice R. Davie, *Refugees in America: Report of the Committee for the Study of Recent Immigration from Europe*, New York, Harper & Bros., 1947; Maurice R. Davie, *World Immigration*, New York, The Macmillan Co., 1936; Carl A. Dawson, *Group Settlement: Ethnic Communities in Western Canada*, Toronto, The Macmillan Co. of Canada, 1936; C. A. Dawson, and Eva R. Younge, *Pioneering in the Prairie Provinces; The Social Side of the Settlement Process*, Toronto, The Macmillan Co. of Canada, 1940; Marcus Lee Hansen, *The Immigrant in American History*, Cambridge, Harvard University Press, 1940; Landis, *Population Problems*, Chs. 21-22; Bruno Lasker, *Asia on the Move*, New York, Henry Holt & Co., 1945; Bruno Lasker, "Post-War Migration Problems; The Far East," *Social Forces*, Vol. 22, December, 1943, pp. 130-136; Milbank Memorial Fund, *Postwar Problems of Migration*, New York, Milbank Memorial Fund, 1947; Smith, *Population Analysis*, Chs. 16 and 17; Donald R. Taft, *Human Migrations: A Study of International Movements*, New York, The Ronald Press Co., 1936; Thompson, *Population Problems*, Ch. 23.

ments throughout American history. The same thing has happened and is happening elsewhere throughout the world, as between regions and communities within the different countries.[23]

By such movements do populations get shuffled and redistributed. The extent of the selectivity factor in migration is not clearly seen and the problem calls for more research. We are certain, however, that migration has significance for social change. As Smith says, "Migration affects directly not only the physical constitution and health of the population but also the social structures and processes of society, and it exerts tremendous influences upon the personalities of individuals." [24] Migration calls for adjustments on the part of the populations that lose through migration as well as on the part of the receiving populations. Institutional structures are forced to accommodate themselves to the effects of emigration and often die out altogether, while the immigrant-receiving communities and regions must accommodate their social organization and life processes to the introduction of new and oftentimes conflicting cultural and ethnic elements.[25] Early migrations represented the expansion of peoples from centers to the unexploited frontiers of the area organized by the market, but modern industry and the growth of cities changed the character of population movements generally so that recent movements, instead of being to the margins of economic areas, have become movements toward centers of dominance, that is, the cities. Instead of producing a diversity of local and tribal cultures, it tends today to bring about urban civilization with its clash and interpenetration of cultures.

Composition and Distribution of Population.—In the discussion of the ecological elements and processes in earlier chapters,[26] the nature and effects of selective distribution were noted. Involved in and materially affected by ecological distribution are the racial, na-

---

[23] On the subject of internal migration, see Jerome S. Bruner, "How Much Post-War Migration?" *Am. J. Sociol.*, Vol. 49, No. 1, July, 1943, pp. 39-45; Margaret L. Bright and Dorothy S. Thomas, "Interstate Migration and Intervening Opportunities," *Am. Sociol. Rev.*, Vol. 6, No. 6, December, 1941, pp. 773-783; Ta Chen, *Population in Modern China*, Chicago, University of Chicago Press, 1946, Ch. 6; Henry Hill Collins, Jr., *America's Own Refugees: Our 4,000,000 Homeless Migrants*, Princeton, Princeton University Press, 1941; Carter Goodrich, et al., *Migration and Economic Opportunity*, Philadelphia, University of Pennsylvania Press, 1936; Landis, *Population Problems*, Chs. 23-24; National Resources Committee, *The Problems of a Changing Population*, Washington, Government Printing Office, 1938, pp. 83-118; Smith, *Population Analysis*, Ch. 18; Thompson, *Population Problems*, Ch. 24; C. Warren Thornthwaite, *Internal Migration in the United States*, Philadelphia, University of Pennsylvania Press, 1934; Rupert B. Vance, *All These People, The Nation's Human Resources in the South*, Chapel Hill, University of North Carolina Press, 1945, Chs. 9 and 10; P. K. Whelpton, *Needed Population Research*, Lancaster, The Science Press Co., 1938, Ch. 5.
[24] Smith, *Population Analysis*, p. 291.
[25] See Chapters 7-9.
[26] Chapters 7-9.

tionality, sex, age, marital, occupational, urban, and rural elements of the population. How and in what ratios these several different categories of a given population's components get placed in space, time, and position with respect to each other affects profoundly their cultural and social relations, their interactional tendencies, and their amenability or resistance to social control and social change.

In this connection the racial composition of a population has a direct bearing on the capacity of the group for social intercourse and accommodative behavior. In Chapters 15 and 16 we discussed certain aspects of interaction between ethnic groups and, though these principles were treated primarily with reference to social interaction, they apply also to social change. Much that belongs in our present discussion has therefore already been said.

The distribution of nationality groups within a given population or of nationalities in a continental or world-wide pattern is a factor of significance in shaping the character of international relations. Large-scale emigration and immigration have resulted in the transplanting of these migrating groups and their cultures in new and ever-shifting patterns of distribution. Consequently, the recipient societies have been thrown into some confusion due to the resultant acceleration of competition, the heightening of tensions, the increase of occasions for conflict, and the difficulties of finding satisfactory bases of accommodation among the diverse nationality elements in their midst. Since the arrangement of nations and nationality groups in a continental or world pattern is recognized as one involving the occupation of territorial units, this factor, among others, greatly affects their relations with one another. Conditions in border areas of government, trade, culture, and nationality are particularly capable of provoking social interaction and social change. Territorial limitations, linked with the rapid growth of populations and with nationalistic policies of expansion, stimulate competition and conflict. In addition, social change in the direction of enhanced nationality-group consciousness, intensified intragroup unity, and active organization of the in-group forces for aggression or defense is greatly increased in such situations.

The sex distribution of the population appears to be another factor in determining social change. A reference back to previous discussions of sex and age may be helpful at this point.[27] Despite some shortcomings in reporting for purposes of the census, it is probably correct to conclude that the sex classification for the total population

---

[27] See Chapter 17.

of the United States is quite reliable. The same cannot be said for many parts of the world. For the population of the United States as a whole, the Census of 1940 showed a ratio of 100.7 males per 100 females, but when factors of age, race, nationality, and place of residence are considered it is found that the distribution of the sexes is not nearly so uniform as the over-all ratio would seem to indicate. It is virtually impossible to get reliable sex ratios by age, somewhat less difficult to obtain those for race and nationality groupings, and easiest of all to secure those by place of residence.

A balanced sex ratio is by no means uniform throughout the country as between urban areas and rural areas and among the several regions. We find a disproportionate number of females concentrated in urban areas and of males in rural areas and on farms, and a high concentration of males in the West, of females in the South, and a fair balance between them in the North. Broken down still further, the distribution reveals that females are preponderant in residential and governmental cities and in regions given over to commercial activities, whereas males are found in larger proportions in centers of heavy industry, mining, lumbering, and shipping by water, as well as in farming districts.[28]

Analysis of the association between the proportion of the sexes and urban and rural residence and in terms of regional variations has been made in earlier chapters. It is in order at this point, however, to analyze the relations between these ecological variables in distribution of the sexes and the problem of social change. It has been shown by some students of population and those of social disorganization that when the composition of a group is seriously skewed in its sex distribution the effects are felt in the cultural realm and in areas of social interaction and organization. If the unbalancing of a previously established sex ratio is extreme, whether approximating equality or not, the cultural equilibrium is disturbed, folkways, mores, and institutional structures and behaviors undergo radical modifications, taboos and ceremonials are drastically altered, and attitudes toward sex itself and behavior associated with it manifest tendencies toward pronounced revision. However, once a settled ratio has been achieved, no matter how disproportionate it may be either in the direction of maleness or of femaleness, it is possible to effect an accommodation, to the end that appropriate cultural norms are established and functionally adequate social relationships are realized. It is conceivable, under certain conditions such as military necessity, religious

28 See: Smith, *Population Analysis*, Ch. 5.

asceticism, prison confinement, and the like, that temporary and even permanent accommodation may be made to life in an all-male or all-female community. One would expect such single-sex societies to manifest little change, however.

What is more significant for social change in the ratio of the sexes in a population is the changing character of the latter, which is due, in the main, to the ebb and flow of population movement. Significantly, this movement was for many hundreds of years, and is still for most people in the world, principally confined to males, since they were the sex with the greater mobility. In former times, females generally moved only when the male members of their families moved; today, in our part of the world, they are much freer to move, geographically and vocationally speaking, than ever before. But it is this movement, previously discussed, which, when correlated with sex distribution among other factors, is influential in setting in action the forces contributive to social change.

The age of a population is also significant for social change. Populations having a majority of young people display greater fluidity, initiative, and energy, than do those having an excess of young children and of old people. There is in them a spirit of hustle, experimentation, and impatience with indecision and inaction. "Age composition determines in large measure the social roles of the population, the degree, range, and direction of their movement, both vertical and geographical, their adaptability to new situations, the extent and nature of their social participation, and the goals for which they strive."[29]

The relation to social change of the proportionate distribution of the married and of the unmarried of the two sexes of marriageable age in the population is not easily determined. That marital status is conditioned to a great extent by the sex ratio and the age ratio, by socio-economic conditions, by shifts or changes in these factors, and by biological and psychological discoveries, is well established by the studies that have been made.[30] But what effect, if any, the marital status of the members of a given population has on the nature, direction, and rate of social change is not well understood. However, observation leads to the belief that where a population has a higher percentage of unmarried than married members fifteen years of age

---

[29] Landis, *Population Problems*, p. 299.
[30] See: E. W. Burgess and H. J. Locke, *The Family*, New York, American Book Co., 1945, Ch. 13; Henry A. Bowman, *Marriage for Moderns*, New York, McGraw-Hill Book Co., Inc., 2nd ed., 1948, Chs. 3-7; J. K. Folsom, *The Family and Democratic Society*, New York, John Wiley & Sons, Inc., 1943, Chs. 4-5; E. R. Groves and W. F. Ogburn, *American Marriage and Family Relationships*, New York, Henry Holt & Co., 1928, particularly Ch. 27. See other works on marriage and the family.

and over, a greater freedom in personal conduct and a larger measure of laxness in societal behavior tend to prevail.

Occupational Variety.—Occupational distribution is an element of particular importance in determining the course of change in standards of living, industrial control, and cooperative action. Where a single occupational group predominates in a community, its practices and code of ethics come to have prestige. If the businessmen control, then the course of social change will be governed largely by their wishes and will be engineered by the chamber of commerce or other organized business groups. If professional men rate high in the community, we may expect a certain amount of leadership and direction of social change to be guided by their outlook and determined by their objectives. When an organized labor group is in the saddle, its ambitions, troubles, and ideals will occupy a large place in the community's thinking and achievement. When no one occupational or economic-interest group exerts pressure on the local situation, social change is likely to be uncertain, weak, and haphazard, competition unrestrained, and factional conflict a fairly regular occurrence.[31]

Any pronounced alteration in the division of labor induced by a new discovery or invention, industrial or other economic reorganization, a shift in population, change in sex ratios or in age distribution, or from whatever cause, will almost certainly effect corresponding and correlative changes in social interaction and social organization. Likewise, radical disturbances to levels of living and to population movements consequent upon economic depression or economic inflation will be followed by repercussions in family life, governmental structures and functions, personal and group statuses, race and other majority-minority group relations, international interaction, and the beliefs and attitudes of many persons. Similarly, many of the ecological factors incident to war, such as mobilization of manpower, acceleration of industrial production, relocation of large segments of the population, novel and arbitrary working schedules, increased mobility for some and decreased freedom of movement for others through curtailment of travel, and rationing—these and other related factors contribute to place new strains and stresses on institutional structures, moral standards and practices, domestic economy and living patterns, age and sex relations, and the like.[32]

---

[31] See: E. A. Ross, *Principles of Sociology,* New York, The Century Co., 1930, Chs. 42-44.
[32] See: Robert C. Angell, *The Family Encounters the Depression,* New York, Charles Scribner's Sons, 1936; E. Wight Bakke, *Citizens Without Work: A Study of the Effects of Unemployment upon the Workers' Social Relations and Practice,* New Haven, Yale University Press, 1940; E. Wight Bakke, *The Unemployed Worker: A Study of the Task of Making a Living Without a Job,* New Haven, Yale University Press, 1940; Howard M. Bell, *Youth Tell Their Story,* Washington, American Council on Education, 1938; S. Bent, *Machine-*

Expansion of Cities.—Social reorganization has not kept pace with the tremendous acceleration of city growth in the United States and Canada in recent years and with the remarkable extension of technical services in modern times. Among the most notable features of urban concentration and expansion have been the influx of large numbers of immigrants, a great invasion of Negroes from the South into urban centers of the North, the very definite movement (somewhat slackened and even reversed in some areas during the economic depression of the 1930's but resumed during World War II) from the agricultural districts, a general decline in the birth rate (temporarily reversed during and immediately following the war years), disproportions in sex and age groups, and the growing freedom of women to enter the occupations.

The gradual and orderly expansion of urban development would result inevitably in social change. This might be expected to take the form of a moderate degree of disorganization. The latter trend would be normal and not unusual and would tend to stimulate social reorganization in ways and to a degree that would make city life more livable and socially satisfying. But the rapidity of urban expansion has been accompanied by an inordinate amount of disorganization, both social and personal. A study of vital and social statistics for American cities shows a decided increase in insanity, disease, crime, vice, suicide, and other "rough indices of social disorganization." [33]

Made Men, New York, Farrar & Rinehart, 1930; James H. S. Bossard, "War and the Family," *Am. Sociol. Rev.*, Vol. 6, No. 3, June, 1941, pp. 330-344; R. T. Bye and R. H. Blodgett, *Getting and Earning*, New York, F. S. Crofts Co., 1937; Ruth S. Cavan, *The Family*, New York, Thomas Y. Crowell Co., 1942, Chs. 12 and 13; Ruth S. Cavan and K. H. Ranck, *The Family and the Depression*, Chicago, University of Chicago Press, 1938; Stuart Chase, *Men and Machines*, New York, The Macmillan Co., 1929; M. C. Elmer, *Family Adjustment and Social Change*, New York, Ray Long and R. R. Smith, 1932, Chs. 4, 5, 9, 10; Dorothy Canfield Fisher, *Our Young Folks*, New York, Harcourt, Brace & Co., 1943; Carey McWilliams, *Factories in the Fields*, Boston, Little, Brown & Co., 1939; Carey McWilliams, *Ill Fares the Land*, Boston, Little, Brown & Co., 1942; Winona L. Morgan, *The Family Meets the Depression*, Minneapolis, University of Minnesota Press, 1939; National Industrial Conference Board, "Idle Men, Idle Machines, Idle Money," *Bull.*, February 9, 1939; L. R. Nierstaedt, *Economic Equilibrium, Employment and Natural Resources*, Bloomington, Ind., The Principia Press, 1942; James E. Pate, "Mobilizing Manpower," *Social Forces*, Vol. 22, December, 1943, pp. 154-162; Harvey W. Peck, "The New Economy and the Machine," *Social Forces*, Vol. 22, October, 1943, pp. 47-55; Ward Shepard, *Food or Famine: The Challenge of Erosion*, New York, The Macmillan Co., 1945; Mapheus Smith, "The Differential Impact of Selective Service Inductions on Occupations in the United States," *Am. Sociol. Rev.*, Vol. 11, No. 5, October, 1946, pp. 567-572; Goodwin Watson, *Youth After Conflict*, New York, Association Press, 1947; Melvin J. Williams, "A Socio-Economic Analysis of the Functions and Attitudes of Wartime Youth," *Social Forces*, Vol. 24, December, 1945, pp. 200-210. For additional references on the social effects of the changing ecology, see bibliographies to chapters in Parts II and III.

[33] R. E. Park and E. W. Burgess, *The City*, Chicago, University of Chicago Press, 1925, p. 57. For more extended treatment of this problem see Burgess' whole article, "The Growth of the City," *ibid.*, pp. 47-62; Niles Carpenter, *The Sociology of City Life*, New York, Longmans, Green & Co., 1931, Chs. 8-10; Mabel A. Elliott and Francis E. Merrill, *Social Disorganization*, New York, Harper & Bros., 1941, Ch. 29, Noel P. Gist and L. A. Halbert, *Urban Society*, New York, Thomas Y. Crowell Co., 1941, Chs. 2, 3, 10, 11, 14; Stuart A. Queen and Lewis F. Thomas, *The City*, New York, McGraw-Hill Book Co., Inc., 1939, Chs. 3, 21.

With the increase of facilities for transportation and communication, the resulting shifting of populations, and the provision of stimulating and diversified interests and activities in the modern city, the foundations of neighborhood solidarity have been greatly shaken and family and other primary-group bonds have been loosened.[34] The controlling influences of neighborhood sentiments and attitudes are dissipated by competition from the outside. The wish for response, once satisfied in the family and the neighborhood, now finds its chief satisfaction in relationships quite remote from these primary groups. When the individual members act against the unity of the group and its fundamental controls, group disorganization is going on. If not checked by the group as a whole, by the efforts of some of its members, or by outside agencies, disintegration will be complete.

The United States Census for 1940 showed over 12 per cent of the population as living in five cities of one million or more, while nearly 30 per cent were living in urban places of 100,000 or more. In accordance with the 1940 Census procedure, one hundred and forty metropolitan districts were outlined, each containing "at least one city of more than 50,000 population and . . . contiguous minor civil divisions with a density of population of 150 or more per square mile." [35] It is interesting to note that the last census revealed a marked tapering-off in the upward slope of urban growth. "For the first time in our history some of the largest cities in the United States failed to register an increase in numbers in a decennial period. In fact, 27 of the 93 cities in our nation that have a population of over 100,000 lost population from 1930 to 1940; and the increase in the total population of incorporated places of 2,500 or over in the last census period was only 7.9 per cent compared with an average gain of 31 per cent in the four decades from 1890 to 1930." [36]

Not only is the pattern of urban growth changing from the trend of the first three decades of the century, but a greater synthesis between city and country appears to be shaping up in the extension of suburbs and rurban fringes. It is obvious from the census data and from the many studies that have been made that the population of the United States is being redistributed as to place of residence at a rapid rate, that the old rural-urban dichotomy is no longer adequate,

---

[34] See: Marion W. Roper, *The City and the Primary Group*, Chicago, University of Chicago Libraries, 1935.

[35] Chauncy D. Harris, "Suburbs," *Am. J. Sociol.*, Vol. 49, No. 1, July, 1943 pp. 1-2. See also R. D. McKenzie, *The Metropolitan Community*, Recent Social Trends in the United States Monograph, New York, McGraw-Hill Book Co., Inc., 1933, in which data from the 1930 Census were used when 96 metropolitan districts were outlined.

[36] Homer Hoyt, "The Structure of American Cities in the Post-War Era," *Am. J. Sociol.*, Vol. 48, No. 4, January, 1943, p. 475. See also J. M. Gillette, "Some Population Shifts in the United States, 1930-1940," *Am. Sociol. Rev.*, Vol. 6, No. 5, October, 1941, pp. 619-628.

that the power of American cities to expand their industry and trade and to attract ever-increasing increments of population is apparently waning, and, until the war, the congestion of residential occupancy near the centers of cities was decreasing as populations tended to move out to the peripheries and to outside, adjacent, industrial and residential fringe-areas along or near the main trunk lines of transportation. While there is no evidence of a back-to-the-land movement in any considerable numbers there is a tendency for more people to combine rurban living and small-scale-farming activities with urban employment.

All this shifting of population, increase of mobility, and occupational redistribution in and around urban centers have made their effects felt in modes of living and on the processes of interaction among persons and groups. Angell's studies of the social integration of American cities, while hypothetical and highly tentative, seem to show that there may be a natural history of social integration, principally in terms of crime and welfare indexes, as a city grows, that there is no significant relation between city size and the incidence of crime, and that the degree of integration of cities is demonstrably correlated with mobility and racial composition of the population.[37] While some cities are losing population or barely holding that which they have, other cities show decided growth in numbers. (This rapid expansion of the growing cities has brought and continues to bring congestion, overcrowding, and housing shortages, excessive burdens upon municipal treasuries and upon supply facilities, and a host of exceedingly difficult problems of organization and administration, but it has brought also acute and challenging problems of institutional inadequacy and malfunctioning and of personal maladjustment.) On the other hand, partly despite certain pathological effects of immoderate city growth and partly because of them, the modern metropolitan community has become the chief testing ground for social, economic, and general cultural experimentation, the reservoir of scientific, educational, and aesthetic values, the "melting pot" of cosmopolitan population groups and culture elements, and the greatest challenge to large-scale, long-range social planning.

Ecological Position and Social Change.—Chapter 17 contained a rather extended discussion of the concept "ecological position" and showed how the "position," place, or niche of a person or group on a

[37] Robert C. Angell, "The Social Integration of Selected American Cities," *Am. J. Sociol.*, Vol. 47, No. 4, January, 1942, pp. 575-592; Robert C. Angell, "The Social Integration of American Cities of More Than 100,000 Population," *Am. Sociol. Rev.*, Vol. 12, No. 3, June, 1947, pp. 335-342.

vertical scale of functionally defined values serves as an important determinant of status. In that connection the different criteria by which position gets defined and the means by which it may be altered were indicated. In addition, the almost inevitable effects on social interaction and organization and, where the position and status of the individual are involved, on personal development and adjustment were discussed. Although there is a tendency for many types of position to become relatively fixed in a specific ecological order and to be regarded by tradition as largely immutable, nevertheless, in the more advanced and dynamic societies they have considerable flexibility. The positions of persons, groups, institutional patterns, other culture traits, and even whole communities and distinct areas within larger communities do change. Such alterations in position in the ecological frame of reference are almost certainly accompanied or followed by corresponding alterations in social values and attitudes and actions.

Since our earlier treatment of "position" in relation to status dealt nearly exclusively with the area of personal and group units in interaction, we will illustrate by the example of a city how a change in ecological position effects changes of a social nature. First, if we consider a city as a whole, we find that at a given time in its history it occupies a number of positions according to a corresponding number of evaluative criteria. If the particular criterion is size, we may discover that a city holding a position in the below-metropolitan class as ranked by the Census of 1930 may have "climbed" into the category of metropolitan area by the Census of 1940. Thus, its position in the rank-order of cities has changed within a decade while its site, location, and name have remained the same. Moreover, it may be hypothesized that during the same period of time and at least partly as a consequence of its increase in size, the city in question may have had its position, relative to other cities, considerably altered in terms of such statistical criteria as the number and capital worth of new industries and businesses, trade, bank clearings, construction, and newspaper circulation. Let us examine what has been happening within the city proper to some of its "natural areas." We find that changes have been occurring in the positions of residential, industrial, and business districts. Principally in response to the city's growth and expansion, the central business district has spread out to incorporate much of what were formerly nondescript slum and small-industry areas, thus pushing out these latter into the adjoining areas of rooming-houses, workingmen's homes, and, to a greater extent than before, to the outskirts of the expanding city.

In this process, some areas acquire positions on the scale that are higher than those previously occupied and others drop down the scale to lower levels, less valuable functionally and economically. A new preferred residential development may supplant a tenement district and a middle-class area of residence may become a boardinghouse and apartment house area. The opening of a new traffic artery or the building of a community shopping center will raise the position of near-by areas for certain purposes and lower it for other uses. It is not necessary to enlarge further on these matters of relative positions and their alterations. However, we should point out that while these changes have been taking place, and primarily because of them, the course of social interaction has changed, as between the city which is our example and other cities of the same class and of classes immediately higher and lower. Still other changes have occurred among the people of the city, as individuals and as status groups, and among the competing institutions and cultural complexes that constitute so large a part of the urban scene. Changes in structure, tempo, and functional interdependence require and stimulate new response tendencies and action patterns, attitudes and habits, sentiments and outlooks on the part of the persons and groups affected by the changes.

In conclusion, it should be kept in mind that ecological interaction and social interaction are divisions of a single on-going process, that ecological factors and social factors act and react upon each other, and that in some situations one set of factors will have precedence and will condition the interaction and in other situations the other set of factors will have priority and will serve as determiners of the interaction.

QUESTIONS

1. The Introduction to Part IV states that "activity and change are ever-present universal facts." Was it always so in man's thinking about his world?

2. What are some of the basic facts of knowledge established by the application of the scientific method to the study of physical and organic nature?

3. Why may it be said that social change is a fact? What are some evidences by way of confirmation?

4. What are indices of social change? What are the two general categories of such indices?

5. What is meant by saying that social interaction and social change are inseparable and coincident?

6. In what ways may ecological changes enter into social change?

7. Of what does the "primary search for balance and order" in the many areas of human experience consist?

8. Explain social change in terms of population growth, population mobility, and the composition and distribution of population.

9. What importance is assumed by population size?

10. What policies and practices have been applied to the regulation of the size of given populations? How does Meadows criticize the policies commonly employed?

11. How may ecological factors sometimes operate to affect indirectly the quality of population?

12. Compare permanence of residence and change of residence in their effects on social and personal growth and functioning.

13. How has man's enhanced mobility influenced culture?

14. How has the great mobility of the modern world contributed to social disorganization?

15. In what ways have institutions been changed in the course of adapting to the impacts attending ecological movement? Discuss specifically the effects on the family institution.

16. Define "migration" and give the conditions underlying migrations.

17. Why does "settlement" serve as an important criterion of true migration?

18. What is the significance of migration for social change?

19. How does the ecological distribution of such population elements as those of race and nationality, urban and rural, occupation, marital, sex and age, affect social interaction and social change?

20. Why is occupational distribution an element of particular importance in determining the course of social change?

21. Explain social change in terms of the expansion of cities.

22. In what ways does the pattern of urban growth appear to be shaping up in the United States and with what effects?

23. Discuss the bearing of ecological position on social change. Make an application to the city as a whole and to its subdivisions or internal natural areas.

BIBLIOGRAPHY

ANDERSON, NELS. *Men on the Move.* Chicago, University of Chicago Press, 1940.

CHASE, STUART. *Rich Land, Poor Land: A Study of Waste in the Natural Resources of America.* New York, McGraw-Hill Book Co., Inc., 1936.

COLLINS, HENRY HILL, JR. *America's Own Refugees: Our 4,000,000 Homeless Migrants.* Princeton, N. J., Princeton University Press, 1941.

COWGILL, DONALD O. *Mobile Homes: A Study in Trailer Life.* Washington, American Council on Public Affairs, 1941.

DANKERT, C. E. "Labor Immobility and Technological Unemployment." *Social Forces,* Vol. 19, March, 1941, pp. 426-434.

DAVIDSON, PERCY E., AND ANDERSON, H. DEWEY. *Occupational Mobility in an American Community.* Stanford University, California, Stanford University Press, 1937.

DAVIE, MAURICE. *Refugees in America: Report of the Committee for the Study of Recent Immigration from Europe.* New York, Harper & Bros., 1947.

DAWSON, CARL A. *Group Settlement: Ethnic Communities in Western Canada.* Vol. VII of *Canadian Frontiers of Settlement,* edited by W. A. Mackintosh and W. L. G. Joerg. Toronto, The Macmillan Co. of Canada, 1936.

DELL, B. N. *Population Resources and Trade.* Boston, Little, Brown & Co., 1938.

ELLIOTT, MABEL A., AND MERRILL, FRANCIS E. *Social Disorganization.* New York, Harper & Bros., 1941. Chs. 12, 13, 29.

FAIRCHILD, HENRY PRATT. *People, the Quantity and Quality of Population.* New York, Henry Holt & Co., 1939.

GIST, NOEL P., AND HALBERT, L. A. *Urban Society.* Rev. ed., New York, Thomas Y. Crowell Co., 1941, Parts I, III.

GLASS, D. V. *Population Policies and Movements in Europe.* Oxford, The Clarendon Press, 1940.

GLASS, D. V. *The Struggle for Population.* New York, Oxford University Press, 1936.

GLOVER, K. *America Begins Again: The Conquest of Waste in Our Natural Resources.* New York, McGraw-Hill Book Co., Inc., 1939.

GOODRICH, CARTER, et al. *Migration and Economic Opportunity: Report on the Study of Population Redistribution.* Philadelphia, University of Pennsylvania Press, 1936.

HANSEN, MARCUS LEE. *The Atlantic Migration, 1607-1860.* Cambridge, Harvard University Press, 1940.

HAUSER, PHILIP M. "Population and Vital Phenomena." *Am. J. Sociol.,* Vol. 48, No. 3, November, 1942, pp. 309-322.

HOBBS, ALBERT HOYT. *Differentials in Internal Migration.* Philadelphia, University of Pennsylvania Press, 1941.

HOBBS, ALBERT HOYT. "Specificity and Selective Migration." *Am. Sociol. Rev.,* Vol. 7, No. 6, December, 1942, pp. 772-781.

ISHII, RYOICHI. *Population Pressure and Economic Life in Japan.* Chicago, University of Chicago Press, 1937.

JAFFE, A. J. "Urbanization and Fertility." *Am. J. Sociol.,* Vol. 48, No. 1, July, 1942, pp. 48-60.

KIRK, DUDLEY. *Europe's Population in Interwar Years.* Princeton, N. J., Princeton University Press, 1947.

KIRK, DUDLEY. "Population Changes and the Postwar World." *Am. Sociol. Rev.,* Vol. 9, No. 1, February, 1944, pp. 28-35.

KIRKPATRICK, CLIFFORD. *Nazi Germany: Its Women and Family Life.* Indianapolis, Bobbs-Merrill Co., 1938.

KLINEBERG, OTTO. "The Intelligence of Migrants." *Am. Sociol. Rev.,* Vol. 3, No. 2, April, 1938, pp. 218-224.

KULISCHER, EUGENE M. *The Displacement of Population.* Montreal, International Labour Office, 1943.

KULISCHER, EUGENE M. *Europe on the Move: War and Population Changes, 1917-1947.* New York, Columbia University Press, 1948.

LANDIS, PAUL H. "Internal Migration by Subsidy." *Social Forces,* Vol. 22, December, 1943, pp. 183-187.

LANDIS, PAUL H. *Population Problems.* New York, American Book Co., 1943, Part V, "Problems of Migration."

LANDIS, PAUL H. "Rural-Urban Migration and the Marriage Rate—An Hypothesis." *Am. Sociol. Rev.,* Vol. 11, No. 2, April, 1946, pp. 155-158.

LAPIERE, RICHARD T. *Sociology.* New York, McGraw-Hill Book Co., Inc., pp. 168-175, 212-271.

LAPIERE, RICHARD T., AND CHENG WANG. "The Incidence of Sequence in Social Change." *Am. J. Sociol.,* Vol. 37, No. 3, November, 1931, pp. 399-409.

LASKER, BRUNO. *Asia on the Move.* New York, Henry Holt & Co., 1945.

LOCKE, HARVEY J. "Mobility and Family Disorganization." *Am. Sociol. Rev.,* Vol. 5, No. 4, August, 1940, pp. 489-494.

LORIMER, FRANK, AND OSBORN, FREDERICK. *Dynamics of Population.* New York, The Macmillan Co., 1934.

LORIMER, FRANK, WINSTON, ELLEN, AND KISER, LOUISE K. *Foundations of American Population Policy.* New York, Harper & Bros., 1940.

McENTYRE, DAVID, et al. *The Migrants: Migration to the Pacific Northwest.* Washington, D. C., Government Printing Office, 1941.

McWILLIAMS, CAREY. *Factories in the Fields.* Boston, Little, Brown & Co., 1939.

MENEFEE, SELDON C. *Mexican Migratory Workers of South Texas.* Washington, D. C., Government Printing Office, 1941.

MILBANK MEMORIAL FUND. *Postwar Problems of Migration.* New York, Milbank Memorial Fund, 1947.

MINEHAN, THOMAS. *Boy and Girl Tramps of America.* New York, Farrar & Rinehart, 1934.

MUKERJEE, RADHAKAMAL. "Mobility, Ecological and Social." *Social Forces,* Vol. 21, December, 1942, pp. 154-159.

MUKERJEE, RADHAKAMAL. "Population Theory and Politics." *Am. Sociol. Rev.,* Vol. 6, No. 6, December, 1941, pp. 784-793.

MUKERJEE, RADHAKAMAL. *Social Ecology.* London and New York, Longmans, Green & Co., n.d., especially Ch. 5, "The Dynamics of Human Aggregation and Circulation"; Ch. 6, "The Ecological Balance of Population"; Ch. 11, "Freedom of Social Mobility."

MYRDAL, ALVA. *Nation and Family.* New York, Harper & Bros., 1942.

MYRDAL, GUNNAR. *Population: A Problem for Democracy.* Cambridge, Harvard University Press, 1940.

NATIONAL COMMITTEE ON IMMIGRATION POLICY. *Immigration and Population Policy.* New York, National Committee on Immigration Policy, 1947.

NATIONAL COMMITTEE ON IMMIGRATION POLICY. *International Migration and One World.* New York, National Committee on Immigration Policy, 1948.

NATIONAL RESOURCES COMMITTEE. *Our Cities: Their Role in the National Economy.* Washington, Government Printing Office, 1937.

NATIONAL RESOURCES COMMITTEE. *Our Energy Resources.* Washington, Government Printing Office, 1939.

NATIONAL RESOURCES COMMITTEE. *The Problems of a Changing Population.* Washington, Government Printing Office, 1938.

OSBORN, FREDERICK. *Preface to Eugenics.* New York, Harper & Bros., 1940.

QUEEN, STUART A., AND THOMAS, L. F. *The City: A Study of Urbanism in the United States.* New York, McGraw-Hill Book Co., Inc., 1939, Chs. 3, 5, 18.

ROTERUS, VICTOR. "Effects of Population Growth and Non-Growth on the Well-Being of Cities." *Am. Sociol. Rev.,* Vol. 11, No. 1, February, 1946, pp. 90-97.

ROUSH, G. A. *Strategic Minerals and World Politics.* New York, McGraw-Hill Book Co., Inc., 1939.

RYAN, PHIL. *Rural Migration and Social Welfare.* New York, Russell Sage Foundation, 1940.

SCHMID, CALVIN F. *Social Trends in Seattle.* Seattle, University of Washington Press, 1944.

SHRYOCK, HENRY S., JR., AND ELDRIDGE, HOPE T. "Internal Migration in Peace and War." *Am. Sociol. Rev.,* Vol. 12, No. 1, February, 1947, pp. 27-39.

SMITH, T. LYNN. *Population Analysis.* New York, McGraw-Hill Book Co., Inc., 1948, Part III, "The Vital Processes"; Part IV, "Migration"; Part V, "The Growth of Population."

Social Forces, Vol. 12, October, 1933, all articles.

SOROKIN, PITIRIM A., AND ZIMMERMAN, CARLE C. *Principles of Rural-Urban Sociology.* New York, Henry Holt & Co., 1929, Chs. 23-26.

SPENGLER, JOSEPH J. *France Faces Depopulation.* Durham, N. C., Duke University Press, 1938.

SPENGLER, JOSEPH J. *French Predecessors of Malthus: A Study of 18th Century Wage and Population Theory.* Durham, N. C., Duke University Press, 1942.

TAFT, DONALD. *Human Migration: A Study of International Movements.* New York, The Ronald Press Co., 1936.

THOMPSON, WARREN S. *Plenty of People.* New York, The Ronald Press Co., 1948.

THOMPSON, WARREN S. *Population and Peace in the Pacific.* Chicago, University of Chicago Press, 1946.

THOMPSON, WARREN S. *Population Problems.* Rev. ed., New York, McGraw-Hill Book Co., Inc., 1942, Chs. 17-26.

THOMPSON, WARREN S. *Population Trends in the United States.* New York, McGraw-Hill Book Co., Inc., 1933.

VANCE, RUPERT B. *All These People: The Nation's Human Resources in the South.* Chapel Hill, University of North Carolina Press, 1945.

VANCE, RUPERT B. "Security and Adjustment: The Return to the Larger Community." *Social Forces,* Vol. 22, May, 1944, pp. 363-370.

VOGT, WILLIAM. *Road to Survival.* New York, William Sloane Associates, 1948.

YOUNG, KIMBALL. "Population and Power: Some Comments on Demographic Changes in Europe." *Social Forces,* Vol. 25, October, 1946, pp. 1-9.

ZIMMERMANN, ERICH. *World Resources and Industries.* New York, Harper & Bros., 1933.

Chapter 22

CULTURAL DYNAMICS OF SOCIAL CHANGE

Cultural Factors in Social Change

Social change is not only dependent upon ecological and demographical frames of reference, which serve to delimit its extent, range, and rate, and in some measure to define its nature, but it is determined also by the kind of culture traits and systems within which the elements and processes of social interaction operate. It is in culture that are found the forms of social organization, the tested and approved mechanisms of control, and the sanctioned values and norms of personal and group behavior. It is through culturally evolved and perpetuated channels of communication; techniques of production and distribution; arts and practices of creative endeavor and modes of consumption; ideas, ideologies, and attitudes of economic and political orders, religious and educational systems; familial structures; and through intra- and inter-group relation patterns, that social life is carried on with a degree of efficiency, regularity, and continuity. These factors give social organization not only an aspect of permanency, but also furnish it with the dynamics for its own rejuvenation and reorganization.

Cultural anthropologists have told us many things about the changes that have occurred in culture. Some have viewed the subject as an evolution and accumulation of culture traits; others have treated the matter in terms of a perspective of values.[1] Recently, some anthropologists have joined the sociologists in trying to analyze the cultural complexes of a technological society, rather than confine their examinations to primitive societies. This conjunction of the two disciplines has already contributed much of value to our knowledge of comparative cultures, and has pointed up also some promising research tasks.[2]

---

[1] W. D. Wallis, *Culture and Progress*, New York, McGraw-Hill Book Co., Inc., 1930, p. 210.

[2] Among anthropologists who have approached the study of cultures from a sociological point of view and with methods partly derived from sociology, particularly from the work

In the second chapter of this book the student was introduced to the concept of culture, to certain facts concerning its origin, its great diversity, its function in group and personal life, and to one of its primary characteristics, namely, persistence. So long as a culture has vitality, it grows and changes, sometimes slowly, as in small and relatively isolated groups, like the Kwakiutl and the Zuñi, and sometimes rapidly, as in modern machine civilization. Cultural change is social change, since all culture is social in its origin, meaning, and usage. But social change is broader in its nature and does not always enter into and integrate with the other elements of culture so as to endure. However, it seems invariably to be true that whatever social change occurs, even of the most ephemeral type, it must be in relation to the environing culture complex. Thus, culture tends to give direction and momentum to social change, and to set limits beyond which social change may not go. For example, recurrent fads represent social change of a sort, but they seldom affect in any lasting way the culture that makes allowance for them.

The fact of cultural differences among groups was clearly emphasized in the presentation in Chapter 3 of Kwakiutl and Zuñi cultures, cultures radically different from our own. In these differences are to be found the cultural factors conditioning differential social change. Not only do these differences among culture complexes affect the course and rate of social change, but within given culture systems there are also differentials in the status structure that determine how, when, and why individuals may and shall interact with others, participate in the culture, realize their expectations, and change from one role to another. Age, sex, and economic factors are common status-determining forces in most cultures, but we have seen how little importance was attached to economic status among the Zuñi, for example, and how very important it was with the Kwakiutl. The importance of economic status in our culture is very apparent.

Culture is both a divisive and an integrating factor in human life and association. "It makes for easy understanding and mutual appreciation among those who share the same heritage; it makes understanding difficult and appreciation rare among peoples of diverse heritages. A common language is necessary to communication. But even with a common language, the degree of understanding is limited except when there is a common background of belief, interest, and sentiment, a background that comes from participation in a common

---

of E. Durkheim, mention may be made of B. Malinowski and A. R. Radcliffe-Brown in Great Britain, and Ruth Benedict, E. D. Chapple, C. S. Coon, John Gillin, C. Kluckhohn, Margaret Mead, H. Miner, R. Redfield, and W. L. Warner in the United States.

life." [3]   However, even with a common language and other traits of a common cultural heritage, the sub-cultural status groups within a society find many grounds for division and misunderstanding, which contribute to disorganization, individualization, and secularization.

A few years ago, Robert Redfield, a cultural anthropologist, undertook to test the hypothesis that there is a causal relationship between physical isolation and homogeneity of culture, on the one hand, and disorganization, individualization, and secularization on the other. He chose for his investigation four communities in the Yucatan peninsula of Mexico.[4]   As Redfield says, "The problem is seen as one of the relation among variables. No one of these is the sole cause of the others, but it is assumed, subject to proof, that, as certain of these vary, so do others." [5]

The isolation and homogeneity of the communities were taken together by Redfield as the independent variable, since it was assumed that a close correlation existed between the two so as to make them one, for practical purposes. The dependent variables chosen were disorganization, individualization, and secularization of culture. The study showed, at least tentatively, that the dependent variables were present to the highest degree in the community characterized by the lowest degree of isolation and homogeneity. Where a community displayed the highest degree of isolation and homogeneity, the reverse effect was found in the dependent variables, whereas the other communities showed intermediate characteristics to the extent that the independent variables were or were not present.

Recently, Neal Gross put the same hypothesis to the test in four contemporary rural communities in the United States that had previously been studied and reported on.[6]   The problem was the same as Redfield's, namely, the relationships between variables in culture. The latter study, however, applied a different set of variables: cultural isolation, system of interaction, and familial, religious, and educational systems. Both studies assumed that the communities selected represented points along a continuum of cultural contrasts. In the Red-

[3] E. B. Reuter, in A. M. Lee (Ed.), *New Outline of the Principles of Sociology,* New York, Barnes & Noble, Inc., 1946, p. 141.

[4] Robert Redfield, *The Folk Culture of Yucatan,* Chicago, University of Chicago Press, 1941.

[5] *Ibid.,* p. 34.

[6] Neal Gross, "Cultural Variables in Rural Communities," *Am. J. Sociol.,* Vol. 53, No. 5, March, 1948, pp. 344-350. The community studies used by Gross were four of the rural life studies prepared under the supervision of Carl C. Taylor and published by the Bureau of Agriculture under the general title *Culture of a Contemporary Rural Community:* No. 1, *El Cerrito, New Mexico,* by Olen Leonard and C. P. Loomis (1941); No. 2, *Sublette, Kansas,* by E. H. Bell (1942); No. 4, *Irwin, Iowa,* by E. O. Moe and C. C. Taylor (1942); and No. 5, *The Old-Order Amish of Lancaster County, Pennsylvania,* by W. M. Kollmorgen (1942).

field study the "highest" and "lowest" degrees of the independent isolation-homogeneity variable represented the poles of the continuum, with the dependent variables ranged along the continuum in relation to them, whereas in the Gross study the only independent variable was "cultural isolation," with contrasting degrees of "high" and "low." In summarizing his conclusions, Gross says in part:

> In terms of developing a more systematic body of knowledge about human interaction and social environments, it is necessary to view the findings of this research in relationship to the conclusions of Redfield's investigation. Redfield found that: "The changes in culture that in Yucatan appear to 'go along with' lessening isolation and homogeneity are seen to be chiefly three: disorganization of the culture, secularization, and individualization." The conclusions of this study tend to support these conclusions.[7]

From the foregoing it appears that research—although admittedly somewhat inconclusive—seems to indicate that social change is dependent, to some extent at least, upon such factors as differences in degree of cultural isolation and cultural homogeneity. This appears to bear out what sociologists and cultural anthropologists have long observed.

A comparison of the manifold cultures of the world reveals many interesting and sharp contrasts. At one extreme stand the cultures of what have come to be termed "folk societies"; at the other extreme are the cultures characteristic of modern urban society.[8] In between are societies having cultures and sub-cultures presenting a great variety of combinations and permutations of culture traits, with each culture approaching one of the ideal types more than it does the other. Although all societies have some traits in common, each differs from others in specific respects. It is in terms of these dissimilarities that we may expect to find the principal contributing factors to the differentials in social change.

Therefore, it seems reasonably safe to draw the general conclusion that the nature of social change will be different and its rate will be slowest in those societies that most nearly approach the ideal-type

[7] Gross, "Cultural Variables in Rural Communities," op. cit., pp. 349-350.

[8] See: Howard Becker, "Ionia and Athens," Ph.D. dissertation, University of Chicago, 1930; E. Durkheim on the Division of Labor, a translation by George Simpson of De la division du travail social, New York, The Macmillan Co., 1933; H. W. Odum, Understanding Society: The Principles of Dynamic Sociology, New York, The Macmillan Co., 1947, Ch. 14, "Folk Culture and Folk Society"; A. R. Radcliffe-Brown, The Andaman Islanders, Cambridge (Eng.) University Press, 1933; Redfield, "The Folk Society," Am. J. Sociol., Vol. 52, No. 4, January, 1947, pp. 293-308; E. Sapir, "Culture, Genuine and Spurious," Am. J. Sociol., Vol. 29, No. 4, January, 1924, pp. 401-429; F. Tönnies, Gemeinschaft und Gesellschaft (1887), translated and edited by C. P. Loomis as Fundamental Concepts of Sociology, New York, American Book Co., 1940; M. Tumin, "Culture, Genuine and Spurious; A Re-evaluation," Am. Sociol. Rev., Vol. 10, No. 2, April, 1945, pp. 199-207.

folk society, characterized as small, isolated, nonliterate, and homogeneous, and with a strong feeling of group solidarity, as compared
with societies that are most cosmopolitan, heterogeneous, literate,
and technologically advanced. Social change in intermediate types of
society will be marked by variations from the two extremes.

CULTURAL DETERMINERS OF SOCIAL CHANGE

Our purpose in that which follows is to show how certain aspects
of culture affect the process of social interaction so as to obstruct or
to hamper it, or to foster changes in the process itself and in its products. Our thesis is that the amount and quality, the direction and the
rate, of social change are determined, in the absence of catastrophe or
other major historic accident, by the character of the existing culture
complex. This generalization holds equally for the Andaman Islands,
the Belgian Congo, and Yucatan, as it does for Western Europe, the
United States, and Canada.

Cultural Inertia.—In the description of the Kwakiutl and the Zuñi
in the third chapter, there were presented what may be termed relatively inert culture complexes. Such culture groups, living for many
generations in comparative isolation, felt no need of change, were
little influenced by impact with other cultures, and did not possess
within the inner processes and mechanisms of their own cultures the
necessary cultural base to serve as a starting point for social change.
As a consequence of such conditions, the cultures of folk who live
remote from the stream of change, being all-sufficient for their felt
needs, display characteristic features of conformity to that which is
old, sacred, familiar, and hence satisfactory.

However, inertia is not invariably correlated with isolation or with
the absence of contacts between cultures. There are numerous cases
of nomadic peoples wandering over extensive territories and no doubt
meeting other peoples, whose cultures show the same tendencies to
persist unchanged as do those of many settled peoples.

It is possible to conceive of the members of such a society as moving
about physically without communicating with members of other groups than
their own. Each of the Indian villages of the midwest highlands of Guatemala is a folk society distinguishable by its customs and even by the physical
type of its members from neighboring villages, yet the people are great
travelers, and in the case of one of the most distinct communities, Chichi-
castenango, most of the men travel far and spend much of their time away
from home. This does not result, however, in much intimate communication

between those traveling villagers and other peoples. The gipsies have moved about among the various peoples of the earth for generations, and yet they retain many of the characteristics of a folk society.[9]

Moreover, there are many examples of two or more cultures functioning side by side with little or no acculturation. This situation is usually due to the fact that the practitioners of the different cultures belong to distinct social entities. As an example of the parallel existence of divergent cultures in contact and intercommunication, but with a minimum of cross-fertilization, John Gillin discusses the case of a town in eastern Guatemala.

. . . the parallel cultures have existed cheek by jowl for several hundred years, and daily primary contact between the respective practitioners is the general rule. . . . These two groups (Indians and Ladinos) are described in conversation and in local official documents as *razas* (races) or *castas* (castes). "Passing" from the Indian to the Ladino group is practically impossible within the community, . . . Each of these two groups has its own culture or set of customs. Although there are certain patterns common to the two cultures—there is some overlapping—the two configurations of custom are clearly distinguishable . . . the Indian and Ladino cultures differ in "content." The differences between the two cultures are even more strikingly brought out if one considers the two respective configurations as wholes. The Indian culture displays a seemingly higher degree of integration within itself than does the Ladino culture. In an excellent article Tumin has characterized the former as "sacred" and the latter as "secular," on the grounds that the content of the Indian culture in contrast to the Ladino is knit together, as it were, by a more or less pervading set of magical and religious beliefs which lend an air of divine sanction to many, if not all, Indian cultural activities. Another way of putting this is to state that the Indian culture shows a higher degree of consistency of all types. . . . [Of the cultural behavior of the Indian group, the auther says:] First, as regards presentation of new items, it would appear superficially that this had been adequate in all respects, considering the close contacts between the members of the two groups. However, presentation of the European aspects of Ladino culture is not complete in at least one important respect. . . . Indian children receive only one or two years of schooling, and . . . Indian adults are either illiterate or use written symbols with difficulty. All Ladinos, on the other hand, are "basically literate" at the least; that is, they read and write without difficulty; . . . Nationality means nothing to the Indians; modern styles are unknown except as infrequently exhibited by local Ladino women; the hierarchical organization of the Church and the approved interpretation of its dogmas are beyond their ken for lack of the symbolic customs and apparatus through

---

[9] Robert Redfield, "The Folk Society," *Am. J. Sociol.*, Vol. 52, No. 4, January, 1947, p. 296.

which they might be presented; written contracts and commercial dealings based on documentary credit instruments cannot find a fully functioning place in the Indian configuration. . . . It is obvious that, to consider no other instances, the stimulus-presentation of Ladino culture has not been by any means complete as regards the Indian group in Jilotepeque and that the Indians have been to a degree isolated from Ladino culture, despite their close contacts with Ladinos.[10]

When inertia to change is not directly attributable to isolation or the absence of intercommunication, one may infer that it is due to the presence of some other independent cultural variable such as homogeneity. Three characteristics of folk-society homogeneity account for this condition: (1) The traits that make up the cultural whole are so inextricably bound together as to form a rigid and impermeable configuration, so that should change be suggested, it would be rejected as a threat to the whole complex. (2) The cultural configuration constitutes the principal basis of the group's unity and security. The group's very life depends upon it, so it is believed. The individual has no identity apart from the single group, the society, and should he desire change, which is almost unthinkable, or should he seek to initiate change, he would be subject to penalty. (3) However, in spite of homogeneity, changes do gradually occur, but because of homogeneity they are initiated and adopted as a corporate matter. Within the society as a whole and by it, innovation may be and has been permitted, but not otherwise.

Even in the most cosmopolitan and rapidly changing societies, inertia is not entirely absent. Instead of characterizing the society as a whole, as in the typical folk society, the inertia stems from attitudes held by individuals and small subcultural groups. It is atypical more than typical of a society whose culture is fragmental, complex, and secular, whose culture themes are numerous and uncircumscribed, and where wide variations in expressing the themes are allowed.[11] Here the factors making for inertia seem to be segregated from the culture as a whole and exist as residual categories, affecting the course of change more by resistance or in the nature of "lag" than by outright obstruction.

Cultural Lag.—Where cultural change occurs it does so unevenly. Some elements of culture have a tendency to change more rapidly than others. For example, material objects of culture, such as machines

---

[10] John Gillin, "Parallel Cultures and the Inhibitions to Acculturation in a Guatemalan Community," *Social Forces*, Vol. 24, October, 1945, pp. 1-14.
[11] M. E. Opler, "Themes as Dynamic Forces in Culture," *Am. J. Sociol.*, Vol. 51, No. 3, November, 1945, pp. 198-206.

and mechanical gadgets, are introduced and accepted more readily than are the social practices which the machines seem to call for. During the last century and a half, Western Europe and America have experienced a revolution in their industrial system from small work-shops to large establishments with power-driven machinery and sometimes immense concentrations of workers. But this development was not accompanied by an equally quick provision of facilities and laws for the housing of the workers, their safety and health, compen-sation for injuries sustained, and recompense during periods of forced unemployment. Here was a cultural lag. Through the years, these responses of the legal system and the social conscience have gradually caught up fairly well with the more rapidly changing technology.

We have retained in practically all of our institutions certain cul-ture traits such as creeds, formulae, and rituals which have lost much, if not all, of the meaning and significance which they had in the past. One part of our culture which is most resistant to social change seems to be religious creeds. Others include certain legal forms and legal-istic decisions, cant and routine in education, stereotyped methods in business, industry, and philanthropy, and the pattern of family organi-zation, which, though changing rather rapidly in recent years and particularly in the urban environment, still retains features of the older patriarchal system.

We may invent or borrow a new culture trait but fail to fit it into our social organization. We had automobiles long before we devel-oped traffic regulations. We now have the atomic fission principle for generating energy on a scale heretofore unknown, but we are still uncertain as to how it will affect our social order. We allowed our cities to grow "like Topsy" and failed to deal adequately with the attendant effects of slum conditions, increasing difficulties in trans-portation of commodities and people, lack of attention to the recre-ational needs of the population, and similar evidences of neglect and absence of foresight and planning. In recent years, cities have awak-ened to some of the consequences of indifference and have undertaken to introduce costly remedies. But many of our cities present grave problems of maladministration, inefficiency, and negligence. There are many other examples of the failure to adjust the many phases of the cultural heritage to each other and to new social situations. This phenomenon is known as "cultural lag." [12]

At a time when the last World War is still a nightmarish memory,

---

[12] W. F. Ogburn, *Social Change*, New York, B. W. Huebsch, 1922, especially Part IV.

and when many persons see in the present course of events certain movement toward another war, it may be well to consider briefly the place of war in modern civilization. Is war an anachronism, something incongruous? Is it a case of culture lag?

Modern technology, though not responsible for war, has made warfare more efficient and terrible than ever before. Whatever the motives making for war—whether economic, political, or other—it is evident that warfare as we know it today and as it is projected for the future, can only be waged where the arts of production and distribution have been developed to a point where they make possible large-scale mobilizations of peoples and resources, vast fleets of ships and planes, highly mobile armies, mass communication mechanisms, unprecedented concentrations of authority, and imperious exercise of controls for the regimentation of civilian populations. These are essential concomitants of modern warfare and they represent the extremities of cultural adjustment to what are regarded as crises in international relations. War serves as a means to cultural productivity when it stimulates new discoveries, inventions, and the creation of new institutions. Temporary or lasting advances in techniques, social organization, sacrificial and loyalty attitudes, and institutional adaptations are offset, however, by the most grievous losses in lives and property destroyed, disastrous economic and political dislocations, harmful stresses and strains on community and family life, and the quite general release of cruel and barbarous impulses. "What we have learned about the effects of war, while it has made peace more desirable, has not made war any less inevitable." [13] A recognition of the problem is only the first step toward its solution. While millions of the world's population long for enduring peace, other millions are conditioned to believe that the art of warfare is a most worthy avocation, if not a truly noble vocation. Although many people think that war is an outmoded, inefficient cultural mechanism for achieving the results its advocates claim for it, it seems equally clear that the way to lasting peace is obstructed by aggressive nationalism, greedy imperialism, selfish ethnocentrism, and the cult of war. These associated attitude complexes, until they are changed, constitute a formidable assortment of lagging cultural elements.

Cultural Formalism.—An extreme phase of "lag" in culture is known as formalism. One evidence of this phenomenon is the continuance, sometimes apparently in full force, of institutions, folkways,

---

13 R. E. Park, "The Social Functions of War," *Am. J. Sociol.*, Vol. 46, No. 4, January, 1941, p. 551.

and mores long after men have ceased to have faith in their social value. Not infrequently, the vital force of the institution may depart from it and perhaps enter into some other cultural element which is better suited to give it expression, but the shell of the outworn institution may remain indefinitely and retain its status, seemingly unaffected by the change. The same function may pass successively from one institution to another. Industry, for example, has passed from a family economy to a guild economy and then to that of capitalistic enterprise. Governmental, educational, to some extent religious, mutual aid, and other functions have been passed along from one type of institutional repository to another. But after the changes, most of which were effected gradually, there have remained many obsolete survivals loath to give place to the new order and often blocking or hindering change.[14]

Such transvaluation of functions does not necessarily mean that the functions are becoming formalized to the point of "ossification," to use an analogue of E. A. Ross.[15] It becomes so when the transfer of function is effected without changing its obvious form or content, and without integration with the other elements of the containing culture. The grip of "the dead hand" and the hard "cake of custom" are signs of a formalism that, if not resisted, may lead to decay.

Of the many examples that might be given, one will suffice. It is well known that the common law is primarily a system of precedents; yet few laymen realize the extent to which that system has buried itself in a mass of printed pages that obscures thought, stifles initiative, and stultifies its practitioners. As one writer says:

It is necessary to realize that the Law not only stands still but is proud and determined to stand still. If a British barrister of two hundred years ago were suddenly to come alive in an American courtroom, he would feel intellectually at home. The clothes would astonish him, the electric lights would astonish him, the architecture would astonish him. But as soon as the lawyers started talking legal talk, he would know that he was among friends. And given a couple of days with law books, he could take the place of any lawyer present—or of the judge—and perform the whole legal mumbo-jumbo as well as they. Imagine by contrast a British surgeon of two hundred years ago plopped into a modern hospital operating room. He would literally understand less of what was going on than would any passer-by brought in from the street at random.[16]

---

14 See: C. H. Cooley, *Social Organization*, New York, Charles Scribner's Sons, 1920, p. 342.
15 E. A. Ross, *Principles of Sociology*, New York, The Century Co., 1930, p. 451.
16 Fred Rodell, *Woe Unto You, Lawyers*, New York, Reynal & Hitchcock, Inc., 1940, pp. 36-37.

While an extremely unresponsive social order is seemingly the opposite of disorganization, it is, in fact, closely identified with it. "One is mechanism supreme, the other mechanism going to pieces; and both are in contrast to that harmony between human nature and its instruments which is desirable." [17] When in a changing social order the elements of conservatism and traditionalism are excessive, they lead to social stagnation. Such a condition provides the incentive for much conflict between the adherents of one phase of culture and the supporters of another; the laggards and reactionaries oppose the progressives. It furnishes excuses for failure and grounds for obstruction in facing new problems. Excessive and long-continued cultural lag, or formalism, has cultural torpidity as its outcome. [18]

Present Breakdown in Culture and Social Organization.—Many of the factors just analyzed are illustrated in the present post-war situation. As we have noted elsewhere, war inevitably and invariably leaves in its train a kind of socio-cultural vacuum into which pour in chaotic fashion a miscellaneous assortment of residual products to form a veritable witch's brew of misunderstanding, chauvinism, persecution, revenge, insecurity, and turmoil. Wartime controls, artificially and hastily contrived and arbitrarily employed, are either too suddenly relaxed under pressure of political expediency or too long continued in defiance of altered circumstance, to the end that there is "confusion worse confounded." The victors tend to fall out among themselves and, if not too exhausted from their war-making efforts, treat the world as a grab bag full of spoils to be haggled over and divided on a first-come-first-served basis.

The internal affairs of national states suffer from lack of consonance between the backlog of demand for full employment, housing requirements, liquidation of indebtedness, consumers' goods of all kinds, and community welfare needs, on the one hand, and ability or willingness on the part of the groups in power to tackle the problems with vision and firmness, on the other hand. Special interests seek and find preference; minority groups (racial, ethnic, religious, and political) are subjected to added persecution. Class struggles assume greater intensity and larger proportions, while sectionalism, political intrigue, and intra-community factionalism contribute to the weakening of the social order. Absence of anything like comprehensive plans for national recovery and world unity make the situation seem nearly hopeless. The infant United Nations is sabotaged from the

---

17 Cooley, *Social Organization*, p. 347.
18 See: Ross, *Principles of Sociology*, Chs. 45-46.

beginning by at least one great power and its feeble efforts are met with increasing pessimism.

Not only are there evidences of cultural lag and deterioration on every hand, but formalism in the shape of *laissez-faire* policies and doctrines of "states' rights," "constitutional powers," "national sovereignty," and "the American way of life" are able to postpone any action drastic enough to cope with the disorganized state of the world and lead to recovery and good will among nations. What the full effects in the way of cultural deterioration, social disorganization, and personal demoralization will be remain to be seen.

Cultural Revival.—This would, indeed, be a gloomy picture of a civilization if it were viewed solely from the standpoint of its lagging, formalized, and decadent elements. While it is true that many culture systems, or sub-cultures within systems, have lacked the vital and energizing forces necessary to their survival, especially when they have been confronted by more virile and dynamic cultures, there are within most cultures some qualities which, if stimulated, may experience a new lease on life. The resisting and conserving qualities may serve for the purpose of survival, but they are impedimenta when social flexibility is required.

A relatively static culture will be identified usually with a relatively stable and, to its members, satisfactory social order so long as the two remain in comparative isolation. But let them come into contact with different cultures and they will be usually stimulated thereby, even though they may be subordinated to strange groups. The interaction involved produces restlessness and discontent; old values get redefined and new values emerge. The many empirical studies of acculturation seem to bear out this statement.[19]

It not infrequently happens under these changed conditions that the old ways, the common speech, the familiar rituals which have long been taken for granted and possibly neglected and allowed to deteriorate, come to have new meaning for the group and take on a more sacred character. In contrast to the new and unfamiliar, the customary behavior patterns and the traditional beliefs come once more to be highly esteemed and cherished. Satisfaction and comfort are found again in the indigenous culture. This fresh interest and enjoyment may be largely the effect of contrast; they may depend upon the vivid sense of contrast between the present and the past, between the culture that is outside the group and that which is inside.

---

[19] See references to the subject in the bibliography at the end of this chapter.

At any rate, the net effect is for the cultural decline to be halted and even to be set in the reverse direction.

Culture reflects the historical experiences of a people. The designated medium for such culture is language. National culture and character are to be discovered in the native folk speech and folk literature. If, for any reason, the national culture pattern is long suppressed, the folk speech and folk literature tend to be forgotten and may even be despised. However, one of the first evidences of a reviving national consciousness is the rediscovery of the native culture traits, including language and literature. Consequently, linguistic and literary revivals tend to mark the early struggles of national rebirth. It appears somewhat strange, if not paradoxical, that despite the rapid development of modern communication, the expansion of trade, and the mingling of peoples, so many nationalistic movements for independence or cultural revival should have happened the world over during the last half century. In that time, the following nationality groups in Europe and elsewhere have had or still have national revivals: the Irish, the Welsh, the Scots, the Icelanders, the Norwegians, the Flemish Belgians, the Finns, the Baltic peoples, the Poles, the Bohemians (the Czechs), the Hungarians, the Rumanians, the Albanians, the Greeks, the Vlachs in Macedonia, the Armenians, the Egyptians, the Afrikander-Dutch in South Africa, and the Catalonians in Spain, to say nothing of the long-drawn struggle in India recently crowned with success.

Parallel and incident to the cultural revival are changes in social organization. New leaders appear, organizations for the furtherance of the revival are inaugurated, ideals and purposes are reformulated in terms of the revived cultural elements, social attitudes conforming to the renewed cultural values are made manifest in new lines of action, and the self-consciousness of the group is invigorated and strengthened. Old and new culture mechanisms are employed for the furtherance of the cause. Sharing in such work in modern society are its schools, churches, press, radio, and motion pictures. Thus a decadent culture may either be revived or may disappear.

Cultural Reorganization.—A culture trait may change its form or content without obvious change of function and *vice versa*. When viewed from different vantage points or from different periods of time, the family institution displays both changes of form and of function. From a certain point of view the family is a family in the functional sense whether it is large or small, patricentric or matricentric, founded on monogamy or polygamy, and so on, whereas the modern American family, characteristically small and monogamous, and appearing, when looked at superficially, to be very little different from the family of colonial times, does reveal change in its functions. Certain functions which the family discharges in varying degree in every culture are still present, but a number of them have been practically dropped, transferred to other social agencies, or modified to suit changed social and economic conditions. The factory, the bakery, the delicatessen, the school, the nursery, the church, the motion picture theater, and a large number of other institutionalized instruments have relieved the modern family, particularly the city-dwelling family, of many of its earlier functions. These transfers of function have required the family to redefine its remaining functions, to reorganize its structure to some extent, and to reconsider its inner resources of affection, sentiment-attitude, habit, etc., in the light of its altered socio-economic position in an ever-changing technological and largely urbanized social world.

The agencies of organized religion have likewise found themselves, in recent years, under the necessity of reorganizing and reorienting their programs, if not their doctrines, to modern secular trends. Urban churches in particular have taken over various secular functions once left to other agencies. Educational programs, motion pictures, dancing, recreational and athletic features, dramatics, and clubs for young people have come to constitute regular parts of the reorganized program of many city churches.[20] Some churches, in order to survive, "so change their activities that they cease to be churches." Some survive by specializing in primitive emotional religion (revival).[21] "On the other hand, non-religious organizations such as the Rotary Club develop ideals of service and fellowship, and often arouse the same 'spiritual' emotions which it was once the peculiar role of the church to stimulate." [22]

Similar adaptations of structure and adjustments of functions may be observed and to some extent measured throughout the whole of the culture complex and of the social order. Some of these changes are results of chance happenings; others are willed. Ross has chosen

20 See: Aaron I. Abell, *The Urban Impact on American Protestantism,* 1865-1900, Cambridge, Harvard University Press, 1943; H. P. Douglass, *The Church in the Changing City,* New York, Doubleday, Doran & Co., 1927, pp. 222-245; J. T. Landis, "Social Action in American Protestant Churches," *Am. J. Sociol.,* Vol. 52, No. 5, May, 1947, pp. 517-522; M. H. Leiffer, *City and Church in Transition,* Chicago, Willett, Clark & Co., 1938; R. S. and H. M. Lynd, *Middletown,* New York, Harcourt, Brace & Co., 1929, pp. 399-407; R. S. and H. M. Lynd, *Middletown in Transition,* New York, Harcourt, Brace & Co., 1937, pp. 295-318.
21 S. C. Kincheloe, "Major Reactions in City Churches," *Religious Education,* Vol. 23, p. 868.
22 J. K. Folsom, *Social Psychology,* New York, Harper & Bros., 1931, p. 587.

to call the former *transformations;* the latter, *reshapings.*[23] Both are forms of reorganization.

Cultural Creation.—There is really no starting point of cultural change; it has neither beginning nor end; it is continuous. Nevertheless, there occur now and then marked and sometimes abrupt alterations and mutations in culture patterns that appear to be starting points. These responses to stimuli from outside or from within the culture take the form either of borrowed elements or of invented ones. In either case they have the characteristics of cultural creations in that, in the process of interaction with other traits of the culture pattern, they exert pressures upon them with the result that the pattern itself is changed and corresponding socio-psychological changes in wishes, attitudes, interests, and behavior are stimulated. Of course, neither a borrowed trait nor an invented one is in reality a starting point because each is the result of previously existing culture elements.

Research has demonstrated that the fundamental traits of cultures, that is the really novel inventions or discovered principles, are obtained much oftener through diffusion or borrowing than through independent, parallel discovery. This fact quite upsets the popular belief. True invention is rare and difficult; diffusion or imitation is easy. Invention is an irregular, unpredictable, chance relationship. Invention is like mutation in biological evolution. It is a unique result of a chance combination of circumstances.[24]

Cultural origins are treated elsewhere in this book.[25] Our interest in them here has to do with the relation of new increments of culture (borrowed and invented) to social change. The cultural changes themselves depend upon the existence of felt needs and proper cultural bases. Where they are borrowed, they depend on contact and communication, and where invented, on a person of requisite ability. The felt needs lie at the junction points between human nature and social situations.

Man's feeling of need depends upon his organic wants and his socialized wishes in their interaction with his particular physical and cultural environments. Included in the latter is the indispensable

---

23 Ross, *Principles of Sociology,* Chs. 47-48.
24 Folsom, *Social Psychology,* pp. 564, 577. See also G. G. Brown, "Missions and Cultural Diffusion," *Am. J. Sociol.,* Vol. 50, No. 3, November, 1944, pp. 214-219; P. F. Cressey, "Chinese Traits in European Civilization: A Study in Diffusion," *Am. Sociol. Rev.,* Vol. 10, No. 5, October, 1945, pp. 595-604; R. B. Dixon. *The Building of Cultures,* New York, Charles Scribner's Sons, 1928; S. C. Gilfillan, *The Sociology of Invention,* Chicago, The Follett Publishing Co., 1935; J. L. and J. P. Gillin, *An Introduction to Sociology,* New York, The Macmillan Co., 1942, pp. 160-169; H. C. Lehman, "The Exponential Increase of Man's Cultural Output," *Social Forces,* Vol. 25, March, 1947, pp. 281-290; Wallis, *op. cit.,* Chs. 4, 7.
25 Chapter 2.

factor of his peculiar cultural base. For example, if the cultural base is that of a typical folk society, which is characteristically conservative and relatively intolerant of innovation, it would be more difficult for a new culture element to be introduced from the outside (and practically impossible for invention to take place inside) than would be the case where the culture base is more secular and responsive to change. Nevertheless, we must remember that the earliest objects of culture, like the wheel, the fire stick, the stone weapon, the crude shelter, and the most elementary cultural practices, such as the spinning of fibre, the domestication of animals, the weaving of baskets, the belief in and use of magic, were the creations of primitive men interacting with a circumscribed and little-understood physical environment and a highly coercive cultural environment. It would seem, then, that when neither of these environments any longer satisfies man's wishes, he grows restive and seeks a remedy for his condition. Fortuitous circumstances or his own search may bring the desired result through cultural borrowing, or he may have to await the slower creation of a means to the wished-for end through invention.

So we see cultural, socio-psychological, and physical factors interwoven and acting as mutually stimulating and responding agents in the course of change. As an example, Folsom cites the case of "lumbering, which is of course a cultural activity," not harmful in itself, but which, when carried to excess of exploitation, "sometimes brings deforestation to a point where the climate and streams change, and society is driven by wood shortage or floods to change its policies." [26] Educational programs, immigration and population policies, administrative adjustments, political strategy, sometimes religious faiths and practices, and a host of other traits may trace their "origins" to the interaction of similar sets of factors.

The usual sequence of events in such changes finds the borrowing or the inventing of the culture trait coming first to be followed by changes in the social organization to comply with the new trait. When the social reorganization is long delayed, it is a case of social lag. The more promptly the latter changes are made, the less disturbing and disrupting will be the effects of innovation. Since the discovery and invention of objects that contribute to the comfort, convenience, and efficiency of people tend to change rather readily and rapidly, and since social structures, ideas, beliefs, opinions, attitudes, and habits tend to be altered rather slowly and reluctantly, a great deal of social disorganization is to be expected as a consequence.

---

[26] Folsom, *Social Psychology*, p. 576.

Many changes in culture consist in changes in the *quantitative proportion* of something, without the introduction of any new trait. This something may be a material trait or human activity. Such changes, for example, include changes in the number of automobiles *per capita,* in the *rate* of robberies, in the *percentage* of home ownership. Such a change in proportion may constitute an actual change in social structure, as does the present decreased proportion of women engaged in domestic service as compared with 1910, or it may not. Such changes play a large part both as causes and effects of other changes.[27]

Change is inevitable. It may be slow or rapid, progressive or retrogressive, and pursue one line of development or several at a time. We have seen, also, how interlinked are cultural and other factors in relation to social change. One factor tends to stimulate and call out the others. A change in one may or may not elicit a corresponding change in the others. The rates of change vary and we note the phenomena of a forging ahead in one field, a lag in another, a slipping back in still another, and so on, with resultant unevenness in cultural development and a correlative disorganization in formal social structure and in personal life. While certain factors in culture and social organization change slowly, others call for rapid change if serious maladjustments are to be avoided.

QUESTIONS

1. What is the relation of culture to social change?
2. What are some differentials among culture systems and within given culture systems that affect the course and rate of change?
3. Discuss: "Culture is both a divisive and an integrating factor in human life and association."
4. What hypothesis did Redfield undertake to test in his investigation of four communities in Yucatan? What independent and what dependent variables did he postulate? What did the study reveal as to the differential functions of these variables?
5. What were the results of Gross' test of the same hypothesis with respect to four rural communities in the United States? What variables were used in the study?
6. What conclusions concerning social change may be drawn from the foregoing researches?
7. Compare the ideal-type folk society with the ideal-typical modern urban society as to differentials in social change.
8. What is meant by "cultural inertia"? What are some factors that seemingly enter into a situation to contribute to this phenomenon?

---

[27] *Ibid.,* p. 580.

9. What characterizes folk-society homogeneity?
10. Why is inertia not entirely absent "in the most cosmopolitan and rapidly changing societies"?
11. Show how maladjusted to each other the different parts of culture may become.
12. Explain Ogburn's phrase "cultural lag." How does it affect social change?
13. Discuss the idea that war is an anachronism, something incongruous, a case of cultural lag.
14. Characterize "cultural formalism." Illustrate.
15. Discuss: "The 'grip of the dead hand' and 'the hard cake of custom' are signs of a formalism that, if not resisted, may lead to decay."
16. What is meant by saying that "formalism is mechanism supreme"? Illustrate.
17. Discuss the nature and effects of cultural deterioration.
18. What parts are played by the resisting and conserving qualities of culture in connection with social interaction?
19. What is the role of language in cultural revival? Explain.
20. What is meant by saying, "Parallel and incident to the cultural revival are changes in social organization"?
21. Discuss cultural reorganization in terms of the family, the church, and other institutional culture patterns.
22. Discuss: "There is really no starting point of cultural change; it has neither beginning nor end; it is continuous."
23. What is meant by "cultural creation"?
24. Explain the significance of the tendency for a change in one culture element to stimulate and call out change in other elements.

BIBLIOGRAPHY

ANSHEN, RUTH N. (Ed.) *Our Emergent Civilization.* New York, Harper & Bros., 1947.

BARNES, HARRY E. *Society in Transition.* New York, Prentice-Hall, Inc., 1939.

BECKER, CARL. *Progress and Power.* Stanford University, Cal., Stanford University Press, 1936.

BECKER, HOWARD. "Sargasso Iceberg: A Study in Cultural Lag and Institutional Disintegration." *Am. J. Sociol.,* Vol. 34, No. 3, November, 1928, pp. 492-506.

BENEDICT, RUTH. *The Chrysanthemum and the Sword.* Boston, Houghton Mifflin Co., 1946.

BENEDICT, RUTH. *Patterns of Culture.* Boston, Houghton Mifflin Co., 1934.

BERGER, C. Q. "The Persistence of Obsolete Usages." *Sociology and Social Research,* Vol. 18, 1933-1934, pp. 258-265.

BLUMER, HERBERT. "Social Disorganization and Individual Disorganization." *Am. J. Sociol.,* Vol. 42, No. 6, May, 1937, pp. 871-877.

BOSSARD, JAMES H. S. *Social Change and Social Problems.* Rev. ed., New York, Harper & Bros., 1938.

BOWERS, RAYMOND V. "Differential Intensity of Intra-Societal Diffusion." *Am. Sociol. Rev.,* Vol. 3, No. 1, February, 1938, pp. 21-31.

BROWN, L. GUY. *Social Pathology.* New York, F. S. Crofts & Co., 1942.

BUELL, BRADLEY, AND ROBINSON, REGINALD. "A Composite Rate of Social Break-down." *Am. J. Sociol.,* Vol. 45, No. 6, May, 1940, pp. 887-898.

BURKE, KENNETH. *Permanence and Change: An Anatomy of Purpose.* New York, New Republic, Inc., 1936.

CAROUSSIS, GEORGE. *Poetopoeia: The Romance of Euripides.* New York, The William-Frederick Press, 1946. Development of city civilization from the earlier folk culture.

CARR, LOWELL J. "Disaster and the Sequence-Pattern Concept of Social Change." *Am. J. Sociol.,* Vol. 38, No. 2, September, 1932, pp. 207-218.

CHAPIN, F. STUART. *Cultural Change.* New York, D. Appleton-Century Co., 1928.

CHOUKAS, MICHAEL. "The Concept of Cultural Lag Reexamined." *Am. Sociol. Rev.,* Vol. 1, No. 5, October, 1936, pp. 752-760.

COCHRAN, THOMAS C., AND MILLER, WILLIAM. *The Age of Enterprise.* New York, The Macmillan Co., 1942.

COOLEY, CHARLES H. *Social Organization.* New York, Charles Scribner's Sons, 1907, Chs. 30-33.

COOLEY, CHARLES H. *Social Process.* New York, Charles Scribner's Sons, 1909.

DEVEREUX, GEORGE, AND LOEB, EDWIN M. "Antagonistic Acculturation." *Am. Sociol. Rev.,* Vol. 8, No. 2, April, 1943, pp. 133-147.

EKIRCH, ARTHUR A., JR. *The Idea of Progress in America.* New York, Columbia University Press, 1944.

ELDRIDGE, SEBA. *New Social Horizons: Design for a Personality Centered Culture.* New York, D. Appleton-Century Co., 1941.

ELLIOTT, MABEL A., AND MERRILL, FRANCIS E. *Social Disorganization.* New York, Harper & Bros., 1941, especially Chs. 1-2.

FARIS, ROBERT E. L. *Social Disorganization.* New York, The Ronald Press Co., 1948.

FOLSOM, JOSEPH K. *Culture and Social Progress.* New York, Longmans, Green & Co., 1928.

GABRIEL, R. H. *The Course of American Democratic Thought.* New York, The Ronald Press Co., 1940.

GILFILLAN, S. C. *The Sociology of Invention.* Chicago, The Follett Publishing Co., 1935.

GOLDENWEISER, A. A. "The Concept of Causality in the Physical and Social Sciences." *Am. Sociol. Rev.,* Vol. 3, No. 5, October, 1938, pp. 624-636.

HARVARD TERCENTENARY PUBLICATION. *Authority and the Individual.* Cambridge, Harvard University Press, 1937. See R. M. MacIver, "The Historical Pattern of Social Change," and John Dewey, "Authority and Social Change."

HERMAN, ABBOTT P. "An Answer to Criticisms of the Lag Concept." *Am. J. Sociol.,* Vol. 43, No. 3, November, 1937, pp. 440-451.

HERSKOVITS, MELVILLE J. *Acculturation.* New York, J. J. Augustin, Inc., 1938.

HSIAO TUNG FEI, AND CHIH-I CHANG. *Earthbound China.* Chicago, University of Chicago Press, 1945.

HUGHES, EVERETT C. *French Canada in Transition.* Chicago, University of Chicago Press, 1943.

JUNEK, OSCAR W. *Isolated Communities: A Study of a Labrador Fishing Village.* New York, American Book Co., 1937.

KEESING, FELIX M. "The Changing Life of Native Peoples in the Pacific Area: A Sketch of Cultural Dynamics." *Am. J. Sociol.,* Vol. 39, No. 4, January, 1934, pp. 443-458.

KELLER, A. G. *Societal Evolution.* Rev. ed., New Haven, Yale University Press, 1947.

KROEBER, A. L. *Configurations of Culture Growth.* Berkeley, Cal., University of California Press, 1944.

KUO-HENG SHIH. *China Enters the Machine Age: A Study of Labor in Chinese War Industry.* Cambridge, Harvard University Press, 1944.

LaPiere, Richard T. *Sociology.* New York, McGraw-Hill Book Co., Inc., 1946, Ch. 15, "Institutional Dynamics."

Lehman, Harvey C. "The Exponential Increase of Man's Cultural Output." *Social Forces,* Vol. 25, March, 1947, pp. 281-290.

Lehman, Harvey C. "National Differences in Creativity." *Am. J. Sociol.,* Vol. 52, No. 6, May, 1947, pp. 475-489.

Linton, Ralph (Ed.). *Acculturation in Seven American Indian Tribes.* New York, D. Appleton-Century Co., 1940.

Lynd, Robert S., and Lynd, Helen M. *Middletown: A Study in Contemporary American Culture,* and *Middletown in Transition: A Study in Cultural Conflicts.* New York, Harcourt, Brace & Co., 1929, 1937.

MacIver, Robert M. *Social Causation.* Boston, Ginn & Co., 1942.

MacIver, Robert M. *Society: Its Structure and Changes.* New York, Ray Long & R. R. Smith, 1931, Part IV.

Malinowski, Bronislaw. *The Dynamics of Culture Change.* New Haven, Yale University Press, 1945.

Mannheim, Karl. *Diagnosis of Our Time.* New York, Oxford University Press, 1944.

Mannheim, Karl. *Man and Society in an Age of Reconstruction.* Translated by Edward Shils. New York, Harcourt, Brace & Co., 1940.

Mayo, Elton. *The Political Problem of Industrial Civilization:* Part I, "The Modernization of a Primitive Community"; Part II, "Change and Its Social Consequences." Cambridge, Harvard University Press, 1947.

Miner, Horace. *St. Denis: A French-Canadian Parish.* Chicago, University of Chicago Press, 1939.

Mowrer, Ernest R. *Disorganization: Personal and Social.* Philadelphia, J. B. Lippincott Co., 1942.

Mueller, John H. "Present Status of the Cultural Lag Hypothesis." *Am. Sociol. Rev.,* Vol. 3, No. 3, June, 1938, pp. 320-327.

Mumford, Lewis. *The Condition of Man.* New York, Harcourt, Brace & Co., 1944.

Mumford, Lewis. *Technics of Civilization.* New York, Harcourt, Brace & Co., 1934.

Noss, Theodore K. *Resistance to Social Innovation as Found in the Literature Regarding Innovations Which Have Proved Successful.* Abstract of Ph.D. dissertation, Chicago, University of Chicago Press, 1944.

Ogburn, William F. "The Influence of Inventions on American Institutions of the Future." *Am. J. Sociol.,* Vol. 43, No. 3, November, 1937, pp. 365-376.

Ogburn, William F. *Social Change.* New York, B. W. Huebsch, 1923. Part III, "Cultural Inertia and Conservatism"; Part IV, "Social Maladjustments."

Ogburn, William F. *The Social Effects of Aviation.* Boston, Houghton Mifflin Co., 1946.

Ogburn, William F. "Sociology and the Atom." *Am. J. Sociol.,* Vol. 51, No. 4, January, 1946, pp. 267-275.

Ogburn, William F. "Stationary and Changing Societies." *Am. J. Sociol.,* Vol. 42, No. 1, July, 1936, pp. 16-31.

Ogburn, William F., and Gilfillan, S. C. "The Influence of Invention and Discovery," Ch. III in *Recent Social Trends.* New York, McGraw-Hill Book Co., Inc., 1933.

Queen, Stuart A., Bodenhafer, W. B., and Harper, Ernest B. *Social Organization and Disorganization.* New York, Thomas Y. Crowell Co., 1935, Ch. 14, "Culture Lag."

Raper, A. F., and Reid, Ira DeA. *Sharecroppers All.* Chapel Hill, University of North Carolina Press, 1941.

Redfield, Robert. *The Folk Culture of Yucatan.* Chicago, University of Chicago Press, 1941.

REPORT OF SUBCOMMITTEE ON TECHNOLOGY, NATIONAL RESOURCES COMMITTEE. *Technological Trends and National Policy.* Washington, Government Printing Office, 1937. Part I, "Social Aspects of Technology."

ROSE, EDWARD. "Innovations in American Culture." *Social Forces,* Vol. 26, March, 1948, pp. 255-272.

ROSEN, S. McKEE, AND ROSEN, LAURA. *Technology and Society: The Influence of Machines in the United States.* New York, The Macmillan Co., 1941.

ROSENQUIST, CARL M. *Social Problems.* New York, Prentice-Hall, Inc., 1940.

SCHNEIDER, JOSEPH. "Cultural Lag: What Is It?" *Am. Sociol. Rev.,* Vol. 10, No. 6, December, 1945, pp. 787-791.

SHERIF, MUZAFER. *An Outline of Social Psychology.* New York, Harper & Bros., 1948, Ch. 15, "The Effects of Technology"; Ch. 16, "Men in Critical Situations."

SIMS, NEWELL L. *The Problem of Social Change.* New York, Thomas Y. Crowell Co., 1939.

SOROKIN, PITIRIM A. *The Crisis of Our Age: The Social and Cultural Outlook.* New York, E. P. Dutton & Co., 1941.

SOROKIN, PITIRIM A. *Man and Society in Calamity.* New York, E. P. Dutton & Co., 1942.

SOROKIN, PITIRIM A. *The Reconstruction of Humanity.* Boston, Beacon Press, 1948.

SOROKIN, PITIRIM A. *Social and Cultural Dynamics,* 4 vols. New York, American Book Co., 1937-1941.

SOROKIN, PITIRIM A. *Society, Culture, and Personality; Their Structure and Dynamics.* New York, Harper & Bros., 1947.

SOROKIN, PITIRIM A. *Sociocultural Causality, Space, Time.* Durham, N. C., Duke University Press, 1943.

STERN, BERNHARD J. *Society and Medical Progress.* Princeton, Princeton University Press, 1941.

THORNTON, JESSE (Compiler). *Science and Social Change.* Washington, The Brookings Institution, 1939.

TOYNBEE, ARNOLD. *The Study of History.* New York, Oxford University Press, Vols. 1-3, 1934; Vols. 4-6, 1939. Abridgement in one volume by D. C. Somervell, New York, Oxford University Press, 1947.

VANCE, RUPERT B. "Toward Social Dynamics." *Am. Sociol. Rev.,* Vol. 10, No. 2, April, 1945, pp. 123-131.

WALLIS, WILSON D. "The Concept of Lag." *Sociol. and Soc. Res.,* Vol. 19, pp. 399-406.

WALLIS, WILSON D. *Culture and Progress.* New York, McGraw-Hill Book Co., Inc., 1930, especially Parts I and III.

WEBER, ALFRED. "The Historical Pattern of Social Change." *J. Soc. Phil.,* Vol. 2, 1936, pp. 35-54.

WOODARD, JAMES W. *Intellectual Realism and Culture Change.* Hanover, N. H., Sociological Press, 1935.

WOODARD, JAMES W. "A New Classification of Culture and a Restatement of the Culture Lag Theory." *Am. Sociol. Rev.,* Vol. 1, No. 1, February, 1936, pp. 89-101.

ZIMMERMAN, CARLE C. *Outline of Social Change and Progress.* Cambridge, Mass., Phillips Book Store, 1946.

Chapter 23

SOCIAL UNREST AND TYPES OF COLLECTIVE BEHAVIOR

Behavioral Trends and Tendencies

In preceding chapters we have undertaken to describe and analyze the component elements of societies, their cultural milieus and organizational structures, the processes by which they emerge and are maintained, and some of the ways in which these factors, in interaction, compete, conflict, accommodate and assimilate. Such configurations are not static. There is no sharp dualism between form or structure, organization or order on the one hand, and movement and change on the other. The distinction is entirely a matter of the viewpoint and objective of the observer.

Despite the difficulty of visualizing or imagining change, it is possible to discover, describe, and explain certain tendencies in the responses of people, as individuals and as groups. It is also possible to ascertain and to appraise some of the numerous control mechanisms used to manipulate the responses and the social units that commonly employ them, and to describe how the response tendencies frequently assume a sequential order of change. Since the processes of personal adjustment were discussed in previous chapters,[1] attention will now be directed to some specific response tendencies in members of groups.

Social change, viewed broadly, may be discerned as a series of movements in the form of fluctuations or undulations, which are not rhythmic and regular, as some would have us believe. At times they are feeble and almost imperceptible, sometimes they are pronounced, and sometimes they are explosive. Some of the movements are of short duration, others are of long duration—sometimes so long that one may study their history through the course of decades or even centuries. Some movements are seemingly without direction or goals, others become organized and led in terms of idealized and ultimate

---

[1] Chapters 5 and 6.

objectives projected imaginatively into some future time. The latter type of movement will receive attention in Chapter 25; the former type will be treated in this chapter.

Both types of movement belong in the category of collective phenomena in that they are interactional responses of numbers of people to the stimulating conditions of their environments. Such movements grow out of and are conditioned by the wishes and attitudes of the people, which, in turn, have their origin in the cultural matrix of their time. Both movements represent efforts toward more satisfying personal adjustments or more efficient social organization, but, in the case of the more ephemeral and directionless movements, the efforts are likely to be largely unselfconscious and irrational. In the case of the organized social movements, the efforts are more consciously purposeful. Under certain conditions the former type may take on rationally defined goals and thus develop the characteristic features of the latter type. In either case, the former represents tendencies toward change—usually random, sporadic, and oftentimes unpredictable—while the latter shows tendencies to form identifiable trends of change.

By *trend* is meant a persistent general movement in the direction of some distant goal as yet undefined or only vaguely held. Entering into every major trend are minor trends or *tendencies,* which are various factors inherent in the situation, such as recurrent types of behavior. As noted above, many behavior responses seemingly manifest themselves without any clear connection with prior or succeeding tendencies; they appear suddenly, have a brief period of expression, and then disappear. That they emerge as reactions to existing conditions in the situation is usually evident, but they appear, disappear, and sometimes reappear with no very apparent relationship to other similar behaviors. Their relation to social change is that of symptoms, commonly symptoms of frustration and discontent, deep-seated but largely unconscious desires, hopes, and aspirations, or fears and -repressions. But, unless such tendencies develop a connection among themselves so that they move together in a unilinear series of causal and effective relations, they do not constitute a trend.

Sometimes tendencies come in to break up a trend, to distract attention from the focal point, to set up tangents and diversions, and to dissipate energies. In these ways they may disrupt the course of orderly social change. At other times, however, they are organizing factors that give meaning to the situation and combine to give consistent direction and momentum to a trend. Some of the trends in social change are so well marked and definite as to make it possible to trace them through their entire course. This is particularly true in the case of organized social movements.

Our immediate attention will be directed to a consideration of those behavior response tendencies of collectivities (groups) that appear to have little or no lasting effect in social change, that arise spontaneously and capriciously in interaction, but that may have rather disturbing effects during their short duration. Perhaps it is their principal function to release tensions, and to disrupt the equilibrium of social organization so as to attract attention to and provide the incentive for social reorganization. Exceptions to this generalization are the societal behaviors treated at the end of the chapter.

We have stated that these trends emerge from situations. The situations are the contexts—the total configurations—in which the interaction takes place. Such situations may be a football game, a classroom, a mass meeting, a "panic," a riot, a family gathering, a war, and the like. While students of the phenomena have been unable heretofore to subject these group situations to the controlled conditions of laboratory experimentation, nevertheless their deductions make it possible to assert that individuals do interact in characteristic fashion in such situations. The details of the behavior will vary, but certain general features of situations are apparent. The reason for this seems to be that each individual member of the group behaves in accordance with cultural patterns, e.g., folkways, mores, conventions, which all accept, and which the presence of each enforces upon the others.

SOCIAL UNREST AND ITS CONTAGION

Before individuals can be brought to behave collectively, they must come under the influence of some incitement that is common and collective. Back of such behavior tendency there is some exciting factor or factors in the situation to bring the individuals involved under the spell of a mood in which each shares and which comes to dominate their behavior. They respond to each other in interaction and manifest like responses to the common stimulus. This results, in part at least, from the fact that an individual, prompted by an inner feeling of need, desire, fear, hate, or other attitude, is in a state of tension. This tension seeks release in ways that are more or less overt and thus is sensed or perceived by other individuals, who themselves may be under similar tension. The wishes, both positive and negative, press for expression and satisfaction. Normally, a wish not yet satisfied, but with a fair prospect of being fulfilled, may provoke no appreciable tension, but a wish that is balked, inhibited, or suppressed—either by real or imaginary personal limitations or by factors resident in the external environment—tends to arouse tension and to excite restless behavior. This restlessness, expressed by one individual, will communicate itself in turn to other individuals, particularly those individuals who are receptive by reason of their own assorted discontents or unmet desires. Thus, sometimes subtly and almost imperceptibly, and sometimes openly and deliberately, restlessness spreads until it affects numbers of persons, who constitute a collectivity. Through interaction the restlessness has now become social unrest, a precondition of collective behavior.

When we think of restlessness it is not necessary to conjure up mental images of individuals running hither and yon, wringing their hands, tearing their hair, screaming or crying out, and otherwise displaying their feeling in violent physical forms. In many cases the restlessness may be largely internalized in the form of mental conflict, or it may show itself overtly in changes of facial expression, "the look in the eyes" or the set of the mouth, in earnest oral expression, or possibly in efforts to find seclusion from human contacts. The individual may actually have only the vaguest notion as to why he is unhappy or dissatisfied. There is also that restlessness expressive of gay and happy moods, of expectancy and eagerness, of hope and ambition, and the like. Whatever the nature of the restlessness and of the reasons for it, the point is that it is communicable and that, under favorable conditions of interaction, it spreads like a contagion to persons who are susceptible, who, by reason of their own sense of need, are set to respond. In some such fashion individuals are brought into a collectivity prepared to behave similarly, if not always alike.

From what has been said it may be concluded that the spread of individual restlessness until it becomes a pervasive social unrest is a selective process, affecting only those persons who are prepared to respond. Superficially, it is not always apparent that this is so. As a matter of fact, there are occasions where the unrest seems to be all-inclusive. Moreover, there appears to be no known criterion by which it can be predicted, in advance of the actual collective behavior, just who will be affected and how. Studies of collective behaviors have shown, however, that not all persons will be influenced by a given stimulus, or will not be affected to the same degree. In some situations, differences in response tendencies seem to be related to certain general categories like sex, age, race, nationality, status, etc., but in other situations they cut across these categories. Also, differences in the constitutional makeup of individuals, as well as differential factors in social experience, may predispose some individuals to one type of response and other individuals to a variant and even contrary one. Observation shows, however, that collective behavior eventuates when there is a conjunction of an exciting situation and a number of suggestible individuals who respond to a common stimulus and to the restive behavior of each other.

COLLECTIVE BEHAVIOR

Collective behavior has been variously defined. The *Dictionary of Sociology* defines this kind of behavior as that "of a group when it is of such a nature as to give the appearance of arising from unity of attitude, feeling, and motivation." In other words, "the type of behavior consistent with the analogical concept of the group as an organism." [2] Park and Burgess say that "collective behavior . . . is the behavior of individuals under the influence of an impulse that is common and collective, an impulse, in other words, that is the result of social interaction." [3]

It may appear that collective behavior is synonymous with all social interaction and with all group behavior. That the former is so may be questioned, but that the latter is true may be accepted without question when that behavior is intra-group rather than inter-group behavior. When individuals behave together as a group, that is collective behavior. When a family moves from one place to another, when a mob storms an industrial plant that is under strike, when an army division moves against the enemy's lines, when an audience rises spontaneously to applaud the performance of an artist, when the wives and children of miners trapped in an exploded mine wait patiently at the mine entrance for fateful news, and when women converge on the bargain counter eager to purchase goods on special sale, we have examples of collective behavior, but they are examples that are not all alike in their forms of interaction on the part of the individuals involved. The characteristic features of a given pattern of behavior that make it collective in its nature are (1) two or more individuals, not necessarily in physical proximity, but (2) in contact through com-

---

2 *Dictionary of Sociology*, edited by H. P. Fairchild, New York, Philosophical Library, 1944, p. 21.

3 Robert E. Park and E. W. Burgess, *Introduction to the Science of Sociology*, Chicago, University of Chicago Press, 1924, p. 865. See also E. B. Reuter and C. W. Hart, *Introduction to Sociology*, New York, McGraw-Hill Book Co., Inc., 1933, p. 438; R. T. La Piere, *Collective Behavior*, New York, McGraw-Hill Book Co., Inc., 1938, p. 3; Herbert Blumer, "The Field of Collective Behavior," in Alfred M. Lee (Ed.), *New Outline of the Principles of Sociology*, New York, Barnes & Noble, Inc., 1946, pp. 167-169.

munication, and (3) behaving in response to a common stimulus in (4) a specific situation, that, as La Piere maintains, has a definite "duration," that is, a beginning and an end. A fifth factor is sometimes present, namely, a common goal or objective. It is the presence of this factor which gives to some patterns of collective behavior the character of organized social movements. The common goal or objective serves as the focal point of activity and contributes to transform the behavior from mere expectant or expressive behavior to one of action.

The phenomena of collective behavior fall into two general classes—collective-emotional behavior and collective-rational behavior. The line of demarcation between them is not always clear and the observer of some particular case might find it difficult to decide from the overt behavior patterns to which class it belonged. Often the two are inextricably mixed in a single situation. Frequently there is unmistakable evidence of high emotional tone, but in many cases the emotional element may be concealed. On the other hand, collective behavior may take the form of acts that are apparently deliberate and rational and with little or no emotional content. However, a surface calm and a set determination to see a thing through may be deceptive in that they may conceal a turbulent and excited emotional state.

If we analyze these phenomena further, we see that collective-emotional behavior consists, for the most part, of those spontaneous forms of collective excitement which manifest themselves in shouts, laughter, weeping, dancing, psychic katatonia, spontaneous jerkings, incoherent babbling, convulsions, acts of violence, and the like. Under such conditions the individual members of the collectivity, even those who under ordinary circumstances are emotionally and intellectually stable, come under the sway of the mass impulse. On the other hand, there are occasions when group decisions must be worked out in the more deliberate forum of public opinion. Exciting incidents may call forth such behavior quite as often as they stimulate the type of behavior referred to above. Which type of behavior ensues depends largely upon the particular object of attention at the moment. A sudden shift in the focus of attention may easily affect the dominant mood and result in an abrupt transition from one type of behavior to the other.

As indicated above, collectivities tend in situations arousing emotional attitudes of fear, anger, surprise, ecstasy, to behavior quite different from that in situations calling for more rational attitudes. In many situations that stimulate collective behavior, habitual attitudes suffice to meet the needs and wishes of the members. All of which suggests that the forms and mechanisms of collective behavior vary with the definition of the situation itself, as that definition is understood and responded to by the members of the collectivity. A number of the mechanisms more commonly experienced singly by individuals in closely knit groups than in less stable collectivities are discussed in the chapter on social control.

The most elementary form of collective behavior seems to be what is ordinarily referred to as "social unrest." Unrest in the individual becomes social when it is transmitted from one individual to another, but more particularly when it produces something akin to the milling process in the herd, so that manifestations of discontent in A communicated to B, and from B reflected back to A, produce the circular reaction.[4]

But social unrest itself is not a form of collective behavior; it is a precondition of collective behavior.

The first requisite to "milling," as in the buffalo herd, is that restless individuals be brought into contact with each other through communication. Physical presence is not essential to human beings, but communication through some one or more of its mechanisms, like face-to-face communication, the press, the radio, the movie, the telephone, and the telegraph, is necessary. Once interaction is started, the individuals begin to "move" mentally, if not physically, in the direction of a collective excitement and a measure of unification. They come to feel mutually responsive to each other and to common symbols and objects. A condition of *rapport* is established. Rapport facilitates the release of responses which under more normal conditions are inhibited or repressed.

As the circular interaction proceeds, attention gets more and more narrowly focused on a common object and the individuals come under the spell of a mood which they share and which tends to dominate their every response. This mood may be either one of *esprit de corps* or one of morale. Esprit de corps is marked by a buoyant, enthusiastic, or even ecstatic attitude, whereas morale represents a rather dogged, determined, do-or-die attitude. The former typifies the situation that is getting defined favorably and which holds out hope for the collectivity; the latter is found in the situation defined negatively as exemplified by reverses, threatened loss, defeat, or catastrophe, but where hope is not irretrievably lost. When hope seems gone, so far as the given situation is concerned, the group may manifest a different mood, one of despair or depression, if not of outright stupor. Still

---

4 Park and Burgess, *Introduction to the Science of Sociology*, p. 866.

another mood that may come to possess a collectivity, especially when confronted by some unexpected and unprepared-for danger or calamity, is panic. This mood may so immobilize the members of the collectivity as to stop all behavior, or it may serve to destroy the collectivity as a unit and cause its members to disperse in disorder, each seeking escape in his individual capacity.

A significant aspect of milling as a form of collective behavior is the tendency for the excitement to mount, until it reaches its zenith. So intense may become the absorption of the members of the collectivity in each other and in the symbols of their common experience that they may lose all self-awareness. Thus individuals come under the spell of each other's behavior and under the control of the object that is the focal point of attention. "In collective excitement, the personal makeup of individuals is more readily broken; and, in this way, the condition is prepared for the formation of new forms of behavior and for the reorganization of the individual. In collective excitement, individuals may embark on lines of conduct which previously they would not likely have thought of, much less dared to undertake. Likewise, under its stress, and with opportunities for the release of tension, individuals may incur significant reorganization in their sentiments, habits, and traits of personality." [5] Consequently, milling and its accompaniment of intense collective excitement may serve to bring about new forms of collective behavior.

BEHAVIOR OF THE CROWD

The crowd, psychologically organized through some such process as that described, was first treated as a significant social phenomenon by Le Bon.[6] In much of his writing he was prone to discredit it and to regard it as a dangerous thing, "a slave to its impulses." Yet he recognized that the crowd might be noble and heroic as well as vicious. It is not our purpose to discuss the crowd as good or bad, but to describe crowd behavior and the different forms it may assume.

It should be emphasized at the outset of a discussion of crowd behavior that what is meant by "crowd" is not always what the crowd is held to be in popular opinion. To illustrate: a street throng is not a crowd as we use the term. It is a number of people passing up and down the street, some of the individuals greeting others whom they recognize as acquaintances, stopping to converse with some, and occasionally pausing to "window shop" or to perform an errand.

---

[5] Blumer, "Collective Behavior," *op. cit.*, p. 175.
[6] Gustave Le Bon, *The Crowd*, London, T. F. Unwin, 1903.

But, unless some exciting event causes them to converge at the place of the happening, to follow the gaze of others skyward to watch a stunting airplane, or otherwise focus their collective attention on some stimulating object, they are no more than the human ingredients from which a crowd may be recruited. The fact of a number of people within a given area, and even the fact that many of them may share a mood, such as the serious attention of office people to their business, or the gaiety of a holiday throng, or the carefree attitude of a throng on Sunday afternoon or in the evening, does not alone serve to make for crowd formation. A common exciting object or purpose and mutual interstimulation or rapport are essential to crowd behavior.

A commonly held conception of the crowd is that it is "a collection of physically proximate individuals." On the contrary, physical proximity is not requisite to crowd formation. What is necessary is that the individuals composing the crowd must be in contact through communication, thus making interaction possible. Actually, members of a crowd may be near to or far from each other, physically and so far as status is concerned. A population at war is a crowd quite as much as is an audience at a concert or a gathering of fans at a football game.

Though crowds are collectivities that display the characteristics enumerated, they are not all alike. There have been several attempts to classify crowds, but for our purpose we shall classify them according to the types of behavior typically manifested by them. In this connection it should be noted, also, that these typical behaviors of crowds not only differentiate one kind of crowd from another, but may designate successive stages in crowd behavior. For instance, according to the classification we shall employ, crowds may be any one of three types: expectant, expressive, or active, but these descriptive terms may quite as well refer to consecutive phases in the natural history of crowd development, as from expectancy to expressiveness and from expressiveness to action. Not all crowds act, but it is reasonable to assume that every crowd holds potentialities for action. In the case presented below there is illustrated a crowd that is at first expectant, then expressive, and, though not becoming active, is at least prepared for action at a time to be decided upon by the leader.

The huge circus building the party had rented for the evening hummed like a beehive. People were crowding the halls and stairways. S. A. men stood everywhere, giving information and ushering the stream of arrivals. Long before the hour of the meeting every place was taken. In feverish anticipation the people sat all the way up to the roof. Tremendous streamers covered the walls and hammered the party slogans into thousands of heads.

Suddenly there was a flourish of martial music. The rhythm infected the expectant crowd, bent it to its hammering beat. Uniformed men were officiously running through the crowd with mysterious and inscrutable faces. [Dobert, the author, and four of his men were appointed as the Honor Guard and marched to the front.] And now I faced the crowd from a corner of the speaker's platform. The music had fallen silent. The waiting was intolerable.

"Attention!" came a mighty voice. I saw ten thousand faces turn toward the entrance. But no Hitler appeared. In his place came a flourish of trumpets.

If he would only come, this Hitler! The air was supercharged with tension incapable of further increase. The hysterical voice of a woman screamed, "Hitler!" Many people laughed, but their laughter sounded forced, tortured. It had grown oppressively hot. I felt like tearing open the tight collar of my uniform. The doors of the hall opened, but a second later they were closed again. Ten more long minutes elapsed.

But now the crowd leaped to its feet. They pushed against the balustrades, stood on their seats. Ten thousand arms shot up. The accumulated supertension was discharged in a single roar, lasting several seconds. I had been watching closely. They had jumped up even before the broad doors opened again, as though they felt his nearness. And now he entered the hall. This was not cheering and enthusiasm that received him; it was a single, gigantic, writhing body. The sustained, inarticulate roar imperceptibly changed into hoarse, rhythmic, panting cries of "Heil!"

Down the center aisle a solitary man walked slowly, step by step, toward me, followed by a forest of flags. Now I recognized the outlines of his face, the characteristic little mustache, the lock of hair, the eyes. They looked at me with a curious absent-mindedness. He came closer. He stood before us, offering his hand to the five of us in his Honor Guard, and passed on. I stood as though cast in bronze, while the flags brushed my face, for the solemn symbols of the movement were borne past on either side.

Slowly, slowly the crowd calmed down. The drums spoke up loudly. The lights in the hall were dimmed, as flourish followed flourish. I looked into ten thousand faces, one little pale circle next to the other, reflecting the radiance from the platform on which stood the Fuehrer. Then the drums, too, fell silent. A dead silence set in.

Above me there suddenly came a clear, powerful voice: "Deutsche Volksgenossen!"

Sentence followed sentence. Now the voice pleaded, almost implored; now it swelled into a wrath that found its echo in the thousands facing me. Now it assumed tones of bitter sarcasm, and I looked into thousands of derisive faces; now it sounded strangely cool and objective, stating facts which for many in the hall could not be facts at all but assertions never before heard. Yet the crowd in front of me no longer seemed to regard anything as impossible; they were ready to believe anything the voice said; for action was not limited to the one person. He played the crowd like a giant organ, pulling all the stops, permitting the listeners to rave and roar, laugh and cry. But inevitably the stream flowed back, until a fiery alternating current welded speaker and listeners into one. The more deeply the crowd was aroused, the mightier came the voice, the more intense the pleading, the more cutting the irony, the more powerful its wrath.[7]

While the behavior described above displays a somewhat higher degree of regimentation than is ordinarily found, the spontaneity so characteristic of most crowd behavior was present, as were the feeling of expectancy, the narrowed focus of attention, the increase of expressive emotional response, the decrease of rationality, and even an incipient impulse to act. Here we have a picture of a collection of individuals, at first, under the strain of attention, waiting for something to happen, on the *qui vive,* expectant; then, under the stimulating circumstances of the total situation—masses of people, music, the blare of trumpets, the roll of drums, the parade of the flags, and, above all, the appearance of the leader—the floodgates of emotion burst open in expressive responses of physical movement, sustained roars of applause, uncontrolled laughter, and the thunderous rhythm of ten thousand Heils! It might as well have been the milling, jostling, yelling, whistling of thousands of fans at an American ball game, or the shrill shrieks of adoring bobby-soxers at a Sinatra performance, or the tumultuous ovation accorded a Paderewski.

When a crowd develops an image of a goal or objective, then suggestion, whether from a leader or from a favorable conjunction of factors in the situation, may operate to construct a plan of action. "Without having an object toward which it might act, the crowd can release its aroused tension and excitement only in physical movement. Stated tersely, the crowd has to act, but it has nothing toward which it can act, and so it merely engages in excited movements. . . . In such a situation the expression of excited feeling becomes an end in itself; the behavior, therefore, may take the form of laughing, weeping, shouting, leaping, and dancing. In its more extreme expression, it may be in the form of uttering gibberish or having violent physical spasms." [8] On the other hand, "when the members of a crowd have a common impulse oriented toward a fixed image and supported by an

    [7] Eitel W. Dobert, *Convert to Freedom,* New York, G. P. Putnam's Sons, 1940, pp. 165-166, as quoted by F. W. Lamberton, "Hitler, the Orator: A Study in Mob Psychology," *Quart. J. Speech,* Vol. 28, April, 1942, pp. 123-124.
    [8] Blumer, "Collective Behavior," *op. cit.,* p. 183.

intense collective feeling, they are ready to act in the aggressive fashion typical of the acting crowd." [9]

Mention has been made of the tendency of expressive behavior to take on a rhythmic pattern once the milling has become speeded up and intensified. Where there is sufficient rapport and repetition of the behavior, behavior assumes a form of united expression akin to dancing. In fact, it may become manifest in the dance, in the measured beat of the feet and the clapping of the hands, in group singing, or in religious ecstasy. These response tendencies often border on collective hysteria and show up in spontaneous manias, or, if brought under some sort of ceremonial control, in the form of ritual, observed as a sacred duty or as an exhilarating exercise. As we shall have occasion to discuss later, such tendencies may lead to the formation of a cult, a sect, or a primitive kind of religion.[10] Every culture has a record of dancing as collective behavior, sometimes emerging from a prevailing unrest that has been generated by some calamity, by a series of mysterious experiences and similar events, which have left the group in a state of expectancy and nervous tension. Conversely, dancing may arise from a feeling of elation and well-being in connection with some fortunate event or festive occasion, or expressing an awesome or worshipful attitude toward the gods of evil or of good.

In 1374, assemblages of men and women were seen at Aix-la-Chapelle who had come out of Germany and who, united by one common delusion, exhibited to the public both in the streets and in the churches the following strange spectacle. They formed circles hand in hand and, appearing to have lost all control over their senses, continued dancing, regardless of the bystanders, for hours together in wild delirium, until at length they fell to the ground in a state of exhaustion. While dancing they neither saw nor heard, being insensible to external impressions through the spirits whose names they shrieked out; and some of them afterward asserted that they felt as if they had been immersed in a stream of blood, which obliged them to leap so high. Others, during the paroxysm, saw the heavens open and the Saviour enthroned with the Virgin Mary, according as the religious notions of the age were strangely and variously reflected in their imaginations.[11]

The dancing mania in Europe in the 12th to the 15th centuries became alarming first at Aix-la-Chapelle. It later spread to Cologne, Metz, and Strasbourg, and into the Netherlands.

As the years passed, dancing manias of a more specialized nature broke out in other European countries. A famous dance procession in honor of St. Willibrord was organized. The shrine was the Monastery of Echternach

9 *Ibid.*, p. 180.
10 See Chapter 25.
11 J. F. C. Hecker, *The Black Death and the Dancing Mania,* translated from the German by B. G. Babington, London, Cassell & Co., 1888, p. 106.

in the Ardennes, and several parishes went to the shrine, observing a rhythmic step: three steps forward and two back—five steps to progress one. As the number of people in the pilgrimage increased each year, music was introduced to keep the crowds in step. In 1814, the pilgrimage included about 10,000 people, and in 1892, 14,000 people were still "dancing" their way to the shrine each year. This pilgrimage almost disappeared several times during the periods of political unrest when the march was prohibited, but each time the conditions of the country improved and the prohibitions were lifted, the pilgrimage was again introduced as a form of penitence.

Another type of dancing grew out of the town of Taranto. It was Tarantism. A bite of a particular species of spider in this vicinity had a narcotic effect, and it became the practice to keep the victim active for twenty-four hours to combat the narcotic effect of the poison. Out of this grew a type of dance. When a person claimed to have been bitten by one of these spiders, musicians were called in to play and encourage the victim to keep moving. As the person became weary, the music rose to faster and faster tempos to keep him aroused. But the music and movement also affected the people who came to watch. Many joined in the dance and others believed that they, too, were affected by the spider bite and so an orgy of dancing continued until all the dancers lost consciousness from sheer exhaustion. . . .

Every summer saw a fresh epidemic of Tarantism. Those who had suffered the distinction of being bitten had recurring attacks. The musicians were known as tarantella players and for 300 years appeared to cure the victims of the spider bite. Their music may still be found among the classics where it has been interpreted as the "tarantella." . . . Finally, however, the mania lost its power and became only a summer festival which is still observed in the district.[12]

Often the most violent and extreme behavior has been displayed in outbursts of religious expression. After the Reformation and particularly during periods of fervent evangelistic preaching, religious ecstasy has been a common phenomenon.

One of the most famous religious revivals in America occurred in Kentucky in 1800, among a population predominantly Scotch-Irish. The center of the revival was Logan County in southwestern Kentucky. The particular revival which started a religious excitement for miles around was held one evening. Several preachers spoke, a Methodist and a Presbyterian included. While the latter spoke, a woman in the house, unable to repress the violence of her emotions, gave vent to them by shouting loud and long. At the close of the sermon the preacher sat down on the floor of the pulpit and there was a solemn weeping all over the house. . . . [The excitement spread and]

---

12 E. Flaig, "Dancing for the Gods of Evil," *Travel Magazine*, Vol. 83, October, 1944, pp. 20-24.

from distances of forty to one hundred miles men came with their families to listen to the group of evangelists who had stirred the congregation at the Red River sacrament. Soon the neighboring forest was used as a temple so as to accommodate all the people. When night came, they were far from surfeited with religious zeal so spread their bed clothes over poles and improvised tents. At dark fires were kindled. The meeting lasted from Friday until Tuesday. Preaching, praying, and singing continued almost without cessation save for a few hours in the early morning.

After that, ten such meetings were held one after another in that region. At these meetings, people fell and continued for hours in an apparently breathless and motionless state, sometimes reviving with a groan or shriek. After lying there for hours they would rise, shouting deliverance. . . . When the frenzy was at its height, these revival crowds were subject to a set of nervous and muscular manifestations "probably as varied and terrible as ever afflicted a population in this world."

Another phenomenon was the "barking" exercise. People gathered on all fours at the foot of a tree, growling and snapping the teeth, a practice designated as "treeing the devil." [13]

Continued religious excitement becomes contagious. People are drawn into a kind of emotional vortex. The impulse is to let oneself go, to yield to the massive and powerful suggestion of the crowd. If the emotions are restrained, they manifest themselves in convulsive reactions as among the Shakers and the Holy Rollers, or they break forth in incoherent speech, glossalalia, or "the gift of tongues." Some forms of emotional expression tend to become conventionalized, as in the jerks, barking, and prophesying. The jerks attack persons who resist the impulses and have, in their turn, a powerful suggestive influence upon the subjects. The effect of the excitement is to break down established character traits and the individual, chastened and softened, is ready to be reformed.

A crowd in movement is a dynamic force, often thrilling and terrific. A crowd standing or sitting, in whatever numbers, has great potential power. The gathering of vast crowds such as assemble spontaneously to cheer a returning hero, to celebrate a victory or the close of a war, those organized and regimented crowds such as the crowd that heard Hitler in Dresden, or those crowds which constitute an impressive psychological technique of the present-day government in Russia, or solemn demonstration like the one presented below, illustrate the latent forces of hysteria and the potential capacities of crowds for action.

As an aftermath of the famous Haymarket riot in Chicago in 1885, five men were executed. The following account is a description of their funeral:

The city permitted these same friends and relatives to hold a public funeral, if they so pleased. Mayor Roche named a series of streets along which the funeral procession might proceed on its way to Waldheim Cemetery. The hours were from twelve to two o'clock. No music except funeral dirges might be played; no arms were to be borne; no signs or banners were to be displayed. It was to be expected, the newspapers said, that even though these men were the proven enemies of society, criminals, murderers, a few hundred people might well turn out to witness the last rites. . . .

On Sunday, the Judge told his wife that he was going out for a stroll; and though Emma suspected where the stroll would take him, she said nothing, nor did she remark that it was curious, his wanting to go out alone on a Sunday morning. As a matter of fact, it was not so curious; making for the line of march, he realized that he was only one of many, many thousands of Chicago citizens; and presently it seemed that nearly half the city would be lined up along the drab, dirty streets, waiting for the procession.

Presently, the funeral procession came into sight. It was not what he might have expected, certainly not what the city authorities expected when they granted permission for the funeral to be held. There was no music, no sound other than the slow tread of feet and the soft sobbing of women. And with that, all other sounds, all other noises appeared to die away, as if a great and woeful pall of silence overhung the whole city.

First, there came a man with a flag, the only flag in the whole procession, a worn and faded Stars and Stripes that had marched proudly at the head of a regiment in the Civil War; and the man who carried it was a veteran, a middle-aged man with a face like gray stone.

Then came the hearses and the caskets; then the carriages in which the families rode. They were old, open carriages. In one of them Altgeld saw Lucy Parsons, sitting with her two children, staring straight ahead of her.

Then come the close friends, the comrades of those who had died. They walked four abreast, and their faces too were gray, like the face of the Civil War veteran.

Then came a group of well-dressed men and women, many of whom Altgeld knew and recognized. They were lawyers, judges, doctors, teachers, small businessmen, and many others who had come into the fight to save the five dead men.

Then came the workers, and to them, apparently, there was no end. They were from the packing houses, the lumber yards, the McCormick plant, and the Pullman plant; they were from the mills, the fertilizer pits, the railyards, and the canneries; they were from the flophouses of the unemployed, from the road, from the wheatfields, from the streets of Chicago and a dozen other cities. Many were in their best, the one good suit, the black suit in which they were married; many had their wives with them; children walked with them too, and some carried children in their arms. But there were enough who had no other clothes than the clothes they worked in, and they wore their overalls, their blue jeans, and their flannel shirts. There were cowhands who had ridden five hundred miles and more to Chicago, thinking that where men believed and willed, this thing could be stopped; and when it had not been stopped, they stayed to walk in the procession in their awkward, high-heeled boots. There were red-faced farmers from the prairies about the city, there were locomotive engineers, and there were sailors from the Great Lakes.

· · · · ·

And still the workers came on. For an hour Altgeld stood there, and still they came, shoulder to shoulder, their faces like stone, the tears running slowly and unwiped. Another hour, yet there was no end to them; how many thousands had passed, he could not guess, nor could he guess how many thousands more were to come; but he knew one thing: that never before in the history of the land, not even when the most beloved of all leaders, Abe Lincoln, had died, was there such a funeral as this.[14]

As the illustration shows, the demonstration may be quite orderly and even formal, but it is more apt than not to present irregular forms of behavior in spite of the efforts of leaders to direct it. More formal demonstrations are characteristic of the audience as distinct from the spontaneous crowd, but the audience may easily become an orgiastic crowd and its function may be changed accordingly.

The more or less spontaneous collective behavior tendencies which we have described have certain common characteristics which may be summarized as follows: They are elemental forms of collective behavior in which the contagious expression of emotion is the most pronounced trait. There is a dominant mood and a condition of rapport which result in responses that are largely irrational. More often than not, there is no goal or objective; the crowd is turned in upon itself, as it were, and the behavior comes to a climax with relative suddenness and then as suddenly subsides. When the expression that arises in such behavior begins to gather a meaning, so that it begins to be sought for or to be made a test, moral or spiritual, then the behavior is on the margin of becoming organized into a movement. Many such behavior tendencies do acquire an objective and thus pass over into one of the types of movement discussed in a later chapter. For example, religious ecstasy, if it comes to have a "sacred" meaning or objective, will assume the form of a religious revival or an incipient sectarian movement. In similar fashion, a demonstrative

---

[14] Howard Fast, *The American*, pp. 109-112. Reprinted by permission of the Publishers, Duell, Sloan and Pearce, Inc., New York. Copyright, 1946, by Howard Fast.

crowd may become a mob bent upon some form of action with respect
to an ideal, an object like the Tuileries or the Bastille, or a suspected
criminal.

BEHAVIOR OF THE MASS

Fundamentally different from the crowd in some respects, but like
it in other ways, is the mass. This type of collectivity is distinguishable by the following characteristics:

First, its members may come from all walks of life, and from all distinguishable social strata; it may include persons of different class position,
of different vocation, of different cultural attainment, and of different wealth.
One can recognize this in the case of the mass of people who follow a murder
trial. *Second,* the mass is an anonymous group, or more exactly, is composed
of anonymous individuals. *Third,* there exists little interaction or exchange
of experience between the members of the mass. They are usually physically
separated from one another, and, being anonymous, do not have the opportunity to mill as do the members of the crowd. *Fourth,* the mass is very
loosely organized and is not able to act with the concertedness or unity that
marks the crowd.[15]

Like the crowd, the individuals composing the mass interact under
the stimulus of a common object of attention. But, unlike the crowd,
their goals remain individual. Although they may be infected by a
similar mood and display similar behavior, they do not lose their
self-awareness as do the members of the crowd. Self-consciousness
is likely to be enhanced in the mass. This fact, among others mentioned, often gives to mass behavior the nature of uncertainty and
confusion. Instances of mass behavior, such as fashion and fad,
crazes and booms, and mass migrations and rushes, readily come to
mind.

Fashion consists of those more or less widespread and sometimes
extreme changes that affect dress, social conduct, tastes, amusements,
and, in fact, nearly every realm of life. It spreads from group to
group and from the higher social levels downward to the lower levels
by a process of social contagion, and introduces changes that are
irrational and usually unpredictable. It finds its basis in human
nature in the desire for novelty (wish for new experience) and the
desire for conformity (wishes for security and recognition).

Less widely accepted and more sporadic and shortlived is the fad.
Ross says, "The fad originates in the surprise or interest excited by
novelty." [16] Teen-age boys and girls are seemingly more susceptible

15 Blumer, "Collective Behavior," pp. 185-186.
16 E. A. Ross, *Social Psychology,* New York, The Macmillan Co., 1915, p. 80.

to fads than are their elders, although those of middle age are not im‧ mune. This suggests that fads are responded to as escape mechanisms from boredom or frustration, or as a result of the sheer weight of prestige and example in peer groups. Among contemporary fads may be mentioned moron jokes, "Confucius say," zoot suits, dietary and health fads, bubble gum, yoyo, dance fads, art and music fads, "Kilroy was here!" and innumerable others. Most of these will be *passé* before this book is in print, but it is certain that there will be others to take their places. Back of fashion and fad are the prestige factors and commercial interests. That which is the fashion will be sought without regard to utility, necessity, or beauty; it is enough that it is different and in vogue.

The craze is another manifestation of collective behavior characterized, in this type, by an addiction to or obsession with some whim, caprice, or fancy, which takes on the proportions of a mass phenomenon. It is of the nature of a popular mania, which, instead of growing out of an interest in the novel or diverting, seems to be more often than not motivated by interest in economic gain. Through, the agency of mass communication media, appeals to an indeterminate mass of anonymous individuals effect the development of a kind of irrational unanimity of interest, which spreads contagiously and takes on the aspect of a psychic epidemic. Historic examples of this type of collective behavior are the tulip craze in Holland in 1634, the Mississippi Bubble, the South Sea Bubble, and numerous periods of financial speculation and crisis. A recent example was the fever of speculation in stocks and bonds during the 1920's, followed by the stock market "crash" in 1929.

Akin to crazes are so-called "booms" marked by wild speculation, usually in real estate, following some discovery, as of oil, or the opening up of a new territory for settlement. A "boom" is correlated with an inflation of economic values, which may be confined to a single economic "good" or to a few, or which may be as pervasive as the whole economy of a local community, or a nation, or even of a considerable part of the world. After World War II, the United States, more than any other nation, entered a "boom" period. Of this period we read:

The Great American Boom is on. There is no measuring it; the old yardsticks won't do. The people and their money behave queerly and very humanly, which is to say contrary to predictions and graphs.

Almost all the curves are up. There is a powerful demand for everything that one can eat, wear, burn, read, drink, see, ride, taste, smell, and rest in. Throughout the nation there is at large a vast force of spending money, surging violently about the economy, like an Olympian bull in an old curiosity shop battering its way in and out of stores and through the banks and into the stock market and off to the black market and on into the amusement industry. Everything is bought up as fast as it appears. Mink coats at $15,000, men's wrist watches at $1000 sell just about as fast as egg beaters and pork chops.

The Boom now under way is an abnormality, far beyond such a peaceful thing as "prosperity." It is the sudden release of an unprecedented amount of money into a market unprecedentedly bare of goods. Yet this is not quite true: there are more goods than ever before, because American peacetime production is at record levels. Yet the catalogue of shortages is fabulous. The country is short of meat, bread, butter, milk, sugar, fats. There are shortages of lumber, coal, steel, X-ray tubes, burlap bags, power cranes, greenhouses, plumbing supplies. There is a shortage of train and plane seats, of hotel rooms, of pharmacists, salesmen, veterinarians, carpenters, gardeners, telephone linemen, painters, and cooks.

The list is endless, almost; the demand is fantastic; every one seems to have money, no one seems to go broke—these are the stigmata of Boom.[17]

Crazes and booms are usually short-lived and not infrequently end with a suddenness that threatens disaster, leaving those who have been caught up in the collective excitement temporarily hopeless and depressed. A panicky state of mind may overwhelm the individuals who are thus affected, with the result that something like a stampede will occur. The shocked and disillusioned members of the collectivity, now that the course of events has redefined the object of their frenzied behavior as an illusion, seek security by whatever means may come to hand. It is interesting to note, as one effect of the fear and disillusionment accompanying such experience, that people, individually and *en masse,* are left especially vulnerable to suggestions of a quite different nature, particularly those with a religious appeal.

Among the collective behavior responses significant for social change are the movements of numbers of people from place to place. While it is true that many such movements have been definitely organized and therefore are not a proper subject for consideration in this discussion, it is even more true that most movements of persons and groups have not been organized, even though their potentialities have been exploited by commercial, governmental, or other interests. Many members of western societies in particular are continuously confronted by conditions that invite, when they do not provoke or compel, mobility. Relatively handy and cheap means of transportation in the presence of situations which are characterized for many by insecurity,

---

17 "The Boom," *Fortune,* Vol. 33, June, 1946, pp. 97, 99. Copyright, *Time,* Inc.

unemployment, broken homes, and similar distracting and discouraging factors, serve to stimulate responses already conditioned by advertising, reading, hearsay, restlessness, and the wanderlust to strike out for parts unknown or to seek one's fortune on the road.

Four types of movement of people interest us in this connection: (1) immigration, (2) rural-urban migration, (3) Negro migration from Southern to Northern industrial centers, and (4) transiency or wandering of individuals and family groups who many times have no destination. That some of the movement in each of these types has been fostered and organized is beside the point; most of it has been undertaken by individuals and small groups as such and on their own initiative, and for reasons best known to themselves. Our interest in these movements concerns their mass character and their effects in terms of cultural transformation, social reorganization, and personal readjustment.

Movement involving change from one cultural setting to another and movement involving a shift from one immediate social situation to another within the same general culture pattern inevitably lead to cultural impacts, comparisons, and contrasts, possibly conflicts and accommodations, and, finally, to a measure of assimilation. Movement in space thus creates new and undefined social situations. If the old-timers and the newcomers in the community do not clash they may face each other, so to speak, without cooperation. Certain opportunities are closed to the invaders, whether temporary or permanent. As a consequence, their participation in the life of the community is limited. Seasonal labor and tenant farm families are notoriously lacking in community attachments and responsibilities and usually take little active part in community affairs. Others who manifest little interest in the place of their temporary residence are tourists, visitors, students, summer or winter boarders, and health seekers. They are in the community, but not of it. However, their presence there is not without its effect. The fact that they are from the outside makes their ways, speech, and dress noticeable and a matter of comment and frequently of emulation. As "strangers" they may enjoy a certain prestige. They may inject new ideas and ways into the local situation so as to challenge the old standards and disturb the continuity of the community's folkways and mores. If they tend to create problems, as they often do, they may also serve as promoters of desirable changes in culture and social organization.

Sometimes the movement of numbers of people is so sudden and precipitous as to be termed a "rush." Frequently a "rush" contributes to a "boom," as in the case of a real-estate development, a gold strike, or some other local situation marked by inflated values, because, as more and more people "rush" to the center of attraction, the demand for scarce commodities mounts and prices rise proportionately until the term "boom" graphically describes the kind of behavior precipitated. In the rush, each individual or family group is drawn by a collective symbol of value, but each seeks his objective in his own way, each tries to get ahead of the other, each has to look out for himself, with the result that there is little feeling of community, cooperation, or loyalty. The forces that make for order and discipline are either non-existent in such a situation or they are largely impotent to meet any crisis. As a result, a rush may easily be transformed into a stampede.

We see in the forms of mass behavior just described the presence of a powerful social contagion, but no shared goal. That is, there is a high susceptibility of the individual to the collective symbol, but each one acts as an individual seeking his own ends. Such behavior may or may not effect lasting change in the mores or in social organization. If severe enough and if repeated often enough in the lifetime of the individual, it may have a permanent effect on personality organization.

There is one more type of mass behavior that needs to be mentioned before we leave this topic: a kind of behavior that has features of the fad, the craze, and the popular mania rolled into one. It has been mistakenly called a "public," as in the instance of the "following" of a celebrity, like a crooner, a baseball player, or a movie star. More often than not, this behavior is eccentric and fanatical, bordering on the hysterical, as witness the following account:

Most of his fans are plain, lonely girls from lower-middle-class homes. They are dazzled by the life Sinatra leads and wish that they could share in it. They insist that they love him, but they do not use the verb in its ordinary sense. As they apply it to him, it is synonymous with "worship" or "idealize."

His fans seemingly will do almost anything he tells them to, and it is fortunate for the rest of the population that he does not have a hankering for, say, arson. Their obedience falters only when he asks them to keep quiet, as he usually does just before a broadcast.

Sinatra fans have a party line, like Communists. Lately they have been preaching self-control. It was once policy to make as much noise as possible, but the older hands now profess to disapprove of squealing unless Frankie does something so wonderful you can't help yourself.

The fans pin club buttons not only over their hearts but also on their socks, and they inscribe his name on sweaters and coats. A girl whose arm he had accidentally brushed while trying to escape from a pack of fans wore a bandage over the spot for two weeks, to prevent anybody else from brushing against it. Another became the envy of her gang, when, after Sinatra had checked out of a hotel room, she got into it before the maids did and escaped with a precious cigarette butt and a half-used packet of matches, both of which she assumed her idol had touched.

One of the few actual cases of coma induced by Sinatra's singing turned out to be simply the result of malnutrition; a young lady had been waiting in line outside a theater all night and then had sat through seven shows without nourishment. Many other girls, however, have obligingly lost consciousness to accommodate photographers.

The most loyal of his fans are those who follow him about whatever city he happens to be in. They usually run in packs of about ten. Lots of these girls, who have been fans of his for two or three years, are now 16 or 17. They consider it poor taste to pester him for autographs, and they rarely try to converse with him, being content merely to stare.

Whenever Sinatra emerges from his hotel and hops into one of the limousines he engages while in town, any girls who are lucky enough to be near a vacant taxi swarm into it and take off after him. Others light out on foot, but they lose track of his car after a block or so. Then breathing heavily, they try to guess where he is eating or—since he almost always goes to the theater after dinner—which of the shows is on his agenda.[18]

BEHAVIOR OF THE PUBLIC

In contrast to the collective-emotional behavior which characterizes crowds and masses, there is the conscious element of rational deliberation in publics. In the latter the individual recognizes that the sentiments and attitudes of others are to some extent at variance with his own. These others do not think and believe as he does. Therefore, the individual in a public is self-conscious in his efforts to conceive a program of group action that considers the interests of others in the collectivity somewhat objectively with his own. Thus the public, unlike the crowd, permits large latitude for the range of individual opinion and expression. If the individual does not sense an underlying relationship between himself and others, he will not participate in public behavior. That is, he will not be in a public and will not have a part in the formulation of a public opinion.

A *public* is formed in the spontaneous interaction of individuals who have a common concern about some specific matter about which they are willing to discuss their differences in a spirit of give and take. The matter uppermost presents an issue for dealing with which there

[18] E. J. Kahn, Jr., *The Voice*, New York, Harper & Bros., 1947, pp. 46-54, 68, 83-84, 121. Based on material that appeared originally in *The New Yorker*.

does not exist an agreed-upon pattern of behavior. Hence the matter must be discussed, either in face-to-face deliberations or through other channels of communication, until the issue is resolved with a degree of consensus. Divergent opinions, through inter-communication in a public, tend to inhibit and modify each other until the matter is thought out more or less dispassionately and a common definition is reached. This shared opinion is termed *public opinion*. The individual's opinions are incorporated, partially if not completely, in the dominant trend of opinion and he acquiesces to this collectively representative judgment with respect to the matter at issue.

Public opinion is just the opinion of individuals plus their differences. There is no public opinion where there is no substantial agreement. But there is no public opinion where there is not disagreement. Public opinion presupposes public discussion. When a matter has reached the stage of public discussion it becomes a matter of public opinion.[19]

It is in the course of discussion, therefore, that the situation is defined by the group—the public—as a whole. Somebody starts the process and it spreads, with more and more interested persons being brought into the interaction, until it may come to pervade large areas and include many people. The following selection will serve to illustrate how a matter of solicitude to a few individuals may become the subject of discussion in small groups and then be extended to other groups in the local community and, finally, from them to the country at large.

When young George Hook and his cousin, Bill Verity, came home from the war to Middletown, Ohio, six months ago, they were troubled by all the ominous talk they heard about the next war. On every side, people seemed to be taking it for granted.

.   .   .   .   .

One night last spring they sat talking in Bill's little white house on the edge of the golf course. Just because the Big Three diplomats couldn't get together, they decided, was no reason why the plain people of the world shouldn't try.

"You and I will have to do something," George said.

Bill agreed. Both men belonged to the local Legion post. The Legion is a power in Middletown; one out of every 11 citizens belongs to it. So at the next meeting the two cousins told their fellow veterans that it was up to them to prevent a third war. Post Commander Hugh Wright appointed a

---

19 R. E. Park, *The Crowd and the Public* (unpublished manuscript), quoted in Park and Burgess, *Introduction to the Science of Sociology*, p. 832.

committee to study the problem of peace or war—not in London, Paris, or Washington, but in little Middletown. It is the kind of committee that can be set up in any of a thousand American towns—the municipal judge, three lawyers, an engineer, two industrial marketers, a lumber dealer, a newspaperman. Bill Verity is its chairman; George Hook and a first-war veteran, Earl Emerson, who lost a son in this war, are its chief spark plugs.

On May 15 Emerson stood before some 400 veterans at a special post meeting. He pointed out the dangers—including atomic bombs—confronting the world and all its Middletowns. We had our choice, he said, between the old methods which had failed so often—balance of power, armament races, military alliances, buffer states—and the new idea of making the United Nations work. U.N. wasn't accomplishing much right now, he admitted, but somehow it must be made to function.

The committee members reached in their own pockets and bought books, haunted the public library, dug into files, read reports. They met nightly and argued over Emery Reves' plan for world government, Einstein's theory for keeping the peace, the Baruch, Lilienthal, Culbertson, and Sumner Welles proposals. They compromised at last on the "Quota Force Plan." This plan recognizes the United Nations, with all its faults, as the best foundation for peace, but it would strengthen the U.N. by adding three amendments to its charter.

These amendments would give smaller nations a larger voice in the Security Council than they now have, without tying the hands of the "Big Three." They would give the Council the power by majority vote to suppress aggression and to limit and control all major weapons everywhere. They would establish a world court to decide whether Council edicts have been violated. They would arm the Council with an international military police powerful enough to enforce its decisions.

When Bill Verity's committee took the plan to the Legion post, the post adopted it unanimously and voted to send it to the state Legion convention for endorsement, hoping to win the support of the Legion's national organization.

"That's fine," said someone, "but we've got to get other organizations interested. Let's tell the whole town about it."

So the plan was explained to luncheon clubs, labor unions, women's organizations, churches, and lodges, and a big meeting was set for the night of July 11.

At eight o'clock on that still, hot evening, every church bell in Middletown began to ring furiously. And the people turned out, rich and poor, black and white, 2000 of them. The Legion hall was packed; 200 citizens stood in the yard and listened through open windows, 200 others crowded the basement to hear the discussion through a loudspeaker. Ely Culbertson, who had been plugging for the Quota Force Plan up and down the land, was there. Congressman E. J. Gardner flew in from Washington. Governor Frank Lausche drove down from Columbus.

The Episcopal rector served as chairman; a Catholic monsignor sat on the platform; a Negro preacher asked the Lord to bless the efforts of the people gathered there. After the veterans had outlined their plan, the meeting was thrown open to questions. Everyone seemed to have something to say, the professor of political science from a nearby university, a taxi driver, the dean of girls at the local high school, a rabbi, a war veteran just back from Germany. The owner of a big manufacturing plant stood shoulder to shoulder with the CIO organizer who had shut his gates, and the two pledged to work with the rest of the town to bring peace to the world.

Verity read a resolution the committee had prepared, urging the U.N. to adopt the Quota Force Plan and supporting the Baruch proposal for safeguarding atomic energy. The gathering roared its approval. After three long hours on the hottest night of the summer the chairman adjourned the meeting. Still the people did not go home. It took another hour for 960 of them to sign the resolution.

Next day the Kiwanis and Rotary clubs, the AFL, and the CIO picked up the torch. Then the local Federation of Women's Clubs, the Veterans of Foreign Wars—23 organizations in all. They sent delegates to their state conventions, still are sending them all over Ohio, working feverishly to secure the adoption by as many people as possible of this scheme to prevent war. The American Legion and the Federation of Labor at their state meetings in August unanimously passed resolutions urging their national conventions to support the plan.

Other midwest cities heard about it and began to fire questions at Bill Verity and George Hook. So committee members from Middletown went to Newark, Monroe, Wilmington, Franklin, and many other Ohio towns, organizing meetings.

Then the larger cities began to take notice: Cincinnati, Dayton, Cleveland, Springfield. Outside the state, Louisville, Ky., has taken up the plan; also Butler, Pa., Des Moines, Iowa, and Indianapolis, Ind. Members of the Legion in Michigan, Kentucky, and Texas are planning "Middletown meetings."

Middletown is convinced that once all American communities hear about it and understand it, this will become a national movement. But they realize that even national solidarity is not enough. They want the people of Great Britain to understand their plan, and the people of France and China and of the South and Central American republics. And above all, the people of Russia—though they haven't figured out yet how to accomplish this last.

The church bells are ringing these fall evenings in cities and towns across the Midwest; people are standing up in meeting and talking from their hearts; plain people have taken into their hands the vexing problem of planning for peace.[20]

---

[20] Karl Detzer, "Middletown vs. World War III," the *Christian Science Monitor, Magazine Section*, October 5, 1946, pp. 3, 19, and as condensed in the *Reader's Digest*, Vol. 49, November, 1946, pp. 50-52. Reprinted by permission of the author, the *Christian Science Monitor*, and the *Reader's Digest*.

The case of Middletown illustrates a relatively elementary form of public behavior. It reminds one of New England town meetings, the mass meetings of political campaigns, or even of the more primary group meetings of folk societies. Under conditions of modern urban life, the process is likely to be more complicated. The group cleavages of society, the great extent of individualization, the high degree of physical and psychic mobility in the population, the importance of group leaders and special pleaders, and the significance of conflicting ideologies, together with the modern agencies of publicity contribute to confuse issues and make the interaction among participants in a public much more involved. At the same time, more people unquestionably are functioning in public behavior. They are doing so in terms of issues of more far-reaching importance than ever before. This means that more people belong to more publics and play a more dynamic role in those publics than at any time in previous history.

The membership of a public is not fixed. Lippmann says on this point:

The public in respect to a railroad strike may be the farmers whom the railroad serves; the public in respect to an agricultural tariff may include the very railroad men who were on strike. The public is not, as I see it, a fixed body of individuals. It is merely those persons who are interested in an affair and can affect it only by supporting or opposing the actors.[21]

It follows, then, that the individual may normally belong to a number of publics. He may be a member of political, religious, scientific, literary, philosophical, occupational, or other publics, possibly simultaneously. Within these circles of influence there are universes of discourse and bodies of belief which enable one individual to understand what another individual means when he expresses his opinion. Sociologically speaking, there is no single or general, all-inclusive public. There are many publics. Which of these an individual will belong to depends on his interest. Each public seeks to make itself articulate and for this purpose employs various means to formulate and disseminate the diverse opinions of the group members and the common opinion of the public as a whole. Thus may a public arrive at and declare its collective opinion.

SOCIETAL BEHAVIOR

Behavior which has to do with a society as such is distinct from that which characterizes a particular collectivity within a society.[22] When behavior, individual or collective, is oriented to well-estab-

---

[21] Walter Lippmann, *The Phantom Public*, p. 77. Copyright, 1925, by Walter Lippmann. Used by permission of The Macmillan Co., publishers.
[22] See Chapter 1 for a treatment of "Society."

lished norms of conduct, to understood situational definitions, and to particular facets of social organization, it can be defined as societal. This type of behavior is distinguishable from the types that have been discussed in the foregoing parts of this chapter. Although he might not agree with our way of classifying such behavior, it seems to us that LaPiere had some such classification of collective behavior in mind in his designations: Institutional, conventional, regimental, formal, exchange, politic, and nomothetic.[23]

Stated in a different context, but for a similar purpose, the following excerpt presents what is here meant by societal behavior:

Reduced to its simplest rudiments, social organization, whatever else it may be, is a system of reciprocal values and usages inherent in a culture which provides the members of society with common attitudes and behavior modes. The simplest element in social organization appears to be a usage-value unit, such as the folkway of shaking hands, observed by all or most members of a group. In their more formal and elaborate aspects, usage-value units become mores, institutions, and ideologies. They serve as a framework on which and within which persons build their common activities. From the viewpoint of society, value-usages are norms which define how a person should act with reference to a social situation. The more or less systematic coordination of these value-usage units with one another and with the culture as a whole enables the members of society to maintain working relations so that joint activities are possible although the participants may be separated in space, time, and function. The common values associated with the usage give it validity, justify it, and enable the group's members to achieve relative consensus. In short, we believe organization and control are inextricable aspects of the process wherein behavior is directed toward groupwise interactional responses so uniform in nature that members of society can predict the responses of their fellows to the situation. The product is the observable order found in every organized group.[24]

In the case of societal behavior, as distinct from other forms of collective behavior, there is a determinate and organized group-structure, which functions as a unit in terms of fairly well adapted means (usages) to relatively well defined ends (values). In such collectivity, the participants are set to conform to the requirements of the given situation, as it gets defined for them in interaction, in terms of the appropriate means to the end sought within the range of their abilities and inclinations and as limited by such differentials as age, sex, race, nationality, and status. The behavior is based on

---

23 LaPiere, *Collective Behavior*, Parts II and IV.
24 A. B. Hollingshead, "The Concept of Social Control," *Am. Sociol. Rev.*, Vol. 6, No. 2, April, 1941, pp. 221-222.

common understandings or traditional norms and shared expectations. Little is left to chance, whim, or impulse. The interaction is brought under institutional pattern.

QUESTIONS

1. How may social change be viewed scientifically?
2. What types of collective phenomena serve as objects of the study of social change? How are they differentiated from each other?
3. Define trends and tendencies. How are they related to social change?
4. What is perhaps the chief function of the more or less ephemeral response tendencies of collectivities of human beings?
5. What is the role of "the situation" in social change?
6. Discuss the respective functions of "common and collective incitement" and "tension" as they enter into social unrest and social contagion.
7. What is the nature of "restlessness" and how may it be accounted for?
8. "The spread of individual restlessness until it becomes a pervasive social unrest is a selective process." Explain.
9. What are the common elements in different definitions of "collective behavior"?
10. Distinguish between collective-emotional behavior and collective-rational behavior.
11. How are the forms and mechanisms of collective behavior related to "the definition of the situation"?
12. Describe and analyze the phenomenon called "milling."
13. Define and explain the functions of the conditions of *rapport, esprit de corps,* and morale.
14. What are some consequences of intensified and prolonged "milling"?
15. Define "the crowd" and characterize "crowd behavior."
16. Classify crowds according to the behavior typically manifested by them.
17. What elements of crowd behavior were manifested in the case of the Nazi crowd described in the text?
18. Discuss the preparation of a crowd for action.
19. Is there significance in the tendency of expressive behavior in the crowd to take on a rhythmic pattern? If so, what is it? What are some of its typical forms of expression?
20. "A crowd in movement is a dynamic force." Illustrate by describing and analyzing the potentialities of the demonstrative crowd.
21. Summarize the common characteristics of spontaneous collective behavior tendencies.
22. How may "the mass" be characterized? In what respects is "the mass" like and in what respects is it unlike the crowd?
23. What are the distinguishing features of fashion, the fad, the craze, the "boom," and the "stampede"?

24. Discuss the significance for social change of "the movements of numbers of people from place to place." What four types of such movement are of interest in this connection?

25. What characterizes "the rush" and what are some of its possible effects?

26. Discuss the phenomenon of "the following" of a celebrity as a form of collective-emotional behavior.

27. Define "the public." In what respects is the role of the individual different in a public from what it is in a crowd?

28. What is public opinion? How is it formed? By whom is it formed —by the few or the many?

29. Discuss: "Under conditions of modern urban life, the process (of public opinion formation) is likely to be complicated."

30. Explain: "Sociologically speaking, there is no single or general, all-inclusive public. Rather are there many publics."

31. What is the meaning of "societal behavior"?

32. In what respects does societal behavior differ from other forms of collective behavior?

BIBLIOGRAPHY

ALBIG, WILLIAM. *Public Opinion.* New York, McGraw-Hill Book Co., Inc., 1939, Chs. 1-7.

BELOFF, MAX. *Public Order and Popular Disturbances, 1660-1714.* New York, Oxford University Press, 1938.

BERNARD, JESSIE. "Normative Collective Behavior: A Classification of Societal Norms." *Am. J. Sociol.,* Vol. 47, No. 1, July, 1941, pp. 24-38.

BERNARD, L. L. *Introduction to Social Psychology.* New York, Henry Holt & Co., 1926, Parts II and IV.

BIRD, GEORGE L., AND MERWIN, FREDERIC E. *The Newspaper and Society.* A Book of Readings. New York, Prentice-Hall, Inc., 1942, Ch. 1, "Concepts of Public Opinion."

BLUMER, HERBERT, in A. M. Lee, *New Outline of the Principles of Sociology.* New York, Barnes & Noble, Inc., 1946, Chs. 19-21, 23.

CANTRIL, HADLEY. *The Invasion from Mars: A Study in the Psychology of Panic,* with the complete script of the famous Orson Welles broadcast. Princeton, Princeton University Press, 1940.

CASTIGLIONI, ARTURO, M.D. *Adventures of the Mind.* New York, Alfred A. Knopf, 1946.

DOOB, LEONARD W. *Public Opinion and Propaganda.* New York, Henry Holt & Co., Chs. 1-10.

DURKHEIM, EMILE. *Elementary Forms of Religious Life.* Translated by Joseph W. Swain. New York, The Macmillan Co., 1915; Glencoe, Ill., The Free Press, 1947.

GREENWOOD, M. *Epidemics and Crowd Epidemics.* London, Williams & Norgate, 1935.

HAWES, ELIZABETH. *Fashion is Spinach.* New York, Random House, 1938.

HECKER, J. F. C. *Black Death: Account of the Great Pestilence of the Fourteenth Century.* New York, Cassell & Co., 1888.

HECKER, J. F. C. *Dancing Mania of the Middle Ages.* New York, J. Fitzgerald & Co., 1885.

HOCKING, WILLIAM E. *Morale and Its Enemies.* New Haven, Yale University Press, 1918.

HOLLINGSWORTH, H. L. *The Psychology of the Audience.* New York, American Book Co., 1935.

HOOK, SIDNEY. *The Hero in History.* New York, John Day Co., 1943.

JOHNSON, GERALD W. *American Heroes and Hero Worship.* New York, Harper & Bros., 1943.

KELLETT, E. E. *Fashion in Literature, A Study in Changing Taste.* London, Routledge, 1931.

LAPIERE, RICHARD T. *Collective Behavior.* New York, McGraw-Hill Book Co., Inc., 1938.

LEBON, GUSTAVE. *The Crowd—A Study of the Popular Mind.* London, T. F. Unwin, 1903, 1920.

LEDERER, EMIL. *State of the Masses: The Threat of the Classless Society.* New York, W. W. Norton & Co., 1940.

LEE, ALFRED McCLUNG. "Social Determinants of Public Opinion." *Int. J. Opinion and Attitude Res.,* Vol. 1, pp. 12-29.

LIPPMANN, WALTER. *The Phantom Public.* New York, Harcourt, Brace & Co., 1925.

LIPPMANN, WALTER. *Public Opinion.* New York, Harcourt, Brace & Co., 1922.

LUNDBERG, GEORGE A. "Public Opinion from a Behavioristic Viewpoint." *Am. J. Sociol.,* Vol. 36, No. 3, November, 1930, pp. 387-405.

MACKAY, CHARLES. *Extraordinary Popular Delusions and the Madness of Crowds.* Boston, L. C. Page & Co., 1932. A reprint of the 1852 edition.

MARTIN, EVERETT D. *The Behavior of Crowds.* New York, Harper & Bros., 1920.

MELVILLE, LEWIS. *The South Sea Bubble.* Boston, Small, Maynard & Co., 1923.

MERTON, ROBERT K. *Mass Persuasion: The Social Psychology of a War Bond Drive.* New York, Harper & Bros., 1946.

"Morale." *Am. J. Sociol.,* Vol. 47, No. 3, November, 1941. All articles deal with the subject of "Morale."

MORRELL, W. P. *The Gold Rushes.* New York, The Macmillan Co., 1941.

NORDHOFF, C. B., AND HALL, J. N. *Mutiny on the Bounty.* Boston, Little, Brown & Co., 1932. A fictionized version of a mutiny on a British ship in the 18th century.

PARK, ROBERT E. "Collective Behavior." *Encycl. of the Social Sciences,* Vol. 3, pp. 631-633.

PARK, ROBERT E. "Human Nature and Collective Behavior." *Am. J. Sociol.,* Vol. 32, No. 5, March, 1927, pp. 733-741.

REICH, WILHELM. *The Mass Psychology of Fascism.* Translated by Theodore F. Wolfe. New York, The Orgone Institute Press, 1946.

REUTER, EDWARD B., AND HART, C. W. *Introduction to Sociology.* New York, McGraw-Hill Book Co., Inc., 1933, Chs. 17-18.

RIEGEL, O. W. *Mobilizing for Chaos: The Story of the New Propaganda.* New Haven, Yale University Press, 1934.

ROSS, EDWARD A. *Social Psychology.* New York, The Macmillan Co., 1915, Chs. 2-6.

SAPIR, EDWARD. "Fashion." *Encycl. of the Social Sciences,* Vol. 6, pp. 139-144.

SIDIS, BORIS. *The Psychology of Suggestion.* New York, D. Appleton & Co., 1898.

SMITH, CHARLES W., JR. *Public Opinion in a Democracy.* New York, Prentice-Hall, Inc., 1939.

STEINER, LEE R. *Where Do People Take Their Troubles?* Boston, Houghton Mifflin Co., 1945.

TARDE, GABRIEL. *Laws of Imitation.* Translated by Elsie Clews Parsons from the 2nd French ed., 1895. New York, Henry Holt & Co., 1903. Especially Ch. 7, "Custom and Fashion."

THORP, W. L. "Speculative Bubbles." *Encycl. of the Social Sciences,* Vol. 3, pp. 24-26.

VAUGHT, E. "Release and Heightening of Individual Reactions in Crowds." *J. Abnorm. Soc. Psychol.,* Vol. 22, 1928, pp. 404-405.

VERRILL, A. *The Inquisition.* New York, D. Appleton & Co., 1932.

WALKER, STANLEY. *Mrs. Astor's Horse.* New York, Frederick Stokes Co., 1936. Includes material on fads and crazes.

YOUNG, KIMBALL. *Social Psychology.* New York, Alfred A. Knopf, 1930, Part V, "The Crowd and the Public."

YOUNG, KIMBALL. *Source Book for Social Psychology.* New York, Alfred A. Knopf, 1927, Part VI, "Collective Behavior."

Chapter 24

MECHANISMS OF SOCIAL ORDER AND CHANGE: SOCIAL CONTROL

———

The Meaning of Social Control

The last three chapters have discussed various factors that together and in interaction are effective in hindering or in facilitating social change. There was also presented the problem of maintaining a social order in conformity with, and sometimes in spite of, social change. It shall be our purpose in this chapter to consider the processes, means, and agencies through which order and social change are effected.

In the whirlpool of modern civilization men strive to keep from being engulfed by rapid change. Some fight, many work, a few play, some govern; but most things needful cannot be realized except through the pursuit of united aims. Status can be maintained only in the preservation of acceptable relationships with those who are like and those who are unlike ourselves. Out of the interplay of divergent forces emerges a common definition of the situation, a common meaning as a basis of social order. Since the social order presents itself as a system of social relations in which individuals and groups, at once similar and diverse, function in pursuit of their several ends, but nevertheless maintain a competitive equilibrium, it is important to see and understand how the balance, or order, is sustained with some degree of stability and, at the same time, is responsive to change. This is held by some to be the central problem of sociology. This is the reason for social control.

A person is everywhere and at all times at the mercy of the socially defining environment. Every act must have a definition; every definition means the affirmation of an existing social value or the creation of a new social value.

Preliminary to any self-determined act of behavior there is always a stage of examination and deliberation which we may call *the definition of the situation*. And actually not only concrete acts are dependent on the definition of the situation, but gradually a whole life-policy and the personality of the individual himself follow from a series of such definitions.

But the child is always born into a group of people among whom all the general types of situations which may arise have already been defined and corresponding rules of conduct developed, and where he has not the slightest chance of making his definitions and following his wishes without interference. Men have always lived together in groups. Whether mankind has a true herd instinct or whether groups are held together because this has worked out to advantage is of no importance. Certainly the wishes in general are such that they can be satisfied only in a society. But we have only to refer to the criminal code to appreciate the variety of ways in which the wishes of the individual may conflict with the wishes of society. And the criminal code takes no account of the many unsanctioned expressions of the wishes which society attempts to regulate by persuasion and gossip.

There is therefore always a rivalry between the spontaneous definitions of the situation made by the member of an organized society and the definitions which his society has provided for him. The individual tends to a hedonistic selection of activity, pleasure first; and society to a utilitarian selection, safety first. Society wishes its member to be laborious, dependable, regular, sober, orderly, self-sacrificing; while the individual wishes less of this and more of new experience. And organized society seeks also to regulate the conflict and competition inevitable between its members in the pursuit of their wishes. The desire to have wealth, for example, or any other socially sanctioned wish, may not be accomplished at the expense of another member of the society—by murder, theft, lying, blackmail, etc.

It is in this connection that a moral code arises, which is a set of rules or behavior norms, regulating the expression of the wishes, and which is built up by successive definitions of the situation. In practice the abuse arises first and the rule is made to prevent its recurrence. Morality is thus the generally accepted definition of the situation, whether expressed in public opinion and the unwritten law, in a formal legal code, or in religious commandments and prohibitions.[1]

Social control does not necessarily imply a deliberate and purposeful coercion on the part of the group; the mere fact that human beings live in groups is in itself evidence of the presence of an interacting process which makes for a regulation of conduct. The great problem of social life is how to bring A and B together for the purpose of securing cooperative action in those situations that require it. As has been stated before, those traits and qualities that we know as distinctly human are acquired through social living. By no process of the imagination can it be demonstrated that individuals come into possession of socially significant meanings or behavior patterns through the magic of some natural intuition or inner urge.

[1] William I. Thomas, *The Unadjusted Girl*, Boston, Little, Brown & Co., 1924, pp. 42-43.

Another way of viewing the problem confronting society, namely, how to get individuals to act corporately and harmoniously, would be to consider that they have never been really apart in a sociological sense. Each is a part of a whole. The child is a part of the father's body and of the mother's body, of the father's nature and of the mother's nature, of the father's life and of the mother's life. Moreover, the child is a part of the family, the play group, the neighborhood, the Sunday School class, the community. So with the adult. He is a part of the crowd, the party, the lodge, the committee, the church, and so on. No crowd ever feels; the individuals in the crowd feel. No committee ever thinks; the individual members of the committee think. And yet when we say that, we leave room for the idea that no individual thinks, feels, or acts without the assistance of others in his group. No one person can do a social act. One person cannot build a ship, organize a bank, run an industry, win a war, play football, and the like. One person may start a social act; someone else must help finish it. The socially functioning individual is merely a part of a social totality. In every instance, before there can be unity of purpose and cooperative behavior, there must be understanding which involves the process of defining and redefining, creating and re-creating, social values. This is a major function of social control.

As Thomas says in the above selection, the child is born into a situation in which there are ready-made definitions for all the ordinary affairs of everyday life. These definitions are in the folkways and mores of all groups that have a history and a tradition and they are inculcated in the thinking and behavior habits of the group members. New circumstances and changed conditions call for new definitions. Social control signifies the social definition of the wishes of the individual and their incorporation in the common attitudes and objectives of the group.

IMPLICIT SOCIAL CONTROL

Ideas come to the child with all the force of infallibility; they are taken over uncritically from the group. At first, all the ideas or definitions we get come in this way.

The family is the smallest social unit and the primary defining agency. As soon as the child has free motion and begins to pull, tear, pry, meddle, and prowl, the parents begin to define the situation through speech and other signs and pressures. "Be quiet," "Sit up straight," "Blow your nose," "Wash your face," "Mind your mother," "Be kind to sister," etc. This is the real significance of Wordsworth's phrase, "Shades of the prison house begin to close upon the growing child." His wishes and activities begin to be inhibited, and gradually, by definitions within the family, by playmates, in the school, in the Sunday School, in the community, through reading, by formal instruction, by informal signs of approval and disapproval, the growing member learns the code of his society.[2]

Much the same thing is true of all simple, face-to-face groups. Therein the members find the meanings of most of their activities. In addition to the family, the small, compact neighborhood and the larger, inclusive community are defining agencies. At least such is their function in simple and homogeneous societies. With us their power for regulating human behavior has been greatly diminished, a fact which has given rise to more formal agencies for control. However, by far the greater part of social defining goes on in the informal, primary-group relationships and the members of the groups continue to take over more or less implicitly these social definitions and to be guided by them. The types and mechanisms of such implicit controls will be reviewed in the following sections.

Control in the Crowd.—Man's motor and vocal mechanisms for the communication of experiences make possible collective action and the accomplishment of common aims. Normally men and women are mobile creatures moving from group to group and from place to place, and each contributing a variety of experiences. These experiences, transformed in the process of communication, do not remain subjective. They are brought under symbols of common meaning. In short, experiences are communicated and, in their interaction with each other, get developed and organized immediately in certain directions. This conceptualization of experience is to be observed in such informal groups as the crowd and the public.

In the preceding chapter we discussed how, by a process of circular interaction called "milling," the crowd is formed and psychologically organized into a unity and prepared for expressive emotional behavior or forms of concerted action. It is now our purpose to describe how the crowd may become a force for control. In order to do this the following selection is inserted to furnish a point of departure for discussion:

A short time ago, while I was principal of a little backwoods high school and a participant-observer in a small town on the Mississippi Delta, I was

---

2 *Ibid.*, p. 43.

caught up in one of the greatest social events ever to befall our little Negro community.

Lo and behold! "Sister President," mother of the church, had died when "she was just getting ready for the annual convention of the missionary society at Jackson." Word-of-mouth reported that she had died one year, one month, and one day later than her husband, "Reverend President," the greatest preacher ever to have circulated in those parts. Rumor had it that a good neighbor upon hearing of Sister President's death immediately fell dead herself.

The staunch church members quickly proceeded with the arrangements for the funeral. Circulars in the form of handbills were printed and distributed throughout the communities of the county, announcing the time of the funeral and the prominent personages to appear on the program. Reverend H— was to officiate, and a prominent singer was to come all the way from Rosedale, a distance of ninety miles, to sing "over" Sister President one of her favorite songs—"Life Is Uncertain, but Death Is Sure."

The day of the funeral finally came. Very few of the persons (if any) went to work that morning and some had driven scores of miles to be present. St. Andrew's Church could not accommodate everyone interested, so as a consequence hundreds of persons were milling around the sides and front of the building.

At about eleven o'clock, shortly after services had begun, the frame walls of the church started to crack under the immense strain of the large numbers within, so someone had the idea of finishing the services at the school.

Shortly I saw great numbers of persons "swarming" over to my institution. Fowls and pigs that heretofore had been walking complacently in the roadway now fluttered, cackled, and bolted in various directions, adding to the confusion. I rushed out to contact the minister or whomever I could to ascertain what was happening, but I was immediately pushed aside. Pretty soon I saw a dozen or more persons running with a casket in the direction of the building. Someone finally told me in a wild-eyed fashion that—"the church is fallin' down—dey gonna finish havin' it at the school."

I rushed back indoors to attempt to dismiss the children, but saw them already scampering in all directions. One of my teachers (a refined, quiet, modest little lady, if ever there was one) jumped out of the classroom window. Children were trampled upon and "shooed" out. Some were crying, others were laughing, and had gone into the auditorium along with the crowd.

After approximately one half hour, the seats were arranged. Additional benches had been brought over from the church and had been placed around the walls. One of the ministers was complaining miserably about his pocketbook containing one hundred dollars that had been stolen as the crowd rushed from the church to the school.

The services got under way again. Eight or ten ministers were seated on the platform together with the combined church choirs. Seated down front were the members of the various mystic burial orders to which Sister President had belonged. Two groups that I recall were the Knights and Daughters of Tabor, and the members of the Order of the Beautiful Star. The Knights carried in their hands cardboard swords, and the members of the Beautiful Star were dressed in white robes having on their heads paper crowns on which were pasted silver stars. They had all filed in ceremoniously and had been allowed to be seated—the crowd being held back. When they had taken their seats the people rushed in and sat on whatever was available. Some of the persons were sitting two and three to a seat, on one another's laps. Others sat on the window ledges and still others reclined against the walls.

The "rattling" of feet began, and as the ministers delivered their sermons various members of the audience would give shrill screams and fall prostrated. Responsive ushers would place these persons out on the lawn and a relative or friend would burn chicken feathers, placing the fumes to the noses of the victims to revive them. (The feathers had been brought along especially for this purpose.)

The eminent singer from Rosedale, an elderly gentleman, was late in arriving and was unable to force his way through the crowd to the platform. News of his presence finally got to the stage and one of the preachers stated that—"if the good brother from Rosedale will go 'round to the side, we might kin get him in through the window." This he did. He was able to sing Sister President's selection.

Occasionally a choir member would get so enraptured through the rendering of a song that she too would be overcome and would have to be carried outside. The pianist cried sadly throughout the services and from time to time she would look mournfully out to the audience, resting her chin downwards on one shoulder. Some of the persons were not quite "out" when they yelled and resisted attempts to remove them. With wild swinging of the arms and with cries of "unloose me," "unloose me," they struggled against anyone attempting to take hold of them. In instances like these the more muscular ushers would "grapple" with the victims and would secure "arm locks" on them, holding them taut until they were subdued.

Finally, the great Reverend H— who had reserved last place on the program for himself, gave his sermon. He started off very piously and soberly, talking of Sister President's wonderful spirit, her achievements, and her general love of humanity. With consistent "egging" from the ministers on the platform and with cries of "come on, come on," Reverend H— too entered into the spirit of the occasion. He snarled, gnashed his teeth (displaying a set of bright yellow gold), gurgled, growled, and gasped, apparently losing control of himself at intervals. Dramatically and with appropriate gestures he likened Sister President to a "great soldier":

> "An' standin' therefo having her loins girt with truth—and havin' on the breas'plate of righteousness. And her feet shod wid the preparation of the gospel of peace—and above all—'bove all—takin' the

shield of faith, and the helmet of salvation and the sword of the spirit, which is the word of God."

This last part of the sermon was repeated over and over again for increased emphasis. One lady sang out from the back of the audience in a high shrill soprano voice—"It's early in the evenin'—and my soul is getting tired." Others remarked, "Well" and "Lord" at heightened intervals. (Words can scarcely express the tension that pervaded the room.)

The audience "rattled" their feet, clapped their hands, and cried out "Amen! Amen!" With much mopping of his brow, Reverend H— (with his coat now hanging partly off) was pulled back to his chair by some of the other ministers, some of whom shook his hands and others of whom patted him on his back. At this time the choir started up a chant of the "Old Ship of Zion." With the first verses being sung, at least a score of persons screamed and cast their arms into the air—"Have mercy, Lord." With each successive verse an increasing number joined in. When they proceeded to the words, "it has landed my dear mother," bedlam broke loose. Some of the people danced if they could find any space, patting themselves on the legs while skipping sidewise, some caressed their neighbors, others slapped someone, and still others were content to just "give out" with piercing yells. This continued for at least twenty minutes, finally coming to an end with grunts and a dwindling of the "rattling" of feet.

The announcement was given that the audience could now "view the remains." As the persons passed the coffin some said "Goodbye, Sister President—I'll be seeing you soon." Others just wept, drying their eyes with one hand, while finishing a sandwich with the other, as food had been brought along. It was well after three o'clock when the "viewing" was over.

When they attempted to inter the remains of Sister President, several persons had to be withheld from jumping into the grave. One person succeeded, and had to be helped out of the excavation.

After the tires that had gone flat were fixed, the mules hitched to the wagons, and the drunken persons "gathered" up, they all made the long trek back home to talk for months about the "time" they had had, and to await with patience the next great occasion.[3]

In the case cited above a collectivity of bereaved and curious individuals were galvanized into an organized crowd under the not wholly spontaneous but rather more conventionalized, ritualistic circumstances. Here one sees how the behavior of group members is facilitated, how the suggestibility of each one is enhanced by the focusing of attention and by the direction of responses by the leaders and by the emergence of a mood that comes to dominate the situation.

---

[3] Joseph H. Douglass, "The Funeral of 'Sister President'," *J. Abnorm. Soc. Psychol.*, Vol. 39, No. 2, April, 1944, pp. 217-220.

Our original impulses get fixed in habit. But habit and impulse do not have a rigid fixation. There are always loose ends to be caught by transitory stimuli. Vagrant impulses slop over old habits. Habits are continually breaking down under the exigencies of conduct, and impulses are thus released to indiscriminate behavior. This mobility of impulse is the key to readjustment and freshness in experience. It is in just this increase of vagrant impulses and the breaking down of customary habits by which control over the environment is maintained that a soil is prepared for crowd behavior.[4]

The persons at "Sister President's" funeral were grieved and depressed. The release which such tensions have to get comes in the collective emotional excitement of the crowd. In the heightened state of rapport, in the mutual responsiveness of the individual members, the person loses self-control. The inhibited sentiments and emotions, which ordinarily control behavior, are lifted and assimilated to those of others in the process of interaction. It is in this circular interaction that a collective impulse is formed which dominates all members of the crowd. Experiences are communicated by subtle as well as by more overt motor dispositions and a common aim is developed spontaneously in the process. It is this complex condition of rapport, the contagious excitement and heightened suggestibility associated with it, the focus of attention, and the impromptu formulation of a common definition and aim, that afford the peculiar unlimited control of the crowd over the individual members.

In describing control in the crowd, Ross says:

Of all the controls that impinge upon the individual that of the crowd is the most aimless, arbitrary, and capricious. The crowd stands for the common man in his most unreasonable mood, and hence its rule is marked by impatience of contradiction, contempt for individual rights, and destruction of personal freedom.[5]

Thus we see that control in the crowd is most elementary, spontaneous, and, by reason of its nature and the circumstances producing it, credulous, irrational, and ephemeral. Once the forces producing the crowd are set in motion and after a certain point in its organization has been reached, it is practically impossible for the individuals to turn back. Their every move is forced by some compelling process outside themselves and their course of action is fatally determined until the final issue.

---

[4] C. A. Dawson, in an unpublished manuscript.
[5] E. A. Ross, *Social Control*, p. 72. Copyright, 1901, by The Macmillan Co., and used with their permission.

In the discussion of war it was suggested that the public, discursive and self-conscious, may be easily converted into the expectant crowd, restless and disturbed by propaganda and agitation, until some sudden crisis precipitates the crowd into action.   The strike, the clash of racial groups, the strife of intra-group and inter-group politics, and the controversies of sects and other dissident groups, are characterized by this peculiar factor in collective behavior. Despite the quotation from Ross, heroic deeds may emerge in crowd behavior. Under the spell of crowd interstimulation the members may be carried to heights of magnanimous service and unselfish sacrifice unthinkable in their individual capacities. Either trend in behavior is possible because in the crowd the symbols of common meaning are elastic and inexact and these allow experiences to coalesce spontaneously. There are no recognized norms because the distinction between the individual and the group has momentarily disappeared. Consequently, it is easy for the sentiments to be fused in any common aim which may chance to be thrust suddenly into the situation. Thus does the crowd dominate the individuals who constitute it.

Folkways and Mores.—Folkways and mores have been defined in earlier chapters. Certain additional observations will be made here concerning them. Sumner points out that "the life of Society consists in making folkways and applying them." [6]   In other words, folkways are coming into existence all the time although they are not intended, planned, or understood in advance. Moreover, it is in the process of making folkways and defining the mores that elementary social phenomena arise. The folkways and mores thus created through social interaction become fixed in the sentiments and attitudes of the group as "true" and "right."   They come to have the authority and prestige of tradition, and constitute a basis of ethnocentrism and societal selection. The folkways, being the customary and traditional ways of a group, become, like the habits of the individual, practically second nature, and are passed down from generation to generation in custom and tradition, and from individual to individual and from group to group among contemporaries. The hold of the folkways upon a people is well illustrated in the following:

"Each individual in India is a slave to the customs of the group to which he belongs. . . . The council of village elders does not command anything; it merely declares what has always been. Nor does it generally declare that which it believes some higher power to have commanded; those most entitled to speak on the subject deny that the natives of India necessarily require

---

[6] W. G. Sumner, *Folkways*, Boston, Ginn & Co., 1906, p. 34.

divine or political authority as the basis of their usages; their antiquity is by itself assumed to be a sufficient reason for obeying them." But "The body of persons to whose memory the customs are committed has always added to the stock of usage by tacitly inventing new rules to apply to cases which are really new."

Now, apropos "of the invention of customary rules to meet cases which are really new" by the council of elders of the Hindoo village, Maine says: "It is always the fact or the fiction that this council merely declares customary law." For instance, the water supplied to village communities by government irrigation canals is distributed according to rules which "do not purport to emanate from the personal authority of their author or authors; nor do they assume to be dictated by a sense of equity: there is always, I am assured, a sort of fiction, under which some customs as to the distribution of water are supposed to have existed from all antiquity, although in fact no artificial supply had been even so much as thought of." [7]

The "law" of the free Anglo-Saxon people was regarded as a thing existing in itself, like the sunlight, or at least existing like a universally accepted custom observed by everyone. It was five hundred years before the notion crept into the minds even of the members of the British Parliaments, that they could make *new* law. What they supposed they did, and what they were understood by the people to do, was merely to declare the law, as it was then and as it had been from time immemorial; the notion always being —and the farther back you go and the more simple the people are, the more they have that notion—that their free laws and customs were something which came from the beginning of the world, which they always held, which were immutable, no more to be changed than the forces of nature; . . . the Parliament never did anything but tell what the law was; and, as I have said, not only what it was then but what it had been, as they supposed, for thousands of years before. The notion of a legislature to make *new* laws is an entirely modern conception of Parliament. . . .

It probably would have surprised the early Englishman if he had been told that either he or anybody else didn't *know* the law—still more that there was ever any need for any Parliament or assembly to tell him what it was. They all knew the law, and they all knew that they knew the law, and the law was a thing that they knew as naturally as they knew fishing and hunting. They had grown up into it. It never occurred to them as an outside thing. [8]

In both cases cited we see the subtle working of the group customs upon the group members. All accept and obey them as if there were no other possible behavior. They are sanctioned by the attitudes

---

[7] E. A. Ross, *Social Control*, pp. 185-186, quoting Sir Henry Maine, *Village Communities in the East*, London, 1895, pp. 13, 68, 75, 110, 116. Copyright, 1901, by The Macmillan Co., New York, and used with their permission.

[8] Frederic J. Stimson, *Popular Law Making*, New York, Charles Scribner's Sons, 1912, pp. 2-4.

of the group and by the social disapproval which follows infractions of them. Group interests overrule individual interests in their development and application. In the folkways and mores there is an implicit "conception and rule of action, which is regarded as right and proper in the circumstances." [9]

Among people living under a simple culture pattern, all the exigencies of life are pervaded and controlled by folkways and mores. Before men began to reflect and to bring reasoned judgment to bear on collective and individual thought and action, they were almost completely regulated by the ways unconsciously begun and pursued by the group. Even in our more sophisticated and rational social world, the established and recognized attitudes of the group or groups to which the individual belongs are reflected in his subconscious mind and constitute an inner control over his conduct.

The folkways and mores, then, comprise important and specific forces for the conditioning of human nature and for the construction of social order.

As has been stated in previous chapters, it is largely by means of the operation of such factors as the folkways and mores upon the plastic original nature of man that native impulses and tendencies are moulded into character. It is through the folkways and mores also that organized human nature is transmitted. In this sense, the folkways and mores include social ritual, ethical judgments, and convention. Social ritual prescribes that certain acts be done in specified ways, as in etiquette, perfunctory duties, and approach to the divinity. Ritual has the value of enforcing precision, of enjoining strict compliance to rule, and of disallowing irregularity or exception. Convention takes account of inexpediencies and inconsistencies in the traditional folkways and gives approval to certain modifications of them, or may set up conditions under which a thing may be tolerated that otherwise would be objectionable. By means of conventionalization, the scanty attire worn at the bathing beach, in the ballroom, or on the stage may pass as decent. Scientific literature and pictures may escape the censor, and the artist may portray the nude without giving offense. In many areas of social life convention operates to sanction variations from current usage.

Closely related to the above is the accumulation of common memories, which is known as tradition. We have already noted how the folkways and mores tend to be traditional, that is, carried along in the sentiments, memories, and rationalizations of the group, from

---

[9] R. E. Park and E. W. Burgess, *Introduction to the Science of Sociology*, Chicago, University of Chicago Press, 1921, p. 799.

generation to generation. Thus certain ways of believing and acting tend to become enshrouded in a bundle of sentiments which get crystallized and thus persist in tradition. Tradition is preserved not merely by being deposited in the minds of the group members, but by inhibiting other memories, by connecting up with natural predispositions, and by working into the web of personality and group organization. It is largely tradition that determines the concentration of individuals into groups other than crowds and it is tradition that intensifies their adherence. The disciplined soldier depends upon the banner (traditional symbol) and the leader (the bearer of military traditions). It is in the intimate circle—the home, the sect, the neighborhood—that traditional ideals are nourished and it is here that social solidarity begins. Tradition, by means of which the folkways are transmitted from generation to generation, constitutes one of the important mechanisms of social heredity and control.

In the traditional forms of society—the family, the tribe, the state, the caste, and the class—tradition predisposes the individuals in the group to a similarity of behavior and thought. Such groups pay homage to specific customs, ceremonies, rites, and beliefs, all of which social factors rest on similarity of function and likeness of tradition.

Units of the same cult or institution—church, lodge, political party, labor union, neighborhood—have inclinations toward certain ways of thinking that make them easily consociated. They react to the same ideas, concepts, and beliefs. They do things according to the same ritual and ceremony. Their emotions can be reached by the same objects and in the same sequence. They notice and ignore the same sights and sounds. Their foreground processes wear a common aspect. Any social factor that tends to unite a human group in everyday life makes of it an especially homogeneous audience and also impresses upon its members a fixed disposition toward subsequent union.[10]

The more significant of the social factors so conditioning behavior are the folkways and mores, and the traditions which give them continuity.

Ceremonial.—Herbert Spencer was the first to point out the importance of ceremonial as a mechanism of control. He declared that "the earliest kind of government, the most general kind of government, and the government which is ever spontaneously recommencing,

---

[10] C. H. Woolbert, "The Audience," in "Studies in Social and General Psychology," M. Bentley (Ed.), *Psychological Monographs*, 1916, Vol. 21, No. 92, p. 41.

is the government of ceremonial observances." [11] Accordingly, it
may be said that ceremonial is the most fundamental kind of government or control. Perhaps the most primitive form of ceremonial is
the dance, not the modern sophisticated dance which "presents itself
to us in every respect as a vestigial organ which has become useless
in consequence of changed conditions of life, and has therefore de-
generated," [12] but the mimetic and gymnastic dances of primitive
tribesmen.

The war dance is one of the most characteristic mimetic dances
of primitive men and one of the most important. In it the emotions
express themselves spontaneously, thus creating *esprit de corps.*

Subjects for mimetic dances are afforded by the two most important events
of human life—love and the battle. Mundy describes a mimic war dance
which he saw in New South Wales. The dancers performed first a series
of complicated and wild movements in which clubs, spears, boomerangs, and
shields were brandished. Then "all at once the mass divided into groups,
and with deafening shrieks and passionate cries they sprang upon one another in hand-to-hand fight. One side was speedily driven out of the field
and pursued into the darkness, whence howls, groans, and the strokes of
clubs could be heard, producing the perfect illusion of a terrible massacre.
Suddenly the whole troupe again came up close to the fire, and having
arranged themselves in two ranks, the time of the music was changed. The
dancers moved in slower rhythm, accompanying every step with stamping
and a grunting sound. Gradually the drum beats and the movements became
more rapid till they attained as nearly a lightning-like velocity as the human
body can reach. Sometimes the dancers all sprang into the air to a surprising
height, and when they struck the ground again the calves of their widely
spreading legs trembled so violently that the stripes of white clay looked
like wriggling snakes, and a loud hissing filled the air." The love dances
of the Australians are passed over in most of the accounts with a few suggestive references. They are hardly suitable for exhaustive descriptions.
"I have seen dances," writes Hodkinson, "which consist of the most repulsive of obscene motions that one can imagine, and, although I was alone in
the darkness, and nobody observed my presence, I was ashamed to be a witness of such abomination." [13]

The rites by which a young man is transferred from a matricentric
to a patricentric group, or from youth to manhood are often accompanied by ceremonial observances by means of which the initiate
is instructed in the secrets of the tribe, and taught habits of self-

---

[11] Herbert Spencer, *Principles of Sociology,* 3rd ed., London, Williams & Norgate, Ltd.,
1906, Vol. II, p. 3.
[12] Ernst Grosse, *The Beginnings of Art,* New York, D. Appleton & Co., 1897, p. 231.
By permission of Appleton-Century-Crofts, Inc., owners of the copyright.
[13] *Ibid.,* p. 585.

restraint and hardihood. Primitive peoples make great use of subtle psychological means of control, including the rites and ceremonies which exercise control not only over their own spiritual natures but also, so they think, over the spirits they believe to be surrounding them and influencing them. They employ charms, magic, and ceremony a great deal more than we do because they live in a less understood and humanly controlled world. But the role of ceremonial is not confined to stirring the imagination, exciting the awe, and concerting the behavior of primitive men. Its impressive function pervades many of the important acts of our self-conscious, intelligent society.

Ceremonial derives its force for control from the fact that it is both a mode of group expression and a type of collective representation. The nature of ceremonial control is such that it does not necessarily determine the attitudes and sentiments but it does prescribe specific acts. Shaking hands, or any act of courtesy, does not reveal the attitudes of persons when they come in contact, but it does automatically determine their actions. The costume of the judge, the kissing of the Bible, and the repeating of certain time-worn phrases are a means of stimulating and maintaining the proper attitude. Moreover, ceremonial control, unlike crowd control, has a backward reference because it alludes to the past experiences of the group. It revives the memory of earlier group action and mobilizes the emotional background of the group. It impresses by its solemnity and stirs the imagination by its symbolism. In a rationalistic age, primitive ceremony is losing its grip, and is being replaced by ceremonial of a more sophisticated kind.

Taboo.—Sumner, in discussing the "rightness" of the folkways, says that "the ways are defined on the negative side by taboos." [14] In other words, acts that are punishable under the mores are taboo, or prohibited. Growing up within the mores and defining certain acts as being contrary to the mores, taboos represent the extreme fixation of attitudes on the negative side. The behavior of the individual tends to follow these predetermined lines of group control. Departure from the prescribed behavior patterns is positively prohibited and any deviation in behavior that goes counter to the taboo is stoutly resisted and is accompanied by intense emotional disturbance.

Present-day folkways of so-called modern cultural groups are not without their restrictive taboos. "Thou shalt nots," both implied and expressed, are everywhere to be found as the guardians of the mores,

---

[14] Sumner, *Folkways*, p. 28.

and the individual is inclined to accept them uncritically. However, it is possible for the individual, living in the highly mobile societies of today, to leave a group if he does not like it and seek status in some other group where the inhibitions are less irksome. Because one is limited to a closed group in primitive societies, attitudes tend to be fixed and the taboos rigid and powerful, resulting in stereotyped behavior.

Primitive ceremonies of initiation take on a variety of forms but, without exception, all impose certain restrictions upon the initiates. The following example will serve to illustrate the form taken by the taboos:

The rule is that during the period of probation the novice is absolutely prohibited from holding any communication with a woman, even his own mother. He must not even look at one, and this prohibition extends to the emu, for the emu is Ngalalbal, the mother of *Daramulun.*

The food restrictions in connection with these ceremonies are that the *Gumbang-ira* (raw-toothed novice) may not eat any of the following: emu, because it is Ngalalbal; any animal, *e.g.,* the wombat, which burrows in the ground, and therefore reminds of the foot-holes; such creatures as have very prominent teeth, such as the kangaroo, because they remind of the tooth itself; any animal that climbs to the tree-tops, like the koala, because it is then near to *Daramulun;* any bird that swims, because it reminds of the final washing ceremony. Other food forbidden is spiny ant-eater, common opossum, lace-lizard, snakes, eels, perch, and others.

Thus the young man during his probation is placed in an artificial state of scarcity as to food, although perhaps surrounded by plenty. Included in the forbidden is the *Budjan* of the novice, although this is becoming more and more disregarded in the younger generations.

The novices were told that if they eat any of the forbidden animals, the Jola belonging to it would get into them and kill them. . . .

In the old times a novice, known to have broken the food rules after initiation, would have been killed by violence.

The strictness with which these food rules are observed by the men affords a measure of their force in the olden times. The old man whom I have mentioned as the Wolgal singer, and who seemed to be about seventy years of age, told me, when we were speaking of these rules, that he had never eaten of the flesh of the emu. He said that he had never been free of its flesh, by someone stealthily rubbing a piece of it, or the fat, on his mouth.[15]

Among the most common taboos are those in regard to food. The notion pervades the whole life of a people.

---

[15] A. W. Howitt, *Native Tribes of South-East Australia.* Copyright, 1904, by The Macmillan Co., and used with their permission, pp. 560-561.

The faith in goblinism produced other-worldly interests which overruled ordinary worldly interests. Foods have often been forbidden which were plentiful, the prohibition of which injuriously lessened the food supply. There is a tribe of Bushmen who will eat no goat's flesh, although goats are the most numerous domestic animals in the district. Where totemism exists it is regularly accompanied by a taboo on eating the totem animal. Whatever may be the real principle in totemism, it overrules the interest in an abundant food supply. "The origin of the sacred regard paid to the cow must be sought in the primitive nomadic life of the Indo-European race," because it is common to Iranians and Indians of Hindostan. The Libyans ate oxen but not cows. The same was true of the Phoenicians and Egyptians. In some cases the sense of a food taboo is not to be learned. It may have been entirely capricious. Mohammed would not eat lizards, because he thought them the offspring of a metamorphosed clan of Israelites. On the other hand, the protective taboo which forbids killing crocodiles, pythons, cobras, and other animal enemies of man was harmful to his interests, whatever the motive. . . . India furnishes a great number of cases of harmful mores. "In India every tendency of humanity seems intensified and exaggerated. No country in the world is so conservative in its traditions, yet no country has undergone so many religious changes and vicissitudes." "Every year thousands perish of disease that might recover if they would take proper nourishment, and drink the medicine that science prescribes, but which they imagine that their religion forbids them to touch." "Men who can scarcely count beyond twenty, and know not the letters of the alphabet, would rather die than eat food which had been prepared by men of lower caste, unless it had been sanctified by being offered to an idol; and would kill their daughters rather than endure the disgrace of having unmarried girls at home beyond twelve or thirteen years of age." [16]

Another characteristic of many taboos is their association with religion.

Rules of holiness in the sense just explained, i.e., a system of restrictions on man's arbitrary use of natural things, enforced by the dread of supernatural penalties, are found among all primitive peoples. It is convenient to have a distinct name for this primitive institution, to mark it off from the later developments of the idea of holiness in advanced religions, and for this purpose the Polynesian term "taboo" has been selected. The field covered by taboos among savage and half-savage races is very wide, for there is no part of life in which the savage does not feel himself to be surrounded by mysterious agencies and recognise the need of walking warily. Moreover all taboos do not belong to religion proper, that is, they are not always rules of conduct for the regulation of man's contact with deities that, when taken in the right way, may be counted on as friendly, but rather appear in many cases to be precautions against the approach of malignant enemies—

---

[16] Sumner, *Folkways*, pp. 26-27.

against contact with evil spirits and the like. Thus alongside of taboos that exactly correspond to rules of holiness, protecting the inviolability of idols and sanctuaries, priest and chiefs, and generally of all persons and things pertaining to the gods and their worship, we find another kind of taboo which in the Semitic field has its parallel in rules of uncleanness. Women after childbirth, men who have touched a dead body, and so forth, are temporarily taboo and separated from human society, just as the same persons are unclean in Semitic religion. In these cases the person under taboo is not regarded as holy, for he is separated from approach to the sanctuary as well as from contact with men; but his act or condition is somehow associated with supernatural dangers, arising according to the common savage explanation, from the presence of formidable spirits which are shunned like an infectious disease. In most savage societies no sharp line seems to be drawn between the two kinds of taboo just indicated, and even in more advanced nations the notions of holiness and uncleanness often touch. Among the Syrians, for example, swine's flesh was taboo, but it was an open question whether this was because the animal was holy or because it was unclean. But though not precise, the distinction between what is holy and what is unclean is real; in rules of holiness the motive is respect for the gods; in rules of uncleanliness it is primarily fear of an unknown or hostile power, though ultimately as we see in the Levitical legislation, the law of clean and unclean may be brought within the sphere of divine ordinances, on the view that uncleanness is hateful to God and must be avoided by all that have to do with Him.[17]

We see that many taboos represent a wish for security from divine ill-will. The very attitude which invested the deities with mystic powers made it perilous for the plebeian or the uninitiated to deal with objects considered sacred or "holy," that is, associated with the supernatural. This same attitude also endowed those who represented the divinities on earth with a "mysterious unapproachableness." "No Tongan durst appropriate the remains of a superior's meal on pain of a sore throat; the cloak discarded by a Maori chief could not with safety be donned by an attendant. A Mangaia pontiff's body could not be tattooed; his equivalent in Tonga could not be either tattooed or circumcised like other men, since no one was competent to touch him with immunity, and when he was buried by his inferiors, as he inevitably had to be, these were reckoned infected for ten months. A number of prohibitions were widely distributed. Thus, no one was allowed to touch a superior's head or pass close behind him or eat in his presence. A Hawaiian whose shadow fell upon the king's house or back, or who climbed over the royal stockade was doomed; to defy

---

[17] From W. W. Smith, *The Religion of the Semites*, New York, The Macmillan Co., 1907, pp. 152 ff.

these taboos was tantamount to asserting oneself an equal or superior." [18]

In pre-literate societies there were innumerable taboos; but with the spread of scientific knowledge and the development of critical attitudes, people began to question the need for and wisdom of taboos and became more and more tolerant of their violation. Nevertheless, we continue to have numerous taboos. They include regulations of dress, speech, sex relations, recreation, and a wide range of reference in addition to food and religious practices. They are group regulators of man's conduct and serve to inhibit his impulses. Because of the differences in them as affecting the sexes, the young, and the aged, and the different classes in society, taboos act selectively and thus affect the course of social development.

Prestige.—Very definitely in the field of implicit controls is that subtle "something" which is designated "prestige." As the history of the word in English usage indicates, *prestige* is in some way associated with the mysterious, the attractive, the incalculable.[19] Professor Cooley remarks: "A sense of power in others seems to involve a sense of their inscrutability; and, on the other hand, so soon as a person becomes plain he ceases to stimulate the imagination; we have seen all around him, so that he no longer appears an open door to new life. . . . The power of mere inscrutability arises from the fact that it gives a vague stimulus to thought and then leaves it to work out the details to suit itself." [20]

Prestige may rest either in the person, the group, in a work, or in an intangible idea. We have seen how prestige among the Kwakiutl was determined by the elaborateness with which the potlatch ceremony was performed, and among the Zuñi by religious participation. In more complex and secular societies, the bases for prestige are more numerous.

Prestige paralyzes the critical faculties of those who come beneath its sway and fills them with wonder and respect. The object of prestige is automatically clothed with authority which precludes discussion or a protecting pathos which precludes criticism. The moment prestige is called in question it disappears. It is supported by success and doomed by failure. It stimulates the emotions of fear and love, it commands the sentiments of esteem and respect, it dictates the

---

[18] Robert H. Lowie, *Primitive Religion*, New York, Boni & Liveright, 1924, p. 79.
[19] See: Lewis Leopold, *Prestige: A Psychological Study of Social Estimates*, London, T. Fisher Unwin, 1913, pp. 16-62.
[20] Charles H. Cooley, *Human Nature and the Social Order*, New York, Charles Scribner's Sons, 1902, pp. 313-315.

attitudes of emulation and obedience. "Prestige is the mainspring of all authority. Neither gods, kings, nor women have ever reigned without it." [21]

A brief analysis of implicit forms of social control will show they have the common traits of being elementary. They are effective through the simple interaction of fundamental social forces and spontaneously mobilize sentiments and emotions around some socially defined object and in terms of definite social situations. In every kind of implicit control the critical and deliberative elements are lacking. In some kinds, for example the taboos, a social philosophy may arise to stave off criticism and to prevent manipulation. Taboos exist for a reason, as, for instance, the desire not to offend the spirits; hence the philosophical element.[22] Moreover, the mores, including the prestige-attitudes, contain judgments as to societal welfare. These implicit controls involve no formulations about causation.

Explicit Social Control

Crises in the experience of the group call for a type of control different from those we have been discussing. As the term is used here, a crisis is any situation that demands attention; it is an interruption in the ongoing of group activity; it raises issues. It need not be an incident producing a violent shock, but it must stir the group from its equanimity, and cause the group to stop and consider. The definition of the problem need not be rational, but it should be plausible. It need not be critical, it need not be relevant, but it must carry conviction. The definition may be shifting and fluctuating, but it follows a general trend and has a purpose.

Among the controls of the essentially explicit sort are myth, legend, and public opinion. These forms have the facility of defining situations in terms of concreteness and objectivity. They are called out by the nature of the situation itself and seek to orient the individual and the group to the immediate conditions. This may be done in accordance with traditional patterns, but always with modifications to fit the present exigencies of time, place, and circumstance.

Myth and Legend.—In connection with the treatment of interaction there was occasion to make use of the concept "myth" and its role in conditioning the behavior of divergent groups.[23] Common

---

[21] Gustave Le Bon, *The World Unbalanced*, New York, Longmans, Green & Co., 1924, p. 148.
[22] See: Sumner, *Folkways*, pp. 30-31.
[23] See pages 329-330, 364-366.

sense makes no clear distinction between myth and legend, but the definitions of common sense are meager and inexact. Both myth and legend grow up uncritically, and both may become conventionalized and steeped in traditional principles. They differ, however, in that myth is more universal than legend and hence more unlimited in its range of influence. Myth, having a distributive aspect, tends to assume somewhat concrete manifestations in different localities where it fuses with other rumors in expanding its content. This distributive aspect, with a well-grounded and permanent local attachment to a place or a person, bearing an autonomy of its own, may be designated a legend. Because of its more universal character and wider area of influence, the myth will receive the burden of our attention in this discussion.

Other distinguishing marks of the myth are its artistic reference, its subtle implication, its idealization, its mysticism. It is often vaguely stated, leaving much to the imagination. Through the agency of the myth the world of fancy supplements those critical periods of stress and thwarted purposes where the world of common sense is barren and unsatisfactory. Wishes come to the front in times of social poverty and restlessness, and man's capacity for living beyond the immediate present of the senses produces highly flavored stories of calamity, deliverance, or prosperity. The myth, then, is fundamentally a form of mass wish-fulfillment. In time of emotional excitement it arises and releases those deep-rooted tensions which tend to be inhibited in the activities of everyday life. Because of its vivid and stirring imagery the myth affords a form of expression that is symbolic. And in its pictorial representativeness all the experiences and memories of all the individuals become embodied in an uncritical formulation, assimilated to a violent emotional tone, and elaborated into "a counterfeit of reality."

The nature and function of the myth can best be presented by considering them under certain types of myth. First is the *aetiological* myth. This type of myth is that which assigns causes. It is one which seeks to explain. Early man began to originate stories to account for all kinds of phenomena—tribal and racial origins, the creation of the universe, ritualistic observances, prosperity and calamity, ghost fear and taboo, and so on through a long list. Sumner tells us that "it is not to be understood that primitive men philosophize about their experiences of life. That is our way; it was not theirs. . . . They made myths, however, in which they often presented conceptions which are deeply philosophical, but they repre-

sented them in concrete, personal, dramatic and graphic ways." [24]
Many explanatory myths are connected with religion, viewed in the
broad sense. To this type belongs the ritual myth.

Each family, and almost every individual, also possessed gods and fetishes, which had been pointed out for their worship by sudden intuition.
They had a place in some corner of the house, or a niche in its walls; lamps
were continually kept burning before them, and small daily offerings were
made to them, over and above what fell to their share on solemn feast-days.
In return, they became the protectors of the household, its guardians, and
its counselors. Appeal was made to them in every exigency of daily life,
and their decisions were no less scrupulously carried out by their little circle
of worshippers than was the will of the feudal god by the inhabitants of
his principality.

The prince was the great high priest. The whole religion of the home
rested upon him, and originally he himself performed its ceremonies. . . .
Hence the officiating priest assumed a formidable responsibility as regarded
his fellows: a slip of memory, the slightest accidental impurity, made him
a bad priest, injurious to himself and harmful to those worshippers who
had entrusted him with their interests before the gods. Since it was vain to
expect ritualistic perfections from a prince constantly troubled with affairs
of state, the custom was established of associating professional priests with
him, personages who devoted all their lives to the study and practice of the
thousand formalities whose sum constituted the local religion. . . .

In addition to its rites and special hierarchy, each of the sacerdotal colleges
thus constituted had a theology in accordance with the nature and attributes
of its god. Its fundamental dogma affirmed the unity of the home god, his
greatness, his supremacy over all the gods of Egypt and of foreign lands—
whose existence was nevertheless admitted, and none dreamed of denying
their reality or contesting their power. The latter also boasted of their unity,
their greatness, their supremacy; but whatever they were, the god of the
home was master of them all—their prince, their ruler, their king. It was
he alone who governed the world, he alone kept it in good order, he alone
had created it. Not that he had evoked it out of nothing; there was as yet no
concept of nothingness, and even to the most subtle and refined of primitive
theologians creation was only a bringing of pre-existent elements into play.
The latent germs of things had always existed, but they had slept for ages
and ages in the bosom of the Nu, of the dark waters. In fulness of time
the god of each home drew them forth, classified them, marshalled them
according to the bent of his particular nature, and made his universe out
of them by methods peculiarly his own. Nit of Saïs, who was a weaver,
had made the world of warp and woof, as the mother of a family weaves
her children's linen. Khumu, the Nile-god of the cataracts, had gathered up

<hr/>

[24] Sumner, *Folkways*, p. 31.

the mud of his waters and therewith moulded his creatures upon a potter's table. In the eastern cities of the Delta these procedures were not so simple. There it was admitted that in the beginning earth and sky were two lovers lost in the Nu, fast locked in each other's embrace, the god lying beneath the goddess. On the day of creation a new god, Shu, came forth from the primaeval waters, slipped between the two, and seizing Nuit with both hands, lifted her above his head with outstretched arms. Though the starry body of the goddess extended in space—her head being to the west and her loins to the east—her feet and hands hung down to the earth. These were the four pillars of the firmament under another form, and four gods of four adjacent principalities were in charge of them. Osiris, or Horus the sparrow-hawk, presided over the southern, and Sit over the northern pillar; Thot over that of the west, and Sapdi, the author of the zodiacal light, over that of the east. . . .

None of these conceptions alone sufficed to explain the whole mechanism of creation, nor the part which the various gods took in it. The priests of Heliopolis appropriated them all, modified some of their details and eliminated others, added several new personages, and thus finally constructed a complete cosmogony, the elements of which were learnedly combined so as to correspond severally with the different operations by which the world had been evoked out of chaos and gradually brought to its present state.[25]

Another common myth is the *hero* myth, sometimes called the "great-man" myth. Carlyle says we are all hero worshippers. It is easy to believe anything about a hero, a deliverer, one we admire or worship. Great men, even while living, are frequently known to the public only through a glorified and fictitious personality. Aeneas, St. George, Napoleon, Washington, Lincoln, and a host of others are epic figures. In most instances the myths are highly laudatory; the heroes become incarnate. Sometimes the myth finds its inspiration in some supernatural visitor or delivering host.[26] In every case of hero mythology the pattern is such that it gives release to the hopes, wishes, and wants of those who come under its controlling influence. The devotees believe in the myth because they want to. They wish to believe that their heroes represent the highest current ideals of goodness and courage. In the myth their wishes are fulfilled. Thus the group morale is lifted and concerted action assured.

But the mythologizing of the worshipful makes for a role difficult of attainment. The leader rarely turns out to be what he is conceived to be. Yet if he is to succeed, he must undertake to conform to the popular conception of his personality. This calls for compromise,

---

25 G. Maspero, *The Dawn of Civilization, Egypt and Chaldea,* 4th ed., London, Society for Promoting Christian Knowledge, 1901, pp. 122-135.
26 See: II Kings XIX, 35; Arthur Machen, *The Bowmen and Other Legends of the War,* New York, G. P. Putnam's Sons, 1915.

which, in turn, may result in the idol's fall, for now the revered leader will likely become the victim of spiteful gossip and the object of derogatory myth-making.

A very common form of myth is the *conflict* myth, that is, the uncritical and emotional expression given to the wishes and sentiments of groups in conflict. To those who threaten group interests and security are automatically ascribed certain traits and courses of conduct which get formulated into exceedingly uncritical concrete definitions of the situation, commonly accepted as true.

Nevertheless, the "Ballad for Americans" does not mention the Japanese (Japanese in the U.S.). We do not feel them to be a part of us as we feel the Czechs, the Poles, the Italians, and, indeed, the Germans to be a part of us. From the point of view of that loyalty which war makes, it would be disloyal to include the Japanese-Americans. For, in a way which Italians and Germans do not represent, the Japanese are our enemies. They are the enemy with whom, in the first months of the war, we met in closest and bitterest combat. The pain we suffered at Pearl Harbor and on Bataan turns again within us when we see a face or hear a name that stands for our Japanese enemies. We distinguish Nazis from Germans. Not all Italians are followers of Mussolini. We know these things and recognize them. *But the Japanese are all "Japs." The Japanese, in the thinking of most of our people, are all one thing; a people fanatically devoted to the destruction of the United States—our enemies, all of them.* The loyalty of war will not allow tender feelings toward anyone felt to be a representative of the Asiatic enemy.[27]

It is not hard to see how such myths could develop in an emotional crisis. On both sides of conflict, fighting men undergoing the baptism of fire are excitable and impressionable. They tend to have extraordinary collective illusions which gain in content as myths spread in the form of rumor from man to man, from company to company, and from army to civilian population. These myths are readily accepted because they articulate the collective emotion of the group and organize its energies for more determined action. The role of the conflict myth has been presented in the discussion of war and its appearance in the contact of different races, groups, and cultures is well known.[28] Groups idealize their own wishes and aspira-

---

[27] Robert Redfield, "The Japanese-Americans," in *American Society in Wartime*, edited by William F. Ogburn, Chicago, University of Chicago Press, 1943, p. 149. Italics added to point up the mythology back of the movement of upwards of 70,000 of our citizens to relocation camps by the U. S. Government. Actually very few Japanese-Americans proved to be disloyal. On the contrary, they cooperated well with the authorities during their internment, the Nisei troops acquitted themselves magnificently in Italy, and, on the whole, the group's conduct was such as largely to dispel this particular conflict myth.

[28] See pp. 329-330, 364-366.

tions in mythical fashion and define those who threaten their security by derogatory myths. These tend to mobilize the respective groups for corporate action.

Finally, there is the *utopian* or futuristic myth. By means of this type of myth "a distant goal takes on the urgency of the present." All myths imply a forward look, but certain myths explicitly set forth a futuristic reference. These latter include such well-known ones as the Messianic hope, the "second coming," the Marxian "catastrophic revolution," the general strike, and others of a similar nature.

The myth of a general strike, for example, is an impressive and moving collective representation portraying a time when the mobilized workers will have power and opportunity to assume control of economic and social affairs.[29] It is not a historical prediction but a program of collective action. Its main purpose is to arouse and enroll in the cause of proletarian freedom those who are not yet affected by the conception. It lacks definiteness as to space and time and thus is prepared to meet all individual and group requirements without disappointment as to their realization.[30] It is only necessary for the masses to believe in it, for the function of the myth is to stir and make contagious a common enthusiasm. Thus it becomes a compelling stimulus to action.

It is apparent at this point that myth and legend are products of social interaction. They are forms of wish-fulfillment for either groups or individuals.[31] For this reason myths and legends have been termed "mass dreams." The development of the myth generally follows a pretty clear pattern: the imagination which acts in a creative capacity, the will to accept and believe, and out of these elements, a concept of reality to which there is impassioned, uncritical response. The main point to remember about the role of the myth and legend as explicit factors in control is that, particularly in times of tension and excitement, persons react to them as to objective facts. This illusion may easily be projected from person to person and become the active mental pattern of the whole group.

Public Opinion.—Up to this point in our treatment of social control we have investigated those factors in social situations which tend to force individuals to act in concert, more or less spontaneously

---

29 See: G. Sorel, *Reflections on Violence*, New York, B. W. Huebsch, 1914, pp. 130-136, for a discussion of this syndicalist myth.
30 See: Vernon Lee (pseud. for Violet Paget), *Vital Lies*, London, John Lane, 1912, p. 80.
31 See: W. A. White, *Mechanisms of Character Formation*, New York, The Macmillan Co., 1916, p. 120.

and uncritically, by bringing about complete rapport and the domination of the individual by the group through a sort of circular process of interaction. In each case the group acts very much as a crowd, impulsive and dogmatic. The concerted action is practically free from conflict and deliberation. The dominant mood stimulated in the interplay of social forces, inner sentiments and feelings, tends to inhibit spontaneously those sentiments and attitudes which do not fit into it immediately. Within it all sentiments are released and fused with each other to form the common aim of the group.

In discussing the behavior of a public in the preceding chapter, it was shown how public opinion tends to form around issues which concern enough people to excite deliberation and to eventuate in some measure of consensus among them. How public opinion, once established, temporarily operates as a force for control was not discussed. The problem of public opinion in control is an intricate and involved one. There are those who regard what they term "public opinion" as one of the most pervasive and one of the surest mechanisms for social control, while others, like Walter Lippmann,[32] consider it to be lacking in dependability and stability and practically worthless so far as its effect for control is concerned. Be that as it may, what a public, especially a widespread and representative public, thinks now and is likely to think in the future about a given question must be of the greatest importance.

In the very process of public opinion formation, the individual is subjected to varying degrees of control through the exercise of pressures by other individuals and groups as he gets drawn more and more into the arena of discussion. All the arts of persuasion and argument may be brought to bear upon him by those who are already members of the public. To these blandishments and reasonings he may oppose his interests and ideas. But, if he is to become a part of a public, he will make compromises and concessions so far as necessary to have his own views heard and accepted. Considerations of status and self-interest, as well as those of broader policy and general welfare, may be sufficient to induce the individual to subordinate his wishes and will to those of the public.

Once public opinion has been shaped to a noticeable extent, its influence begins to be felt in other and more significant ways. As more people are brought within its orbit, its weight tends to accumulate, partly in terms of sheer numbers of persons sharing in a particular opinion. The business of gauging or measuring the

32 Walter Lippmann, *The Phantom Public*, New York, The Macmillan Company, 1925.

opinions of given publics in modern societies [33] on specific issues has taken on the proportions of a major enterprise. To the extent that "the man in the street" accepts the results of public opinion polls at their face value, he may allow his personal opinion to be affected thereby. Just what the measuring techniques—polls, questionnaires, and interviews—measure is not very clear, but, whether valid tests of the opinion of publics or not, one effect of their use and the announcement of the results is to enlist the interest of more people in the issue that is the focal point of collective attention.

A public, as such, is not an active agent for the dissemination of its opinion, for the assertion of its will, or for carrying out its decisions in social action. A public is merely a deliberative body, usually quite amorphous, and does not possess the machinery for positive action. When action is in order, the time for discussion is past. Accordingly, the public, having decided that action is called for, must either be transmuted into a body equipped and organized for action, like a crowd, or it must create, or at least lend its support to, special agencies prepared to act in its name. Such agencies may be those which are already established and functioning, like governmental, religious, educational, publicity, or other institutional units, or they may be opportunistic bodies, like pressure groups, propaganda experts, and the like, having special interests to be served, but representing their interests to be those of a much larger and more inclusive public. We may say, then, that public opinion is effective to the extent that it is organized and expressed indirectly through media of communication, legislatures, administrators, farm and labor organizations, and churches. "Leaders of organized groups may and often do have more to say about policy than The People. A one man poll of the Farm Bureau's Ed O'Neill might yield more legitimate insight into future tariff schedules than would a careful sampling of the total population." [34]

There are some characteristics of public opinion that lead many persons to be skeptical about its value as a guide to conduct. Among these a few may be mentioned. First, it is held that public opinion is a kind of fetish, a catch phrase, a stereotype, and therefore un-

---

[33] George Gallup, "Testing Public Opinion," *Public Opinion in a Democracy*, Supplement to *Public Opinion Quart.*, Vol. 2, January, 1938, pp. 8-14; George Gallup and Saul F. Rae, *The Pulse of Democracy: The Public-Opinion Poll and How It Works*, New York, Simon & Schuster, 1940; "The Public Opinion Polls: Dr. Jekyll or Mr. Hyde" (A symposium), *Public Opinion Quart.*, Vol. 4, June, 1940, pp. 212-284; John C. Ranney, "Do the Polls Serve Democracy?" *Public Opinion Quart.*, Vol. 10, 1946-1947, pp. 349-360; Paul Studenski, "How Polls Can Mislead," *Harper's Magazine*, Vol. 180, December, 1939, pp. 80-83.

[34] Jerome S. Bruner, "Public Opinion and America's Foreign Policy," *Am. Sociol. Rev.*, Vol. 9, No. 1, February, 1944, p. 50.

worthy of the acquiescence of realistic, intelligent persons. This conception is gradually disappearing, however, as more scientific methods are brought to bear on its study and manipulation.[35] Secondly, public opinion is often confused with press opinion.[36] Where those who hold this view think that "you can't believe what you read in the newspapers," it is logical for the two terms to be considered as indistinguishable, and for public opinion to be regarded as not dependable. Third, public opinion is said to be too vague and indefinite for the individual or group to look to it for guidance. There is a measure of truth in this contention. But

It should be recognized that opinion is always relative to definite situations, and that therefore what appears to be inconsistent or erratic public opinion on a subject is frequently merely reaction to different situations. If a political party or other public declares itself vigorously in favor of improving the condition of the farmer during the campaign and after the election ignores the practical measures of agricultural relief, it does not necessarily prove either that the announced platform was not the "true" opinion of the group at the time of the campaign, or that their opinion has undergone a change in the meantime. The two situations are different both as regards the ends to be achieved and the means whereby they are to be attained. In the first case, the principal end is to capture the farmers' votes and the means are verbal promises. After the election the practical program involves many considerations not present in the first situation. The opinion has changed because the situation has changed.[37]

Fourth, it is sometimes contended that public opinion is fickle, subject to "every passing wind that blows," and hence unreliable. Such apparent capriciousness may be illusory or it may be due to a misapprehension of what constitutes public opinion. Political "landslides," the sudden desertion of one leader or line of discussion for another, and the abrupt loss of interest in an issue are not necessarily evidences of the changeableness of public opinion but rather marks of mass or crowd behavior. Fifth, and closely related to the last point, is the fairly common belief that public opinion is not trustworthy because it cannot be sustained over extended periods of time and that it fails in a crisis. In many instances this criticism is justified. For example, public opinion frequently abates when confronted by a *fait accompli*. The less personal the issue, the more likely is this to be true.[38] In the presence of crisis, especially one

---

[35] Alfred McClung Lee, "Public Opinion," in J. S. Roucek (Ed.), *Social Control*, New York, D. Van Nostrand Co., Inc., 1947, p. 385.

[36] *Ibid.*, pp. 385-386.

[37] George A. Lundberg, "Public Opinion from a Behavioristic Viewpoint," *Am. J. Sociol.*, Vol. 36, No. 3, November, 1930, pp. 403-404.

[38] Bruner, "Public Opinion and America's Foreign Policy," *op. cit.*, p. 50.

that strikes close to the security of the individual or his immediate family or business, personal interest is likely to take precedence, temporarily, over public interest. In addition, many issues are quite incomprehensible to the average citizen.

Sixth, and finally, some persons say they prefer to rely on their own judgment rather than on that of a public. The assumption is that the judgment of the individual, particularly if you are that individual, is superior to the judgment of the many. While there is virtue oftentimes in relying on one's own judgment, nevertheless there is in this idea an excellent example of self-deception, for little does the person realize, or else he is unwilling to admit, that whatever his opinion on the subject at issue may be, it is not wholly unique and that the individual and the public are not mutually exclusive entities in a specific situation.

Despite the real and imagined shortcomings of public opinion as a mechanism for social control, the fact remains that it is a very potent force in society, especially a democratic one. Indeed, there can be no democracy without free and responsible public discussion and a wholesome respect for and maximum adherence to public will. The only alternatives are dictatorship or anarchy. The individual may have divergent views on this or that matter of public concern and, on occasion, he may pit his opinion against that of a large and representative public. But once a given opinion has the ascendency he will subscribe to it or suffer public disapproval and possible loss of status. Despite the opinions of an individual, his acts—at least those that enter into social interaction—will be likely to conform to patterns sanctioned by public opinion. Even the leader, whose opinions may have more weight in shaping public opinion than those of other people, will be guided by what his public considers to be for the public welfare, if he wishes to succeed and survive as leader. Moreover, in democracy, it is enlightened public opinion that generates, sustains, and revises most of the other mechanism for social control, such as the law, governmental administration, religion, education, and civilization itself.

In order to keep the social order intact many devices for control have been invented and utilized. Some specific ones are flattery and praise; epithets like "scab," "upstart," "tattletale," "libertine," "Red," "traitor," "warmonger," and the like; complimentary titles, such as "hero," "master," "your honor," "judge," and "patriot"; advertising, slogans, and propaganda; satire, laughter, and threats: and unequivocal measures in the form of commands and specified penalties.[39]

---

[39] See: F. E. Lumley, *Means of Social Control*, New York, The Century Co., 1925.

Perhaps no means of defining the situation is more powerful than gossip, especially in the small, primary community. Thomas relates how he asked a Polish peasant what was the extent of the Polish neighborhood and received the reply that "it reaches as far as the report of a man reaches—as far as a man is talked about." [40] This is significant, for it indicates how the community tends to regulate its members by talking about them. Such talk is not necessarily vicious and untrue; hence gossip is not always bad. Sometimes it is quite the opposite. Gossip has value as a socializing and organizing medium. Within the rather narrow confines of the area encompassed by what may properly be termed *gossip,* the status of the individual and of his family is pretty largely determined.

Formal Means of Control

As social life expands and civilization grows, the number of things that are taken out of the realm of informal control steadily increases. Under the changing conditions of social life the process of secularization proceeds, and institutionalization advances until much that was naïve and implicit in the more elemental forms of control has been lost. Rules of action that were implicitly defined in custom and tradition tend to become more explicitly defined under the searching scrutiny and testing of public opinion. At this stage a new element enters the picture, namely, deliberation. In the crowd and under the sway of custom no allowance is made for individuals or groups holding ideas and attitudes that diverge from the dominant mood of the crowd or the dictates of custom. It is in the public that these divergent individuals and groups interact upon one another in terms of propaganda, if not of truth and fact. The crowd tends to ignore facts.

Folkways, mores, and ceremonial recognize only the facts in the immediate situations, under which they grew up, and myth and legend, though frequently in possession of the facts, may lightly pass them by. In public opinion there is a disposition to weigh facts somewhat objectively. However, it is not until impartial structures develop out of definite social situations, and thereby embody ideas and furnish instrumentalities for the purpose of resolving conflicts and interpreting matters in dispute, that society reaches a stage of development where control passes under positive enactment and even-handed jurisdiction.

---

[40] Thomas, *The Unadjusted Girl,* p. 44.

In earlier chapters,[41] the process of institutionalization was given extensive treatment. There it was shown how groups satisfy certain definite and fundamental interests through the medium of specific complex culture mechanisms. They are more or less consistent with the informal mechanisms of concerted group activity out of which they emerge and upon which they rely for support. How they function as powerful engines of control will now receive attention.

Law.—Social groups define acts which they fear will disturb the social order or will menace the security of the group. As societies become more complex, more formal and authoritative controls are needed. Organized government emerges to fulfil this need. Under governmental systems of control a certain amount of direction is permitted to remain with the family, the school, the military, and a few other agencies, while, in major matters of community concern, the government takes over the role of defining anti-social acts and of attaching and enforcing penalties.[42] The acts are defined as either crimes or misdemeanors, according to the degree of seriousness with which they are regarded. The social mechanisms in which they get defined and the penalties stated are laws.[43]

The person who behaves in a manner which his society has defined as anti-social goes through the process of having his acts defined spontaneously for him, first, in personal, informal terms, by face-to-face, intimate groups, until he reaches the age of social responsibility as it is currently understood by his society and specified by the state. From that time on, he receives his definitions in the more formal statements of legal terminology and judicial formulations. The "ordering and forbidding attitude," according to Thomas and Znaniecki, "is the oldest and most persistent form of social technique."

Law is society's most formidable instrument of social control. The theory is that law arose, not to supplant the more informal mechanisms of control, but rather to translate them into more unmistakable and specific terms. The relation of this institutionalized form of control to the less formal forms is incisively stated by Sumner where he says:

---

41 Chapters 11 and 12.

42 See: N. S. Timasheff, "The Sociological Place of Law," *Am. J. Sociol.*, Vol. 44, No. 2, September, 1938, pp. 206-221. See also references to "law" at the end of this chapter.

43 In the United States the practice has developed of giving court decisions the effect of laws. In so far as this is a practice it has bestowed upon the judiciary a remarkable amount of legislative function and power. Indeed, the American practice exalts Federal judges of the Supreme Court to positions of political irresponsibility with a life tenure, and able, with impunity, to nullify the laws of the people's legislature by declaring such laws unconstitutional. This is not so in England where, since the beginning of the eighteenth century, the judges have been responsible to Parliament.

Acts of legislation come out of the mores. In low civilization all societal regulations are customs and taboos, the origin of which is unknown.
Positive laws are impossible until the stage of verification, reflection, and
criticism is reached. Until that point is reached there is only customary
law, or common law. The customary law may be codified and systematized
with respect to some philosophical principles, and yet remain customary.
The codes of Manu and Justinian are examples. Enactment is not possible
until reverence for ancestors has been so much weakened that it is no longer
thought wrong to interfere with traditional customs by positive enactment.
Even then there is reluctance to make enactments, and there is a stage of
transition during which traditional customs are extended by interpretations
to cover new cases and to prevent evils. Legislation, however, has to seek
standing ground on the existing mores, and it soon becomes apparent that
legislation, to be strong, must be consistent with the mores. Things which
have been in the mores are put under police regulation and later under
positive law. It is sometimes said that "public opinion" must ratify and
approve police regulations, but this statement rests on an imperfect analysis.
The regulations must conform to the mores, so that the public will not think
them too lax or too strict. The mores of our urban and rural populations
are not the same; consequently legislation . . . which is made for one of these
sections of the population does not succeed when applied to the other. The
regulation of drinking places, gambling places, and disorderly houses has
passed through the above mentioned stages. It is always a question of expediency whether to leave a subject under the mores, or to make a police
regulation for it, or to put it into the criminal law. . . . When an enactment
is made there is a sacrifice of the elasticity and automatic self-adaptation of
custom, but an enactment is specific and is provided with sanctions. Enactments come into use when conscious purposes are formed, and it is believed
that specific devices can be framed by which to realize such purposes in the
society. Then also prohibitions take the place of taboos, and punishments are
planned to be deterrent rather than revengeful. The mores of different
societies, or of different ages, are characterized by greater or less readiness
and confidence in regard to the use of positive enactments for the realization
of societal purposes.[44]

The earlier conception of law was that of common or customary
law and this *was* the law for hundreds of years and until comparatively recent times.[45] Statute law, recent as it is, has come to assume
in our thinking the main bulk of the concept of law. Indeed, our
statutes have become so bulky that they are confusing, with the result
that they have tended to lose prestige and to be disregarded by an
increasingly large number of people. The outpouring of legislative

[44] Sumner, *Folkways*, pp. 55-56.
[45] See p. 640.

enactments and court decisions has been so great that our era has come to be called "the day of universal law" in America. Every time Congress and the legislatures meet it may be expected that thousands of laws will be passed, not to speak of resolutions, joint resolutions, and concurrent resolutions.

In attempting to secure conformity to the social patterns of behavior law has laid down, it is usual to employ force or the threat of coercion. Law defines an act as an offense, annexes a penalty for disobedience, and dictates by decisions. It aims at an incisive, definite technique of control. The fundamental theory of law holds that justice under the law must be impartial and even-handed. Thus it would differ from the so-called "unwritten law" applied by vigilantes or by the lynching party. Nevertheless, law is definitely punitive and only to a very little extent corrective. However, law is changing, or rather its use in administration is being altered. The methods of the Juvenile Court, instituted to deal with youthful delinquents, are gradually being employed in modified form in the handling of adult offenders. These methods seek to define the situation in each individual case in terms of all the factors present and to temper justice with mercy wherever the facts seem to warrant such procedure. Under this technique the offender is treated as a personality, as the product of a complexity of individual and social factors. The social responsibility for the young individual is defined and the mode of his entire social conditioning is being considered more and more by the enlightened public and the understanding judiciary. The word of the law may be altered tardily, but its spirit is being changed gradually in the direction of a sympathetic treatment of the transgressor. It is becoming evident that there are persons whose attitude can be changed much more effectively by other than legal processes.

Religion.—Originally law was closely related to religion. In earliest law, which was largely customary, the function was to enforce the religious taboos. The first crimes punished by the community as a whole were those involving a disrespect for or neglect of the rites associated with the worship of deities who were thought to be offended by such oversight or indignity. It was the purpose of punishment to ward off any direful calamity that might befall the community because of divine wrath. Early Roman law was founded on a conception of social organization in which the worship of ancestors prevailed. During the Middle Ages, because of the power of the Church, law was dominated by the belief in divine authority. Only recently, with the separation of church and state, has law come to rest on an almost purely secular culture-base.　In spite of their separateness in theory, in practice they go in and out the areas of social life and together include all the sanctions and inhibitions which society authorizes and imposes upon its members.

It has already been indicated how the religious act tends to become institutionalized and how the religious institution functions as a unit of social organization.　In the same connection it was pointed out how the religious movement becomes articulate through practice, myth, doctrine, dogma, and creed.[46]　Our purpose here is to attempt an objective analysis of the mechanisms of religious behavior through which it exerts the control necessary for its survival.

One can distinguish, in theory if not in practice, between individual religious experience and socialized religious behavior.　Some writers on religion put the emphasis on the reality and intensity of the individual experience, others prefer to see in religion a purely social pattern, an institution on which the individual must draw in order to have religious experience at all. The contrast between these two points of view is probably more apparent than real.　The suggestions for religious behavior will always be found to be of social origin; it is the validation of this behavior in individual or in social terms that may be thought to vary.　This is equivalent to saying that some societies tend to seek the most intense expression of religious experience in individual behavior (including introspection under that term), while others tend toward a collective orthodoxy, reaching an equivalent intensity of life in forms of behavior in which the individual is subordinated to a collective symbol.　Religions that conform to the first tendency may be called evangelistic, and those of the second type ritualistic.[47]

If we strip "religion" of its accoutrements, we see it to be simply a type of behavior in which fundamental ideals and ultimate values are defined and emotionalized.　As expressed, it assumes, among other forms, a shared quest for a good life.　It is the task of science to analyze and understand facts, that of philosophy to organize the norms of conduct on the basis of these facts, and that of religion to mysticize and emotionalize these norms of behavior.

Confronted by factors in the social situation which inspire in him a potent fear of the unknown—natural phenomena of a startling nature, pestilence, death, the enigma of a future after death, defeat, and the like—the individual naturally wishes for a way of escape, assurance, and inward peace.　He searches his environment for an answer

46 See pp. 273-274, 282-284.
47 Edward Sapir, "The Meaning of Religion," *American Mercury*, Vol. 15, September, 1928, p. 74.

to his problem. Somehow he must become accommodated to an ideal order which for the present is mysterious and inscrutable and beyond the verification of science.

It is possible for the individual in such a situation to have an uniquely individual experience with the unknown, which defines the situation for him, provides him with a deep emotional thrill, and becomes immediately a sacred value to be cherished throughout life. Such an experience is a religious experience in the truest sense. The vision quests of the Crow Indians and other North American tribesmen are cases in point.[48] So are the visions that came to Saint Paul on the Damascus road and to Saint John on the island of Patmos.

Usually, however, the individual—perplexed, fearful, or sorely tried—finds ready-made definitions in his social world to answer his need. In every social group there exist notions about deity, heaven, hell, devils, and angels, which are inevitably forced upon the attention of the individual. He may respond positively or negatively towards them, but he must respond. How these group notions get formally accepted and acted upon by the group has been related elsewhere.[49] How they are taken over and incorporated into the behavior of the individual will receive consideration at this point.

The child is born into a worshipping community just as truly as he is born into a family, a neighborhood, a farming, or industrial community. Sooner or later he will come under the influence of one or more of the traditional culture complexes in which reside the elements of the behavior patterns that go back to the fundamental ideals and ultimate values of life. These patterns are constantly confronting and stimulating him. His every social act is checked up in terms of an ideal mystical relationship of man to man, brother to brother, spirit to spirit. In such situations he comes to the conviction that his conduct requires a superhuman sanction, if it is to be effective.

It is the primary function of religion, then, to elevate the levels of human conduct by redefining and accommodating attitudes on a basis of ideals. That which inspires a devotion to a cause, a principle, an ideal, no matter whether these are immersed in the traditional lore of the past or projected into the realm of futuristic goals to be striven for, is religion in the broadest sense. It is a dynamic force which emerges from social interaction, becomes emotionalized in terms of an immediate felt need, and receives the united support of the group through the medium of an institutional pattern.

---

48 See: Lowie, *Primitive Religion*, pp. 1-14, 171; Ruth F. Benedict, "The Concept of the Guardian Spirit in North America," *Memoirs Am. Anthrop. Ass.*, 1923, No. 29, pp. 20 ff.
49 See Chapter 12.

Education.—It is a recognized function of education, broadly considered, to acquaint people with the findings of social studies of limited scope and significance, the conclusions of research pursued in accordance with the scientific method and attitude, and the generalizations or laws of pure science. Also, it properly includes those bodies of thought, such as history, literature, philosophy, and aesthetics, which are not scientific, but which may be equally justified for the purpose of common life. On the respective values for society of the discipline of science and the inspiration of the non-scientific, Windelband made this pertinent statement:

This raises the question: What is the more valuable for the purpose of knowledge in general, a knowledge of law (scientific) or a knowledge of events? As far as that is concerned, both scientific procedures may be equally justified. The knowledge of the universal laws has everywhere a practical value in so far as they make possible man's purposeful intervention in the natural processes. That is quite as true of the movements of the inner as of the outer world. In the latter case knowledge of nature's laws has made it possible to create those tools through which the control of mankind over external nature is steadily being extended.

Not less for the purposes of the common life are we dependent upon the results of historical knowledge. Man is, to change the ancient form of the expression, the animal who has a history. His cultural life rests on the transmission from generation to generation of a constantly increasing body of historical memories. Whoever proposes to take an active part in this cultural process must have an understanding of history. Wherever the thread is once broken—as history itself proves—it must be painfully gathered up and knitted again into the historical fabric. . . .

On the other hand it is certain that all interest and values of life are concerned with what is unique in men and events. Consider how quickly our appreciation is deadened as some object is multiplied or is regarded as one case in a thousand. "She is not the first," is one of the cruel passages in *Faust*. It is in the individuality and the uniqueness of an object that all our sense of value has its roots. It is upon this fact that Spinoza's doctrine of the conquest of the passions by knowledge rests, since for him knowledge is the submergence of the individual in the universal, the "once for all" into the eternal.[50]

Unfortunate, perhaps, is the emphasis on past events and idealized future goals which marks the present trend of education. Life is a continuous process, but this fact is generally lost sight of by the remarkable lack of attention paid in education to present facts and forces. On this point, Dewey remarks:

[50] Translated from Wilhelm Windelband and quoted by **Park** and **Burgess**, *Introduction to the Science of Sociology*, pp. 9-10.

As traditionally conducted, it [education] strikingly exhibits a subordination of the living present to a remote and precarious future. To prepare, to get ready, is its keynote. The actual outcome is lack of adequate preparation, of intelligent adaptation. The professed exaltation of the future turns out in practice a blind following of tradition, a rule of thumb muddling along from day to day; or, as in some of the projects called industrial education, a determined effort on the part of one class of the community to secure its future at the expense of another class. If education were conducted as a process of fullest utilization of present resources, liberating and guiding capacities that are now urgent, it goes without saying that the lives of the young would be much richer in meaning than they are now. It also follows that intelligence would be kept busy in studying all indications of power, all obstacles and perversions, all products of the past that throw light upon present capacity and in forecasting the future career of impulse and habit now active—not for the sake of subordinating the latter but in order to treat them intelligently. As a consequence whatever fortification and expansion of the future that is possible will be achieved—as it is now dismally unattained.[51]

In so far as education stresses aims and neglects the means to the attainment of these ends it is a failure. From the point of view of sociology, it is not the principal business of education to inform or to instruct in terms of ideals, but to furnish an equipment, a technique for meeting the varied exigencies of life. Educational institutions have an influence in shaping attitudes, in defining situations, and in creating new social values to the extent that they open the mind, stimulate mental curiosity, encourage intellectual activity, train in critical analysis and interpretation, and provide tested instruments by which socially idealized goals may be realized.

CONTROL ON A BASIS OF FACT

Lack of accuracy and loose thinking, tendencies to economize effort and follow lines of least resistance, to act rather than to think, to respond spontaneously to suggestion without discrimination, and to ignore facts are traits of the average human being. This is not an attempt to evaluate such behavior as "good" or "bad," socially "desirable" or "undesirable." Whether it is or not depends upon the circumstances of the situations in which it is found. Exhaustive and persevering observation in many areas of life is an essentially modern procedure and, for the masses of the people, has yet to estab-

---

[51] John Dewey, *Human Nature and Conduct*, 1922, pp. 269-270. Copyright, 1922, Henry Holt and Co., Inc. For a discussion of some of the functions and problems of present-day education, see *Am. J. Sociol.*, Vol. 48, No. 6, May, 1943, and *Survey Graphic*, Vol. 36, November, 1947.

lish itself as a technique worthy of emulation and confidence. However, it seems reasonably certain that future social change will become increasingly dependent upon the continued and extended definition of situations and formation of attitudes in terms of data critically analyzed and verified. We will now direct our attention to some of the fields whence come controls on a basis of fact.

News.—This has been called "the age of the newspaper," and so it is if one may judge, not by numbers and circulation alone, but also by content and the influence exerted by the press. While the newspaper is by no means the only medium of communication nor the sole dispenser of "news," it is undoubtedly the chief one, especially in urban areas. Professor Park, in discussing public opinion as a force for social control, says of the newspaper:

> In any attempt to understand the nature of public opinion and its relation to social control it is important to investigate first of all the agencies and devices which have come into practical use in the effort to control, enlighten, and exploit it.
> The first and the most important of these is the press, that is, the daily newspaper and other forms of current literature, including books classed as current.
> The newspaper is the great medium of communication within the city, and it is on the basis of the information which it supplies that public opinion rests. The first function which a newspaper supplies is that which formerly was performed by the village gossip.[52]

Walter Lippmann, who is at once dubious about public opinion and skeptical of the press as a force for generating and directing a public opinion, says:

> Everywhere today men are conscious that somehow they must deal with questions more intricate than any that church or school had prepared them to understand. Increasingly they know that they cannot understand them if the facts are not quickly and steadily available. Increasingly they are baffled because the facts are not available; and they are wondering whether government by consent can survive in a time when the manufacture of consent is an unregulated private enterprise. For in an exact sense the present crisis of western democracy is a crisis in journalism.
> . . . So long as there is interposed between the ordinary citizen and the facts a news organization determining by entirely private and unexamined

52 Robert E. Park, "Human Behavior in the Urban Environment," in Park and Burgess, *The City*, Chicago, University of Chicago Press, 1925, pp. 38-39. See also Robert E. Park, "News as a Form of Knowledge: A Chapter in the Sociology of Knowledge," *Am. J. Sociol.*, Vol. 45, No. 5, March, 1940, pp. 669-686, and Robert E. Park, "News and the Power of the Press," *Am. J. Sociol.*, Vol. 47, No. 1, July, 1941, pp. 1-11.

standards, no matter how lofty, what he shall know, and hence what he shall believe, no one will be able to say that the substance of democratic government is secure. "The theory of our constitution," says Mr. Justice Holmes, "is that truth is the only ground upon which men's wishes safely can be carried out. In so far as those who purvey the news make of their own beliefs a higher law than truth, they are attacking the foundations of our constitutional system. There can be no higher law in journalism than to tell the truth and shame the devil." [53]

In spite of its deficiencies, the newspaper is reaching more people, providing for more varied tastes, and exerting more influence than ever in its history and in ways possible to no other single medium. Moreover, it does carry the news. It may not be all the news and it may be biased, distorted, or untruthful but it is practically all the news the majority of citizens get. Whether it is good, bad, or indifferent is beside the point in this discussion. The important fact is that it reaches the people, gives them information on every subject, and stimulates public thought and action. The ethics of the newspaper interest some people, but the sociologist is primarily interested in its natural history, policies, and content in so far as these help to determine its socializing function and its force for social control. Without doubt the newspaper will continue indefinitely as the principal guide to the formation of opinion on matters of public interest.

Social Survey.—The forerunners of the modern social survey movement were of the nature of social description and census-taking, and it is practically impossible to locate their precise origins. The social survey in the modern sense was adopted as a technique of investigation into community problems, when communities began to be group-conscious with respect to the presence, prevalence, and seriousness of such factors in community life as poverty, disease, unsanitary conditions, crime, and other undesirable features of society. The survey is the outgrowth of an expressed desire on the part of the people to ascertain what is in need of correction and improvement in their community. It is a study which applies a more or less scientific method to social and economic phenomena for the purpose of obtaining data upon which to formulate a sound program for future community development. It is a sort of inventory, a taking of stock, and a method of social diagnosis. Gradually, the scope of the survey has been expanded to include all kinds of data about a community, assets as well as liabilities.

---

[53] Walter Lippmann, *Liberty and the News.* Copyright, 1920, by Walter Lippmann. Used by permission of The Macmillan Co., publishers, New York.

The facts which the survey reveals are made available to the public chiefly concerned and may be made accessible to a wider public. Many channels of publicity are utilized for getting the information to the people. These include the newspaper, the graphic exhibit, the public platform, the radio broadcast, the published bulletin, the magazine and periodical press, the pageant or play, the motion picture, and a full report in book form. The social survey is at once a technique of investigation on a broad scale and a means of influencing social change. The test of the survey as a method of fact-finding, publicity, and social control is found in the action which follows it.[54]

Research.—"The typical American survey is an essentially practical measure, directed toward the immediate solution of a present problem; research, on the other hand, deals with general data divorced from time and place; it seeks to test a general hypothesis." [55] In recent years, social research has received a tremendous impetus from the public approval and practical application of its findings. Vast sums of money have been contributed for its support and to insure its future on a substantial financial basis. Foundations with large financial resources at their disposal have launched on the gigantic task of searching out the facts in the many broad fields of human affairs.

In the fields of industry, business, public health, education, church, and state, researchers are at work finding the facts and giving them publicity. Organizations like the Metropolitan Life Insurance Company, and foundations, like those bearing the names of Rockefeller, Russell Sage, Carnegie, and other financiers, maintain staffs of experts to extend research and education in a variety of areas of life. Some of these, e.g., the Rockefeller Foundation, have created subsidiary agencies to carry out specific programs.

The ways in which the factual results of research are affecting social control are many and varied. So rapid and far-reaching have been the gains in scientific knowledge that men have come to accept its guidance in many of the important affairs of human life. Some spheres of human activity remain practically untouched by the research influence, however, because of its failure to meet certain human needs and because of the tendency of human beings to be more readily moved by their emotions and preconceptions than by carefully ascertained facts. In some fields of study and at some times in our recent

---

[54] Allen Eaton, and Shelby M. Harrison, *A Bibliography of Social Surveys*, New York, Russell Sage Foundation, 1930; Joanna C. Colcord, *Your Community*, New York, Russell Sage Foundation, 1947; Manuel C. Elmer, *Technique of Social Surveys*, Los Angeles, J. R. Miller, 1927; Shelby M. Harrison, *The Social Survey, New York*, Russell Sage Foundation, 1931.

[55] Harriett M. Bartlett, "The Social Survey and the Charity Organization Movement," *Am. J. Sociol.*, Vol. 34, No. 2, September, 1928, p. 331.

history, scientific dicta have been discredited and repudiated. Nevertheless, the margin of error in human judgments and programs for present and future action has been reduced by the systematic application of scientific data. The influence of scientific knowledge is slow in making its way, even though it has truth on its side. Scientists are thinkers and workers in special and generally narrow fields and are sometimes not equipped in themselves to carry their theories into the specific problem and there put them to the test of practical experience. Until the gap between the scholar and the layman is more fully bridged, the discovery of new facts and the formulation of new theories will have a limited application in directing social change.[56]

Control on a basis of fact, on the whole, is devoid of the emotional and traditional drives of the other forms of control. The attitudes which it defines are without sentiment. They are convincing but not inspiring. They affect the enlightened minority but make little impression in a positive way upon the masses. They are listened to by some who see them as being practical; they are suspected by others as being "modern," "high-brow," or "impractical." They rely upon ideas rather than ideals.

Since facts are neither ethical nor non-ethical they bear no ethical sanctions and their rapid and general ascendance might be expected to result in a moral crisis. They foster individualism and a free spirit and may thereby weaken the social unity and loosen the bonds of control. If, on the other hand, they are restricted to a minority, they are apt to encourage an autocracy of learning. Under the assault of facts certain of the more regulative controls are giving way and the theological and other doctrinaire systems they nourished are being subordinated to knowledge. If by means of broad and systematic education the control of knowable facts can be introduced subtly and gradually into the thinking habits and behavior patterns of the group as a leavening influence rather than as destructive criticism, there is reason to hope that, when the group has mastered the new technique, out of it may be constructed a rejuvenated and more satisfying social order.

SOCIAL POLICY AND SOCIAL ENGINEERING

A shift of interest from the description and understanding of phenomena to attempts to make those phenomena subservient to some practical end marks the transition from scientific research to tech-

---

[56] Sociological research methods will receive attention in Chapter 27.

nology. Technology is applied science. When the scientific principles of physics are applied to the design of a bridge or a machine, for example, we have technology. Similarly, when the scientific data of sociology or of other social sciences are used to work out plans affecting functions of government, the rate of crime, the layout of a community, or the incidence of unemployment, we have social technology. When the plans so worked out are put into effect for the purpose of changing conditions, we have social engineering, that is, to the extent that the principles of social technology are actually employed.[57]

The field of city planning affords a good illustration of social technology. In this field various commissions of experts are at work on the task of "deepening and spreading the investigations basic to it." Social and economic factors are receiving quite as much attention as the more purely geographic. The Regional Plan of New York and Its Environs, completed in 1928, is at once the most extensive and intensive project of the kind ever undertaken.[58] Throughout America and in Europe, whence the impetus for city planning came, cities are undertaking the task of making themselves over to conform to standards of beauty, convenience, health, sanitation, housing, recreation, efficiency, and the like, which have emerged from researches into a complexity of engineering, economic, social, legal, and other factors.[59] Social engineering is used where programs of slum clearance, construction and financing of low-cost housing, playground development, parking, and landscaping are put into effective operation.

A fundamental prerequisite of social planning is a social philosophy. In other words, planned social reorganization must have aims, goals, and objectives. Since very early times many thinkers have been pondering such questions as "Whither are we going?" "Is man capable of shaping his own destiny?" "What kind of society do we want?" and "If we should succeed in shaping our culture and social action to our present needs, what kind of society would we have?" Many and varied have been the answers to these questions, propounded through the ages. But when such answers have come from

---

[57] See: C. H. Cooley, R. C. Angell, and L. J. Carr, *Introductory Sociology*, New York, Charles Scribner's Sons, 1933, pp. 481-482.

[58] R. L. Duffus, *Mastering a Metropolis*, New York, Harper & Bros., 1930; *Regional Survey of New York and Its Environs*, New York, Regional Plan Association, Inc., 8 vols., 1927-1931.

[59] Alfred Bettman, *City and Regional Planning Papers*, Cambridge, Harvard University Press, 1946; Harold M. Lewis, *City Planning, Why and How*, New York, Longmans, Green & Co., 1931; Public Administration Service, Chicago, *Action for Cities: A Guide for Community Planning*, Chicago, Public Administration Service, 1943; S. E. Sanders and A. J. Rabuck, *New City Patterns*, New York, Reinhold Publishing Corp., 1946; Camillo Sitte, *The Art of Building Cities*, New York, Reinhold Publishing Corp., 1945; Mabel I. Walker, *Urban Blight and Slums*, Cambridge, Harvard University Press, 1937.

mere speculative philosophy—a very common occurrence—they have usually assumed the character of grandiose schemes, utopian formulations, and easy rationalizations about "social evolution," "social progress," and "social betterment." Such assumptions and prognostications hold sway over men's minds and imaginations for a time, but are discredited as impractical, visionary, other-worldly, and unscientific.

In the introduction to Part IV it was pointed out that change is universal and inevitable. This fact is held as one of the chief tenets of all science. If this be true, it follows that social technology and social engineering cannot set for themselves fixed goals. The objectives aimed at must consist of those qualities that inhere in changing human nature, in our shifting cultural patterns, and in our constantly forming and reforming social organization. Only painstaking, scientific investigation can determine what these qualities are and what discernible and measurable tendencies and trends of change they display.[60]

SOCIAL CONTROL AS THE INTEGRATION OF THE NEEDS OF THE PERSON AND THE REQUIREMENTS OF SOCIETY

Throughout this chapter we have been dealing with persons and the social controls which are always impinging on them. The individual is, from the start, subject to defining social environments. The process, sometimes conscious and intentional and sometimes unconscious and unintentional, by which the defining goes on, involves the interaction of social forces operating in the capacity of means of social control.

Group life in great measure depends upon predictable, routine behavior on the part of persons. Yet individuals are never quite alike in their emotional needs, their objectives, and their judgments of self-interest. As a consequence, they tend to behave in ways that occa-

---

[60] See: C. C. Bouglé, *The Evolution of Values,* New York, Henry Holt & Co., 1926; C. M. Case, *Social Process and Human Progress,* New York, Harcourt, Brace & Co., 1931; F. Stuart Chapin, "Social Theory and Social Action," *Am. Sociol. Rev.,* Vol. 1, No. 1, February, 1936, pp. 1-11; Charles H. Cooley, *Human Nature and the Social Order,* New York, Charles Scribner's Sons, 1902, Ch. 12; Charles H. Cooley, R. C. Angell, and L. J. Carr, *Introductory Sociology,* New York, Charles Scribner's Sons, 1933, Ch. 29; Paul H. Landis, *Social Policies in the Making,* Boston, D. C. Heath & Co., 1947; Lewis Mumford, *The Story of Utopias,* New York, Boni & Liveright, 1922; Lewis Mumford, *Technics and Civilization,* New York, Harcourt, Brace & Co., 1934; C. C. North, *Social Problems and Social Planning,* New York, McGraw-Hill Book Co., Inc., 1932, Ch. 19; Howard W. Odum, "The Case for Regional-National Planning," *Social Forces,* Vol. 13, October, 1934, pp. 6-23; Frederick B. Parker, "Social Control and Technology," *Social Forces,* Vol. 22, December, 1943, pp. 163-168; Talcott Parsons, "The Role of Ideas in Social Action," *Am. Sociol. Rev.,* Vol. 3, No. 5, October, 1938, pp. 652-664; Pitirim A. Sorokin, "Is Accurate Social Planning Possible?" *Am. Sociol. Rev.,* Vol. 1, No. 1, February, 1936, pp. 12-24.

sionally disrupt group routines. Also, group routines tend to hinder the activities of some individuals. Out of these conflict situations there emerges the need for social control. Individuals and groups must be induced to conform or to change in ways consistent with the sentiments, interests, and objectives of other individuals or other groups with a view to maintaining existing kinds of order or to achieving specific kinds of change. Thus it is seen that what has been said in this chapter about the mechanisms of social control and the processes by which they function to define situations and to determine behavior in conformity with societal requirements and ideals, applies to the development of personality and of group status with about equal validity.

QUESTIONS

1. What is held by some sociologists to be the central problem of sociology?
2. How does social interaction serve to set up the mechanisms of social control?
3. "No one person can do a social act." Explain.
4. What are the meaning and function of social control?
5. What characterizes social control that we call "implicit"?
6. Analyze the process by which control is exercised by the crowd.
7. Explain in terms of sociological concepts what happened in the story of the funeral of "Sister President."
8. Why may it be said of control in the crowd that it is "most aimless, arbitrary, and capricious"?
9. How do you account for the control exercised by the folkways and mores?
10. In what ways is tradition a factor in social control?
11. Why do savage peoples make great use of subtle and psychological means of control?
12. What are the characteristics of ceremonial and ritual that make them effective in social control?
13. What is meant by saying that "taboos represent the extreme fixation of attitudes on the negative side"?
14. Mention some present-day taboos and attempt to explain them in terms of the "wishes."
15. Wherein lies the force of prestige for control?
16. Summarize the characteristic traits of implicit forms of social control.
17. Why are explicit controls called for and in what essential respects do they differ from the implicit forms?
18. Differentiate between myth and legend.
19. What are the distinguishing characteristics of the four classes of myths? Illustrate.

20. What aspects of myths and legends have led to their characterization as "mass dreams"?
21. What makes the problem of public opinion in control an intricate and involved one?
22. Discuss the mechanisms for control employed by publics.
23. What has led many people to be skeptical of public opinion as a guide to conduct?
24. "There can be no democracy without free and responsible discussion and a wholesome respect for and maximum adherence to public will." Discuss.
25. What are some miscellaneous devices originated and utilized for the purpose of maintaining the social order?
26. Explain the process by which formal means of control arise.
27. How are delinquency and crime explained in terms of "the social definitions"? What are the usual defining agencies?
28. How is law related to the less formal means of control?
29. What is the usual method of law in attempting to secure conformity to the social patterns of behavior it has laid down? Discuss.
30. Analyze the mechanisms of religious behavior through which it exerts the control necessary for its survival.
31. What is the primary function of religion?
32. What is generally recognized as being the primary function of education?
33. Compare the estimates of Park and Lippmann as to the functions and reliability of the press. What are the inferences for social control?
34. Advance arguments both for and against the newspaper as an agency for control.
35. What is the social survey and how does it influence behavior?
36. What and how does research contribute to a factual basis of conduct?
37. What can be said in favor of social control on a basis of fact?
38. Evaluate the efforts at scientific prevision in human affairs.
39. Differentiate between social policy, social technology, and social engineering. Though different from one another, how are they interrelated?
40. Discuss social control as the integration of the needs of the person and the requirements of society.

BIBLIOGRAPHY

ALBIG, WILLIAM. *Public Opinion.* New York, McGraw-Hill Book Co., Inc., 1939, Chs. 8-23.

ALLPORT, GORDON W., AND POSTMAN, LEO. *The Psychology of Rumor.* New York, Henry Holt & Co., 1947.

ARNOLD, THURMAN. *The Symbols of Government.* New Haven, Yale University Press, 1935.

BENDIX, REINHARD. "Bureaucracy: The Problem and Its Setting." *Am. Sociol. Rev.*, Vol. 12, No. 5, October, 1947, pp. 493-507.

BERNARD, L. L. *Social Control in Its Sociological Aspects.* New York, The Macmillan Co., 1939.

BETH, MARIAN W. "The Elite and the Elites." *Am. J. Sociol.*, Vol. 47, No. 5, March, 1942, pp. 746-755.

BIRD, GEORGE L., AND MERWIN, FREDERIC E. *The Newspaper and Society: A Book of Readings.* New York, Prentice-Hall, Inc., 1942, Part II, "The Newspaper at Work in Society"; Part III, "The Newspaper, A Product of Many Forces."

BURNHAM, JAMES. *The Machiavellians: Defenders of Freedom.* New York, John Day Co., 1943.

CARROLL, WALLACE. *Persuade or Perish.* Boston, Houghton Mifflin Co., 1948.

CHASE, STUART. *Democracy Under Pressure: Special Interests vs. the Public Welfare.* New York, Twentieth Century Fund, 1945.

CHASE, STUART. *The Tyranny of Words.* New York, Harcourt, Brace & Co., 1938. `

CHILDS, HARWOOD L. *An Introduction to Public Opinion.* New York, John Wiley & Sons, 1940.

COOLEY, CHARLES H. *Social Organization.* New York, Charles Scribner's Sons, 1909, Part VI, "Public Will."

DOOB, LEONARD W. *The Plans of Men.* New Haven, Yale University Press, 1940.

DOOB, LEONARD W. *Public Opinion and Propaganda.* New York, Henry Holt & Co., 1948.

DOWD, JEROME. *Control in Human Societies.* New York, D. Appleton-Century Co., 1935.

EHRLICH, EUGEN. *Fundamental Principles of the Sociology of Law.* Cambridge, Harvard University Press, 1936.

ELIOT, THOMAS D. "Human Controls as Situation Processes." *Am. Sociol. Rev.*, Vol. 8, No. 4, August, 1943, pp. 380-388.

FRAZER, SIR JAMES G. *The Golden Bough.* London, 1911. Part II, "Taboo and the Perils of the Soul."

GALLOWAY, GEORGE, AND ASSOCIATES. *Planning for America.* New York, Henry Holt & Co., 1941.

GARBER, WILLIAM. "Propaganda Analysis—To What End?" *Am. J. Sociol.*, Vol. 48, No. 2, September, 1942, pp. 240-245.

GELLERMAN, WILLIAM. *The American Legion as Educator.* New York, Teachers College, Columbia University, 1938.

GOODMAN, PERCIVAL, AND GOODMAN, PAUL. *Communitas: Means of Livelihood and Ways of Life.* Chicago, University of Chicago Press, 1947.

GURVITCH, GEORGES. *Sociology of Law.* New York, Philosophical Library, 1942.

GURVITCH, GEORGES, AND MOORE, WILBERT E. *Twentieth Century Sociology.* New York, Philosophical Library, 1945, Ch. 10, "Social Control," by G. Gurvitch; Ch. 11, "Sociology of Law," by Roscoe Pound; Ch. 13, "Sociology of Knowledge," by Robert K. Merton; Ch. 14, "Sociology of Religion," by Joachim Wach.

HERRING, E. PENDLETON. *Public Administration and the Public Interest.* New York, McGraw-Hill Book Co., Inc., 1936.

HERSKOWITS, MELVILLE J. "Education and Cultural Dynamics." *Am. J. Sociol.*, Vol. 48, No. 6, May, 1943, pp. 737-749.

HOLLINGSHEAD, AUGUST B. "The Concept of Social Control." *Am. Sociol. Rev.*, Vol. 6, No. 2, April, 1941, pp. 217-224.

HUGHES, HELEN McGILL. *News and the Human Interest Story.* Chicago, University of Chicago Press, 1940.

JAMES, E. O. *The Social Function of Religion.* Nashville, Cokesbury Press, 1940.

KELLETT, E. E. *The Story of Dictatorship from Earliest Times Till Today.* New York, E. P. Dutton Co., 1937.

LANDIS, PAUL H. *Social Control: Social Organization and Disorganization in Process.* Philadelphia, J. B. Lippincott Co., 1939.

LANGENHOVE, FERAND VAN. The Growth of a Legend. New York, G. P. Putnam's Sons, 1916.

LASSWELL, HAROLD D., AND BLUMENSTOCK, DOROTHY. *World Revolutionary Propaganda: A Chicago Study.* New York, Alfred A. Knopf, 1939.

LEE, ALFRED McCLUNG. "The Analysis of Propaganda: A Clinical Summary." *Am. J. Sociol.,* Vol. 51, No. 2, September, 1945, pp. 126-135.

LEE, ALFRED McCLUNG. *The Daily Newspaper in America.* New York, The Macmillan Co., 1937.

LEIGHTON, ALEXANDER H. *The Governing of Men.* Princeton, Princeton University Press, 1945.

LEMERT, EDWIN M. "The Folkways and Social Control." *Am. Sociol. Rev.,* Vol. 7, No. 3, June, 1942, pp. 394-399.

LEOPOLD, LEWIS. *Prestige: A Psychological Study of Social Estimates.* London, T. Fisher Unwin, 1913.

LUMLEY, FREDERICK E. *Means of Social Control.* New York, The Century Co., 1925.

MACCURDY, J. T. *The Structure of Morale.* New York, The Macmillan Co., 1943.

MACIVER, ROBERT M. *The Web of Government.* New York, The Macmillan Co., 1947, Part I, "The Emergence of Government"; Part II, "The Bases of Authority."

MACKENZIE, FINDLAY (Ed.). *Planned Society: Yesterday, Today and Tomorrow.* New York, Prentice-Hall, Inc., 1937.

MEAD, GEORGE H. "The Genesis of the Self and Social Control." *Int. J. of Ethics,* Vol. 35, pp. 251-277.

MERRIAM, CHARLES E. *The Role of Politics in Social Change.* New York, New York University Press, 1936.

MERTON, ROBERT K. "Bureaucratic Structure and Personality." *Social Forces,* Vol. 18, 1940, pp. 1-10.

MERTON, ROBERT K., FISKE, MARJORIE, AND CURTIS, ALBERTA. *Mass Persuasion; Social Psychology of a War Bond Drive.* New York, Harper & Bros., 1946.

MURPHY, GARDNER, AND LIKERT, RENSIS. *Public Opinion and the Individual.* New York, Harper & Bros., 1938.

MYERS, ALONZO F., AND WILLIAMS, CLARENCE O. *Education in a Democracy.* New York, Prentice-Hall, Inc., 1937.

NEWMAN, JAMES R., AND MILLER, BYRON S. *The Control of Atomic Energy: A Study of Its Social, Economic and Political Implications.* New York, McGraw-Hill Book Co., Inc., 1948.

ODEGARD, PETER H., AND HELMS, E. ELLEN. *American Politics—A Study in Political Dynamics.* New York, Harper & Bros., 1938.

PARK, ROBERT E. "News as a Form of Knowledge: A Chapter in the Sociology of Knowledge." *Am. J. Sociol.,* Vol. 45, No. 5, March, 1940, pp. 669-686.

PARK, ROBERT E. "News and the Power of the Press." *Am. J. Sociol.,* Vol. 47, No. 1, July, 1941, pp. 1-11.

PARK, ROBERT E., AND BURGESS, E. W. *Introduction to the Science of Sociology.* Chicago, University of Chicago Press, 1921, Ch. 12, "Social Control."

PARKER, FREDERICK B. "Social Control and the Technicways." *Social Forces,* Vol. 22, December, 1943, pp. 163-168.

POUND, ROSCOE. *Social Control Through Law.* New Haven, Yale University Press, 1942.

QUEEN, STUART A., AND THOMAS, L. F. *The City: A Study of Urbanism in the United States.* New York, McGraw-Hill Book Co., Inc., 1939, Part V, "Prediction and Control."

RADCLIFFE-BROWN, A. R. *Taboo.* London, Cambridge University Press, 1939.

RANKIN, ROBERT S. *When Civil Law Fails: Martial Law and Its Legal Basis in the United States.* Durham, N. C., Duke University Press, 1939.

RIVERS, W. H. R. "The Sociological Significance of Myth." *Folklore,* Vol. 23, No. 3, September, 1912, pp. 307-331.

ROSS, EDWARD A. *Social Control: A Survey of the Foundations of Order.* New York, The Macmillan Co., 1915, 1929.

ROUCEK, JOSEPH S. (Ed.). *Social Control.* New York, D. Van Nostrand Co., Inc., 1947.

SALMON, LUCY. *The Newspaper and Authority.* New York, Oxford University Press, 1924.

SEAGLE, WILLIAM. *Men of Law from Hammurabi to Holmes.* New York, The Macmillan Co., 1947.

SIMPSON, SIDNEY P., AND STONE, JULIUS. *Cases and Readings on Law and Society.* St. Paul, Minn., West Publishing Co., 1948, Part I, "Law in a Kin-Organized Society"; Part II, "Law in an Emergent Political Society."

SMITH, BRUCE, LASSWELL, HAROLD D., AND CASEY, RALPH D. *Propaganda, Communication and Public Opinion: A Complete Reference Guide.* Princeton, Princeton University Press, 1946.

SOREL, GEORGES. *Reflections on Violence.* Translated from the French by T. E. Hulme. New York, B. W. Huebsch, 1912, Ch. 4, "The Proletarian Strike." An example of the Utopian myth.

STOLPER, GUSTAV. *This Age of Fable: The Political and Economic World We Live In.* New York, Reynal & Hitchcock, 1942.

SUMNER, W. G. *Folkways.* Boston, Ginn & Co., 1906, Chs. I, II, V, XVII.

TAYLOR, EDMUND. *The Strategy of Terror.* Boston, Houghton Mifflin Co., 1940.

TIMASHEFF, N. S. *An Introduction to the Sociology of Law.* Cambridge, Harvard University Committee on Research in the Social Sciences, 1939.

WACH, JOACHIM. *Sociology of Religion.* Chicago, University of Chicago Press, 1944.

WALLIS, WILSON D. *Religion in Primitive Society.* New York, F. S. Crofts & Co., 1939.

WAPLES, DOUGLAS (Ed.). *Print, Radio and Film in a Democracy.* Chicago, University of Chicago Press, 1942.

WEBSTER, HUTTON. *Taboo: A Sociological Study.* Stanford University, Stanford University Press, 1942.

WEST, REYNARD. *Conscience and Society: A Study of the Psychological Prerequisites of Law and Order.* New York, Emerson Books, Inc., 1945.

YINGER, MILTON. *Religion in the Struggle for Power: A Study in the Sociology of Religion.* Durham, N. C., Duke University Press, 1946.

Chapter 25

TRENDS OF SOCIAL CHANGE: SOCIAL MOVEMENTS

Social change is dependent upon a combination of tendencies into fairly definite trends. Tendencies and trends there are in all changes, but they effect major changes principally through their functioning in what have been called "social movements." It is through the objective study of such movements that an understanding of the evidences and mechanisms of social change in the direction of social reorganization may be obtained. Such a study must involve the classification of movements and the analysis of concrete cases in an attempt to formulate principles operating in the natural history of social movements, both general and specific. At present the field is largely untouched and is open for scientific exploration.

In the chapter on "Social Unrest and Types of Collective Behavior," we examined some of the more or less primitive expressions of collective behavior. In that connection it was stated that the amorphous, poorly organized, and largely aimless collective responses discussed are indicative of social change, that they imply the disintegration of the old and the emergence of the new, and that they may affect the course of change in the direction of social reorganization to the extent that they combine to constitute trends. Thus, they have a dual role in social change: as symptoms of unrest and disorganization and as possible tendencies which may cumulate to establish trends of change toward a new order of life. If and when collective response tendencies begin to assume cumulative aspects, to take a rather definite direction toward some more or less clearly defined goal, and to display other than elementary, spontaneous mechanisms of control, there is evidence of the beginning of the development of a social movement. As a social movement is advanced, it takes on the characteristics of societal behavior.[1]

Social movements are relatively slow in their development and the participants have a fairly clear consciousness of group unity, of a purpose or an objective, and of a common means or program for achieving that end. There is concerted action because there are

---

[1] See Chapter 23.

common mechanisms and a common goal. In the beginning, however, it is not always possible to determine whether the tendencies at
work are shaping up to form a trend of social movement or are merely
the spontaneous and ephemeral symptoms of restless collectivities
without organization and common objective. Now and then, also, a
social movement of considerable proportions and duration may flare
up in expressive form, thus revealing its abortive nature or its inability to survive opposition from without or schism within its structure.
Furthermore, there are instances where two or more movements
merge and become one, and there are other instances where one
strong movement absorbs one or more weaker movements. The
former possibility is illustrated by the temporary merging of the
incipient labor movement with the Chartist movement in England in
1842; the latter possibility is manifested in the not infrequent absorption of protest political movements by one or another of the older,
well established political parties. History is replete with examples
of organized social movements, sometimes well along in the course
of their development and sometimes definitely established as going
concerns, which experience division into two or more lesser movements. In fact, it seems safe to conclude that most social movements
start with the breakup of the institutional structures of an old social
order and represent the efforts of dissident sects or other schismatic
groups to inaugurate a new scheme of life.

TYPES OF ORGANIZED SOCIAL MOVEMENT

Generally speaking, the kinds of collective behavior that characterize the progress of a social movement from its incipiency to its
culmination in institutional form range all the way from the elementary process of milling, at one extreme, to societal behavior, at
the other extreme. It may be added, also, that the mechanisms of
control employed in the development of a social movement may vary
all the way from the informal and implicit ones to those of a formal
kind. What particular kinds of response tendencies and what specific
mechanisms for controlling behavior get selected in a given social
movement will depend upon the nature of the total situation in that
particular movement and not upon a general rule. The different types
of social movement do tend, however, to display their own peculiar
behavior patterns and mechanisms for control. Types of social movement are to be distinguished and classified, though not so much in
terms of these features as in terms of their differentiating end-values,
the objectives which they seek to accomplish. The means employed

are generally selected to achieve rather definite ends and are usually justified accordingly.

"Social movements can be viewed as collective enterprises to establish a new order of life." [2] This definition by Blumer suggests the essential features of a social movement which differentiate it from other forms of collective behavior discussed in Chapter 23, namely, by implication at least, its organized character, and the presence of a purpose. As mentioned before, however, the organization is something that is acquired by the movement as it develops an increasingly clear conception of a goal or objective. It is in terms of their consciously held objectives that organized social movements may be classified and differentiated.

The types of organized social movements which we shall discuss fall into two broad categories : cultural and political. The former seek objectives that will embody the inner sentiments of the aspiring group; the primary objective of the latter is a modification of the social order in some specific regard or a complete overturning of the social order. This means that essentially political movements are of two classes— reformative and revolutionary. Of these two classes, those with more or less reformative aims seek to change fundamental institutions and conditions to bring them into conformity with the existing mores; they aim to change policy and administration. On the other hand, those with revolutionary aims seek to change the mores and institutions by destroying the existing social order and by setting up a new social order. A third type of organized movement—movement of organized groups from place to place—has been included in some classifications. Careful investigation of movements such as the Crusades of the eleventh, twelfth, and thirteenth centuries, tribal migrations, the treks of such sectarian groups as the Mormons, the Mennonites, the Dukhobors, and other similar bodies, seems to show that while they differ in motivation and in their organized character from the mass migrations described earlier,[3] they are little more than incidental phases of one of the two inclusive types of organized social movement mentioned above. Their mechanisms of operation will be treated in what follows, but only as incidental to our discussion of social movements.

Cultural Movements.—While the motives actuating all social movements, the stages through which they pass, and the goals they hope to attain are determined by the dominant values of the culture

---

[2] H. Blumer, in Alfred M. Lee (Ed.), *New Outline of the Principles of Sociology,* New York, Barnes & Noble, Inc., 1946, p. 199.

[3] Chapter 21.

and the character of the social organization of the time and place in question, there are certain social movements which may be designated "cultural" as distinct from those which are chiefly "political," although, as we shall see, a cultural movement may serve as a prelude to one that is political. The principal distinguishing mark of a cultural social movement is that its purpose is not one of changing the objective nature of the social order or of any of its component parts, but rather one of seeking through collective endeavor a larger measure of satisfaction of the sentiments, moral principles, or otherwise conceived ideals, values, and emotional aspects of traditional cultural patterns. The participants in such movements may or may not strive for social change, but, whether they do or do not, they find release in expressive behavior which, if continued or repeated to the point of becoming crystallized, may affect the persons involved and make an impress on the social order.[4]

Typical of cultural movements are revivals, such as sectarian (religious and political) and nationalistic (linguistic and literary and otherwise cultural), some kinds of crusades, fashion movements, and festivals (folk dancing, anniversary celebrations, etc.). Given social conditions in which earlier dispositions—nationalistic, artistic, political, or religious—have been suppressed, thus leading to tension and unrest, there is a tendency for these dispositions to be revived and to take possession of the group.

A revival indicates a return to the soul-stirring experiences that belonged to the earlier life of the individual or of the group. The memories of the group members are revivified, the attention gets centered once more on the sacred symbols associated with the past, rapport and *esprit de corps* are renewed, old rituals and ceremonials are revitalized, and a new sense of unity and power takes possession of the group. Under the urgency of the collective excitement, which is in most respects that of the ecstatic religious or dancing crowd, the external conditions of the moment fade into insignificance by comparison. Such behavior, when repeated and sought for, marks the beginning of a social movement, be it nationalistic, aesthetic, or sectarian in either a religious or a political sense.

Revivalism of any kind is an apparent consequence of such situational factors as changing community structure, disturbance in institutional organization, dislocations of population through migration, acute social and personal maladjustment, and a widespread feeling of insecurity and frustration on the one hand, and of vague

---

4 See: Blumer, *op. cit.*, p. 214.

hope on the other. Holt is inclined to account for the phenomenal growth of the Holiness and Pentecostal denominations or sects in the southeastern United States as "largely the natural product of the social disorganization and cultural conflict which have attended the over-rapid urbanward migration and concomitant urbanization of an intensely rural, and among other things, religiously fundamentalist population."[5] He states further:

The movement is typically a social movement in that it is an attempt on the part of certain groups experiencing acute social maladjustment to recapture their sense of security through religious revival and reform. Their present attempt at social adjustment and reintegration tends to be reactionary and reformist rather than revolutionary or constructive in character, and does not promise to help eradicate the maladjustment which brought it forth. Its beliefs and ethics are drawn from a disintegrating rural agricultural tradition. However, they are successful in inspiring hope and a type of behavior in individuals which may raise their individual or group status above that of their class.[6]

Similar unsettled and unsatisfactory conditions seem to have surrounded most revivalistic movements of a sectarian character at the time and place of their inception. Once such a movement gets set on a definite course, whether that of worshipful behavior or political action, it tends to center its collective emotions on a body of beliefs and rites which become its creed and its ritual, to emphasize its peculiarities, and to follow its delegated or charismatic leaders.

Elsewhere we had occasion to point out that revivals of folk speech, folk literature, and other aspects of native culture frequently mark the beginning of a movement which may develop into an organized struggle for national autonomy and status.[7] The culture of a nationality group finds its principal medium in the native language and it is in the folk speech and folk literature that a people discovers its national culture and national character. This is particularly true of a people that is oppressed or so thinks of itself. When the historic moment arrives, an acute nationalistic movement is born. Such was the case in South Africa following the Anglo-Boer War.

The South African situation appears as a parallelism between the national movement and the linguistic and literary revival movement. The former may be regarded as a general political and cultural movement; the latter appears as a special cultural movement. The former stimulated the latter

---

5 John B. Holt, "Holiness Religion: Cultural Shock and Social Disorganization," *Am. Sociol. Rev.*, Vol. 5, No. 5, October, 1940, p. 741.
6 *Ibid.*
7 See pp. 324, 590-591.

and in turn was stimulated by it. This reciprocal relation is also observed in the rise of nationalism in Europe. The smaller nationalities are similar cases to South Africa. The movement of nationalism gives rise to special culture movements and linguistic revivals.[8]

It is in the psychologically organized crowd that desires and impulses that have been suppressed come to the surface. They are released and accompanied unconsciously by the images connected with the activity and associated with the memories of earlier days. In the revival the impressions received in early life are recalled by the suggestion of common symbols and there is a turning back, temporarily at least, to the freshness and spontaneity of less highly conventionalized modes of behavior.

In the beginning, these revivalistic and many other cultural movements take on the essential features of cults. To be a cult there must be a collective devotion to some particular person, thing, theory, idea, or the like. In the case of religious cults it is some peculiar object or manner of worship that holds the center of attention and around which the entire worshipping community revolves. But there are many cults that are not commonly regarded as religious in nature, although, as a matter of fact, they may possess the essential qualities of religious systems, if by religious is meant conscientious devotion to the object of devotion. Cultism is as old as primitive man and as modern as the present. Limitations of space preclude the listing of more than a few of the things that have been the objects to which innumerable cults have been dedicated within recent times. These include such values as success, freedom, reason, the simple life, nudity, Nature, humanism, health, enlightenment or "culture," modernity, contentment, Utopia, and the like.[9]

---

[8] G. S. H. Rossouw, *Nationalism and Language*, Ph.D. thesis, University of Chicago, 1922, p. 90.

[9] As the cults have flourished, so has the literature about them. Only a few references can be given here. E. R. Bentley, *A Century of Hero-Worship*, Philadelphia, J. B. Lippincott Co., 1944; C. S. Braden, "Why Are the Cults Growing," *Christian Century*, Vol. 61, July-December, 1943, pp. 45-47, 78-80, 108-110, 137-140; Dale Carnegie, *How to Win Friends and Influence People*, New York, Simon & Schuster, 1937; Christopher Dawson, *The Spirit of the Oxford Movement*, London, Sheed & Ward, 1934; Paul H. DeKruif, *Health Is Wealth*, New York, Harcourt, Brace & Co., 1940; A. H. Fauset, *Black Gods of the Metropolis: Negro Religious Cults of the Urban North*, Philadelphia, University of Pennsylvania Press, 1944; Norman Foerster, *Humanism and America*, New York, Farrar & Rinehart, 1930; A. W. Griswold, "New Thought: A Cult of Success," *Am. J. Sociol.*, Vol. 40, No. 3, November, 1934, pp. 309-319; A. E. Haydon, "Modernism as a World-Wide Movement," *J. Religion*, Vol. 5, No. 4, January, 1925, pp. 1-13; F. E. Johnson, *The Foundations of Democracy* (a symposium), New York, Harper & Bros., 1947; G. A. Koch, *Republican Religion: The American Revolution and the Cult of Reason*, New York, Henry Holt & Co., 1933; Helmut Kuhn, *Freedom Forgotten and Remembered*, Chapel Hill, University of North Carolina Press, 1943; Gay MacLaren. *Morally We Roll Along* (Chautauqua movement), Boston, Little, Brown & Co., 1938; Jacques Maritain, *True Humanism*, New York, Charles Scribner's Sons, 1938; M. F. Melcher, *The Shaker Adventure: An Experiment in Contented Living*, Princeton, Princeton University Press, 1941; F. and M. Merrill, *Among*

Cults bear a resemblance to fads, crazes, and fashions [10] but differ from such mass phenomena in that the latter arise and spread in terms of extrinsic values alone, whereas cults appear and grow in terms of intrinsic values. In the cult the participants tend toward fanaticism, while such behavior is not so generally called out by the other phenomena. Finally, and importantly, cults generate among their adherents a definite group-consciousness, a morale, and an impulse to group action. Moreover, although fads, crazes, and fashions no doubt have their leaders, such as the so-called "leaders of fashion," these leaders are usually anonymous and remain unknown to the "followers" *en masse*, while in the cult the leader more often than not occupies a most important position in the estimation of the devotees. In fact, in a great many instances, the leader is of the type designated "charismatic." The authority or domination of the charismatic leader is based on the direct personal allegiance of the followers by virtue of that individual's dynamic and creative personality, in contrast to the leader whose power rests on traditional, legal, or institutional elements. Not infrequently the cult leader is self-appointed; he is the creator of the movement, its high priest, if not its demi-god.[11]

Like fads, crazes, fashions, and popular manias, the cult typically originates at some place, under cultural and immanent conditions favorable to its rise, and spreads from this center, first along class or other status levels and eventually downward and upward across lines of status difference. Interestingly, cults show a tendency to emerge out of precisely the same type of environment that gives birth to the forms of mass phenomena just mentioned, namely, economically unstable, highly mobile, culturally variable, and socially disorganized communities and regions.[12]

Cults come and go. The movement wanes and may disappear when the particular setting which evoked and facilitated the move-

the Nudists, New York, Garden City Publishing Co., 1933; Arthur E. Morgan, *Nowhere Was Somewhere* (Utopia), Chapel Hill, University of North Carolina Press, 1946; Louis S. Reed, *The Healing Cults: A Study of Sectarian Medical Practice*, Chicago, University of Chicago Press, 1932; J. A. Richardson, *The Groups Movement* (Oxford Group movement), New York, Morehouse Publishing Co., 1935; D. W. Riddle, *Early Christian Life: As Reflected in Its Literature*, Chicago, Willett, Clark & Co., 1936; J. Strange, *Adventures in Nakedness* (nudism), New York, Alfred A. Knopf, 1934; H. H. Stroup, *The Jehovah's Witnesses*, New York, Columbia University Press, 1945; R. B. Tozier, "A Short Life-History of the Chautauqua," *Am. J. Sociol.*, Vol. 40, No. 1, July, 1934, pp. 69-73.

[10] See pp. 616-618.

[11] Examples of charismatic sectarian leaders are Joseph Smith of the Mormons, Benjamin Purnell of the House of David, Ann O'Delia Diss Debar of Spiritualism, Aimee Semple McPherson of The Four-Square Gospel, Mme. Helena P. Blavatsky of Theosophy, Ann Lee of Shakerism, Dr. Frank N. D. Buchman of The Oxford Group, to name only a few.

[12] See p. 606. See also Carey McWilliams, *Southern California Country*, New York, Duell, Sloan & Pearce, Inc., 1946, pp. 273-313; Carey McWilliams, "Mecca of the Miraculous," *Holiday Magazine*, January, 1947, pp. 41 ff.; Luther Whiteman and Samuel L. Lewis, *Glory Roads: The Psychological State of California*, New York, Thomas Y. Crowell, 1936.

ment is changed appreciably. It may die out if the leader dies or if
he, by his conduct, loses the respect and confidence of the followers.
This may also happen if the followers, either through boredom or the
finding of greater satisfaction elsewhere, desert the cause or become
indifferent to its claims. On the other hand, if the protagonists of
the movement succeed in outgrowing their essentially emotional,
moralistic, and inwardly directed sentimental attitudes, in modifying
or eliminating the more fantastic and bizarre features of their behavior, and in acquiring a sense of their destiny in a better world
outside the narrow confines of the cult's ideology and structure, then
the cult, like the revivalistic movement, may evolve into a political
movement.

Similar in certain respects to the cult is a type of movement sometimes referred to as the crusade. Crusades display the same religious
fervor and fanaticism as that expressed in the revival and the cult,
but, unlike the latter, they are usually conducted, not toward the
satisfaction of the spiritual, intellectual, aesthetic, or other inner
needs of their participants, but rather toward some external condition
or situation which is interpreted as inimical to the realization of broad,
if not universal, human interests. The appeal of the crusade is to
direct action, in behalf of the masses or of a particular segment of the
population. In this respect it resembles a political movement of
reform or revolution, of which it may be, in fact, a precursor. While
the ideals of and participants in a cult may be confined to a more
or less self-appointed elite, the "elect," a "chosen people," the crusade
is usually gauged to the experiences and interests comprehended by
the common man. Crusaders are reformers or revolutionists in belief
and will, but frequently they never evolve beyond the stage of indict-
ing what they consider in need of reform to the point of moving
actively against the object of their displeasure. In many ways crusaders constitute no more than a restless, discontented, and expressive
public.

The turn of the century witnessed in the United States a series of
"muckraking" episodes in which a considerable "literature of exposure" figured to focus attention upon "the shame of our cities," the
corruption of municipal politics, the laxity of morals, "how the other
half lives," and similar "evils" of life in America. In no more than
a few instances, however, did the persons who inveighed against such
conditions consciously and actively lead a popular crusade, although
their efforts were admittedly not without effect.[13] For a crusade to

---

[13] Names that come to mind are those of Jacob Riis, Josiah Strong, Ida Tarbell, Brand
Whitlock, Lincoln Steffens, Washington Gladden, and David Graham Phillips.

pass beyond the phase of agitation and fervent evangelism and to become a full-fledged political movement, it has to receive popular approval and support, to develop a program of action, and to acquire and use mechanisms to implement the program.

Not very different from the Crusades of the Christians against the hated Turks in the eleventh and twelfth centuries are the Woman's Temperance Crusades after 1873, the Holy War of the Sudan, and certain missionary movements in which the "primer and blackboard" figure instead of the sword. For many who entered World War I it took on the aspect of a holy crusade against the "barbarous Hun." Crusading enterprises of recent years include Dr. Townsend's Old Age Revolving Pension (OARP) movement, Rochedale cooperatives and related barter undertakings, including Tradex (California), Upton Sinclair's EPIC, the revived Ku Klux Klan, Silver Shirts, the Black Legion (centering in Detroit), and others of the same kind. With few exceptions, the above-mentioned movements imply mass regimentation and a totalitarian ideology. On a different plane may be mentioned crusades for birth control, prison reform, socialized medicine, adequate housing, prevention of delinquency, world peace and world federation, peacetime preparedness for defense, and community planning. Most of these movements have borne fruit in social organization and action, but many of them are under the necessity of continuing their crusading efforts because, despite advances made in the direction of their objectives, they see their ultimate goals unrealized.

Another cultural movement of considerable importance for social change is that of fashion. The mass behavior aspects of fashion were briefly discussed in an earlier chapter; [14] here we must treat the movements of fashion more fully. In the words of Blumer,

Fashion behaves as a movement, and on this basis it is different from custom which, by comparison, is static. This is due to the fact that fashion is based fundamentally on differentiation and emulation. In a class society, the upper classes or so-called social elite are not able to differentiate themselves by *fixed* symbols or badges. Hence the more external features of their life and behavior are likely to be imitated by classes immediately subjacent to them, who, in turn, are imitated by groups immediately below them in the social structure. This process gives to fashion a vertical descent. However, the elite class finds that it is no longer distinguishable, by reason of the imitation made by others, and hence is led to adopt new differentiating cri-

---

14 Chapter 23.

teria, only to displace these as they in turn are imitated. It is primarily this feature that makes fashion into a movement and which has led one writer to remark that fashion, once launched, marches to its doom.

As a movement, fashion shows little resemblance to any of the other movements which we have considered. While it occurs spontaneously and moves along in a characteristic cycle, it involves little in the way of crowd behavior and it is not dependent upon the discussion process and the resulting public opinion. It does not depend upon the mechanisms of which we have spoken. The participants are not recruited through agitation or proselyting. No *esprit de corps* or morale is built up among them. Nor does the fashion movement have, or require, an ideology. Further, since it does not have a leadership imparting *conscious* direction to the movement, it does not build up a set of tactics. People participate in the fashion movement voluntarily and in response to the interesting and powerful kind of control which fashion imposes on them.

Nevertheless, the movement of fashion is an important form of collective behavior with very significant results for the social order. First, it should be noted that the fashion movement is a genuine expressive movement. It does not have a conscious goal which people are trying to reach through collective action, . . . nor does it represent the release of excitement and tension generated in a dancing crowd situation. It is expressive, however, of certain fundamental impulses and tendencies, such as an inclination toward novel experience, a desire for distinction, and an urge to conform. Fashion is important especially in providing a means for the expression of developing tastes and dispositions; this feature establishes it as a form of expressive behavior.

The latter remark provides a cue for understanding the role of fashion and the way in which it contributes to the formation of a new social order. In a changing society, such as is necessarily presupposed for the operation of fashion, people are continually having their subjective lives upset; they experience new dispositions and tastes which, however, are vague and ill-defined. It seems quite clear that fashion, by providing an opportunity for the expression of dispositions and tastes, serves to make them definite and to channelize them and, consequently, to fix and solidify them. To understand this, one should appreciate the fact that the movement and success of fashion are dependent upon the acceptance of the given style or pattern. In turn, this acceptance is based not merely upon the prestige attached to the style but also upon whether the style meets and answers to the dispositions and developing tastes of people. (The notorious failures that attend efforts to make styles fashionable upon the basis of mere prestige provide some support for this point.) From this point of view, we can regard fashion as arising and flourishing in response to new subjective demands. In providing means for the expression of these dispositions and tastes, fashion acts, as suggested before, to shape and crystallize these tastes. In the long run fashion aids, in this manner, to construct a *Zeitgeist* or a common subjective life, and in doing so, helps to lay the foundation for a new social order.[15]

To the cultural type of social movements belong, also, certain more or less formal observances intended to revive the memories and stir the emotions of the group, such as folk dancing (which has now become a fad, if not a fashion, in the United States), the war dance of primitive tribesmen, and anniversary occasions. Some occasions take on a somewhat sacred character and are memorialized in holidays (holy days) and festivals, upon which occasions characteristic forms of behavior have become matters of tradition in which the whole group shares. From a certain point of view the establishment of holidays is a rational act in that it gives a needed period of relaxation and relief from work. Actually, however, the holy days of the church were intended to afford the individual an opportunity to participate in religious observances rather than to provide him with surcease from toil. But the holiday interval tends always to become a time of relaxation and release of tension, often becoming orgiastic. Moreover, with a rapid multiplication of holy days it became emotionally difficult, if not practically impossible, to maintain them all, with the result that a process of secularization set in and only a few genuinely holy days, rooted in tradition, survive. When such collective behavior patterns, whether sacred or secular, take on a ritualistic character and are associated with ceremonial occasions, they mark a trend of change in the direction of institutionalization and contribute interest and zest to the subjective life of the social group.

Political Movements.—The word "political," as it will be used here, has a somewhat different connotation from that commonly understood. It does not pertain to a science of government nor to a particular system of government; rather, it relates to those forms of concerted behavior and action which seek to effect changes in a given social order as a whole or in some specific segment thereof. In a political movement, then, a group of persons, who desire to achieve certain purposes thought to lie in large measure outside their own personal interests or needs, organize and work for these ends which, as we have seen, may be either those of reform or of revolution. Also mentioned previously is the fact that many political movements are initially cultural movements projected "outward" from the group toward alterations in the social order. They are movements both *for* a "better" way of social life in general or in some specific segment of that life, and *against* whatever it is in the existing order, in whole or

---

15 Blumer, *op. cit.*, pp. 217-218.

in part, that seems to the group as undesirable and as standing in the way of the desired objective. Political movements with more or less reformative aims include sectarian religious and political ones like prohibition, Christian Science, and feminism; nationalistic movements; international movements, as for peace and disarmament; economic movements, such as agrarian reform, and labor organization; educational movements, as for adult education, religious education, and so-called liberal education; social welfare movements, such as public health, child welfare, and so on. Movements that seek to establish new social orders include such efforts as insurrections, rebellions, some strikes (the general strike, for example), as well as revolutions proper.

The limits of space will not permit us to discuss the several kinds of political movement just mentioned. There will follow, however, a fairly detailed exposition of the natural history of one such social movement. With this discussion to guide him, the student may find it profitable to trace through their various phases the natural development of other specific social movements.

THE NATURAL HISTORY OF SOCIAL MOVEMENTS

The "natural history" of social movements calls for explanation. A significant feature of the development of sociological theory and methodology in recent years has been the emphasis placed on what has been called the "natural history" approach, as distinct from the one-time commonly employed historical or descriptive method, which was confined largely to the collection and publication of generalizations and narratives subjected to preliminary, common-sense verification. *Natural history* undertakes to investigate and record all pertinent facts about type phenomena, to describe in conceptual terms the processes by which these phenomena take place, to analyze the mechanisms operative in the changing character of the phenomena, and to furnish valid explanations of the events so that prediction and control may be possible. Natural history takes account of social change; in fact, it is "nothing more nor less than an account of an evolutionary process—a process by which not the individual but the type evolves." [16] Fundamental differences are not ignored; neither are relevant similarities. Particularities are valuable only as they serve for comparative purposes or as they contribute to an understanding of that which is typical through their quantitative treatment.

---

[16] R. E. Park, in Introduction to L. P. Edwards, *The Natural History of Revolution*, Chicago, University of Chicago Press, 1927, p. xi.

Any person, group, institution, or social movement may be treated by the methods of natural history. Case studies and life histories constitute the principal documentary material of natural history. Each case is treated with reference to a particular purpose, excluding what is believed to be unique or atypical, and with special attention to what is considered to be characteristic of the type being studied. Single case studies or life-history documents do not constitute in themselves sufficient type data for generalization and prediction. But many cases carefully selected, recorded, and compared do furnish bases for the formulation of generalized conclusions about the social, institutional, or personality types studied.[17]

Manifestly, there is not space in an introductory text to include a number of natural histories of a specific type of social movement in order that they might be compared, analyzed, and interpreted for the purpose of generalization. It will suffice for our purpose to present a single case history, very much abbreviated, in order to show some of the more outstanding characteristic features of such a movement, the course of its development, the changing roles of its functionaries, and some of the main mechanisms employed.

It is here postulated that organized social movements follow a fairly uniform pattern in their natural history, though they vary from that pattern in certain details. Practically all of them tend to pass through four definite stages in their development—the preliminary stage of social unrest, the popular stage of collective excitement, the stage of formal organization, and finally, the stage of institutionalization. Further study will have to be undertaken before one can say how generally applicable this hypothesis is.

All movements do not pass through the series of stages just presented; some are balked or die out in the early stages. Each stage appears to be marked by its own distinctive characteristics, leaders, aims, mechanisms of control, and each passes over into the next stage by almost imperceptible changes. The particular movement we have selected for the purpose of illustrating our description and analysis

---

17 Illustrations of the use of the natural history method are: from anthropology, B. Malinowski's *Crime and Custom in Savage Society, The Family among Australian Aborigines,* and *The Sexual Life of Savages;* Margaret Mead's *Coming of Age in Samoa* and *Growing Up in New Guinea;* John and Mavis Biesanz's *Costa Rican Life;* Cora DuBois's *The People of Alor;* Verrier Elwin's *The Baiga;* S. W. Hall's *Tangier Island;* Clyde Kluckhohn and D. Leighton's *The Navaho;* A. H. and D. C. Leighton's *The Navaho Door;* A. R. Radcliffe-Brown's *The Andaman Islanders* and *The Social Organization of Australian Tribes;* and R. Redfield's *Chan Kom* and *Tepoztlan;* from economics, N. S. B. Gras' *Introduction to Economic History;* from sociology, L. P. Edwards, *The Natural History of Revolution;* R. E. Park and H. A. Miller, *Old World Traits Transplanted;* C. R. Shaw, *The Jack Roller* and *The Natural History of a Delinquent Career;* W. I. Thomas and F. Znaniecki, *The Polish Peasant in Europe and America;* W. L. Warner and associates, *The Yankee City* series.

of the natural history of social movements is one belonging to the sectarian type. It is one that was initially set in the direction of reform and then, by force of circumstances, was transmuted into a revolution. In it, we believe, all the essential features are exemplified in serial fashion step by step throughout the entire natural history process.

The Preliminary Stage of Social Unrest.—The Christian movement was a revolutionary movement in a broad, inclusive sense. Christianity began as a sect and became institutionalized as a major world-wide religious system. Within it, as within most religious movements, there occurred through the centuries numerous sectarian movements of which the Methodist movement was one of the most colorful and significant. This specific movement we have selected as the subject of our present study.

The history of England, following the Restoration, is marked by remarkable changes in the direction of great parliamentary reforms, but these were offset to a considerable extent by a decline in the manners and morals of English society. The general decadence is thus described by Stevens:

The vigor of its (Puritanism's) Commonwealth has illustrated the name of England in the history of the world; but its reaction under the Restoration spread over the country greater demoralization than had preceded it under the Papal reigns. The court became a royal brothel. The play-house became the temple of England. The drama of the day could not now be exhibited, nor even privately read without blushes. Many of the most learned and devoted clergymen, whose writings are imperishable in our religious literature, were either silenced or displaced. The ministrations of the Church grew formal and ineffective. The Puritan churches themselves at last fell into general decay, while Natural religion was the favorite study of the clergy, and of the learned generally, and included most of their theology. . . . The decayed state of the English Church, in which Methodism was about to have its birth, was, in fine, the cause, direct or indirect, of most of the infidelity of the age, both at home and abroad. . . . The higher classes laughed at piety, and prided themselves on being above what they called its fanaticism; the lower classes were grossly ignorant, and abandoned to vice, while the Church, enervated by a universal decline, was unable longer to give countenance to the downfallen cause of truth.[18]

The time was ripe for the emergence of some kind of movement. It happened that the movement in this instance was religious in char-

---

[18] Abel Stevens, *The History of the Religious Movement of the Eighteenth Century Called Methodism*, New York, Carlton & Porter, 1858, 3 vols., Vol. I, pp. 21-27.

acter. Methodism may have saved England from a much more catastrophic revolution.

The corruption of manners which had been general since the Restoration was combated by societies for the "Reformation of Manners," which in the last years of the seventeenth century acquired extraordinary dimensions. They began in certain private societies which arose in the reign of James II, chiefly under the auspices of Beveridge and Bishop Horneck. These societies were at first purely devotional, and they appear to have been almost identical in character with those of the early Methodists. They held prayer meetings, weekly communions, and Bible-readings, they sustained charities and distributed religious books and they cultivated a warmer and more ascetic type of devotion than was common in the church. Societies of this description sprang up in almost every conceivable city in England and even in several of those of Ireland. In the last years of the seventeenth century we find no less than ten of them in Dublin. Without, however, altogether discarding their first character, they assumed, about 1695, new and very important functions. They divided themselves into several distinct groups, undertaking the discovery and suppression of houses of ill-fame, and the prosecution of swearers, drunkards, and Sabbath-breakers. They became a kind of voluntary police, acting largely as spies, and enforcing the laws against religious offences. The energy with which this scheme was carried out is very remarkable. As many as seventy or eighty persons were often prosecuted in London and Westminster for cursing and swearing, in a single week. Sunday markets, which had hitherto been not uncommon, were effectually suppressed. Hundreds of disorderly houses were closed. Forty or fifty night-walkers were sent every week to the Bridewell, and numbers were induced to emigrate to the colonies. A great part of the fines levied for these offences was bestowed on the poor. In the fortieth annual report of the "Societies for the Reformation of Manners" which appeared in 1735, it was stated that the number of prosecutions for debauchery and profaneness in London and Westminster alone, since the foundation of the Societies, had been 99,380.

The Methodist movement was a purely religious one. All explanations which ascribe it to the ambition of its leaders, or to merely intellectual causes, are at variance with the facts of the case. The term Methodist was a college nickname bestowed upon a small society of students at Oxford, who met together between 1729 and 1735 for the purpose of mutual improvement. They were accustomed to communicate every week, to fast regularly on Wednesdays and Fridays, and on most days during Lent; to read and discuss the Bible in common, to abstain from most forms of amusement and luxury, and to visit sick persons, and prisoners in the gaol. John Wesley, the master-spirit of this society, and the future leader of the religious revival of the eighteenth century, was born in 1703, and was the second surviving son of Samuel Wesley, the Rector of Epworth, in Lincolnshire.

The society hardly numbered more than fifteen members, and was the object of much ridicule in the university; but it included some men who afterwards played considerable parts in the world. Among them was Charles, the younger brother of John Wesley, whose hymns became the favourite poetry of the sect, and whose gentler, more submissive, and more amiable character, though less fitted than that of his brother for the great conflicts of public life, was very useful in moderating the movement, and in drawing converts to it by personal influence. Charles Wesley appears to have been the first to originate the society at Oxford; he brought Whitefield into its pale, and besides being the most popular poet he was one of the most persuasive preachers of the movement.

There, too, above all, was George Whitefield, in after years the greatest pulpit orator of England. He was born in 1714, in Gloucester, in the Bell Inn, of which his mother was proprietor, and where upon the decline of her fortune he was for some time employed in servile functions. In 1733, he came in contact with Charles Wesley, who brought him into the society. To a work called "The Life of God in the Soul of Man," which Charles Wesley put into his hands, he ascribed his first conviction of that doctrine of free salvation which he afterwards made it the great object of his life to teach.

With the exception of a short period in which he was assisting his father at Epworth, John Wesley continued at Oxford till the death of his father in 1735, when the society was dispersed.[19]

The evidences of social unrest which precede a social movement appear first in the restless behavior of individuals, in local disorders, wandering individuals, and crimes of passion, in the increase of vice, of insanity, and of agitation. The restlessness tends to spread and become social; tensions increase; attention wanders and fixes itself first on one individual, object, or line of action, and then on another. At this stage there is no organization except in the most rudimentary sense. There is no discipline, merely a loose association of individuals whose action pattern is being set up by means of their interaction. They make random, tentative gestures, groping to find some basis for corporate action.

It should be noted further that the preliminary stage in the development of this movement was marked by governmental and ecclesiastical inefficiency, if not outright corruption; by a condition in which men of ability, including "the most learned and devoted clergymen," were shut out of careers of importance; by a move on the part of intellectuals toward a Natural-religion cult; and by a general cultural

19 From W. E. H. Lecky, *A History of England in the Eighteenth Century*, New York, D. Appleton & Co., 1882, 4 vols., Vol. II, pp. 594-602. By permission of Appleton-Century-Crofts, Inc.

drift in the direction of revolutionary change. These are characteristics typical of the beginning phase of social movement.

The leaders in this period of growing unrest—if leaders they can
be called—are of the agitator type. The function of agitation is very
important at the beginning and during the early stages of a social
movement for, as the term suggests, "agitation operates to arouse
people and so make them possible recruits for the movement. It is
essentially a means of exciting people and of awakening within them
new impulses and ideas which make them restless and dissatisfied.
Consequently, it acts to loosen the hold on them of their previous
attachments, and to break down their previous ways of thinking and
acting." [20] Blumer points out that agitation operates in two kinds
of situations: that characterized by injustice and corruption which,
if sensed at all, are only vaguely realized, and that situation in which
the people are already aroused but where agitation is needed to give
impetus and direction to their discontent.

These two kinds of situation call for correspondingly different
types of agitators. The one type, suited to the first kind of situation,
is, in Blumer's words, "more calm, quiet, and dignified. He stirs
people not by what he does, but what he says. He is likely to be a
man sparing in his words, but capable of saying very caustic, incisive,
and biting things—things which get 'under the skin' of people and
force them to view things in a new light." Of the other type, Blumer
says: "he is an excitable, restless, and aggressive individual. His
dynamic and energetic behavior attracts the attention of people to
him; and the excitement and restlessness of his behavior tend to
infect them. . . . His appearance and behavior foster the contagion
of unrest and excitement." [21]

During this pre-revolutionary stage the mechanisms employed to
influence behavior, that is to effect control, may be of considerable
variety, depending on "the dominant socio-psychological conditions"
surrounding the incipient movement and on the mood which comes
to prevail.[22] In the record of the early history of Methodism we note
certain mechanisms such as meetings held at regular intervals, prayer

---

[20] Blumer, *op. cit.*, pp. 203-204.
[21] *Ibid.*, pp. 204-205.
[22] R. D. Hopper, in *The Struggle for Independence in Latin America; a Sociological
Interpretation,* unpublished Ph.D. dissertation, The University of Texas, 1943, has presented
a very satisfactory, though admittedly tentative, table of characteristics typical of the four
stages of a revolutionary movement which is something other than a miscellaneous collection
of items. For each stage he outlines the following characteristics: socio-psychological conditions or frame of reference, leadership, mechanisms used to control or influence behavior,
processes that operate, and the form or "mold" in which behavior is cast. Dr. Hopper's
material will be drawn on throughout the rest of this chapter, with appropriate footnote
citations.

and Bible reading, fasting, the practice of philanthropy, and the like, all useful in building up a proper mood and in generating and maintaining a favorable attitude toward drastic action on the part of the group members.

Typically, the interactional process so characteristic of this stage of a social movement is what we have elsewhere discussed as "milling," [23] or what Blumer has called "circular reaction." [24] "It is sufficient," says Hopper, "to point out that 'milling' results from vaguely apprehended unrest on the one hand and from confusion regarding goals on the other." [25] The social form or mold within which the behavior is cast during this first stage is typically that of a "psychological mass," or at most, that of an association. Although the small group of ascetics of the case under discussion constituted what they called a Society, the record shows little structure and behavior present in the situation that can be called societary. The organization of the group was obviously tenuous, and without established leadership, customs, or traditions, and the behavior was expressive of tension, which the group was unable to release in the direction of some actual change in the social order, with mere expressive behavior as the only alternative.

As the wishes of the persons involved in the interaction come to possess new formulations and as the restlessness is communicated through the contagious extension of the several signs of unrest, there is a tendency for attention to be more narrowly focused on some object or aim, for the state of expectancy to be heightened, and for activity to increase. These features indicate that the movement is entering its second phase, the popular stage.

The Popular Stage.—This stage is one of great collective excitement.

In the course of 1738 the chief elements of the movement were already formed. Whitefield had returned from Georgia. Charles Wesley had begun to preach the doctrine with extraordinary effect to the criminals in Newgate and from every pulpit into which he was admitted. Methodist societies had sprung up under Moravian influence. They were in part a continuation of the society at Oxford, in part a revival of those religious societies that have already been noticed as so common after the Revolution. The design of each was to be a church within a church, a seed plot of a more energetic propagandism than existed in religious communities at large. In these societies the old Christian custom of love-feasts was revived. The members some-

---

23 Pages 606-607.
24 Blumer, *op. cit.*, pp. 170-171.
25 Hopper, *The Struggle for Independence in Latin America.*

times passed almost the whole night in the most passionate devotions, and voluntarily submitted to a spiritual tyranny that could hardly be surpassed in a Catholic monastery. They were to meet every week, to make an open and particular confession of every frailty, to submit to be cross-examined on all their thoughts, words, and deeds. The following among others were the questions asked at every meeting: "What known sin have you committed since our last meeting? What temptations have you met with? How were you delivered? What have you thought, said, or done which you doubt whether it be sin or not? Have you nothing you desire to keep secret?"

Such rules could only have been accepted under the influence of an overpowering religious enthusiasm, and there was much truth in the judgment which the elder brother of John Wesley passed upon them in 1739. "Their societies," he wrote to their mother, "are sufficient to dissolve all other societies but their own. Will any man of common sense or spirit suffer any domestic to be in a band engaged to relate to five or ten people everything without reserve that concerns the person's conscience how much soever it may concern the family? Ought any married persons to be there unless husband and wife be there together?

PROPAGANDIZING THE FAITH

From this time the leaders of the movement became the most active of missionaries. Without any fixed parishes they wandered from place to place, proclaiming their new doctrine in every pulpit to which they were admitted, and they speedily awoke a passionate enthusiasm and a bitter hostility in the church. Nothing, indeed, could appear more irregular to the ordinary parochial clergyman than those itinerant ministers who broke away violently from the settled habits of their profession, who belonged to and worshipped in small religious societies that bore a suspicious resemblance to conventicles, and whose whole tone and manner of preaching were utterly unlike any thing to which he was accustomed. The Methodist preacher came to an Anglican parish in the spirit, and with the language, of a missionary going to the most ignorant heathens; and he asked the clergyman of the parish to lend him his pulpit, in order that he might instruct the parishioners—perhaps for the first time—in the true gospel of Christ. It is not surprising that the clergy should have resented such a movement, and the manner of the missionary was as startling as his matter. The sermons of the time were, as I have said, almost always written, and the prevailing taste was cold, polished, and fastidious. The new preachers preached extempore, with the most intense fervor of language and gesture, and usually with a complete disregard for the conventionalities of their profession. Wesley frequently mounted the pulpit without even knowing from what text he would preach, believing that when he opened his Bible at random the Divine Spirit would guide him infallibly in his choice. The oratory of Whitefield was so impassioned that the preacher was scarcely able to proceed for his tears, while half the audience was convulsed with sobs. The love of order, routine, and decorum, which was the strongest feeling in the clerical mind, was violently shocked. The regular congregation was displaced by an agitated throng, who had never before been seen within the precincts of the church. The usual quiet worship was disturbed by violent enthusiasm or violent opposition, by hysterical paroxysms of devotion or remorse, and when the preacher had left the parish he seldom failed to leave behind him the elements of agitation and division.

We may blame, but we can hardly, I think, wonder at the hostility all this aroused among the clergy. It is, indeed, certain that Wesley and Whitefield were at this time doing more than any other contemporary clergymen to kindle a living piety among the people. Yet before the end of 1738 the Methodist leaders were excluded from most of the pulpits of the church, and were thus compelled, unless they consented to relinquish what they considered a Divine mission, to take steps in the direction of separation.

MOVEMENT TOWARD SEPARATION

Two important measures of this nature were taken in 1739. One of them was the creation of Methodist chapels, which were intended not to oppose or replace, but to be supplemental and ancillary to the churches, and to secure that the doctrine of the new birth should be faithfully taught to the people. The other, and still more important event, was the institution by Whitefield of field-preaching. The idea had occurred to him in London, where he found congregations too numerous for the church in which he preached, but the first actual step was taken in the neighborhood of Bristol. At a time when he was himself excluded from the pulpits of Bristol, and was thus deprived of the chief normal means of exercising his talents, his attention was called to the condition of the colliers of Kingswood. He was filled with horror and compassion at finding in the heart of a Christian country, and in the immediate neighborhood of a great city, a population of many thousands, sunk in the most brutal ignorance and vice, and entirely excluded from the ordinances of religion. Moved by such feelings, he resolved to address the colliers in their own haunts. The resolution was a bold one, for field-preaching was then utterly unknown in England, and it needed no common courage to brave all the obloquy and derision it must provoke, and to commence the experiment in the center of a half-savage population. Whitefield, however, had a just confidence in his cause and in his powers. Standing himself upon a hillside, he took for his text the first words of the sermon which was spoken from the Mount, and he addressed with his accustomed fire an astonished audience of some 200 men. The fame of his eloquence spread far and wide. On successive occasions, five, ten, fifteen, even twenty thousand were present. It was February, but the winter sun shone clear and bright. The lanes were filled with the carriages of the more wealthy citizens, whom curiosity had drawn from Bristol. The trees and hedges were crowded with humbler listeners, and the fields were darkened by the compact mass. The voice of the great preacher pealed with a thrilling power to the very outskirts of that mighty throng. The picturesque novelty of the occasion and of the scene, the contagious emotion of so great a multitude, a deep sense of the condition of his hearers and of the momentous importance of the step he was taking, gave an additional solemnity to his eloquence. His rude auditors were electrified. They stood for a time in rapt and motionless attention. Soon tears might be seen forming white gutters down cheeks blackened from the coal-mine. Then sobs and groans told how hard hearts were melting at his words. A Fire was kindled among the outcasts of Kingswood, which burnt long and fiercely, and was destined in a few years to overspread the land.

It was only with great difficulty that Whitefield could persuade the Wesleys to join him in his new phase of missionary labour. The picturesque scenes and the striking contrasts which out-of-door preaching furnished added to the effect, and the great multitude who were attracted by his eloquence gave in turn to that eloquence an additional power. A contagion of excitement was aroused, and an irresistible wave of sympathetic feeling rolled through the mighty host.

THE REQUISITE LEADERSHIP

But for the simultaneous appearance of a great orator and a great statesman, Methodism would probably have smouldered and at last perished like the very similar religious societies of the preceding century. Whitefield was utterly destitute of the organizing skill which could alone give a permanence to the movement, and no talent is naturally more ephemeral than popular oratory; while Wesley, though a great and impressive preacher, could scarcely have kindled a general enthusiasm had he not been assisted by an orator who had an unrivalled power of moving the passions of the ignorant. The institution of field-preaching by Whitefield in the February of 1739 carried the impulse through the great masses of the poor, while the foundation by Wesley, in the May of the same year, of the first Methodist chapel was the beginning of an organized body capable of securing and perpetuating the results that had been achieved.

From the time of the institution of lay preachers Methodism became in a great degree independent of the Established Church. Its chapels multiplied in the great towns, and its itinerant missionaries penetrated to the most secluded districts. They were accustomed to preach in fields and gardens, in streets and lecture-rooms, in market-places and church-yards. On one occasion we find Whitefield at a fair mounting a stage which had been erected for some wrestlers, and there denouncing the pleasures of the world; on another, preaching against the mountebanks at Moorfields; on a third, attracting around his pulpit 10,000 of the spectators at a racecourse; on a fourth, standing beside the gallows at an execution to speak of death and of eternity. In this manner the Methodist preachers came in contact with the most savage elements of the population, and there were few forms of mob violence they did not experience. In 1741 one of their preachers named Seward, after repeated ill-treatment in Wales, was at last struck on the head while preaching at Monmouth, and died of the blow. In a riot, while Wheatley was preaching at Norwich, a poor woman with child perished from the kicks and blows of the mob. At Dublin Whitefield was almost stoned to death. At Exeter he was stoned in the very presence of the bishop. At Plymouth he was violently assaulted and his life seriously threatened by a naval officer.

Scenes of this kind were of continual occurrence, and they were interspersed with other persecutions of a less dangerous description. Drums were beaten, horns blown, guns let off, and blacksmiths hired to ply their noisy trade in order to drown the voices of the preachers. Once, at the very moment when Whitefield announced his text, the belfry gave out a peal loud enough to make him inaudible. On other occasions packs of hounds were brought with the same object, and once, in order to excite the dogs to fury, a live cat in a cage was placed in their midst. Fire-engines poured streams of fetid water upon the congregation. Stones fell so thickly that the faces of many grew crimson with blood. The magistrates, who knew by experience that the presence of a Methodist preacher was the usual precursor of disturbance or riot, looked on them with the greatest disfavor, and often scandalously connived at the persecution they underwent.

EFFECTS OF CROWD EXCITEMENT

It was frequently observed by Wesley that his preaching rarely affected the rich and the educated. It was over the ignorant and credulous that it exercised its most appalling power, and it is difficult to overrate the mental anguish it must sometimes have produced. Timid and desponding natures unable to convince themselves that they had undergone a supernatural change, gentle and affectionate natures who believed that those who were dearest to them were descending into everlasting fire, must have often experienced pangs compared with which the torments of the martyr were insignificant. The confident assertions of the Methodist preacher and the ghastly images he continually evoked poisoned their imaginations, haunted them in every hour of weakness or depression, discoloured all their judgments of the world, and added a ten-fold horror to the darkness of the grave. Sufferings of this description, though among the most real and the most terrible that superstition can inflict, are so hidden in their nature that they leave few traces in history; but it is impossible to read the journals of Wesley without feeling that they were most widely diffused. Many were thrown into paroxysms of extreme, though usually transient, agony; many doubtless nursed a secret sorrow which corroded all the happiness of their lives, while not a few became literally insane. Religious madness, which from the nature of its hallucinations is usually the most miserable of all the forms of insanity, was in this as in many later revivals of no unfrequent occurrence.

In the intense religious enthusiasm that was generated, many of the ties of life were snapped in twain. Children treated with contempt the commands of their parents, students the rules of their colleges, clergymen the discipline of their church. The whole structure of society, and almost all the amusements of life, appeared criminal. The fairs, the mountebanks, the public rejoicings of the people, were all Satanic. It was sinful for a woman to wear any gold ornament or any brilliant dress. It was even sinful for a man to exercise the common prudence of laying by a certain portion of his income. When Whitefield proposed to a lady to marry him, he thought it necessary to say, "I bless God, if I know anything of my own heart, I am free from that foolish passion which the world calls love." "I trust I love you only for God, and desire to be joined to you only by His commands, and for His sake." It is perhaps not very surprising that Whitefield's marriage, like that of Wesley, proved very unhappy. Theatres and the reading of plays were absolutely condemned, and the Methodists employed all their influence with the authorities to prevent the erection of the former. It seems to have been regarded as a Divine judgment that once, when "Macbeth" was being acted in Drury Lane, a real thunderstorm mingled with the mimic thunder in the witch scene. Dancing was, if possible, even worse than the theatre. "Dances," said Whitefield, "please the devil at every step"; and it was said that his visit to a town usually put "a stop to the dancing-school, the assemblies, and every pleasant thing." He made it his mission to "bear testimony against the detestable diversions of this generation"; and he declared that "no recreations, considered as such, can be innocent." A poor Kingswood collier was noted for his skill in playing the violin. He passed under Methodist influence, and at once consigned his instrument to the flames.

Accompanying this asceticism we find an extraordinary revival of the grossest superstition. It was a natural consequence of the essentially emotional character of Methodism that its disciples should imagine that every strong feeling or impulse within them was a direct inspiration of God or Satan. The language of Whitefield—the language in a great degree of all the members of the sect—was that of men who were at once continually inspired, and the continual objects of miraculous interposition. In every perplexity they imagined that, by casting lots or opening their Bibles at random, they could obtain a supernatural answer to their inquiries. Wesley again and again reiterated, with the utmost emphasis, his belief in witchcraft, and again and again attributed its downfall to religious scepticism. He had no doubt that the physical contortions into which so many of his hearers fell were due to the direct agency of Satan, who tore the converts as they were coming to Christ. He had himself seen men and women who were literally possessed by devils; he had witnessed forms of madness which were not affections which resulted from supernatural agency. On the other hand, if Satanic agencies continually convulsed those who were coming to the faith, Divine judgments as frequently struck down those who opposed it. Every illness, every misfortune that befell an opponent was believed to be supernatural. Molther, the Moravian minister, shortly after the Methodists had separated from the Moravians, was seized by a passing illness. "I believe," wrote Wesley, "it was the hand of God that was upon him."

Numerous cases were cited of sudden and fearful judgments which fell upon the adversaries of the cause. By such anecdotes and by such beliefs a fever of enthusiasm was sustained.

LIMITED ACCEPTANCE AT THIS STAGE

But with all its divisions and defects the movement was unquestionably effecting a great moral revolution in England. It was essentially a popular movement, exercising its deepest influence over the lower and middle classes. Some of its leaders were men of real genius, but in general the Methodist teacher had little sympathy with the more educated of his fellow-countrymen. To an ordinarily cultivated mind there was something extremely repulsive in his tears and groans and amorous ejaculations, in the coarse anthropomorphic familiarity and the unwavering dogmatism with which he dealt with the most sacred subjects, in the narrowness of his theory of life and his utter insensibility to many of the influences that expand and embellish it, in the mingled credulity and self-confidence with which he imagined that the whole course of nature was altered for his convenience. But the very qualities that impaired his influence in one sphere enhanced it in another. His impassioned prayers and exhortations stirred the hearts of multitudes whom a more decorous teaching had left absolutely callous. The supernatural atmosphere of miracles, judgments, and inspirations, in which he moved, invested the most prosaic life with a halo of romance. The doctrines he taught, the theory of life he enforced, proved themselves capable of arousing in great masses of men an enthusiasm of piety which was hardly surpassed in the first days of Christianity, of eradicating inveterate vice, of fixing and directing impulsive and tempestuous natures that were rapidly hastening towards the abyss. Out of the profligate slave-dealer, John Newton, Methodism formed one of the purest and most unselfish of saints. It taught criminals in Newgate to mount the gallows in an ecstacy of rapturous devotion. It planted a fervid and enduring religious sentiment in the midst of the most brutal and most neglected portions of the population, and whatever may have been its vices or its defects, it undoubtedly emancipated great numbers from the fear of death, and imparted a warmer tone to the devotion and a greater energy to the philanthropy of every denomination both in England and the colonies.[26]

The developments in the movement recorded in the above document may be regarded as characteristic of the popular stage of a sectarian movement. In this particular case the unrest which developed as a reaction to the general situation became fairly well coordinated in the tentative objective—"a church within a church, a seed plot of a more fervent piety, the center of a stricter discipline and a

[26] From Lecky, *A History of England in the Eighteenth Century,* Vol. II, pp. 608-653. By permission of Appleton-Century-Crofts, Inc.

more energetic propagandism." This objective, as yet nebulous and temporary, served to focus the attention and to become for the group the representation of an object of action and an outlet for its restlessness. Social movements in general are characterized at this stage by the tendency of those participating in them to formulate some ideal end which is sufficiently remote as to have a more or less universal appeal.

The case further displays a common characteristic in the appearance of other representations in the form of collective illusions, myths, superstitions, and peculiar doctrines, which serve to strengthen the group's purpose and to rally others to its support. Similar in function and equally characteristic of this stage is the appearance of conflict. Forensic groups are formed to counter the movements of opposition and thus does the group come to rationalize its position and its aim. The group becomes in this manner increasingly self-conscious and, if it survives this period of criticism and overt hostility, it is likely to move on to the next or formal stage.

As in every case, the conditions of the time and the requirements of the special situation determine the type of leadership. Characteristically, leadership in the popular stage is that of the prophet and reformer types. The agitator has done his work; the prophet and reformer now take over and carry on. It may happen, as in the case of Methodism, that the role of prophet or reformer may be taken by the one who has been agitator, but such is not always the case. As leader, the prophet feels a sense of possession. He has a feeling that he has special and separate knowledge concerning the causes of unrest and of what is necessary to remedy the situation. He speaks with confidence, an air of authority. He is a revealer of a message, of a new philosophy of life. He uses the sense of authority to make articulate the hopes and wishes of the people and to add weight and prestige to their direction. There is a feeling that he is not himself; someone else speaks through him.

The reformer, though functioning in this same period, is a somewhat different type, although there have been instances where the prophetic and reformer roles were combined in one individual. The reformer is produced by and is reacting to the same basic conditions, but the nature of his reaction to them is different. It is conceived by him to be his function to lead in attacks on specific evils. Thus, he has a more clearly defined program than that of the agitator or of the prophet. He is determined to change conditions in conformity with conventional and traditional moral standards of an ideal type. Social movements in general are piloted through this stage by these types of leaders, though with some variation according to the type of movement.

As for the mechanisms employed, agitation, suggestion, imitation, and milling are continued, but there are some rather fundamental changes in their use. "There is a focusing of attention on a tentative objective to be realized that was absent in the earlier stage. This change results in giving new direction to mechanisms and processes already in operation as well as in calling into play certain additional mechanisms and processes." [27] First, a marked effort to develop *esprit de corps* is present. This has been described by Blumer as "the organizing of feelings on behalf of the movement. In itself, it is the sense which people have of belonging together and of being identified with one another in a common undertaking. Its basis is constituted by a condition of rapport." [28] A second new mechanism in the form of what Edwards has called the "social myth" generally appears at this time.[29] In order to mobilize unrest and discontent and prepare the people for active response to the leaders' appeal, the people must be furnished with an incentive, a belief in the cause with which they are being asked to identify themselves, a hope for the future, which the myth helps to make articulate for them. In addition to these two major devices and as aids to their realization, other mechanisms may be employed as the leaders decide and as the situation seems to demand. For instance, in the case of the Methodist movement, it was the unusual character of its methods, including in particular the "bold experiment" of field-preaching instituted by Whitefield, that led the sect to adopt the name of Methodist, a name which may have been used first in derision by their opponents.

The processes functioning in this stage include an intensification of the "milling" process of the preliminary stage, with a tendency for it to be not quite so random and aimless and for it to take on the character of "collective excitement," which, as it spreads, assumes the form of social contagion, the relatively rapid, unwitting, and nonrational dissemination of a mood, impulse, or form of conduct. These processes serve to integrate the unrest, break down old behavior patterns, and prepare the way for new forms of behavior.

The above brings us to the consideration of the form which the collectivity takes in this popular stage. The most obvious change from the initial stage to this one is to be found in the fact that the

---

27 Hopper, *The Struggle for Independence in Latin America.*
28 Blumer, *op. cit.,* pp. 205-206.
29 See: L. P. Edwards, *The Natural History of Revolution,* Chicago, University of Chicago Press, 1927, pp. 90-96.

mass has evolved into the *crowd*. In the organized crowd there is a very uncritical objectification of experience. Only those tendencies to respond that meet the demands of the dominant mood are expressed; those that would inhibit such response are in abeyance. The individual members of the religious crowd see visions, give vent to inspired utterances, dance, sing, shout, pray.[30] In religious revivals there is a sort of ceremonial reproduction of the contagion and the collective excitement in which the sect was born and through which it continues to propagate itself. The sect perpetuates the religious crowd. As Sighele says, the sect is a chronic crowd.

Social issues arise when the movement has developed to the point where its aims, now becoming defined with clarity, are challenged. There is no issue while the movement is inchoate and unformed. The issue comes when the collective representations and leadership clash with other forces of public opinion. In fact, the crisis may be said to occur when the program of action is decided upon; in the case cited it was when the Methodist leaders decided to take steps in the direction of separation. From this point on, the movement gradually passes over into the next stage of its natural history—the stage of formal organization.

The Stage of Formal Organization.—The next developments in the history of Methodism are typical of this stage.

It is interesting to trace the successive stages in its progress. The colonial work devolved chiefly on Whitefield, who, in his many expeditions to Georgia, revived something of the old spirit of the Pilgrim fathers. He made, however, no attempt to form a separate community, and the first Methodist Society in America was created at New York in 1776, by some Irish emigrants, under a local preacher named Embury. America Whitefield regarded with a peculiar fondness; he became a fervent advocate of its independence, and he at last left his bones in its soil. The clergy in the colony were far more favorable to Evangelical preaching than those in England; but in the perhaps somewhat partial judgment of Wesley, the impression made upon the people was more transient. This judgment, however, was not justified by the event. Methodism in America grew and flourished beyond all its rivals. . . .

In England, as we have seen, the most brutal scenes of violence occurred among the miners of Staffordshire and Cornwall, but their untaught and passionate natures soon felt the attraction of Methodism; and before the close of his career, Wesley preached to overflowing multitudes, and amid perfect silence, at Wednesbury, Newcastle, Bolton, Wigan, and St. Ives.

---

[30] See pp. 608-616, for a description of the expressive behavior of the psychologically organized crowd.

Early in the present century a severe censor of the Methodists acknowledged that "all mines and subterranean places belong to them." In general in England the preachers made least impression in the agricultural districts, and were most favourably received in the seaport towns.

In Wales Methodism became completely triumphant, but it triumphed only after a long and fierce struggle, attended with many striking and instructive incidents. In Scotland the Methodist movement was much less important than in other parts of the island. It had not there to dispel the same ignorance or the same apathy, and it found a people accustomed to a higher standard of dogmatic preaching than in England. Ireland, on the other hand, he [Wesley] found a soil pre-eminently suited for his seed.

But Methodism, or at least that Evangelical movement which grew out of it, soon left a deep impress upon the literature of its time. Cowper, the greatest English poet of the closing years of the eighteenth century, devoted his graceful and tender genius to its service. It contributed powerfully to the popularity of the "Night-Thoughts" of Young; and it appeared prominently in the "Fool of Quality" of Henry Brooke, and in all the writings of Harvey and Hannah More. Its special literature has now probably few readers among the highly educated classes and has scarcely obtained an adequate recognition in literary history. The "Ecclesiastical History" of Milner, and the "Biblical Commentaries" of Scott, are perhaps its most conspicuous monuments, but there was also a vast literature of purely devotional works which have awakened an echo in the hearts of thousands. The "Cardiphonia" of Newton, the "Life of Faith" of Romaine, the "Force of Truth" of Scott, the "Devout Exercises" of Jay, the "Village Dialogues" of Rowland Hill, "The Complete Duty of Man" by Venn, the "Olney Hymns," the "Practical View" of Wilberforce, as well as the innumerable sermons and religious biographies emanating from the same school, have exercised a deep and lasting influence upon the character and opinions of large sections of the English people. In hymns the movement was especially rich. Both of the Wesleys, as well as Newton, Berridge, Shirley, and Rowland Hill, were hymn-writers. Both Madan and Gambold sometimes showed traces of a high order of poetry, and Toplady has left two or three of the most beautiful hymns in the language.

The progress of Evangelical opinions among the higher orders, though perhaps less sincere, and certainly less lasting than among the poor, was also considerable. Several ladies and a few men of great position were greatly impressed with the new teaching. By the exertions of all these patrons, Methodism for a time became almost fashionable. "If you ever think of returning to England," wrote Horace Walpole to Sir Horace Mann, "as I hope it will not be long, you must prepare yourself for Methodism. I really believe by that time it will be necessary; this sect increases as fast as almost ever any religious nonsense did." Lady Fanny Shirley opened her drawing-rooms for preaching in London, and Evangelical opinions gradually spread to the fashionable watering-places; the social position of Lady

Huntingdon at once introduced Methodism into Bath society. A chapel was erected, and Shirley, Venn, and Jay made many converts. Cheltenham, which was just rising into a great watering-place, became in time one of the most Evangelical towns in the kingdom. At Tunbridge Wells occasional preachings were held in the house of Sir Thomas I'Anson. The eminently religious character of George III, though generally very inimical to everything approaching Dissent, more than once spoke with warm admiration of the Methodists.[31]

By this time the motives which inspire the movement have become fixed and the aim definitely established. The movement is now organized around its leaders and a program. It has developed a structure and is supported by a body of traditions. As a reaction to criticism, it has developed a set of norms which find their formal statement in creed or dogma and their formal expression in ritual.

The leaders of this stage are usually of the statesman type. They are the ones who formulate policies and attempt to develop social policy into an art. It is they who gauge the forces in the current mores and perceive and evaluate their tendencies. They are the ones who undertake to understand and voice the convictions which have become established, to state the ideology of the movement, and to propose measures which will realize the interests of which the group has become conscious. The agitator of the period of unrest and the prophet and the reformer of the stage of popular excitement may become the statesmen of this more formal stage, but they do not commonly do so because they are unable, as a rule, to make the necessary adjustment to the changing order. Usually, a statesman is thought of as one concerned with affairs of state. Literally, this is true. But there are church statesmen, educator statesmen, economic statesmen, and other statesmen as well.

In general it may be said that the mechanisms that characterize this stage are those devices that are effective in developing morale and group ideology. Morale is dependent upon a set of convictions which hold that the purpose of the movement is eminently right, that the goal will ultimately be attained, and that the movement is charged with a sacred responsibility which it must accomplish. The ideology consists of the body of belief, doctrine, and myth, without which the movement would lack direction and be unable to withstand the opposition of out-groups. Prominent among the mechanisms of this stage is propaganda, "a deliberately evoked and guided campaign to induce people to accept a given view, sentiment, or value." [32]

[31] From Lecky, *A History of England in the Eighteenth Century,* Vol. II, pp. 653-673. By permission of Appleton-Century-Crofts, Inc.
[32] Blumer, *op. cit.,* p. 193.

A complete list of possible mechanisms cannot be given here. Suffice it to say that various types of leaders and various types of mechanisms combine to facilitate the process of formalization. Historians, apologists, poets, hymnologists, and propagandists, as well as those in the role of statesmen, make use of the press, pamphlets, books, the stage, the movie, the platform and pulpit, cartoons, posters, slogans, banners, insignia, to further the cause of the movement. In the establishment of Methodism, many of these devices were employed. Every social movement tends to develop a literature of its own as well as to influence literature in general.

Collective excitement and social contagion are not adequate to serve as the processual foundation for enduring social change. For this, the formulation of issues and the formalization of procedures are demanded. In brief, the roots of the movement must strike deeper than sentimentalism, sensationalism, fashion, and fad. It must come to appeal to the essential wishes and felt needs of the people—one of the supreme tests of any movement. If it does not possess sufficient human-nature elements, it may not survive the test and may, instead, become quixotic and be dissipated to its destruction.

During this stage the issues around which the movement arose must be resolved if the movement is to endure. This means that differences of opinion get thrashed out in discussion and deliberation. A premium is placed on more or less rational consideration of relevant facts, arguments are advanced, criticized, and met by counterarguments. "In the give and take of argument over and critical analysis of possible lines of action with reference to the issues under examination, policies begin to take shape and programs are 'formulated.' As the movement proceeds, . . . wishes that have been reformulated, goals that have emerged, and policies that have been developed get worked into the mores of the participants and become a 'formal' part of their behavior." [33] It is in this period, also, that there is most likely to occur a "transfer of allegiance of the intellectuals," one of the "master symptoms" of impending revolution identified by Edwards, from the "oppressors" to the cause of the "oppressed." [34] This is a highly significant occurrence in that it indicates that the movement has "arrived," so to speak, that it has gained the active adherence and loyal support of persons of influence.

As has already been intimated, the process of discussion and deliberation, of formulation and formalization, goes on in a *public,* the form which the collectivity has assumed by this time. If the move-

---

[33] Hopper, *The Struggle for Independence in Latin America.*
[34] Edwards, Chapter 4.

ment survives to the point where it finds acceptance in public opinion and support from the current mores, it has established itself as an institution.

The Institutional Stage.—Lecky observes

If Wesley had not been very credulous and very dogmatic, utterly incapable of a suspended judgment, and utterly insensible to some of the highest intellectual tendencies of his time, it may be safely asserted that his work would have been far less. He does not rank in the first line of the great religious creators and reformers, and a large part of the work with which he is associated was accomplished by others; but it is no exaggeration to say that he has had a wider constructive influence in the sphere of practical religion than any other man who has appeared since the sixteenth century. He lived to see the sect which he founded numbering more than 70,000 souls upon British soil, and about 300 itinerant and 1,000 local preachers raised up from his own people. . . . They (the Methodists) have already far outnumbered every other Nonconformist body in England and every other religious body in the United States, and they are probably destined largely to increase, while the influence of the movement transformed for a time the whole spirit of the Established Church, and has been more or less felt in every Protestant community speaking the English language.[35]

Under favorable conditions a movement may terminate in the form of a lasting organization—a labor union, a nation, a denomination, or similar organization. These culminations of successful social movements become established as institutional forms. In the case cited, the Methodist sectarian movement passed through all the characteristic stages of a social movement and ended with the group organized on an accommodation basis in the form of a powerful, socially recognized denomination. It started as a reform effort and, principally because of the refusal of the Established Church to be reformed, ended by staging a revolution and becoming organized as a separatist body along radically novel lines.

The successful leader in this final stage is the administrator. He is the one who translates the policy of the movement into action. Every institutional agency has its functionaries and on certain of these rest the business of direction and the responsibility of getting the organization to operate effectively with respect to its policies. Administration may devolve upon persons, as officers, or upon groups, as boards, cabinets, synods, and the like, or upon both. The agitator, the prophet, and the reformer have no place in this formal arrangement. Personal ascendency, however, is less essential to this relatively stable

---

[35] Lecky, *A History of England in the Eighteenth Century,* Vol. II, p. 687. By permission of Appleton-Century-Crofts, Inc.

and established order than the impersonal instruments it has forged for itself—its laws, disciplines, faiths, dogmas, and ideals. As Sighele has said:

> The members of a stable and legitimate association are more cultured, more calm, more settled, more reflective than are the members of a sect or crowd. Personal appeal has less grasp upon them; with them the centers of control are more active; reason directs and checks sentiment, and immediate and complete adherence to a single man is rare and difficult.[36]

Thus, we are told, mechanisms and established procedures take precedence over personalities. The process of accommodation initiated in the formal stage of the movement has now become a condition, a "recognition and acceptance of a set of relationships that defines the status of the person in the group or of the group in the more inclusive social organization." [37]

We have seen that the mass, the crowd, and the public were the dominant forms of organization corresponding to the first, second, and third stages of an evolving social movement. These are all forms of elementary, more or less spontaneous collective behavior. But by the development of the fourth stage the movement "acquires organization and form, a body of customs and traditions, established leadership, an enduring division of labor, social rules and social values—in short, a culture, a social organization, and a new scheme of life." [38]

SOCIAL MOVEMENTS AND SOCIAL CHANGE

With the emergence of an established institutional pattern out of an evolving social movement, the latter has reached the concluding stage of its life history. The more spectacular and what are probably the more significant modes of social change come about through the reorganization and transformation wrought by types of social movements similar in their natural history to the one just analyzed.[39] The termination of a social movement in a new social order or in a reformed institution indicates that the change is complete and relatively permanent and will remain so until the time when fresh social contacts and accelerated interaction result in a new state of unrest and an increase in social and personal disorganization. Then a new trend of social change in the form of a movement will occur. In this con-

---

[36] S. Sighele, *La Psychologie des Sectes,* Paris, M. Giard et Cie., 1898, p. 79.
[37] E. B. Reuter and C. W. Hart, *Introduction to Sociology,* New York, McGraw-Hill Book Co., Inc., 1933, p. 320.
[38] Blumer, *op. cit.,* p. 199.
[39] Less spectacular and enduring forms of social change have been dealt with in preceding chapters.

nection, mention should be made of frequent incidental consequences of social movements. For example, the Puritan movement in the late sixteenth and early seventeenth centuries set up currents of agitation and propaganda that helped prepare the stage for the parliamentary rebellion, the radicalism of the Levellers, the founding of New England, sectarian divisions, and an incipient bourgeois ethic, all effects hardly intended by the Puritan leaders.[40]

The content of a social movement—its meaning for those who participate in it—is of primary interest to history but not to sociology. The concern of sociology is to understand the processes and mechanisms involved, the more formal aspects of the movement, and its role in effecting social change. In other words, sociology seeks to understand the natural history and not the history of social movements and social change.

QUESTIONS

1. What place is held by social movements in the general course of social change?
2. What kinds of collective behavior and what mechanisms for social control characterize the progress of social movements from their incipiency to their culmination in institutional form?
3. Discuss: "Social movements can be viewed as collective enterprises to establish a new order of life."
4. Into what two broad categories may social movements be classified? Differentiate between them.
5. If a third type of social movement is added, what is it and what, if any, is its significance?
6. What is the distinguishing mark of the cultural type of movement?
7. Name and describe the subtypes of cultural movement.
8. Account for the nature, occurrence, and consequences of revivalism.
9. Discuss cults and cultism as to their nature and manifold expressions.
10. How are cults different from fads, crazes, and fashions, which they resemble in some respects?
11. Under what circumstances and by what means may a cult evolve into a political movement?
12. What are crusades? How do they differ from revivals and cults?
13. Discuss: "Crusaders are reformers or revolutionists in belief and will."
14. Discuss fashion as a social movement.
15. What are some of the more or less formal observances, intended to revive the memories and stir the emotions, which belong to the cultural type of social movement?

---

[40] William Haller, *The Rise of Puritanism, 1570-1643*, New York, Columbia University Press, 1938.

16. How is the term "political" to be understood as the designation for a particular type of social movement? What are some examples of political movements?

17. What is the "natural history" approach as developed in sociological theory and methodology?

18. What significance do case studies and life histories have in the natural history approach?

19. Upon what hypothesis is the study of the natural history of organized social movements based?

20. What are the four definite stages through which organized social movements pass in the course of their natural history?

21. Discuss the main characteristics of the several stages in terms of the Methodist movement.

22. What is the sociology of the emergence of leadership and the roles it plays?

23. Discuss in some detail the characteristic features of the following types of leader: agitator, prophet, reformer, statesman, and administrator.

24. Discuss the mechanisms employed in each stage to influence behavior.

25. Describe the different phases of the interactional process as they appear in the several stages.

26. Describe the forms or structural organizations which characterize the different stages.

27. What are social issues? How do they develop? What are the functions of issues in social movements? Illustrate from the Methodist movement.

28. How does truly significant social change come about in society? What is the part played by organized social movements in social change?

29. What difference is there between the history and the sociology of a social movement?

BIBLIOGRAPHY

ADAMS, BROOKS. *The Theory of Social Revolutions.* New York, The Macmillan Co., 1913.

ADAMS, GRACE, AND HUTTER, EDWARD. *The Mad Forties.* New York, Harper & Bros., 1942.

ALINSKY, SAUL D. *Reveille for Radicals.* Chicago, University of Chicago Press, 1946.

ATKINS, GAIUS G. *Modern Religious Cults and Movements.* New York, Fleming H. Revell Co., 1923.

BALABANOFF, ANGELICA. *My Life as a Rebel.* New York, Harper & Bros., 1938.

BARBER, BERNARD. "Acculturation and Messianic Movements." *Am. Sociol. Rev.,* Vol. 6, No. 5, October, 1941, pp. 663-669.

BARNES, HARRY E. "Social Reform Programs and Movements—Their Historical Development." *Encycl. Americana,* Vol. 25, pp. 166-186.

BERNAYS, E. L. *Propaganda.* New York, Liveright Publishing Corp., 1938.

BILLINGTON, RAY O. *The Protestant Crusade, 1800-1860: A Study of the Origins of American Nativism.* New York, The Macmillan Co., 1938.

BLUMER, HERBERT. "Social Movements," in Alfred M. Lee (Ed.), *New Outline of the Principles of Sociology.* New York, Barnes & Noble, Inc., 1946, pp. 199-219.

BOGARDUS, EMORY S. *Leaders and Leadership.* New York, D. Appleton-Century Co., 1934.

BRINTON, CRANE. *The Anatomy of Revolution.* New York, W. W. Norton & Co., 1938.

BUCHANAN, J. R. *The Story of a Labor Agitator.* New York, The Outlook Company, 1903.

BUNYAN, JAMES. *Intervention, Civil War and Communism in Russia, April-December, 1918: Documents and Materials.* Baltimore, Johns Hopkins Press, 1936.

BURGESS, J. STEWART. "The Study of Modern Social Movements as a Means for Clarifying the Process of Social Action." *Social Forces,* Vol. 22, March, 1944, pp. 269-275.

BURNS, C. DELISLE. *The Principles of Revolution.* New York, Oxford University Press, 1921.

CANTRIL, HADLEY. *The Psychology of Social Movements.* New York, John Wiley & Sons, 1941.

CHADWICK, H. MUNRO. *The Nationalities of Europe and the Growth of National Ideologies.* New York, The Macmillan Co., 1945.

CHAMBERLAIN, JOHN. *Farewell to Reform.* New York, John Day Co., 1933.

CHAMBERLAIN, WILLIAM HENRY. *The Russian Revolution, 1917-1921.* New York, The Macmillan Co., 1935.

CHEYNEY, EDWARD P. *Modern English Reform.* Philadelphia, University of Pennsylvania Press, 1931. Especially Chs. 2-6.

COLTON, ETHAN. *Four Patterns of Revolution.* New York, Association Press, 1935.

CREEL, GEORGE. *Rebel at Large.* New York, G. P. Putnam's Sons, 1947.

DAVENPORT, F. M. *Primitive Traits in Religious Revivals.* New York, The Macmillan Co., 1905.

DAVIS, JEROME. *Contemporary Social Movements.* New York, The Century Co., 1930.

DAVIS, MICHAEL M. *America Organizes Medicine.* New York, Harper & Bros., 1941.

DAWSON, CHRISTOPHER. *The Spirit of the Oxford Movement.* New York, Sheed & Ward, Inc., 1934.

EARHART, MARY. *Frances Willard: From Prayers to Politics.* Chicago, University of Chicago Press, 1944.

EDWARDS, LYFORD P. *The Natural History of Revolution.* Chicago, University of Chicago Press, 1927.

ELLIOTT, MABEL A., AND MERRILL, FRANCIS E. *Social Disorganization.* New York, Harper & Bros., 1941, Part V, "World Disorganization."

FERGUSON, C. W. *The Confusion of Tongues.* New York, Garden City Press, 1929. Sectarian and cultist movements in the United States.

FISHER, VARDIS. *Children of God.* New York, Harper & Bros., 1939. An epic of the Mormon migration and settlement in Utah.

GOTTSCHALK, LOUIS. "Causes of Revolution." *Am. J. Sociol.,* Vol. 50, No. 1., July, 1944, pp. 1-8.

HALLER, WILLIAM. *The Rise of Puritanism, 1570-1643.* New York, Columbia University Press, 1938.

HALLGREN, M. *Seeds of Revolt.* New York, Alfred A. Knopf, 1933.

HERTZLER, J. O. *The History of Utopian Thought.* New York, The Macmillan Co., 1926.

HULETT, J. E., JR. "The Kenny Healing Cult: Preliminary Analysis of Leadership and Patterns of Interaction." *Am. Sociol. Rev.*, Vol. 10, No. 3, June, 1945, pp. 364-372.

HUNTER, ROBERT. *Revolution: Why, How, When?* New York, Harper & Bros., 1940.

JAMESON, J. FRANKLIN. *The American Revolution Considered as a Social Movement.* Princeton, Princeton University Press, 1940.

JENNINGS, HELEN H. *Sociometry of Leadership.* New York, Boston, Beacon House, 1947.

JOHNSON, GERALD W. *American Heroes and Hero Worship.* New York, Harper & Bros., 1943.

JORDAN, W. K. *Men of Substance: A Study of the Thought of Two English Revolutionaries.* Chicago, University of Chicago Press, 1942.

KASTEIN, J. *The Messiah of Ismir: Sabbatai Zevi.* New York, The Viking Press, 1931.

KOCH, G. ADOLPH. *Republican Religion: The American Revolution and the Cult of Reason.* New York, Henry Holt & Co., 1933.

KOHN, HANS. *Prophets and Peoples.* New York, The Macmillan Co., 1946.

KOHN, HANS. *Revolutions and Dictatorships.* Cambridge, Harvard University Press, 1939.

KRESS, ANDREW J. *Introduction to the Cooperative Movement.* New York, Harper & Bros., 1941.

KUHN, HELMUT. *Freedom Forgotten and Remembered.* Chapel Hill, University of North Carolina Press, 1943.

LAIDLER, HARRY W. *Social-Economic Movements.* New York, Thomas Y. Crowell Co., 1944.

LASKI, HAROLD J. *Reflections on the Revolution of Our Time.* New York, The Viking Press, 1943.

LEBON, GUSTAVE. *The Psychology of Revolution.* New York, G. P. Putnam's Sons, 1913.

LEE, ALFRED MCCLUNG. "Techniques of Social Reform: An Analysis of the New Prohibition Drive." *Am. Sociol. Rev.* Vol. 9, No. 1, February, 1944, pp. 65-77.

LOUD, G. C. *Evangelized America.* New York, The Dial Press, 1928.

MANNHEIM, KARL. *Ideology and Utopia.* New York, Harcourt, Brace & Co., 1936.

MARTIN, EVERETT D. *Farewell to Revolution.* New York, W. W. Norton & Co., 1935.

MAZOUR, ANATOLE G. *The First Russian Revolution, 1825: The Decembrist Movement.* Berkeley, University of California Press, 1937.

MEADOWS, PAUL. "Sequence in Revolution." *Am. Sociol. Rev.*, Vol. 6, No. 5, October, 1942, pp. 702-709.

MECKLIN, JOHN M. *The Passing of the Saint.* Chicago, University of Chicago Press, 1941.

MECKLIN, JOHN M. *The Story of American Dissent.* New York, Harcourt, Brace & Co., 1934.

MERRIMAN, ROGER B. *Six Contemporaneous Revolutions.* London, The Clarendon Press, 1938.

MURRAY, ROBERT H. *Group Movements Throughout the Ages.* New York, Harper & Bros., 1936.

The Nazi Primer: Official Handbook for Schooling the Hitler Youth. Translation and Preface by Harwood L. Childs. New York, Harper & Bros., 1938.

NEUMANN, SIGMUND. *Permanent Revolution.* New York, Harper & Bros., 1942.

NYSTROM, PAUL. *The Economics of Fashion.* New York, The Ronald Press Co., 1928.

ORTEGA Y GASSET, J. *The Revolt of the Masses.* New York, W. W. Norton & Co., 1932.

PALMER, R. R. *Twelve Who Ruled: The Committee of Public Safety during the Terror.* Princeton, Princeton University Press, 1941.

PARKER, R. A. *The Incredible Messiah.* Boston, Little, Brown & Co., 1937.

PIGORS, PAUL. *Leadership or Domination.* Boston, Houghton Mifflin Co., 1935.

POSTGATE, RAYMOND. *How to Make a Revolution.* New York, Vanguard Press, 1934.

RIDDLE, DONALD W. *Early Christian Life, as Reflected in Its Literature.* Chicago, Willett, Clark & Co., 1936. The orderly, natural development of a cult.

ROSENSTOCK-HUESSY, EUGENE. *Out of Revolution: Autobiography of Western Man.* New York, William Morrow & Co., 1938.

SEARS, CLARA E. *Days of Delusion.* Boston, Houghton Mifflin Co., 1924.

SMITH, JOHN M. P. *The Prophet and His Problems.* New York, Charles Scribner's Sons, 1914.

SMITH, MORTIMER B. *Evangels of Reform.* New York, Round Table Press, 1934.

SOROKIN, PITIRIM A. *Social and Cultural Dynamics.* 4 vols., New York, American Book Co., 1937, 1941, Vol. 3.

SOROKIN, PITIRIM A. *The Sociology of Revolution.* Philadelphia, J. B. Lippincott Co., 1925.

SOULE, GEORGE. *The Coming American Revolution.* New York, The Macmillan Co., 1934.

SWEET, WILLIAM W. *Revivalism in America: Its Origin, Growth and Decline.* New York, Charles Scribner's Sons, 1944.

VON MARTIN, ALFRED. *Sociology of the Renaissance.* Trans. by W. L. Luetkens, New York, Oxford University Press, 1944.

WAGNER, DONALD O. *Social Reformers: Adam Smith to John Dewey.* New York, The Macmillan Co., 1934.

WAGNER, R. *Leadership in a Changing World.* New York, Harper & Bros., 1935.

WALLIS, WILSON D. *Messiahs: Their Role in Civilization.* Washington, American Council on Public Affairs, 1943.

WARNER, REX. *The Cult of Power.* Philadelphia, J. B. Lippincott Co., 1947.

WARNER, WELLMAN J. *The Wesleyan Movement in the Industrial Revolution.* New York, Longmans, Green & Co., 1930.

WESTMEYER, RUSSELL E. *Modern Economic and Social Systems.* New York, Farrar & Rinehart, 1940.

WOOLSTON, HOWARD B. "American Intellectuals and Social Reform." *Am. Sociol. Rev.,* Vol. 1, No. 3, June, 1936, pp. 363-372.

ZIMAND, SAVEL. *Modern Social Movements.* New York, H. W. Wilson Co., 1921.

PART V

LINES OF SOCIOLOGICAL DEVELOPMENT

Chapter 26

THE SOCIOLOGICAL MOVEMENT

It is now fitting that brief attention should be given to the development of the science which this volume has introduced to the student. Sociology, as a special subject, emerged from a long series of significant episodes in social and political thinking. In our discussion, however, we shall be limited to the briefest consideration of two major phases of the sociological movement: pre-sociology in Europe and the United States, and sociology as it has developed into a more or less independent discipline during the last half century.

PRE-SOCIOLOGY IN EUROPE

The Historians and Social Economists of Germany.—Pre-sociological theory had its origin in Germany in political science. Significant in this connection was the work of the Cameralists, falling between 1555 and 1765. The Cameralists considered themselves possessed of a science whose purpose was to provide officers of state with rules for procedure. Behind this theory was the supreme welfare of the state, which, to the early Cameralists at least, meant the welfare of the prince and his ability to control efficiently. Since money was necessary for this purpose, "the beginnings of German social science in general then, and of political science in particular, was fiscal science, or ways and means of supplying the public treasury." [1] Thus we see that the social thought of this period was chiefly political science, with some slight attention paid to economics. The historical technique of the ancients was lost during the Middle Ages and revived later.

Among the historians of the pre-sociological period there are, according to Professor Small, four men who characterize the drive toward objectivity. [2] These men are Friedrich Karl von Savigny (1779-1861), K. F. Eichhorn (1781-1854), B. G. Niebuhr (1776-1831), and Leopold von Ranke (1795-1886). Savigny introduced the notion that every object, including human beings and institutions,

---

[1] A. W. Small, *Origins of Sociology*, Chicago, University of Chicago Press, 1924, p. 115.
[2] *Ibid.*, pp. 37-101.

is an incident in a causal series of human experiences (continuity) ; Eichhorn emphasized the complexity and interrelationship of many influences.[3] Niebuhr appeared with a more critical technique for "subjecting alleged historical evidence to the severest scrutiny,"[4] in which were included: the necessity for excluding mythology, the comparison of all versions for the purpose of discovering common material and common sources, the examination into the credibility of sources, and the use of circumstantial evidence. It remained for von Ranke to insist upon the verification of historical data by documentation. The result of this historical movement was the substitution of social and economic history for pure political history.

During this time there were some fragmentary essays which might be termed sociological, but men interested in sociology found no place in economics, political science, or history. They therefore had to formulate a science of their own.[5]

The Social Philosophers of France.—Auguste Comte (1798-1857), while sometimes called "the father of sociology," was clearly a social philosopher who belongs properly in the pre-sociological period. Condorcet, Montesquieu, Saint-Simon, and Voltaire were in some sense predecessors of Comte, who was indebted to Saint-Simon for much for which he himself receives credit. Saint-Simon lacked the power of synthesis and the force of Comte, who espoused the cause of a positive philosophy and worked out a classification of the sciences from the simple and more general to the complex. In this hierarchy of the sciences Comte placed sociology (he is the first to use the name) as the last in time but the first in importance. What he wanted to do was to make history and philosophy positive sciences. This he would do through sociology. Not only did he coin the term sociology, but he was first to correlate the different aspects of social life, unify them, and treat them as a whole. He believed that the object of science was to discover natural law, which for him meant a statement of how things work.

Comte regarded society as a "collective organism." For him the social consensus existing between the parts of society was more close and vital than the physiological interdependence of the parts of the animal organism. Comte was not so much a maker of sociology as he was a prophet who pointed the way to it.[6]

---

[3] *Ibid.*, p. 65.
[4] *Ibid.*, p. 80.
[5] Some early German contributors to sociology, as such, were: Paul von Lilienfeld (1829-1903), Ludwig Gumplowicz (1838-1909), and Gustav Ratzenhofer (1842-1904).
[6] Chief among the works of Comte are: *Cours de philosophie positive*, Paris, Bachelier, 1830-1842; *Système de politique positive*, Paris, M. Giard et E. Brière, 1851-1854; and

Essentially economic in his philosophy, Frederic Le Play (1806-1882) emphasized geographical determinism in his theory of social organization. His greatest contributions, perhaps, were the importance he attached to the family institution, which he saw chiefly as a business unit, his face-to-face method of collecting data, and his methodical monographic presentation of facts.[7] René Worms (1869-1926), though a contemporary of the sociological movement proper, followed a philosophical rather than an empirical approach. He subscribed wholeheartedly to biological analogies in explaining human society.[8]

The Social Philosophers of England.—Chief among the English social philosophers of the pre-sociological period was Herbert Spencer (1820-1903). Like Comte, Spencer was an organicist, but, unlike Comte, emphasized the analogy between society and a physical organism, disregarding the dissimilarities. Spencer conceived society as an entity, and association of discrete units. According to him, individuals are the social units and he does not consider how they get together. In other words, there is in society no "social sensorium," no social sensations. His is a mechanical theory and his sociology is primarily structural and not functional. Both Spencer and Comte had similar aims—to correlate all knowledge; each in his way emphasized the organic principle.[9]

Other English social thinkers of this same period include Henry Thomas Buckle (1821-1862), writer of a *History of Civilization,* who was a leading advocate of the influence of environment on human society; Henry S. Maine (1822-1888), best known for his book on *Ancient Law,* who was a pioneer in the study of the natural history of institutions; and Walter Bagehot (1826-1877), who, in his *Physics and Politics* (1872), emphasized the use of conflict, showing that social struggle is a group struggle and that the compact groups are superior in struggle. Bagehot also formulated a law of progress in terms of the differences that break up "the cake of custom." He stressed the importance of cultural factors as over against Buckle's

Synthèse subjective, ou système universel des conceptions propres à l'état normal de l'humanité, Paris, M. Giard et E. Brière, 1856.

[7] Le Play is best known for his works entitled *Les Ouvriers européens,* Paris, 1855; *La Organisation de la famille,* Tours, A. Mame et fils, 1871; and the magazine, *La Réforme Sociale,* published by the Le Play School, Paris, 1864.

[8] Typical of the writings of Worms are: *Organisme et société,* Paris, M. Giard et E. Brière, 1896; articles in the *Revue internationale de sociologie,* of which he was founder and editor; *Philosophie des sciences sociales,* 3 vols., Paris, M. Giard et Cie., 1903-1907; *La sociologie, sa nature, son contenu, ses attaches,* Paris, M. Giard et Cie., 1921.

[9] Spencer's works include: *Principles of Sociology,* 3rd ed., 3 vols., New York, D. Appleton & Co., 1880-1896; *Social Statics,* 5th ed., New York, D. Appleton & Co., 1903; and *Study of Sociology,* New York, D. Appleton & Co., 1878.

emphasis on physical forces, and formulated a theory of imitation (of personal leaders) which antedated, and was possibly the source of, Tarde's theory.[10]

The Speculative Treatises of Lester F. Ward.—Ranking with Comte and Spencer as forerunners of sociology was Lester F. Ward (1841-1913). Like them, he attempted to make sociology all-inclusive. He considered that his work offered the following new contributions: (1) a differentiation between social aggregation and social evolution, (2) a theory of social forces, and (3) the superiority of artificial or teleological processes over natural or genetic processes. Ward was the first American to suggest a psychological basis for sociology. His main theories were borrowed from Comte and his data were drawn largely from Spencer. His whole system was built on a hedonistic philosophy and it is clearly more metaphysical than sociological.

The first edition of Ward's *Dynamic Sociology* was published in 1883, and a second edition appeared in 1897. With the exception of Spencer, this was the first significant English contribution to social theory. It is a lengthy, two-volume outline of cosmic philosophy, a justification for sociology, which category he took for granted; a conception of sociology as "dynamic" in regard to all phenomena in which there is motion with respect to evolutionary aspects; an intellectual conception of social causation, particularly social change, in which he conceived of society as coming into being only when people will it; and an attempt to set up a fundamental classification of social forces, desires, etc.

Ward's *Pure Sociology* (1903) defends the position taken in his earlier writings. Again, he is a philosophical monist—the reformer rather than the scientist. He does indicate uncertainty as to methodology and expresses a need for some investigational devices. His contributions to present-day sociology are almost negligible. They gave an impetus, however, to sociological study and teaching.

Sociology and Social Problems.—Contemporary with the beginnings of sociology in the United States was the philanthropic movement, with its interest in poverty, crime, and other social ills, and its organization of charities to combat these evils. Sociological antecedents in this country also felt the influence of the German *Verein*

---

[10] Gabriel Tarde, *Laws of Imitation*, translated from the second French ed. by Elsie Clews Parsons, New York, Henry Holt & Co., 1903.

für Sozialpolitik (1873).   Indeed, so close were these two movements to each other that the earliest impetus to the spread of so-called sociology in the curricula of American universities was through the study of "social problems."   This tendency was so marked that early volumes of the *American Journal of Sociology,* founded in 1895, are filled with articles on social work tinctured with *a priori* sociology. At this time little distinction was made between social work, labor legislation, and sociology.   This emphasis upon social problems and organized philanthropy has continued until recently, and still occupies a considerable place in sociological thinking.[11]

Social Politics.—As might be expected, many who were styled sociologists leaned heavily in the direction of social reforms.   They were in reality social politicians intent upon utopian schemes for social betterment.   No method having been evolved for getting the facts necessary for a social science, attention was turned to *a priori* philosophical generalizations about the world as it had been and about society as it ought to be, ethically, economically, and politically.   Pronounced trends on behalf of "welfare" interests in the United States were largely responsible for these more or less general and discursive social philosophies.   Emphasis began to be placed upon the organization of welfare programs and functions, both public and private, and upon the training for professional service in the fields of social-welfare action.   This interest has been continuous and still holds the major part of attention in some sociology departments.

TYPICAL ATTEMPTS TO DEFINE SOCIOLOGY

In so far as the early sociologists presented other than a philosophy of history, which meant an attempt to trace or plot the graphic equivalent of the course of history through time, sociology was little more than a body of generalizations about society arrived at *a priori*. It was not until the beginning of the twentieth century that a definition of the aim and scope of sociology was undertaken on the basis

11 E. T. Devine, *Misery and Its Causes,* New York, The Macmillan Co., 1909; C. A. Ellwood, *Sociology and Modern Social Problems,* New York, American Book Co., 1913; J. M. Gillette and J. M. Reinhardt, *Current Social Problems,* New York, American Book Co., 1933, 1937; J. L. Gillin, *Poverty and Dependency: Their Relief and Prevention,* New York, The Century Co., 1925; Gillin, Dittmer, and Colbert, *Social Problems,* New York, D. Appleton-Century Co., 1928, 1943; C. R. Henderson, *Introduction to the Study of the Dependent, Defective, and Delinquent Classes, and of Their Social Treatment,* Boston, D. C. Heath & Co., 1908; H. W. Odum, *American Social Problems,* New York, Henry Holt & Co., 1939, 1945; Maurice Parmalee, *Poverty and Social Progress,* New York, The Macmillan Co., 1916; Harold A. Phelps, *Contemporary Social Problems,* New York, Prentice-Hall, Inc., 1932; C. M. Rosenquist, *Social Problems,* New York, Prentice-Hall, Inc., 1940; P. W. Paustian and J. J. Oppenheimer, *Problems of Modern Society,* New York, McGraw-Hill Book Co., Inc. 1938.

of the objective and comparative study of social group phenomena. Sumner and Thomas in America made such a start in the study of ethnographic data.[12] Sumner's ultimate aim was to draft a sociological treatise.[13] His purpose was to make clear one of the fundamental preconceptions necessary for a sociological system, i.e., the mores. He marked an advance in that he attempted to explain data in terms of timeless, psychological theory. Thomas' work is broader in scope, showing that he was interested in the whole field of culture. He dealt with the subjective side of culture, while Sumner was more interested in objective phenomena. Both approaches have found their way into sociology and psychology.

Prior to the appearance of these works, the trend of sociology was moving away from the organic theory and in the direction of a more pluralistic and conceptual notion of the science. The abstract concept "society" was giving way to the "group" concept and emphasis began to be placed on the "process" concept. Leaders in this trend in America were Giddings, Small, Ross, and Cooley. Ludwig Gumplowicz (1838-1909), G. Ratzenhofer (1842-1904), and G. De Greef (1842-1924) were the leading spirits in the movement in Europe.[14]

Franklin H. Giddings (1855-1931) considered sociology an elementary, coordinating, inclusive, fundamental social science. To him social phenomena appeared as the product of the situation and pluralistic behavior; when participants in pluralistic behavior become differentiated "consciousness of kind" develops. This leads to conscious discriminative association and social pressure. Giddings advanced the notion that society organizes itself for collective endeavor; differences lead to division of labor. Organized society, by approvals and disapprovals, pressures and achievements, attempts to select and perpetuate the socially adequate.[15]

Second in importance to the work of Ward and Giddings was that of Albion W. Small (1854-1926). His contributions were primarily in the history of social theory. His conception of sociology changed from time to time, but latterly he came to regard it as the technique

---

[12] W. G. Sumner, *Folkways*, New York, Ginn & Co., 1906; W. I. Thomas, *Source-Book for Social Origins*, Boston, R. G. Badger, 1909.

[13] This aim was partially realized, posthumously, in the publication of W. G. Sumner and A. G. Keller, *Science of Society*, 4 vols., New Haven, Yale University Press, 1927.

[14] See: L. Gumplowicz, *Der Rassenkampf*, Innsbruck, Wagner'oche Univ. Bundhandlung, 1883; and *Outlines of Sociology*, Philadelphia, American Academy of Political and Social Science, 1899; G. Ratzenhofer, *Wesen und Zweck der Politik*, 3 vols., Leipzig, F. A. Brockhaus, 1893; and *Die Soziologische Erkenntnis*, Leipzig. F. A. Brockhaus, 1898; G. De Greef, *Introduction à la sociologie*, Paris, Félix Alcan, 1886. All of these men stress the importance of the conflict process.

[15] The principal works of Giddings include: *Principles of Sociology*, New York, The Macmillan Co., 1896; *Elements of Sociology*, New York, The Macmillan Co., 1898; *Studies in the Theory of Human Society*, New York, The Macmillan Co., 1922; and *The Scientific Study of Human Society*, Chapel Hill, University of North Carolina Press, 1924.

which approaches the study of human experience through the investigation of group life. Small stressed methodology, by which he meant an attitude towards or results gained from social analysis.[16]

Edward A. Ross (1866-   ) made his largest contribution to the developing science by his treatment of the subject of social control. Social order offered a problem for solution and it was the aim of Ross to show by what mechanisms and devices this order is maintained. He saw the social order as a finished product rather than as a growth, and in essentially didactic fashion he presented his theory of control as being of two kinds—political or external, and moral or through the mores.[17]

More introspective in his approach is Charles H. Cooley (1864-1929). His work shows the organic influence, but utilizes a more observational method than that employed by most of his predecessors. Running through Cooley's writings is a growing tendency to point out the universal aspects of human nature as developed in primary groups; the individual remains an abstraction and has no existence apart from the social milieu in which he is placed. Cooley introduced the sociological conceptions of personality and the "self," that is, the "looking-glass self." With Ross and Ellwood,[18] he had much to do with starting the trend of contemporary sociology in the direction of social psychology.[19]

In England, L. T. Hobhouse (1858-1929) was advancing his theory of political and social evolution and presenting sociology as the science of human progress.[20] According to Hobhouse, progress is the harmonious adjustment of man to society, of different types of social organization to each other, and of society as a whole to its environment. Another English social scientist interested in the evolu-

---

16 The chief writings of Small include: *Introduction to the Study of Society*, as co-author with George E. Vincent, New York, American Book Co., 1894; *General Sociology*, Chicago, University of Chicago Press, 1905; *Adam Smith and Modern Sociology*, Chicago, University of Chicago Press, 1907; and *Origins of Sociology*, Chicago, University of Chicago Press, 1924.

17 *Social Control*, New York, The Macmillan Co., 1901, Ch. 30. Other works by Ross include: *Social Psychology*, New York, The Macmillan Co., 1908, showing in a pronounced way the influence of Tarde's "laws of imitation"; *Foundations of Sociology*, New York, The Macmillan Co., 1905; and *Principles of Sociology*, New York, The Century Co., 1920, rev. ed. 1930.

18 C. A. Ellwood, *Prolegomena to Social Psychology*, Ph.D. thesis, University of Chicago, 1901; *Sociology in Its Psychological Aspects*, New York, D. Appleton & Co., 1912; *An Introduction to Social Psychology*, New York, D. Appleton & Co., 1917; *The Psychology of Human Society*, New York, D. Appleton & Co., 1925.

19 These men drew largely from such psychologists as Dewey, Mead, Sidis, Baldwin, and G. Stanley Hall. However, there is reason to believe that they, in turn, contributed significant insights to these other men. Cooley's outstanding works include: *Human Nature and the Social Order*, New York, Charles Scribner's Sons, 1902; *Social Organization*, New York, Charles Scribner's Sons, 1909; *The Social Process*, New York, Charles Scribner's Sons, 1918; *Sociological Theory and Social Research*, New York, Henry Holt & Co., 1930.

20 *Social Evolution and Political Theory*, New York, Columbia University Press, 1917, Chs. 1-4. See also his *Morals in Evolution*, London, Chapman and Hall, Ltd., 1906.

tionary principle is Edward Westermarck (1862-1939), who defends the theory of cultural "evolution" from independent origins as against the "diffusion" theory, although he undertakes to reconcile the two.[21] As an anthropologist he was especially interested in the use of ethnological data in a study of the mind (or "innate ideas") of primitive man, expecting thereby to add to the understanding of original nature.[22] Perhaps the most significant work of Westermarck, from the standpoint of sociology, is his *History of Human Marriage* (1901), an early attempt to study the natural history of an institution. He employed the comparative method of Spencer and his followers, which marked a definite step in the advance of a scientific sociological method. However, much of the value of Westermarck's data was lost by reason of their being extracted from and explained without reference to their cultural setting.

On the Continent, at the opening of this century, two men stand out as leaders in making sociology a science in fact as well as in name. They are Georg Simmel (1858-1918) in Germany, and Emile Durkheim (1858-1917) in France. Simmel narrowed the field of sociological investigation to include merely the forms of interaction; that is, the ways in which individuals form into groups. He was not concerned with the content or meaning of human associations. His was a kind of social geometry. This he held to be the specific, definite field of sociology. History, economics, political science, and psychology could investigate the content; sociology must trace out and describe the formal structure of groups. According to Simmel, origins and evolution have no place in the science of sociology. This emphasis shows him to be far away from the biological school of social scientists. Though he condemns the use of psychology by sociologists, his whole work is shot through with psychological explanations.[23] Moreover, in spite of his dicta to the contrary, Simmel always implied the subjective processes by going into their origins and development, and considered the content as well as the form of human association. In spite of his inconsistencies, no one went into the influence of association on the individual as did Simmel and his impress on modern sociology in Germany and America was pronounced.

21 *History of Human Marriage,* 5th ed., London, Macmillan & Co., Ltd., 1922, Vol. 1, pp. 1-25.
22 *The Origin and Development of Moral Ideas,* London & New York, The Macmillan Co., 1908.
23 See Small's translations of chapters from Simmel's *Soziologie,* 1908, especially Ch. 3, "Superiority and Subordination," *Am. J. Sociol.,* Vol. 2, No. 2, September, 1896, pp. 167-189, and Vol. 2, No. 3, November, 1896, pp. 392-415; and Ch. 4, "Sociology of Conflict," *Am. J. Sociol.,* Vol. 9, No. 4, January, 1904, pp. 490-525; Vol. 9, No. 5, March, 1904, pp. 672-689; Vol. 9, No. 6, May, 1904, pp. 798-811.

Ferdinand Tönnies (1855-1936) and Max Weber (1864-1920) are two other German sociologists who made a deep impression on American sociological thought. The former is best known for his most important work entitled *Gemeinschaft und Gesellschaft* in which he analyzed contrasting ideal types of human associations, the "community" and "society," the former as found in the isolated peasant village, or folk society, and the latter as found in the highly accessible urban center.[24] Weber was another exponent of the ideal-typical kind of sociological interpretation.[25] He stressed the importance of rationally purposeful social action, but recognized that much human action is emotional and not always intelligible. His analyses of such concepts as those of "class," "status group," and "party" have been receiving considerable favorable attention recently, and his insistence upon scientific objectivity and the avoidance of value-judgments on the part of sociologists has not been overlooked in these latter years.

Durkheim had an influence on French sociology comparable to that of Simmel in Germany. The significance of his work is due primarily to the emphasis he gave to the social phenomenon of progressive socialization and its accompanying increase of interdependence.[26] As against Giddings' notions of "like-mindedness" and "consciousness of kind" Durkheim showed that unity is as much dependent upon diversity as upon similarity. This idea was not original with Durkheim—it is found in Spencer—but he gave it a fresher formulation and made it more acceptable. Durkheim laid great stress upon the concept "social mind," by which he meant that a society or group has a "mind" that controls the minds of the individuals composing the group or society, and does so through collective symbols, words, ceremonies, and the like, which he called "collective representations." Another feature of Durkheim's sociology, while not original with him, was the importance he placed upon sociological method. He in-

---

[24] See: *Gemeinschaft und Gesellschaft*, Leipzig, Fues's Verlag (R. Reisland), 1887, with numerous subsequent editions. The two concepts introduced by Tönnies are to be regarded as typological constructs, not existing in pure form but simply as "models." They are not antithetical but merely classificatory terms which are in the same genre as the similar concepts at present in vogue in sociology, e.g., "sacred" and "secular," "rural" and "urban," "folk society" and "civilization," "familistic" and "contractual," etc.

[25] Max Weber, *Die protestantische Ethik und der Geist des Kapitalismus*, 1904-1905, translated by Talcott Parsons as *The Protestant Ethic and the Spirit of Capitalism*, London, George Allen & Unwin, Ltd., 1930. See also his *Religionssoziologie*, 3 vols., Tübingen, J. C. B. Mohr (P. Siebeck), 1920-1921, and *Wissenschaftslehre*, Tübingen, J. C. B. Mohr (P. Siebeck), 1922. Among American sociologists who have been considerably influenced by Weber, and who have had a great deal to do with bringing his theories to the attention of American students, are H. H. Gerth and C. Wright Mills, *From Max Weber: Essays in Sociology*, New York, Oxford University Press, 1946; Talcott Parsons, *Max Weber: The Theory of Social and Economic Organization*, New York, Oxford University Press, 1947; Talcott Parsons, *The Structure of Social Action*, New York, McGraw-Hill Book Co., Inc., 1937.

[26] See his *De la division du travail social*, Paris, Félix Alcan, 1893.

sisted that this method must be objective, statistical, and devoid of introspection and the personal element. He demonstrated his method in his ethnological studies of elementary religious phenomena and in his monographic work on suicide.[27]

More and more, method has come to be regarded as fundamental by sociologists in the United States. Among the first to give primary attention to it were W. I. Thomas (1863-1947) and Florian Znaniecki—no doubt influenced by Dewey—in their monumental work, *The Polish Peasant in Europe and America*.[28] The "Methodological Note" [29] undoubtedly represents the chief object of the authors. They were not interested in social ethics or policy or concrete problems as such. To these men, the fundamental methodological postulates and techniques include: (1) the object matter taken for study is essentially what is known as culture, in the scientific sense; (2) the technique most satisfactory for use includes documents, letters, life histories, and the like; and (3) the scheme of analysis is in terms of attitudes and values, the former being defined as the tendency to act and the latter as the object toward which such tendency expresses itself. Such a method works from concrete data to abstract descriptions and generalizations. The desired objective is the discovery of the timeless elements in social phenomena. Up to date, no one has felt ready to go all the way in forming a complete abstract set of concepts and hypotheses except persons dominated by ethical and political preconceptions. In addition to the work of Thomas and Znaniecki, there is a general tendency to get away from metaphysical deductions and to make use of the case-study method for developing conclusions. The urban studies made at the University of Chicago [30] illustrate this trend, as do Thomas' *The Unadjusted Girl*,[31] and Park and Miller's *Old Traits Transplanted*.[32]

The current trends in sociological consensus appear to be along the following rather definite lines: toward a standardization of fundamental concepts in meaning and in use; a growing interest in several

---

[27] *The Elementary Forms of Religious Life,* translated by J. W. Swain, London, Macmillan & Co., Ltd., 1914; and *Le suicide,* Paris, Félix Alcan, 1887. His ideas on methodology are incorporated in *Règles de la méthode sociologique,* Paris, Félix Alcan, 1895, translated as *The Rules of the Sociological Method* by Sarah A. Solovay and John H. Mueller, Chicago, University of Chicago Press, 1938.

[28] Published in five volumes, Boston, R. G. Badger, 1918-1921, and in two volumes, New York, Alfred A. Knopf, 1927.

[29] Vol. I, pp. 1-86, in both editions.

[30] Nels Anderson, *The Hobo,* 1923; R. E. Park and E. W. Burgess, *The City,* 1925; Frederic Thrasher, *The Gang,* 1927; Louis Wirth, *The Ghetto,* 1928; Harvey Zorbaugh, *The Gold Coast and the Slum,* 1929. These five works were all published by the University of Chicago Press.

[31] W. I. Thomas, *The Unadjusted Girl,* Boston, Little, Brown & Co., 1923.

[32] R. E. Park and H. A. Miller, *Old World Traits Transplanted,* New York, Harper & Bros., 1921.

special fields of sociological importance, such as human ecology, social stratification, and sociological method and analysis as applied to industrial organization, political behavior, law, religion, and education; an objective approach to the study of group phenomena and to the investigation of personality development and adjustment in a variety of group and cultural situations; and the formulation of tentative, generalized hypotheses on the basis of concrete data and in terms of their timeless and universal aspects. There will be differences of opinion among sociologists, but this seems to be what is occurring in the sociology field today in Europe and America. Above all else, there is an increasing emphasis upon methods of research, including mensuration and investigations in the field, that is, in the community, the region, and other measurable areas.

QUESTIONS

1. What were the significant contributions of von Savigny, Eichhorn, Niebuhr, and von Ranke to pre-sociological thought?
2. How did Cameralism affect social theory?
3. What purpose did Comte have in placing sociology in his hierarchy of the sciences? Why did he place it "last in time but first in importance"?
4. What was Comte's conception of society?
5. What positions were held by Le Play and Worms with respect to a science of society?
6. "There is in society no 'social sensorium,' no social sensations." What is the implication of this Spencerian doctrine?
7. How does Spencer's conception of society differ from that of Comte?
8. What did Buckle, Maine, and Bagehot contribute to the development of social theory?
9. For what reasons is Ward regarded as of first rank among sociologists? Would you criticize his theories? If so, how and why?
10. Is sociology interested in "social problems" as such?
11. Why the marked tendency to make of sociology a study of the pathological features of social life?
12. Can you account for the tendency to substitute notions of social ethics for a science of sociology?
13. Who were the early leaders in Europe and America in the direction of "a more pluralistic and conceptional notion of the science" of sociology?
14. How did Giddings, Small, Ross, and Cooley promote the development of a scientific sociology?
15. For what are Hobhouse and Westermarck known in the furtherance of the sociological movement?

16. What is meant by saying that Simmel's idea of sociology was "a kind of social geometry"? Explain.

17. What contributions to sociological theory were made by Tönnies and Max Weber?

18. In what respects did Durkheim take the lead in French sociology? What estimate is made of his influence?

19. What were considered by Thomas and Znaniecki to be the fundamental methodological postulates and techniques in sociology?

20. What are the major current trends in sociology?

BIBLIOGRAPHY

ABEL, THEODORE. *Systematic Sociology in Germany: A Critical Analysis of Some Attempts to Establish Sociology as an Independent Science.* New York, Columbia University Press, 1929.

ALPERT, HARRY. *Emile Durkheim and His Sociology.* New York, Columbia University Press, 1939.

American Journal of Sociology, Special Semicentennial Issue. Vol. 50, No. 6, May, 1945. Commemorative of the completion of the first fifty years of the publication of the *Journal.*

BARNES, HARRY E. *An Introduction to the History of Sociology.* Chicago, University of Chicago Press, 1948.

BARNES, HARRY E., AND BECKER, HOWARD. *Social Thought from Lore to Science.* 2 vols. Boston, D. C. Heath & Co., 1938.

BARNES, HARRY E., BECKER, HOWARD, AND BECKER, FRANCES B. *Contemporary Social Theory.* New York, D. Appleton-Century Co., 1940.

BEACH, WALTER G. *The Growth of Social Thought.* New York, Charles Scribner's Sons, 1939.

BECKER, HOWARD. *Systematic Sociology: On the Basis of the Beziehungslehre and Gebildelehre of Leopold von Wiese.* New York, John Wiley & Sons, Inc., 1932.

BENDIX, REINHARD. "Max Weber's Interpretation of Conduct and History." *Am. J. Sociol.,* Vol. 51, No. 6, May, 1946, pp. 518-526.

BERNARD, L. L., AND BERNARD, JESSIE. *Origins of American Sociology.* New York, Thomas Y. Crowell Co., 1943.

BOGARDUS, EMORY S. *The Development of Social Thought.* New York, Longmans, Green & Co., 1947.

DAVIE, MAURICE R. (Ed.). *Sumner Today: Selected Essays by William Graham Sumner.* New Haven, Yale University Press, 1940.

DEGRANGE, McQUILKIN. "Comte's Sociologies." *Am. Sociol. Rev.,* Vol. 4, No. 1, February, 1939, pp. 17-26.

GERTH, H. H., AND MILLS, C. WRIGHT. *From Max Weber: Essays in Sociology.* New York, Oxford University Press, 1946.

GINSBERG, MORRIS. *Reason and Unreason in Society.* Cambridge, Harvard University Press, 1948. Chs. 2-5.

HERTZLER, J. O. *The Social Thought of the Ancient Civilizations.* New York, McGraw-Hill Book Co., Inc., 1936.

HOUSE, FLOYD N. *Development of Sociology.* New York, McGraw-Hill Book Co., 1936.

JANDY, E. C. *Charles Horton Cooley: His Life and His Social Theory.* New York, The Dryden Press, 1942.

KROUT, M. H. "The Development of Small's Sociological Theory." *J. Appl. Sociol.,* Vol. 11, 1926-1927, pp. 216-232.

Lundberg, George A., Bain, Read, and Anderson, Nels. (Eds.). *Trends in American Sociology.* New York, Harper & Bros., 1929.

Merton, Robert K. "Durkheim's Division of Labor in Society." *Am. J. Sociol.,* Vol. 40, No. 3, November, 1934, pp. 319-328.

Parsons, Talcott. *Max Weber: The Theory of Social and Economic Organization.* New York, Oxford University Press, 1947.

Parsons, Talcott. *The Structure of Social Action.* New York, McGraw-Hill Book Co., Inc., 1937.

Small, Albion W. *Origins of Sociology.* Chicago, University of Chicago Press, 1924.

Sorokin, Pitirim A. *Contemporary Sociological Theories.* New York, Harper & Bros., 1928.

Spykman, Nicholas J. *The Social Theory of Georg Simmel.* Chicago, University of Chicago Press, 1925.

Tönnies, Ferdinand. *Fundamental Concepts of Sociology.* Translated and supplemented by Charles P. Loomis. New York, American Book Co., 1940.

Wirth, Louis "Modern German Conceptions of Sociology." *Am. J. Sociol.,* Vol. 32, No. 3, November, 1926, pp. 461-470.

Wirth, Louis. "The Sociology of Ferdinand Tönnies." *Am. J. Sociol.,* Vol. 32, No. 3, November, 1926, pp. 412-422.

Chapter 27

SOCIOLOGY: ITS THEORY, METHODS, AND APPLICATIONS

SOCIOLOGICAL THEORY

The previous chapter sketched briefly the history of the development of sociological theory from historical, philosophical, and reformist-ideological beginnings. But a study of the more or less highly generalized synthetic theories of the past cannot prove very profitable to the student who wishes to understand current trends in sociological thought and method. For every synthesizer in the field today there are a score or more of individual researchers and writers who, while they are in fair agreement concerning certain major sociological premises, are at work on their individual empirical studies, which, in toto, range widely but which, it may be expected, will make their respective contributions to the development of a single major conceptual structure.[1]

Like any "young and little more than fledgling" science, we may expect that sociology will display in its theoretical assumptions and in some of its conclusions a certain lack of clarity in and agreement on some of the problems of conceptualization and systematization. Nevertheless, there is a considerable sociological heritage which shows that progress has been made toward the solution of these and related problems of method and interpretation.

It is apparent that human beings always and everywhere have lived in groups, have developed institutions that served them as guides for concerted action, and have been subject to their control. Out of the sociological movement have come certain so far unchallenged propositions concerning which sociologists are in unanimous agreement. Among these is the generalization that the social group is central and, furthermore, that group action is achieved chiefly, if

---

[1] Talcott Parsons, "The Position of Sociological Theory," *Am. Sociol. Rev.*, Vol. 13, No. 2, April, 1948, p. 157. See also, Robert K. Merton, "Sociological Theory," *Am. J. Sociol.*, Vol. 50, No. 6, May, 1945, pp. 462-473; Talcott Parsons and Bernard Barber, "Sociology, 1941-1946," *Am. J. Sociol.*, Vol. 53, No. 4, January, 1948, pp. 245-257.

not exclusively, through patterns of behavior that have become institutionalized. Moreover, consideration of the relation of the individual to the group and to its institutions has brought the sociologist face to face with social values and social attitudes, the respectively objective and subjective sides of cultural and social organization. The person and his attitudes are quite as much the products of social interaction as are the major institutions. Any comprehensive study of the latter involves the former. To be sure, one may take the organic point of view with respect to an institution and study its natural history without a close scrutiny of individuals, for an institution has an existence and momentum of its own which surmount and persist regardless of the functioning of any given set of individuals. Group, institution, person, attitude, and value constitute the main units in the sociological heritage.

The scope of sociology as a scientific discipline has been the subject of much debate. By some its field has been defined as that of an over-all generalizing social science, while by others it is held to be that of a specialty among the social sciences. The data of sociology are studied in the total social situation. The general methodological approach now most in favor is the empirical one of all mature science. The particular form it will take is determined by the situation under investigation, the purpose to be served, and the limits of the data to be studied.

The data with which sociology has to deal are those which are at once functional units in and end products of social interaction. As we have seen, human beings are affected by the presence and behavior of each other, and the *group* comes into existence at the moment when there is interaction between two or more persons, whether they are near or remote in space. The process of interaction, in its several phases, and the mechanisms involved in the process, set up in the course of time relatively permanent patterns which enable the members of the group to act concertedly in given social situations. In their elementary form, these patterns are called *folkways*. As the group becomes more conscious of itself and of its welfare, certain group behavior patterns become incorporated in what are called the *mores*, which may or may not comport in all respects with group-held ideal patterns of conduct which serve as *moral standards*. An *institution* is a still more elaborate and relatively fixed complex of expected behavior patterns whereby the energies of persons are focused on a major objective and a well-established structuralized means of reaching it. In addition to the fundamental institutions are those forms of social organization which relate institutions to each other in a given social system. Each of the devices which integrate the colliding activities of human beings is termed a *social mechanism*. Each of these mechanisms may be isolated, its natural history revealed, and its function described and explained.

Since persons and groups act and interact within the framework of the content and meaning of social situations, these latter factors become highly significant objects of sociological theory and investigation. Generally speaking, a situation embraces certain aspects of a physical environment as well as persons who are actors in the situation. However, analysis of a total situation need not be made, invariably, from the standpoint of the physical or biological sciences simply because of its physical-environmental features. Rather, it should be made in terms of the meaning which these features have for the human components in the situation. However, the ecological aspects of physical structures and other environing factors, their spatial distribution, and their influence on the interaction will enter into consideration. Of great importance are the definitions of the parts of the situation, as well as of the total situation as these are formulated and held by the active participants as residues of their own unique experiences and as elements in the culturally-held value system. It is in accord with such definitions of the situation that persons and groups act and interact.

The exposition and analysis of culture systems is primarily the province of cultural anthropology. The sociological theorist is greatly indebted to modern cultural anthropology for furnishing him with valuable data from these complex entities for use in his own comparative analysis of present-day institutional patterns and social systems. Equally important is the relation between sociology and so-called social psychology. In this book no attempt has been made to treat the two disciplines as separate and distinct. The sociologist does not rely to any appreciable degree on concepts of individual psychology but does utilize to some extent certain concepts which are germane to the interaction of persons, groups, and institutions. When he pushes his study of institutions in certain directions he finds that he is dealing with mass behavior or with what is sometimes called group psychology. If he pursues his study of institutions in another direction he finds that he is dealing with group incorporation of the person and his attitudes. But the concepts of individual psychology are not suitable for the analysis of this problem because the objectives and methods of sociology and general psychology are different. The sociologist studies the person, his organization and disorganization, in relation to the groups of which he is a member.

The relations of these groups to each other affect the personalities of their members profoundly. In these connections, it is a fine question as to where sociology begins and where it ends so far as its relation to social psychology is concerned. Both sociologists and psychologists have had a hand in developing the marginal field of social psychology.

SOCIOLOGY AS A SCIENCE

The question is often raised: "Is sociology a science?" Perhaps the typical representatives of the physical sciences would answer this question in the negative. The other social sciences also would be denied scientific status according to the standards of the natural and physical sciences. Fortunately there is no *de facto* monopoly of the objectives, methods, or spirit of science. The scientist in whatever field observes phenomena, classifies them, and develops hypotheses to explain the data he has collected. But these procedures alone are insufficient to make a science. Merton has called interpretations so based *"post factum* interpretations." Concerning them, he writes in part as follows:

. . . This procedure in which the observations are at hand and the interpretations are subsequently applied to the data has the logical structure of clinical inquiry. The observations may be case-history or statistical in character. The defining characteristic of this procedure is the introduction of an interpretation *after* the observations have been made rather than the empirical testing of a predesignated hypothesis. The implicit assumption is that a body of generalized propositions has been so fully established that it can be appropriately applied to the data in hand.

Such *post factum* explanations, designed to "explain" given observations, differ in logical function from speciously similar procedures where the observational materials are utilized in order to *derive* fresh hypotheses to be confirmed by *new* observations.

Post factum explanations remain at the level of *plausibility* (low evidential value) rather than leading to "compelling evidence" (a high degree of confirmation). Plausibility, in distinction to compelling evidence, is found when an interpretation is consistent with one set of data (which typically has, indeed, given rise to the decision to utilize one, rather than another, interpretation). It also implies that alternative interpretations equally consistent with these data have not been systematically explored and that inferences drawn from the interpretation have not been tested by new observations.

The logical fallacy underlying the *post factum* explanation rests in the fact that there is available a variety of crude hypotheses, each with some measure of confirmation but designed to account for quite contradictory sets of affairs. . . . The basis for "plausibility" rests in the consistency between the interpretation and the data; the absence of compelling evidence stems from the failure to provide distinctive tests of the interpretations apart from their consistency with the initial observations. The analysis is fitted to the facts, and there is no indication of just which data would be taken to contravene the interpretations. As a consequence, the documentary evidence merely illustrates rather than tests the theory.[2]

The inadequate logic of the *post factum* procedure lies in the all-too-common tendency of those who employ it to seek phenomena that will confirm their theoretic assumptions, to avoid "an explicit formulation of the conditions under which the hypotheses will be found to hold true," [3] and to draw sweeping generalizations from sets of data characteristic of unique or atypical situations.

To the extent that workers in the field of sociology succeed in correcting and testing their procedures and interpretations against repeatedly verified specific theories, and work inductively from such theoretical orientations either for the purpose of validating or of invalidating *ad hoc* propositions, then it may be said that sociology is on its way to becoming truly scientific. Many of the most valuable contributions of science have been the unanticipated results of inquiry carried out along these lines. While sociology is still in its infancy as a science, it is evident from the work of many sociologists during the last two or three decades that sociology is achieving a place of recognition and importance in the family of the sciences.

SOCIOLOGICAL METHODS

In spite of what has just been said, sociology still bears some resemblance to one of its predecessors, the philosophy of history. It is frequently speculative and its conclusions are often remote from the theoretically oriented and tested interpretations of science. Exceptions are pushed aside in the interest of some highly artificial logical construction. In the last twenty years or so, however, the trend in sociology has been away from armchair philosophizing and in the direction of scientific research. The major sociological hypotheses and generalizations are being tested in actual concrete social situations where the methods of observation, mensuration, analysis, and theoretical orientation are being more carefully controlled. Thus, sociological research is coming to play a dominant role in the development of sociological theory and there is a very evident shift of emphasis from knowledge *about* social life to knowledge *of* social life.

---

2 Merton, "Sociological Theory," *op. cit.*, pp. 467-469.
3 *Ibid.*, p. 468.

Recent years have witnessed a vast amount of attention devoted by sociologists to research and to a proliferation of books and courses of study on methods of research. Merton suggests that this "reflects the growing-pains of an immature discipline." Be that as it may, it is indicative of a state of affairs in the development of the science which recognizes the many and varied problems to be investigated and the need for their consideration at the hands of persons equipped with the best research procedures that may be devised. The student who has the aptitude, interest, and training for research will find in the sociological field ample opportunity for his research efforts. But, as implied in what has been said, the approach to research in this area of science, as in any other, should be from the vantage point of a thorough and sound theoretical preparation.

Some Applications of Sociology

Many students raise the question, "What can I do with sociology?" This perfectly legitimate question calls for thoughtful consideration by sociologists and students alike. Sociologists are inclined to believe that most students can benefit from some sociological training, whatever their future life work may be. The problems of the modern social world and of persons seeking to find satisfactory adjustments to the complex conditions of this world call for knowledge and understanding of the social process and of human nature, which sociology is prepared to give in large measure. Moreover, the special insights and skills required to meet successfully the requirements of specialized activities and professional duties practically demand that those who would be prepared for such tasks know at least the basic principles upon which present-day social life and organization are grounded and the relations of these principles to the development and integration of personalities. Sociology undertakes, through research and instruction, to make these generalizations and relationships known and to indicate their significance for modern life and work.

As a subject for study in the liberal arts programs of colleges and universities, sociology takes its place beside the social sciences: history, human geography, economics, philosophy, political science, and social psychology. Moreover, the prospective student in medicine, law, engineering, business administration, education, or theology should derive considerable valuable social orientation for his life work by including, whenever possible, some sociology in his pre-professional training. Persons contemplating entrance into one of the service occupations, such as social work, personnel work, recreation leadership, social research, community organization, management in housing development (public or private), or feature writing, will find preparation in sociology an essential qualification. Sociology does not train professionally for these fields, but it does furnish a background of information, an understanding of social situations and pertinent research.

QUESTIONS

1. What facts are central in the sociological heritage? Elaborate.
2. What constitute the field and general methodological approach of sociology?
3. Why are the content and meaning of social situations important objects of sociological theory and investigation?
4. How are cultural anthropology, sociology, and social psychology mutually indebted to each other? How do they differ from one another?
5. What are the procedures of science? Does sociology undertake to comply with these procedures?
6. Discuss Merton's criticism of "*post factum* interpretations."
7. Wherein lies the logical inadequacy of such interpretations?
8. What are some problems and possibilities incident to sociological research?
9. What may sociology afford the student who wants a general education? What has the discipline to offer to the student who wishes to specialize in the direction of professional training?

BIBLIOGRAPHY

ARGOW, WALTER W. "The Practical Application of Sociology." *Am. Sociol. Rev.,* Vol. 6, No. 1, February, 1941, pp. 37-40.

BAIN, READ. "Measurement in Sociology." *Am. J. Sociol.,* Vol. 40, No. 4, January, 1935, pp. 481-488.

BAIN, READ. "Sociology as a Natural Science." *Am. J. Sociol.,* Vol. 53, No. 1, July, 1947, pp. 9-16.

BERNARD, L. L. (Ed.). *The Fields and Methods of Sociology.* New York, Farrar & Rinehart, 1934.

BLUMER, HERBERT. "Sociological Theory in Industrial Relations." *Am. Sociol. Rev.,* Vol. 12, No. 3, June, 1947, pp. 271-278.

BOWERS, RAYMOND V. "Conceptual Integration and Social Research." *Am. Sociol. Rev.,* Vol. 3, No. 3, June, 1938, pp. 307-319.

BURGESS, ERNEST W. "Sociological Research Methods." *Am. J. Sociol.,* Vol. 50, No. 6, May, 1945, pp. 474-482.

CARR, LOWELL J. "Situational Sociology." *Am. J. Sociol.,* Vol. 51, No. 2, September, 1945, pp. 136-141.

CHAPIN, F. STUART. *Experimental Designs in Sociological Research.* New York, Harper & Bros., 1947.

CHAPIN, F. STUART. *Field Work and Social Research.* New York, The Century Co., 1929.

COOLEY, CHARLES H. *Sociological Theories and Social Research*. New York, Henry Holt & Co., 1930.

COTTRELL, LEONARD S., JR. "Analysis of Situational Fields—A Theoretical Orientation for Social Psychology." *Am. Sociol. Rev.*, Vol. 7, No. 3, June, 1942, pp. 370-383.

DODD, STUART C. *Dimensions of Society: A Quantitative Systematics for the Social Sciences*. New York, The Macmillan Co., 1942.

DURKHEIM, EMILE. *The Rules of the Sociological Method*. Trans. by Sarah A. Solovay and John H. Mueller. Chicago, University of Chicago Press, 1938.

EUBANK, EARLE E. *The Concepts of Sociology*. Boston, D. C. Heath & Co., 1931.

FARIS, ELLSWORTH. "The Promise of Sociology." *Am. Sociol. Rev.*, Vol. 3, No. 1, February, 1938, pp. 1-12.

GARDNER, BURLEIGH, AND WHYTE, WILLIAM FOOTE. "Methods for the Study of Human Relations in Industry," *Am. Sociol. Rev.*, Vol. 11, No. 5, October, 1946, pp. 506-512.

GOTTSCHALK, LOUIS, KLUCKHOHN, CLYDE, AND ANGELL, ROBERT C. *The Use of Personal Documents in History, Anthropology, and Sociology*. New York, Social Science Research Council, 1945.

GREENWOOD, ERNEST. *Experimental Sociology: A Study in Method*. New York, King's Crown Press, 1944.

GURVITCH, GEORGES, AND MOORE, WILBERT E. (Eds.). *Twentieth Century Sociology*. New York, The Philosophical Library, 1945. Ch. 1, "Sociology and the Social Sciences," by Huntington Cairns; Ch. 2, "Research Methods in Sociology," by Ernest W. Burgess; Ch. 3, "The Present Position and Prospects of Systematic Theory in Sociology," by Talcott Parsons; Ch. 4, "Interpretive Sociology and Constructive Typology," by Howard Becker.

HAGOOD, MARGARET J. *Statistics for Sociologists*. New York, Reynal & Hitchcock, Inc., 1941.

HENDERSON, WILLIAM, AND AGINSKY, B. W. "A Social Science Field Laboratory." *Am. Sociol. Rev.*, Vol. 6, No. 1, February, 1941, pp. 41-44.

HOUSE, FLOYD N. "Measurement in Sociology." *Am. J. Sociol.*, Vol. 40, No. 1, July, 1934, pp. 1-11.

HOUSE, FLOYD N. *The Range of Social Theory*. New York, Henry Holt & Co., 1929.

LINTON, RALPH. *The Science of Man in the World Crisis*. New York, Columbia University Press, 1944.

LUNDBERG, GEORGE A. *Foundations of Sociology*. New York, The Macmillan Co., 1939.

LUNDBERG, GEORGE A. "The Proximate Future of Sociology: The Growth of Scientific Method." *Am. J. Sociol.*, Vol. 50, No. 6, May, 1945, pp. 502-513.

LUNDBERG, GEORGE A. *Social Research: A Study in Methods of Gathering Data*. New York, Longmans, Green & Co., 1942.

MERTON, ROBERT K. "Science and the Social Order." *Philosophy of Science*, Vol. 5, July, 1938, pp. 321-337.

MERTON, ROBERT K. "Sociological Theory." *Am. J. Sociol.*, Vol. 50, No. 6, May, 1945, pp. 462-473.

MORENO, J. L. "Contributions of Sociometry to Research Methodology in Sociology." *Am. Sociol. Rev.*, Vol. 12, No. 3, June, 1947, pp. 287-292.

MOWRER, ERNEST R. "Methodological Problems in Social Disorganization." *Am. Sociol. Rev.*, Vol. 6, No. 6, December, 1941, pp. 839-852.

NORTHROP, F. S. C. *The Logic of the Sciences and the Humanities*. New York, The Macmillan Co., 1948.

ODUM, HOWARD W. "Sociology in the Contemporary World of Today and Tomorrow." *Social Forces*, Vol. 21, May, 1943, pp. 390-396.

ODUM, HOWARD W., AND MOORE, HARRY E. *American Regionalism*. New York, Henry Holt & Co., 1938.

OGBURN, WILLIAM F., AND GOLDENWEISER, A. A. (Eds.). *The Social Sciences*. Boston, Houghton Mifflin Co., 1927.

PALMER, VIVIEN M. *Field Studies in Sociology*. Chicago, University of Chicago Press, 1928.

PARETO, VILFREDO. *The Mind and Society*. 4 vols. New York, Harcourt, Brace & Co., 1935.

PARK, ROBERT E., AND BURGESS, ERNEST W. *An Introduction to the Science of Sociology*. Chicago, University of Chicago Press, 1921, 1924, Ch. 1, "Sociology and the Social Sciences."

PARSONS, TALCOTT. "The Role of Theory in Social Research." *Am. Sociol. Rev.*, Vol. 3, No. 1, February, 1938, pp. 13-20.

PARSONS, TALCOTT, AND BARBER, BERNARD. "Sociology, 1941-1946." *Am. J. Sociol.*, Vol. 53, No. 4, January, 1948, pp. 245-257.

PHELPS, HAROLD A. *Principles and Laws of Sociology*. New York, John Wiley & Sons, 1936.

QUEEN, STUART A. "Some Problems of the Situational Approach." *Social Forces*, Vol. 9, June, 1931, pp. 480-481.

RECKLESS, WALTER C. "The Implications of Prediction in Sociology." *Am. Sociol. Rev.*, Vol. 6, No. 4, August, 1941, pp. 471-477.

RICE, STUART A. (Ed.). *Methods in Social Science*. Chicago, University of Chicago Press, 1931.

THOMAS, W. I. "The Behavior Pattern and the Situation." *Pubs., Am. Sociol. Soc.*, Vol. 22, 1928, pp. 1-13.

THOMAS, W. I., AND ZNANIECKI, FLORIAN. *The Polish Peasant in Europe and America*. New York, Alfred A. Knopf, 1927, Vol. 1, pp. 1-86, "Methodological Note."

VAN KLEEK, MARY. "Toward an Industrial Sociology." *Am. Sociol. Rev.*, Vol. 11, No. 5, October, 1946, pp. 501-505.

WIRTH, LOUIS. "Clinical Sociology." *Am. J. Sociol.*, Vol. 37, No. 1, July, 1931, pp. 49-66.

WOLFF, KURT H. "Notes toward a Sociocultural Interpretation of American Sociology." *Am. Sociol. Rev.*, Vol. 11, No. 5, October, 1946, pp. 545-553.

YOUNG, DONALD. "Memorandum on Suggestions for Research in the Field of Social Adjustment." *Am. J. Sociol.*, Vol. 46, No. 6, May, 1941, pp. 873-886.

YOUNG, KIMBALL. "The Proximate Future of American Sociology: Research in a Changing Society." *Am. J. Sociol.*, Vol. 50, No. 6, May, 1945, pp. 493-501.

YOUNG, PAULINE V. *Scientific Social Surveys and Research: An Introduction to the Background, Content, Methods and Analysis of Social Studies*. New York, Prentice-Hall, Inc., 1939.

ZNANIECKI, FLORIAN. *The Method of Sociology*. New York, Farrar & Rinehart, 1934.

ZNANIECKI, FLORIAN. "The Proximate Future of American Sociology: Controversies in Doctrine and Method." *Am. J. Sociol.*, Vol. 50, No. 6, May, 1945, pp. 514-521.

AUTHOR INDEX

739

AUTHOR INDEX

SUBJECT INDEX

Boss, the political, 474-476
Bride capture, 265
Bride price, 265
Burgess hypothesis, regarding zonal structure of urban communities, 138-139
Bushman, the, 264

Caste, and class in terms of race differences, 455-457
Center of dominance, as a center of centers, 168; the concept of the, 154-158; defined, 154; at focal point of transportation and communication, 154-155; in Hawaii, 204; industrial development in the, 165-166; joint stock companies in the, 163; London as a, 158-170; New York as a, 158; in relation to frontiers, 156; the rise of the new, 156-158; and subordinate areas, 155-156; symbiotic unity of a, 156; in terms of specialization, 220 (See also Centralization, Dominance)
Centralization, defined, 216; as an ecological process, 216-218; gives form to the community, 217; and the region, 217-218; in the urban community, 216-217 (See also Center of dominance)
Ceremony, the role of, in social control, 642-644
Change, cultural, 30-32; in South Africa, 207, 209-210; necessity of, in old age, 123-124; technological, and unemployment, 114-115 (See also Social change)
Child, acquisition of social patterns by the, 14; adjustment of the, 103-106; the case of the only, 105-106; in the family, 14-17, 102-103; and institutional participation, 104; and the play group, 104-105; and relationships to parents, 100-102; in time of bereavement, 121
China, class structure in, 196-197; the community system in, 196; the family unit as primary in, 196; industrialization in, 194-195, 197-200; labor surplus in rural, 195-196; overpopulation in, 195; social stratification in, 196-197; and Western technology, 194-200
Church (See Religion)
City, centralization in the, 216-218; concentration in the, 215-216; the culture of the, 498-499; the dominance of the, and its effects, 505-507, 508; the expansion of the, 570-572; as product of natural processes of growth, 213-214; segregation in the, 218-219; selective distribution of population in the, 238-241
City planning, 276; the function of, 229
Civilization, defined, 16
Clan, marriage outside the, 264-265; of the Zuñi, 70-71
Class, and caste in terms of race differences, 455-457; three-fold categories of, 281; characteristic behavior in terms of, 281-282; denial of the existence of divisions, 422-423; determination of the social, 16; as a determiner of status, 422-424, 438-439; differentiation by social, 281; divisions of society, 9-10; as a factor in party politics, 483-485; function of, structure, 282; meaning of, 422, 423-424; the so-called "middle," 439-440, 448, 453, 455; the Negro in terms of,

structure, 455-457; the non-landholding in St. Denis, 191-192; open-, system, 457-458; status, role, and the, structure, 259-260; structure in China, 196-197; the so-called, struggle, 426-429, 440; types of, groupings, 424-426; the weakening of, barriers, 439-440 (See also Position, Status, Stratification)
Clique, defined, 280
Cocopa Indians, 29
Collective behavior, definitions of, 604-605; develops a rhythmic character, 611-612; distinguished from societal behavior, 626-627; in the form of fashion, fad, craze, etc., 616-618, 620; in the form of hero worship, 620-621; as manifested in the crowd, 607-616; of the mass, 616-621; mass migration as a form of, 618-620; the milling aspect of, 606-607, 695, 703; of the public, 621-625; regimented form of, 608-610; relation of, to social movements, 678-680, 709; and social change, 602; social unrest and types of, Ch. 23, bibliography, 628-630; spontaneous character of much, 615-616; types of, 605
Collective excitement, 695, 704, 707; effects of, 699
Collective representations, characteristic of a developing social movement, 702; in mobilization for war, 329-331
Communication, as affected by inventions, 93; facilitation of, 91; as focal point of a center of dominance, 154-155, 167-168; necessary to conflict, 297; symbols of, 91-92
Communism, the point of view of, 325; and the so-called class struggle, 427-428
Community, Ch. 10, bibliography, 246-248; changing, functions and activities, 515-516; characteristic features of the immigrant, 392-394; classification of, types, 497; defined, 220; different from region, 215-216, 217-218, 220; division of labor in the, 214; ecological forces of the, 220-241; ecological processes in the urban, 215-220; the effects of industrial conflict on the, 434; interaction between aliens and the, 394-395; interaction involving inter- and intra-, relations, Ch. 19, bibliography, 526-528; inter-, competition, 498; intra-, interaction, 509-516; organization, 516; population selection in the urban, 238-241; the rural, described, 499-500; system in China, 196; the urban, described, 498-499
Competition, centers of, in the city, 216; defined, 213; and the ecological forces, 213-220; the idea of, basic to human ecology, 214; inter-community, 498; selection by means of, 241, 245-246; for space in New York City, 229-238
Compromise, as an accommodative mechanism, 400; of divergent moral principles, 546; in industrial relations, 435; in international relations, 344-345; in politics, 478-479
Concentration, defined, 215; as an ecological process, 215-216; industrial, 165, 168-170; of masses of mankind, 140; regional, 215-216; of urban populations, 175-176,

215-216; zones of active and passive, 151-152

Conciliation, defined, 345; in international relations, 345

Conflict, and accommodation, 299-300, 303-304; areas of economic, 437-439; contact and communication necessary to, 297; defined, 297; effects of, on the individual, 297-298; effects of industrial, 433-434; emergence of, in social movements, 702, 704, 707; in everyday life, 298; factional, 520-521; the feud as a form of, 522-524; forms of, 298; industrial, 285-286, 429-434; the inevitability of, 524-525; interest in, 299; international, apart from war, 343; between invaders and natives, 407; the judicial form of, 521-522; between the learned and the unlearned, 534-535; marital, 269-270; numbers in relation to race, 355-356; between parents and children, 448-449; political party, 467-478; sectarian, described, 488-490; sectarian, illustrated, 486-488; the so-called, between classes, 426-429; in terms of incongruous moral principles, 541-543; urban-rural, 508; war as a form of, 315

Contacts, between great culture areas, 310-312; direct and indirect, in race relations, 358-360; initial, between invaders and native peoples, 390-391; necessary to conflict, 297; reconciliation in primary and personal, 391-392, 400; reconciliation in secondary and impersonal, 390-391; resulting from invasion, 401-404; typical reactions to, in race relations, 360-361

Contract, the marriage, 264-266

Control (See Social control)

Conventionalization, where moral principles are involved, 544

Conventions, as behavioral phenomena, 540

Conversion, as an accommodative mechanism, 400; the nature of, 491-492

Cooperation, interracial, 383-384

Courtship, personal adjustment to, 117-118

Craze, and the cult, 684; as a form of collective behavior, 617

Crime, among the Zuñi, 76

Crisis, adjustment to personal, 125-126; involving divorce and desertion, 122-123; involved in the occurrence of death, 121; of unemployment, 116-117

Crowd, behavior of the, 607-616; classification of, types, 608, 610-611; defined, 607-608; develops a plan of action, 610-611; the dynamism of the, 613; and the mass, 616; process of, formation, 638; the psychologically organized, 683, 703-704, 709; social control in the, 634-639; the war-making, 334-335

Crusade, as a type of social movement, 685-686

Cult, the nature of the, 683; the Sun, of the Zuñi, 65; as a type of social movement, 683-685; the war, 327-328; the War, of the Zuñi, 65, 69; the Masked Gods of the Zuñi, 66-67

Cultural, borrowing by the Zuñi, 72-73; breakdown and social organization, 589-590; change, 30-32; creation, 593-595; formalism, 587-589; inertia, 583-585;

lag, 585-587; reorganization, 591-593; revival, 590-591; unevenness of, change, 585-587, 595

Cultural dynamics of social change, Ch. 22, bibliography, 596-599

Cultural integration, in specific societies, Chs. 3 and 4, bibliography, 77-79; themes of, 43-44

Cultural lag, as lack of integration in culture, 127-128; 585-587

Cultural movements, 680-688 (See also Social movements)

Cultural responses, Malinowski's categories of, 35-40

Cultural survivals, 28-29

Culture, Ch. 2, bibliography, 77-79; an abstraction, 27-28; adjustment to the nature and integration of, 127-129; and change, 30-32, 580; characteristics of, 27-34; the comparative study of, 42-44; as a continuum, 32; contradictions in, 127-129; and the creation of needs, 29-30, 40; in the solution of needs, 32-35; defined, 40; differences in, 580; distinguishing characteristics of rural, 499-501; distinguishing characteristics of the urban, 498-499; dynamic quality of, 30; of four Yucatan communities, 581; functions of, 580-581; group, and personality, Part I; homogeneity of, 581-583; independent of individuals, 32; an integration, 28; of the Kwakiutl Indians, Ch. 3; lack of integration in, 127-128; and levels of social behavior, 539-540; major status universes in every, 454-455; of minorities, 346-347; origins of, 32-34; overelaboration of, 29, 58-59; people as intermediaries of, 279-280; personality and, 81-82, 95-97; rewarding and frustrating effects of, 30; rural, brought to the cities, 509; the sacred, of China, 194-195; selective cumulativeness of, 28; sex in, 127; social interaction channelized by, 312; a social phenomenon, 27; of St. Denis, 188-192, 193-194; survivals of, 28-29; themes of, 44; traits of, 45; urban, brought to the rural folk, 507-508; variability in, and social change, 581-582; in the war-making role, 322-323; of the Zuñi, 62, 66

Culture-complex, defined, 45; Kwakiutl potlatch, a kind of super, 45

Cultures, selective distribution of peoples and, Chs. 7 and 8, bibliography, 182-184, Ch. 9, bibliography, 211-212

Cycle, of race relations, 387-388

Death, personal adjustment to, 120-122

Decentralization, of certain functions in New York City, 233-234; of factories, 230-233

Deliberation, an accommodative mechanism in industrial relations, 436, in international relations, 342-343

Demonstration, described, 613-615

Density, of population, 140, 142, 145, 148

Desertion, 269; family adjustment to, 123; personal adjustment to, 122-123

Disorganization, as an aftermath of war, 589-590; defined, 271; family, 269-271; social, as prerequisite to organized so-